P9-DUD-742

CONTENTS

PREFACE   vii

PART 1: THE DYNAMICS OF FASHION   1

  1. The Nature of Fashion   3
  2. Environmental Influences on Fashion Interest and Demand 16
  3. The Movement of Fashion   33
  4. Fashion Leaders and Followers   50

PART 2: MARKETERS OF FASHION   67

  5. The Materials of Fashion: Textile Fibers and Fabrics   69
  6. The Materials of Fashion: Leather and Fur   88
  7. Manufacturers of Women's Fashion Apparel   101
  8. Manufacturers of Menswear   119
  9. Manufacturers of Fashion Accessories   136
 10. Foreign Fashion Market Centers   158
 11. Retail Distributors of Fashion   175

PART 3: RETAIL MERCHANDISING OF FASHION   199

 12. Interpreting Customer Demand   201
 13. The Dollar Merchandise Plan   217
 14. Planning the Fashion Merchandise Assortment   236
 15. Controlling Fashion Assortments: Unit Control   253
 16. Controlling Fashion Assortments: Inventory Control   272
 17. Selecting Fashion Merchandise for Resale   291
 18. Promoting Fashions: Advertising and Display   313
 19. Promoting Fashions: Publicity and Personal Selling   334
 20. Fashion Coordination   351
 21. Developing a Fashion Image   369

APPENDIX: Career Opportunities in Fashion   382

GLOSSARY   401

BIBLIOGRAPHY   410

INDEX   415

FASHION MERCHANDISING

SECOND EDITION

MARY D. TROXELL

ASSOCIATE PROFESSOR
COORDINATOR, MERCHANDISING OPTION
IOWA STATE UNIVERSITY

GREGG DIVISION
McGRAW-HILL BOOK COMPANY

New York   St. Louis   Dallas   San Francisco
Auckland   Düsseldorf   Johannesburg   Kuala Lumpur
London   Mexico   Montreal   New Delhi
Panama   Paris   São Paulo
Singapore   Sydney   Tokyo   Toronto

Library of Congress Cataloging in Publication Data

Troxell, Mary D.
  Fashion Merchandising

  (The Gregg/McGraw-Hill marketing series)
  Bibliography: p.
  Includes index.
  1. Clothing trade—United States. 2. Fashion.
I. Title.
HD9940.U4T74 1976 658.8'09'68775-16484.
ISBN 0-07-065278-3

Fashion Merchandising
Second Edition

1 2 3 4 5 6 7 8 9 0 MURM 7 8 3 2 1 0 9 8 7 6

The editors for this book were Lawrence A. Walsh and
Cynthia Newby, the designer was Victoria Wong, and
the production supervisor was Phyllis D. Lemkowitz. It
was set in Bodoni Book by York Graphic Services, Inc.
Part 1 photographs: *Top,* The Granger Collection, New
York. *Bottom,* New York Couture Business Council;
André Courréges, Paris; Victor Joris for V & J Design,
a division of Cuddle Coat. Part 2 photographs: *Top,*
J. P. Stevens & Co., Inc.; Hush Puppies Division of
Wolverine World Wide Inc. *Bottom,* Paul Laszlo, Paul
Laszlo Associates. Part 3 photograph: Macy's Herald
Square.
Printed by the Murray Printing Company and bound
by Rand McNally & Company.

PREFACE

Fashion Merchandising is a comprehensive, factual text that explores and explains both the subject of fashion and the fashion industry. It provides an up-to-date guide to the fundamentals of fashion and the application of these fundamentals to the merchandising of fashion apparel and accessories.

The text is intended primarily to be used by college-level students in preparation for entry-level jobs throughout the fashion industry in general and for such jobs as assistant buyer, merchandising trainee, and assistant fashion coordinator in the merchandising sectors of the industry in particular. In addition, the detailed coverage of the book makes it a useful guide and reference for those already employed at all levels in the fashion industry.

Fashion Merchandising presents, in sequential learning order:

- The basic principles of fashion; how fashions begin, move, and disseminate; and how fashions may be predicted
- The history and development, methods of operation, merchandising activities, and current industry trends at all levels within the fashion industry, from the producers of raw materials to the retail distributors of consumer goods
- A detailed, step-by-step description and explanation of the planning and control procedures used on the job in today's retail merchandising of fashion goods

This second edition represents a complete revision of the material that appeared in the first edition. In addition, some important new material has been added:

- A chapter on the *Manufacturers of Menswear.* This is a detailed coverage of the history, organization and operation, merchandising activities, and industry trends within this increasingly important sector of fashion apparel and accessories. The new chapter is reinforced by the insertion of useful and pertinent menswear references and examples throughout the general material of the book.
- A chapter on *Foreign Fashion Market Centers.* This chapter explores the developing fashion market centers throughout the world, their importance in relation to the American fashion industry, and the growing importance of fashion products in international trade. Discussed are the fashion industries of the world, how they have developed, the specific products for which each major country or geographic area is known, and the important market centers

for fashion products within that country or area. This chapter is unique; in no other place can this material be found in such a concise, compact form.

- A thorough updating of the industry trends and their implications in each of the major sectors of the fashion industry.
- An expansion and updating of the "nuts and bolts" merchandise planning and control section, intended to give students a well-grounded understanding of the systems and techniques they must know to work in this area.

To reinforce students' understanding, each chapter of *Fashion Merchandising* ends with three types of activities. "Merchandising Vocabulary" lists important terms and asks students to define them. The basic questions in "Merchandising Review" cover the key concepts of each chapter. Finally, "Merchandising Digest" requires students to use analytic skills in framing answers to more difficult questions. An instructor's manual and key is available to the instructor.

Fashion Merchandising is consumer-oriented. The information in the text is organized and presented in terms of the basic marketing concept: that customers alone create fashions through their acceptance or rejection of offered styles. Fashion producers and retailers alike, and all those who work in this industry, are successful only to the degree that they recognize and operate on this basis.

ACKNOWLEDGMENTS

Many people helped in the preparation of this edition of *Fashion Merchandising*. Thanks go to those in business and education who so generously shared their valuable and pertinent information and experience. Special thanks go to the hundreds of students who field-tested experimental versions of the text, and whose enthusiastic response and interest provided the incentive needed to complete this revision. A special debt of gratitude is owed to Catherine Spurr, who contributed so much dedicated effort, professional skill, and human understanding throughout the development of this edition.

Mary D. Troxell

FASHION MERCHANDISING

PART 1
THE DYNAMICS
OF FASHION

Dynamics refers to any basic forces and the laws relating to them that explain the pattern of change or growth of those forces. Fashion is one of the great basic forces in present-day life, and there are very specific, proven laws concerning fashion.

The knowledge of fashion is a science. It does not involve artistic whims and happenstance; it involves known facts and the prediction of actions and reactions based on those facts.

An understanding of any subject involves study. The study of fashion, like the study of all subjects, begins with fundamentals. Unlike the fundamentals of some other subjects, the study of fashion touches on many different bodies of knowledge, including psychology, economics, sociology, art, history, and religion.

Part 1 of this book concentrates on these fundamentals of fashion. The four chapters discuss:

- The basic vocabulary of fashion; the components of fashion; the intangible elements of fashion; and the basic principles relating to fashion and its movement
- The environmental factors—economic, sociological, and psychological—that influence fashion interest and demand, and the impact of that influence
- How fashions change, and how an understanding of the movement of fashion can be used to analyze and predict fashion trends
- How fashions begin, and how they disseminate

An understanding of these fundamentals of fashion is a basic requirement for success in any area of the fashion business. Dr. Paul Nystrom, who was among the first to treat the study of fashion as a practical science, said:

A correct understanding of fashion and how to work with it is obviously of importance to every business owner, executive, and employee who has any constructive activity to carry on in the production or marketing of fashion goods. The artist or designer who combines beauty and individuality with current fashions in the creation of styles also needs the facts concerning fashions and their trends. In this group may be mentioned the factory manager who executes the designs in such detail as to convey the precise feeling of the fashions; the salesman of the firm who must be able to discuss the fashionableness, as well as other qualities of the merchandise, in intelligent terms; the retail store buyer who wants to be assured that the stock purchased and carried in his store shall be what his customers will want; and, finally, the salespeople of the store, who should have at least a rudimentary acquaintance with the nature of fashion and how it works.[1]

Part 1 of this book offers a basic and thorough discussion of exactly that: the nature of fashion and how it works. An understanding of this general knowledge is needed before specialized study of a particular area of fashion is undertaken. It is important background information for those interested in such aspects of fashion as costume history or design. It is essential information for those interested in merchandising fashion goods at either the wholesale or retail level.

[1] Nystrom, Paul H., *Fashion Merchandising*. New York: Ronald Press, 1932, pp. 37–38.

1
THE NATURE OF FASHION

A powerful force touches every facet of our lives. It influences what we wear, what we eat, where we live, what furnishings we have in our homes, how we travel, what we do for amusement. It involves each of us individually, frequently, personally; some use it to highlight personality and individuality, while others find in it an armor that builds self-confidence and assurance.

This same force has given a strong thrust to the vast expansion of industry and trade since the seventeenth century. Because of the spotlight of popularity it puts first on one product and then on another, it encourages manufacturers to produce, marketers to sell, and businesses of all kinds to hire at an ever increasing rate. With its aid, the standard of living moves constantly higher.

The name of this potent force is fashion.

In dresses and dinner jackets, neckties and nightgowns, in automobiles and apartment houses, fashion plays an important role in product design, in sales promotion and advertising, in merchandise presentation, in every phase of marketing.

Despite the growing importance of the role fashion plays in the lives of most of us, several misconceptions about it continue to exist. The most common misconception is that fashions are dictated by designers and retailers who decide what the fashions will be and then force these decisions on helpless consumers. Instead, consumers themselves dictate fashion, by their acceptance or rejection of the styles offered.

A second misconception is that only women are influenced by fashion. But men are increasingly responsive to it, too. Fashion is the force that causes women to change their skirt lengths or hair colors and men to adopt or abandon vests, to grow or shave off mustaches and beards.

A third misconception is that fashion is mysterious and unpredictable. Yet there are no unfathomable mysteries about the workings of fashion. Its direction can be detected, and its changes can be predicted with remarkable accuracy by those who understand the fundamentals of fashion.

Fashion touches the daily lives of nearly everyone, and that touch can be measured and evaluated. Fashion merchandising has become a science as well as an art.

THE TERMINOLOGY OF FASHION

In studying the exciting and complex subject of fashion, certain words and phrases are used over and over again: high fashion and mass fashion, style, design, apparel, taste, classic, and fad. The words seem simple, but they are used differently by different people in different contexts. Their exact meanings within the field of fashion merchandising have to be understood if the field itself is to be understood.

The study of fashion merchandising as a science as well as an art is relatively new. It requires the exact definition of the fashion vocabulary so that concepts can be discussed and described without any misunderstanding of the terms. One of the major pioneers in this field was Dr. Paul H. Nystrom. The definitions in this section are those established by him, and they have become generally accepted for the academic study of fashion.[1]

Fashion

The prevailing style accepted and used by the majority of a group at any given time is a *fashion.* Full skirts, high heels, long hair, natural make-up—each has been a fashion, and no doubt each will be again when it is once more the style accepted by the majority of a group with similar interests or similar characteristics. For instance, college students form one group, young married couples another.

Different groups often adopt different fashions, and fashions are often divided according to the group to which they appeal. *High fashion* refers to those styles or designs accepted by a limited group of fashion leaders, the elite among the consumers, those who are first to accept fashion change. In general, high fashion styles or designs are newly introduced and are produced and sold in small quantities, generally at high to fairly high prices. *Mass fashion* or *volume fashion* refers to those styles or designs that are widely accepted. Such fashions usually are produced and sold in large quantities, generally at moderate to low prices.

Style

A *style* is a characteristic or distinctive mode of presentation or conceptualization in the field of some art. There are styles in writing, in speaking, in home decorating, in table manners. In apparel, style is the characteristic or distinctive way a garment looks, the sum of the features that make it different from other garments. For example, skirts are one style of women's apparel, while pants have become another. Men's tailored jackets are one style, while sport jackets are another.

Styles come and go in fashion acceptance, but a specific style always remains a style, whether or not it is currently in fashion. Also, several styles may be in fashion at one time. For instance, pantsuits and dresses, which are completely different styles, may both be fashionable at the same time for many of the same occasions.

Styles are often named for the period of history in which they originated, and a style that has faded from the scene frequently returns to fashion again at a later date. This has happened with such styles as the Grecian, Roman, Renaissance, and Empire. When such styles return to fashion, their basic elements remain the same, but minor details are altered to reflect the taste or needs of the new era in which they reappear. Thus the Empire style of the early nineteenth century featured a waistline cinched high up under the bust, and that style can still be bought today. In today's version, however, the characteristic details associated with the style's design are modified to reflect those in current fashion acceptance.

Design

A specific or individual interpretation or version of a style is a *design.* For example, pants are a distinctive style in women's apparel. Designs are the countless variations in which women's pants are available, such as tapered or bell-bottomed slacks, short shorts or bermuda-length shorts, culottes, and pantsuits. A coatdress is a style. Variations in skirt length and width and in sleeve and neckline treatment form different designs of that style.

Each manufacturer is apt to produce several designs or variations of a popular style. If platform shoes are a current fashion, each shoe manufacturer will offer several different designs of that style varying in color, material, or decoration.

In the fashion trade, however, manufacturers and retailers refer to what technically is a design as a "style" or "style number" or simply a "number." When a buyer says, "I'm going to reorder that style," or "I'm going to mark down that number," the buyer usually is talking about a specific design, about an individual interpretation or version of a style.

Taste

An individual's ability to recognize what is and what is not attractive and appropriate is referred to as *taste*. Good taste in fashion implies sensitivity not only to what is artistic but also to what prevailing fashion says is appropriate for a specific occasion. Styles may be artistically beautiful, but if they are not appropriate, they may not be in good taste. For instance, even after pantsuits were widely accepted as appropriate for many occasions, some exclusive restaurants would not serve women wearing pantsuits. Pantsuits simply were not—and in some places still are not—considered in good taste for formal dining. The same is true of whether men are expected to wear neckties in formal restaurants.

Dr. Nystrom pinpointed the relationship between taste and fashion this way: "Good taste essentially is making the most artistic use of current fashion . . . bridging the gap between good art and common usage."[2]

Timing, too, makes a difference in what is considered good or bad taste. James Laver, the British costume authority, saw the relationship as a cycle through which a style goes. Whether or not a style is in good taste depends upon the place it has reached in that cycle at a particular time. A style, he said, is thought to be:

"indecent"	10 years before its time
"shameless"	5 years before its time
"outré"	1 year before its time
"smart"	in its time
"dowdy"	1 year after its time
"hideous"	10 years after its time
"ridiculous"	20 years after its time[3]

While the actual amount of time covered may be greatly expanded or condensed for different styles, the cycle itself is a valid concept. A new

*One hundred years
(1850, 1925, 1959)
of swimwear fashions.*
Cole of California

style is first considered daring and often in dubious taste, then is gradually accepted, then is widely accepted, and finally is gradually discarded.

A Classic

Some styles or designs remain in good taste over a long period, proving an exception to the increasingly rapid movement of styles through their fashion life cycles. A *classic* is a style or design that remains in general fashion acceptance for an extended time.

Everyone's wardrobe has some classics in it, while some wardrobes are made up mainly of classics. A classic is characterized by simplicity of design and by the length of time it stays in fashion and is considered acceptable and in good taste. The shirtwaist dress has been a classic for many years. So has the simple pump.

A Fad

A short-lived fashion is called a *fad*. Fads usually affect only a narrow group within the total population and generally are concerned with some detail of design. Young people are especially susceptible to fads, but adults are not totally immune. Fads have also been called "miniature fashions," following the same cycle as a fashion but completing that cycle much more quickly. A fad can come and go in a single season.

Some fads that have followed the pattern of appeal to a narrow group, with quick ascent and descent in popularity, include the Nehru jacket for men and granny dresses for children. For brief periods, teenagers experimented with micromini skirts and with gaudily decorated jeans and T-shirts. Clogs were fads worn not only by women but also by some men.

Occasionally what first appears to be a fad later develops into a classic. The bikini, a shocking Riviera fad of the early 1950s, gradually grew into an accepted beach fashion. Today the name has lost its capital letter, and the garment has lost its power to shock.

Another example is the sack or chemise dress, which flared into instant popularity in the late 1950s. Although it quickly passed from the fashion scene, it was reborn within a few years as the shift. In 1974, the chemise again made its appearance in the Paris collections, this time with certain of its former disadvantages eliminated. The style was quickly reproduced by a number of American producers in several versions and at a wide variety of prices. Only time will tell whether the chemise style will be just another fad or a style that goes through a complete fashion cycle, or whether it becomes a classic in the last half of the twentieth century.

COMPONENTS OF FASHION

Creating a fashion design is a complex process. The great designers of apparel do not produce by a hit-or-miss technique. Instead, the finished look of a fashion style or design is a blend, a composition, of four basic elements or components, each one contributing to the total effect. These four elements with which all apparel fashions are concerned are silhouette, details, texture, and color. Any change in fashion acceptance involves a change in one or more of these elements. This is true of all fashion-influenced products, from refrigerators to automobiles, from office buildings to apartment houses, from apparel to accessories.

Silhouette

The *silhouette* of a costume is its overall outline or contour. Silhouette is also frequently referred to as "shape" or "form."

To a casual observer it may appear that women have worn countless silhouettes throughout the centuries. According to authorities, however, there are really only three basic types, each with many variations: the straight or tubular, the bell-shaped or bouffant, and the bustle or back-fullness.[4] Since the mid-eighteenth century, these basic silhouettes have consistently followed each other in fashion acceptance in the same sequence, each recurring once in approximately 100 years and lasting for about a 35-year period. Research indicates that the change in fashion acceptance of the three basic types of women's apparel silhouettes has followed this same general pattern for almost three hundred years. Widespread sociological change and rapid technological developments that are occurring in the last half of the twentieth century may, however, alter both the traditional life span and sequence of these silhouettes in the future.

Details

The individual parts that give form to the silhouette or make up its structure are called *details.* These include trimmings, skirt length and width, or shoulder, waist, and sleeve treatment.

Changes in detail, especially in the skirt, are steps leading toward a change in silhouette. Silhouettes evolve gradually, from one to another, through changes in detail. When the trend in a detail reaches an extreme, a reversal of the trend takes place. For example, skirt lengths reached an extreme in brevity in the late 1960s, and the reversal began to show itself in the increasing number of longer-length styles available in the 1970s. Men's ties grew narrower during the 1960s, then widened again in the early 1970s. The changes are usually predictable, although the speed at which they take place varies.

Variations in detail offer both designer and consumer unlimited opportunity to express individuality within the framework of an accepted fashion silhouette. For example, for a natural-waistline silhouette a slender woman might choose a simple, wide belt, a heavily decorated belt, or a belt in a contrasting color to suit either her personality or the occasion. A woman who wants to de-emphasize a wide waist might choose either a narrow or a noncontrasting belt, or perhaps wear no belt at all, preferring seams that suggest a natural waistline.

Texture

One of the most significant components of fashion is texture. *Texture* is the look and feel of all types of material, woven or nonwoven.

Texture can influence the appearance of the silhouette by making it appear bulkier or more slender, depending on the roughness or smoothness of the materials used. A woman dressed in a rough tweed dress and a bulky knit sweater is likely to look larger and squarer than she does in a dress of identical lines executed in smooth jersey and worn with a cashmere sweater. When the bulky look is popular, the popular textures include shaggy tweeds, mohairs, cable-stitched and other heavily ribbed knit fabrics, and rough-textured materials. When sleek lines are the fashion, rough textures yield to smooth surfaces and simple flat weaves and knits.

Texture influences the drape of a garment because different textures of material drape differently when cut and sewn. Chiffon clings and flows, making it a good choice for soft feminine styles, while corduroy has a stiffness and bulk that make it a good choice for more casual garments.

Texture can influence the quality of color in a fabric by causing the surface either to reflect or to absorb light. Rough textures absorb light, causing the colors to appear dull; smooth textures reflect light, causing colors to appear brighter. Anyone who has tried to match colors soon discovers that a color which appears extremely bright in a shiny vinyl, satin, or high-gloss enamel paint seems subdued in a rough wool, a suede, or on a wall finished in stucco. Pile surfaces like velvet both reflect and absorb light, making colors look richer and deeper than they would on flat, smooth surfaces.

Color

In women's clothing, color has always been a major consideration. In men's clothing, especially since the end of World War II, color has been regaining the importance it had in previous centuries but had lost in more recent times. Today color is a key factor in apparel selection for both sexes. It is important not only in apparel fashions but in advertising, packaging, and store decor as well.

Historically, colors have been used to denote rank and profession. Purple, for instance, was associated with royalty, and in some areas during some periods could be worn only by those of noble birth. Black became the ordinary wear for the clergy and for most businessmen.

What a color denotes often varies with geographical location. White, for example, is the Western world's symbol of purity, worn by brides and used in communion dresses, whereas in India, white is the color of mourning.

Color has been affected by progress in technology. Better ways of tanning leather and dyeing and finishing fabrics have resulted in a wider variety of colors and color combinations for fashion designers to work with than ever before. In addition, colors today are more permanent, more resistant to fading or changing, and thus more acceptable to consumers.

Today, a fashion designer's color palette changes with consumers' diverse preferences. In some seasons, all is brightness and sharp contrast, and no color is too powerful to be worn. In other seasons, only subdued colors appeal. Fashion merchants soon develop an eye for color, not just for the specific hues and values popular in a given season but also for indications of possible trends in consumer preference.

THE INTANGIBLES OF FASHION

The definition of fashion, remember, is "the prevailing style accepted and used by the majority of a group at any given time." A style is tangible, made up of silhouette and details of design. Fashion, however, is a matter of intangibles, such as group acceptance and constant change.

"Accepted" is part of the definition; to be a fashion, a style must be accepted. Fashion, therefore, is acceptance. "Prevailing" and "at any given time" indicate the need to identify a style with a particular period of time, for fashion moves, fashion is change. "A group" relates fashion to specific people living a specific lifestyle in a specific place and time.

Acceptance

Group acceptance or approval is implied in any discussion of fashion. A style must be adopted by a major portion of a single group or a major segment of the whole population before it becomes a fashion. An article of clothing may be breathtakingly new and aesthetically flawless, yet it may not be called a fashion until it has been accepted and used by a substantial number of people. Acceptance, rather than novelty or beauty, is required for a style to become a fashion.

Acceptance need not be universal, however. A style may be adopted by one group, thus becoming a fashion for that group, even though other segments of the population ignore it. Country club fashions are rarely popular with the college crowd; business wardrobes often bear little or no relationship to those accepted by either country club or college groups.

Similarly, a style may be accepted and become a fashion in one part of the world, while it is ignored or rejected elsewhere. The igloo of the Eskimos, the thatched hut of the African tribespeople, or the ranch house of the American suburbanites are all considered fashionable—but each by its own inhabitants. In the same way, some ethnic and religious groups have unique fashions. In this country, the Amish and the Mennonites are groups whose members still can be recognized by their apparel.

Acceptance also means that a fashion must be considered appropriate to the occasion and purpose for which it is worn. Clothes considered appropriate for classroom wear by college students, for example, would not be acceptable by the same body of students for formal social events.

The group that adopts or rejects a specific style decides what is appropriate for the time, the place, and the occasion; it therefore determines what is acceptable. For example, once the accepted style for women to wear when traveling on a train or plane used to be a dress or a suit. Accessories then included a hat, gloves, and a handbag. Today, pantsuits have been accepted as both comfortable and sensible attire, and hats and gloves are rarely worn.

Men's fashions also provide many illustrations of styles considered appropriate in their day. When the term "white-collar class" was born, the collar that gave it its name was fashionably high and stiffly starched, and a man never removed his coat or tie in company. Today, fashions for men are much more relaxed, even in office wear. The stiff collar is gone. The dark, tailored suit jacket has given way to a patterned, more casual sport jacket. The white shirt is often replaced by colored or patterned shirts, some even being worn without a tie.

Regardless of the suitability of a style from any practical standpoint, however, if it is accepted by the majority of a specific group at a given time and place for a specific occasion, it is considered a fashion. Therefore, many fashions can and do exist side by side at any given period of time because of the preferences of different consumer groups and the variety of activities in which each participates.

Change

Fashion is subject to constant change, sometimes rapidly, sometimes slowly. As soon as a fashion is fully accepted, it is apt to begin to look too ordinary to some people, and they seek something different, something new. The emphasis on change, however, is neither peculiar to the fashion field nor new. More than 2,500 years ago a Greek philosopher said, "The only eternal truth in the history of the universe is change."

What is new is the speed at which fashion change takes place. There has been a marked acceleration in the rate of change in women's clothes during the past 100 years and in men's clothes since World War II.

The invention of the sewing machine and the development of man-made fibers have played important parts in this acceleration, giving designers and the garment industry faster ways of turning out garments and a much greater variety of materials to work with. For consumers, a mass-produced dress bought "off the rack" at a moderate price is much easier to discard than a hand-sewn or hand-knitted creation representing weeks or even months of work. The new fibers and fabrics encourage such discarding, too, for each new fiber or blend of fibers seems to offer more than the last.

Another major factor responsible for an accelerated rate of fashion change is modern communications. The mass media spread fashion news throughout the world in hours. Something new that an acknowledged fashion leader wore to a party one evening is pictured and described in newspapers the next day, and what is being worn by public figures is on view every time the television set is turned on. Thus even slight changes in fashion are given faster and wider publicity than ever before, and the consumers who decide they like those changes demand them from the merchants, who in turn demand them from producers.

Historically, women's apparel has always showed the most rapid change. Men's fashions have changed at a slower rate until recently. Home furnishing fashions have changed at a still slower rate, and fashions in architecture have changed still more slowly.

The Futility of Forcing Change Since fashion changes are outgrowths of changes in consumers' needs, it is seldom possible to force or hold back fashion change. Efforts to alter the course of fashion have been made from time to time, but they usually fail. Fashion is a power, a potent force, whose very definition includes its support by the majority.

A recent example occurred in the late 1960s, when designers and retailers decided that skirts had reached their limit in brevity and that women would soon be seeking change. So the designers designed and the retailers stocked and promoted the midi, which featured a midcalf-length skirt. The designers and retailers were right in theory but wrong in timing and choice of skirt length. But consumers found the midi too sudden and radical a change

Christian Dior's New Look, 1947.

Copyright © 1947 (renewed 1974) by The Condé Nast Publications Inc.

During World War II, the United States government controlled the kind and amount of fabric that could be used in consumer goods. One World War II regulation, for instance, prohibited anything but slit pockets on women's garments, to avoid using the extra material that patch pockets require. Skirts, of necessity, were short, and silhouettes were narrow, reflecting the scarcity of material.

Meeting the Demand for Change After the war, a reaction toward a freer line and a more feminine garment was to be expected. A new French designer, Christian Dior, caught and expressed this feeling in his first collection and achieved instant fashion success. Using fabric with a lavishness that had been impossible in Europe or America during the war years, he created his New Look, with long, full skirts, fitted waistlines, and feminine curves.

Dior did not change the course of fashion. He simply recognized and interpreted the deep need women felt at the time to get out of stiff, narrow, unfeminine clothes and into soft, free, feminine ones. Consumers wanted the change, and the lifting of wartime restrictions made it possible to meet their demand.

Another example of a consumer demand for change occurred in the menswear area just before World War II. Year after year, manufacturers had been turning out versions of a style that had long been popular in England, a padded-shoulder draped suit. A number of young men attending well-known Northeastern colleges—some of them from very influential families—became tired of that look. They wanted a change. They took their objections to New Haven clothing manufacturers, and the result was the natural-shoulder Ivy League suit that achieved widespread popularity for the next 15 to 20 years.

A Mirror of the Times

Fashions are molded by the force of an era. They mirror the times by reflecting how people think and live—or thought and lived. The modesty of Vic-

and did not accept or buy the style in sufficient numbers at that time to make it a fashion.

Occasionally, necessity and government regulation can interrupt the course of a fashion.

torian women was reflected in covered-up fashions with their bulk and concealment, for instance, while the sexual emancipation and equality felt by flappers of the 1920s was obvious in short skirts, short hair, and a flattened figure.

Fashions mirror the times by reflecting the values of each social level in the prevailing class structure of a given era. For example, traditional European peasant costumes reflected the fact that strong, sturdy wives were needed and admired. The characteristic puffy sleeves, laced bodices, and full skirts, which make even a slender girl look plump and sturdy, attest to this fact. European peasants wore such costumes at the same time that women of the wealthy classes had adopted fashions that emphasized delicacy.

Fashions also mirror the times by reflecting the degree of rigidity within the class structure of any era. Throughout much of history, certain apparel fashions were limited in their use to members of rigidly defined social classes. At times, sumptuary laws regulating both the type and ornateness of apparel that could be worn were enacted to achieve distinctions between various classes. At other times, certain fashions provided mute but obvious evidence of well-defined social classes. For example, during the nineteenth century the constricted waist of Western women and the bound feet of high-caste Chinese women reflected the material success and high social standing of the male head of the household. The way delicacy is emphasized in the faces, hands, and figures of women in medieval tapestries shows that the wealthy of that era maintained their women in leisure—their feminine fashions emphasized slenderness and delicacy and concealed any bulk under gracefully full skirts and sleeves.

Today, however, social classes are far less structured and increasingly mobile. As a result, many apparel fashions exist simultaneously. Anyone is free to adopt the fashions of any class with which one wishes to be associated, be it lower or higher. Those who reject current conventions in an effort to form societies of their own, establish their own modes and standards of dress, which thereby be-

An American look for fall 1975.

Morty Sussman for the Mollie Parnis Boutique

come fashions for each group. There were typical fashions that identified the beatniks and hippies of the 1960s, just as there were fashions that identified their earlier counterparts, the Bohemians of the 1920s.

Hide and Chic

(America's newest fashion game)

If you've got the "chic," we've got the "hides." So come play leather coat with us. It's no challenge to find a winner from our collection of beauties. Never before, in fact, have we had such a super collection of leather coats and jackets. Peanut-buttery suedes, sleek calfskins, split pigskins. New shapes, new lengths, new everything. Leather is so important this Fall, we can't keep it down on the country farm for another day, so we've opened a whole new shop to house them in.

Now should you think the tab is steep, we have a smashing way for you to rationalize your purchase. First of all, you never give a good leather coat away. You keep them at least ten years. So simply divide the price by ten and you'll see it costs you tops 26.00 a year to own the most beautiful coat of your life.

So wend your way to the new **Leather and Suede Shop.** Come play hide and chic at Altman's. To save you time on what to seek, take a look at all the fashion pointers right here on this page.

(We think it's so exciting, we've done our Fifth Avenue windows that way.)

softest calfskin

terra cotta

very new stow-it necker

8 to 14 sizes

new length important

the front is divine

Captain's epaulettes

Turn up collar

newest trench-boxy

fantastic detail

8 to 14 sizes

buttery suede pigskin   260.00

bitter chocolate

44" long – important!

hoodwinking hood

silk print lining

split pigskin

the shirt cuff

8 to 14 sizes

deep slip pockets

dreamy taupey   135.00

B. Altman & Co

The Leather and Suede Shop, third floor
Fifth Avenue, White Plains, Manhasset, N.Y.,
Short Hills, Ridgewood, Paramus, N.J., St. Davids, Pa.

Altman's used all four elements: silhouette, details, color, and texture, to tell its fashion story in this advertisement.
B. Altman & Co.

Fashions also mirror the times by reflecting both the type and diversity of activities in which people of an era participate. The ornate styling that dominated the apparel of both men and women associated with royal courts during most of the seventeenth and eighteenth centuries was evidence of the importance of court-centered social activities during those periods. The Industrial Revolution in the late eighteenth and early nineteenth centuries created a new working class, and men's fashions as a result became considerably less colorful and more functional.

Today, too, men's and women's wardrobes contain obvious evidence of both the type and diversity of their activities. Those with home-centered interests and activities are apt to live casually and dress functionally. The wardrobes of those who are business centered are likely to include apparel for business wear, for leisure wear, and for more formal social occasions. And active sports enthusiasts are likely to have wardrobes that include fashions considered appropriate for the sports in which they participate, such as tennis, golf, or boating.

PRINCIPLES OF FASHION

There are five fundamental principles of fashion. These do not change from season to season or from year to year. They were as valid yesterday as they are today, and they will be just as valid tomorrow.

These principles are the foundations upon which the body of knowledge about fashion is built, whether that knowledge concerns the history of fashion, how fashions disseminate, or the techniques of fashion merchandising. Therefore, these principles must be the basis of any study of fashion. Some of the five principles have already been mentioned; each will be referred to throughout this book; each is stated and explained below.

1   Consumers make fashions by their acceptance or rejection of offered styles

Contrary to what some believe, fashions are not created by designers or producers or retailers. Con-

sumers—customers—create fashion. They decide when a style no longer appeals and they choose what new style will be favored.

Designers create hundreds of new styles each season, basing their designs on what they think may attract consumers. From among those many styles, manufacturers choose what they think will be successful, discarding many more than they select. Retailers choose from the manufacturers' offerings those styles they believe their customers will want. Then consumers make the vital, really important choice. By accepting one style and rejecting another, they—and only they—dictate what styles will become fashions.

2   Fashions are not dependent upon price

The price tag on an item of apparel or an accessory does not determine whether the item is currently "in fashion." It is the look of the item and the degree of acceptance that look has achieved.

While it is true that new styles which eventually become fashionable are often introduced at high prices, this is less true than it once was. One new style may enter the fashion picture from the high-priced salon of a name designer, as the "BigDress" did in the mid-1970s. But another may come into fashion from a chain-store catalog or Army-Navy store stock, as blue jeans recently did.

In addition, even items that originally carry high price tags are quickly made available in a variety of price lines. A Paris dress style, for instance, may be introduced in a hand-sewn model with a price of over $1,000 for a custom-made copy. A few weeks later, stores may offer ready-to-wear copies of that style in a wide range of prices, even at budget prices. The fabric, trimmings, and workmanship will be different, but the style will appear essentially the same.

3   Fashions are evolutionary in nature; they are rarely revolutionary

There probably have been only two real revolutions in fashion styles throughout history, and only one occurred during the twentieth century: the Dior New Look of 1947. Fashions usually evolve gradually from one style to another. Skirt lengths go up or down an inch at a time, season after season. Suit lapels narrow or widen gradually, not suddenly.

Fashion designers both understand and accept this principle. When developing new design ideas, they always keep the currently accepted fashion look in mind. They know that few people could or would buy a whole new wardrobe every season, and that the success of their designs depends on ultimate sales. Consumers today buy apparel and accessories to supplement and update the wardrobe they already own, some of which was purchased last year, some the year before, some the year before that, and so on. In most cases, consumers will buy only if the purchase complements the wardrobe already owned and does not depart too radically from last year's purchases.

4 No amount of sales promotion can change the direction in which fashions are moving

A producer's or retailer's promotional efforts cannot dictate what consumers will buy. The few times that fashion merchants have tried to promote a radical change in fashion, they have not been successful.

For example, a strong promotional effort was used to introduce the long-skirted midi in 1969 and 1970. But consumers were not ready for so radical a change in skirt lengths, and they did not buy the midi in sufficient quantities to make it more than a fad.

In the same way, promotional effort cannot renew life in a fading fashion unless enough change is made so that the fashion has an altogether new appeal. This is why stores have special-price sales. When the sales of a particular style start slumping, stores know they must clear out as much of that stock as possible, even at much lower prices, to make room for newer styles in which consumers have indicated greater interest.

5 All fashions end in excess

This saying is sometimes attributed to Paul Poiret, a top Paris designer of the 1920s. There are many examples of its truth. Eighteenth-century hoop skirts ballooned out to 8 feet in diameter, which made even moving from room to room a complicated maneuver. Similarly, miniskirts of the 1960s finally became so short that the slightest movement caused a major problem in modesty.

Once the extreme, the excess in styling, has been reached, a fashion is nearing its end. The attraction of the fashion palls, and people begin to seek a different look, a new fashion.

REFERENCES

[1] Nystrom, *Economics of Fashion,* pp. 3–7; and *Fashion Merchandising,* pp. 33–34.
[2] Nystrom, *Economics of Fashion,* p. 7.
[3] Laver, *Taste and Fashion,* p. 202.
[4] Young, *Recurring Cycles of Fashion,* p. 92.

MERCHANDISING VOCABULARY

Define or briefly explain the following terms:

Fashion	Classic
High fashion	Fad
Mass or volume fashion	Silhouette
Style	Details
Design	Texture
Taste	

MERCHANDISING REVIEW

1. What are the three most commonly held misconceptions about fashion? Do you agree or disagree with them? Why?
2. Describe several apparel styles that are named for the period of history in which they originated.
3. Describe several apparel styles (for men, women, or children) which are in fashion today and can be considered classics.
4. Distinguish between (a) style and fashion, (b) style and design, (c) classic and fad.
5. What are the four components of all fashions? Briefly explain their interrelationships.
6. Is it possible to force an unwanted fashion on consumers? Defend your answer.
7. What factors have contributed to the acceleration of fashion apparel change during the last 100 years? In your opinion, which factors have had the greatest impact, and why?
8. In what respects do "fashions mirror the times"? Give examples to illustrate your answer.
9. What are the five basic principles relating to fashion? Discuss the implications for fashion merchants of any two of these principles.
10. Name at least three types of consumer products, other than apparel or accessories, in which you believe fashion plays a dominant role today. What fashion element(s) or component(s) are featured in each?

MERCHANDISING DIGEST

The following statements are from the text. Discuss the significance of each, citing specific examples to illustrate how each applies to the merchandising of fashion goods.

1. "Acceptance . . . means that a fashion must be considered appropriate to the occasion and purpose for which it is worn."
2. "Today color is a key factor in apparel selection for both sexes."
3. "Today, . . . many apparel fashions exist simultaneously."

2
ENVIRONMENTAL INFLUENCES ON FASHION INTEREST AND DEMAND

Just as fashion touches so many facets of living, so in turn does the environment, in which that living takes place, influence fashion. *Environment* is the sum of the conditions that surround and influence a person. Fashion develops more readily in some environments than in others. Among static and ingrown societies, the demand for fashion is slight, and its opportunities to thrive are minimal; but fashion flourishes in societies with considerable physical, economic, and social mobility.

In general, the major environmental influences on fashion interest and demand in any era are

- The degree of economic development of a country or an area
- The sociological characteristics of the class structure, its mobility, and the size of its middle class
- The psychological attitudes of consumers

ECONOMIC FACTORS

A high level of economic development is essential to the growth of fashion demand since it supplies both the means of production and the strong purchasing power needed for growth. This principle is clearly demonstrated by comparing the dress of people in economically advanced countries like the United States with the prevailing dress in less developed nations.

Quentin Bell, in *On Human Finery*,[1] underscored the relationship between economic progress and fashion by showing that economically backward countries retained national costumes long after more economically advanced nations had discarded theirs. England, which led the Western world into the Industrial Revolution, was the first country to abandon traditional national dress. Bell points out that Greece, Russia, Spain, and Persia (now Iran), which had little in common with one another except lagging economic development, retained a national costume when countries with more progressive economies, such as Germany, Belgium, Denmark, and Japan, were abandoning theirs.

In the twentieth century, the Soviet Union provides a dramatic example of how a country moving swiftly in economic development also moves ahead in fashion. In the first few decades following the 1917 Revolution, clothing was drab and utilitarian. By the mid-1950s, however, the Soviet economy had advanced to a point where it was able to place greater emphasis on production of consumer goods, and the influence of fashion, particularly in clothing, increased. Today, Soviet consumers have a fairly wide choice of apparel, in comparison with earlier years. They are able to accept or reject styles, to create or discard a fashion. In fact, at one point in the early 1970s, a government source chided Soviet consumers for being so fashion-conscious, saying that such an interest did not serve a socialistic society.

Consumer Income

Consumers living in the highly developed economy of the United States have their choice of a wide variety of goods. Most consumers also have the money with which to buy those goods.

Consumer income is measured in a variety of ways, most importantly by personal income, disposable income, and discretionary income. All these income measurements have shown sharp increases in recent years. Their relative importance, however, depends in part on what changes occur in the purchasing power of a dollar in any given period.

Personal Income   The total, or gross, amount of income received from all sources by the population as a whole is called *personal income.* It consists of wages, salaries, interest, and all other income for everyone in the country. Divide personal income by the number of people in the population, and the result is per capita personal income.

As Table 2-1 shows, over the years there has been a steady increase in personal income on a per capita basis (or on an "average per person basis"). For instance, the average income in the United States in 1950 was about $1,500. In 1973, it was $5,041, or more than three times as much.

Disposable Income   The amount a person has left to spend or save after paying taxes is called

TABLE 2-1
Personal Income and Disposable Personal Income

YEAR	PERSONAL INCOME	DISPOSABLE PERSONAL INCOME	DISPOSABLE INCOME AS % OF PERSONAL INCOME
1950	$1,501	$1,364	91
1955	1,881	1,666	89
1960	2,219	1,937	87
1965	2,773	2,436	88
1970	3,966	3,366	86
1972	4,549	3,807	85
1973	5,041	—	—

Figures are in current dollars, obtained by dividing total personal income and total disposable personal income by total population figures.

Source: U.S. Bureau of the Census.

disposable personal income. It is roughly equivalent to what an employee calls "take-home pay" and provides an approximation of the purchasing power of each consumer during any given year. Table 2-1 indicates that disposable personal income in the United States has risen steadily, but not quite as rapidly as personal income.

Discretionary Income   The money that an individual or family can spend or save after buying necessities such as food, clothing, shelter, and basic transportation is called *discretionary income.* Of course, the distinction between "necessities" and "luxuries," or between "needs" and "wants," is a subjective one.

Purchasing Power of a Dollar   While Table 2-1 shows that income has gone up each year, it does not mean that people have had an equivalent increase in purchasing power each year. Purchasing power has increased, but not nearly so much as the table might suggest. That is because the value of a dollar, its purchasing power, what it will buy, has declined.

A decline in the purchasing power of money is caused by inflation. This country, and much of the world, has been in an inflationary period for a number of years. And beginning in 1973 and 1974, inflation increased sharply. During inflation, wages usually increase, but so do taxes and prices. Thus, in an inflationary period, people may earn more money each year, but higher taxes and higher prices leave them with less disposable and discretionary income.

Table 2-1 shows that while both personal income and disposable personal income increased, the latter increased more slowly than the former. This was because taxes took a larger percentage out of the total personal income each year. In 1950, the average amount of disposable income—the income left after taxes—was 91 percent of personal income. In 1972, the average amount of disposable income was 85 percent of personal income.

Table 2-2 shows how inflation affects the prices of various products. Even though family income

TABLE 2-2
Purchasing Power: Prices and Income, 1948–1974

ITEM	PRICE IN				PERCENT CHANGE, 1948–1974
	1948	1958	1968	1974	
Ranch mink coat	$4,200	$4,000	$4,200	$4,500	+7.1
Family-sized Chevrolet	$1,255	$2,081	$2,656	$4,119	+228.2
Pair of blue jeans	$3.95	$3.75	$5.29	$11.25	+226.1
Gallon of gasoline	25.9¢	30.4¢	33.7¢	55.6¢	+114.8
Pair of men's shoes	$9.95	$11.95	$16.95	$21.95	+120.6
Year's tuition at Harvard	$455	$1,250	$2,000	$3,400	+647.3
Hospital cost per in-patient day	$13.09	$28.17	$61.38	$114.90	+777.8
Phone call, New York to Topeka, Kansas	$1.90	$1.80	$1.40	$1.25	−34.2
Pound of chicken	61.2¢	46.5¢	39.8¢	55.7¢	−9.0
Pound of round steak	90.5¢	$1.04	$1.14	$1.81	+100.1
Median family income*	$3,187	$5,087	$8,632	$12,700	+298.5

*Half the families in the country earned more, half earned less.

Source: Adapted from a table in the *New York Times*, Aug. 25, 1974.

increased nearly 300 percent between 1948 and 1974, the price of a pair of blue jeans also increased almost as much. Thus, in 1972, a person had to work almost the same number of hours to earn the price of a pair of blue jeans as in 1948. Note, however, that there is no uniformity among price changes for the various items in Table 2-2. Food prices didn't rise as rapidly as clothing prices did, but the cost of a college education and health care went up much more rapidly.

Effect on Fashion Marketing Not only the year-to-year trends but even the month-to-month trends in income and prices give fashion merchants important clues about what consumers will buy. In an inflationary period (and in a depression as well), basic necessities eat up more of the disposable income, and less discretionary income is available to consumers. The amount of discretionary income available is a vital consideration in fashion merchandising.

When money is "tight," as it is in either an inflation or a depression, those hardest hit are low-income groups, and those least affected are high-income groups; yet these two groups are small when compared with middle-income groups. A fashion merchant's greatest concern is how middle-income groups will react to any economic squeeze, because middle-income groups make up the biggest and most important market for fashion goods.

When money is tight, some middle-income groups react by buying less. A man who had planned to buy a new coat and a new suit may settle for the suit and put off purchasing the coat for another year. Some react by buying more conservative styles. A woman who was thinking of getting a velvet pantsuit that she could wear only occasionally may decide to buy a dress in a classic style, reasoning that the dress will have a longer life as an acceptable style and be more suitable for a greater variety of occasions. Some react by seeking lower prices. Steady customers of the better specialty stores may begin to visit them only when special-price sales are being held and may investigate the more moderately priced department stores and discount stores.

Thus, while income and price tables may seem dull, they are important guides for a fashion merchant. Merchants who watch the trends and customers' reactions can adjust stock to meet customers' changing needs and wants. Merchants who ignore them may find themselves with too much stock in relation to sales, with the inevitable result of higher markdowns and lower profit.

Population

The majority of the population of the United States has some discretionary income and thus can influence the course of fashion. Two factors relating to population, however, have an important bearing on the extent of fashion demand.

The first important population factor is the size of the total population and the rate of its growth. The size of the population relates to the extent of current fashion demand, while the rate of its growth suggests what tomorrow's market may be.

The second important factor is the age-mix of the population, and its projection into the future, which determines some characteristics of current fashion demand and suggests what they may be like in the future.

Size of Population In 1915, the United States had a population of about 100 million people. Fifty years later, the population had almost doubled. Estimates for the year 2000, or 85 years after the 100-million mark was reached, range from a conservative 250 million to an impressive 300 million.

While the birthrate in this country has dropped sharply in recent years, the population is growing and is expected to continue to grow. Barring significant downturns in the economy and reversal of present trends in consumer income, there should be an ever-increasing number of consumers with the money to spend on fashion.

Age-mix The rate of growth, however, is not the same for all age groups within the population, nor is it identical for both sexes (see Table 2-3). Variations in the age-mix both today and tomorrow are important clues to fashion demand because not all age groups are equally enthusiastic consumers of fashion. In addition, each age group has its own fashion interests.

A group to watch is the 15-to-24 year olds. Although not as large as most other age groups at this time, it is the one most responsive to change and most eager for the new. It is also an age group, particularly among its younger members, with fewer

TABLE 2-3
Estimates and Projections of the Population of the United States: 1970, 1980, 1990, 2000 (in thousands)

	1970	1980	1990	2000
Males				
Under 14 years	29,841	28,194	33,431	34,096
15 to 24 years	18,451	20,950	18,176	22,214
25 to 44 years	23,826	30,989	39,418	39,223
45 to 64 years	20,053	20,557	21,346	28,081
65 and older	8,450	9,710	11,081	11,503
Total	100,621	110,400	123,452	135,117
Females				
Under 14 years	28,374	27,047	32,018	32,642
15 to 24 years	18,042	20,338	17,603	21,437
25 to 44 years	24,586	31,345	39,274	38,858
45 to 64 years	21,885	22,932	23,629	30,158
65 and older	11,727	14,343	16,687	17,338
Total	104,614	116,005	129,211	140,433
Median Age	28.0	29.3	31.3	32.5

Source: U.S. Bureau of the Census.

restrictions imposed on its spending because of family responsibilities or on its choice of styles because of figure problems. New fashions thrive among these consumers, and when their numbers increase, fashion change is likely to accelerate.

Senior citizens, or the over-65 group, represent a growing and increasingly influential age group. Earlier retirement, longer life expectancy, and increased retirement income place today's senior citizen in an increasingly important position to affect fashion. Although not as large and powerful a group as younger consumers, the senior citizens' ideas about fashion warrant careful consideration by designers and marketers alike.

Technological Advances

Without competition, we would be clinging to the clumsy and antiquated processes of farming

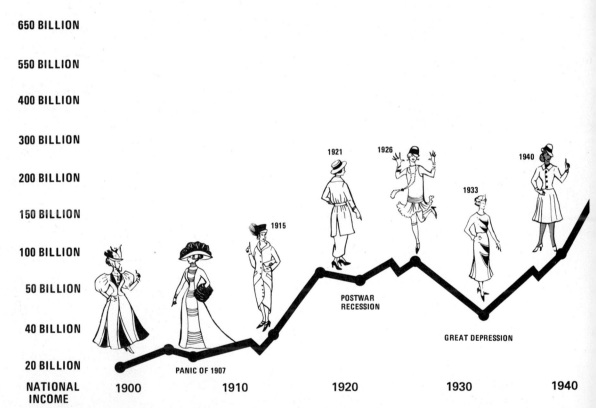

650 BILLION

550 BILLION

400 BILLION

300 BILLION

200 BILLION

150 BILLION

100 BILLION

50 BILLION

40 BILLION

20 BILLION

NATIONAL INCOME

1900   1910   1920   1930   1940

PANIC OF 1907

1915

1921

POSTWAR RECESSION

1926

1933

GREAT DEPRESSION

1940

Skirt lengths have tended to reflect the state of the economy, rising in good times and falling in bad times.

The H. W. Gossard Co.

and manufacture and the methods of business of long ago, and the twentieth would be no further advanced than the eighteenth century.

So said President William McKinley at the beginning of the twentieth century.

In few if any countries has business competition grown as rapidly and been as keen as in the United States. The competition has fostered many technological advances, many of which have had impact on the fashion field. Technological advances have increased the demand for new fashions because of the increase in both variety and availability of new products.

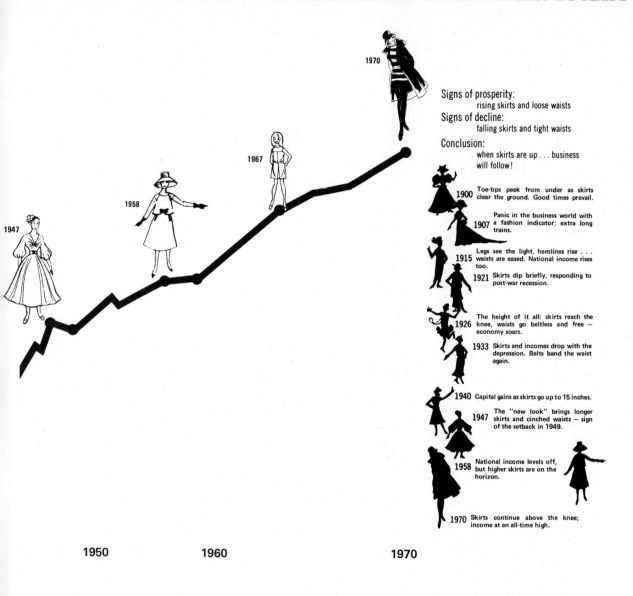

Signs of prosperity:
rising skirts and loose waists
Signs of decline:
falling skirts and tight waists
Conclusion:
when skirts are up . . . business
will follow!

1900 Toe-tips peek from under as skirts clear the ground. Good times prevail.

1907 Panic in the business world with a fashion indicator; extra long trains.

1915 Legs see the light, hemlines rise . . . waists are eased. National income rises too.

1921 Skirts dip briefly, responding to post-war recession.

1926 The height of it all: skirts reach the knee, waists go beltless and free — economy soars.

1933 Skirts and incomes drop with the depression. Belts band the waist again.

1940 Capital gains as skirts go up to 15 inches.

1947 The "new look" brings longer skirts and cinched waists — sign of the setback in 1949.

1958 National income levels off, but higher skirts are on the horizon.

1970 Skirts continue above the knee; income at an all-time high.

1950   1960   1970

Manufacturing Equipment and Processes
Improved spinning and weaving machines helped start the entire Industrial Revolution. Within the fashion industry, the mechanical sewing machine was the next advance, in the mid-1800s. Today, almost every phase of fabric and apparel manufacture is mechanized, sometimes automated.

Modern sewing machines are powered and operate at high speeds; some specialized machines can produce 5,000 to 6,000 stitches a minute. There are high-speed knitting machines. Embroidery machines can be programmed to stitch different patterns at a turn of a dial and can produce the design on many pieces of cloth at one time.

Hems can be power-stitched at high speed or even "welded" by ultrasonic waves. There are bonding machines for welding two thicknesses of cloth; some can also weld fibers into new types of nonwoven fabrics that are more supple and delicate than felt, the original nonwoven fabric.

New processes have burgeoned, too. These include ways to make and use a wide variety of man-made fibers, separately or in blends. The industry also is producing blends of man-made and natural fibers for improved quality, appearance, and performance.

The development of new ways for treating fabrics has made possible many fashions that could not have been introduced in the past. Bright colors were more readily accepted when they became resistant to fading from sun, rain, and laundry soaps. Pleats became more popular when they were treated to retain their crease through many washings. Bulky fashions met lessened resistance when the bulk was achieved without weight. High boots became practical for indoor wear when they could be made from supple, easily cleaned vinyl.

Agriculture   Agricultural developments have affected the fashion field most strongly in the areas of cotton, wool, fur, and leather. In general, improved agricultural techniques have resulted in more and better quality products.

Improved seed strains and better control of insect pests and plant diseases have helped increase the amount of cotton grown on an acre, as well as its quality. Mechanized equipment helps farmers plant the crop, tend it, and harvest it more efficiently and with less labor. Scientific breeding has produced sheep that yield increasingly better grades of wool. It also has increased the amount of wool that can be clipped from each animal. Improved methods of fur farming and ranching have contributed to better pelts and hides for the fur and leather industries.

Communications   Yesterday, when communication was slower, fashion change was necessarily slower. Word of "what they are wearing" often took months to travel from one part of the country to another, and fashion trends moved at as leisurely a pace as the news. Today communication is not only infinitely faster, but there are immense quantities and many varieties of it.

Television has become an important medium for transmitting fashion information, for the apparel worn by well-known personalities on network shows has a demonstrated fashion impact. The clothes of actors and actresses, of notables and other people seen in commercials and on news programs, also have impact. Fashion information is transmitted, too, through televised fashion shows and through advertisements.

Radio still does its share, too, because it is an excellent medium for a merchant to tell a local audience about a special fashion event.

Transportation   Improved trucks, superhighways, faster rail service, and the growth of the air-freight business all bring the producer of fashion goods and the stores that sell those goods much closer together. Instead of taking weeks, the transportation of goods from vendor to store now takes days—sometimes only hours, if the speed is worth the cost. Consolidated shipping, where two or more shippers put together a truckload or carload, helps get merchandise to the stores more quickly, and reduces transportation costs slightly.

Developments in transportation have also influenced fashion. The earliest automobiles created a need for dusters, veils, and gauntlets. This influence is still apparent today: Sports cars and motorcycles encourage the wearing of pantsuits, scarfs, and short or divided skirts. Air travel, which makes any part of the world and any climate accessible in only a matter of hours, sets up a demand for travel and vacation clothes far more varied and versatile than those needed when a vacation meant a trip to a nearby beach or lake.

SOCIOLOGICAL FACTORS

To understand fashion, it is necessary to understand the sociological background against which fashion trends develop, live, and die. Fashion itself is a social phenomenon that reflects what Cecil Beaton called "the same continuum of change that rides through any given age."[2] Changes in fashion, he emphasized, "correspond with the subtle and often hidden network of forces that operate on society. . . . In this sense, fashion is a symbol."[3]

Thus changes in the social patterns of the times cause changes in the attitudes of consumers, which in turn cause changes in fashion.

Leisure Time

An average citizen in the United States today has far more leisure time than a citizen a half-century ago. In addition to paid holidays, paid vacations, and early retirement, the workweek has been steadily shrinking and apparently will continue to do so.

At the turn of the century, workers put in from 10 to 12 hours a day, six days a week. By 1970, the typical office workweek was 35 hours, the typical factory workweek was 40 hours, and both were based on a five-day week. In the early 1970s, some industries were already experimenting with a four-day week.

Shortening the workweek has given people more time for recreation, travel, self-improvement, or even a second job. Increased leisure has initiated many changes in values, in standards of living, and in scope of activities. Whole new markets have opened up as a result of these changes. New and diverse activities, resulting from the availability of more leisure time, have led to a demand for larger and more varied wardrobes.

Casual Living In fashion, the impact of greater leisure time is most clearly indicated by the growth of interest in sportswear or casual clothes. Sportswear has become an important part of that larger and more varied wardrobe.

Sports clothes were on the fashion scene even in the early 1900s, although the clothes that women wore then for tennis or golf were quite similar to what was later considered ordinary streetwear. By the 1920s many people had leisure time for active

sports or to loll in the sun, and they wanted appropriate apparel that permitted greater freedom of movement.

Today's casual apparel did not reach full acceptance until the 1950s, when the great trek to the suburbs was in full swing. Casual wear bloomed in the suburbs, but rapidly spread to the cities. It became commonplace, rather than shocking, to see women wearing slacks on city streets. This eventually led to the acceptance of pantsuits as almost all-occasion wear.

Retirement Leisure Leisure of a somewhat different type is enjoyed by a special segment of the population. This is the leisure of retired people, whose numbers are increasing rapidly. Because of medical advances, pensions, and intelligent planning, those who have retired from full-time jobs now have both the life expectancy and the means to afford a wide range of interests and activities. Instead of spending their retirement years quietly at home, many modern people are healthy enough and interested enough to take up second or even third careers, to involve themselves in charitable and civic affairs, to travel, to buy new homes, or to take up new studies.

These people introduce a new element into the impact that leisure time is having on fashion demand. They want apparel that both suits their ages and figures and is appropriate for their new interests and activities.

Status of Minority Groups

A major sociological change in recent years has occurred in the status of nonwhite groups. Blacks and other non-Caucasians, including Mexican-Americans, American Indians, Orientals, and Puerto Ricans, account for approximately one-eighth of the country's population today, according to figures from the Bureau of the Census.

Until the late 1950s, more than half the population of these groups earned incomes below the poverty mark, a much larger percentage than in the

Increased leisure time has expanded markets for sportswear and vacation wear.

Left: Bermuda News Bureau
Top: The McCall Pattern Company

African influences on American headwear.
Ashanti Bazaar

white group. Their purchases were dictated by need, not choice; their interest in and influence on fashion were almost nil. They dressed as Caucasians did and tried to achieve the look of the dominant, successful white group.

Since then, however, new laws and dedicated work on the part of many groups and individuals have brought more education, better jobs, and new pride to these groups. In addition, they have increasingly more money to spend.

Fashion has reflected the change, particularly among the black group. Afro hairstyles were widely adopted among black men and women; black self-awareness was expressed in men's clothes patterned after native African dress, and women's clothes were either made of or inspired by African fabrics. New cosmetics for blacks appeared on the market, designed to emphasize rather than camouflage the beauty of dark coloring.

Some fashion ideas began to cross ethnic lines. Many white people found the traditional African styles, fabrics, and patterns captivating and fresh. Others, mainly the long-haired young, adopted the

American Indian's headband and jewelry. These are interesting reversals of the situation that prevailed when for many years white culture alone set the fashion.

Wars and Disasters

Wars and widespread disasters shake people's lives and focus attention on ideas, events, and places that may be utterly new. Because of changes in their lives resulting from war or disaster, people develop a need for fashions that are compatible with their altered attitudes and environments.

This process is most obvious in changes that took place in this century in women's activities and in fashions as a result of the two world wars. World War I brought women into the business world in significant numbers, whetted their appetites for independence and suffrage, and gave them reason to welcome styles that restricted physical movement less. World War II drew women into such traditionally masculine jobs as riveting, for which they had previously not been considered strong enough;

it put them into war plants on night shifts; it even brought women other than nurses into the military services for the first time in the country's history. All these changes encouraged and gave rise to the adoption by many women of fashions previously considered appropriate only for men, such as slacks, sport shirts, and jeans.

The Depression of the 1930s, however, was a widespread disaster with a different effect on fashions. Because jobs were scarce, considerably fewer were offered to women. They went back into the home and adopted more feminine clothes. And because money was also scarce during the Depression, wardrobes became skimpier; often a single style was made to serve a large number of social occasions.

Status of Women

The status, interests, and activities of women in the United States have changed profoundly since the beginning of the twentieth century. These changes have had their effect not only on fashion but on the entire field of marketing. In some ways, it could be said that women have gained some of the goals that the minority groups are now in the process of gaining.

It is almost impossible for a modern woman—accustomed to making her own decisions, managing her own money, and deciding what fashions she is going to accept—to put herself in the place of a woman at the turn of the century. In those days, she could not vote, or serve on a jury, or earn a living in other than a very few kinds of occupations. Her husband or father controlled the purse strings, and she dressed to please him and reflect his status. All that has changed. And today's women's movement is bringing about even more changes.

Jobs and Money Today, more women than ever before are working in almost every kind of job imaginable. Because these women spend a large part of each day away from home, their interest in fashion has accelerated. A woman at work, particularly in a white-collar occupation, is susceptible to fashion influences. She meets people. She

sees and is seen. She is able to shop, with cash or charge plate, during her lunch hour and on her way home. The incentive, the opportunity, and the means to respond to the appeal of fashion are all present.

In addition, women today have money of their own, earned or unearned, and the freedom to spend it. In 1970, approximately three women in every five, among those 14 years of age and older, had incomes of their own. With more women employed outside the home and more money to spend, their acceptance or rejection of offered styles takes on new fashion significance.

Education "Fashion is custom in the guise of departure from custom," says Sapir.[4] He considers fashion a resolution of conflict between people's revolt against adherence to custom and their reluctance to appear lacking in good taste. A major factor favoring fashion change, according to Sapir, is education.

Women of today are receiving more education than ever before, a factor that has definite repercussions on fashion. Education gives women wider exposure to other cultures and people of different backgrounds than their mothers or grandmothers had. All of this is reflected in their willingness to try new fashions more readily, thus accelerating fashion change.

Social Freedom Most marked, perhaps, of all the differences in the status of women since the early 1900s is the degree of social freedom they now enjoy. Young women today are free to apply for a job, to earn and spend or save their own money. They are free to go unescorted to a restaurant, theater, or other public place. Women travel more frequently, to more distant locations, at a younger age, often alone. If they can afford it, they may maintain an apartment or share one with others. They are free to come and go, frequently in their own cars.

Short skirts, like those in the 1920s, the early 1940s, and again in the 1960s, are commonly interpreted as a reflection of women's freedom. So, too, is the simplicity of the styles that prevailed in these periods: chemises, sacks, tents, shifts, and other variations of loose-hanging dresses—and, now, slacks and pantsuits.

Conjecture and proof, however, do not always go hand in hand on this point. One can theorize that stiff, unyielding corsets went out with a stiff, unyielding moral code—or that they were replaced, with no special significance, by more flexible materials that could mold the figure without discomfort. One can theorize that slacks and pantsuits are expressions of women's freedom—or that these same garments have become fashionable because they are suitable for hopping in and out of the indispensable automobile.

On one point, however, the relationship between fashion and women's "place" seems clear and firm: With ever greater activities, women eagerly accept fashions that grant them freedom of movement. Crinolines, hobble skirts, and corsets of the "iron maiden" variety are clearly not compatible with the on-the-go lifestyles of modern women.

Social Mobility

There are classes within almost all societies, and individuals choose either to stand out from or to conform to their actual or aspired-to class. Quentin Bell sees the mainspring of fashion in the process "whereby members of one class imitate those of another, who, in their turn, are driven to ever new expedients of fashionable change." [5]

Bell considers the history of fashion inexplicable without social classes. He is not alone in his thinking. Other sociologists relate fashion change to changes in social mobility and to the effort to associate with a higher class by imitation.

Social Fluidity The United States is sometimes called a classless society, but this description is valid only in that there are no hereditary ranks, royalty, or untouchables. Classes do exist, but they are based largely upon occupation, income, education, or avocation, and their boundaries are becoming increasingly fluid.

Fashion can help cross class lines. Ski enthusiasts illustrate this point. There are active ski fash-

ions and après-ski clothes within the reach of every income, and when once donned, only the choice of a ski area is likely to distinguish one class group from another. Concentration is on the sport itself and the social life surrounding that sport.

Middle-class Growth Most fashion authorities agree there is a direct relationship between the growth and strength of the middle class and the growth and strength of fashion demand. The middle class has the highest physical, social, and financial mobility. The middle class, because it is the largest class, has the majority vote in the adoption of fashions. Members of the middle class tend to be followers, not leaders, of fashion; but the strength of their following pumps money into the fashion industry, and the persistence of their following often spurs the fashion leaders to seek still newer and more different fashions of their own.

The United States has such a middle class, with both fashion interest and the money to indulge it. The size of that middle class is very large and, as a proportion of the total population, is growing, thanks to the determination of this country to bring all its population up to a reasonable standard of living. That growth means a widespread increase in consumer buying power, which in turn generates increased fashion demand.

Physical Mobility

Physical mobility, like social mobility, encourages the demand for and response to fashion. One effect of travel is "cross-pollenization" of cultures. After seeing how other people live, travelers bring home a desire to adopt or adapt some of what they observed and make it part of their environment.

Thus Marco Polo brought gunpowder, silks, and spices from the Orient, introducing new products to medieval Europe. Much later, travelers brought touches of Asian and African fashions to Western dress and home furnishings. Later still, Latin American and pre-Columbian influences were introduced into North America, thereby dramatically changing fashion's direction and emphasis in this country.

In the United States, people enjoy physical mobility of several kinds. There is life on wheels, for example, the daily routine for so many people. Both those who drive to work, often in a different city, and those who drive to a shopping center are exposed to a broad range of influences during their daily trips. Among these influences is the opportunity to observe the fashions of others and the fashion offerings of retail distributors.

A second form of physical mobility popular among Americans is vacation travel, which takes people to a nearby lake or around the world. Not only does each trip expose travelers to many different fashion influences, but the trip itself demands special fashions. Those who live out of suitcases for a while, whether for a few days or a few months, want clothes that are easy to pack, wrinkle-resistant, suitable for a variety of occasions, and easy to keep in order.

A third form of physical mobility is change of residence, which, like travel, exposes an individual to new contacts, new environments, and new fashion influences. According to annual statistics of the Bureau of the Census, about one person out of five changes residence in any given year. This has been the statistical pattern since 1948, when the first such study was made. Among those who move, nearly 20 percent go to a different county within the same state, and another 20 percent move to a different state. These people bring some old fashion ideas to their new residences, and they adopt or reject some of the new fashions they find in the new locations.

PSYCHOLOGICAL FACTORS

Many psychological factors influence fashion demand. "Fashion promises many things to many people," says economist Dr. Rachel Dardis. "It can be and is used to attract others, to indicate success, both social and economic, to indicate leadership, and to identify with a particular social group. . . ."[6] Prevailing psychological attitudes also have an important bearing on the extent of fashion interest at any time.

Basic Psychological Factors

Perhaps the most basic psychological factors relating to human nature that influence fashion demand are boredom, curiosity, reaction to convention, need for self-assurance, and desire for companionship.[7] These factors are responsible for a large share of people's basic actions and reactions.

Boredom It is a human tendency to become bored with fashions too long in use, and boredom leads to restlessness. Garments that have been worn throughout a season have tired both the eye and the sense of touch of the wearer. The comments heard toward the end of any season illustrate that: "I can't wait to get out of these wools." "I'm tired of that heavy coat." "My clothes simply seem stale."

Boredom and its resulting restlessness are particularly noticeable in the case of strong colors, dramatic accessories, and outstanding designs. The color, the style, the design begin to grate on both the eyes and the nerves of the wearer. That is why classics, styles that remain popular, are seldom extreme in design or color; their appeal is pleasant and satisfying but muted and undemanding.

Boredom sets in particularly quickly among people who have a concentrated interest in fashion and fashion-dominated products, whether these are clothes, home furnishings, or other articles. As soon as a product loses its first luster and excitement, when something newer appears on the market, these people become bored with what they have and restless to have something new and different.

When boredom and restlessness are felt, people seek change. In fashion, the desire for change expresses itself in a demand for something new and satisfyingly different from what one already has. Boredom and restlessness, therefore, feed fashion demand.

Curiosity Curiosity is like boredom in that it creates restlessness and encourages change for its own sake. Many people like to experiment. They want to know what is around the next corner, what oil and water really will do when poured together, and what a garment will look like if its line were changed or certain details added. Curiosity and the need to experiment permeate fashion demand.

Hector Escobosa, former head of the fashionable specialty store I. Magnin's, once described fashion as a "constantly evolving tide, seldom capricious, and generally orderly in its constant evolution." He said that fashion "feeds on new designs, and new designs are created by a dynamic compulsion that keeps creators constantly experimenting, striving for something newer, more exciting, more beautiful." [8]

Curiosity, the desire for new sensations and the spirit of adventure that leads to experimenting, is a psychological motive that sometimes conflicts with generally accepted ideas of what is beautiful and harmonious. Thus the desire to break away from what has been customary and to try something new in order to appease one's curiosity sometimes encourages adoption of fashion styles that are not in accordance with currently popular principles of art. If the new becomes accepted, then it becomes true fashion. If it flames and then dies away, its only fashion significance is as a fad.

Individuals with highly developed senses of curiosity often find satisfaction in launching new fashions. These are the women and men who are quick to experiment with styles and color combinations in apparel, with new accessories and new ways to wear them.

There is some streak of curiosity in everyone. Some may respond less dramatically than others to its proddings, but curiosity is there, and it keeps fashion demand alive.

Reaction to Convention One of the most basic psychological factors influencing fashion demand is the manner in which people react to convention. Their reactions take one of two forms: rebellion against convention, or adherence to it.

Rebellion against convention is characteristic of young people. This involves more than boredom or curiosity; it is a positive rejection of what exists and a search for something new.

Generally, young people from 15 to 24 are the most rebellious, the group that finds adjustment to custom most difficult. One manifestation of youth's rebellion is the rejection of fashions worn by one's parents. Clothing styles popular among young people are often radically different from those worn by older groups.

By the age of 25, most people tend to settle down, to accept the responsibilities of family and career, and to make whatever compromises with custom may be necessary. As they mature, those who once rebelled often become the adherents to custom and convention.

While rebellion creates new fashions, adherence to convention builds strength in current fashions. For instance, the wearing of slacks by women as ordinary streetwear began to be accepted by young women in the mid-1960s. At that time, a majority of people did not consider pants proper streetwear for women. Yet their acceptance continued to grow. By the late 1960s and early 1970s, slacks and pantsuits were being worn by women of all ages and classes for many different occasions. They thus became conventional, and their wide acceptance built up a stronger demand for the style than the youth market alone could have built.

Acceptance by the majority, remember, is an important part of the definition of fashion. The majority tend to adhere to convention, either within their own group or class or in general. If a new style adopted by a few does not grow in acceptance, it remains, at best, a fad. It has to win the approval of the majority of a group to become a true fashion. And if it wins enough support as well as conventional acceptance for a long enough time, it is on its way to becoming a classic fashion.

Self-Assurance The need for self-assurance, or confidence, is the human desire that gives fashion demand one of its strongest thrusts. Often it is based on the need to overcome feelings of inferiority or of disappointment. And often these needs can be satisfied through apparel. People who consider themselves to be well and fashionably dressed have an armor that gives them protection and self-assurance. Those who know that their clothes are dated are at a psychological disadvantage.

Change in dress often helps to create an illusion of change in personality, a way to overcome feelings of inferiority or of disappointment. The homemakers or workers who change into after-five apparel lay aside their everyday personalities and are transformed in their own eyes into more glamorous individuals.

Women are believed to have more need for the reassurance that fashion provides than men are. A highly successful marketer of cosmetics credited his spectacular rise to his recognition of this element in the feminine character. "We don't sell cosmetics," he said, "we sell hope." And the need for hope, he explained, grows out of woman's perennial need for assurance, for recognition. Cosmetics, as this producer advertises them, provide that assurance.

Companionship The desire for companionship is fundamental in human beings. The instinct for survival of the species drives an individual to seek a mate, who is one kind of companion, and the gregarious nature of humans encourages them also to seek other companions. Fashion plays its part in all human seekings for companionship.

Fashion certainly plays a part when men or women want to attract each other. Women then dress to please and interest a man, and men dress to impress and interest a woman. Both carefully choose fashions that emphasize what they consider their best points and play down what they consider their faults. The care and concentration with which a woman dresses to go to meet the man of her choice, or a man dresses to go to meet the woman of his choice, are proof of this.

Companionship, however, has broader meanings. In its broader sense, it implies the formation of groups, each of which requires conformity of its members in dress as in other respects. College campuses are a good example, for each campus has its own approved mode of dress for students, determined by the undergraduate influentials. Within the framework of college dress, which is generally quite informal, one campus may favor slacks for women, another shorts, and still another skirts.

In the business world, companionship often expresses itself by the acceptance within a particular field of work of a particular style of dress. In the late 1950s and the very early 1960s, the gray flannel suit was so widely worn by young executives in advertising and related fields that the phrase "gray flannel suit" identified the young man on his way up in one of these fields. In the mid-1960s, however, nonconformity became an important distinguishing mark for creative people, both in advertising and in other fields, and art directors and copy chiefs of advertising agencies seemed to vie with each other in wearing unusual and colorful working costumes.

Flamboyant or subdued, the mode of dress can be a bid for companionship as well as the symbol of acceptance within a particular group.

General Psychological Attitudes

The general psychological attitudes of consumers also exert an important influence on both fashion interest and fashion demand. When the economy is developing at a rapid rate, with incomes rising, population increasing, and technological advances accelerating, most consumers are optimistic about the future and tend to spend more freely. They are less concerned about the utilitarian nature of goods, and they buy more on the basis of "want" than of "need." Thus fashion interest and demand run high, and fashion change accelerates.

In periods of economic uncertainty, however, when taxes and bank interest rates are high, when incomes increase more slowly than do prices, when unemployment escalates and productivity declines, consumers then become pessimistic about the future and tend to spend less freely. Under these conditions, they are more likely to be concerned with the utilitarian or lasting qualities of goods they buy, and they buy more on the basis of "need" than of "want." As a result, fashion interest and demand lag, and fashions change at a slower pace.

War negatively affects fashion interest and demand. It diverts the production of many consumer goods into the production of war-related goods, thus reducing or limiting the availability of many fashion goods. Consumer interest and attention become more centered on war-related activities, on national interests rather than on individual desires or wants. Civilian apparel takes on the styling of service uniforms. Red, a symbol of blood and patriotism, becomes a favored color. Discretionary income is invested in war bonds instead of new apparel and home furnishings.

As mentioned before, periods of inflation also have their psychological effect. With prices of all goods increasing much more rapidly than wages and salaries, consumers tend to buy more on the basis of "need" than "want," thus depressing fashion interest, fashion demand, and fashion's rate of change.

REFERENCES

[1] Bell, *On Human Finery,* p. 72.
[2] Beaton, *The Glass of Fashion,* p. 335.
[3] Ibid., pp. 379–381.
[4] Sapir, *Fashion,* p. 140.
[5] Bell, op. cit., p. 72.
[6] Dardis, *The Power of Fashion,* pp. 16–17.
[7] Nystrom, *Economics of Fashion,* pp. 66–81.
[8] Escobosa, "Heartbeat of Retailing," *Readings in Modern Retailing,* p. 390.

MERCHANDISING VOCABULARY

Define or briefly explain the following terms:

Environment   Disposable personal income
Personal income   Discretionary income

MERCHANDISING REVIEW

1. What are the three major environmental influences on fashion interest and demand in any era?
2. How does the size and age-mix of a population affect fashion demand?
3. How have technological advances in agriculture affected fashion products?
4. How has the changing status of minority groups affected fashion interest and demand?
5. In what ways does a higher level of education affect fashion interest and demand?
6. What is meant by the term "social mobility"? How does the degree of social mobility affect fashion interest and demand? Give examples to illustrate your answer.
7. Why is it more difficult to identify classes in this country's social structure than it is in many other countries? Upon what factors are classes in the United States largely based?

8. Name three kinds of physical mobility that people in this country enjoy today. How does each influence fashion demand?

9. Name the five basic psychological factors relating to human nature that influence fashion demand. How does each affect fashion interest and demand?

10. How do consumers' psychological attitudes at any particular time influence fashion interest and demand?

MERCHANDISING DIGEST

1. Discuss how technological advances in the following areas have affected fashion interest and the rate of fashion change: (a) manufacturing equipment and processes, (b) communications, (c) transportation.

2. The text states that "changes in the social patterns of the times cause changes in the attitudes of consumers, which in turn cause changes in fashion." Discuss how the following have brought about changes in fashion demand: (a) increased leisure time, (b) increased employment of women outside the home, (c) wars and disasters.

3. In what ways has the status of women significantly changed in the twentieth century? How has each of these changes affected fashion interest and demand?

3
THE MOVEMENT OF FASHION

Fashion is constantly in motion. Its movements may be rapid and obvious or slow and barely discernible, depending on the social, political, and economic environment. The movements, however, have both meaning and definite direction. From designer to consumer, everyone involved with fashion is concerned with interpreting those movements and estimating their speed and direction.

Textile producers are concerned. They have to decide which designs, textures, and colors to offer each season 12 to 18 months before they show their lines to manufacturers. Apparel manufacturers are concerned. They have to decide which styles to include in a seasonal line, as well as which fabrics to use in producing those styles, three to nine months before showing that line to buyers. Retail buyers are concerned. They have to select from manufacturers' lines two to six months before the goods will be on the sales floor. Most consumers are concerned. Unless they have an unlimited wardrobe budget, they will be looking for fashions that will serve more than one purpose and last more than one season. For example, in shopping for a winter coat, they will want to make sure that it can be worn for several years and for different kinds of occasions and still be considered fashionable.

THE CYCLING OF FASHION

All fashions move in cycles. The term *fashion cycle* refers to the rise, widespread popularity, and then decline in acceptance of a style. Although the word "cycle" suggests a circle, in fashion usage it is represented by a bell-shaped curve (see Graph 3-1). Some authorities compare the fashion cycle to a wave: first a slow swell, then a crest, and finally a swift fall.

Unlike waves, however, fashion cycles do not follow each other in regular, measured order. Some take a short time to crest; others take a long time. The length of the cycle from swell to fall may be short or long. And, again unlike waves, fashion cycles overlap.

Stages of the Fashion Cycle

Fashion cycles are best understood by concentrating on the evolution of a style and learning to recognize each stage of its development. There is an orderliness about this development that permits it to be traced and even predicted, on a short-range basis at least, with considerable accuracy. This forward movement of a fashion cycle passes through five stages:

- Introduction
- Rise
- Culmination
- Decline
- Obsolescence

These stages parallel, to some extent, the timetable suggested by Laver (see Chapter 1). A style that Laver would term in its "shameless" or "outré" period would be in the introductory and

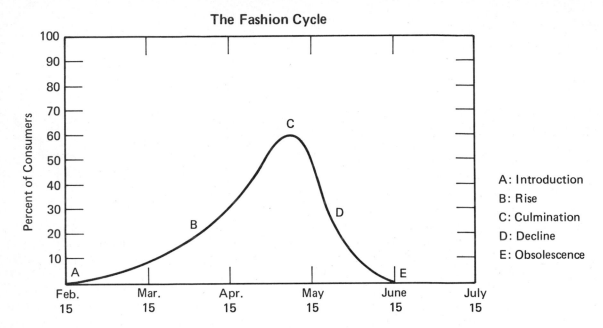

The Fashion Cycle

A: Introduction
B: Rise
C: Culmination
D: Decline
E: Obsolescence

early rise stages of its cycle. It is considered "smart" when it achieves its culmination. As the fashion goes into decline and obsolescence, it passes through the "dowdy," "hideous," and "ridiculous" stages as identified by Laver.

Introduction When a producer offers a new style, color, or texture for consumer approval, a potential fashion is introduced. The new style may be a squared-toe shoe when points prevail, for instance, or a full skirt when most are straight, or white and black in the midst of a color orgy.

Today most new designs are introduced in higher-priced merchandise. Mass production and its resultant savings are not possible at this stage; therefore, production costs are high. Allowance must also be made for the risks entailed. There is always some possibility of failure when a producer or seller is experimenting with a new style; therefore, prices must be high enough on those styles that are sold to cover losses on those that are not. Furthermore, people who are quick to embrace the new often patronize only the more expensive stores. They would be unlikely to seek new fashions in a bargain-basement atmosphere.

Rise The acceptance of either the original design or its adaptations by an increasing number of consumers is referred to as its *rise*. Prices in this phase are lower generally than at the introductory stage because production is now on a larger scale. There are also adaptations or exact copies of an original style, made of less expensive materials, and employing less meticulous workmanship.

For example, a wealthy woman may pay over $1,000 for an "original" dress from a Paris couture house. The style she chooses is made to her measurements, often from fabric unavailable elsewhere, and stitched throughout by hand. Meantime, an American ready-to-wear manufacturer may produce *line-for-line copies* of that style. These are exact duplicates of the original style, using less expensive materials, machine stitching, and standard size measurements. The copy may sell for $200 to $300, or even below $100.

Finally, *adaptations* appear. These are designs that reflect the dominant features of the style that inspired them but make no pretense of being exact copies. A broad or narrow shoulder, a full or slim skirt or sleeve, a cinched or eased waist, a bright or subdued color, a smooth or rough texture—any or all of the distinguishing features of the original may be used in adaptations.

Culmination That period when a fashion is at the height of its popularity and use is known as the *culmination* or *plateau*, of its cycle. The fashion then is in such demand that it can be mass produced, mass distributed, and sold at prices within the reach of most consumers. This stage may be long or brief, depending upon how long the peak in popularity lasts. The miniskirts that became a uniform for young women during the 1960s was an example of such a culmination. Just about everyone who wanted the style owned one or more versions of it.

The culmination stage of a fashion may be extended in two ways: (1) If a fashion becomes accepted as a classic, it settles into a fairly steady pattern of sales. (2) If new details of design, color, or texture are continually introduced, interest in the fashion may be kept alive longer. An example is pantyhose; both sales and interest have been maintained by the introduction of seamless pantyhose, support styles, and many variations in weight, construction, and color.

Decline The decrease in consumer demand, because of boredom resulting from widespread use of a fashion, as stated in Chapter 1, is referred to as the *decline*. One principle of fashion is that all fashions end in excess. The reverse of this statement is also true: Excess ends all fashions.

When a fashion's decline sets in, consumers may still be wearing it, but they are no longer willing to buy it at regular prices. They are now experimenting with other styles that are still in the earlier stages of their cycles. Stores that lead the fashion parade abandon the style; more traditional stores mark down their existing stock to make room for newer goods; bargain stores still offer it, but at prices well below those that prevailed during the style's culmination stage. Production of the particular style has stopped or is coming to a halt.

There is no predictable timetable for completion of a fashion cycle, since each fashion proceeds at its own speed. One element of timing can always be counted upon, however: The decline is fast, and the drop to obsolescence is much steeper than the rise to culmination.

Obsolescence When revulsion has set in and a style can no longer be sold at any price, the fashion is in its *obsolescence* stage. In merchandising parlance, "you can't give it away."

Length of Cycles

The cycle of innovation, rise in demand, widespread acceptance, and then rejection applies to many different kinds of products. It is as true of menswear as of women's apparel. It is also true for refrigerators, automobiles, and architecture. A designer has a new idea. It is introduced in product form. It gathers interest, and the rise in its acceptance begins. It gains in popularity and is seen everywhere. Then its popularity declines—usually because a newer design idea has begun to catch people's attention. All fashions follow the same cyclical pattern of movement. All that varies is the speed with which each passes from one stage to the next in its development, and the length of time required for each to complete its entire cycle.

No recent studies have been made of the time required for fashion cycles to run their course, but experience indicates that it is steadily decreasing. Among the reasons for this speedup are fast-changing environmental factors, intensified competition among manufacturers and retailers for consumers' patronage, and consumers' desire for constantly changing assortments from which to select. In addition, rapid technological developments tend to make current fashions obsolete more quickly.

Consumers are constantly exposed to a multiplicity of new styles for their acceptance or rejection. Some of these win enough acceptance for a discernible cycle to get underway, and therefore achieve fashion status. Many more are rejected right at the start. Each new fashion presses hard at the heels of existing ones, and so the time required today for a fashion to complete its cycle is noticeably shorter than a few decades ago.

Breaks in the Cycle

It sometimes happens that the normal progress of a fashion cycle is broken abruptly by an outside influence. It can be something as simple as unfavorable weather for certain seasonal goods; or it can be something much more dramatic, such as widespread economic depression or war.

Although no formal studies have been made of this phenomenon, producers and merchants hold that the broken cycle tends to pick up where it left off, once conditions return to normal, or once the season that was cut short reopens the following year. Women's boots, as an element of the outdoor-indoor costume, offer an excellent example of a cycle broken by unfavorable weather for certain seasonal goods. Boots were at their introductory phase in 1957. Each summer after that, their progress was halted; each winter, it resumed, gaining strength. Popularity continued into the 1970s, when either knee-high boots or the "boot look" (achieved by color-matched shoes and hosiery) was widely used for both indoor and outdoor wear with skirts. Also, in the early 1970s, short boots were introduced for wear with increasingly popular pants, thus helping to extend the life of the boot fashion cycle.

Widespread economic depressions and wars also temporarily interrupt the normal progress of a fashion cycle. Throughout most of the 1930s, for instance, the United States and much of the world was struggling through the Great Depression. For nearly 10 years after the stock market crash of 1929, a third of this country's labor force was unemployed and in desperate want. Against such a background, fashion slowed its pace. Similarly, World War II halted almost all fashion development because of redirected interests and restrictions on consumers' use of fabrics.

Just before the stock market crash in 1929 and the economic depression that followed, the trend in women's apparel was towards fuller skirts.

Interrupted first by the Depression and then by World War II, the fashion trend picked up in 1947, where it had abruptly left off in 1928, with Dior's New Look.

Long-run and Short-run Fashions

The length of time it takes for individual fashions to complete their cycles varies widely. The terms *long-run* and *short-run* are used to describe fashions that take either more seasons or fewer seasons to complete their cycles than what might be considered their average life expectancy.

Some fashions tend to rise in popular acceptance more slowly than do others, thereby prolonging their life. Some stay in popular demand much longer than others do. The decline in popular demand for some fashions may be slower than for others.

Silhouettes, colors and textures, accessories, classics and fads—all vary widely in how long each takes to complete a full demand cycle because of their specific and individual characteristics. In addition, the level of technological development, existing lifestyles, and psychological reactions to prevailing social and economic conditions all influence the time it takes for various fashions to complete their cycles.

Silhouettes and Details   Because they change slowly and gradually as a result of changes in styling details, silhouettes are considered long-run fashions. Silhouettes have been found to change completely approximately every 35 years. However, this change is not abrupt: Silhouettes evolve from one to another through a series of changes in detail from one selling season to another. So subtle are some of these changes that last year's garment may not look out of fashion. As a result of a series of almost imperceptible changes over a period of four or five years, however, older apparel may begin to look badly proportioned and out of fashion.

As a general rule, the more detailed an item of apparel, the sooner it becomes dated. It is interesting to note that many foreign and domestic high-fashion designers express pride in the fact that some of their styles remain fashionably correct sometimes as long as 10 or 15 years.

Colors and Textures   More superficial elements of fashion, such as colors and textures, used to be considered short-run fashions, mainly because their popularity often was restricted to a single season. In recent years, however, their life spans have tended to lengthen.

In the late 1950s, for example, white, which formerly had been considered solely a summer color, was introduced as a fashionable color for winter holiday apparel. In 1962, *Harper's Bazaar* helped to popularize white as a year-round apparel color. Later it also became popular as a background color for prints and plaids. A possible explanation for this may be traced to technological developments in fibers and fabrics that have made it considerably less of a chore than it used to be to keep white garments fresh and sparkling. Black, formerly a winter staple, was displaced from the fashion scene in the early 1960s, yielding to a variety of bright colors. It did not stage a fashion comeback until the 1970s.

Textures, too, have become less seasonally oriented than they used to be. Here again, due to technological advances in fiber and fabric treatments, various textures may continue in popularity without respect to seasonal changes in climate. Cotton, wool, and synthetics may be worn the year around. Cotton fabrics may be smooth or nubby, crisp or soft, sheer or opaque. Wool may be rough or smooth, crisp or soft, heavy or tissue weight. Synthetics may have the appearance and texture of cottons, wools, silks, linens.

Accessories   Scarfs, shoes, handbags, belts, cosmetics, costume jewelry, millinery, and gloves are accessories to apparel and tend to have short-run or seasonal cycles. In recent years, however, their life spans, like those of colors and textures, have tended to lengthen. They are worn—or not worn—to complete and carry out the effect created by apparel. At the culmination of the straight or tubular silhouette in the early 1960s, for example, belts were conspicuously absent from the fashion picture. Not until the second half of that decade, when figure-skimming garments and the waistline began to return to fashion, was there any interest in this accessory. Gradually belts came to be used more often. They grew wider and more ornate. Only recently has there been a trend toward less ornate belts.

Until recently, scarfs were considered of only minor fashion importance because of the popularity of the simple, pared-down look in women's apparel. In the mid-1970s, however, with the return to favor of more feminine styling, scarfs exploded on the fashion scene. In a wide variety of sizes, lengths, and fabrics, they were used to achieve the then favored bulky or layered look. They were worn as belts or sashes with tent-dresses or chemise styles, and they were worn as functional as well as decorative head coverings.

Jewelry is worn to accent the apparel styling of the season. In winter, long chains may be worn with heavy turtleneck sweaters. The lower, looser necklines of summer encourage the use of a decorative pin or a single-strand necklace or no jewelry at all.

Classics   At the long end of the time scale are classics, those fashions with cycles that seem permanently arrested at the culmination stage. Classics are usually practical and universally appealing. Among classics are such items as the shirtwaist dress, cardigan sweater, plain pump, neutral hosiery shades for women, and the oxford-type shoe and sport jacket for men.

Classics change, but only superficially. Material, texture, detail, and even silhouette may vary, but the style itself continues in fashion. A woman's pump may be made of any leather, fabric, or plastic; it may have a blunt or a pointed toe, high or low heel; it may be made in a single color or a combination of colors. Although it changes superficially to relate to current fashions, it remains a pump—not an oxford, a loafer, or a T-strap. Similarly, a shirtwaist dress, whatever its fabric, color, sleeve length, and skirt fullness, remains a shirtwaist.

Fads The shortest of short-run fashions are fads. Their rise is spectacular, and their decline even more so. Occasionally, however, fads fool the experts. Some of them start, as usual, among a limited group, but instead of rapidly reaching saturation and dying abruptly, they spread to general public acceptance and become full-fledged fashions.

Two interesting modern examples of fads that became fashions are the chemise and the wig. The chemise, as previously noted, made its bow in the late 1950s, skyrocketing among younger wearers of inexpensive dresses, and then fizzing out. A few years later it returned as the shift and became the important dress fashion of the 1960s. In 1974, the chemise again returned to the fashion scene, first in the Paris collections and shortly thereafter in ready-to-wear adaptations.

The wig began as high fashion early in the 1960s. Costing at least $300, it was strictly a fad that only the wealthy could afford. As less expensive methods of making and selling wigs were devised,

they became fun fads for people of various ages and income brackets. More recently, they have become almost a classic among certain groups of active women. Wigs and hairpieces have also been adopted by some men, particularly those who frequently appear in public, such as television personalities and actors.

Consumer Buying and the Fashion Cycle

Each fashion has both a consumer buying cycle and a consumer use cycle (see Graph 3-2). The consumer buying cycle curve usually rises directly with the rise of the consumer use cycle, but when the fashion reaches its peak, consumer buying tends to decline more rapidly than consumer use. Just as different segments of society respond to and tire of a fashion at different times, so different groups continue to wear fashions for varying lengths of time after they have ceased buying them. While each class of consumer is using and enjoying a fashion, the producer and merchant serving that group are already abandoning the style and seeking something newer. Their efforts in this direction are

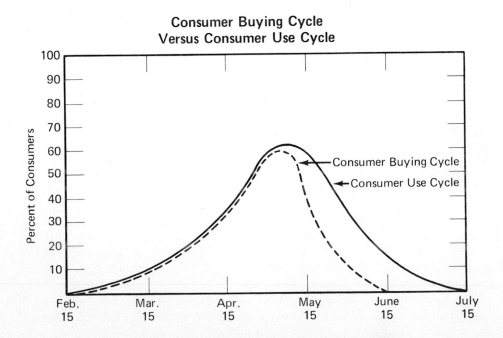

**Consumer Buying Cycle
Versus Consumer Use Cycle**

most profitable when they anticipate, rather than follow, the trend of consumer demand.

Consumer buying is often halted prematurely because producers and sellers no longer wish to risk making and stocking any item they believe will soon decline in popularity. Instead, they concentrate their resources on new items with better prospects of longevity. This procedure is familiar to anyone who has tried to buy summer clothes in late August or ski wear in March.

FACTORS INFLUENCING FASHION MOVEMENT

The fashion cycle has been compared to a force of nature because, in Laver's words, "nothing seems to be able to turn it back until it has spent itself, until it has provoked a reaction by its very excess."[1] Nevertheless, there are factors that can accelerate or retard the movement of fashion, just as wind can spread a forest fire and rain can slow or halt it.

Accelerating Factors

The influences that exert an accelerating effect on fashion cycles are more widespread buying power, increased leisure, more education, improved status of women, technological advances, sales promotion, and the changes of seasons.

Increasingly Widespread Buying Power More widely diffused discretionary income means there are more people with the financial means to respond to a fashion change. The more consumers who flock to a new fashion, the sooner it will reach its culmination; the more widespread the financial ability of consumers to turn to a yet newer fashion, the sooner the current fashion will plunge into obsolescence.

Increased Leisure Long hours of work and little leisure permitted scant attention to fashion in the past. More leisure time usually means more time to buy and enjoy fashion of many kinds. In the

last 20 years, sharp decreases in working hours and increases in paid vacations have encouraged more use of at-home wear, casual clothes, sports apparel, travel clothes, and different types of ordinary business dress. The increased purchases of these types of apparel give impetus to their fashion cycles.

More Education The increasingly higher level of education in the United States helps to speed up fashion cycles in two ways: First, more people's horizons have been broadened to include new interests and new wants; and second, more people are equipped by education to earn the money to satisfy those wants. These interests and wants, accompanied by the means to obtain them, provide a significant push toward the adoption of new fashions.

Improved Status of Women In a society with few artificial social barriers, women with discretionary income can spend it as they choose. No law or barrier of custom forces any woman of means to refrain from buying the newest and most prestigious styles in dresses, hats, or shoes, thus giving impetus to a fashion cycle in its earliest phases. The steady decrease in sex discrimination in the job market and the steady increase in social acceptance of women who manage both homes and jobs have given today's women more discretionary income; they are influencing the speed of fashion cycles by how they are using that income.

Technological Advances News, including fashion news, races around the world today. Improved production techniques speed up the manufacturing process. Fast transportation overland, by sea, and by air brings finished goods promptly to retail stores. Little or no time is lost between the moment when the consumer is psychologically and financially ready to add a forward push to the fashion cycle and the time when the goods are available for purchase. The development of new fibers, finishes, and materials also speeds up cycles. Many of these not only add utility but also reduce the prices of fashion goods, enabling people of more limited means to buy. The combination of durability and low price encourages those purchases, pushing fashion along in its cycle.

Sales Promotion Publicity and promotion by producers and retailers cannot force acceptance of a new fashion or revitalize a dying or dead one. They have, however, repeatedly accelerated the progress of an acceptable fashion. The publicity given miniskirts early in their cycle is an example. Even as late as 1965, most women were protesting that they would not be seen in above-the-knee skirts. Meantime, thigh-high hems were shown in fashion magazines, on television, in store displays, and in public places by those who had adopted the fashion in its early stages. By the late 1960s, the eyes of even the most conservative women had grown accustomed to skirt brevity, and it was hard to find a woman whose knees did not show. Without publicity and promotion, the fashion cycle for miniskirts might have taken considerably longer to reach its culmination.

Seasonal Change Consumers demand fashion change in direct response to the changing calendar, varying the weight and look of their garments according to seasonal patterns. Warm-weather clothes tend to be lighter in both color and weight. Cool-weather clothes tend to be darker and heavier. This remains true even though central heating and air conditioning have made an indoor physical need for these changes less real than several decades ago.

Increased travel and vacation needs also can have a seasonal impact on speeding up change. For instance, when a man intends to travel from New York to Florida for a January vacation, he may decide to pick up a new pair of summer slacks just before the trip. He may find a selection in resort assortments, often forerunners of the styles that will be found in the regular seasonal assortments the following spring and summer.

Even in areas where seasonal change does not bring much change in temperature, as in Florida and Hawaii, many people still tend to change their wardrobes with the season. Boredom alone is a major factor in keeping them from being content to wear a single wardrobe the year around.

Retarding Factors

Factors that retard the development of fashion cycles by discouraging people from adopting incoming styles or that encourage them to continue to use styles that might be considered on the decline include not only the reverse of the accelerating factors but also habit and custom, religion, sumptuary laws, the nature of the merchandise, and reductions in consumers' buying power.

Habit and Custom By slowing acceptance of new styles and prolonging the life spans of those already accepted, habit and custom exert a braking effect on fashion movement. The restraining hand of habit is at work slowing the adoption of new skirt lengths, silhouettes, necklines, or colors whenever shoppers unconsciously select styles that do not differ perceptibly from those already owned. It is easy for an individual to let habit take over. Some consumers are more susceptible to this tendency than others; their loyalty to an established style is not so much a matter of fashion judgment as it is a natural attraction toward something that has become familiar.

Custom slows progress in the fashion cycle by permitting vestiges of past fashions, status symbols, taboos, or special needs to continue past their utility in modern dress. Custom is responsible for such details as buttons on the sleeves of men's suits, vents in their jackets, and the sharp creases down the front of their trousers. Custom usually requires a degree of formality in dress for religious services. The trend toward similarity of dress for men and women in this country has permitted women to wear trousers, but custom still frowns on men in skirts.

A classic example of the influence of custom is the placement of buttons: They are on the right side for men, originating from the need to have the weapon arm available while dressing and undressing; and they are on the left for women, who tend to hold babies on that side and can more conveniently use the right hand for buttons. The stitching on the backs of gloves is another example; it dates back to a time when sizes were adjusted by lacing at these points.

Religion Religious leaders have historically championed custom and demonstrated their sanction of the old in ceremonial apparel. They have tended to associate fashion with temptation and have urged their followers to turn their backs on both. Religion today, however, exerts much less of a retarding influence on fashion. Examples of this may be found in the modernization of women's dress among many religious orders and the fact that women no longer consider a hat obligatory when in church.

Sumptuary Laws The law is one of the few forces that usually can slow or halt a fashion cycle by command. Height of headdress, length of train, width of sleeve, value and weight of material, and color of dress have all been restricted at times to specific classes by law. Such laws were aimed at keeping each class in its place in a rigidly stratified society.[2]

Other laws attempted to keep a society's collective mind on a high level by condemning frippery, as the Puritans did. For instance, an order passed in 1638 by the General Court of Massachusetts stated:

No garment shall be made with short sleeves, and such as have garments already made with short sleeves shall not wear same unless they cover the arm to the wrist; and hereafter no person whatever shall make any garment for women with sleeves more than half an ell wide.[3]

And in the eighteenth century, a bill was proposed (but rejected) that stated:

All women of whatever age, rank, profession, or degree, whether virgin, maid, or widow, that shall impose upon, seduce, and betray into matrimony any of His Majesty's subjects by scents,

paints, cosmetic washes, artificial teeth, false hair, Spanish wool, iron stays, hoops, high-heeled shoes, or bolstered hips, shall incur the penalty of the law now in force against witchcraft and the like demeanours, and that marriage, upon conviction, shall stand null and void.[4]

Local ordinances, however, have a way of being ignored if they conflict with a fashion cycle that is gathering strength. In New York during the 1930s, fines could be imposed if men or women appeared on the streets in tennis shorts, or if the shoulder straps of bathing suits were not in place on public beaches. What was considered indecent exposure then is commonplace today: shorts for streetwear and strapless bathing suits.

Nature of the Merchandise The nature of the merchandise concerned is sometimes a factor in slowing the rate at which a fashion cycle moves. Silhouettes change more slowly than do colors, textures, and details. Apparel moves in slower cycles than accessories. Men's fashion cycles have traditionally been slower than women's, but are gradually speeding up.

Reductions in Consumers' Buying Power Just as increasing spending power can speed up a fashion cycle, so can any decrease in spending power—as a result of economic depression, high taxes and interest rates, inflation, strikes, or a high percentage of unemployment—retard the forward movement of fashion cycles. Similarly, any increase in the number of economically deprived consumers slows down the cycles of fashion. The poor are bystanders in matters of fashion, and bystanders do not keep cycles moving. Laver noted this when he wrote that nothing can make a style permanent other than poverty.

RECURRING FASHIONS

Styles reoccur in fashion acceptance. Occasionally an entire "look" is reborn, as in the 1960s, when

The three basic silhouettes: bell-shaped or bouffant, bustle or back-fullness, and straight or tubular.

Sometimes a single costume component or a minor detail that earlier exhausted its welcome stages a comeback. At other times, a single article of clothing, like the sandals of the ancient Greeks, returns to popularity.

Research indicates that, at least in the past, similar silhouettes and details of design in women's apparel have recurred with remarkable regularity.

Agnes Brooks Young, in *Recurring Cycles of Fashion*,[5] undertook a study of skirt silhouettes and their variations in connection with her primary interest in theatrical costumes. From data she collected on the 177-year period from 1760 to 1937, she concluded that, despite widely held opinions to the contrary, there were actually only three basic silhouettes: the bell-shaped or bouffant, the bustle or back-fullness, and the straight or tubular. Moreover, her data indicated that these three basic silhouettes followed each other in regular sequence, and each recurred about once every 100 years.

Each silhouette, with all its variations, dominated the fashion scene for a period of approximately 35 years. Having reached an excess in styling, it declined in popularity and yielded to the next different silhouette in regular sequence.

Conclusions reached by A. L. Kroeber, anthropologist, from his study of changes in women's apparel over the 330-year period from 1605 to 1936 tended to confirm Young's findings that similar silhouettes recur in fashion acceptance approximately once every 100 years. In addition, Kroeber also found that similar neck widths recurred every 100 years and similar skirt lengths every 35 years.

PLAYING THE APPAREL FASHION GAME

According to Madge Garland, a well-known English fashion authority, "Every woman is born with a built-in hobby: the adornment of her person. The tricks she can play with it, the shapes she can make of it, the different portions she displays at various times, the coverings she uses or discards . . ."[6] all add up to fashion.

Many clothing authorities read a clear message into this alternate exposure and covering of various

the prevailing straight lines and short skirts strikingly resembled the 1920s fashions. In the late 1960s and early 1970s, nostalgic interest developed in Edwardian styles and those of the 1930s. The Edwardian influence was seen in elegant clothes and full heads of hair and sideburns for men. The 1930s influence was obvious in fluid, clinging lines in women's clothes, in fluffy curls, and in bright lipstick.

parts of the body: sex. Flügel sees sexual attraction as the dominant motive for wearing clothes. Laver suggests that those portions of the body which it is no longer fashionable to expose are "sterilized" and no longer sexually attractive, whereas those which are newly exposed are *erogenous,* or sexually stimulating. He sees fashion pursuing the ever-shifting erogenous zone, but never quite catching up with it. "If you really catch up," he warns, "you are immediately arrested for indecent exposure. If you almost catch up, you are celebrated as a leader of fashion."[7]

Men's apparel has long played the fashion game, too, but since the Industrial Revolution in a less dramatic manner than women's. Whereas women's fashions have tended to concentrate mainly on different ways to convey sexual appeal, men's fashions have been designed to emphasize such various attributes as strength, power, bravery, and high social rank. When a male style did emphasize sex, it was intended to project an overall impression of virility.

Pieces of the Game

The pieces with which the women's fashion game is played are the various portions of the female body. Historically, as each part of the anatomy reached a saturation point of interest, it has withdrawn from the fashion spotlight to be replaced by some other portion.

In the Middle Ages, asceticism was fashionable, and women's clothes were designed to play down, rather than emphasize, femininity. The Renaissance, however, was a period of greater sexual freedom. Women's apparel during this period highlighted the breasts and the abdomen, particularly the latter.

By the eighteenth century, however, the abdomen had lost its appeal. Although the bosom continued to get emphasis, the abdomen was flattened, and heels were raised to facilitate upright carriage. The Empire period also stressed the bosom with a high waistline, but the entire body was emphasized with sheer and scanty dresses, some so sheer

they could be pulled through a ring. Some advocates of this fashion even wet their apparel so that it would cling to the figure when worn.

During the nineteenth century, fashion interest shifted to the hips, and thus skirts billowed. Later, the posterior was accented with bustles and trains.

Early in the twentieth century, emphasis switched from the trunk to the limbs, through short skirts and sleeveless or tight-sleeved dresses. Flügel interpreted accent on the limbs, together with an underdeveloped torso, as an idealization of youth. He foresaw continued emphasis on youth and boyishness, attributable to women's participation in varied activities, the steady march of democracy, and increasing sexual freedom.[8]

Fifty years later, emphasis switched back to the trunk of the body. Legs were covered with pants or long skirts, and arms with full, wrist-length sleeves, but midriffs were bared and wide, and plunging necklines scarcely concealed bare bosoms. These fashions continue to prove Flügel's theory, in that more recent fashions also emphasize youth because only women with slim, youthful figures can look attractive in such styles.

The Waist   As far back as 3000 B.C., women used corsets in some form to diminish their waist measurements. Accentuation of the waist has taken various forms: cinching, padding above and below, and baring the area, as in modern halter tops and bikinis.

The Shoulders   Baring one or both shoulders in evening wear and on the beach is considered so commonplace now that it is hard to imagine the furor caused by the strapless gown of the 1930s. Madge Garland points out that the Victorians exposed shoulders "shamelessly," and Edwardians "covered them hypocritically with wisps of chiffon."[9] In more recent decades, strapless brassieres, or wearing no bra at all, have made it possible for women to expose as much of their shoulders as they choose, particularly in evening and at-home apparel. At the same time, however, fashion emphasis on shoulders was accomplished in street and

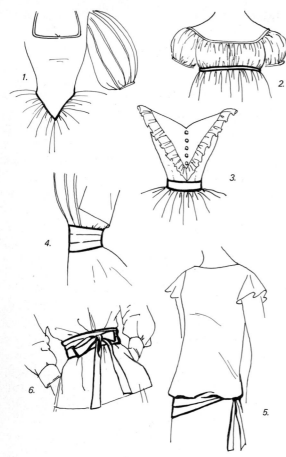

Nearly 400 years of waistlines: 1. 1600, 2. 1815, 3. 1850, 4. 1880, 5. 1925, 6. 1975.

outerwear through fitted yokes, dropped or extended shoulder lines, and bulky scarfs draped loosely over the shoulders.

The Bosom   Ancient Minoan women exposed their breasts, as did Renaissance ladies. In more recent times, women called attention to the bosom with padding, or deep cleavage, rather than nudity. In midcentury, padded bras added inches to the measurements of young women, and clinging sweaters and plunging necklines heightened the effect. Popular movie actresses posed for publicity photographs that revealed their generous dimen-

sions and increased the popularity of the high-bosomed look.

As the 1960s drew to a close, disenchantment with the excesses in skirt brevity set in, and fashion interest shifted to the upper part of the body, mainly the bosom. By the early 1970s, the natural look was in; padding and the high-bosomed look were out. Undergarments became less structured and restrictive. The "no-bra" brassiere was followed by the molded brassiere and the form-fitting body suit to help achieve the increasingly popular natural look. By the mid-1970s, many women were dressing without bras, and apparel for evening and at-home wear featured bare bosoms only slightly concealed beneath see-through fabrics or necklines unfastened to the waist.

The Hips   In the 1920s, a desire for boyish slimness replaced the former popularity of prominent hips. Two decades later, however, hips were again in the fashion spotlight. In 1947, Dior reportedly padded the hips of his models to make their waists appear smaller. Balenciaga's full skirts and cinched waists in 1954 achieved the same effect. But eventually the unfitted styles triumphed. Whenever the major fashion trend favors the slim, youthful look, hips have small claim to fashion importance.

The Neckline   Early in the twentieth century, the V neck was a daring innovation; women were still accustomed to collars that rose to their ears. As years passed, the V went deeper, at times plunging to the waist. In recent years, necklines for daytime wear have shown infinite variety, with scoop necks, backless halter tops, and turtlenecks being worn alongside primly buttoned shirtwaists or wide necklines unfastened to the waist.

The Feet and Legs   For thousands of years, fashion kept women's feet and legs well hidden. Only in the twentieth century did ankles appear. Once exposed, however, women's legs began to steal the fashion scene. Skirts rose, and by the 1920s knees were exposed. Then down came the skirt lengths (but never to their earlier length) until the 1960s, when they reversed and moved up to midthigh. Having reached that extreme in brevity, a reaction set in. Skirt lengths began to drop, and leg-covering pants became almost a uniform for women of all ages. By the mid-1970s, fashionable evening skirts were ankle-length, while those for day wear ended 1 or 2 inches below the knee, with some interest shown in longer lengths.

The Figure as a Whole According to Garland, the fashions of the 1950s and 1960s showed off the entire figure:

> *The modern girl manages at the same time to bare her shoulders, accentuate her bust, pull in her waist, and show her legs to above the knees. It is a triumph of personal publicity over the taboos of the past and the previous limitations of fashion.*[10]

This "triumph of personal publicity" in the late 1960s called attention to feet clad only in sandals or low-heeled shoes, to legs sheathed in textured, fishnet, or decorated pantyhose, and to skirts stopping at midthigh. It ignored the waist much of the time but accentuated it in sportswear with bare midriffs, bikinis, and hip-huggers. Sleeveless dresses, natural-line bras, wide but high cowled collars, drop earrings, wigs, and tinted hair long and flowing or dramatically cut and arranged gave the eye much to observe. Areas that were normally covered made their bid for attention, too, with cutouts in dresses and gloves. Unlike previous fashion eras, in which attention centered on only certain parts of the body, fashions during the 1960s tended to emphasize all parts.

Although fashion interest in the 1970s may have shifted from the legs to the upper torso, the general trend in women's apparel fashions is toward softer, less structured styling that emphasizes the body as a whole, thereby reflecting new attitudes regarding exhibitionism and modesty. Although some parts of the body may be exposed and, therefore, considered erotic, other parts of the body are equally as seductive when covered by fabrics that softly follow their contours without actually revealing them.

Rules of the Game

The game of emphasizing different areas of the female anatomy at different times has its rules. The first and fundamental rule is that fashion does not flit. Its attention lights on one area of the body and stays with that area, intensifying concentration upon it until every last possibility for excitement has been exhausted.

Laver explains fashion's anatomical emphasis in terms of the sexuality of the body. "Fashion really began," he says, "with the discovery in the fifteenth century that clothes could be used as a compromise between exhibitionism and modesty."[11] Exposure of any part of the feminine body focuses erotic attention on that part. The aim of fashion thus has been to emphasize various portions of the body in sequence. When one part of the body has been overemphasized, it loses power to excite, and fashion concentration shifts to another area.

This shift occurs, however, only after fashion has gone as far as it can in emphasizing that one area. Crinolines and hoops reached impossible diameters before skirts became narrower. Tight lacing grew tighter until health was endangered before the practice was abandoned.

The excesses reached in exposing one part of the body prepare the way for its retreat from the fashion scene. A staleness develops; the overemphasized area becomes sterile, or unable to excite, and a new erogenous zone is found.

Garland has suggested a second rule for this fashion merry-go-round: Only certain parts of the body can be exposed at any given time.[12] Recent fashions provide ample illustrations: turtlenecks on sleeveless dresses or sweaters, miniskirted dresses with high necklines and long sleeves, plunging necklines on ankle-length evening gowns.

The third rule of the fashion game is that its movement is always forward, never in reverse. As Robinson has said, "A fashion can never retreat gradually and in good order. Like a dictator it must always expand its aggressions or collapse. Old fashions never fade away; they die suddenly and arbitrarily."[13] This is as true of the pieces of the fashion game as it is of fashion itself.

PREDICTING THE MOVEMENT OF FASHION

The tastes and fashion preferences of the public follow certain well-defined channels. Everyone who hopes to make or sell fashion goods at a profit is constantly using whatever means possible to identify these channels and direct efforts along the indicated courses.

Fashions move constantly, but at varying individual speeds, toward culmination and inevitably toward decline. Predicting which among current fashions will enjoy pronounced consumer demand in the future requires the forecaster (1) to distinguish what the current fashions are; (2) to estimate how widespread they are; and (3) to determine at what point in time these fashions will appeal to the firm's target customer groups. With information on these three points, the projection into the future of current trends, a prime requisite in successful fashion merchandising, becomes possible.

Identifying Trends

A *fashion trend* is the direction in which fashion is moving. If manufacturers or merchants correctly recognize that direction, and determine whether it is toward or away from maximum acceptance, then they can decide whether to actively promote the fashion, or to bide time, or to abandon it.

For example, a recognized fashion trend may be for sleeveless daytime dresses. At the introductory and rising stages, retailers will stock and promote a progressively larger proportion of sleeveless designs. When it seems that customers are reaching a point of saturation with bared arms, retailers will begin introducing sleeves into their stock in progressively larger numbers. If they have correctly anticipated the timing of the downturn with respect to customer demand, they will have few sleeveless styles on hand when decline in demand occurs. Customers may still be wearing the sleeveless styles, but they will not be buying them, at least at regular prices; and retailers will have abandoned the fashion, foreseeing its rapid descent into obsolescence.

Sources of Data

The ways in which successful producers or retailers determine the strength and direction of fashion trends among their customers have little to do with intuition or clairvoyance. Good, solid facts about consumer acceptance are behind most successful merchandising decisions, not that rather vague talent often called "fashion sense." Successful merchants collect data by checking their sales records; by observing what is being worn, both generally and by their own customers; and by determining where each fashion is in its life cycle and when it is likely to be of interest to their customers.

Sales Data   Automated methods of collecting sales data, both punch-card and electronic, are a boon to fashion merchants. Some stores have completely automated systems that start right at the cash register. To complete a sale, the salesperson punches into the register not only the price but also several other numbers that appear on the price ticket. These numbers identify the category of merchandise, the style, perhaps the color, fabric, or size. The system can be used to collect information about almost any fashion element that the merchant thinks important to watch.

Automated systems not only give merchants more accurate details about sales and stock on hand, but they also make those figures available for study much more quickly than ever before. This speed is very important in fashion merchandising. It means that results from the testing of new styles and colors are available to the merchant almost immediately. Changes in customers' preferences can be identified quickly, and the rate of sale of affected styles can be charted and evaluated. The speed of automated systems enables buyers to make quick, more accurate decisions about reorders.

Observations   Observations of what is being generally worn augment what merchants can learn from their own sales and from what others say about their sales experience. Actual counts may be made of women at, say, an important charity event to ascertain who and how many wear a new style. These women are often the fashion leaders, and what they choose to wear may signify the beginning of a new fashion trend. When pantsuits were new, in the winter of 1966–1967, *Women's Wear Daily* frequently reported how many pantsuits were seen at each of the fashionable New York restaurants.

A fashion merchant's dependence on observation rather than intuition is by no means new. As far back as 1928, Nystrom pointed out:

Changes in fashions may be checked and their trends determined by the simple process of making successive periodic counts of the same styles, among the same classes of people, comparing the result from one period to another, and taking note of the change.[14]

Since fashion is a complex phenomenon involving many elements, observations are most helpful if they are made in terms of each of the four elements of fashion: silhouette, detail, texture, and color. Thus, in a given season, successive observations may show bright colors predominating, but brown on the rise and black making a tentative entry upon the scene. A concurrent series of counts might each time show fewer women wearing the jewel neckline and more wearing turtlenecks and shirt collars.

In addition, observations should take into consideration the characteristics of customers as well as the characteristics of a style. The strength and direction of a trend varies in different age and income groups, in groups with different interests, in groups in different areas. What young suburbanites wear to a club luncheon is not necessarily what urbanites wear to a fashionable restaurant. Successful fashion forecasting requires that merchants first pinpoint what their target group of customers are wearing today in order to determine what they are likely to wear tomorrow.

Most merchants do not depend solely on their own observations, however. They consult sources of information about the buying and use habits of consumers other than their own. In attempting to predict the course of fashion trends, they look at both the local picture and the total picture, their own sales experience and that of others, and base decisions on both their own judgment and that of others. In fashion forecasting, wise merchants draw information from every available source, and they then coordinate the data in terms of the fashion preferences of their specific target customers.

Interpreting Influential Factors

To interpret the data they have collected and organized, fashion forecasters, whether merchants, producers, or designers, must put their knowledge of fashion and fashion principles to work. They not only examine the data and the pattern they show, but also take into consideration certain factors which serve to accelerate or retard a fashion cycle among the target group of customers. These factors include current events, the appearance of prophetic styles, sales promotion efforts, and the current canons of taste.

Current Events Items in the news can influence consumers and affect their response to fashion. For instance, former President Nixon's visit to the People's Republic of China in 1972 focused attention on that large and ancient country. There was a rapid growth of interest in Chinese goods of all kinds. Fashion ads began to talk about silks, the fabric most closely associated with China. Variations of the coolie coat and the mandarin collar appeared in new apparel styling. There was even a short panda fad, ranging from small stuffed pandas to panda prints on T-shirts, caused by the popularity of the pair of pandas presented by the Chinese government to this country.

Prophetic Styles Good fashion forecasters keep a sharp watch for what they call *prophetic styles*, particularly interesting new styles that are still in the introductory phase of their fashion cycle. Taken up enthusiastically by the socially prominent or by the flamboyant young, they may gather momentum very rapidly. Or they may prove to be nonstarters. Whatever their future course, the degree of acceptance of these very new ideas provides information of interest to qualified observers.

Sales Promotion Efforts Along with the records of past sales, fashion forecasters give thought to the kind and amount of promotion that helped stimulate interest in prophetic styles, as well as the kind and amount of additional sales promotion they can look forward to. A fiber producer's powerful advertising and publicity efforts may have helped turn a slight interest in a product into a much stronger interest during a corresponding period last year. The forecaster's problem is to estimate how far the trend might have developed without those promotional activities, how much momentum remains from last year's push to carry it forward this year, and how much promotional support can be looked for in the future. The promotional effort that the forecaster's own organization plans to expend is only one part of the story; outside efforts, sometimes industrywide, also must be considered in forecasting fashions.

Canons of Taste In judging the impact of new styles, a forecaster relates them to currently accepted canons of taste and utility. In an era of uninhibited exposure of much of the body, one would not expect to sell many "long johns" to young women. In an era of clear, vibrant color, pastels and misty tones often seem to have few advocates. When pastels have their day, bold colors seem crude and inappropriate.

According to Nystrom, fashions that are in accord with currently accepted canons of art, custom, modesty, and utility are most easily accepted, go furthest, and last longest.

Importance of Timing

Successful merchants must determine what their particular target group of customers are wearing now, and what they are likely to be wearing a month or three months from now. Therefore, they collect information that enables them not only to identify current fashions but to dissect each fashion in terms of who is wearing it and what point it has reached in its life cycle. Since merchants know at what point in a fashion's cycle their customers are most likely to be attracted, they can determine whether a current fashion is one to stock now, or a month from now, or three months from now.

For instance, in 1966 and 1967, pantsuits were a newly introduced style at the beginning of their cycle. Specialty shops that catered to fashion leaders rushed to get pantsuits in stock. Department stores, whose customers were more conservative fashion followers, took note of the new style but were in no hurry to add pantsuits to their inventory. They waited until statistics and observations showed that the fashion was building strength and widening its appeal. Then they bought small stocks of pantsuits to test acceptance among their own customers. When acceptance was proved, the number and variety of pantsuits on the racks increased. Today, pantsuits occupy dominant sections in many ready-to-wear departments.

REFERENCES

[1] Laver, *Taste and Fashion*, p. 52.
[2] Binder, *Muffs and Morals*, pp. 162–164.
[3] McClellan, *History of American Costume*, p. 82.
[4] Taylor, *It's a Small, Medium, and Outsize World*, p. 39.
[5] Young, *Recurring Cycles of Fashion*, p. 92.
[6] Garland, *Fashion*, p. 11.
[7] Laver, op. cit., p. 201.
[8] Flügel, *The Psychology of Clothes*, p. 163.
[9] Garland, op. cit., p. 18.
[10] Ibid., p. 20.
[11] Laver, op. cit., p. 200.
[12] Garland, op. cit., p. 11.

[13] Robinson, "Fashion Theory and Product Design," p. 128.
[14] Nystrom, *Fashion Merchandising*, p. 84.

MERCHANDISING VOCABULARY
Define or briefly explain the following terms:

Fashion cycle	Culmination stage	Short-run fashion
Rise stage	Long-run fashion	Erogenous
Line-for-line copies	Decline stage	Fashion trend
Adaptations	Obsolescence stage	Prophetic styles

MERCHANDISING REVIEW
1. Name and explain the five phases of a fashion's life cycle.
2. How do adaptations differ from line-for-line copies?
3. What are the two ways in which the culmination stage of a fashion can be extended?
4. What can disrupt the normal progress of a fashion cycle? Once disrupted, can the cycle be resumed? Cite examples to illustrate your answer.
5. Differentiate between long-run and short-run fashions and give examples of each.
6. How does the consumer use cycle differ from the consumer buying cycle? What implications does this have for fashion merchants?
7. What conclusions did Agnes Brook Young reach in her study of skirt silhouettes from 1760 to 1937?
8. List the "pieces" with which the women's fashion game is played, according to Madge Garland.
9. What are the three basic rules that govern the fashion game, according to leading fashion authorities?
10. How does one predict fashion trends? From what resources can a fashion merchant collect data that will help determine fashion trends?

MERCHANDISING DIGEST
1. Discuss the various factors that tend to accelerate the forward movement of fashions through their cycles, giving at least one example of how each factor has an accelerating effect.
2. Discuss the factors that tend to retard the development of fashion cycles by discouraging the adoption of newly introduced styles. Give at least one example of how each factor exerts a braking influence on fashion development.
3. From your study and appraisal of currently popular women's apparel styles, do you see any signs which indicate that a new and different silhouette is in the making? If so, what would that silhouette be? Give examples to defend your answer.

4
FASHION LEADERS
AND FOLLOWERS

Earlier chapters explained how styles have mirrored class distinctions that existed during a particular period. Today, however, even people of modest means can wear clothes of practically the same design as those worn by the wealthy. Increased, more evenly distributed discretionary income now enables most people to purchase goods on the basis of fashion appeal. Improved technology makes mass production and mass distribution of fashion goods economically possible and highly profitable. Speedier communications, better education, and a thriving middle class encourage people to want and to accept the new more readily than did their grandparents. Finally, the leisure to enjoy fashion, to become bored with prevailing styles, and to seek the refreshment of new ones today prevails among most consumers in the United States.

These factors have caused fashion to move at breakneck speed in the second half of the twentieth century. As one watches the quick march of new fashions, a few questions arise:

Who starts fashions? Where do they begin? Who sponsors them? Who influences consumers so that a style gains wide acceptance? The answers involve designers, manufacturers, retailers, and, most important of all, consumers.

Consumers demand change because of changing interests, changing wants, and changing ideas of what is appropriate and acceptable. Sometimes consumers demand change simply for the sake of change. Designers, manufacturers, and retailers try to chart, forecast, and meet consumers' demands.

BIRTH OF A FASHION

Neither designers nor manufacturers make a fashion or create fashion change. They simply spread before the public their interpretations of current consumer ideas and attitudes. They influence fashion in one important way, however: They provide consumers with an unending series of new styles and thus allow them to choose styles that best express their individual lifestyles.

Designers and manufacturers are by no means infallible in the choice of designs they believe will win consumer acceptance. There are times when their interpretations may be more extreme than consumers are willing to accept. At other times they may introduce new designs too early, before the public is quite ready to accept them. It has been estimated that at least two thirds of the new designs introduced by the fashion industries each season fail to become fashions.

There are also times when manufacturers and their designers make the mistake of thinking that all consumers will go along with a commonly accepted trend. They fail to allow for pockets of resistance in certain areas of the country. In the early 1970s, for example, when fashion-conscious women in cities like New York, Chicago, and San Francisco were receptive to skirt lengths at or below the knee, women in less urban areas still wore much shorter skirts. In the mid 1970s, urban women were moving toward skirts, but pantsuits remained the important fashion for women outside the cities.

A designer has to study many styling features and trends to determine what tomorrow's customer will want.
Bonnie Cashin and Philip Sills

The Designer's Role

A *fashion designer* creates styles, thereby giving concrete expression to fashion ideas. There is a widely held misconception that designers are involved solely in the creation of aesthetically beautiful art objects. Nothing could be further from the truth. Their efforts are always influenced and limited by such mundane business considerations as availability and cost of materials, by labor costs, by available production techniques, by the requirement that their designs can be profitably produced within the employer firm's established and somewhat narrow wholesale price range. Furthermore, unless designers own their own firms, their designs must conform at all times to the particular image the employer firm chooses to maintain.

Successful designers do not live and work in an ivory tower. They must continually study the lifestyles of the consumers to whom their designs are meant to appeal. Months before the goods are actually available to prospective customers, they must interpret fashion trends in terms of how specific groups are apt to react. They must be alert at all times to the effects on consumer demand of current events, of socioeconomic conditions, and of psychological attitudes toward fashion.

Types of Designers In general, there are three types of American designers. At the top is the

couture, or high-fashion, designer (sometimes referred to as a "name designer"). A couture designer
is responsible not only for creating new styles but
also for choosing the materials in which to execute
those styles. Often a couture designer actively
participates in the promotion of the firm's line.

A couture designer may be the head of a firm
or may work for a manufacturing firm as chief
designer, with a staff of assistants. Examples of
some well-known American couture designers are
James Galanos, Oscar de la Renta, Adele Simpson,
Geoffrey Beene, Bill Blass, Bonnie Cashin, and
Calvin Klein.

Until recently, couture designers' names were
associated only with certain types of apparel at
expensive prices. Today, however, all that is changing. More and more couture designers now work
with an increasing variety of apparel and accessories, in a wider variety of price lines, and with
products other than apparel.

A second type of designer, sometimes called
a stylist, makes adaptations of others' successful
designs. A stylist usually is responsible for choosing
the materials to be used in producing the designs,
but rarely is involved in promoting the firm's products. Usually a stylist's work is produced in moder-
ate-to-low price lines, rather than expensive ones. A
stylist may be the only creative person in a
manufacturing firm, or a creative executive with a
staff of assistants. Many stylists work in the fabric
industry, as well as in the apparel and accessories
industries.

A third type of designer is a free lancer, who
sells sketches to manufacturers. The designs done
by a free lancer may be original styles, or they may
be adaptations. The sketches may reflect the free
lancer's own ideas, or they may be drawn to a
manufacturer's specifications. With the delivery of
the sketch to the manufacturer, a free lancer's job
is finished.

Insight and Intuition A designer takes a fashion idea and embodies it in new styles. Even the
most creative designers, however, are frank to dis-
claim any power to force acceptance of their styles.

Few have said so more effectively than did Paul
Poiret, one of the twentieth century's great Parisian
couturiers, who once told an American audience:

*I know you think me a king of fashion. . . .
It is a reception which cannot but flatter me and
of which I cannot complain. All the same, I
must undeceive you with regard to the powers
of a king of fashion. We are not capricious des-
pots such as wake up one fine day, decide upon
a change in habits, abolish a neckline, or puff
out a sleeve. We are neither arbiters nor dicta-
tors. Rather we are to be thought of as the
blindly obedient servants of woman, who for her
part is always enamoured of change and athirst
for novelty. It is our role, and our duty, to be
on the watch for the moment at which she becomes bored with what she is wearing, that we
may suggest at the right instant something else
which will meet her taste and needs. It is therefore with a pair of antennae and not a rod of
iron that I come before you, and not as a master
that I speak, but as a slave . . . who must divine
your innermost thoughts.*[1]

Insight and intuition, then, play a large part
in a designer's success. He or she must constantly
experiment with new ideas. When one fashion is
reaching that excess which marks its approaching
demise, a designer must have new candidates ready
and waiting for the public's favor.

On occasion a style or design takes such firm
hold on the consumer's affections that it continues
to be popular for many seasons. Designers then give
it apparent freshness each season by using new
details or new materials. Thus, in the early 1970s,
when denim jeans were so widely accepted as to
have become almost a uniform, designers added
variety and a new look through trimmings such as
beads, sequins, decals, and embroidery.

Sources of Design Inspiration Even while a
fashion is at its height, the restless minds of creative
designers are seeking inspiration for new fashions
to follow it. That inspiration can come from a

variety of sources. For instance, events of the early 1970s concentrated attention on the Far East, and so designers looked to the Far East for fashion ideas. The mandarin collar, the slit skirt, the coolie coat, and even the coolie hat found their way into new Western styles. Silk and silklike fabrics became popular, as did batiks.

Movies and television also have an influence on design. The first half of the 1970s brought a number of movies and television shows about the 1920s and 1930s. Soon, modern adaptations of the styles popular in those decades began to appear in some designer collections. Among the popular movies were *The Godfather, The Great Gatsby,* and *The Sting.* Edith Head, noted Hollywood costume designer, won her eighth Academy Award for her costumes for *The Sting,* the first time the Oscar was ever given for the design of men's clothes. Some of the 1920s and 1930s styles she used were the snap-brimmed hat and the vest.

Popular entertainers also have their impact on fashion ideas. For instance, popular music groups have strongly influenced the styles preferred by young people, and therefore the designers who design for them. When music groups were "mod" in dress, so were their admirers. When the former adopted long hair and work clothes, the high school and college crowds reflected that look. When hair began to be cut a little shorter and clothes fitted a little more carefully, designers for the young group picked up the neater look in the styles they offered.

A designer's reactions to what he or she sees and feels do not, in themselves, launch a new trend. They simply act as a catalyst that helps the designer crystallize in new styles the very ideas which the public is trying to express.

In their search for inspiration, however, designers always keep the immediate past in mind, as well as what currently is interesting people. As profitable as it would be if people cleaned out their entire wardrobes and started with new clothes each season, designers know this doesn't happen. Each season, consumers are eager for something new—but whatever it is will have to blend in, to some

degree, with what they already have in their closets. Only rarely is a revolutionary new style successful. It is the evolutionary new style that usually becomes the best-selling fashion.

The Manufacturer's Role

Manufacturers would agree with Robinson that "every market into which the consumer's fashion sense has insinuated itself is, by that very token, subject to [the] common, compelling need for unceasing change in the styling of its goods."[2]

Even in such prosaic items as paper napkins, the need for change has produced rainbows of pastels on grocery shelves, augmented by brilliant deep shades and whites with dainty prints. Similarly, in basics such as bedsheets or men's dress shirts, the once traditional white has yielded to a variety of colors, stripes, and prints. There is scarcely an industry serving consumers today in which the manufacturer's success does not depend in part upon an ability to attune styling to fashion interest and demand.

Types of Manufacturers In general, manufacturers of fashion goods can be divided into three groups. One group is made up of firms that produce innovative, high-fashion apparel; it is usually identified as the "better market." A second group is made up of firms that sometimes produce originals but usually turn out adaptations of styles which have survived the introductory stage and are gaining increased acceptance—in other words, styles which are in the rise stage of their fashion life cycle. This group of firms is usually identified as the "moderate-priced market." A third group of manufacturers makes no attempt to offer new or unusual styling. Rather, these firms mass-produce close copies or adaptations of styles that have proved their acceptance in higher-priced markets. Such firms are usually identified as the "budget market."

Fashion Influence In the field of women's apparel, manufacturers historically are committed to producing several new lines a year. A *line* is an assortment of new designs, some actually new in every sense of the word and others merely adaptations of currently popular styles. Producers hope that a few of the designs in a given line will prove "hot"—be so precisely in step with demand that their sales will be profitably large.

Occasionally, manufacturers' styles may be too advanced for the fashion tastes of customers. Such producers neither accelerate nor retard fashion; their goods simply do not get wide distribution and have little or no impact upon the public.

For the most part, the fashion industries are made up of manufacturers whose ability to anticipate the public's response to styles is excellent. Those who do badly in this respect, even for a single season, usually reap small sales and large losses—and unless they are unusually well financed, they quickly find themselves out of business. In the fashion business, the survival of the fittest means the survival of those who give the most able assistance in the birth and growth of fashions that consumers want.

The Retailer's Role

Retailers are in much the same position as producers. They do not create fashion, but they can encourage or retard its progress by the degree of accuracy with which they gauge their customers' interests and preferences. A retailer's function is to anticipate the demands of a target group or groups of customers and to seek out in the market styles that are most likely to win acceptance.

Types of Retailers There are many ways to classify retail firms. However, when evaluating their roles as far as fashion leadership is concerned, they tend to fall into three main categories.

First there are firms that are considered fashion leaders. They feature newly introduced styles that have only limited production and distribution and are usually expensive. A second group of retailers—by far the largest in number—features fashions that have captured consumer interest in their introductory stage and are in the late-rise or

early-culmination stage of their life cycles. Since these styles are usually widely produced by this time, they are most often offered at moderate prices. A third group of retailers, often called "mass merchants," features widely accepted fashions that are firmly in the culmination phase of their life cycles. Since fashions at this stage of development are usually mass-produced, mass merchants can and do offer fashions at moderately low to low prices.

Fashion Influence Occasionally, retailers are so intuitive or creative that they are a step ahead of their suppliers in anticipating the styles their customers will accept. Such retailers accelerate the introduction and progress of new fashions by persuading manufacturers to produce styles that answer the latent demand which retailers sense.

Normally, however, retailers simply select from what is offered by producers in the market. To do a good job, retailers must carefully shop the markets, selecting styles they feel sure will be of special interest to their customers. They must have the styles in their stores when customers are ready to buy. On the other hand, retailers can hold back a good incoming fashion by failing to stock styles that customers would buy if given the opportunity. Conversely, they can make the mistake of exposing new styles prematurely—that is, before their customers are ready to accept them. No amount of retail effort can make customers buy styles in which they have lost interest or in which they have not yet developed interest, and stocking such merchandise simply means lost sales and probable markdowns.

The more accurately a retailer understands customers' fashion preferences, and the more accurately that understanding is reflected in the assortments purchased, stocked, shown, and promoted, the more successful the operation, and the more important the retailer's fashion role within the community.

THEORIES OF FASHION ADOPTION

Fashions are accepted by a few of any group before they are accepted by the majority. Isolating and

We found our Belle in San Francisco

Last Wednesday, we were on the verge
of sending an S.O.S. to bring Mr. Keen,
Tracer of Lost Persons, out of retirement.

We wanted to talk to the clever woman
who did this costume and get all the
what/why/where/when/who details so we
could give you a good,
well-rounded fashion report.

Five hours later, we still hadn't found
the "who", designer Belle Saunders.

"She's out of town," her office told us.

"I had lunch with her yesterday and
she didn't mention any trip," said our buyer.

Finally, we called **Abe Schrader**,
prexy of the company she creates for,
and he spilled the beans.
Seems she had left work the night before
humming "Open up that Golden Gate".

But it was worth all the worry
when we finally tracked her down in S.F.
Belle Saunders is a charming lady, even on a coast-to-coast
phone, and answered all our **Big Five** Questions brightly.

what is her fashion credo?
"Uncluttered," she answered immediately.
Not gimmicky. I think clothes should have a
natural ease. They should be becoming to all
shapes, not just will-o'-the-wisps or
towering **Valkyries**.
And clothes should have no age."

why does she especially believe
in the dress-and-jacket costume?
"I think it's perfect for those days that start
at 9 a.m. and go on through cocktails and
dinner. And with the outfit Altman's
chose for instance, a woman
won't stand for ten minutes staring into
her closet and wondering what goes
with what. She slips into the slim black
dress, pops on the black and white
cardigan, swings the scarf around
her throat. And there she has it,
perfectly put together."

We told her this particular two-piecer is our favorite.
We like the sharp, black-and-white of it. Comes in
pure, carefree polyester for misses' sizes, 158.00.

where, we asked, does Ms. Saunders
get ideas? "Not sitting in an office all the time.
(She didn't have to tell us that.) Sitting in an office
doesn't generate the mind. I go all over the world.
To Europe, of course, for the couturier shows.
To museums, to **art galleries**. Anywhere
there's something new to learn."

"when," we said finally, "are you ever
coming home?" "See you on Wednesday, 'bye now."

who So it's all arranged. Come meet our who's-
fashion designer. (and world traveler and wife
and mother and painter and very busy lady).
Belle Saunders will be in our Americana Shop tomorrow from 12:30 till 2.
We'll have informal modeling and you can see her entire spring collection.
No matter how busy you are, you owe it to yourself to drop by.
It'll save you time in the long run.

B. Altman & Co

Stores often feature designers in their fashion advertising.
B. Altman & Co.

Three Theories of Fashion Dissemination

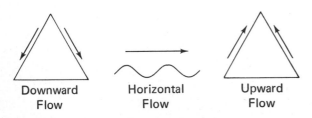

Downward Flow   Horizontal Flow   Upward Flow

identifying those few, and keeping track of their preferences, is an important step in fashion forecasting—anticipating which styles are most likely to succeed as fashions and how widely and by whom each will be accepted.

Three theories have been advanced to explain the "social contagion" of fashion adoption: the "downward-flow" theory, the "horizontal-flow" or mass-market theory, and the "upward-flow" theory. Each attempts to explain the course a fashion travels or is likely to travel, and each has its own claim to validity in reference to particular fashions or social environments.

Downward-flow Theory

The oldest theory of fashion adoption, the *downward-flow theory* (or the "trickle-down theory") maintains that in order to be identified as a true fashion, a style must first be adopted by people at the top of the social pyramid; the style then gradually wins acceptance at progressively lower social levels.

This theory assumes the existence of a social hierarchy in which lower classes seek identification with levels above them, while those at the top seek disassociation from those they consider socially inferior. The theory suggests that fashions are accepted by lower classes only if, and after, they are accepted by upper classes, and that upper classes will reject a fashion once it has flowed down to below their own social level.

Early economists, such as Roe in 1834 and Foley and Veblen at the turn of this century, were among the first to observe this type of social behav-

ior and its effect upon fashion. In 1903, a French sociologist, Gabriel Tarde, compared the spread of fashion to a social water tower from which a continuous fall of imitation could descend.[3] The German sociologist Georg Simmel, one of the first of his discipline to undertake a serious study of fashion, wrote in 1904:

Social forms, apparel, aesthetic judgment, the whole style of human expression, are constantly being transformed by fashion in [a way that] . . . affects only the upper classes. Just as soon as the lower classes begin to copy their styles, thereby crossing the line of demarcation the upper classes have drawn and destroying their coherence, the upper classes turn away from this style and adopt a new one. . . . The same process is at work as between the different sets within the upper classes, although it is not always visible here.[4]

The theory that fashions disseminate or flow downward from upper to lower social classes has had among its twentieth-century proponents such authorities as Robinson, Laver, Sapir, and Flügel. Flügel, in fact, suggests that sumptuary laws originated in the reluctance of upper classes to abandon the sartorial distinctiveness that to them represented superiority.[5]

To some extent, this theory has validity, but more so in the past than recently. Some fashions may appear first among the socially elite, but if a style becomes popular, eager manufacturers quickly mass-produce lower-priced copies of it which many consumers can then afford to adopt, and the elite seek newer styles.

Today, because of radical change in our social structure, this theory has few adherents. The downward-flow theory of fashion dissemination can apply only when a society resembles a pyramid, with people of wealth and position at the apex and followers at successively lower levels. The social structure today, however, is more like a group of rolling hills than it is a pyramid. There are many social groups and many directions other than straight down in which fashion can and does travel.

This changed pattern of fashion acceptance is also a result of the speed with which fashion news travels now, so that all social groups know about fashion innovation at practically the same time. Moreover, accelerated mass production and mass distribution of fashion goods have broadened acceptance of styles by making them available less expensively and more quickly than ever before.

For these reasons, today's mass producers are less likely to wait cautiously for upper-class approval of newly introduced styles. As soon as significant signs of an interesting new style appear, they are ready to offer adaptations or even copies to the public.

Horizontal-flow Theory

A newer theory, called the *horizontal-flow theory* or mass-market theory of fashion adoption, holds that fashions move horizontally between groups on similar social levels rather than vertically from one level to another. Chief exponent of this theory is Dr. Charles W. King, whose research has mainly concerned the adoption of millinery fashions.

King believes that the modern social environment, including rapid mass communications and the promotional efforts of manufacturers and retailers, results in introducing new styles to the fashion leaders of all social groups at approximately the same time. He notes that there is almost no lag between the adoption of a fashion by one social group and another, citing the way Paris fashions are now bought and copied for mass distribution sometimes even before the originals are available to the more elite markets. Trade buyers at couturier openings ship the models they have purchased home by air and get copies into retail stores often before the custom client—whose garments are made to order by the same couturiers—has had a chance to wear the new clothes.

The incidence of this horizontal flow also has been observed by some modern supporters of the older downward-flow theory. Robinson, for example, recognizes horizontal movement within a particular social stratum when he says that any given group or cluster of groups forming a class takes its cues from those contiguous with it. He claims fashions therefore radiate from a center.[6]

Implications for Merchandising The theory of horizontal fashion movement has great significance for merchandising. It points out the fallacy of assuming that there is a single homogeneous fashion public in this country. In reality, a number of distinctly different groups make up the fashion public. Each group has its own characteristics and its own fashion ideas and needs. The horizontal-flow theory recognizes that what wealthy society people are wearing today is not necessarily what suburbanites, college students, or office workers will wear tomorrow or will wait until tomorrow to accept. It admits that there are separate markets in fashion goods as in any other type of merchandise.

Retailers who apply the horizontal-flow theory will watch their customers closely rather than be guided solely by what more exclusive stores may be selling. They will seek to identify the groups into which customers can be divided in terms of income, age, education, and lifestyle. Among their customers, they will look for the innovators (and their style choices) as well as the influentials (and their selections). King defines a *fashion innovator* as a person who is quicker than his or her associates to try out a new style. A *fashion influential* is a person whose advice is sought by associates; a fashion influential's adoption of a new style gives it prestige among a group. The two roles may or may not be played by the same individual within a specific group.

The news that socially prominent women are wearing plunging necklines in exclusive New York restaurants will have less significance for the retailers of a small Midwestern city than the observation that the leader of the country club set in their community is abandoning bright colors for black on formal occasions. If the latter is a fashion influential in the community, her dress is the more important weathervane for them than what is being worn in New York.

Industry Practice King draws a distinction between the spread of a fashion within the industry itself and its adoption by consumers. A vertical flow definitely operates within the industry, he concedes: "Exclusive and famous designers are watched closely and emulated by lesser designers. Major manufacturers are studied and copied by smaller and less expert competitors."[7] And, as any reader of *Women's Wear Daily* can testify, there is no hotter news in the industry than information about what the top designers and the top producers are showing.

King points out, moreover, that the innovation process in the industry represents a "great filtering system." From an almost infinite number of possibilities, manufacturers select a finite number of styles. From these, trade buyers select a smaller sampling. Finally, consumers choose from among retailers' selections, thereby endorsing certain ones as accepted fashions.

This process, King maintains, is quite different from the consumer reaction outlined by Simmel and other proponents of the downward-flow theory. The difference lies in the fact that today the mass market does not await the approval of the class market before it adopts a fashion.

Upward-flow Theory

The third theory to explain the process of fashion adoption is relatively new. It reflects the enormous social changes that have occurred in the past decade or two and are continuing to occur. Because the process of fashion dissemination that has evolved in the 1960s and 1970s is exactly opposite to that which prevailed throughout much of recorded history, this theory has important implications for producers and retailers alike.

This theory of fashion adoption, called the *upward-flow theory*, holds that the young, particularly those of low-income families as well as those in higher income groups who adopt low-income life styles, are quicker than any other social group to create or adopt new and different fashions. As its name implies, this theory is exactly the opposite of the downward-flow theory; it holds that fashion adoption begins among the young of lower classes and then moves upward, into higher social levels.

Perhaps the most obvious example of the upward-flow theory in action is the worldwide popularity of blue jeans, denim, and even denimlike material. Acceptance of this fashion began in the 1960s and grew steadily stronger well into the 1970s. Blue jeans and denim jackets, traditionally the working clothes of those who did manual labor, were first worn as street clothes by teenagers who were members of lower-income groups or who chose to be associated with those groups. The jeans fashion spread rapidly among all young people, regardless of income, and then moved almost as rapidly up the age scale. By the early 1970s, fashionable pantsuits and even evening dresses were made of denim or of costly materials dyed to resemble denim.

Fashions such as long hair, leather and peasant apparel, and styles and designs associated with various minority groups have followed the same pattern: a young and lower lifestyle beginning, quickly followed by adoption among older people with different lifestyles. In the mid-1970s, the "western look" was beginning to follow a similar pattern, particularly in men's and boys' apparel.

For producers and retailers, this new direction of fashion flow implies radical changes in traditional methods of charting and forecasting fashion trends. No longer can producers and retailers look solely to name designers and socially prominent fashion leaders for ideas that will become tomorrow's best-selling fashions. Instead, they also must pay considerable attention to what young people favor, for the young have now become a large, independent group that can exert considerable influence on fashion styles.

As a result, today fewer retailers and manufacturers attend European couture showings that were once considered fashion's most important source of design inspiration. Now producers and retailers alike are more interested in ready-to-wear showings, where they look for styles and design details that reflect trends with more fashion relevance for the youth of the United States.

It would appear that fashion will never again flow in only one direction. However, while there will always be customers for high fashion as well as for conservative fashion, producers and retailers must now accept that they will be doing a considerable proportion of their business in fashions created or adopted first by the lower-income young and by those who choose to be allied with them.

FASHION LEADERS AND FASHION FOLLOWERS

Each of the three theories of fashion adoption recognizes the existence of leaders and followers in fashion acceptance. The downward-flow theory casts persons of social, political, and economic prominence in the role of leaders. The horizontal-flow theory recognizes individuals whose personal prestige makes them leaders within their own circles, whether or not they are known elsewhere. The upward-flow theory points to the fact that the young as well as people with lower incomes have played an important fashion role in the last half of the twentieth century.

Fashion Leaders

The theories of fashion adoption stress that the fashion leader is not the creator of the fashion; nor does merely wearing the fashion make a person a fashion leader. As Quentin Bell explains: "The leader of fashion does not come into existence until the fashion is itself created . . . a king or person of great eminence may indeed lead the fashion, but he leads only in the general direction which it has already adopted."[8] In effect, if a fashion parade is forming, fashion leaders may head it and even quicken its pace. They cannot, however, simply by marching down the street, bring about a procession, nor can they, by snapping their fingers, reverse an existing procession.

Innovators and Influentials Famous people are not necessarily fashion leaders, even if they do influence an individual style. Their influence, in

The Dutchess of Windsor, a fashion leader for 40 years.
Wide World Photos

such cases, usually affects only one striking style, one attribute, one set of circumstances. The true fashion leader is a person constantly seeking distinction and therefore likely to launch a succession of fashions rather than just one. A person like Beau Brummel, who made a career of dressing fashionably, or the Duchess of Windsor, whose wardrobe has been front-page fashion news for decades, influences fashion on a much broader scale.

What makes a person a fashion leader? Flügel explains: "Inasmuch as we are artistically minded and dare to assert our own individuality by being different, we are leaders of fashion."[9] King, however, makes it clear that more than just daring to be different is required. In his analysis, a person eager for the new is merely an innovator or early buyer. To be a leader, one must be influential, sought after for advice within a proscribed coterie. An influential person, says King, sets the appropriate dress for a specific occasion in a particular circle. Within that circle, an innovator presents current offerings and is the earliest visual communicator of a new style.[10]

Social Leaders Leaders of whatever group is considered "society" are prime candidates for positions of fashion leadership. The glamour and publicity that surround them cause an average person to notice what they wear, or even to daydream that some of their luster will rub off on him or her if their fashions are imitated.

Royalty in the past has played a major role in introducing and encouraging new fashions. Among the eighteenth- and nineteenth-century royal families of Europe, Marie Antoinette and Empress Eugénie were undoubtedly the outstanding fashion leaders. As democracies replaced monarchies, members of the wealthy and international sets stepped into the spotlight and thus into fashion leadership. Lists of best-dressed men and women today rarely include kings or queens, princes or princesses; instead, the names are those of the families of prominent industrialists and political figures, with occasionally a stage, screen, or television personality.

Whenever such people attend a ball, a dinner party, or even a quiet lunch at a smart restaurant, the press reports details of what they wear. So far as fashion is concerned, these people are not just in the news; they *are* the news. Should they go skiing and buy sweaters in a local shop, the purchase is publicized. When they view designers' collections, newspapers announce their selections, if the information can possibly be extracted from those concerned.

Consciously or subconsciously, the public is influenced by what these social leaders wear. If in no other way, an average person is affected because so many manufacturers and retailers of fashion take their cue from these elite. Right or wrong, people in the fashion business count on the fashion sense of these leaders. They also rely on the exposure given social leaders' clothes in news media to encourage people of ordinary means to adopt similar styles.

People in the News It is not always necessary, however, for people to be socially prominent or wealthy to influence fashion. Fashion is affected by people whose names appear on the front pages of newspapers, whether or not they appear on the society pages as well.

Stars of stage and screen, by their great exposure to the public, have also influenced fashion but to a greater extent in earlier days than today. Greta Garbo and Marlene Dietrich, in the 1930s, stimulated the then daring new fashion for slacks. In the 1960s, actresses Marilyn Monroe and Jayne Mansfield encouraged styles that featured a large bosom and a plunging neckline.

From time to time, both sports and the professionals who participate in them have had a powerful impact on fashion. For instance, as tennis gradually overtook golf as the country's most popular participation sport in the mid-1970s, white, the traditional color for tennis costumes, showed a rapid growth in acceptance for all kinds of apparel for both men and women. White became particularly popular in casual sportswear and streetwear. At the same time, however, some of the best-known tennis stars, such

Chris Evert is among those who influenced tennis fashions in the 1970s.

Todd Friedman

as Chris Evert, Billie Jean King, and Margaret Court, began to appear at matches in colored, patterned, and frilled tennis outfits. Soon these untraditional styles of active sportswear appeared in the sports departments of retail stores and on many enthusiastic amateurs who were taking up the game. In resort areas, shops cut the amount of rack space devoted to golf outfits and increased their stocks of tennis outfits.

An example of how the clothes worn by those in the public eye influence those later purchased by less well-known people was provided early in the 1960s when three women, each prominent in a different field, were photographed, each wearing a leopard coat. They were Queen Elizabeth II of

England, the then Mrs. John F. Kennedy, and actress Elizabeth Taylor. Immediately a fashion was firmly launched. With simultaneous sponsorship in such varied groups as each of these women represented, spotted-fur fashions caught on and spread rapidly. Those who could afford leopard coats bought them; others bought fabric dyed to resemble leopard. Spotted-fur accessories and trims were much in evidence. Even fabrics for garments completely unrelated to outerwear, such as lingerie and sleepwear, took on a leopard look. Home-furnishings fabrics were also printed with leopard spots.

Interest in this particular fashion has remained high. Today, although laws forbid the importation and, in some states, the sale of leopard or ocelot, many apparel and home-furnishings fabrics are still available in prints that resemble spotted furs.

History provides many examples of fashions associated with prominent individuals, even though these individuals were not otherwise considered fashion leaders. General Dwight D. Eisenhower, commanding the Allied Forces in Europe during World War II, adopted the short jacket that has been known ever since as the Eisenhower jacket. The semifitted velvet-collared coat style adopted by the Earl of Chesterfield in the nineteenth century has ever since been widely known simply as a Chesterfield.

Fashion Followers

While some people prefer the excitement and risk of fashion leadership, others prefer to be followers. Followers are in the majority within any group or cluster of groups. Without followers the fashion industry certainly would collapse. Mass production and distribution can be profitable only when merchandise is accepted by many consumers.

By observing fashion leaders, manufacturers and retailers can predict fairly well what the majority of customers, as fashion followers, will want in the foreseeable future. This element of predictability in fashion demand has helped make possible the vast ready-to-wear business in this country.

Fashion leaders may be stimulating and exciting customers for the fashion industries to serve but fashion followers are the "bread-and-butter" customers of these industries. Almost 90 percent of the dresses produced for ready-to-wear in the United States each year are made to retail at under $38. At that price level, there is little room for fashion experimentation. These dresses, and some at slightly higher prices, are for the followers rather than the innovators.

Reasons for Following Fashion Theories about why people follow rather than lead in fashion are plentiful. Among the explanations are feelings of inferiority, admiration of others, lack of interest, and ambivalence about the new.

Inferiority Flügel writes, "Inasmuch as we feel our own inferiority and the need for conformity to the standards set by others, we are followers of fashion."[11] For example, high school boys and girls are at a notably insecure stage of life and therefore are more susceptible than any other age group to the appeal of fads. A woman about to face a difficult interview or attend her first meeting with a new group carefully selects new clothes and reveals her insecurity by asking anxiously, "How do I look?" Often an inner feeling of inadequacy can be hidden by wearing a style that others have already approved as appropriate and acceptable.

Admiration Flügel also maintains that it is a fundamental human trait to imitate those who are admired or envied. A natural and symbolic way to do this is to copy their clothes. An outstanding illustration of his theory was provided in the 1960s by the then Mrs. John F. Kennedy. First as the wife and then as the widow of the president, her clothes and hairstyles were copied instantly among many different groups throughout this country. On a different level, the young girl who copies the hairstyle of her best friend, older sister, or favorite aunt demonstrates the same principle; so do college students who model their appearance after that of campus leaders.

Lack of Interest Sapir suggests that many people are insensitive to fashion and follow it only because

"they realize that not to fall in with it would be to declare themselves members of a past generation, or dull people who cannot keep up with their neighbors."[12] Their response to fashion, he says, is a sullen surrender, not by any means an eager following of the Pied Piper.

Ambivalence Another theory holds that many people are ambivalent in their attitudes toward the new; they both want it and fear it. For most, it is easier to choose what is already familiar. Such individuals need time and exposure to new styles before they accept them.

Varying Rates of Response Individuals vary in the speed with which they respond to a new idea, especially when fashion change is radical and dramatic. Some fashion followers apparently just need time to adjust to new ideas. Merchants exploit this point when they buy a few "window pieces" of styles too advanced for their own clientele, then expose these new styles in windows and fashion shows to allow customers time to get used to them. Only after a period of exposure to the new styles do the fashion followers accept them.

An example may be found in the fashion cycle of women's pantsuits during the 1960s. Norman Norell had introduced a culotte suit in his 1960 collection and a suit with long pants in 1964. Dior had shown a pants-skirt in 1962. Yet, in July 1964, *Women's Wear Daily* still reported reservations about pants among members of the Paris fashion industry. A Dior spokesman was quoted as saying that pants were for around the house but not for every day. A St. Laurent spokesman said, "Absolutely not here. Pants aren't anything great." Yet by 1966, pantsuits were featured in the *New York Times* in an article appropriately titled, "Now Everyone Wears the Pants"; and by 1968, Eugenia Sheppard, in her syndicated column, was writing, "Anything but pantsuits is square." By that time there were pants for daytime, evening, or at-home wear, and for all shapes and ages. Shock, resistance, and reservations had finally given way to enthusiastic acceptance.

FASHION AS AN EXPRESSION OF INDIVIDUALITY

A remarkable feature of today's mass-produced fashions is that, although styles in apparel and accessories may be made by the hundreds or thousands, one rarely sees two people dressed exactly alike. Dress may meet identical dress, and suit may meet identical suit, but the same apparel will be worn with distinctive touches imparted by each wearer. Within the framework of fashion conformity, each person attempts to remain individual. Social scientists see in this situation a paradox, an endless conflict between the desire to conform and the desire to remain apart, or individual.

Long before the world reached its present impersonal age of numbers—social security, ZIP Code, bank account, automobile registration, time clock, and the like—sociologists and psychologists, as well as fashion authorities, had witnessed the individual's refusal to merge entirely into the mass. Purchasers of fashion apparel in the United States usually go along with general fashion styles rather than risk seeming out of step with the times. However, they continue to assert their individuality in such touches as how they combine colors and textures, how they wear accessories, and how they wear their hair.

Fashion editor Jessica Daves summed up the miracle of modern ready-to-wear fashion by saying that it offers "the possibility for some women to create a design for themselves . . . to choose the color and shape in clothes that will present them as they would like to see themselves."[13]

The same possibility for carving individuality out of conformity is present today in men's fashions. In the late 1960s, turtlenecks began to be widely worn, but they were given individuality by choice of color, texture, and accessories. Some men wore medallions; others wore beads; some left the garment unadorned. Similarly, although the fashion for fuller and longer hair was adopted quite generally among young men during that period, each interpreted the fashion to suit his own personality:

bushy sideburns, back hair below the collar, or full head of hair, full beard, and mustache.

The Paradox of Conformity and Individuality

For decades, experts have tried to explain why people seek both conformity and individuality in fashion. Simmel suggests that two opposing social tendencies are at war: the need for union and the need for isolation. The individual, he reasons, derives satisfaction from knowing that the way in which he or she expresses a fashion represents something special. At the same time, people gain support from seeing others favor the same style.[14]

Flügel interprets the paradox in terms of a person's feelings of superiority and inferiority. The individual wants to be like others "insofar as he regards them as superior, but unlike them, in the sense of being more 'fashionable' insofar as he thinks they are below him."[15]

Sapir ties the conflict to a revolt against custom and a desire to break away from slavish acceptance of fashion. Slight changes from the established form of dress and behavior "seem for the moment to give victory to the individual, while the fact that one's fellows revolt in the same direction gives one a feeling of adventurous safety."[16] He also ties the assertion of individuality to the need to affirm one's self in a functionally powerful society in which the individual has ceased to be a measure of the society itself.

One example of this conflict may be found in the off-duty dress of people required to wear uniforms of one kind or another during working hours, such as nurses, police, and mail carriers. A second example is the apparel worn by many present day bankers. While retaining the customary shirt and tie, many have abandoned the traditional "banker's gray" suit for more individual and often colorful sport jackets and slacks.

Retailers know that although some people like to lead and some like to follow in fashion, most people buy fashion to express personality or to identify with a particular group. To belong, they follow fashion; to express their personality, they find ways to individualize it.

Fashion and Self-expression

Increasing importance is being placed on fashion individuality—on "doing your own thing," or expressing your personality, or refusing to be cast in a mold. Instead of slavish adoption of any one look, today's young person seeks to create an individual effect through the way he or she combines various fashion components. For instance, if a young woman thinks a denim skirt, ankle-length woolen coat, and heavy turtlenecked sweater represent her personality, they are considered acceptable among her group.

Forward-looking designers recognize this desire for self-expression. Designers say that basic wardrobe components should be made available, but that consumers should be encouraged to combine them as they see fit. For instance, they advise women to wear pants or skirts, long or short, according to how they feel, not according to what past tradition has considered proper for an occasion. They suggest that men make the same choice among tailored suits, leisure suits, and slacks to find the styles that express their personalities.

Having experienced such fashion freedom, young people may never conform again. Yet the young experimenters have this in common despite individual differences in their dress: a deep-rooted desire to dress differently from the older generations with whom they live and associate.

For most people—particularly for those who lack the time, funds, and vital flair for combining different components into a strictly personal look—the tendency continues to be to accept a fashion or effect as a whole. A touch of novelty in accessories, color, line, or texture within the framework of prevailing fashion is enough to satisfy the feeling of individuality that the average consumer craves.

The fashion merchandising rules as expounded by Nystrom years ago thus continue to prove themselves valid in both theory and practice.

REFERENCES

[1] Quoted in Bell, *On Human Finery*, pp. 48–49.

[2] Robinson, "Fashion Theory and Product Design," p. 29.

[3] Tarde, *The Laws of Imitation*, p. 221.

[4] Simmel, "Fashion," p. 140.

[5] Flügel, *The Psychology of Clothes*, p. 139.

[6] Robinson, "Economics of Fashion Demand," p. 383.

[7] King, "Fashion Adoption," pp. 114–115.

[8] Bell, op. cit., p. 46.

[9] Flügel, op. cit., p. 140.

[10] King, op. cit., p. 124.

[11] Flügel, op. cit., p. 140.

[12] Sapir, "Fashion," p. 140.

[13] Daves, *Ready-made Miracle*, pp. 231–232.

[14] Simmel, op. cit., pp. 137, 140.

[15] Flügel, op. cit., p. 140.

[16] Sapir, op. cit., p. 140.

MERCHANDISING VOCABULARY
Define or briefly explain the following terms:

Fashion designer	Fashion innovator
Line	Fashion influential
Downward-flow theory	Upward-flow theory
Horizontal-flow theory	

MERCHANDISING REVIEW
1. Name the three types of designers most commonly serving the American fashion industry today. What are the responsibilities of each?
2. What are the major sources of inspiration for many fashion designers? Give an example of how the designs of a modern apparel designer have been influenced by one such source of inspiration.
3. Into what three groups may fashion manufacturers be classified? Indicate the general identifying characteristics of each group.
4. What are the three groups or classifications into which most fashion retail firms fall? What are the basic identifying characteristics of each?
5. Briefly explain the downward-flow theory of fashion adoption. How valid is this theory today? Why?
6. Briefly explain the horizontal-flow theory of fashion adoption. Discuss its implications for today's fashion merchants.
7. Briefly explain the upward-flow theory of fashion adoption. What are its implications for modern fashion merchants?
8. Why are the following prime candidates for positions of fashion leadership: (a) social leaders, (b) people in the news, (c) sports professionals?
9. For what four reasons do most people follow, rather than lead, in matters relating to fashion? Briefly explain the meaning of each.
10. How can an individual use fashion as a means of self-expression?

MERCHANDISING DIGEST
1. Discuss the implications of the following quotation from the text: "Successful designers do not live and work in an ivory tower." To be successful, how must they live and work? Cite examples to support your answer.
2. The text states that "famous people are not necessarily fashion leaders, even if they do influence an individual style." Discuss this statement and its implications for the fashion industry. Name at least one recently famous person who has *not* been a fashion leader or influential and at least one who *has* been a fashion leader or influential and a specific style for which the latter has become famous.
3. Discuss why people today seek both conformity and individuality in fashion and the implications this has for the fashion retailer.

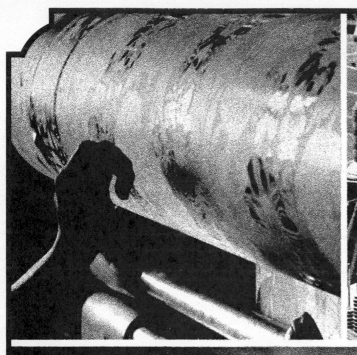

PART 2
MARKETERS OF FASHION

Few consumers are aware of the numerous processes or stages through which raw materials must go to become the finished fashion products that retail merchants stock and promote. The purpose of Part 2 of this text is to familiarize readers with the whole series of business activities necessary to make fashion goods available to consumers in such form that they can be used immediately.

Marketing refers to the performance of business activities that direct the flow of goods from producers to consumers. All the various processes or series of activities involved in converting raw materials into such form that they can be used by ultimate consumers, without further commercial processing, is known as the *marketing process*. This is how the marketing process looks in chart form, in terms of fashion goods:

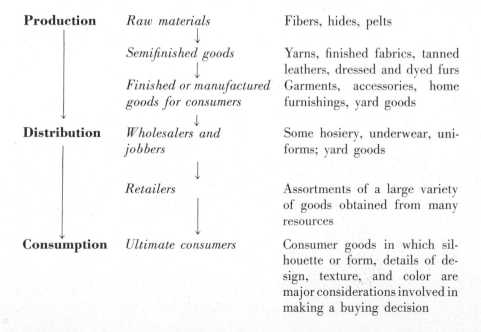

Production	*Raw materials*	Fibers, hides, pelts
	Semifinished goods	Yarns, finished fabrics, tanned leathers, dressed and dyed furs
	Finished or manufactured goods for consumers	Garments, accessories, home furnishings, yard goods
Distribution	*Wholesalers and jobbers*	Some hosiery, underwear, uniforms; yard goods
	Retailers	Assortments of a large variety of goods obtained from many resources
Consumption	*Ultimate consumers*	Consumer goods in which silhouette or form, details of design, texture, and color are major considerations involved in making a buying decision

Merchandising is an important marketing activity. At each stage of the marketing process, business firms operating at that particular stage "merchandise" their products to potential consumers. Producers and distributors alike need to have the right goods, at the right time, in the right quantities, in the right place, and at right prices if they expect customers to patronize them in an increasingly competitive market. The term *market,* as used in this context, refers to a group of potential customers. In another context, *market* refers to the place or area in which buyers and sellers congregate to transact business.

Part 2, Marketers of Fashion, explores and discusses the various industries involved in marketing fashion goods. It explains the history and development of these industries, their organization and operation, the merchandising activities they engage in, and the trends that seem to influence what these industries will be like in the future. The industries discussed are those that produce the raw materials of fashion, those that produce semifinished or finished fashion goods, and those that distribute the fashion goods to ultimate consumers. Domestic and foreign fashion market centers are also discussed.

5
THE MATERIALS OF FASHION: TEXTILE FIBERS AND FABRICS

Fashions and the materials from which they are made are inseparable. When designers work out their ideas, they think not only in terms of silhouettes and shapes but also in terms of materials best suited for each silhouette and shape, like the crisp assertion of a taffeta, for instance, or the soft cling of a jersey. Materials are vital to manufacturers, too; selection of materials is a major operating decision, and their cost is a major investment. Retailers must also carefully consider the materials from which apparel fashions are made because they play a significant role in influencing customers' buying decisions.

More fashion garments and accessories are made of textiles than of any other kind of material. Fashion textiles are the product of a network of primary industries, such as the cotton industry, the wool industry, the various industries producing man-made fibers, and the fabric industry.

A basic knowledge of each of these industries is important to those engaged in the merchandising of fashion. Such knowledge not only explains the origin and background of the fabrics themselves, but also shows just how, and how quickly, each industry can be expected to respond to fashion trends in apparel. Such knowledge also makes it possible to evaluate the fashion guidance provided by these industries to apparel producers, retailers, and consumers.

Changes in the textile industries have been rapid and important, particularly in recent years. Not only have there been radical new methods of producing and blending fibers, but advances have also been made in methods of making and finishing fabrics. All have contributed to an increasing variety of fashion goods and greater excitement in the world of fashion.

THE TEXTILE FIBER INDUSTRIES

A *fiber* is a hairlike unit of raw material from which textile fabric is made. The fibers that are spun into yarn and woven or knitted into fabric influence fashion by determining the possibilities ultimately available in the color, weight, texture, and other qualities of the finished garment.

Fibers are divided into two main categories: natural and man-made. *Natural fibers* are derived from plant or animal sources. *Man-made fibers* are produced in chemical plants.

Considering the wide variety available today, it is difficult to imagine the narrow selection of fibers offered to manufacturers and consumers a century ago. At that time, for instance, it was impossible to produce winter clothing in clear, light colors. Of the fibers then available, wool was the only one with built-in warmth, but because of the often creamy or uneven coloring of wool fibers, plus the limited knowledge of dyeing techniques, woolen fabrics usually were available only in dark colors. In the same way, fashions that required a person's figure to be subtly instead of forceably controlled by undergarments would not have been possible even 50 years ago, because such man-made fibers as spandex had not yet been developed.

History and Development

The fiber industries are of vastly different ages and backgrounds. The natural fiber industries are so old that even primitive human beings are believed to have gathered flax to make yarn for fabrics. The man-made fiber industries, on the other hand, are so young that the oldest among them, rayon, has not yet rounded out its first century. Thus natural fibers have had a very long history of extremely slow development, which has speeded up only in recent years, while man-made fibers have had a very short history of amazingly rapid development.

The Natural Fibers Industries The principal natural fibers used in the production of textile fabrics include *cotton,* a vegetable fiber from the cotton boll of the cotton plant; *wool,* an animal fiber from the hair of sheep; *silk,* an animal fiber from the cocoons spun by silkworms; and *linen,* a vegetable fiber from the woody stalk of the flax plant.

Cotton Cotton, the most extensively used of the natural fibers, thrives in various sections of the United States, one of the world's major cotton producers. It is also grown in the Soviet Union, Brazil, China, Egypt, India, Hawaii, Japan, Mexico, Peru, and the West Indies. It is one of the world's major money crops.

The oldest bit of cotton cloth yet found, at an archaeological site in Mexico, is estimated to have been woven about 7,000 years ago. A 3,500-year-old Hindu hymn mentions cotton; and 2,500 years ago, a Greek historian described how Indian women picked the cotton bolls and carded and spun the fiber into yarn. Until a few decades ago, most of the world's cotton crop was still picked by hand. Today, however, while manual labor still prevails in many cotton-producing countries, the United States, because of its technological advances, harvests three-quarters of its crop by mechanical pickers and strippers.

Cotton fibers are of various lengths, depending upon the plant strain and the climate in which it is grown. The longest and finest fibers are used for sheer cotton fabric; shorter fibers go into coarser goods; the very short fibers, called *linters,* that remain on the seed are used mainly in the manufacture of rayon and for such nonfashion products as paper and absorbent cotton.

Wool Wool for use in apparel comes from Australia, New Zealand, England, Scotland, South Africa, Uruguay, and the United States—those areas that have good grazing conditions for sheep. In colder climates, sheep are likely to have coarser coats more suitable for carpet wool than for apparel.

Early people domesticated sheep and goats for their hair. There are records going back to 4200 B.C. that mention weavers, dyers, and wool merchants, and the wool industry continued thereafter as one of the most powerful in the textile field. In England, for example, wool had no rival until the eighteenth century, when cotton became important.

The first United States wool mill was established in Massachusetts in the late 1600s. Today, the states that count wool-bearing sheep important as farm income include Utah, Nevada, and Colorado. The majority of the woolen mills, however, have remained on the Atlantic coast, about half of them in the Northeast and the other half in the Southeast.

Silk The diet and climate preferences of the silkworm have made Japan, Italy, and China the world's principal producers of silk fiber. The industry began in China, considerably more than 4,000 years ago. Even then silk was considered such an important fiber for fashion fabrics that the Chinese guarded its production with a decree of death for anyone who told the secret to the unauthorized. The silkworm and its culture, called sericulture, came west during the late Middle Ages, and France, Italy, and Spain became the important silk centers in Europe. Cortez tried to bring the silkworm to the Americas in the sixteenth century, but failed, and that failure has been repeated on several later occasions. Various sericultural experiments have been tried in this country, but none have proved

This mechanical picker picks cotton bolls from two rows of plants at a time.

International Harvester

successful. All the silk fiber used annually by United States mills is imported.

Silk is the only natural fiber created in a continuous filament, rather than in short fibers that have to be spun together. The cocoons spun by the silkworm yield filaments that are from 800 to 1,300 yards in length.

Silk has always been considered a luxury fiber. In the Middle Ages and during the Renaissance, the sumptuary laws of many countries restricted the use of silk to royalty and members of the elite classes. Even today, silk is used mainly in dressy apparel and usually in higher-priced designs.

Silk used to be a thriving fabric business in the United States but is no longer. World War II abruptly cut off silk fiber supplies, and by the time the war had ended, the market for silk fabrics made in this country had all but vanished. Those man-made fibers most directly competitive with silk had made an important place for themselves by combining strength, sheerness, and washability. Silk fabrics produced in countries where labor is less expensive fill the small demand for this material at prices lower than domestic suppliers can profitably meet. Today, silk fabrics represent a minute part, about one six-thousandth, of the United States fiber consumption, just as silk represents an infinitesimal part of a fashion market it once dominated, women's hosiery.

Linen Linen fiber for fashion fabrics comes principally from the flax plants of Ireland and Belgium. Other producers include Egypt, France, Germany, Holland, Italy, Poland, and the Soviet Union, the latter being the world's chief producer of flax fiber. In the United States, the flax plant is grown mainly for the oil yielded by its seeds.

Flax may have been cultivated by man first for its food value, but it was soon used for its fiber as well. It probably was first grown in the Mediterranean area. Materials made of flax fibers have been found in Stone Age ruins in Switzerland; the ancient Egyptians used linen for wrapping mummies. Eventually, flax cultivation spread throughout Europe, into Asia, and across the Atlantic to the Americas. Flax was a popular fiber crop during the colonial period in this country, but dwindled rapidly in importance after the invention of the cotton gin in 1792, which made cotton a cheaper fiber to produce. The United States, therefore, imports most of its flax fiber for apparel purposes, and uses about 6 million pounds a year in its mills.

The Man-made Fiber Industries Like the medieval alchemists who sought to transform base metal into gold, European chemists of the eighteenth and nineteenth centuries sought to create artificial silk. Unlike the alchemists' dream, this dream came true. After a number of contributions by various scientists, the French Count Hilaire de Chardonnet started commercial production in the world's first artificial silk plant in 1891. The first such plant in the United States was established at Marcus Hook, Pennsylvania, in 1910.

At first, the new fiber was called "artificial silk" or "art silk." By 1924, however, the National Retail Dry Goods Association (now the National Retail Merchants Association) recognized that the new fiber needed an identity of its own. The Association coined the word "rayon," and registered it internationally. Man-made fibers had come of age; they could now be given names of their own and be accepted on their own merits.

The earliest man-made fibers, rayon and acetate, are the "cellulose fibers," for they use as their base such natural cellulose products as wood pulp or cotton linters. Nylon, the first of the truly man-made fibers and the first of the "polymers," appeared in 1938. It was followed in the years after World War II by other polymers such as the polyesters (Dacron was a leader), the acrylics (Orlon was the first big one), and the elasticlike spandex fibers. Polymers are so named because they are made by a chemical process called "polymerization," a way of combining simple chemicals into a complex group or fiber with definite characteristics of its own.

Man-made fibers start out as thick liquids. Then fibers of varying lengths are produced by forcing the liquid through the tiny holes of a me-

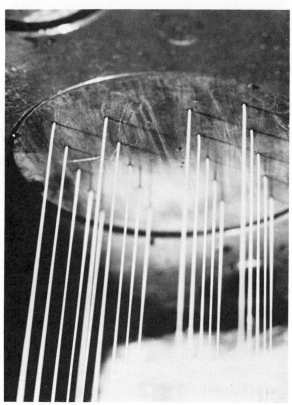

Thick liquids are forced through a spinerette to form synthetic fibers.

Celanese Fibers Marketing Co.

chanical device known as a *spinnerette*, in much the same way that spaghetti is made out of dough.

In the last few decades, man-made fibers have become very important in the production of fashion apparel. In 1972, for example, United States mills used over 6 billion pounds of man-made fibers. Table 5-1 compares the United States mill consumption of natural and man-made fibers; Table 5-2 shows the United States mill use of fibers in terms of some of the major apparel categories.

Organization and Operation

Because of the vast differences in the origin and characteristics of the various fibers, the fiber industries do not have uniform patterns of organization or operation. Although there may be similarity within groups, the practices of the natural fibers industry differ markedly from those of the man-made fibers industry. It is the difference, again, between something obtained from living plants and animals and something produced in a laboratory.

In spite of the differences, however, the goal of both groups is the same: to produce as efficiently as possible the fibers favored by consumers and thus needed by the textile fabric field.

The Natural Fibers Industries Cotton and wool, the major natural fibers, are produced where climate and terrain are favorable. The primary pro-

TABLE 5-1
United States Mill Consumption of Natural and Man-made Fibers
(Pounds Consumed Per Capita, Selected Years, 1950–1972)

YEAR	COTTON	WOOL	FLAX	SILK	RAYON AND ACETATE	OTHER MAN-MADE
1950	30.9	4.2	0.07	0.07	9.1	1.0
1955	26.5	2.5	0.05	0.07	8.8	2.7
1960	23.2	2.3	0.03	0.04	6.0	4.4
1965	23.0	2.0	0.04	0.03	8.2	10.4
1970	18.6	1.2	0.03	0.01	7.0	19.9
1972	18.4	1.0	0.03	0.01	6.8	29.4

Source: U.S. Department of Agriculture, Economic Research Service.

TABLE 5-2
United States Mill Consumption of Fiber in Selected End-use Categories, 1972
(millions of pounds)

CATEGORY	COTTON	WOOL	RAYON AND ACETATE	OTHER MAN-MADE	TOTAL
Women's dresses and playsuits	128.0	10.0	185.9	434.1	758.0
Men's suits, slacks, and coats	325.0	20.0	24.2	355.1	724.3
Women's suits, skirts, slacks, coats	200.0	55.0	41.0	285.0	581.0
Men's shirts	200.0	1.3	27.7	212.7	441.7
Women's lingerie	108.6	1.0	61.0	145.0	315.6
Women's blouses and shirts	73.5	0.5	45.5	98.8	218.3
Utility and career apparel	165.0	4.0	4.8	125.3	299.1
Men's underwear and nightwear	203.2	0.8	2.7	34.7	241.4

Source: Textile Organon, November 1972.

ducers of these fibers tend to be many in number and small in size.

There are four major areas of cotton production in the United States. In the Southeast, a considerable quantity of cotton is grown in the Carolinas, in Georgia, and in Alabama, but few farms have even as many as 20 acres under cultivation. In the Mississippi Delta land, particularly in Arkansas, Mississippi, and Louisiana, cotton is an important crop, and many farms are larger than 100 acres. In the Southwest, in areas of Texas and Oklahoma, cotton is a valuable crop, and the land under cultivation by each farmer is apt to be more than 100 acres. In the newest cotton-growing region, New Mexico, Arizona, and particularly California, there are both big farms and high yields per acre.

Much of the wool produced in this country comes from the Utah, Nevada, and Colorado ranges of relatively small ranchers.

Nearly all the natural fiber producers sell their product in local markets, either to mill representatives or, far more likely, to wholesalers. Wholesalers then do their bargaining at the central markets. The important central markets in this country for cotton are in Memphis, New Orleans, Dallas, and Houston, with New York and Chicago also handling a number of transactions although without having the physical goods on hand. Boston is the major central market for wool in the United States, and also handles most of the import transactions, so important to the wool industry. The many small producers of the natural fiber industries tend to compete with each other only in the sense that each strives to produce the maximum yield from resources. Each tries to cultivate those characteristics in the product that will command the best prices in the market. The cotton farmer tries to grow more cotton, of a better quality, on each acre. The sheep farmer tries to develop a hardier herd that will produce larger quantities of quality wool per clipping.

The Man-made Fibers Industries A man-made fiber can be produced wherever a chemical company erects a plant, which is apt to be where the supplies of raw chemicals, power, and labor are readily available. Thus there are plants up and down the Atlantic coast, with an increasing emphasis on the Southern states, where labor and other expenses are still somewhat lower than in the North. There is also an increasing number of plants along the West Coast, and concentrations in the interior of the country wherever companies have found good sources of raw materials or efficient railroads and waterways to facilitate easy shipping of those materials.

These plants, in contrast to the farms and

ranches of the natural fiber producers, are huge in size. In addition, sometimes the producing company serves as its own market, not only making the fiber but also spinning it into yarn and knitting or weaving it into fabrics.

Fiber Development Limited quantities of a new or modified man-made fiber are usually first produced in a pilot plant on an experimental basis. If research indicates that both industry and consumers will accept the new product, additional plant capacity is devoted to it, new applications of the fiber are explored, and new industries are consulted and encouraged to use it.

While this procedure is going on in one chemical company, there is always the possibility that another company may be working along similar lines to develop a competitive fiber. The company that is first to develop a new fiber has no assurance that it will have the field to itself for long. For example, there are many brands of such man-made fibers as nylon, rayon, and acetate already on the market, and quite a roster of companies producing various acrylics, polyesters, and other man-made fibers.

One reason why each important man-made fiber is produced by several chemical companies at almost the same time is that these fibers are engineered to provide whatever characteristics are currently in demand by industry and the consumer. Popular demand for a particular attribute—such as locked-in color, warmth without weight, or imperviousness to wrinkles—sets the same problem before the research laboratories of all fiber producers at the same time. Many of them come up with similar answers.

Consumer products in which textile fibers are incorporated are required by federal law (the Textile Fibers Products Identification Act of 1960) to bear labels specifying their fiber content by generic name and percentage of each that is used. The brand name or trademark of any of the fibers contained may also be stated, although this is not required by law. Some of these brand names and trademarks, however, have been given exposure to consumers over the years at considerable expense to the producer, and the producer is naturally concerned that these branded fibers should be handled by fabric manufacturers in ways that will enhance and not endanger the brand's acceptance.

Fiber Distribution There are three ways in which producers of man-made fibers usually sell their fibers to fabric manufacturers:

- As unbranded products, with no restrictions placed on their end use and no implied or required standards of performance claimed.
- As branded or trademarked fibers, with assurance to consumers that the quality of the fiber has been controlled by its producer but not necessarily with assurance as to either implied or required standards of performance in the end product.
- Under a licensing agreement, whereby the use of the fiber trademark concerned is permitted only to those manufacturers whose fabrics or other end products pass tests set up by the fiber producer for their specific end uses or applications.

Licensing programs set up by different fiber producers and by processors of yarn vary considerably in scope. The more comprehensive programs entail extensive end-use testing to back up the licensing agreement, exercise considerable control over fabric products that have been licensed, and offer technical services wherever needed to help correct situations in which a given fabric fails to pass a qualifying test. Trademarks used under such licensing agreements are referred to as *licensed trademarks*. Celanese's Fortrel is an example of a licensed trademark.

Licensing programs may involve wear tests as well as laboratory tests. They also may specify blend levels, such as when a required minimum percentage of the designated fiber must be contained in the yarn to qualify the product for licensing. Checking products periodically through retail shopping is not unusual.

Merchandising Activities

No matter how familiar fashion fabric and apparel producers and consumers may be with the inherent qualities of each fiber, there is always the need to disseminate information about the newest modifications and their application to fashion merchandise. To do this, producers of both natural and man-made fibers make extensive use of advertising and publicity and market research, and extend various customer services to manufacturers, retailers, and consumers.

Usually the producer of man-made fibers undertake these activities on behalf of their own individual brands and companies although the Man-Made Fiber Producers Association also carries on a very active program of consumer education about man-made fibers in general. Producers of natural fibers, on the other hand, carry on related activities through trade associations, each representing a particular natural fiber, such as the National Cotton Council (the central organization of the cotton industry); Cotton Incorporated (the group specializing in promoting the use of cotton by designers and manufacturers); the American Wool Council; the Wool Bureau; the Mohair Council of America; plus organizations promoting the use of fibers from other countries, such as the Irish Linen Guild and the Belgian Linen Association.

Advertising and Publicity While both man-made fibers and natural fibers are given advertising and publicity, man-made fiber producers put considerably more dollars into this merchandising effort than do natural fiber trade associations. They maintain a continuous flow of competitive advertising and publicity directed at both the trade and consumers. Sometimes an advertising and publicity effort will concern the entire range of textile fibers made by a single producer. Sometimes it will concentrate on a single fiber and its characteristics.

Among the trade media used by the man-made fiber producers are such publications as *Women's Wear Daily, Men's Wear,* and *Daily News Record.* Among the consumer media used are mass-circulation magazines and newspapers, as well as radio and television. Today some giant man-made fiber producers use national television spectaculars to publicize their brand names and get their fashion message across to consumers, although not to the extent that such spectaculars were used in the 1960s.

Since the names of major fibers are relatively well known today, an increasing number of man-made fiber producers now emphasize the qualities of their products rather than concentrating on the names of fibers. An outstanding example is Monsanto. The company has used almost every medium, including television, to publicize its "Wear-Dated" licensed trademark program. The basis of this program is a guarantee that not only the fabric, but also the buttons, belts, buckles, zippers, lining, padding, thread, and all other appurtenances used in the construction of a garment labeled "Wear-Dated" will give satisfactory normal wear for one full year, or Monsanto will provide the customer with either a refund or a replacement of the garment.

Although natural fibers are not advertised and promoted as aggressively as man-made fibers, some natural fiber groups are putting more effort and money into campaigns to meet the growing domination of man-made fibers. Because these campaigns are mainly handled by trade groups, they promote the fiber itself, not the products of an individual natural fiber producer. One of the most eye-catching campaigns of the mid-1970s, for instance, was Cotton Incorporated's ads and posters that not only underlined cotton's advantageous characteristics as a fiber but also pointed to the cotton industry's importance in the economy, to its interest in ecology, and even to its aid in the fuel crisis ("Cotton: less energy to produce; fed by earth; powered by sun"). At the time, all of these subjects were front-page news and billboard topics.

Fiber sources also provide garment producers and retailers with various aids that facilitate mention of their fibers in the advertising of consumer goods. This procedure adds to the impact of the recognition already achieved by the producer's name, trademark, slogan, or logotype. For example, the Wool Bureau encourages the use of its ball-of-yarn logotype in producer and retailer advertising of all-wool merchandise, as well as in displays of such goods.

To help spread the textile fiber fashion story, producers and trade associations continually provide the press with newsworthy information, background material, and photographs for editorial features, to facilitate mention of fashion and fiber in the media. Some of this publicity effort is accomplished by direct contact with the press; some of it is done by supplying garment producers and retailers with glossy photographs and other materials to enhance the effect of their own efforts. A familiar example of fashion publicity on behalf of a natural fiber is the National Cotton Council's annual Maid of Cotton program, the selection of a beauty queen to make appearances throughout the country in a fashionable cotton wardrobe made up of designs supplied by famous designers. An example of fashion publicity on behalf of a man-made fiber was furnished when Du Pont introduced Qiana, a new form of nylon, in 1968. First, members of the Paris couture were encouraged to present dresses in fabrics made entirely of this fiber; then, intensive trade advertising stressed the use by outstanding United States and European designers of fabrics made from Qiana. Later, Qiana was advertised and publicized as being used in the production of a wide variety of moderate-priced men's and women's apparel and accessories.

Another form of fiber advertising and publicity is the development of seasonal fashion presentations for use by retail stores. Publicity kits and programs specially prepared for local markets are developed. The objective is to support promotions during peak retail selling periods. Producers may also supply fashion experts to commentate fashion shows, to participate in television "talk" programs, or to address local consumer groups and retail sales personnel. Films about fibers and fabrics also may be utilized to further dramatize the fiber story.

Another promotional effort is the advertising undertaken by fiber producers in cooperation with fabric and garment manufacturers and retailers.

Such *cooperative advertising,* which is retail advertising for which the costs are shared by a store and a manufacturer on terms agreed to by both, benefits the fiber in two ways. First, consumers begin to associate the fiber name with other names already familiar, from the name of the fiber source to the name of the retail store selling the garment. This is particularly important when a fiber is man-made and still new. Second, fabric and garment producers, as well as retailers, are encouraged to use and promote the fiber because of the fringe benefit they receive in the form of subsidized local or national advertising. However, because of changing market conditions, there was considerably less cooperative advertising money available from producers in the 1970s than there had been during the 1960s, when so many new fibers were being introduced.

Research and Development   Both natural fiber producers and man-made fiber producers are constantly seeking ways to improve their products. The large man-made fiber producers handle research and development mainly on an individual company basis. The natural fiber producers, because of the small size of the average company, often work through group efforts.

The research facilities of the giant chemical companies develop new fibers, evaluate them, and engineer both existing and new fibers to meet the fashion and performance demands of their expanding and varied markets. The producers of man-made fibers are particularly active in instructing the fabric industry in the manipulation of new yarns, in developing optimum blends and constructions, in improving dyeing and finishing techniques, and in evaluating consumer reaction to the fabrics made from their fibers. Technical bulletins on the proper methods of processing their fibers are issued to the trade and are supplemented by the availability of expert advice on specific problems relating to yarn, fabric, or garment production.

Research into fabric styling and development is also undertaken by most major producers of man-made fibers. Working with fabric producers, these companies develop experimental constructions and sample weavings and knittings well in advance of each new season. They also make available to their fabric customers the services of fabric construction specialists, stylists, print consultants, color experts, and fashion and market experts.

Producers of natural fibers have increased their research activities in recent years in attempts to develop various methods of imparting to their fibers or to the yarns and textile fabrics made from these fibers such qualities as dimensional stability, crease retention, wrinkle resistance, luster or matte finish, washability, and any other characteristics that improve their acceptance. While some man-made fibers offer dimensional stability, for instance, wool and cotton can also offer the same characteristic when woven into cloth if the fabric is preshrunk. Similarly, wash-and-wear and crease-resistant properties, formerly found only in fabrics made from certain man-made fibers, can now be offered in fabrics made of cotton, wool, and linen.

Historically, producers of natural fibers have shown little interest in the various stages through which their products go in the process of being transformed into consumer products. The producers of man-made fibers, on the other hand, are interested in all the stages through which their products will go: yarn, fabric, garments, retail distribution, and ultimate use by consumers.

Customer Services All major producers of man-made fibers and many smaller firms offer a number of services to direct and secondary users of their products. Producers of natural fibers, working through their associations, also offer many such services. These include:

- Technical advice to yarn and textile mills, as well as to garment producers.
- Assistance to textile and garment producers and retailers in locating sources of supply.
- "Libraries" of fabrics that can be examined by manufacturers, retailers, and the fashion press, with information supplied about where to buy these fabrics, what to pay for them, and what delivery to expect.

- Fashion advice and information to the textile industry, retailers, and the public.
- Fashion exhibits for manufacturers and retailers, which, in some instances, are also open to the public.
- Extensive literature for manufacturers, retailers, educators, and consumers about fiber properties, use, and care.
- Fashion experts and clothing and textile home economists to address groups of manufacturers, retailers, or consumers, staging appropriate fashion shows and demonstrations.
- Educational films and audiovisual aids for use by the trade, schools, and consumer groups.
- Assistance to retail stores in staging promotions of garments in which one or more of the promoted fibers are used. Such assistance may include finding sources of supply; staging fashion shows; developing customized retail-oriented promotional programs for department and specialty stores, resident buying offices, chain and mail-order outlets; supplying speakers and retail merchandising representatives to interested groups; providing publicity releases and suggested advertising copy; cooperating with retail stores in the cost of local advertising; advising on store displays; and conducting consumer demonstrations and sales training meetings in stores.
- Textile processing experts to help solve fabric production problems; similarly qualified experts to help solve problems in the production of apparel and accessories.

THE TEXTILE FABRIC INDUSTRY

Between the fiber and the apparel fashion lies the fabric, the basic material out of which the garment or accessory is made. *Textile fabric* is cloth or material made from fibers by one of the following methods: weaving, knitting, braiding, felting, crocheting, knotting, laminating, or bonding. Sometimes one particular method may be in fashion. At other times, there may be a trend in favor of a combination of methods. In general, however, most textile fabrics are either woven or knitted.

Hand-screen printing is one of the reasons for the distinctive quality of
Marimekko's famous fabrics.

Marimekko (*Design Research International, Inc.*)

The textile fabric industry is comprised of a
network of secondary industries, each accom-
plishing one of the steps required to turn fibers into
finished fabrics. Fibers are made up into yarns.
Yarns are made into *greige goods,* or unfinished
fabrics. Greige goods are converted into finished
fabrics intended for either consumer or industrial
use.

The textile fabric industry, like the textile
fiber industries, has felt the impact of great technological changes, ranging from increased diversification of products to more expert anticipation of
fashion trends.

History and Development

The production of most fabrics begins with the
production of yarn. *Yarn* is a continuous thread
formed by spinning or twisting fibers together. The
earliest step toward mechanization in the textile
fabric industry was in the production of yarn, when
the spinning wheel was introduced into Europe
from India around the sixth century. Spinning remained a slow, tedious process and a home occupation for centuries thereafter, until the British, in
the eighteenth century, worked out mechanical
ways of spinning cotton fibers into yarn. By 1779,

Hargreaves, Arkwright, and Crompton each had made a contribution toward the modern factory production of yarn.

Next came mechanization of the loom, the tool that weaves the yarn into cloth. When the British worked out machine methods of spinning fibers into yarns, they were confronted with an output of yarn much larger than hand-operated looms could handle. The first power loom was invented by an English clergyman, Dr. Edward Cartwright, and patented in 1785. It used water as a source of energy.

The same sequence of mechanization was true on this side of the Atlantic. In 1790, Samuel Slater established a yarn mill in Pawtucket, Rhode Island. A present-day giant in the textile field, J. P. Stevens and Company, is descended from Slater's famous mill. Fabric production remained both a hand operation and a home industry, however, totally inadequate to meet the demand for apparel fabrics. Then, a New Englander, Francis Cabot Lowell, visited a textile factory in England and memorized the detailed specifications of its power-operated machinery. In 1814 Lowell built the first successful power loom and the first textile fabric mill in the United States.

The demands of a rapidly growing country provided an eager market for the output of United States textile mills, and as a result the young industry flourished. Automation and mechanization techniques, developed both here and abroad, have advanced production procedures to a point where it is now possible for a single operator to oversee as many as 100 weaving machines if the fabric is plain.

Organization and Operation

The textile fabric industry in the United States today is composed of between 6,000 and 7,000 mills employing about 900,000 workers. Some of these mills produce yarn; some weave or knit cloth for apparel and other purposes; some do finishing. All are part of an industry that, in the mid-1970s, delivered about $25 billion worth of goods annu-

ally. Even this rate of production, however, has proved insufficient to satisfy this country's appetite for textile products; in the mid-1970s about $1.5 billion worth of textile products were being imported annually, while only half that amount were exported.

Textile mills are widely dispersed throughout the country, partly as a result of the industry's tendency to seek areas where labor and land costs are low and partly because there has been little advantage in concentrating production in any one area through the construction of giant mills or complexes. A small mill can operate about as efficiently as a large one, since textile machinery has a long useful life and its output can be increased by working two or three shifts. There used to be some concentration of textile mills in the northeastern states, but in recent years the southeastern part of the country offers less expensive labor and land.

Because it is necessary for the textile fabric industry to commit itself far in advance to specific weaves, colors, and finishes, it is extremely well informed about fashion and alert to incoming trends. But, because they are geared to mass-production methods, most mills are loathe to produce short, experimental runs for individual designers.

The market centers for textile fabrics are not at the mills but in the fashion capital of the country, New York City. There, on the doorstep of the garment industry, every mill of importance has a salesroom. A fabric buyer or designer for a garment maker, or a retail store apparel buyer or fashion coordinator, seeking firsthand information on what the fabric market offers, only has to walk a block or two to obtain all the information wanted.

Types of Mills Some mills sort and select the fibers to be used, spin them into yarn, then weave or knit them and finish the fabric. Finishing may include dyeing, napping, and pressing, or treating the fabric to ensure such attributes as nonshrinkage and permanent press. Fashion influences decisions every step of the way.

Some mills produce only the yarn. Others

weave or knit fabric from purchased yarn but do not carry the process beyond the greige, or unfinished, state. There are also plants that bleach, dye, preshrink, print, or in other ways impart desired characteristics to fabrics produced by other mills. The plants that handle the various stages may or may not be under common ownership, and they may or may not be geographically close.

For certain effects, yarns may be dyed before being woven or knitted (yarn dyed); for others, fabrics are knitted or woven first and then dyed (vat dyed); in some instances, either the warp or the weft (filling) yarns alone are dyed before weaving, and then the completed fabric is dyed to get a cross-dyed effect.

Many mills no longer limit themselves to working with yarns made of a single fiber. Fibers may be used alone or with other fibers, as demand dictates. Any of the types of mills described above may combine a natural fiber with another natural fiber, or more commonly, a natural fiber with a man-made fiber, to achieve a desired effect. Examination of the fiber content labels on garments will show how widespread the man-made fibers are, and how rayon, in particular, is combined with almost any other fiber to achieve a specific effect.

The Converter   The converter was a dominant figure in the textile fabric industry before World War II, particularly in the cotton industry. A *textile converter,* who often was well capitalized but owned no looms or mills, bought fabrics in the greige and contracted to have them finished (dyed, bleached, printed, or subjected to other treatments) in plants specializing in each operation. Converters were often their own selling agents.

Through close contact with the apparel trades, converters usually knew, almost from day to day, what colors, textures, and types of fabrics would be in demand. They spared the mills the expense and risk of having to style their lines down to the last detail, or even having to study the fashion market. The mills concentrated on production.

During World War II, conditions made this separation of functions unprofitable. Mills acquired finishing plants; finishers purchased mills; sales agents who had once functioned on commission for textile producers also became part of the new combinations that were forming.

The converter, however, is by no means a creature of the past. As an independent operator or as a division of a giant textile corporation, the textile converter continues to take basic greige goods and give them characteristics that make them readily salable to the fashion industries. In recent years, the converter's fashion "knowhow" has become increasingly important in helping American textile producers meet the competition of foreign textile producers who often offer more fashion-oriented goods in small yardages. Converters can and do supply apparel producers with shorter runs (fewer yards) of selected fabrics than can the larger fabric mills that must produce tremendous yardages of a designated pattern or design in order to maintain a profitable operation.

Merchandising Activities

It is said that fabric precedes the fashion. This means that dress designers, for example, cannot create a garment unless they find cloth that will drape the way they want it to and will have the colors and textures needed to give the desired form to designs.

Since the textile fabric industry must work several seasons ahead of consumer demand, it must be early in recognizing the direction that fashion is taking. Textile firms employ staffs of fashion experts who attend market openings around the world and work with designers to create fabrics in those weights, textures, colors, and patterns that it is anticipated consumers will want, in advance of when they are expected to want them. And they do this two or three seasons, or some 12 to 18 months, before the garments made of those fabrics will appear in stores. Should the textile producers fail to identify and act upon a trend, retailers and apparel producers can be frustrated in their efforts to serve the fashion consumer.

Advertising and Publicity   Large fabric manufacturers advertise lavishly, featuring the brand names of their products and frequently the names of specific apparel manufacturers who use their goods. Either with the cooperation of fiber sources or on their own, these fabric houses sponsor radio and television programs, run full-color advertisements in a wide variety of mass-circulation magazines and newspapers, cooperate in the cost of brand advertising run by retail stores. Their advertising generally makes consumers aware of new apparel styles, the fabrics of which they are made, and often the names of retail stores where they may be purchased.

MANUFACTURER'S NAME
(serves as a means of identification
for future purchases and complaints)

FIBER CONTENT
(identification by generic fiber type in
percentages — required by federal law)

LICENSED
TRADEMARK

CARE
RECOMMENDATIONS

REGISTERED TRADEMARK

*Today's labels are designed to give consumers
maximum information.*
Celanese Fibers Marketing Co.

Fabric producers compete among themselves for the business of apparel producers, for recognition among retail store buyers, and for acceptance by consumers of products made of their goods. They publicize brand names, stage seasonal fashion shows in market areas for retailers and the fashion press, and provide hang tags for the use of garment manufacturers. These tags may bear not only the brand name of the fabric but also instructions relating to its care. In addition, in accordance with federal regulation, fabric producers supply manufacturers with the required care labels that must be permanently sewn into all garments. Many fabric firms also make educational materials available to schools, consumer groups, and retail sales personnel, and supply information to consumers and the trade press, as a means of publicizing fashion news, fabric developments, and products.

Research and Development   Fabric producers, like fiber producers, now devote attention to exploring the market potential of their products and anticipating the needs of their customers. Success in the fashion industry depends on supplying consumers with what they want. Fashion causes swift changes. Anticipation of such changes requires closeness to the market and a scientific study of trends.

Many of the large fabric producers maintain product and market research divisions. Their experts work closely with both the trade and consumer markets in studying fabric performance characteristics; many provide garment manufacturers with sample runs of new fabrics for experimental purposes. The market researchers conduct consumer studies relating to the demand for or acceptance of finishes, blends, and other desired characteristics. Such studies also help fabric and garment producers to determine what consumers will want in the future, where and when they will want it, and in what quantities.

Customer Services   Today's well-integrated and diversified textile companies speak with great fashion authority. They also employ merchandising and marketing staffs whose expertise on fashion trends is available to apparel manufacturers, retailers, the fashion press, and frequently to consumers. Fashion staffs attend foreign and domestic market openings; issue seasonal fashion forecasts; provide traveling representatives who conduct in-store sales training programs and address consumer groups; stage fashion shows for the trade and press; help retail stores arrange fashion shows and storewide promotions featuring their products; and assist buyers in locating resources for merchandise made from their fabrics. These fashion merchandising experts not only carry the company's fashion message to trade customers but also reach retailers and consumers as well.

TRENDS IN THE TEXTILE INDUSTRY

Major trends in the textile industry, as in all industries, are influenced by the economy in general and the balance of supply and demand within the industry in particular. In the 1960s, the economy was generally healthy, and the supply of textile fibers and fabrics was balanced by a demand strong enough to result in a profitable market for most producers. In the 1970s, however, the picture has changed. Costs of both labor and raw materials have risen sharply. Competition from foreign firms has increased, particularly in fashion-oriented fabrics. There have been and probably will continue to be some scarcities of the raw materials needed to produce some of the man-made fibers. There have been and probably will continue to be shifts in demand for certain types of fibers and fabrics.

In the mid-1970s, major trends influencing the future growth and development of the textile industry are much the same as those influencing other industries that produce consumer goods, namely; expanding use of mechanization and automation; improved technology; a continued trend toward giantism; increased foreign expansion; greater diversification of products; and increased government regulation.

Expanding Use of Mechanization and Automation

The trend toward expanding use of machinery and less labor is apparent at all levels in the production of textile fibers and fabrics.

In the cotton fields, the goal is a savings in labor costs and a speed-up of harvesting time. A mechanical striper can harvest 50 times as many bolls of cotton as a worker who snaps off the bolls by hand. A mechanical picker can harvest 500 times as much cotton lint as a worker who picks the lint from the plants by hand.

In the mills, machines for mixing fibers for conversion into yarn enable one worker to mix the same amount of fiber in the same amount of time it formerly took four workers. In addition, machines make possible greater standardization of product. New high-speed mechanized yarn twisters are twice as productive as conventional twisters. Automated weaving and knitting machines operate at increasingly higher speeds and require fewer operators, most of whom have been trained by the machinery producers in how to repair the machines should problems develop. Automated knitting machines, capable of producing fabrics with cutting patterns outlined on them in knitted thread, are being developed. Machines for recycling products and converting former waste into usable materials are also in the developmental stage.

During the first half of the 1970s, sophisticated electronic equipment for high-speed preparation of designs on fabric had become so commonplace that more than 75 percent of the total gross knitted fabric output used this technique—which performed in seconds an operation that formerly took hours. At the same time, but still in the laboratory stage, was an incredibly fast system for dyeing and printing fabrics by using a computerized design terminal and reproducing the computerized designs from a television screen directly on to fabrics.

New electronic systems for printing designs on fabric "read" a design and produce a hard copy in the form of a special croque and color separation negative. These negatives are electronically scanned; in a single hour, screen or engrave rollers—which used to take the printing industry 100 hours to make—are produced. Other electronic systems make it possible for a firm's management to determine the cost price of fabrics before they are knitted or woven. Still other systems provide a fabric firm's management with daily and cumulative figures, for year-to-date or season-to-date as compared with previous year, detailed as to orders, stock on hand, and quantities on order; shipments broken down by individual accounts; and other pertinent data the firm may require to keep stock in a desired ratio to sales.

All of this means a reduction in labor costs; a reduction in human-error factors; a reduction in the time required for production; improved productivity per work hour; greater standardization of product; and better quality control.

Improved Technology

Understanding that healthy sales depend upon having what ultimate consumers want, the textile industry is putting increased effort into developing processes that will give products the characteristics consumers find both practical and inviting. New processes have been developed at every level of fiber and fabric production, but some of the most interesting are in the dyeing and finishing areas.

There are both improved methods of dyeing and improved dyes. Some produce better dyeing of fibers and fiber blends that formerly were difficult to dye. Some produce sharper colors; some more subtle colors. Some produce colors that are more resistant to fading or changing under sunlight or after repeated washings. In the 1970s, heat-transfer printing became big news as the way to print designs on this decade's biggest fiber, polyester.

A number of improved or new finishes turn out fabrics that have more consumer appeal. Some increase soil-resistance. Some reduce the static-electricity problem that knits can have, or their snagging problems. Some produce a fabric that feels like suede. The newest finishes in the mid-1970s

were those designed to make fabric more flame-retardant.

Continued Trend toward Giantism

Mergers, acquisitions, and the trend toward giantism continue. Firms have been expanding horizontally. *Horizontal integration* means absorbing other companies that function at the same level of production, such as the merger of two fabric producers. Firms have also been expanding vertically. *Vertical integration* means absorbing or merging with companies at other levels of production, such as the merger of a fiber mill with a fabric firm.

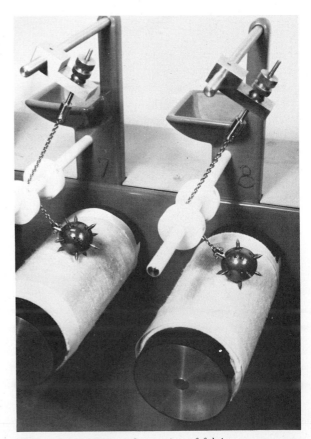

Mace test for pilling and snagging of fabrics.
Celanese Fibers Marketing Co.

As a result, the textile industry shows a decline in the total number of firms but an increase in the number and size of large firms. Burlington Industries, for example, passed the billion-dollar mark in sales early in the 1960s, and the two-billion-dollar mark in 1973. Its more than 30 divisions operate plants in 15 states, 8 foreign countries, and Puerto Rico.

Increased Foreign Expansion

Another trend, one limited to fabric producers rather than fiber producers, is toward the acquisition or establishment of mills abroad. Such foreign-based mills may be wholly owned by a United States firm or may be jointly owned by a United States firm and a host-country firm. Most are located close to fiber sources. To this convenience are added the facilities, fashion knowledge, and technical skill of their United States owners or part-owners. The engineers may be American or American-trained, but the rest of the plant is usually staffed by local labor who are paid according to local wage scales. By producing some goods abroad, domestic manufacturers defend themselves against the competition of foreign-made fabrics and also put themselves in a more favorable position to sell in countries where tariff walls limit or keep out goods made in the United States.

In reverse, several foreign business firms, mainly Japanese, are buying into fabric or finishing plants here or are becoming partners in or sole owners of new facilities being built here. At least one Japanese firm was said to be thinking of moving into cotton cultivation in the southern United States to secure a long-term, stable supply.

Greater Diversification of Products

Today, the textile industry produces a more diversified range of fibers and fabrics than ever before. The specialization that once divided the industry into separate segments, each producing fabrics from only a single fiber, has all but faded. To meet the needs of consumers, it is often necessary to blend together two or more fibers into a yarn or to combine a warp yarn of one fiber with a weft yarn of another fiber. Mills are learning to adjust their operations to any new and wanted fiber or combination of fibers. Illustrating the importance of blends was Cotton Incorporated's introduction of a new trademark to be used on fabrics that contain 60 percent or more cotton fiber but are not 100 percent cotton, and the Wool Bureau's introduction of a trademark for fabrics made of a fiber blend of at least 50 percent wool.

Two of the largest firms in the field illustrate how the industry is moving toward greater diversification of product. Burlington, originally a rayon mill specializing in bedspreads, now produces and sells spun and textured yarns of both natural and man-made fibers; a wide variety of finished woven and knitted fabrics; some unfinished fabrics; hosiery for men, women, and children; and a wide variety of domestics and home furnishings, ranging from bed linens to rugs and furniture. Under the J. P. Stevens banner are cotton and woolen mills, some producing spun and textured yarns, others producing finished fabrics both for over-the-counter selling and for apparel manufacture, and still others producing women's hosiery. Both companies use the major natural fibers and a large number of the man-made fibers available in this country.

Increased Government Regulation

Until recently, federal regulation of the textile industry was mainly concerned with the fiber-content labeling of fabrics and products made of those fabrics. In 1954, a Flammable Fabrics Act was passed, but it served only to ban a few very ignitable fabrics, and apparel made from those fabrics, from the market. The increasing strength and direction of the consumerism movement, however, is showing itself in the increasing amount of government regulation of the textile industry, not only on the federal level but also on the state level.

July 1972 was the month when two important changes in federal textile regulations became effective: the FTC's rule concerning "Care Labeling of

Textile Wearing Apparel," and the revision of the Flammable Fabrics Act.

The FTC's care-labeling rule requires that all fabrics, including piece goods as well as apparel and accessories made of fabric, be labeled to show the type of care the fabric requires. The label must indicate whether the fabric can be washed or should be drycleaned. If the fabric can be washed, the label must indicate the temperature at which it should be washed, whether ironing is required, and if so, the temperature the iron should be. The labeling job is the responsibility of the manufacturer of the piece goods or the item made of fabric. In the case of apparel, the manufacturer must sew a permanent label into each garment.

In 1970, the Department of Commerce published its findings that there was a possible need for regulation of the flammability of fabric used in children's sleepwear and dresses. This initiated a series of regulations that will probably continue to be issued for some time to come. By 1973, carpets, mattresses, and, most important, all children's sleepwear in sizes 0 to 6X were required to be made of fabrics that meet federal flammability standards. In addition, federal standards for fabric used in other children's wear, in men's and women's apparel, and in blankets and mattresses had been proposed and were being considered.

Leading authorities predict the following trends in the textile industry as a result of government environmental and consumer regulations concerning fibers and fabrics:

- Fibers and textile products will be made by larger producers with a resulting decrease in the number of small concerns and marginal operations, mainly because of the higher production costs related to complying with the new government regulations and the greater capital investment required to stay competitive in a period of continually rising costs.
- Manufacturing operations will function at higher efficiencies, recycling as much product as possible and converting waste to energy.
- Fibers having built-in environmental disadvantages will slowly give way to more suitable replacements, or new processing techniques will be devised to allow their continued use.
- Transfer printing may be an important way to reduce some of the dye-house stream-pollution problems.
- Consumers will be increasingly protected, with particular emphasis on children's apparel and home furnishings.
- Consumers will be better advised on the characteristics of their purchases.

MERCHANDISING VOCABULARY

Define or explain each of the following terms:

Fiber	Licensed trademark
Natural fibers	Cooperative advertising
Man-made fibers	Textile fabric
Cotton	Greige goods
Wool	Yarn
Silk	Textile converter
Linen	Horizontal integration
Linters	Vertical integration
Spinerette	

MERCHANDISING REVIEW

1. Why is it necessary for a student of fashion merchandising to have a basic knowledge of textile fibers and fabrics and of their respective industries?

2. Name the four natural fibers. From what source is each obtained? Indicate at least two countries that are principal sources for each.

3. Compare or contrast natural and man-made fibers on the basis of the following: (a) relative size of their producers; (b) capital investment required; (c) location of production facilities; (d) predictability of supply; and (c) consistent uniformity of product.

4. Trace the steps or stages through which a completely new or newly modified man-made fiber goes from its conception to its general availability. Why are fibers with similar characteristics usually available from more than one producer at almost the same time?

5. Name and explain the three ways in which producers of man-made fibers usually sell their products to fabric manufacturers.

6. What are the various methods used for converting fibers into fabrics? Which methods are in most common use today?

7. Trace the historical development of the textile industry in the United States. What specific technological advances have been of major importance in its development?

8. Through what processes do fibers usually go in being transformed into fabrics?

9. What is the function of a textile converter? What are the advantages to (a) a fabric mill and (b) the apparel trade of dealing with a converter?

10. Name and describe the provisions of three government regulations that have importantly affected the American textile industry in the past 20 years.

MERCHANDISING DIGEST

1. Compare or contrast the methods employed by natural and man-made fiber producers in carrying out their advertising and publicity activities.

2. Discuss current trends in the textile industry as they relate to (a) expanding use of mechanization and automation; (b) increased foreign expansion; and (c) greater diversification of products.

6
THE MATERIALS OF FASHION: LEATHER AND FUR

Human beings used leather and fur for clothing thousands of years before they developed textiles. These materials still play an important part in the fashion picture. Leather is particularly important in some of the fashion accessory fields, such as shoes, handbags, and gloves, and is developing increasing strength as an apparel material. Fur is primarily an apparel material, used either for the basic garment or for its trim.

In contrast to the methods used for producing textiles, the processing of leather and fur appears primitive and slow. Thus the response of the leather and fur industries to fashion demand is necessarily slow, and fashion trends have to be spotted particularly early. Yet changes are taking place in the industries, largely in improved production methods and techniques, and these changes are giving designers a wider range of products to work with. In addition, these changes may be indicators of the course that fashions in leather and furs may take in the future.

THE LEATHER INDUSTRY

The process of transforming animal skins into leather is known as *tanning*. "Tanning" comes from the Latin word for oak bark, the earliest known material used to treat the skins of animals. It is the oldest craft known. Primitive people not only killed animals for food, but they also devised ways to treat the skins for use as body covering and a host of other purposes. Modern people slaughter animals that are raised for milk, meat, or wool, and convert their skins to leather; or they may kill animals, except those protected by governmental regulations, for the primary or even sole purpose of transforming their skins into leather.

History and Development

The use of leather for apparel and other purposes was commonplace in North America long before the first European settlers arrived. The earliest known tanners in what is now the United States were Indians, who made clothing, moccasins, and tents from deerskins. Although they lacked the knowledge to produce leathers of today's variety and quality, they developed tanning techniques that met their own needs.

The first commercial tannery in the American Colonies was established in 1623 in Plymouth by Experience Miller, an Englishman. Peter Minuit, Governor of New Amsterdam, invented the first machinery used for tanning in the Colonies, a horse-driven stone mill to grind the oak bark then used in converting animal skins into leather.

Mechanization of the industry took a long step forward in 1809 when Samuel Parker invented a machine that split heavy steer hides 25 times faster than was possible by hand. Split hides produce lighter, more supple leather, desirable in shoes, boots, and other apparel.

Yet mechanization, which developed at about the same rate on both sides of the Atlantic, has not appreciably reduced the time required for the actual tanning process. Hides and skins require prolonged exposure to a series of treatments before they become leather. To produce kid leather, for example, requires a number of weeks for the actual tanning process itself, in addition to the time required to purchase the skins, ship them to the tannery, receive and inspect them, and start them on their way through the tanning process. However, mechanization has reduced much of the heavy manual labor previously required to stir soaking hides and skins, and to dehair and flesh them. In addition to splitting hides, there are also machines now that emboss patterns and perform other processes formerly done by hand.

Chemistry has made a great contribution to tanning methods by providing new tanning agents that reduce the time required to transform hides and skins into leather and that achieve greater variety of qualities in leather. Modern instruments control solutions for temperature and other factors to assure uniformity of product.

Organization and Operation

What was once a household industry, and still is one in some of the less-developed areas of the world, has today become relatively big business in the United States. Nearly 25,000 workers are employed in this country's tanneries, turning out 800 million dollars' worth of leathers a year for widely divergent uses.

The tanning processes which are the heart of this industry are basically the same as those followed for thousands of years. Although the grease and brains of an animal are no longer used to treat its pelt, tanners still soak pelts to soften them, remove any flesh or hair that may adhere to them, and treat them to retard putrefaction. As recently as a century or two ago tanners still relied principally on such natural materials as oak or hemlock bark to process skins, but today there is a vast range of chemical and natural agents at their disposal: chrome salts, alum, and oils, for example. As a result, the variety of colors, textures, and finishes available to the fashion industries today is infinitely greater than it was even 50 years ago. So is the variety of animals whose skins are used.

Organization The leather industry in this country is divided into three major types of companies: regular tanneries, converters, and contract tanneries. *Regular tanneries* are those companies that purchase and process hides and skins and sell the finished leather. *Converters* buy hides and skins, farm out the processing to contract tanneries, and sell the finished product. *Contract tanneries* process hides and skins to the specifications of converters and are not involved in the sale of the finished product. About half the firms in the industry are regular tanneries. The other half is made up of contractors and converters.

The leather industry is necessarily characterized by specialization because the methods and materials employed vary according to the nature of hides or skins being treated and the end product for which each is intended. Tanners of calfskin do not normally tan kidskins; tanners of glove leathers do not normally produce sole leather.

Although the leather industry is composed mainly of small firms, there are some giants in the field. For example, the A. C. Lawrence Leather Company—which works mainly with calfskin, sheepskin, and cowhides—is the world's largest tanning firm and produces as many as 1,500 different types and colors of leather in a single year.

Mergers, consolidations, and affiliations, prevalent in the textile industry during and immediately following World War II, have also taken place in the leather industry. In 1870 there were 4,500 tanneries in operation in the United States; today there are fewer than 500. Additional mergers and a continuing trend toward fewer and larger plants may be possible, but other dramatic changes are unlikely.

Vertical integration, which made possible giantism in the textile industry, has gone about as far as it can go in the leather industry. For years, some of the country's largest tanneries have been subsidiaries of meat packers. For example, the A. C. Lawrence Leather Company is a division of Swift and Company. Other tanneries have integrated with their main sources of supply.

Because leather is still largely a by-product of the milk-, meat-, or wool-producing industries, it is lower in cost than it would be if animals were raised for their skins alone.

Most United States tanneries are located in the Northeast and North Central states. In these regions also cluster the industry's major customers, such as shoe and glove manufacturers. Like textile producers, however, most leather firms maintain sales offices or representatives in New York City for the convenience of their customers.

Sources of Leather Supply

Although most leather comes from the cow and calf, fashion uses the hides and skins of many other animals from all parts of the world. Kid and goatskins come from Europe, Asia, Africa, and South America; capeskin comes from a special breed of sheep raised in South Africa and South America; pigskin comes from the peccary, a wild hog native to Mexico and South America; buffalo comes from Asia and eastern Europe.

The variety of leathers used in making gloves alone illustrates how worldwide are their sources:

- *Cabretta* from South American sheep
- *Calfskin* from young calves of the United States and elsewhere
- *Goatskin* from South America, South Africa, India, Spain
- *Kidskin* from Europe
- *Pigskin* from Central and South America, Mexico
- *Buckskin* from deer and elk in South and Central America, People's Republic of China, Mexico
- *Mocha* from Asian and African sheep

In the United States in a recent year, imports of hides and skins exceeded $65 million, but exports were nearly $300 million. In the United States, however, the great bulk of supply of raw materials for leather comes from domestic meat-packing industries.

Leather Processing

The leather trade divides animal skins into three classes according to weight. Animal skins that weigh 15 pounds or less when shipped to the tannery are referred to as *skins*. Calves, goats, pigs, sheep, and deer are among the animals producing skins. Animal skins weighing from 15 to 25 pounds, such as those from young horses and cattle, are referred to as *kips*. Animal skins weighing over 25 pounds each, such as those from cows, oxen, buffalo, and horses, are referred to as *hides*.

The process by which skins, kips, and hides become leather is a lengthy one, one of the many reasons why the leather industry has to work well in advance of demand. Three to six months are usually required for the tanning of hides. The time is shorter for kips and skins, but the processes are more numerous, requiring more extensive equipment and more highly skilled labor.

Tanning methods may involve using oils, vegetable materials, minerals, or chemicals as the tanning agent. The choice of tanning agent mainly depends upon the end use for which the leather is being prepared.

Oil Processing with oil is one of the oldest ways of turning raw animal skins into leather. A fish oil, usually codfish, is used. Today, oil tanning is used to produce chamois, doeskin, and buckskin, relatively soft and pliable leathers for use in making gloves and jackets. Besides being soft and pliable, oil-tanned leather has the characteristics of having a somewhat slimy feel when dry and a somewhat oily feel when wet.

Vegetable Materials Also an old method, vegetable tanning uses such agents as tannic acids from the bark, wood, or nuts of various trees and shrubs and from tea leaves. Vegetable tanning is used on cow, steer, horse, and buffalo hides. The product is a heavy, often relatively stiff, leather used for the soles of shoes, some shoe uppers, some handbags and belts. Vegetable-tanned leather can be identified by a dark center streak in the cut edge. It is resistant to moisture and can be cleaned by sponging.

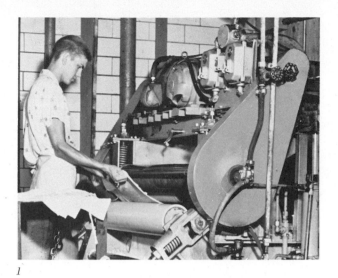

1

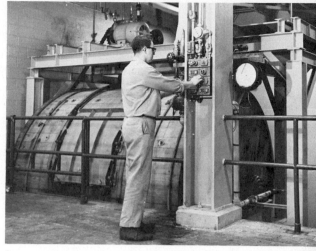

2

In preparing leather, skins are (1) *fleshed* to remove all unwanted substances, (2) *tanned* in large vats, (3) *pressed* to wring out water and wrinkles, (4) *sanded* to remove the grain, and (5) *sorted* into grades.

Hush Puppies Division of Wolverine World Wide, Inc.

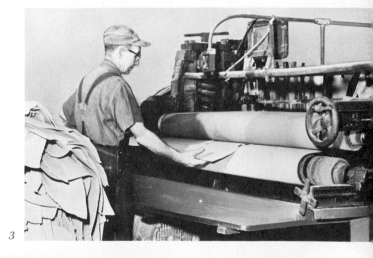

3

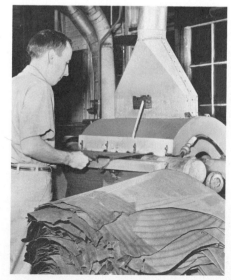

4

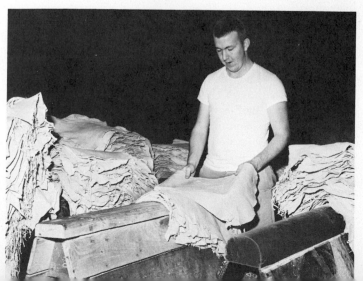

5

Minerals There are two important tanning methods that use minerals. One uses alum; the other uses chrome salts. Alum was used by the ancient Egyptians to make writing paper. Today it is used mainly to make kidskin for gloves. Alum-tanned kidskin is white when tanned, and soft and pliable to the touch. It is not washable, and if it becomes wet it dries stiff and wrinkled. Chrome-tanning, a much newer method introduced in 1893, is now used to process nearly two-thirds of all leather produced in this country. This is a fast method that produces a leather used for shoe uppers, gloves, handbags, and so forth. Chrome-tanned leather can be identified by the pale blue-gray color in the center of the cut edge. It is slippery when wet. It is usually washable, or at least can be cleaned by sponging.

Chemical Another relatively new process uses formaldehyde for tanning. This is a quicker method of tanning. The leather is white when tanned, and so it can be dyed easily, and the tanned leather is washable. Leather tanned by formaldehyde is often used for gloves and children's shoe uppers.

Combinations It is possible to combine tanning agents. Alum and formaldehyde is one combination that is used. Oil and chrome is another. Such combinations give leather better qualities.

Merchandising Activities

Because tanning is such a slow process, leather producers cannot merely stay abreast of fashion, they must keep ahead of it. As a result, they are among the best and most experienced forecasters in the fashion business. They have to be—especially those who work with the skins or hides of foreign animals. Months before other fashion industries have to commit themselves on matters of color and texture, leather producers have already made their decisions and have started the search for precisely the right dyes and treatments to produce what they expect future fashion will want. The time consumed in transforming skins and kips and hides to leather requires tanneries to project fashion demand several seasons into the future.

Fashion Information Services Having made their assessments of fashion trends very early, leather tanners, like fiber and fabric producers, share their conclusions with their customers. Individually or through industry associations, tanners retain fashion experts to disseminate this information and advise manufacturers, editors, and retailers on future fashion trends in leather.

A typical activity of leather producers is the preparation of fashion booklets for distribution to manufacturers, retailers, the press, and other interested persons. Such booklets are sometimes available a year before the consumer is likely to wear or use the leather products described. Contents would include comments on the general fashion trend; the leather colors and textures suitable for classics, boutique merchandise, and promotional use; swatches of important textures and looks in leather.

Another typical activity, either of individual producers or of industry associations, is the assignment of a fashion expert to work with retailers, manufacturers, and the press to help them crystallize their fashion thinking. This service might take the form of individual conferences, of membership on a committee of producers or retailers, of making fashion presentations to industry, retail, or consumer groups, and similar undertakings.

Yet with all this activity, individual tanners are not known by name to the public. A fashion editor describing a leather garment, glove, or shoe is not likely to mention the leather producer. Nor is the leather producer likely to be named in retail store advertising or in the advertising placed by the manufacturers of the finished products. As a result, the consumer who may possibly recall names of several fabric and fiber producers would probably have a hard time naming even one tanner.

Trade Associations Tanners work together to promote their products. Their industry supports associations whose function is to disseminate technical and fashion information to producers, consumers, and the press. Some associations, like the Calf Tanners Association, strive to promote a particular kind of leather; others, such as the Tanners Council, function on an industrywide basis, working to promote all kinds of leather.

Formerly such associations were primarily concerned with serving segments of the market that were already customers. Today the major effort is to broaden the market for all types of leathers. Markets that once exclusively used leather, such as the shoe industry, are now shared with other products, making it necessary for the industry to defend its frontiers. Markets that traditionally never used leather, such as dresses, skirts, and coats, now are being actively cultivated by the leather industry.

At the retail level, the leather industry's associations are a valuable source of information in fashion planning and selection. They are also an important source of fashion and technical information for salespeople. For the customer, promotional efforts of the industry associations are reflected in fashion and technical material made available to schools, distributed with merchandise purchased in retail stores, and publicized through the fashion press.

Research and Development   Leather retains and expands its markets by adapting its products to fashion's changing requirements. Before World War II, relatively few colors and types of leather were available in any one season, and each usually had a fashion life of several years. Today, a major tannery may turn out hundreds of leather colors and types each season, meanwhile preparing to produce more new colors and textures for the next season.

To protect and expand their markets, leather producers constantly broaden their range of colors, weights, and textures and introduce improvements that will make their output more acceptable where it now has either limited use or no use at all.

Leather has the weight of tradition behind it; people for centuries have regarded fine leather as a symbol of luxury. But today leather shares its hold on the fashion field with other and newer materials.

Producers are attempting to meet the competition not only of other leathers but also of other materials through product research and development. Leathers that can be powdered and then reconstituted in the form of sheets of standardized widths and lengths, like textile fabrics, are already a reality.

Industry Trends

Until just a few decades ago, the leather industry concerned itself primarily with meeting the needs of relatively few segments of the fashion industries, such as shoes, gloves, belts, handbags, and small leathergoods. Apparel use was restricted largely to a few items of outerwear, such as jackets and coats that were stiff, bulky, and primarily functional in appeal.

Today, the leather industry is changing. These changes are the result of several trends: enlarging market opportunities, increased competition from synthetics, and increased foreign trade.

Enlarging Markets   Improved methods of tanning are turning out better, more versatile leathers with improved fashion characteristics. In general, these fashion characteristics are of two types: (1) The new leathers are softer and more pliable; (2) they can be dyed more successfully in a greater number of fashion colors.

As a result, an increasing amount of leather is going into apparel. In 1968, 11 percent of all leather produced in this country was used to produce apparel. By 1973, that figure had increased to 18 percent. Today, leather is being used to make jackets, coats, skirts, dresses, and vests. In the mid-1970s, apparel manufacturers were reporting steady and sometimes spectacular increases in sales of leather apparel.

Competition from Synthetics   Some of the potential market for leather is being taken away by synthetic materials. For instance, synthetics are replacing leather in some shoe parts. The traditional leather heel lift is now almost always made of plastic. Synthetics are also replacing leather in other accessories. Synthetics are used in making handbags that look and feel like leather but are less susceptible to scratches and can be cleaned more easily. Synthetics are even taking over some of the potential leather apparel market. Today fabrics made of natural and man-made fibers look and feel like various types of leather but are easier to clean and care for.

At least one former giant among the tanneries is meeting the challenge of synthetics by diversifying its product line. The Allied Kid Company, traditionally known as the world's largest goatskin tanner, today is called the "Allied Leather Company" and is a giant producer of various kinds of natural leathers, man-made leathers, and fabrics. While its products are primarily intended for the shoe industry, some are used to manufacture apparel and accessories.

Increased Foreign Trade The demand for leather throughout the world keeps increasing. United States producers, able to get higher prices for their hides from tanneries in countries where demand outstrips supply, have sharply increased their export of hides. As a result, prices have gone up sharply. Many of this country's tanneries, caught between a shortage of hides and increased prices, have had to curtail production or even close. In turn, because of higher domestic prices, United States retailers have been turning to other countries for leather and leather products, buying from Spain, Israel, Italy, South America, Greece, and recently, Canada.

However, government intervention may change this trend. For example, foreign producers had won almost 40 percent of the American shoe market by the end of 1973. Then the Treasury Department increased duties on shoes from some countries and talked about such action for footwear from other countries; imports dropped by 7 percent by late 1974. If the export-import balance becomes too hard on American tanneries and leather producers, it is likely that export-import quotas may be established.

THE FUR INDUSTRY

The wearing of fur as a symbol of wealth and prestige dates back to earliest recorded history. High-ranking Chinese are known to have worn furs 3,500 years ago. Greeks and Romans also dramatized rank by fur trim on their clothing. In medieval Europe, fur was a prime status symbol: Italian cardinals wore ermine as a symbol of purity; English nobles wore it as a symbol of power. By the sixteenth century, Europe's demand for luxury furs was far greater than that continent could supply. Pressure to find new sources played an important role in encouraging exploration and trade and greatly influenced the early development of North America.

The fur industry, even today, is a craft industry, involving small firms and highly skilled workers. Advances in technology have produced new colors and less expensive furs. But technology has had less impact on the fur industry than on others producing fashion materials.

History and Development

Fur trappers and traders were among the earliest explorers of North America. Their work was the original basis of the Colonies' foreign trade; some of the continent's largest cities were originally founded by trappers.

The English and Dutch organized companies to deal with the Indians for furs, which were often traded for colored beads and cheap alcohol. Trading posts that were set up to handle the Indian's catch were the first centers of colonization in various parts of what is now the United States. Major cities like Chicago, Detroit, St. Paul, Spokane, and St. Louis grew from such beginnings. In Canada, the French were just as eager to buy furs; as early as 1580 they had 150 ships engaged in transporting furs obtained from the North American Indians.

The colonists themselves and, later, their descendants, used fur for apparel and other purposes. Daniel Boone's coonskin cap and the

TABLE 6-1
United States Foreign Trade in Furs

U.S. BUYS	FROM
Mink	Canada, Denmark, Sweden, Norway, Finland, Poland, East Germany, Japan, Netherlands, United Kingdom, and 25 other countries
Persian lamb and Caracul	Afghanistan, Republic of South Africa, U.S.S.R., and 11 other countries
Rabbit	France, Australia, Belgium, West Germany, and 19 other countries
Squirrel	U.S.S.R. and 5 other countries
Marten	Canada, Czechoslovakia, West Germany, France, and 16 other countries
Sable	U.S.S.R. and Canada
Otter	Brazil, Colombia, Bolivia, and 17 other countries

U.S. SELLS	TO
Muskrat	United Kingdom, West Germany, Sweden, Canada, Italy
Raccoon	Canada, West Germany, and 10 other countries
Mink	United Kingdom, Canada, Switzerland, West Germany, France, Italy, Belgium, Australia, and 18 other countries
Skunk	France, West Germany, and 3 other countries
Opossum	West Germany, United Kingdom, France, and 10 other countries

U.S. RE-EXPORTS*	TO
Persian and other lamb	West Germany, Canada, United Kingdom, Belgium, Italy, and 9 other countries
Mink	Canada, France, Italy, and 8 other countries

*Foreign merchandise, i.e., imported merchandise which has *not* been changed in condition in the United States, including merchandise withdrawn from bonded storage warehouses for exportation.

Source: U.S. Department of Commerce, BDSA, *Fur Facts and Figures: A Survey of the United States Fur Industry,* 1966, p. 20.

bearskin rug are examples of early uses of furs by settlers. For the most part, however, the young country used furs for export purposes, to buy from more developed countries those articles it could not yet produce for itself.

The history of the fur business in the United States is one of growth more than change. Fur traders still send their agents to areas around the world where desirable animals are to be found. There they buy directly from trappers or local fur merchants.

Today fur trading is an international venture. Important fur-bearing animals native to or raised in the United States include mink, muskrat, fox, beaver, chinchilla, and racoon, some of which are exported to other countries. This country's chief imports from other countries are mink and Persian lamb. (See Table 6-1.)

Organization and Operation

The fur industry in the United States can be divided into three groups: (1) the trappers, farmers, and ranchers who produce the pelts; (2) the fur processing firms; and (3) the firms manufacturing fur products for consumers.

Obtaining the Pelts   The first step in the production of fur merchandise is to obtain the necessary pelts. A *pelt* is the skin of a fur-bearing animal. Trappers are the major source of supply of wild-animal pelts, which must be taken only at the coldest season of the year to be of prime quality. The trapper sells pelts to nearby country stores or directly to itinerant buyers. In some areas, collectors or receiving houses accept furs for resale on consignment from trappers or local merchants. When enough pelts have been gathered, a fur merchant may export them or send them to an auction house. Private sale or sales through a broker may also take place.

A fairly recent development in the fur industry, and an increasingly important source of pelts, is *fur farming,* or the raising and breeding of fur-

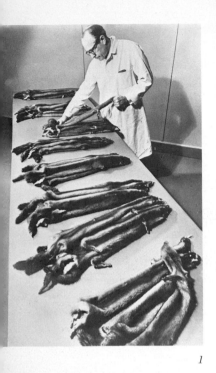

1

2   3

In fur apparel production, pelts are (1) graded by color, size, and hair length to obtain maximum uniformity, (2) "let out" by skilled cutters, (3) sewn into long strips (4) which are wetted and tacked to a board in the exact shape required by the pattern, and then (5) carefully made up into the finished garment.

Fur Information and Fashion Council

4

5

bearing animals under controlled conditions. This began in 1880 with silver-fox fur farming on Prince Edward Island, off the eastern coast of Canada. Chinchilla, Persian lamb, fox, and nutria farms, as well as mink ranches, have grown rapidly throughout the United States during the past 50 years. By careful breeding, strains most likely to win fashion and financial success have been evolved. Some of the most beautiful and exotic colors in fur pelts today are the result of breeding to develop colors and markings that meet the changing demands of fashion. Fur farmers and ranchers usually sell their pelts directly to auction houses.

At auctions, fur buyers and manufacturers bid for the pelts, which are sold in bundles. Those who plan to make garments seek matched bundles of skins similar in color and quality which will form a garment of uniform beauty.

The auction trail is an international one that attracts United States fur buyers to England, Scandinavia, and Russia, as well as to various fur market centers in the United States itself and Canada. European fur buyers visit New York, Greensville, St. Louis, Seattle, Minneapolis, and cities in Canada to obtain pelts of animals native to North America. Except for London, each auction center handles primarily the pelts of its own country. (See Table 6-1.)

Many people in the United States do some trapping of wild animals every year, although, for most, such trapping represents a very seasonal and minor source of income. The several thousand fur farms and ranches in this country produce by far the greatest number of pelts. Together fur trappers and farmers in this country "harvested" some 3,200,000 pelts of various kinds in 1973, which were sold for a wholesale price of about $64 million. Of these, some $22 million worth were exported; the rest were sold to domestic buyers, who, in addition, bought about $50 million worth of pelts from other countries of the world.

Fur Processing After fur goods manufacturers buy the pelts at auctions or from wholesale mer-chants, they contract with fur dressing and dyeing firms to process the pelts.

The job of fur dressers is to make pelts suitable for use in consumer products. First the pelts are softened, both by soaking and by mechanical means. Then the "flesher" removes with a blade any unwanted substances from the inner surface of the skin. For less expensive furs, this process may be performed by roller-type machines. At this point, the pelts are treated with tanning solutions that tan the skin side of the pelt into a pliable leather. At this stage, the fur side of the pelt may be processed, either by plucking unwanted guard hairs or by shearing the underfur to make the fur lighter in weight and the pelt still more pliable. Finally, the pelt is cleaned again. Although fur dressing has traditionally been a handcraft industry, modern technology has turned it into a more mechanized process.

After dressing, the pelts may go to a dyer. Fur dyes once were derived from vegetable matter, but today they consist largely of complicated chemical compounds. New dyes are constantly developed, making it possible to dye fur more successfully and in more shades than ever before.

Fur Goods Manufacturing Fur goods manufacturing is basically a handcraft industry, made up mainly of small, independently owned and operated shops. This is because of the nature of the basic material with which the industry works. No two animals are quite alike, and neither are two pelts. A pelt, moreover, varies in color and quality of hair from one section of the body to another.

Because of the skills and judgments required in working with pelts, the production of fur garments lends itself neither to mass-production methods nor to large-scale operation. After the processing that all fur pelts undergo, the following steps are required to transform pelts into finished garments:

- Sketching a design of the garment
- Making a canvas pattern of the garment

- Cutting the skins to conform to the designer's sketch, to exhibit the fur to its best advantage, and to minimize waste
- Sewing the cut skins together
- Wetting the skins and nailing them to a board so that they dry in a permanently set shape
- Sewing the garment sections together
- Lining and finishing
- Inspection

Nearly all the above steps are done by hand, with consideration for each pelt's peculiarities and the differences in color and hair quality in the various parts of each skin. This is in sharp contrast to the mass-production methods of those apparel makers who cut and sew fabrics.

For some more luxurious furs, the cutting operation may be extremely complex in order to "let out" short skins to a length adequate for garment purposes. Letting out mink, for example, involves cutting each skin down the center of the dark vertical stripe running lengthwise of the skin. Each half-skin is then cut at an angle into diagonal strips one-eighth to three-sixteenths of an inch wide, after which each tiny strip is resewn at an angle to the strip above and below it in order to make the skin longer and narrower. The other half-skin is resewn in like manner. The two halves are then joined, resulting in a longer, slimmer pelt, which is more beautiful than the original. Ten miles of thread may sometimes be needed to join the let-out strips for a single coat. The nailing process may require as many as 1,200 nails.

In 1971, a census of manufacturers showed that there were somewhat less than 1,000 fur goods producers, employing some 5,000 workers, and doing an annual wholesale business of about $180 million. This is an output considerably less than that of a single, good-sized textile firm. The center of the fur industry is in New York City.

Retail Distribution of Fur Garments   The line between manufacturing and retailing is less clear in furs than in other industries. Retail fur merchants may maintain an assortment of finished garments to show or sell to customers who buy off the rack, but they will also have a supply of skins and a fur workroom so that they can make up custom garments as well.

Most fur garments are retailed in one of two ways: through leased departments or through consignment selling. Both types of operation permit a retail store to offer its customers a large selection of fur and garment types without tying up vast quantities of capital in inventory.

A *leased department* is one ostensibly operated by the store in which it is found but which is actually run by an outsider who pays a percentage of sales to the store as rent. In a leased department, the operator, or lessee, rather than the store, owns the stock. The lessee may also run departments in other stores and can, if necessary, move garments and skins from one location to another. The lessee, a retailer of a special kind, is usually well capitalized and has expert knowledge of both furs and retailing. In *consignment selling,* a manufacturer places merchandise in a retail store for resale but permits any unsold portion, together with payment for those garments that have been sold, to be returned to the wholesale source by a specified date. In consignment selling, the garment producer, in effect, lends stock to a store. If not sold, the furs are returned to the producer for possible sale elsewhere. Producers who sell furs on consignment usually maintain large enough inventories so that they can afford to consign stock to retailers who prefer to operate their fur departments on this basis.

Merchandising Activities

In contrast to other industries, the fur industry, because it is made up almost entirely of small firms, relies to a considerable extent upon group efforts rather than those of individual entrepreneurs for its merchandising and promotional activities. In some instances, the labor unions, as well as fur traders, dressers, and garment producers, work together to encourage the public's acceptance of furs.

Trade Associations   The fur industry relies mainly on the efforts of its trade associations to impress upon consumers the fashion and luxury values of its product. Trade associations also assist retailers in promoting fur to the public. The Fur Information and Industry Council does this for the industry as a whole. Individual types of furs are promoted by such specialized associations as EMBA (organized as the Eastern Mink Breeders Association and now nationwide); GLMA (the Great Lakes Mink Association, a much smaller group than EMBA, specializing in ranch mink); and ECBC (the Empress Chinchilla Breeders Cooperative). EMBA is by far the biggest and most important of these trade groups. It disseminates publicity and produces educational booklets for retailers, schools, and the general public.

Labeling To capitalize on the consumer's interest in whatever furs are currently fashionable, the industry finds ways to treat one type of fur so that it resembles another, more desirable or more expensive one. For the consumer's protection, the Federal Trade Commission, through the Fur Products Labeling Act of 1952 and various rules issued since then, has established definite requirements for the labeling of articles made of fur.

By law, the following must be stated, both on a label attached to the merchandise and in all advertising of fur products: (1) the English name of the animal; (2) the country of origin; (3) the type of processing, including dyeing, to which the pelts may have been subjected; and (4) if paws or tails have been used or if parts from used garments have been re-used. Thus, a customer who buys a Persian lamb coat made from the most desirable sections of the pelts and a customer who buys a coat made of paws alone both know exactly what they are paying for. And a customer who bought a "Hudson seal" generations ago would be told today that it is dyed muskrat.

Industry Trends

Demand for furs is generally related to a country's economic conditions. During the Depression of the 1930s, fur sales dropped off drastically. In the period immediately following World War II, when the public had money and very little consumer merchandise was available, fur sales boomed. More recently, however, the fur industry had been plagued by a lessened interest in furs among consumers and by campaigns of the ecologically minded against the use of some wild furs.

However, in the early 1970s, the ebbing of the fur market slowed, and 1973 saw the beginning of a reversal of the sales decline. New fashion interest, increased foreign trade, and new legislation are the major trends influencing the sales of fur products in the 1970s.

Fashion Interest Fashion demand in recent years has led to an increase in the variety of fur garments. Where once nearly all fur garments were full-length coats, today stoles, scarfs, and jackets have widespread acceptance. Furs are now used to line outerwear, such as cloth coats and raincoats. Fur suits, fur vests, fur evening skirts, and fur hats are all gaining in popularity.

Increased interest in fur apparel is found not only among older customers, who form the traditional market for furs, but also among young customers as well. Neither is it limited to women's apparel; there is a greatly increased use of fur coats and hats among men.

Name designers are helping to put new fashion interest into furs. Calvin Klein, Stephen Burrows, Halston, Oscar de la Renta, Bonnie Cashin, and Bill Blass are a few well-known apparel designers who now work in fur as well as fabric.

New Legislation While the Federal Trade Commission and the fur industry are perpetually engaged in discussions about changes in the fur labeling rules, the most important fur legislation of recent years concerned the so-called "endangered species," those species of animals in danger of becoming extinct. In 1973, the federal Endangered Species Act was passed, forbidding the importation or transporting across state lines of a variety of animals or products made from those animals. Among those classified as endangered species are a number formerly used in making fur products, including major varieties of leopard, tiger, ocelot, cheetah, jaguar, vicuna, and a few types of wolf.

MERCHANDISING VOCABULARY
Define or briefly explain the following terms:

Tanning	Hides
Regular tanneries	Pelt
Converters	Fur farming
Contract tanneries	Leased department
Skins	Consignment selling
Kips	

MERCHANDISING REVIEW
1. In what ways have technological advances in machinery and chemistry benefited the leather industry?
2. Name and describe the three major types of firms into which this country's leather industry is divided.
3. Why does specialization prevail throughout the leather industry in this country? Give examples of such specialization.
4. Name the five major agents or methods used for tanning leather. Briefly describe the characteristics of leather tanned by each of these agents or methods. For what consumer products is each of these best suited?
5. Describe the fashion information services provided by leather producers and/or their trade associations.
6. Why is product research and development so important today in the leather industry? What specific benefits to the consumer have resulted from such product research and development?
7. Describe the history and development of the fur industry in this country.
8. Into what three groups is the fur industry in this country divided? Briefly describe the function of each.
9. What is meant by the term "fur farming"? Discuss its importance in the fur industry today.
10. Differentiate between "leased departments" and "consignment selling" as these terms apply to retail distribution of fur garments. What major advantages does each have for retail merchants?

MERCHANDISING DIGEST
1. Discuss the following statement from the text and its implications for leather merchandising: "Leather producers cannot merely stay abreast of fashion, they must keep ahead of it."
2. Discuss current trends in the leather industry as they relate to: (a) enlarging markets, (b) competition from synthetics, and (c) increased foreign trade.
3. Discuss: (a) the provisions of the Fur Labeling Act of 1952 and how it protects the consumer, and (b) recent legislation relating to furs.

7
MANUFACTURERS OF WOMEN'S FASHION APPAREL

Women's apparel manufacturing is a major industry in the United States. The industry employs about 1.3 million people, or one out of approximately every 14 people employed in manufacturing in this country. The combined wages and salaries of these people exceed $6.5 billion a year. The total annual output of the industry exceeds $25 billion at wholesale values.

In the production of women's ready-to-wear apparel fashions, the subject of this chapter, the United States leads the world. Its apparel industry has no peer in size, in efficient production methods, in workers' pay, or in ability to provide attractive fashions quickly and economically to women in every walk of life.

The term *ready-to-wear* refers to apparel made in factories to standard-size measurements. This is in contrast to custom-made apparel produced by professional dressmakers or by home sewers to the exact measurements of the individual who is going to wear the garment.

The women's ready-to-wear industry is relatively young; it was little more than an infant at the turn of the century. The industry has gained flexibility and grown rapidly in size since then. Whereas once Paris was the sole source of fashion inspiration, today the industry gathers its design ideas from all over the world. Whereas once a rigid pattern of seasonal offerings prevailed, today the industry is attempting to meet consumer demand with a continuous flow of new styles. Whereas once fashion and marketing decisions were based largely on guesswork, today market research and computerized operations prevail.

Ready-to-wear is a fast-moving, complex industry in which patterns of operation, as well as styling and timing, must constantly adjust to the changing tastes and preferences of consumers. Only producers who interpret and satisfy changing tastes and preferences succeed.

HISTORY OF THE INDUSTRY

Historically, the making of apparel for the entire family was a household job, usually the responsibility of the women. This has been true in most cultures ever since the family home was a cave and garments were often animal skins sewed together with leather thongs.

Although women traditionally did the sewing, men became the first professional producers of apparel. For many centuries, professional tailors have made a business of producing custom-made clothes for men. It was only a few centuries ago that professional dressmakers began producing custom-made women's apparel. Today, the demand for custom tailoring and dressmaking has shifted toward less-expensive factory-produced ready-to-wear in great variety.

Growth of the Ready-to-wear Industry

As will be discussed in Chapter 8, the first ready-to-wear clothing in the United States was made for

Working conditions in the garment factories of the early 1900s were crowded, uncomfortable, often unsafe—and hours were long.
International Ladies Garment Workers Union

men. During the first half of the 1800s, apparel manufacturing was limited to men's clothes. Only after the Civil War did women's apparel begin to be made on a commercial basis. The first garments turned out on a ready-to-wear basis were cloaks and mantles, neither of which required the careful fit that most other women's garments need.

By the turn of the century, however, limited quantities of women's suits, skirts, and blouses were made in factories. Within a decade, some manufacturer had the idea of sewing a blouse and a skirt together, and the first ready-to-wear dresses were produced.

By the end of World War I, the women's apparel business—today the heart of the fashion business—had passed the $1 billion mark in prod-

uct value. By 1970, the factory value of all shipments made by the women's apparel industries
totaled over $7 billion.

Unionization

An important element in the growth of the women's
ready-to-wear industry in this country was that
labor of the right type was available at the right
time and in the right place. In the nineteenth and
early twentieth centuries, millions of Europeans
sought refuge in the United States, particularly in
big cities along the eastern seaboard. They needed
to earn a living. Many, trained as dressmakers or
tailors in their homelands, turned naturally to the
growing apparel industry for jobs.

However, working conditions in the apparel
trades at the turn of the century were appalling.
Hours were long, pay was little, and factories were
overcrowded, dark, unsanitary, and unsafe.

In 1900, workers formed the International
Ladies' Garment Workers' Union (ILGWU), the
major union in the women's apparel trade today.
Strikes in 1909 and 1910 helped pave the way for
collective bargaining in the women's garment trade.
The tragic Triangle Shirtwaist Factory fire of 1911,
which killed 146 workers, rallied support around
the workers and eventually led to improved building codes and revised labor laws.

Characteristic of today's union activities is the
ILGWU's participation in joint employer-union
committees to set prices for piecework on individual
garments, depending on the elements of work involved in each style.

However, the ILGWU has developed into
more than a collective bargaining agency. This
union has contributed funds for promoting New
York as an industry fashion center and has helped
develop schools to train technical workers, designers, and other skilled employees needed in the
industry. In addition, ILGWU has subsidized housing and vacation resorts and provided other benefits
to make it easier and more pleasant for employees
to remain in the city and in the garment industry.

ORGANIZATION AND OPERATION OF THE INDUSTRY

The apparel industry is unusual among major
manufacturing industries in the United States in
that it is dominated by small firms. There are a
few giants, but the output of each is relatively
modest in comparison with the giants in other industries.

Producers of women's apparel have developed
a pattern of operation capable of rapid response to
the changing demands of fashion. Manufacturers
can contract or expand their facilities almost at a
moment's notice, depending on how well their
styles are accepted. New talents can enter the industry with minimum capital and sometimes sky-
rocket to a size that places them in the ranks of
the few giants.

Certain patterns of organization and operation
prevail within the apparel industry. First, not all
producers of apparel actually perform all the various
processes necessary to turn out finished garments.
Second, firms within the industry have traditionally
been highly specialized in terms of their production.
Third, new lines, or assortments of styles, are developed for each selling season of the year.

Types of Producers

The fashion apparel industry consists of three types
of producers: manufacturers, jobbers, and contractors. A *manufacturer* is one who performs all
the operations required to produce apparel from
buying the fabric to selling and shipping the finished
garments. A *jobber* handles the designing, the planning, the purchasing, usually the cutting, the selling, and the shipping, but does not handle the
actual sewing operation. The *contractor* is one whose
sole function is to supply sewing services to the
industry.

Manufacturers The greater New York area in
general and New York City in particular are home
to many of the women's apparel manufacturers.

Apparel manufacturing today is mechanized, specialized, and efficient, as illustrated by this Hawaiian factory.
Kamehameha Garment Company, Ltd.

More than 60 percent of the women's apparel produced in this country is made in the greater New York area.

In recent years some manufacturers have set up sewing plants of their own far from New York City. In upstate New York, in Alabama, or in any area where people with sewing skills are available for employment, small plants have been built. The training, supervision, and planning requirements of such plants are minimal compared with those of a main plant. Producers already experiencing labor shortages at their headquarters location find this a practical and economical way to expand sewing operations. However, even when a manufacturer moves production facilities out of New York, designers and the major showroom are usually kept within the city.

Manufacturers, by definition, are producers who handle all phases of a garment's production. Their staff produces the original design or buys an acceptable design from a free-lance designer. Each line is planned by the company executives. The company purchases the fabric and trimmings needed. The cutting and sewing are done in the company's factories. The company's sales force and traffic department handle the selling and shipping of the finished goods. One great advantage to this type of operation is that close quality control can be maintained. When producers contract out some part of their work, they cannot as effectively monitor its quality standards.

Jobbers Apparel jobbers handle all phases of the production of a garment except for the actual sewing and sometimes the cutting. A jobber firm may employ a design staff to create various seasonal lines or may buy acceptable sketches from free-lance designers. The jobber's staff buys the fabric and trimmings necessary to produce the styles in each line, makes up samples, and grades the patterns.

In most cases, the staff also cuts the fabric for the various parts of each garment to be produced. The sales staff takes orders for garments in each line, and the shipping department fills store orders from the finished garments returned by the contractor. Jobbers, however, do not actually sew and finish garments. Instead, they arrange with outside factories run by contractors to perform these manufacturing operations.

Contractors Contractors specialize in just one phase of the production of a garment: sewing. In some cases, contractors also perform the cutting operation from patterns submitted by a jobber or manufacturer. Contractors developed early in the history of the fashion industry, with the beginning of mass-production techniques. Contractors serve those producers who have little or no sewing capability of their own as well as those whose current business exceeds their own sewing capacity.

If a contractor is used, cut pieces of the garment are provided by the jobber or, in some cases, by the manufacturer. For an agreed price per garment, the article is sewn, finished, inspected, and returned to the jobber or manufacturer for shipment to retail store purchasers. The price charged by the contractor is largely determined by the union, which, in collaboration with management, sets the piece rates for labor.

In the mass production of ready-to-wear a single sewing machine operator rarely makes a complete garment. Each operator sews only a certain section of the garment, such as a sleeve or its hem. This division of labor, called *section work,* makes it unnecessary for an operator to switch from one highly specialized machine to another or to make adjustments on the machine. Any change or adjustment in equipment takes time and increases labor costs. In the fashion trade, time lost in making such changes also causes delays in getting a style to consumers. Delays in production could mean the loss of timeliness and sales appeal before an article reaches its market.

Contractors may arrange to work exclusively with one or more jobbers or manufacturers, reserving the right to work for others whenever their facilities are not fully employed. Such agreements are necessarily reciprocal; if a contractor agrees to give preference to a particular jobber's or manufacturer's work, the jobber or manufacturer gives preference to that contractor in placing sewing orders.

The major advantages of the contractor system to manufacturers and jobbers are:

• Large amounts of capital are not required for investment in equipment which may soon become obsolete.
• It minimizes difficulties in the hiring and training of suitable workers.
• It greatly reduces the amount of capital necessary to meet regular payrolls.
• It speeds up delivery of orders by providing additional manufacturing facilities in periods of peak demand.

The contractor system has the disadvantages common to most assembly-line productions. No individual has full responsibility for the finished product, and so the quality of workmanship and inspection may tend to be uneven.

Once, most contractors were located in the metropolitan New York City area. Today, they may be located anywhere in the world where labor is abundant; where wages, taxes, and land costs or rents are lower; and where modern facilities and good transportation are available. Today, it sometimes has proved more profitable to ship fashion goods from New York to contractors in, say, Hong Kong for sewing and finishing and then return them to New York for shipment to customers, than if those same goods were sewn and finished in metropolitan New York.

Size of Producers

Most firms producing women's apparel are small to relatively small in size. For instance, in the dress business alone there are about 5,000 firms whose output totaled $3 billion in 1970. In contrast, the radio and television receiving-set production industry had an output of almost the identical dollar value, while that industry comprised only about three hundred firms.

Publicly owned giants in the fashion industries do exist, however. One of the largest is Jonathan Logan, which in the early 1960s was first in the industry to pass the $100 million mark in sales. Other large publicly owned producers include Bobbie Brooks, Leslie Fay, and L'Aiglon.

But despite the presence of giants, it is possible for a small firm to set up shop and remain in the apparel business with only a modest investment and without the full range of talents and facilities required to process garments from original conception to ultimate distribution. A designer can function as a one-person custom business until attracting a manufacturer with the capital and productive capacity to bring the attention of a larger clientele. Producers with limited capital, but with a wanted product, a good distribution setup, and a price level that is in demand, can use free-lance designers and farm out sewing to contractors, thus stretching their capital.

Specialization by Product

Traditionally, women's apparel firms were divided into distinct and very narrow groups according to categories of apparel, size ranges, and price zones. A blouse manufacturer seldom made dresses as well. A dress manufacturer seldom turned out both women's and juniors' sizes. A coat and suit manufacturer seldom produced both expensive and popular-priced lines.

Today, however, the industry is much less specialized. An increasing number of firms are developing diversified lines and crossing previously established price and product lines.

Nevertheless, both producers and retail buyers still have to think and work in terms of product specialization. For instance, a producer will pick an inexpensive fabric for a popular-priced line, a more expensive fabric for a better-priced line. A retail buyer will shop one group of resources for

women's half-sizes and another group of resources for juniors' regular and petite sizes.

Categories Following are the traditional basic categories in women's apparel and the types of garments generally included in each category:

- Outerwear (coats, suits, rainwear, jackets)
- Dresses (one or two pieces; ensembles, meaning a dress with a jacket or coat)
- Sportswear and separates (active, contemporary, town-and-country, and spectator sportswear, including slacks, shorts, tops, swimsuits and cover-ups, bathing caps, beachbags, sweaters, shirts, jackets, tennis dresses, casual dresses, pantsuits)
- After-five and evening (dressy apparel)
- Brides and bridesmaids
- Blouses (including both dressy and tailored)
- Uniforms and aprons (including housedresses and sometimes career apparel)

Size Ranges Women's apparel is divided into several size ranges. Unfortunately, the industry has not yet developed standard industrywide size measurements for each of these ranges, although exploratory work has been undertaken in this direction. This is why one manufacturer's misses' size 12 is likely to fit quite differently than another manufacturer's misses' size 12 in a similar style. The traditional size ranges are:

- Women's (including even half sizes $12\frac{1}{2}$ to $26\frac{1}{2}$; straight sizes 36 to 52)
- Misses' (including regular even sizes 6 to 20; tall sizes 12 to 20; and some producers making sizes as small as 2)
- Juniors' (regular sizes 5 to 17; petite sizes 3 to 15)

Wholesale Price Zones Women's apparel is produced and marketed at a wide range of wholesale prices. Major factors contributing to the wholesale price of garments are: (1) the quality of materials used; (2) the quality of workmanship

Behind the Price Tag of a $110 Summer Dress

Cotton and polyester dress: Wholesale price $59.75
Retail price $110.00

Manufacturer's Cost

Fabric
(2¹¹/₁₆ yards
at $1.60)   **$4.30**

Lining
(1 ¾ yards at .75,
plus interlining,
¾ yards at .60)   **1.54**

Belt
(Including covered
snaps, elastic)   **2.28**

Labor, wages
(Operator, finisher,
presser)   **21.03**

**Labor,
fringe benefits**
(Health and welfare,
Social Security,
vacation, pension)   **6.73**

Overhead
(Rent, insurance,
utilities, salaries,
costs of samples,
trade discounts, etc.)   **19.87**

Total cost   **$55.75**

Taxes   **2.00**

Profit   **2.00**

**Wholesale cost
of dress**   **$59.75**

Retailer's Cost

$59.75 less discount for
prompt payment   **$55.00**

Markdowns
(Averaged over all
dresses in stock)   **$11.00**

**Shortages,
pilferage, etc.**   2.00

Alterations
(Cost of maintaining
department
averaged out)   2.00

Salaries
Sales staff   5.00

**Merchandising and
buying staff**
(Including expenses)   3.00

Clerical and stock room
(Receiving, marking,
deliveries, etc.;
including expenses)   3.00

**Advertising, display,
sales promotion**   4.00

Administrative
(Executives, credit and
accounting offices,
including expenses)   8.00

**Employe fringe
benefits**   2.00

Overhead
(Rent, insurance, utilities,
cleaning, security)   9.00

Miscellaneous   **2.00**

Total   **$106.00**

Taxes   2.00
Profit   2.00

Selling price   **$110.00**
(plus tax)

employed; and (3) the amount and type of labor required in the production process.

Within this wide range of prices, however, there are certain *price zones,* or series of somewhat contiguous price lines, that are of major appeal to specific target groups of customers. For this reason, the women's apparel market has traditionally been divided into the following three price zones:

- Better (usually the higher priced; sometimes referred to as the "prestige" market).
- Moderate (usually the medium priced; sometimes referred to as the "volume" market). Today, this category also usually includes the "boutique" lines produced by the traditionally considered "better" designers, such as Geoffrey Beene's Beene Bag and Bill Blass's Blassport line.

A pattern is laid out on a length of fabric.

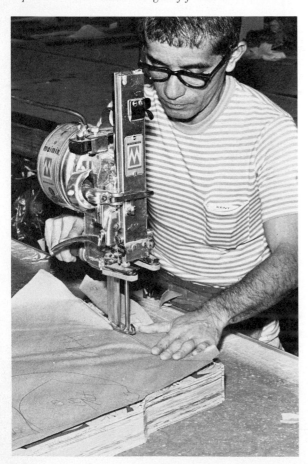

A marker is used as a guide in cutting through layers of material.
Kamehameha Garment Company, Ltd.

- Popular (usually low priced; sometimes referred to as the "promotional," "mass," or "budget" market).

Developing a Line

From 2 to 4 months before apparel for a specific season's selling reaches the retail store, the store's buyers are in the wholesale markets, viewing the lines of manufacturers and making their selections. From 6 to 12 months before that time, manufacturers begin creating their future seasonal lines. This means that the development of a line may begin as much as a year and a half before consumers have their first look at new seasonal merchandise on a store's selling floor.

Creating a Line   First, the designer charged with creating the line reviews all available information on trends, materials, and previous fashion successes and failures, in order to form some idea of what the coming season's line should include. Each design is first sketched or developed in muslin. The design is then considered both on its own merits and for its suitability to the line as a whole. Many designs may be discarded at this point.

Designs that seem most likely to succeed are then made up into a finished garment by a *sample hand,* a designer's assistant who is an all-round seamstress. Various executives of the firm (sales, purchasing, and production heads, cost experts, and others) then examine the samples. At this point, several more designs may be discarded while others may go back to the design room for modification.

Producing a Line

After a design has survived these preliminary challenges, a patternmaker makes a production pattern for it in whatever garment size the firm uses for its samples. From this pattern, one or more samples are cut and sewn. If the sample is acceptable, its production costs are carefully figured, a wholesale price is determined, the design is given a style number, and it becomes part of the manufacturer's line.

After buyers have viewed a line and placed their orders, the manufacturer usually finds that some style offerings have received considerable buyer interest while others have not. Those in the first group are scheduled for production; those in the second group are usually dropped from the line.

For every style that is to be produced, the original pattern is graded or "sloped" to adjust it to each of the various sizes in which the style will be made. Next, the pieces of the pattern in all its sizes are carefully laid out on a long piece of paper, or *marker*, that corresponds in width to the width of the fabric to be used.

One of the most important operations in the mass production of apparel is that of cutting through many thicknesses of material in one operation. Its success depends on the accuracy with which each layer of material is laid on top of the one directly underneath. Selvages must be laid together exactly: Each part of a design must be laid out immediately over the same part of the design on the material directly below. A machine called a "laying-up machine" carries the material back and forth along a guide on either side of the cutting table, spreading the material evenly from end to end. On top of this pile of laid-out material, which may be anywhere from 50 to 100 layers in depth, the marker is laid to serve as a cutting pattern, and the material and marker are secured by clamps at either end and at intervals along the material's selvaged edges.

The cutting of the material around the edges of individual pieces of the pattern's marker is done either by electric knife or sometimes, more recently, by lazer beam. Individual pieces of each pattern, still with the paper marker on top, are then tied up in bundles according to size and passed along to the sewing operators, either in the same plant or in a contractor's shop. After sewing, finishing, pressing, and inspection, the finished garments are ready for shipment.

As the season progresses, retailers reorder popular numbers, and manufacturers may recut them. However, producers recut only on the "hottest" or best-selling numbers in their lines and drop any others for which there have been only scattered reorders.

DOMESTIC FASHION MARKET CENTERS

United States' firms produce over $25 billion worth of fashion apparel and accessories a year, figured in terms of factory shipments. Only a small fraction of this output is exported. Even though an increasing amount of apparel and accessories is imported, well over 90 percent of the vast array of fashion goods spread out before American consumers is made by American producers.

For this reason, domestic market centers are of greatest importance to most American retail store buyers. In these market centers, fashion buyers select most of the merchandise that will be offered for sale in retail stores.

In spite of the influential role that foreign designers have played in the history of fashion, no longer does all fashion inspiration originate outside this country. Today, American producers, as well as some foreign producers, look to American designers for fashion leadership.

Even before World War II, which violently disrupted the traditional pattern and flow of fashion inspiration, designers in this country had begun to fill fashion apparel needs that foreign designers neither understood nor could design for. Prominent among American fashion creators of the past was the late Claire McCardell. Ignoring Paris, so long considered the world's fashion center, she made clothes of special appeal to women in this country, introducing the easy lines that made the most of their figures and also permitted freedom of movement. Among the casual clothes that this world-famous designer created before World War II are types that have continued in popularity throughout the years: shirtwaist dresses, for example, and skirts with unpressed pleats.

American designers have no protection against design piracy, though many of them would welcome such protective laws. Regulations that shelter the French couture world would violate antitrust laws here. Even without such protection, and without the glamour of a centuries-old reputation such as Paris designers enjoy, their American counterparts continue to flourish because their interpretations of fashion appear to be in close harmony with what people want.

The New York Market

New York City is not only the fashion apparel production center of the United States, from which goods are shipped to stores throughout the country; it is also the sales headquarters for manufacturers whose design and production facilities may be located in any of the 50 states. The hub of the "garment district," as the women's apparel market is called, is Seventh Avenue. The garment district itself is that section of the city bounded by Ninth Avenue on the west, the Avenue of the Americas (Sixth Avenue) on the east, 35th Street on the south, and 41st Street on the north.

Within this area are literally thousands of showrooms displaying various types and price lines of women's fashion apparel. Many of these showrooms are maintained by New York producers, but in others the lines of manufacturers located around the world are shown.

Because merchants and their buyers have only limited time to spend away from their stores, they find it advantageous to do all their purchasing in one city. New York can provide many buyers with a one-stop shopping center that saves them both time and travel expense. Furthermore, most major fiber and fabric producers, consumer and fashion periodicals, and trade associations maintain offices and/or showrooms in New York City. These are additional sources of valuable fashion trend information to a merchant on a buying trip.

In many respects, New York is more expensive and more difficult to work in than any other area in which fashion producers have developed businesses. But despite the disadvantages—crowding; the high cost of space, labor, and living—many segments of the fashion industry continue to operate there. Most of those whose headquarters are located elsewhere consider it essential to show their lines in New York City because so many retailers travel there to buy.

The Dallas Market

The Southwest United States today is one of the fastest-growing areas in terms of population, industry, and wealth. It is also the home of several minority ethnic groups, such as American Indians and Mexican-Americans, whose cultural contributions to apparel are evident in some of the typically regional dress and accessories that are widely accepted today. The prevailing climate in the Southwest is conducive to more casual lifestyles, and preferred apparel for such lifestyles is sportswear.

It is primarily for these reasons that Dallas, the largest city in that geographic area, has developed into both an apparel production center and also a very important domestic fashion market center. It is the third largest market center in this country and advertises itself as being "Where New York and California Meet."

The Dallas Apparel Mart is the newest and largest building in the privately owned Dallas Market Center complex, which also includes a Decorative Center, the Dallas Home Furnishings Mart, the Dallas Trade Mart, and Market Hall. The Apparel Mart houses 1,200 permanent showrooms of producers of men's, women's, and children's apparel and accessories, shoes, and textiles. An additional 350 showrooms are available for rent during major market weeks.

Seasonal lines of women's and children's wear are shown at the Dallas Apparel Mart: in late January for the midsummer season, in early April for early fall, in late May for fall, in mid-August for midwinter, and in late October for spring. A fall shoe show is held in mid-March. Market weeks for men's and boys' wear are held in January for spring

The Apparel Mart, Dallas

Market center contrasts: above, The Apparel Mart, Dallas, right, Seventh Avenue, New York City.

The Denver Merchandise Mart

The Denver Merchandise Mart

Buyers flock to the permanent (left) or temporary (lower left) showrooms of producers during seasonal market weeks.

The Apparel Mart, Dallas

and summer, in early February for spring tailored clothing, in mid-April for fall and back-to-school, in August for fall tailored clothing, and in early October for spring and holiday.

Many retailers, particularly those located in the mid-South, Southwest, and Midwest, find buying trips to the Dallas market not only less expensive and less time consuming but also far less overwhelming than trips to the New York market.

The California Market

California apparel producers, in many cases, were more alert than those in the East to sense certain trends in the American lifestyle, particularly the trend toward more casual living. In the 1930s, when sportswear was beginning to find a place in most women's wardrobes, it was being produced almost entirely by California firms. Major fashion retailers throughout the country sent their buyers to check the California offerings and purchase merchandise that would satisfy their customers' demand for casual apparel.

The California market is centered in the huge California Mart, housing more than 1,500 permanent showrooms of domestic and international producers of men's, women's, and children's apparel and accessories, as well as textiles. This mart is open from 9 A.M. to 5 P.M. daily, 52 weeks of the year. Seasonal lines of women's apparel producers open at the California Mart in mid-January for summer, in mid-August for holiday, and in mid-October for spring. A California boutique show is held the first week in January.

Although the California market was perhaps best known originally for women's sportswear and various types of active sportswear, now it has become an important market center for a wide variety of men's, women's, and children's apparel, as well as boutique and textile merchandise.

The Denver Market

Denver is the major market center of the 14 Rocky Mountain and Plains states (roughly one-third of the continental United States). It serves as a clearinghouse for goods and services for the entire region. The Denver Merchandise Mart is one of the four major marts in this country; in fact, two of the mart's shows—the Men's Dress and Western Apparel Show and the Ski Show—have become the largest trade shows of their kind.

The Denver Mart houses 400 permanent showrooms of local, national, and a few foreign producers of men's, women's, and children's apparel and accessories, as well as textiles. A recently added exposition building houses a huge hall and 170 additional temporary showrooms.

Regular seasonal market weeks for women's and children's apparel and accessories, as well as for textiles, are held in November for spring, in January for summer, in August for holiday, and in May for fall. Mens-, boys-, and western-wear weeks are held in September for holiday and spring and in April for fall. The famous Men's Dress and Western Dress market week is held each January. Two shoe shows are also held in the Denver Mart, in September for spring and in April for fall. In addition, an Apparel Extravaganza is held in April, a Ski Show in April, Gift and Jewelry Shows in March and August, and a Home Furnishings Show in February.

The Carolina-Virginia Market

With an unmistakable movement of apparel and accessories production facilities from the northeast region of this country to the mid-Atlantic and mid-South regions, as well as a population movement to these areas, it is inevitable that an important apparel and accessories market should develop.

The Carolina Trade Mart, in Charlotte, North Carolina, houses over 400 permanent showrooms of producers of women's and children's apparel and accessories. An additional 100 producers take temporary booth space for the regular market weeks held in January, late March, May, late August, and October. Local firms exhibiting during these market weeks account for only about 3 percent of the more than 1,000 participating firms or their sales representatives. Other domestic firms represent 96 percent, and about 1 percent are foreign firms.

The Miami Market

Miami, long famous as a winter resort, has more recently become an important fashion market center serving retailers located mainly in the Southern United States, the Caribbean, and South America.

A three-story Miami Merchandise Mart houses between 250 and 300 permanent showrooms of local and other domestic producers. Thirteen annual apparel and accessories seasonal markets are held. Seasonal lines of women's apparel and accessories are shown in mid-October and January and in early April, June, and August. Infants' and children's markets are held in late November and in early June, September, and December. Men's and boy's markets are held in late January and April and in early September.

The Chicago Mart

A new Apparel Center, adjacent to Chicago's famous Merchandise Mart, is scheduled to open in 1976. It is claimed that the 25-story center will be the largest women's and children's apparel complex under one roof with a 52-week, year-round market. It will contain 11 floors of permanent showrooms featuring merchandise from 3,500 resources, an exhibition hall, a 10-story hotel, and a model retail store featuring the latest in in-store display techniques and merchandising concepts. This new Apparel Center is expected to provide five times the space now devoted to women's and children's apparel and accessories in the present Merchandise Mart.

Other Domestic Fashion Market Centers

In recent years, merchandise marts have been built in a number of this country's larger cities that have become important regional trade centers. Like the marts already described, these house the permanent showrooms of local, national, and some foreign fashion producers. Similarly, regularly scheduled market weeks are held in these marts, usually under the sponsorship of various salesmen's associations, such as Style Exhibitors, Inc., the American Fashion

Association, Shoe Travelers' Association, and Men's and Boy's Apparel Association.

Other domestic merchandise marts that serve as regional fashion market centers are the Atlanta Apparel Mart (Atlanta, Ga.), the Northeast Trade Center (Woburn, Mass.), the San Francisco Mart (San Francisco, Calif.), the Radisson Center (Minneapolis, Minn.), and the Kansas City Trade Center (Kansas City, Mo.).

MERCHANDISING ACTIVITIES

Most fashion producers sell directly to retail stores rather than through intermediaries. The pace of fashion in all but a few more staple items is much too fast to allow time for the selling, reselling, or warehousing activities of wholesale distributors or jobbers.

Women's apparel producers aim their sales promotion efforts at both retailers and consumers. Such efforts take the form of advertising, publicity, and a number of promotional aids they may make available to retailers who buy their products.

Advertising

Today, much retail advertising of women's fashion apparel carries the name of its producer. As late as the 1930s, however, nearly all retailers refused to allow any tags or labels other than their own on the fashion goods they offered. A series of government regulations, in addition to merchandise shortages during World War II, helped reverse this situation, however. Today, most merchants capitalize on the producers' national advertising by leaving producers' labels attached, featuring producer names in their own advertising and displays, and sometimes by setting up special sections within their stores for individual producers' lines.

The apparel manufacturing industry spends less than 1 percent of its annual sales total on advertising, but the exposure given to its products is impressive. Some exposure is obtained through ads placed by apparel firms in consumer publications, including both fashion and general magazines as well as newspapers. Some is obtained through ads in trade publications. Another important source of exposure is cooperative advertising with retail stores.

Publicity

Whether they spend money on advertising or not, apparel producers have many opportunities at their disposal to familiarize the public with their brand names through publicity. To obtain maximum publicity, producers sometimes hire a public relations person or firm. Photographs of some of their best-selling styles may be distributed to newspapers and magazines. They may supply television and sports personalities with items of apparel in an attempt to attract public attention.

In addition to the individual efforts of firms to secure publicity, the major women's couture firms located in New York City show their collections at semiannual Press Weeks. There are two Press Weeks each January and two each June. One is organized by the New York Couture Group, the public relations arm of the New York Couture Business Council. The other is called the American Designers Showings, and is an activity of a public relations firm, Eleanor Lambert, Inc. Both give the fashion editors (newspaper, magazine, radio, and television) of the country an opportunity to examine the latest designer collections and make available to them the photographs, prepared stories, and interview opportunities they need to tell the fashion story to their audiences.

Early Press Weeks exhibited merchandise lines that ran the entire gamut of price levels, from lowest to highest. Gradually, however, lower-priced merchandise was eliminated until in recent years New York Press Weeks now feature almost exclusively the lines of higher-priced producers.

In addition, semiannual Press-Week showings are now held in Los Angeles under the sponsorship of the California Fashion Creators.

Promotional Aids

To assist retailers and to speed the sale of their merchandise, many apparel manufacturers provide a variety of promotional aids. The range is vast, and a single firm's offerings may include any or all of the following:

- Display ideas
- Display and stock fixtures
- Advertising aids
- Suggestions for departmental layout and fixturing
- Reorder forms and assistance in checking stock for reorder purposes
- Educational booklets for salespeople and customers
- Talks to salespeople by producers' representatives
- Assistance from producers' fashion experts in training salespeople, staging fashion shows, addressing customers
- Statement enclosures or other mailing pieces for stores to send to customers
- Special retail promotions to tie in with producers' national advertising campaigns

Typical of what can be achieved by close cooperation between producers and retailers was the assistance offered by a sportswear producer to any store that would stage a travel promotion using the firm's merchandise. A major airline joined in the effort; its stewardesses were available to show customers how to pack and to advise them on clothing needs in various vacation spots served by that airline. The producer's fashion experts planned minimum wardrobes to meet maximum travel demands. The producer, the store, and the airline all contributed to the promotion, and each profited by the interest generated.

More recently, one apparel producer offered a limited number of his retail store customers a 20-minute color videotape featuring his current line. The taped fashion show, using four live models and commentated by the producer, was intended to help educate fashion sales personnel about fabrics, colors, silhouettes, and skirt lengths in the producer's line, as well as the accessories necessary to complete his fashion message.

INDUSTRY TRENDS

The women's apparel manufacturing industry is going through a period of dramatic change. Trends in the industry reflect producers' reactions to changing economic climate, market conditions, and customer demands. Which of today's trends will be most significant in shaping the future of the industry cannot yet be determined, but it will probably be one or more of the ones discussed here.

Growth in Size of Firms

The number of firms producing women's apparel keeps decreasing, and yet the volume of goods produced keeps increasing. This is because small firms, although still the backbone of the industry, are more often faced with the choice of going out of business or being absorbed by larger firms. Large firms, still proportionately only a small fraction of the total number of women's apparel producers, are growing bigger and bigger, mainly through acquisitions and mergers.

There are four basic ways by which giant firms are created and by which large firms became even larger. First, a firm can expand by *going public,* which means turning a privately owned company into a public corporation and issuing stock for sale. This enables a company to substantially increase the amount of capital it has available for modernization and expansion purposes.

Second, a firm can expand through horizontal integration—by merging with or acquiring other firms that make similar products at the same marketing level. This enables a company to increase its size without having to learn the intricacies of making or selling a different kind of product. For example, when a producer of misses' dresses acquires a firm making junior apparel, or a producer of daywear dresses acquires a firm making casual knitwear, this is horizontal integration.

Third, a firm can expand through vertical integration—by merging with or acquiring firms at different marketing levels. For instance, a dress manufacturer might seek a merger with a producer of the kinds of fabrics the manufacturer uses or with a chain of specialty stores that sell the manufacturer's type of dresses. Vertical integration enables a company to gain control of all or part of the development, production, and marketing of a product.

Fourth, a firm can expand through the formation of *conglomerates,* which are groups of companies that may or may not be related in terms of product and marketing level. In fact, the parent company usually seeks to acquire companies that are different in terms of product, seasonal demand, and market level. Thus it protects itself against such hazards as great fluctuations or changes in demand or possible setbacks in any one of its activities.

Decentralization of Production Facilities

A mid-1974 report in the *New York Times* estimated that there were 23 percent fewer apparel manufacturing firms in New York City than there had been eight years earlier. While some of the decrease was probably caused by mergers and bankruptcies of small firms, another significant factor probably was the number of firms who have moved their production facilities out of the city. This trend toward decentralization is occurring in all the big metropolitan areas of the East coast, where such apparel firms originally had been clustered.

Producers are leaving the large metropolitan areas for three reasons. First, it is at best difficult and expensive, and sometimes even impossible, to modernize or expand present production facilities in the center of crowded urban areas. There isn't enough space available, and the space that is available is usually too old or too expensive to modernize. Modern, well-designed, efficient plants can be built in other areas of the country where both land and construction costs are lower.

Second, traffic congestion in major cities today makes both deliveries and shipments a serious problem for producers. Moving from the city increases shipping distances, but the actual time involved in moving goods over greater distances on a network of superhighways is often no greater than transporting such goods through crowded urban streets.

Third, labor, taxes, and other operating costs are high in cities. These costs are much less expensive in suburban and rural areas. This is why an increasing number of producers have established factories in the smaller towns of the mid-Atlantic and Southern states. Manufacturing facilities are still less expensive to maintain in such places as Taiwan, Korea, Hong Kong, and the Philippines. And this is why some firms send greige goods abroad for finishing, while others have garments cut and sewn abroad under contract, shipping the finished garments back here for distribution. Some producers even have set up their own factories in foreign countries, taking advantage of lower operating costs.

Decreasing Emphasis on Seasonal Lines

Traditionally, women's apparel producers created two lines a year, one for the spring–summer season, one for the fall–winter season. Rarely were new styles available until the next semiannual line was introduced. Buyers simply reordered those styles that sold well.

However, because of consumer demand, producers gradually began introducing minor seasonal lines (such as holiday, resort and cruise, and transitional wear) between regular semiannual lines. These helped stores bring new styles and new interest to their selling floors throughout the year.

The trend away from strictly seasonal lines is continuing. Although producers of better apparel still tend to develop strictly seasonal lines, producers of moderate-priced apparel keep adding new styles to their lines throughout each season. In addition, producers of popular-priced apparel have just about dropped seasonal lines and instead concentrate on producing a continuous series of lower-priced items that are copies or adaptations of styles at higher prices.

Diversification of Product

Traditionally, as mentioned above, women's apparel producers were specialized in terms of the categories, size ranges, and price zones of apparel they produced. Producers of better-quality misses' coats and suits made just those categories in a specific size range and at a specific level of quality; they produced nothing else. Today, producers are broadening their offerings. For instance, dress houses may add sportswear lines. Producers traditionally known for producing higher-priced goods may add moderate-priced lines, often in the form of boutique merchandise. Producers that once specialized in making one range of sizes now may increase the number of sizes they offer.

Internationalization of Apparel Marketing

A few American producers are selling their products directly to foreign consumers, sometimes through boutiques. Import and export duties as well as fluctuating currency exchange rates have kept this kind of business small so far, but the international flow probably will increase. Other American producers are working out multinational marketing arrangements with foreign firms, enabling the Americans to market through the foreign firms' distribution channels.

The flow is in both directions. An increasing number of foreign designers and producers are showing their goods in the United States. They no longer wait for American buyers to make a trip to their market centers. Instead, they bring their lines here and exhibit them in either temporary or permanent showrooms in one or more domestic market centers. In addition, a few foreign producers have opened boutiques here to sell directly to American consumers.

Proliferation of Licensing Arrangements

Diversification does not always require the use of one's own capital; neither does expansion. Some companies expand and diversify by *licensing,* which is an arrangement whereby firms are given permission to produce and market merchandise in the name of a licensor, who is paid a percentage of the sales for permitting his or her name to be used. Many well-known women's apparel designers are licensing either their designs or the use of their names for a wide variety of goods. A designer's name formerly associated only with couture fashions now may be found on swimwear, sunglasses, accessories, leisurewear, even domestics and home furnishings.

Licensing is also crossing international borders. An increasing number of American designers are working out licensing arrangements with foreign producers.

Automation in Apparel Production

The tremendous technological explosion that is affecting business, industry, and individuals alike is bringing some radical changes to the women's apparel industry. Earlier advances, such as the power sewing machine and the electric cutting knife, were big steps in their time. Some changes now on the drawing boards or being tried in pilot programs, or actually in use today, are even bigger. All are aimed at increasing productivity, reducing labor costs, and achieving standardization of product and better quality control.

Cutting and Sewing Procedures Lazer-beam fabric-cutting systems, first introduced in the menswear manufacturing industry, are now being adapted for use in the more complicated cutting work required in the production of women's apparel. A lazer beam can cut fabric more quickly and more accurately than an electric knife. In addition, since this method cuts by burning, it eliminates raw edges that might unravel.

Equipment is being developed that will automatically lay out a pattern so that the least amount of fabric is used, thus permitting maximum usage of each bolt of fabric. Also on the drawing boards is equipment that will record apparel patterns on electronic tape so that the patterns can be stored easily and safely and can be located quickly. Some equipment in experimental use makes sample duplicates at the same time the original sample pattern is made.

More automation in sewing plants is being explored, too, in terms of electronic scanners that optically guide a sewing machine head to stitch the pieces of a cut pattern in a programmed way. Also being worked on are conveyor belts that will carry the pieces of a garment from one machine to another in the order in which they are to be sewed together. Machines that fuse seams by heat instead of by stitching, thus saving time as well as eliminating raw edges, have already been introduced. Equipment that fits a section of tubular fabric over a three-dimensional metal form, heat-setting the fabric, then cooling it, is claimed to reduce the labor now involved in the sewing of apparel by 30 to 40 percent.

Sales and Inventory Reports A few smaller and many larger women's apparel producers are using daily or weekly computer printouts to keep their inventories of piece goods in better balance with unit sales of each style number. Printouts also provide them with up-to-date information on the number of units, by style, size, and color, that are on hand, in work, and on order by each of their retail store customers. Computerized reports can also tell producers the dollar volume of business they are doing this year with each of their retail accounts as compared to that in previous years.

Some larger retailers and producers are experimenting with daily or semiweekly transmittal of sales information. Sales are fed into store computers, sorted by style and producer, and producers are sent a rundown on the activity of their styles. This enables both stores and producers to keep close track of changes in consumer demand.

For instance, with such current information at their fingertips, producers can update production plans and fabric commitments to correspond with demand trends. Their design departments can keep close track of the acceptance or rejection of individual styles and use this information in their planning of new styles. Their sales staffs can be given more useful and detailed information so that they can tell store buyers about the firm's best-selling styles, fabrics, and colors.

MERCHANDISING VOCABULARY
Define or briefly explain the following terms:

Ready-to-wear	Section work	Going public
Manufacturer	Price zone	Conglomerates
Jobber	Sample hand	Licensing
Contractor	Marker	

MERCHANDISING REVIEW
1. Discuss the effect of extensive immigration on the development of the apparel industry in the United States.
2. What is the name of the major union in the women's apparel industry? List the benefits this union has achieved for its members.
3. In what three ways does the apparel industry in this country differ from other industries also producing consumer goods?
4. Name and describe the function of each of the three types of apparel producers found in the United States today.
5. What is meant by the term *section work?* What are its advantages in the production of fashion apparel?
6. What are the major advantages and disadvantages of the contractor system?
7. Describe the steps involved in developing a line of women's apparel.
8. Why is New York City considered the major fashion market center in the United States?
9. Describe the advertising and publicity activities of fashion apparel producers, indicating specific methods they may use in each activity.
10. Name at least five types of promotional aids that many women's apparel producers provide to their retail store customers.

MERCHANDISING DIGEST
1. Describe the three basic areas into which women's apparel-producing firms have traditionally been subdivided. What changes are currently taking place with respect to such specialization by product?
2. Where are fashion market centers located in this country besides New York City? Discuss at least two market centers, indicating the distinctive characteristics and services each offers retail store buyers.
3. "The women's apparel manufacturing industry is going through a period of dramatic change." Indicate seven significant industry trends and discuss three in detail.

8
MANUFACTURERS OF MENSWEAR

Twenty years ago, the menswear industry in the United States was organized and operated according to a conservative pattern in which changes, both in styling and in production methods, took place slowly and only after due deliberation. Today, as an article in a trade publication said, "There is a kind of fervor in the [industry] that borders on the same kind of day-to-day insanities women's wear goes through every time a 'hot body' moves out of a test store."[1] The single major factor that turned a traditionally conservative industry into an arena of confusion and change has been increasing consumer demand for a return to real fashion in menswear.

Throughout history and until relatively recent times, fashion interest centered around men's apparel rather than around women's. Not only was male dress more distinctive and "stylish" than female dress, but much of it—particularly that worn for ceremonial occasions—was more colorful. Males were the acknowledged dominant sex, and their apparel was intended to bear witness to that fact.

While in earlier times both custom and royal decree often dictated that apparel clearly indicate the social class of its wearer, men's clothes also boasted of bravery, strength, manliness, and a superior role. The apparel of medieval knights shows this. So, too, does the apparel worn by men in the French royal courts of the seventeenth and eighteenth centuries, which emphasized high social status from the top of the curled wigs to the cascades of lace and ribbons on the breeches.

Then came the Industrial Revolution. Power, both in terms of money and of influence, gradually moved from upper classes into the hands of the clever and the hard-working. As a result, a new class of "industrial riche" was created. However, many of the newly powerful chose to identify with the Puritan work ethic; instead of publicizing their newly acquired wealth and power through elegant apparel, they dressed soberly and discretely.

Gradually, even those not connected with the growth of industry wore subdued clothing styles, too. They found it wiser, more practical, and more in tune with the times to dress as an accountant than as a gallant. Women encouraged this change. While it was fine to have a brave and handsome husband, these two qualities did not necessarily result in security. But a good position in industry did, and industrial leaders tended to dress conservatively.

And so, almost all menswear became conservative. It remained conservative for over two hundred years. During this period, men were content to see their wives and daughters become the fashion plates. Women's clothes were styled not only to show off the attributes of the wearer but also to signal the social class, financial achievement, and social success of husbands and fathers.

During this long period of conservatism in men's fashions, the menswear industry was born and took shape. Menswear is the oldest and most traditional of the domestic apparel industries. And though it is the industry where custom-tailoring retained its importance longest, it is also where ready-to-wear got its start.

On the runway, a model in the kind of casual attire that Halston, long known for better women's apparel, showed in his first menswear line.

Halston

HISTORY AND DEVELOPMENT

Until the late 1700s, all men's apparel made in this country was custom-tailored. The rich patronized tailors' shops. Those who could not afford tailor-made clothing wore clothing made at home.

The first ready-to-wear clothing produced here probably was made by tailors in ports in the Northeast. Seamen off ships stopping in these ports needed city clothes while on shore, but they lacked the time or money to spend on tailor-made clothes. To meet the seamen's needs, a few tailors in waterfront cities such as New Bedford, Boston, New York, Philadelphia, and Baltimore began anticipating sales. They made suits in advance so that sailors could put them on as soon as they stepped on shore.

These first ready-to-wear shops were called "slop shops," and in comparison with today's apparel, the name was appropriate for the product they sold. These ready-to-wear suits offered none of the careful fit and detail work found in custom-tailored suits. However, sailors had seldom worn anything except homemade clothes, and so the ready-to-wear suits were acceptable, and the prices were right.

Some of today's leading menswear retail organizations got their start in those early days. For instance, Brooks Brothers' first store was a shop opened by Henry Brooks in 1818 in downtown New York; and Jacob Reed's Sons' first store was opened by Jacob Reed in 1824 near the waterfront in Philadelphia.

During this period, industrialization resulted in a population movement to urban areas, where people settled around or near factories. Often the adults and older children of a family worked in a nearby factory. Factory work left neither time nor anyone at home to make the family's clothing. Still, it did provide enough income so that the head of the house could buy a ready-made suit.

Industrialization also created a rapidly growing new middle class of white-collar factory supervisors, managers, and junior executives. These newcomers to the middle class did not have the income to pay for custom-tailored clothes, but they did want wardrobes that would show off their new class status. To meet this new demand, tailors improved the quality, fit, and variety of ready-to-wear apparel.

Soon, the slop shops had become respectable men's clothing stores. By the mid-1800s, the upper classes still would not consider buying clothes off a rack, but the middle class—always most important in terms of fashion acceptance—patronized these stores.

The sewing machine, invented by Elias Howe in 1846, helped speed up production of men's ready-to-wear. The Gold Rush of 1848 increased the demand for male ready-to-wear. One name connected with menswear during the Gold Rush is Levi Strauss. He went to the gold fields of California with heavy fabric to sell to miners for tents; instead, he turned it into the pants and overalls the miners needed more than tents. The Civil War increased the demand for ready-to-wear even more, this time in the form of uniforms. In addition, the specifications given factories for the production of Civil War uniforms gradually led to the development of standard measurements and a better fit in men's ready-to-wear.

"Store-bought clothes" succeeded in breaking the final class barrier near the end of the 1800s. Several financial crises during that period caused men who had formerly worn only custom-made clothes to patronize ready-to-wear clothing stores. Their patronage helped ready-to-wear to spread throughout the class structure and gain widespread acceptance. Even though custom tailoring remained a vital part of the industry until recently, it gradually declined to its present status as a minor segment of the menswear industry.

Dual Distribution

One operating policy connected with the menswear ready-to-wear industry since its early history has been *dual distribution*, which refers to manufacturers' policy of selling goods at both wholesale and retail. This practice has been far more prevalent in the menswear industry than in women's apparel.

Dual distribution of menswear got its start in the early and middle 1800s, when the ready-to-wear business was expanding along with the country's population. New ready-to-wear factories were concentrated in the North, but since population was growing rapidly in the South, particularly in port cities, good business was to be found there.

At first, ready-to-wear clothing manufacturers were content to sell goods to independent clothing stores in the South. However, producers soon decided that it would be doubly profitable to own some of those Southern retail outlets. By the 1830s, a number of New York manufacturers had outlets in New Orleans, then the second largest port in the United States, and in other Southern population centers. At the same time, other manufacturers continued to sell goods on a wholesale basis to independent clothing stores where they did not have outlets of their own.

This was the start of the menswear industry's involvement with dual distribution. The involvement has waxed and waned over the decades. In general, the policy has paid off in prosperous times but has been disastrous during economic recession or depression.

Contractors

As the men's ready-to-wear business grew, so did its attractiveness as a profitable investment. But going into business as a menswear manufacturer required considerable capital in terms of factory construction, equipment, and labor costs. This situation led to the birth of the contractor business described in Chapter 7. By hiring a contractor to do the sewing, and sometimes the cutting as well, manufacturers did not need factories or sewing machines or a labor force.

Contractors of menswear handled their work in one of two ways. Usually, they set up their own factories where the sewing was done. But sometimes they distributed work to operators who sewed at home, either on their own machines or on machines rented from contractors. These workers were paid on a piecework basis.

Thus, right after the Civil War and for the next two decades or so, menswear was manufactured in three different ways: (1) in *inside shops*, where garments were made in factories owned and operated by manufacturers; (2) in contract shops, where garments were produced for manufacturers in contractors' factories; (3) in homes, where home workers made garments on a piecework basis, usually for contractors but sometimes for manufacturers.

A contractor's most important value in apparel manufacturing is the ability to turn out short runs of a style quickly and inexpensively. (A *short run* is the production of a limited number of units of a particular item, fewer than would normally be considered an average number to produce.) Because short runs are a contractor's specialty, contracting remained an important factor in women's apparel manufacturing, but it gradually was abandoned by menswear manufacturers until recently, when it again became important in producing sportswear.

Traditional menswear manufacturers turned away from contractors and stayed away until recently for several reasons. First, the menswear industry had a pattern of very slow style change, and contracting was not as economical as inside-shop production. Second, improved equipment and cheaper electric power helped make production in inside shops more practical and efficient. Third, as quality became increasingly important, menswear manufacturers found it easier to control work within their own factories than in the contractors' factories.

Unions

As the menswear market and industry grew, so did competition among manufacturers. Factory employees became the victims. To produce ready-to-wear clothing at competitive prices, manufacturers and contractors demanded long hours from workers, and yet they paid low wages. In addition, factory working conditions, which had never been good, deteriorated further. Contractors were particularly guilty, and their factories deserved their designation as "sweat shops" or "sweaters." According to an official New York State inspection report of 1887:

The workshops occupied by these contracting manufacturers of clothing, or "sweaters" as they are commonly called, are foul in the extreme. Noxious gases emanate from all corners. The buildings are ill smelling from cellar to garret. The water-closets are used by males and females, and usually stand in the room where the work is done. The people are huddled together too closely for comfort, even if all other conditions were excellent.[2]

The outcome was inevitable. Workers finally rebelled against working conditions, hours, and pay.

Local employee unions had existed in the industry since the early 1800s, but none had lasted long or wielded much power. The Journeymen Tailors' National Union, formed in 1883, functioned (and still functions today) mainly as a craft union. A union representing all apparel industry workers, the United Garment Workers of America, was organized in 1891, but it had little power and soon collapsed. Finally, in 1914, the Amalgamated Clothing Workers of America was formed. It has remained the major union of the menswear industry.

Workers in tailored clothing plants make up the backbone of the Amalgamated, and thus the union is a strong force in menswear manufacturing in the North. However, its influence in factories producing men's work clothes, furnishings, and sportswear in the South and other parts of the country was almost nonexistent until the mid-1970s, when a drive to organize support in the South gave the union its first toe-hold in these areas.

ORGANIZATION AND OPERATION OF THE INDUSTRY

The menswear industry traditionally has been divided into firms making five kinds of clothing:

- Tailored clothing (suits, overcoats, topcoats, sport coats, separate trousers)
- Furnishings (shirts, neckwear, sweaters, knit tops, underwear, socks, robes, pajamas)

- Heavy outerwear (windbreakers, snowsuits, ski jackets, parkas, related items)
- Work clothes (work shirts, work pants, overalls, related items)
- Other (uniforms, hats, miscellaneous items)

For many years, the Federal Bureau of Labor Statistics did not recognize these divisions within the industry but instead combined all production data under the general heading of "men's apparel" or "men's garments." Since 1947, however, because of strong urging from tailored clothing firms, the federal government has used these five classifications. In the trade, *tailored clothing* firms are those producing structured or semistructured suits, overcoats, topcoats, sport coats, and separate slacks in which a specific number of hand-tailoring operations are required. Tailored clothing firms once dominated the menswear market, both in unit production and in sales. However, in recent years, there has been a steady decline in demand for tailored clothing and a steady growth in demand for sportswear, or more casual apparel that is less structured and involves fewer (if any) hand-tailoring operations.

For years, a number of firms in the menswear industry, usually furnishings or work clothes firms, have traditionally produced limited quantities of so-called sportswear items. But as a result of an increasing demand for more varied types of casual apparel, a new type of firm, the sportswear house, has entered the picture and become an established part of the menswear industry. In the menswear industry, a sportswear house is a firm that concentrates on production of men's casual attire, including sport jackets, slacks, shirts, and *leisure suits* (a suit consisting of a matching jacket and slacks designed in a casual style).

Size and Location of Manufacturers

Unlike women's apparel manufacturing, menswear manufacturing is dominated by large firms. Even though there are well over 3,000 menswear manu-

The leisure suit, big news in menswear in the mid-1970s. Celanese Fibers Marketing Co.

facturers and some 80 percent of them are small (with fewer than 250 employees), the giants in the field do a much larger percentage of the total business than do the giants in women's apparel.

However, few if any of these giants are among the new category of sportswear firms, which are still relatively young and still quite small. Still, the growing sportswear market is not entirely supplied by small firms. Some giant firms that traditionally have been classified as tailored clothing or furnishings manufacturers are now producing large quantities of sportswear—if we expand the term to include any item that emphasizes more casual styling and a bolder use of color. For instance, Arrow, the country's biggest shirt producer, estimates that in 1965 more than 80 percent of the shirts it sold were solid white with button-down collars. In 1970, 80 percent of its shirt sales were in solid colors or had colored patterns, and only 2 percent had button-down collars.[3]

Although there are menswear manufacturers in almost every section of the country, the largest number of plants are in the mid-Atlantic states. New York, New Jersey, and Pennsylvania form the center of the tailored clothing industry, and traditionally over 40 percent of all menswear manufacturers have been located in this area.

However, the industry's center is gradually moving South. A number of Northeastern manufacturers have set up plant facilities in the South, where both land and labor are less expensive. These include not only apparel manufacturers from the mid-Atlantic states but even some men's shoe manufacturers, who once were found almost exclusively in New England.

Some menswear manufacturers have always been located in the South. For instance, separate trouser firms, a part of the tailored clothing segment of the industry, have always been centered in the South, as have many firms making men's shirts, underwear, and work clothes.

There is also a steadily growing number of firms located in the West and the Southwest. Most of these plants produce sportswear or casual attire.

Designing a Line

For generations, tailored clothing manufacturers in the United States were known as slow but painstakingly careful followers, rather than leaders, in menswear styling. The typical tailored clothing manufacturer had a staff of designers or bought free-lance designs. Designers' names were known only within the trade and were seldom considered important by consumers.

Traditionally, the leading fashion influence was English styling. Designers in this country would study the styles currently popular in England, decide which might be acceptable here, and gradually develop a line based on those styles. Production was a slow process because of the amount of handwork involved in producing tailored clothing. Usually a full year passed from the time a style was developed until a finished product was delivered to a retail store.

The first signs of male rebellion against traditional styling came during the late 1940s and early 1950s. As described earlier, year after year manufacturers had been turning out versions of a style that had long been popular in England, a padded-shoulder draped suit based originally on the broad-chested uniform of the Brigade of Guards. A number of young men attending well-known Northeastern colleges became tired of the traditional look. They took their objections to New Haven clothing manufacturers, and the result was the natural-shoulder Ivy League suit.

Influence of Name Designers   In the second half of the 1950s, men again became restless about styling. They began turning away from tailored clothing and were more attracted to sportswear because of its more innovative styling and more imaginative use of colors and fabrics. Many of the styles they liked were created by well-known foreign designers of women's couture apparel. It was during this period that Pierre Cardin opened a men's shop in Paris; and in England, Hardy Amies branched out into men's fashions.

More and more well-known designers, originally known for their work in women's apparel, joined the ranks of menswear designers. Bill Blass won the first Coty Award ever given for menswear. John Weitz opened this country's first men's shop run by a name designer. Oleg Cassini, Geoffrey Beene, Oscar de la Renta, and Yves St. Laurent soon were selling designs or design ideas to men's apparel manufacturers. Today, there are very few name designers in the women's apparel field who do not turn out some men's apparel designs as well.

However, not all design talent has flowed from the women's area into the menswear area. Ralph Lauren, first known for menswear designs, moved into women's apparel in the early 1970s and won the Coty Award in 1974. Emmett Cash, who began as a menswear designer, today works in both fields and is known for the wardrobes he has designed for various celebrities, including Barbra Streisand and Tom Jones. And as the decade advanced, other menswear designers and manufacturers extended their talents to include the production of women's apparel.

Producing a Line

A generation ago, it might have been possible to identify tailored clothing as office or formal wear, and sportswear as weekend or vacation wear. Today, the only real difference between the two types of apparel is a matter of construction, not of styling, colors, or fabrics.

A tailored sport coat is "three-dimensional," or "structured." Its construction involves many different hand-tailoring operations. These give it a shape of its own even when not being worn. A sport jacket is "unstructured." Its construction involves few if any hand-tailoring operations. It often lacks padding, binding, and lining. It takes its shape in part from the person who wears it.

For this reason, two distinctly different production methods currently are used to produce menswear. One is the older tailored clothing method, which traditionally has been slow to react

to consumer demand. The other is the newer sportswear method, developed specifically because it can respond quickly to demands for style change.

Tailored Clothing Production   Tailored clothing in general and suit production in particular have long been considered the backbone of the menswear manufacturing industry. Suits made by tailored clothing firms are graded according to the number of hand-tailoring operations required for their production. The grades, from lowest to highest, are 1, 2, 4, 4+, 6, and 6+. The grade-1 suit represents the lowest quality of tailored suit carried by a store that features popular prices. A grade-6+ suit, which requires between 120 and 150 separate hand-tailoring operations, is the top line of tailored suits carried in a prestige store.

The typical tailored suit firm usually makes only one grade of suit. For instance, the Hickey-Freeman label is identified with grade-6 or grade-6+ suits; Hart Schaffner and Marx suits are grade 4 or 4+; suits sold by Bond and by Robert Hall are usually made by manufacturers of grade-2 suits. Tailored clothing firms making suits of more than one grade are likely to produce each grade in a separate factory.

Until recently, each menswear manufacturer tended to produce only one type of apparel, such as coats, or suits, or shirts. If a large firm produced more than one kind of apparel, each was likely to be made in a separate factory. For example, the firm would produce coats in one factory and sport coats in another. Today, many large firms are producing various types of menswear, although usually each type is usually still produced in a separate factory.

Production of tailored clothing is usually a long and complicated process. After selecting the styles to be featured in the next line, a manufacturer orders the fabric in which the various styles are to be made up. Once the line is set up, the manufacturer shows it to store buyers. Delivery of the fabric may take up to nine months. Even after the fabric is delivered, however, the manufacturer

If you've got Dad's sign, we've got his scent!

PACO
(Dec. 22 – Jan. 20)
Paco is pure Capricorn.
Forceful, conservative,
steady as a rock, but
kicky just the same.
Paco Rabanne Pour Homme
Cologne, 2 oz. 8.00, 4 oz. 12.00.

CANOE
(Jan. 21 – Feb. 18)
Aquarians have trail blazing
minds, are inventive and are
progressive. Never leave him
upstream without his Canoe by Dana.
Eau de Cologne, 3-11/16 oz. 6.00,
8-7/16 oz. 9.00.
Atomizer Spray, 4 oz. 7.00.

CARDIN
(Feb. 19 – Mar. 20)
Pisces people are intuitive —
often the power behind
the thrones. Pierre Cardin
rules the waves for them.
Cologne, 2 oz. 6.00, 4 oz. 9.00.
Spray Cologne, 2-1/2 oz. 9.00.

NOMADE
(Mar. 21 – Apr. 20)
Aries spawns the pioneer types
who love to roam.
Emilio Pucci Nomade
scorns danger, is filled with
ardent emotion. Eau de Toilette,
2 oz. 8.50, 4 oz. 15.00.

BRUT
(Apr. 21 – May 21)
Taurus is a practical,
persistent, dogged person,
who will love the
rugged vitality of Brut
All-purpose Lotion,
3.2 oz. 6.50, 6.4 oz. 10.00.

BRAGGI
(May 22 – June 21)
Geminis are quick thinkers,
talented and tend to be Braggi-docio.
Braggi by Charles Revson
is a perfect counterpart
to Gemini. Cologne, 4 oz. 8.00,
Cologne Spray, 3 oz. 8.00.

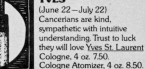

YVES
(June 22 – July 22)
Cancerians are kind,
sympathetic with intuitive
understanding. Trust to luck
they will love Yves St. Laurent
Cologne, 4 oz. 7.50.
Cologne Atomizer, 4 oz. 8.50.

EAU SAUVAGE
(July 23 – Aug. 23)
Leo the lions are born leaders,
love bold, energetic scents.
Eau Sauvage by Christian Dior
is all this and more.
Eau de Toilette, 3-7/8 oz. 8.00.
Atomizer Cologne, 4 oz. 9.00.

COPENHAGEN
(Aug. 24 – Sept. 23)
A logical, precise, Virile
Virgo-ian scent in the
tradition of the Great Danes.
Royal Copenhagen
Cologne, 4 oz. 8.00.
6 oz. 10.00.

BLASS
(Sept. 24 – Oct. 23)
Libras are artistic, fashionable
as all get out, sensitive
and idealistic. They fit the
Bill Blass image every which way.
100 Strength Cologne and
Cologne Spray, 10.00 each.

TABAC
(Oct. 24 – Nov. 22)
Scorpios are the shrewdies.
Capable of intense concentration.
Have a penchant for magnetic
personalities mainly of the
opposite sex. Tabac Original
Cologne, 3-1/5 oz. 5.00,
5-7/8 oz. 7.50, 10-2/5 oz. 11.00.

ARAMIS
(Nov. 23 – Dec. 21)
Sagittarians are enthusiastic,
inspirational and total optimists.
That's why they love the
peppery, sensuous spray mist
of Aramis, 4 oz. 8.50.
Cologne, 4 oz. 8.50, 8 oz. 14.50.

STAFF
(Jan. 1 – Dec. 31)
Let our staff of experts chart
your Daddy-Day present.
Just check out his birth date,
read the clues here and forge
right on down to Altmans.
He'll thank his lucky stars
we have such good scents.

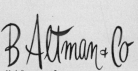

B. Altman & Co

Men's Store — street floor
Fifth Avenue, White Plains, Manhasset, N.Y.,
Short Hills, Ridgewood/Paramus, N.J., St. Davids, Pa.

This Father's Day ad emphasizes the growing interest in men's cosmetics.
B. Altman & Co.

does not start to cut a style until enough store orders are accumulated for that style to make its production profitable. This is because making up a single style in, say, a man's suit involves cutting a great many sizes, considerably more than are involved in producing a woman's dress style.

For instance, a typical suit manufacturer may be prepared to cut a single style in these sizes:

- Shorts: 36–44
- Regulars: 35–48
- Longs: 37–48
- Extra longs: 38–48
- Portlies: 39–50
- Portly shorts: 39–48
- Big sizes: 46, 48, 50

While it is unlikely that a manufacturer will receive orders that require a single style to be cut in this entire range of proportioned sizes, it is likely that the most popular styles will have to be cut in at least half or more of them.

Even after the cutting is done, the work goes slowly. For instance, a 6+ suit may require as much as 15 hours of an experienced tailor's time, and it may take between 1 and $1\frac{1}{2}$ hours just to press a 6+ suit before it leaves the factory. This is why the cost of labor makes up approximately two-thirds the entire cost of producing an item of tailored clothing. Most tailored clothing firms own their own production facilities. The quality control that such construction requires can only be maintained in an inside shop.

Sportswear Production In contrast, many sportswear firms use contractors in exactly the same way and for the same reasons that women's apparel producers do. Sportswear manufacturers, unlike tailored clothing manufacturers, are interested in short runs and quick response to customer demand. The quality of workmanship is much less important in this area than having the styles, colors, and fabrics that customers want when they want them. It is the style, color, and fabric of a sport jacket that sells it, not the way its lapel is constructed.

In addition, unstructured sportswear, regardless of what kind of firm produces it, is likely to be made up in a much narrower size range than tailored clothing. For instance, a sport shirt is not produced in the wide variety of neck sizes, sleeve lengths, and collar and cuff styles in which a dress shirt is made. Instead, a sport shirt is usually produced in four basic sizes (small, medium, large, and extralarge) and sometimes with a choice between short and long sleeves.

This is the kind of production work that contractors handle most successfully. When contractors are used, the sportswear manufacturer may be the designer, or a designer may be hired, or a design may be bought. The manufacturer buys the needed fabric. Then both the cutting and the sewing are usually done by the contractor, exactly as in the women's apparel field. Finally, the finished goods are returned to the manufacturer, who handles the distribution.

Contractors' plants are located wherever production costs can be kept low. There are many in different locations in this country, and an increasing number of American sportswear manufacturers are

TABLE 8-1
Suit and Sport Coat Cuttings, 1961–1974
(*millions of units*)

YEAR	SUITS	SPORT COATS
1950	23.0	0.7
1961	18.7	9.7
1962	20.3	11.3
1963	20.5	11.1
1964	20.3	10.8
1965	22.5	12.4
1966	20.7	13.1
1967	18.9	12.6
1968	19.6	14.0
1969	21.8	14.3
1970	16.0	10.9
1971	16.2	11.5
1972	16.8	16.8
1973	15.6	17.7

Source: U.S. Department of Commerce.

using contractors in other countries. The use of the contractor system allows the sportswear manufacturers to provide a steady flow of new styles at moderate prices.

Market Centers

New York is the traditional and still by far the largest market center for all kinds of menswear, including tailored clothing, sportswear, and furnishings. Regional markets in other parts of the country—Chicago, Los Angeles, Dallas—are growing in importance; but the biggest shows and the largest number of permanent showrooms are still located in New York.

The Clothing Manufacturers Association, the trade association of the tailored clothing industry, holds two market weeks a year in New York. Fall lines are shown in February, spring lines in late August or early September.

The National Association of Men's Sportswear Buyers, a membership organization founded by sportswear buyers but now including independent store owners, retail buyers, and merchandise managers, holds two week-long showings a year in New York. Fall lines are shown in late March or early April, spring lines in October. These showings include lines from manufacturers of all types of menswear, including tailored clothing as well as sportswear firms. It is claimed that these showings bring together the offerings of more menswear producers than any other show in the world.

In addition, numerous small regional shows are held around the country. Nearly every area has a Men's Apparel Guild which stages regular seasonal showings in regional market centers.

The delivery terms offered by firms when taking orders during these market weeks afford an additional contrast between tailored clothing firms and sportswear firms, although the former are slowly changing. Tailored clothing firms traditionally deliver all merchandise ordered from a seasonal line in one shipment. Sportswear firms are moving toward successive deliveries of a seasonal line, sometimes with slight style changes from month to month.

Distribution

Menswear producers have always been interested in the profit potential of dual distribution. As mentioned earlier, it was a popular trend for a few decades in the early 1800s, again in the boom years after World War I, and again in the years right after World War II. Each time interest lasted for a few years and then sagged.

The most recent rebirth of interest in dual distribution was seen in the latter half of the 1960s, when producers again began building chains of retail outlets. By the mid-1970s, however, the trend

TABLE 8-2
Market Share of Dollar Sales by Selected Apparel Category, 1973

APPAREL CATEGORY	DEPARTMENT STORES	SPECIALTY STORES	DISCOUNT STORES	CHAINS
Suits	21%	53%	7%	11%
Sports coats	23	43	14	14
Pants	29	28	13	20
Jeans	29	18	16	23
Knit sport shirts	33	22	14	21
Woven sport shirts	30	19	20	25
Dress shirts	33	28	14	21

Note: Figures do not total 100 percent because miscellaneous retail outlets are not included.
Source: Men's Wear, Feb. 14, 1975.

had passed. One reason for this was the economic scene. The rule was holding true: In good times, dual distribution has been attractive; in bad times, it has been dangerously costly. Another reason (which probably will keep manufacturers from ever again becoming involved with dual distribution) is the increasing possibility of violating federal anti-trust laws, which frown upon one-company domination of any specific segment of an industry.

The number of stores owned and operated by menswear producers has never been large, nor is it now, in comparison with the total number of menswear retail outlets. However, the best of the quality outlets in many major metropolitan areas are owned by manufacturers and are likely to remain so. This limited dual distribution does not violate federal laws, and, in most cases, is a source of additional profits.

MERCHANDISING ACTIVITIES

Menswear producers, like women's apparel producers, back their offerings with both advertising and publicity. Various fiber firms and associations often cooperate in these endeavors, as discussed in Chapter 7. Advertising is usually done by individual producers or by producers working in cooperation with fiber firms or associations. Publicity is handled mainly by various trade associations.

Advertising

Men's apparel producers turned to advertising in the latter 1800s, when they used trade advertising to establish direct contacts with retailers. As a result, the business relationships between manufacturers and stores soon became very strong and stable. In most large towns and small cities, each major menswear retailer had an exclusive arrangement with a separate manufacturer. That tie often continued for generations. As a result of this long relationship, most menswear manufacturers in general, and tailored clothing firms in particular, have not felt it necessary to do much national consumer advertising. Instead, they have tended to put adver-

tising money into cooperative programs with established retail accounts. This remains the trend among many long-established firms. Cooperative advertising is still an important merchandising activity of the tailored clothing segment of the industry. Today, tailored clothing firms not only prepare newspaper and magazine ads and provide mats of various kinds for use by retail store customers but some also provide the necessary material for radio and television commercials as well.

The sportswear houses, however, are relatively new and have not yet built strong retail ties. Sportswear manufacturers have to compete for retail accounts much as women's apparel manufacturers do. Thus they use little cooperative advertising. Instead, they concentrate on building brand recognition and acceptance by advertising nationally. Some of the ads are aimed at consumers. Others, placed in the trade press, are aimed at retail stores.

Publicity

While most large menswear manufacturers have publicity departments, the major publicity efforts in the menswear industry are organized and carried out by two trade groups, the National Association of Men's Sportswear Buyers (NAMSB) and the Men's Fashion Association of America (MFA). The former handles trade publicity within the trade: between manufacturers and retailers. The latter handles external publicity: between the trade and consumers.

NAMSB The main purpose of the National Association of Men's Sportswear Buyers is to help retailers learn what producers are offering. In addition to its Show Weeks, NAMSB also provides members with a steady stream of pertinent information about developments within the menswear industry. For instance, it distributes a detailed monthly newsletter about fashion trends in menswear to Association members. Twice a year, it prepares fashion-trend slide kits that members can rent for a nominal fee. NAMSB also has a college scholarship program for children of retail members and

Men's furnishings and accessories are prominently featured in fashion ads.
Saks Fifth Avenue

their employees, intended to encourage young people "to consider menswear retailing as a career."

MFA The Men's Fashion Association of America, which represents all segments of the menswear manufacturing industry, aims its publicity and public relations efforts at consumers by providing consumer media with information about the menswear industry in general and about menswear trends in particular.

The MFA holds three major Press Previews a year. In February, it holds a Press Preview in a major Southwestern or West Coast city, such as Houston, Dallas, or Los Angeles, to cover spring–summer trends. In June, it holds a Press Preview in the New York area to cover fall–winter trends. The third Press Preview, added to the schedule in the mid-1970s, is held in the Southwest or on the West Coast in September or October.

Each Press Preview lasts between three and four days. It consists of fashion shows, slide presentations, seminars, and other events intended to tell media representatives about major trends in menswear fashions. These previews became so popular that, in the mid-1970s, the MFA began limiting attendance at the meetings to the country's major media representatives.

In addition, the MFA sends regular publicity to the media in the form of press kits, feature articles, photographs, and even slide shows that can be used on television talk shows and women's programs.

INDUSTRY TRENDS

The menswear manufacturing industry is in transition. It is vastly different from what it was 20 years ago; it probably will be vastly different in another 20 years. The single most important factor causing much of the change is the increasingly strong consumer demand that fashion become a real force in menswear again, after more than 200 years of neglect. This manifests itself by customer demand for more imaginative styling and for more innovative use of color and fabric and for more frequent style, color, and fabric changes. At the same time, the industry is trying to cope with and profit from—or survive in spite of—changing economic conditions, changing technology, and changing market conditions.

Perhaps the biggest trend created by these factors is the increased diversification of products offered by individual producers. In addition, there is a strong trend toward production automation, mainly among larger firms; a trend toward an increase in foreign production and foreign sales; and an increase in government regulation.

Diversification of Product

Just as in the women's apparel manufacturing industry, many menswear manufacturers are increasing the types of apparel they offer. Traditionally, a firm in this industry produced only a single type of garment and sometimes only a single grade of that garment. Now menswear producers are beginning to ignore the traditional specialization of product that both manufacturers and retail stores have abided by for so long.

For example, some of the biggest changes have been in an area that once was the most rigid: work clothes. For generations, firms like H. D. Lee and Levi Strauss had turned out overalls, work pants, and work shirts using approximately the same patterns and the same fabrics season after season. Now casual clothes have become popular, and the big-name work clothes producers have found themselves producing fashion goods. In addition to jeans, which had almost completely saturated the market by the mid-1970s, these manufacturers are also producing a wide range of slacks, casual pants, and jackets. These are available in different styles, colors, and fabrics, all carefully selected to sell to today's sportswear-conscious male—and female. By the mid-1970s, H. D. Lee and Levi Strauss were as much interested in style sales reports as they were in unit sales reports.

Suits are another example. In the past, traditional suit manufacturers turned out a selection of styles in one or two grades of suits. Today, the trade calls the traditional tailored suit a "suit-suit" because so many other types of suits have gained in fashion importance.

Some manufacturers have diversified by simply buying into other types of business. Manhattan Industries is a good example. For more than 100 years, Manhattan produced shirts. Today, mainly through the acquisition of other companies, Manhattan produces a variety of men's, women's, and children's apparel, and is in the retail business, too. In 1966, Manhattan had a sales volume of $58 million, nearly all from shirt sales. Six years later, in 1972, Manhattan's sales volume was about $210 million, one-third derived from its production of menswear, one-third from production of women's and children's apparel, and one-third from its retail operations.

Automation of Production

Advances in technology have affected every industry. In menswear, new equipment and systems are helping manufacturers combat one of the most serious problems faced by all apparel producers today: the slow but steady shrinkage of an available labor force. Every year, it becomes increasingly difficult to find a sufficient supply of workers. Turnover in the industry is tremendous, averaging between 60 and 70 percent in recent years. The time required to train workers has become a crucial factor in estimating productivity.

For these reasons, and because of the increased productivity and quality control it can introduce into the manufacturing process, the industry is gradually turning to automation through the introduction of new equipment and systems.

Automated production of a man's jacket.

However, this trend is found only among larger firms. Much of the equipment is still too expensive for smaller manufacturers. It also is capable of working at faster production speeds, which smaller manufacturers do not need.

One way that major companies are handling the labor problem is by establishing "clusters" of plants in the South and other areas where land costs are low and labor is relatively cheap. A large central plant turns out the main segments of a garment, such as various parts of a shirt, and then bundles of those parts are trucked to small satellite plants in nearby communities for machine stitching. Since the more intricate work has already been done in the central plant, the work handled at the satellite plants is simple, and the labor cost is relatively low. The satellite plants attract workers because they provide a home-town source of income, with minimum training required, and workers do not have to travel long distances each day, as would be required to earn slightly more at more distant plants.

It is in the central plant of such a cluster, and in other large apparel manufacturing plants, that automation is beginning to be developed. This is being achieved through the installation of equipment that (1) does jobs by machine that formerly had to be done by hand, (2) cuts down on the number of workers needed to do a specific job, and (3) cuts down on the amount of training and skill that workers need.

For instance, "pocket-setters" sew a pocket on a shirt automatically. "Sequential buttonhole sewers" stitch all buttonholes on a shirt in a single automated operation. "Collar-makers" reduce the number of workers needed to make a collar on a production-line basis from eight to two. In addition, since the equipment is programmed to follow a set pattern of operations and only a few simple tasks are left to the operators, operators can be trained to run such collar-making equipment in 2 weeks instead of the 10 to 12 weeks it used to take to teach workers to handle the manual collar-making operations.

In general, the industry is gradually becoming more machine-oriented than operator-oriented. This is a vast change for an industry that, throughout most of its history, prided itself on the individual workmanship that went into many of its products.

Foreign Production

Price competition is very strong in the menswear market. A very important factor in setting prices at wholesale is the cost of labor. Because of this, an increasing number of menswear producers, particularly sportswear firms, are building plants or contracting to have work done in areas outside the country where land and labor costs are lower.

The amount and kind of work done outside the country varies greatly. Some firms handle everything except the sewing in their domestic plants, and contract to have the sewing done in plants outside the United States. Some have both the cutting and sewing done outside the country. Some ship greige goods to one country for dyeing and finishing, and then to another country for cutting the goods and sewing the garments. Some buy fabric outside the country, have the garments cut and sewn outside the country, and never actually see any step of the production process until the finished goods are delivered to this country for distribution.

The disadvantages of foreign production include sometimes uncertain quality control and a longer wait for delivery of finished garments. Advantages, as discussed in earlier chapters, include lower production costs because of lower costs of building or renting facilities and lower costs of labor. This enables manufacturers to charge lower wholesale prices, and retailers to pass savings on in lower retail prices. However, since goods produced in foreign countries are subject to import duties, savings are possible only when import duties are relatively low. In late 1974, worried by the amount of foreign production in the menswear industry, menswear production workers in this country began demonstrating to get duties raised on imports of menswear from several key areas of foreign production.

Government Regulations

As consumerism emerged as a potent force in the late 1960s and early 1970s, one result was to encourage the federal and state governments to take an increasing interest in monitoring industries that produce consumer goods. In the menswear manufacturing industry, as in the women's apparel manufacturing industry, such goverment concern is now concentrated on more stringent flammability regulations, care labeling, occupational safety regulations, and consumer warranties. In 1974, one industry spokesman said, "The predominant force that will shape business for the next 10 years will be consumerism and social responsibility." For the menswear industry in particular, he might have added a second force: the male consumer's changing ideas about fashion.

REFERENCES

[1] "Tailored Sportcoats: Falling Behind," *Clothes*, May 15, 1974, p. 65.
[2] Quoted in Cobrin, *The Men's Clothing Industry*, p. 67.
[3] *Fortune*, February 1971, p. 70.

MERCHANDISING VOCABULARY

Define or briefly explain the following terms:

✔ Dual distribution   Tailored clothing firms
Inside shops   Leisure suits
Short run

MERCHANDISING REVIEW

1. What effect did the Industrial Revolution have on male apparel? On female apparel? What socioeconomic factors were responsible for the drastic changes that occurred?
2. What four developments in the nineteenth century were largely responsible for the development of the men's ready-to-wear industry in this country? How did each help to accelerate those developments?
3. Name and describe the three ways in which menswear was manufactured in this country in the latter part of the nineteenth century.
4. For what three reasons did early manufacturers of men's tailored clothing give up the use of contractors?
5. What is the name of the major union in the menswear industry today? Briefly review the conditions that led to unionization within the industry.
6. Name the different segments into which the menswear industry is subdivided, on the basis of the type of product lines each produces. What specific products are produced by each segment?

7. Describe the differences between a tailored sportcoat and a sport jacket, from a manufacturing standpoint.
8. Contrast the advertising policies of men's tailored clothing firms with those of firms producing sportswear.
9. What are the names of the two major menswear trade associations? Describe the function and activities of each.
10. What is the single greatest problem facing producers of menswear today? How are producers attempting to alleviate this problem?

MERCHANDISING DIGEST

1. Discuss the following statement from the text and cite examples to illustrate it: "Throughout history, and until relatively recent times, fashion interest centered around men's apparel rather than around women's."
2. What is meant by "dual distribution" in the menswear industry? Discuss dual distribution on the basis of its (a) history, (b) development, and (c) extent of implementation today.
3. Discuss and give examples of how diversification of product lines, as an increasingly important industry trend, has affected (a) menswear production, and (b) the retailing of menswear.
4. Discuss the increased use of foreign production facilities as a menswear industry trend. What are its advantages? Disadvantages?

9
MANUFACTURERS OF FASHION ACCESSORIES

Fashion is not just a dress or a coat; it is a total "look." To achieve a desired total look, fashion customers need to accessorize their apparel with coordinated gloves, jewelry, hosiery, shoes, handbag, facial cosmetics, and proper intimate apparel. Certain style features of such accessories are classics, always in demand, always a part of fashion. Others have brief periods of wide acceptance and then decline in popularity, depending upon what current fashion favors in achieving a total effect.

When fashion emphasis is on the waistline, for instance, belts become popular, as do intimate apparel items that minimize the waist. Short skirts that expose long lengths of leg encourage decorative hosiery but require shoes that are flat and simple. When longer, fuller skirts with plenty of movement are in style, hosiery is less emphasized, and shoes acquire higher heels and more feminine looks.

Today, apparel and accessories cannot have a fashion existence apart from each other. Producers of accessories need to be well informed on such fashion trends in apparel as silhouette, color, texture, and details of design if they are to successfully produce accessory lines that will complement those fashions. Retailers need to be well informed about all types of fashion accessories in order to coordinate their accessories assortments with their apparel assortments, so that customers can find what is needed to achieve certain desired fashion looks.

Today, customers expect apparel salespeople and store displays to suggest appropriate accessories; they also expect accessory departments to relate their merchandise to the apparel with which it will be worn. In addition, today's fashion customers are paying increased attention to one-stop shopping: They want an opportunity to purchase coordinated fashion apparel and accessories in a single shop or department of a store, where everything with a given look or feeling has been brought together.

Thus, although each fashion accessory is produced by separate segments of the industry, all should be coordinated with each other and related to current apparel fashions. Fashion today emphasizes the total look, and accessories are an essential part of that look.

INTIMATE APPAREL

Intimate apparel, sometimes referred to as "inner fashions" or "body fashions," is the trade term for women's foundations, lingerie, and loungewear. As a rule, intimate apparel is not usually considered a fashion accessory by producers, retailers, or even customers. However, it is being so considered in this chapter because these garments play as important a role in achieving a desired look or effect as do more readily identifiable apparel accessories such as handbags or shoes. Furthermore, in the past two decades, both sleepwear and loungewear have developed extensive fashion interest and relevance of their own.

Over the centuries, fashion has made some unrealistic demands of the female figure. Ever since the time of the Cretan civilization thousands of years before Christ, women have endured tight lacing, unyielding stays, bulky padding, layers of petticoats, and an assortment of other discomforts to achieve whatever look was considered fashionable at the time.

The fashion silhouette regularly goes through cycles of change; most human figures have to be coaxed to change with it. Women, moreover, do not come in uniform shapes and sizes. Whatever silhouette is dominant at a given time is wearable readily only by a minority of women; the majority have to amplify or constrict their figures to wear the current fashion.

Historically, women's intimate apparel was produced by three separate industries: the foundations industry, the lingerie industry, and the robe industry. Today, however, the close fashion relationship between foundation garments, lingerie, and robes (now called "loungewear") has brought the industries closer together and encouraged mergers among firms that formerly specialized in only one type of intimate apparel.

The Foundations Industry

Classified as *foundations* are such undergarments as brassieres, girdles, panty-girdles, garter belts, corsets, and corselettes (one-piece garments with a brassiere top and a girdle bottom).

The retail value of foundation garments currently produced in the United States exceeds $1 billion a year. The industry employs some 40,000 workers in more than 350 factories, two-thirds of which are in the New York City area.

History and Development The foundations industry began with the factory production of corsets just after the Civil War, when Warner Brothers opened its first plant in Bridgeport, Connecticut. At that time, the bell-shaped silhouette was at the height of its popularity. To achieve the tiny waist required by the fashionable bell silhouette (and its successors, the bustle-back silhouette and the "Gibson Girl" look), women wore foundations of sturdy, unyielding cotton reinforced with whalebone or steel "bones" which were actually vertical stays.

Front or back lacing permitted varying degrees of waist constriction to achieve the desired effect.

The foundations industry experienced a drastic change in customer demand in the 1920s, when the fashion shifted to straight, loose styles in apparel. These required little corseting but did demand flattening of the bosom. Bandagelike bras were worn to minimize the bust, while girdles controlled any conspicuous bulges below the waistline.

In the 1930s, the silhouette again became more feminine and softly curved. Women coaxed their figures into the appropriate lines with two new types of foundations more comfortable than anything available before: the two-way stretch girdle and the cup-type brassiere. These innovations heralded a trend toward foundations that molded the figure gently while permitting freedom of movement. They also reflected the fashion for easy fit in outerwear, with definite but not exaggerated curves. In the past three decades, further technological advances have enabled the foundations industry to produce softer, more comfortable, and lighter-weight undergarments, with better shape-retention properties, in a wider assortment of styles for various figure types.

Brassieres are a good example of the radical style changes that have occurred in foundation garments in the last 50 years. During this period, brassiere styling developed from the original bandage type, to cup form, to fiber-filled, to wire-supported, to the "no-bra" bra, to the molded rather than the seamed bra.

Today, foundation garments coax or mold a body; they do not harness it. Moreover, they can be comfortable, light, soft, and pretty, all at the same time.

Market Centers Like nearly all other fashion-influenced industries, the foundations industry has its principal market center in New York City, where major firms in the industry maintain permanent showrooms. The industry's trade association, the Corset and Brassiere Association of America, schedules and publicizes market weeks in January and in June.

Merchandising Activities Brand names have always been important in the foundations industry, and much of the industry's merchandising activity has been directed toward the promotion of brand names. The major foundations producers widely advertise their brand names—such as Lily of France, Formfit, and Warner—in both trade and consumer publications. Ads in consumer publications often mention the names of retail stores that stock the featured merchandise. In addition, many firms offer cooperative advertising arrangements to their retail store customers. Merchants use such cooperative allowances to stretch their own advertising budgets and to tie in at the local level with national advertising of the brands they carry.

Historically, the foundations industry has supplied many services to its retail store customers. Producers have helped train retail salespeople and have offered retail store buyers assistance in planning assortments and controlling stocks.

Industry Trends Trends in the foundations industry are similar to those of other fashion-related industries, but of a somewhat more recent origin. The trend toward mergers in other industries during and immediately following World War II did not develop in the intimate apparel industries until the late 1950s. At that time customers began demanding color-coordinated foundation garments. Many small firms that made either brassieres or girdles saw an advantage in joining with one another to produce matched colors. In time, many such collaborating firms merged their ownership and operations in order to meet the competition of larger firms. Some merged with lingerie producers, others explored the advantages of merging with ready-to-wear producers. Since the introduction of figure-control features in bathing suits, some foundations firms have merged with swimsuit makers or set up their own swimsuit divisions. In addition, some are making "body suits," control garments that are completely made of stretch material, with a panty-type bottom and a T-shirt or camisole-type top. Although intended as undergarments, if done in attractive materials they closely

resemble and often can be used as ready-to-wear "body shirts."

Many technological changes are taking place in the industry. New equipment has been developed to produce molded brassiere cups that are in turn shipped to other firms to be made into brassieres. New man-made fibers have been developed with improved stretch and resiliency features. Cotton, once the basic material of bras, is being replaced by cotton stretch-fiber blends.

The Lingerie and Loungewear Industries

Lingerie is the undergarment category that includes slips, petticoats, panties of all types, nightgowns, and pajamas. Slips, petticoats, and panties are considered "daywear," while nightgowns and pajamas are classified as "sleepwear." *Loungewear* is the trade term for the category that includes robes, bed jackets, and housecoats. However, since some lingerie firms have expanded and diversified their product lines to include loungewear items and some lingerie and loungewear firms have merged, it is sometimes difficult to draw a clear-cut distinction between the two industries.

The Lingerie Industry The lingerie industry's annual output has a retail value of $1.6 billion a year and employs more than 75,000 people in over 1,000 plants. More than half of these factories are in New York state, with a fourth in contiguous states.

Originally lingerie and loungewear, like other apparel, were made in the home. Factory production developed slowly and did not reach proportions that justified considering it a separate industry until 1935. Before that, reports of the Census of Manufacturers included lingerie output and sales data with those of women's apparel.

Mass-production methods in the lingerie industry are very similar to those for apparel. A third of the plants producing lingerie are contractors, who provide sewing services for firms that design and distribute the merchandise.

Until the 1930s, most mass-produced lingerie

and loungewear was purely functional, with little variety in style or seasonal change. Cotton was the principal fabric, but wool was also used in extremely cold climates. Silk appeared only in luxury styles. In the 1930s rayon began to be used extensively and remained a basic fabric material throughout the 1940s. During all of this time, lingerie and loungewear were considered staple items, relatively untouched by fashion and produced in limited styles and colors.

The introduction of easy-care man-made textile fibers in the 1950s revolutionized the industries, and lingerie and loungewear stepped into the fashion spotlight. Previously, only the largest companies had sent fashion experts to the Paris openings to report on the lines and colors featured in new apparel styles. As fashion interest began to center around a total look or fashion theme, women began to develop a feeling for color and design harmony in everything they wore. Consequently, the lingerie and loungewear industries became increasingly aware of the need to keep in close touch with the total fashion picture.

Creative lingerie firms today employ top designing talent, often recruiting them from the apparel field. Styling in all three categories—daywear, sleepwear, and loungewear—closely follows that of apparel. For example, when silver touches are important in evening and after-five apparel, silvery gowns and negligees are shown in the more expensive lingerie lines. When color-mad prints predominated in apparel, wildly patterned slips, sleepwear, robes, and panties are featured.

Market Centers   Like the foundations industry, the principal market center of the lingerie and loungewear industries is New York City. Major firms of the latter industries publicize market weeks on the same dates in January and June that the foundations industry holds its market weeks. Market dates are coordinated for the convenience of store buyers. Since many of them buy all three types of merchandise, concurrent market weeks enable them to plan and coordinate purchases and promotions simultaneously. If stores employ separate buyers for these categories, those buyers usually work closely with one another in the market, coordinating their purchases and promotional plans for the coming season.

Merchandising Activities   Brands are as important in the lingerie and loungewear industries as they are in the foundations industry. In fact, store purchases of lingerie and loungewear are often figured in terms of brand resources rather than categories of merchandise. Like the foundations industry, lingerie and loungewear firms widely advertise their branded lines in both trade and consumer publications, and most offer cooperative advertising arrangements to their retail store customers.

In contrast to the foundations industry, however, the lingerie and loungewear industries were slow in offering services to retail accounts. Because lingerie presented no major fitting problems, producers saw little reason to interest themselves in the retail merchandising of their products. They simply held semiannual showings of their lines and left sales promotion techniques to retailers.

When fashion replaced function as the key factor in intimate apparel, the whole pattern of cooperation with retail stores changed. Lingerie-foundation producers began offering fashion and merchandising advisory assistance and services to the stores. Today manufacturers help stores to stage shows using live models to show how ready-to-wear and intimate apparel relate to one another. Many lingerie firms now assist stores with the layout of retail departments, with suggestions relating to display, sales-training materials, and other devices designed to help sell merchandise.

Both industries cover the major United States and European fashion markets today and provide seasonal color and style charts to stores, together with suggestions for relating intimate apparel styles and colors to those of ready-to-wear. Some of the firms offer assistance in planning and controlling retail assortments and in staging retail sales promotion events, often in cooperation with a textile fiber or fabric producer.

Industry Trends Trends in the lingerie and loungewear industries parallel those in the foundations industry. There have been an increasing number of mergers, both between lingerie and loungewear firms and between these types of firms and foundation producers. There also has been an increasing emphasis on fashion-oriented styling and use of fabrics, including such apparel fabrics as chiffon, satin, and panne velvet.

Another trend has been the strong diversification and expansion of product lines. Daywear has now been expanded to include body shirts, chemises, camisole tops, and packaged "little nothings," which are bras, bikinis, and halters that are "nonconstructed" in contrast to the more conventional "constructed" brassieres and foundations. Sleepwear has added matching robes and hostess gowns, some of which can be worn for social occasions outside the home as well as for at-home parties. Loungewear has added matching robes and lounging pajamas, both of which can be worn outside the home as well as for at-home occasions.

Increasing quantities of bras, panties, and bikini sets of the unconstructed type are being produced and packaged for sale on self-selection racks in both conventional and mass-merchandising stores. These enable the stores to increase unit sales without increasing selling expenses.

Fashion continues to be the major competitive tool in the marketing of intimate apparel. Vast quantities of intimate apparel, nevertheless, are still sold on the basis of function, in slowly changing styles that involve minimum risk for producer and retailer and minimum price to the consumer. But in the medium to upper price brackets, fashion, rather than intrinsic value, is the motivating element. It is in these categories that the work of name designers is beginning to appear. Stephen Burrows, Halston, Stan Herman, and Donald Brooks have all designed or sponsored the design of lines of women's lingerie and loungewear in recent years.

Keeping in step with fashion has multiplied the industries' problems but has also enlarged their opportunities to sell more goods at higher prices while at the same time giving greater satisfaction to consumers.

HOSIERY

Until the twentieth century was well underway, women's legs were concealed under floor-length skirts, and women's hosiery served a functional rather than a fashion purpose. As skirts moved higher, during and after World War I, women suddenly became interested in the appearance of their legs.

The success of the hosiery industry as a fashion business is very recent, and has been the result both of product improvements to meet consumer demand and of new products and styles to complement current apparel fashions.

Although an increasing amount of basic hosiery is sold through supermarkets, drugstores, and vending machines, customers interested in fashion turn to established hosiery departments, where display and personal selling techniques encourage them to try more adventurous styles, shades, and textures.

History and Development

For the first two decades of this century, women wore full-fashioned silk or cotton stockings. In the late 1920s, cotton gave way to rayon, which had been introduced to the fiber market in 1924. With the introduction of nylon in 1938, limited quantities of hosiery made from this new fiber were sold, and because of its novelty, easier care, and durability, the new hosiery was eagerly accepted by those who could afford it.

The entry of the United States into World War II restricted nylon to war purposes and made silk unavailable. The only fibers left for women's hosiery were cotton and some rayons of unstable quality, which most women found unattractive. After the war, nylon fiber sources, along with yarn producers and hosiery mills, turned their attention to the development of sheerer deniers, more elastic yarns, and seamless hosiery.

Fashion entered the hosiery picture in the 1950s, with the introduction of colors other than flesh tones, and soon demonstrated its tremendous power to influence sales. As skirts shortened in the 1960s, the spotlight was thrown on legs, and hosiery became a major fashion accessory. Colors, textures, and weights were created in immense variety; and pantyhose were introduced for wear with the miniskirts and microminis of the late 1960s.

The growing popularity of pants in the first half of the 1970s brought a number of developments in the hosiery scene. These included the introduction of completely seamless pantyhose and pantyhose with figure-control features. Also introduced for use with pants were knee-high nylons, which had not been popular for several decades. By the mid-1970s, knee-highs were the fastest growing hosiery category, and they and pantyhose captured the major share of the hosiery market.

Organization and Operation

In the United States, the hosiery industry annually produces close to three billion pairs of socks and stockings for men, women, and children. About 40 percent of this output is in women's hosiery.

By far the largest number of plants engaged in the knitting, dyeing, and finishing of hosiery are located in North Carolina. Most other plants are located in Southern states or in Pennsylvania.

Most hosiery mills perform all the steps necessary to the production of finished hosiery, although some smaller mills may perform the knitting operation only, contracting out the finishing processes.

Full-fashioned hosiery is flat-knit to size and length specifications on high-speed machines that shape the stocking as it is knitted. The outer edges

"Boarding" is the heat-setting process through which hosiery acquires its permanent shape.
Hanes Hosiery, Inc.

are then stitched together on special sewing machines, after which the stocking is dyed. Each stocking acquires permanent shape through a heat-setting process called "boarding." Then stockings are carefully matched into pairs, their welts stamped with a brand name or other appropriate information, and the pairs packaged.

Seamless hosiery and pantyhose are circular-knit to size and length specifications on high-speed machines that shape the item during the knitting process. Subsequent steps are dyeing, boarding, pairing, stamping, and packaging, as for full-fashioned hosiery.

Most hosiery producers manufacture both branded and unbranded hosiery in the same mill, employing the same manufacturing procedures for all goods. Some small mills manufacture unbranded goods only, selling their output to brand manufacturers, to owners of private brands, or to retail stores for special price promotions.

Market Centers

Although hosiery is produced far from New York City, it is not necessary for buyers to visit mills in order to see the various lines and discuss fashion trends. All of the larger mills maintain permanent showrooms and sales staffs in New York City, where semiannual seasonal lines of new colors, textures, and other developments are shown. Smaller mills frequently employ the services of selling agents who maintain offices in New York City for closer contact with the retail and fashion markets.

Merchandising Activities

Traditionally, the women's hosiery industry concentrated its merchandising activities almost exclusively on the promotion and sale of nationally advertised brands. In recent years, however, the industry has become involved in merchandising its products for private labeling and for sale as packaged products in vending machines and other types of self-service fixtures in supermarkets and drugstores.

National Brands Major hosiery producers aggressively advertise their brand lines on a national basis and sell them to a wide variety of retail stores across the country. They also usually supply advertising, display, and fashion assistance to help promote retail sales.

Until recently, branded lines dominated the retail distribution of women's hosiery. Some producers were highly selective of their outlets; others attempted to maintain tight control over prices at which their merchandise could be sold; still others attempted to dictate the amount of stock a retailer should carry.

Today, most of these practices have been discontinued. Control of retail selling prices, once permitted, now is likely to bring action against a producer by the Federal Trade Commission. As a result of increased production and the concomitant need for increased sales, selectivity in retail distribution has largely been eliminated. Customer demand has replaced producer ultimatum as a basis for determining the amount of inventory a store should carry.

Private Brands Chain organizations, groups of retail stores, and some individual stores have developed their own private brands in competition with nationally advertised brands of hosiery.

Retailers realize many advantages by having their own brand of hosiery. To begin with, the cost is usually less, since the price they pay does not include the cost of national brand advertising and promotion. In addition, they can be more selective of colors and constructions and can build assortments around those specific characteristics most requested by customers. Usually they can offer hosiery at lower prices than those of comparable branded goods. Finally, merchants can develop stronger customer loyalty by offering a product that is unobtainable elsewhere.

Mass-merchandised Brands For some time, limited quantities of women's packaged hosiery have been available in vending machines, but usually in only one basic style and color. This hosiery is either unbranded or bears the private label of the jobber servicing the machines. More recently, however, two of the industry's best-known producers of women's better branded hosiery have each developed a low-priced brand of packaged pantyhose which they sell directly to supermarkets and drugstores. Each of these brands offers a fairly wide choice of styles and colors. Each producer supplies attractive self-service stock fixtures, and they each promote their brand through national advertising.

Industry Trends

As in many other divisions of the fashion industry, there has been a blurring of seasonal lines in hosiery and a growing need to launch new developments whenever fashion, rather than the traditional calendar of market dates, requires them. Retailers are eager to present appropriate hosiery at times that coincide with the introduction of new apparel styles. They apply pressure on the industry for earlier showings so that seasonal merchandise can be shipped soon enough to make coordinated presentation of apparel and hosiery possible.

During the first half of the 1970s, hosiery manufacturers were devoting increased time and money to product research and development, with particular emphasis on finding new styles and designs of pantyhose that would win consumer acceptance, and on experimentation with fibers other than nylon. These efforts, plus the development of improved self-service packaging for hosiery, were being made in an attempt to strengthen the sagging unit sales of women's hosiery due primarily to drastic changes in women's apparel fashions.

SHOES

For centuries, fashion paid little attention to women's shoes. Their purpose was regarded as purely functional. Shoes were both high and heavy, worn mainly as a protection against uneven terrain, bad weather, or other hazards. It was considered immodest to expose the feminine ankle, so usually only the tip of a lady's shoe could be seen below her long skirts.

Since the 1920s, however, women's feet have been plainly visible, and shoes have developed both fashion importance and variety. They have run the fashion gamut from pointed to squared toes, from high to flat heels, and from mere shells to thigh-high boots. In the last few decades, women's shoes have developed into a major fashion accessory.

Shoes showed little fashion versatility, however, until after World War II. Up until then, almost the only material used was leather, and the leather industry, in the first half of this century, was principally absorbed in the needs of men's footwear. The women's shoe industry relied on calf, kid, suede, and an occasional reptile. Shoe colors were mainly black and brown for winter, white for summer, and beige and navy for spring. Shoe styling was conservative. A single pair of all-purpose shoes often met the needs of an entire season's wardrobe.

Then fashion invaded the women's shoe industry. Leather manufacturers developed softer, more flexible leathers. New plastic and fabric materials were used to give shoes far more interesting and comfortable characteristics than was previously possible. New and varied textures and an ever-increasing range of colors produced styles that could keep pace with changes in apparel.

Organization and Operation

Footwear production is a major industry in the United States today. The major centers are in New England, where the industry had its origin, in the Great Lakes region, and in the St. Louis region. The westward movement of the industry came when the importance of the Midwest as a source of hide supplies and cheaper labor was recognized.

For each type and size of shoe in a producer's line, there must be a *last,* or wooden form in the shape of a foot, over which the shoes are built. The variety of lasts, the quality of materials, and the number and type of manufacturing operations required determine the quality and price of the finished shoe. As many as 200 to 300 operations may be performed by highly skilled workmen in the making of an expensive, high-quality shoe.

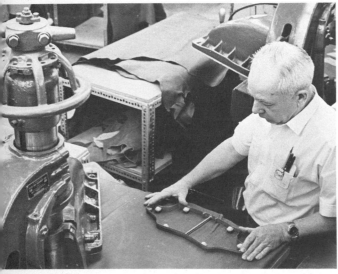
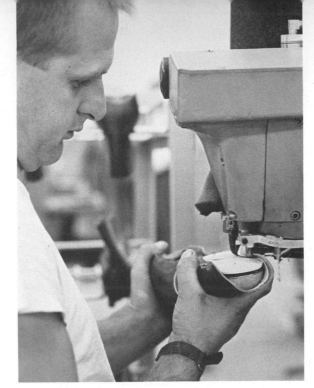

1 2

To transform pigskin into shoes (1) the leather is cut, (2) the parts of the shoe are assembled, (3) heels are attached, and (4) the shoes are paired and inspected.

Hush Puppies Division of Wolverine World Wide, Inc.

3 4

The range of sizes that shoe manufacturers must produce is enormous. The normal range of women's shoe sizes involves 103 width and length combinations—and this does not include sizes shorter than "4," longer than "11," or wider than "D." Even if manufacturers limit production to only the best-selling length and width combinations, their inventory, production problems, and investment are enormous compared with those of a dress manufacturer who makes a style in only five or six standard sizes. Under such conditions, it is not surprising that giants dominate the industry. One-fourth of the total shoe output in the United States is produced by only four manufacturers.

However, opportunity for smaller producers does exist in the shoe industry. For instance, unlike manufacturers in most other industries, shoe producers do not have to invest in machinery if they do not want to. Instead they can lease equipment, thus keeping the major portion of capital available for materials and merchandising activities. Nor do they any longer have to produce lasts, since other firms now perform this function. Neither do they have to make every part of the shoe in their own plants; specialists produce many of the standard components, particularly heels.

Market Centers

As it is for other fashion industries, New York City is the major market center for shoes. Most producers maintain permanent showrooms for their lines in New York, regardless of where their manufacturing facilities may be located. Twice a year, seasonal lines are shown to store buyers and the fashion press. Capsule shoe showings are held in other cities too, for the benefit of local merchants, but virtually every maker in the industry participates in the New York showings.

Merchandising Activities

The shoe industry has an active national trade association, known as the National Shoe Manufacturers' Association. Together with the National Shoe Retailers' Association, it disseminates technical, statistical, and fashion trend information on shoes, sometimes winning extensive publicity for footwear. In addition, the leather industry and its associations operate as sources of fashion information for buyers and other retail store executives.

Brand names are important in the shoe industry, and manufacturers advertise extensively in national consumer and fashion publications.

In contrast with most other fashion industries, many of the larger shoe manufacturers operate retail chain organizations of their own, a practice known as dual distribution (see Chapter 8). Frequently these retail chains augment their shoe stock with related accessories like hosiery and handbags. For example, one such operation, I. Miller Shoes, has diversified its retail assortments to include, in addition to I. Miller and David Evins shoes, boutique apparel and accessories, such as dresses, coats, belts, and scarfs.

Some shoe manufacturers are also involved in the retail field through the operation of leased departments in department and specialty stores. Because of the tremendous amount of capital required to stock a shoe department, as well as the expertise needed to fit and sell shoes, many stores lease their shoe departments to manufacturers or other companies specializing in this type of merchandise. Surveys made by the National Retail Merchants Association have repeatedly shown that women's shoe departments are among those most commonly leased by its member stores.

Industry Trends

Mergers have been fairly common for several years in the shoe industry. Manufacturers of men's shoes have merged with manufacturers of women's shoes. Shoe-machinery manufacturers have acquired shoe producers. A recent trend is toward the merging of shoe producers with apparel producers. In some instances, such mergers are merely financial, in the interests of diversification; in others, the purpose is to make available to retailers and consumers shoes that complete the "look" of the apparel itself.

Shoe manufacturers are experimenting with new materials and methods of production in order to enlarge their market potential and meet the problems faced by foreign competitors. Some of the largest companies have established separate merchandising and marketing divisions as a means of searching out new markets and offering additional services to their customers.

Greater emphasis on fashion continues to be the major trend in the shoe industry. Designers and other key personnel regularly attend European apparel openings, to gather information on trends in apparel and to observe the styling of European shoe manufacturers, many of whom design special models for the French and Italian coutures. In addition, an increasing number of domestic shoe firms have shoes produced abroad to their specifications and shipped back for sale in this country.

More and more, fashion influences both the styling and color of footwear. For example, for artistic balance, short skirts and geometric lines in apparel require shoes with low heels and broad toes. Longer, fuller skirts and apparel that follow the contour of the body more closely require shoes with higher heels and more pointed toes. When color is rampant in apparel, shoes are shown in lively colors and color combinations to match, blend, or contrast with apparel. With pantsuits, chunky shoe shapes are worn. Shoes and apparel depend upon one another for the total, coordinated look that consumers demand.

COSMETICS

Cosmetics include products used by both men and women. As defined by the Federal Trade Commission, *cosmetics* include articles other than soap that are intended to be rubbed, poured, sprinkled, or sprayed on the person for purposes of cleansing, beautifying, promoting attractiveness, or altering the appearance. For such products, the public spends nearly $5 billion a year, plus almost another $4 billion for beauty and barber shop services.

Cosmetics have been used by both men and women throughout history. Primitive people often used paint to frighten off enemies, deceive avenging ghosts, or advertise rank. Modern men and women use cosmetics to enhance their attractiveness as well as to conform to current fashion.

As examples of the relationship between cosmetics and apparel fashion, some authorities believe that the heavily made-up look is apt to be matched with exposed and skimpy apparel fashions, and that the more natural look in make-up is apt to be matched with more romantic apparel fashions.

Organization and Operation

Cosmetics is a multibillion-dollar industry, dominated by giant producers of well-advertised brand lines but also including many smaller firms. Also part of the industry are the so-called "private label" houses, which produce merchandise to the specifications and under the labels of chain organizations, national brands, or small independent firms. Most of the major producers maintain foreign as well as domestic plants.

The largest brand-name cosmetics firms, such as Estee Lauder, Elizabeth Arden, Helena Rubinstein, and Revlon, produce hundreds of items. It therefore becomes necessary to relate preparations into broad categories for sales and inventory purposes. The typical order form of one such firm, for example, lists all the company's products in the various sizes or colors available, under such end-use categories as facial make-up, nail care, bath preparations, hair care, fragrances, eye products, body care, and so on. If a firm produces men's as well as women's cosmetics, each of the two lines is given its own distinctive brand name, and separate sales and inventory records are kept for each brand line.

Chemicals are the basis of most cosmetics products. Major ingredients of cosmetics at any price level are fats, oil, waxes, talc, alcohol, glycerine, borax, coloring matter, and perfumes. The industry is restricted from using potentially harmful ingredients and from making exaggerated claims about the efficiency of its products by federal law: the Food, Drug, and Cosmetic Act of 1939.

Bob Pitsus — Revlon (Maxfau)
Bay Area Dist. (Claireol P.
Chris Mahn — Geil Mlane Kennn d Lord S.

CHAPTER 9   MANUFACTURERS OF FASHION ACCESSORIES   147

*The ultramodern cosmetics department in Hall's Crown Center store,
Kansas City.*

Paul Laszlo, Architects

Merchandising Activities

Brand competition is tremendously keen in the
cosmetics and toiletries industry, whether consumer
sales take place in retail stores or in the home. To
popularize and sell its brands, the industry spends
enormous amounts on national advertising. In
1972, its outlay for television alone was close to
$500 million; another $117 million was spent on

magazine advertising. Most firms also engage in
cooperative advertising with retail store customers.
Few industries spend more on advertising than does
cosmetics.

Toiletries, such as after-shave lotions, deodor-
ants, shampoos, and some cosmetics that bear
nationally advertised brand names, are often sold
through stores of many kinds, including neighborhood drugstores and supermarkets. The more

fashion-oriented cosmetics lines, however, are distributed on a more selective basis, since skilled personal selling is required to demonstrate their use to consumers. In large retail stores, much of the selling is done by trained cosmeticians, known as *brand-line representatives,* each of whom advises customers in the selection and use of products within a specific brand line. A brand-line representative is usually trained in how to sell its products and how to merchandise its stocks and counter displays by the producer of the line. The producer of each line concerned usually contributes toward a representative's salary by making an allowance for this purpose to the store.

In smaller stores, where the volume of business done in any one brand is not large, cosmetics counters are generally staffed with salespeople who are knowledgeable about cosmetics in general but not specialized in any one line and who sell any or all of the brands carried by the store. Producers may or may not contribute toward the salary of such salespeople, but in most cases they do assist in training by providing leaflets, samples, color charts, and other appropriate aids.

Most major cosmetics producers employ traveling representatives who are available to their larger retailer accounts as consultants. These representatives usually spend a few days to a week in each store, advising customers, conducting clinics, promoting the sale of new products in the line, and generally assisting in the training and retraining of store personnel responsible for selling the brand line.

Industry Trends

Competition in the cosmetics industry is extremely keen. Product obsolescence is rapid, and new products or ideas must constantly be introduced.

With current interest focused on youth, whole new markets are being developed among mature consumers who seek a more youthful appearance. Another market which has developed as a result of the youth market is a growing demand for skin care and treatment products by adolescents who formerly were not regarded as important cosmetics consumers. Similarly, expanding use of color in apparel has increased the demand for facial and nail cosmetics in a wide range of colors cued to wardrobe colors.

Cosmetics manufacturers have also capitalized on the fashion potential of famous designer names in promoting the sale of their products, principally fragrances. In the mid-1970s, the sales volume of perfumes bearing French couture designers' names amounted to $600 million at wholesale prices. Chanel, Balmain, Lanvin, and Schiaparelli are among the famous French designers long associated with perfumes and colognes. Other well-known designers, such as Dior, Givenchy, St. Laurent, Valentino, Adele Simpson, Halston, and Norell, have entered the fragrance field more recently, mainly through licensing arrangements with manufacturers.

By far the most significant current trend in the cosmetics industry is the development of whole new lines of men's cosmetics, toiletries, and fragrances. Whereas once the male market was extremely small and restricted to a few toiletries products, today practically every brand-line producer of women's cosmetics has developed, or is in the process of developing, complete lines of cosmetics, toiletries, and fragrances for men. Retail sales of men's fragrances alone amounted to more than $770 million in 1972, according to an industry spokesman. This burgeoning market represents extensive new business volume for manufacturers and stores alike. Currently there are installations of complete men's cosmetics boutiques in an increasing number of department and specialty stores throughout the country.

After years of steady growth, several of the major cosmetics firms are beginning to embark upon ambitious diversification programs. Some are broadening their markets by acquiring foreign firms and facilities, or through licensing agreements. Others have diversified by acquiring pharmaceutical firms. Still others have moved into the fashion apparel field by acquiring European boutiques or even by obtaining financial control of major European couture houses.

In the 1970s, there has been interest and activity on the part of such federal regulatory agencies as the Food and Drug Administration and the Consumer Products Safety Commission in both the production and marketing of cosmetics. Consideration is being given to expanded and more definite regulation of some previously unregulated areas, such as market testing of cosmetic safety and efficacy, ingredient labeling, health hazards, and open quality-control records and complaint files.

JEWELRY

Since early days, jewelry has served as adornment, as a status symbol, as a form of currency, and as a medium for religious expression. Men as well as women have worn necklaces, bracelets, and other decorative ornaments throughout history. The chains and medallions worn by some men in the last decade are no great departure from the protective amulets that men in ancient Rome wore as necklaces; Tibetan Buddhists wore court necklaces derived from Lamaist rosaries; and Renaissance portraits frequently show men wearing heavy gold necklaces.

Organization and Operation

Modern methods of making jewelry may be less arduous than those of earlier times, but essentially they are much the same. Modern jewelry makers melt and shape metal, cut or carve stones, and string beads and shells. Jewelry designers still use enamel, ceramics, and many other materials to express their creative ideas.

The jewelry industry in the United States is subdivided into two separate groups, mainly on the basis of intrinsic value or quality of product. One group is referred to as fine jewelry, and the other is termed costume jewelry or fashion jewelry.

Fine Jewelry The counterpart of haute couture apparel is *fine jewelry*. Only such precious metals as gold and all members of the platinum family (palladium, rhodium, and iridium) are used to make fine jewelry. Silver, although actually a precious metal, is much less expensive, does not hold stones successfully, tarnishes easily, and is therefore not widely used for making fine jewelry. Precious metals in their pure state are too soft to be used alone, and therefore are combined with one or more other metals to produce an alloy of the necessary hardness to retain a desired shape and securely hold stones.

Stones used in fine jewelry are known as gemstones to distinguish them from those that are less attractive or suitable only for industrial use. *Gemstones* are natural stones classified as either precious or semiprecious. *Precious stones* include the rare and more costly diamond, emerald, ruby, sapphire, and real or Oriental pearl. *Semiprecious stones* include the amethyst, garnet, opal, jade, cultured pearl, and other natural stones that are less rare and costly than precious stones. In recent years, chemists have succeeded in creating synthetic rubies, sapphires, and diamonds, but none as yet has been pronounced suitable for use in what is known as "fine jewelry."

The fine jewelry industry is essentially a handcraft industry. The lapidary, or stonecutter, is a craftsman who transforms dull-looking stones into gems of beauty by cutting or carving them according to their size, nature, and the type of setting in which each will be used. Workers in precious metals create unusual and beautiful shapes, often to the specifications of individual customers.

Among the creative fine jewelry houses, as among the haute couture apparel houses, one usually finds design, production, and retail sales all taking place under one roof and one management. Many fine jewelry firms sell only the merchandise they manufacture, much of which is custom designed. Others supplement their original designs with merchandise purchased from other specialized manufacturers.

Costume Jewelry *Costume*, or *fashion, jewelry* may be compared to mass-produced apparel. Materials used in the manufacture of costume jewelry are plastics, wood, glass, brass, or other base metals (such as aluminum, copper, tin, lead, and chromium), some of which may be coated with more costly metals like gold, rhodium, or silver. Stones and simulated pearls used in costume jewelry are made from clay, glass, or plastic, and while attractive and interesting in surface appearance, are less costly and have none of the more desired properties of natural stones.

Most of the large, popular-priced costume jewelry houses employ stylists who design seasonal lines or adapt styles from higher-priced lines. The majority of this type of jewelry is produced in New England and the Middle Atlantic states, with Providence, Rhode Island, as the major production center of the costume jewelry industry. Concentrated mass-production facilities there produce jewelry to the specifications of individual firms much the same as apparel contractors work with apparel manufacturers and jobbers. Mass-production methods prevail. In contrast to the hand-shaping of metal used in fine jewelry, the metal used in costume jewelry is usually cast by first melting it and then pouring the molten metal into molds to harden. Finally, designs may be applied to the hardened metal by painting on colored enamel or etching the metal by machine.

Although most costume jewelry is mass-produced, there are some exceptions. Individuals with creative talent may set up small retail or wholesale operations catering to customers primarily interested in individualized styling. Some who started from such small beginnings have become large-scale producers. Others prefer to remain small, working mainly in one medium, such as copper or ceramics. The smaller companies serve only a limited clientele and often design jewelry items to the specific requirements of their customers.

Marketing Centers

New York City is the principal market center for both fine and costume jewelry. Major firms maintain permanent showrooms there as a convenience to store buyers and also to keep in close contact with developments in other segments of the fashion industry.

Seasonal showings, held semiannually, are sponsored by the industry's trade association, the Jewelry Industry Council. Retailers of both fine and costume jewelry attend these showings to preview fashion trends for the coming season, to keep abreast of developments in the industry, and to buy for their seasonal needs.

Merchandising Activities

Fine jewelry firms traditionally have concentrated their merchandising activities on providing a wide range of fairly basic items, such as diamond rings and watches. They provide their store customers with a wide range of services and, in many cases, some form of advertising assistance. With the exception of watches, brand names are relatively unknown in this branch of the jewelry industry.

Leased jewelry departments are fairly common in the merchandising of fine jewelry. A large amount of capital is required to provide adequate assortments, and specialized knowledge is needed to sell this merchandise. Therefore, large-scale operators, who in many cases are also manufacturers, provide retail stores with stock, trained personnel, and advertising, returning a percentage of sales as rent to the host store.

The larger costume jewelry firms offer seasonal lines so broad that they can easily adapt to whatever trend fashion may be taking. Because they contract the production of most of their merchandise, emphasis can swiftly be switched from less popular items to production of those in greater demand. The larger firms also market much of their merchandise under brand names and advertise widely in national consumer publications.

Some of the larger costume jewelry firms offer advertising assistance in the form of advertising mats or cooperative advertising allowances. Some help to plan and maintain retail store assortments. Some supply display fixtures. Some offer fashion guidance and traveling representatives to help train retail salespeople and to serve customers on the retail selling floor.

Industry Trends

Today, both branches of the jewelry industry are placing greater emphasis on producing designs that complement current apparel fashions. As an example, when turtlenecks became popular, jewelry producers began designing and offering long chains and pendants that looked graceful on high necklines. When sleeveless apparel is in fashion, bracelets are prominent in producers' lines. When prints are popular in apparel, more tailored jewelry styles are usually featured.

Some fine jewelry firms are broadening their lines. Traditionally known for prompt service, fine workmanship, and high prices, several such firms today also offer costume jewelry of original design and excellent quality at modest prices.

Some of the larger costume jewelry manufacturers, especially in the men's field, have begun to adopt a "big business" attitude toward diversification of product, although this is not yet a general industry practice. For example, Speidel, traditionally a watchband producer, has had excellent response to men's colognes; Swank, traditionally a producer of men's cuff links, tie tacs, tie clasps, and related jewelry items, has diversified into colognes, sunglasses, travel accessories, and a variety of men's gifts.

GLOVES

Historically, gloves have served many purposes besides the obvious ones of protection and warmth. At one time, an English knight going into battle carried his lady's glove on his sleeve as a good luck charm. In the exchange of property, the giving of a glove once symbolized good faith in the transaction. Gloves have also been used to denote rank or status; prior to the sixteenth century, for instance, only men of the clergy or of noble rank wore gloves.

Today, gloves are worn both as a costume accessory and for protection and warmth. To be in fashion gloves must closely relate to current apparel fashions in styling, detail, and color. For example, fashions in glove lengths are largely determined by the fashionable length of sleeves, particularly coat and suit sleeves, and fashionable apparel trimmings also often find their counterparts in glove ornamentation. Just as there are classic styles in apparel, so, too, there are classic styles in gloves: the untrimmed white wrist-length glove, for wear on dress occasions, and the "suit" glove, which extends a few inches beyond the wrist, for more general wear.

Organization and Operation

In the early days of the twentieth century, fashion interest focused on the well-gloved hand, and the glove business flourished in the United States. The glove material most favored by fashion at that time was leather. Today, however, knit and woven fabric gloves dominate the field.

In the production of leather gloves, most of the manufacturing operations are hand-guided or, in some cases, done completely by hand. As a result, glove factories have remained small, few machines are required, and comparatively few workers are employed in any one factory. Moreover, producers tend to specialize, performing just one manufacturing operation, such as cutting or stitching, and farming out the other operations to nearby plants, each of which performs its own specialty.

In contrast to the methods employed in the production of leather gloves, much of the production of fabric gloves is mechanized. The most favored and most durable glove fabric used today is a double-woven fabric. It is possible to use almost any fiber in producing this particular type of fabric. Knit gloves are usually made of woolen, acrylic, or cotton string yarns.

Although fabric gloves are produced in various parts of the country today, Gloversville, New York, remains the major production center for fabric as well as leather gloves, with a few plants producing both types.

Market Centers

The major market center for both leather and fabric gloves is in New York City. Many glove firms maintain permanent showrooms there, where they show seasonal lines to store and resident office buyers. The typical glove firm offers a very wide and versatile assortment of both domestic and imported gloves in a rather wide range of prices.

Merchandising Activities

The merchandising activities of the women's glove industry, as a whole, have tended to lag behind those of other fashion accessories industries. Compared with the dollars spent on consumer advertising by other segments of the fashion industry, outlays for glove advertising are quite modest. Only a few large producers with nationally distributed brand lines have actively promoted their products or offered even limited merchandising services to their retail store customers. In recent years, however, because of stagnating sales and competition from imports (particularly of leather gloves), many glove producers have begun to re-evaluate their merchandising techniques. For example, some producers are now experimenting with packaging limited styles of stretch gloves that can be sold from self-service fixtures.

Although most of the larger producers of women's gloves employ fashion stylists, few have made their services available to retail store accounts except on rare occasions. Sales-training aids have been limited mainly to color charts.

For years the glove industry has maintained a trade association known as the National Association of Glove Manufacturers, with headquarters in Gloversville, New York. This association's activities, however, have concentrated mainly on tariff questions and federal agency regulations and rulings rather than on publicizing the industry and its product.

Industry Trends

Sales of domestically produced leather gloves have suffered considerably in recent years from the competition of less expensive imports. To meet this challenge, the industry is trying to improve manufacturing procedures in order to reduce production costs. In addition, improved materials, resulting from product research and development in the leather industry, are expected to increase the market potential of domestically produced leather gloves. For example, many leather gloves today are hand washable and come in a wide range of fashion colors.

HANDBAGS

Receptacles to hold money have been in use ever since coins, as a medium of exchange, were first used. The modern handbag, however, developed from the *reticule*, a small drawstring bag introduced in the late eighteenth century when close-fitting dress fashions provided little or no room for pockets.

The modern handbag is much more than a utilitarian carryall, however. It is an essential addition to the attire of well-dressed women, harmonizing with, dramatizing, or contrasting with their other apparel.

Organization and Operation

The handbag industry is quite small compared with some other fashion industries. The total industry output is about $250 million at factory prices.

Firms producing handbags are also quite small. Fewer than half employ as many as 20 people each. Manufacturing is concentrated in the metropolitan New York area, where more than two-thirds of the industry's factories are located.

Leather, once the most important handbag material, has lost much of its eminence, except for finer-quality handbags in calfskin, goatskin, and lizard. Some heavy-duty tote bags are still made of leather, but today that material is used in only a small percentage of the handbag industry's output.

Handbags are also made of plastic, fabric, metal, straw, beads, string, and whatever other materials lend themselves readily to the demands of current fashion.

Fashion and personal taste decree whether a handbag should blend or contrast with the costume color. Shapes may be small or large, pouch or swagger, draped or boxlike; but in general they are designed to harmonize with the currently popular apparel silhouette. Textures may be rough or smooth, dull or shiny, according to the current fashion look or the individual's own interpretation of that look.

Materials required for the 20 to 40 different parts of a handbag are usually cut by dies or by hand, much as shoe parts are cut. The various parts of the bag are then machine-stitched together. Liners, fillers, and stay materials are glued into the bags and, as a final process, the necessary fasteners are attached. In most cases, the frame is the most important and costly part of the handbag.

Market Centers

The handbag market center is New York City, close to the major garment industries. Permanent showrooms are maintained there, and seasonal lines may be viewed at least twice a year.

Merchandising Activities

Brand names are relatively unimportant in the handbag industry. Fashion is the keynote. Industry sales rise or fall according to how successfully individual producers have anticipated trends and succeeded in preparing to meet fashion demand.

Furthermore, few producers are large enough to advertise on a significant scale or engage in much cooperative advertising with retail stores. Even those who do advertise tend to emphasize dependable quality rather than fashion importance. The customer's impression of what is fashionable in handbags is gained primarily from the assortments offered in retail departments, in store displays, and in "total look" newspaper advertising and fashion publication advertising.

Today, handbag styles range from the most casual to the most formal.
Liberty House, Honolulu

Industry Trends

The handbag industry devotes little concerted effort to improving marketing techniques. There is a trade association, the National Authority for the Ladies' Handbag Industry, but it is not a fashion spokesman for the industry. Manufacturers prefer working as individuals in determining and interpreting fashion trends rather than pooling technical and fashion information and market research.

A few handbag manufacturers have diversified their lines in recent years to include styles for men. Large enough to also serve as briefcases, men's handbags are usually designed to be carried over the shoulder. Although men's handbags have not achieved as much acceptence in the United States as they have in Europe, this fashion trend appears to merit watchful attention by the domestic handbag industry.

Some of the larger manufacturers of handbags have recently diversified their product lines to include luggage, as well as personal leather goods such as wallets and key cases. Through advertising and promotion of new colors, textures, patterns, and shapes in these related lines, attention indirectly underscores the fashion importance of the handbag as a fashion accessory. Some of these efforts are being undertaken in an attempt to combat the increasing competition of imported handbags. Retail store buyers are finding good-quality handbags at lower prices than domestic producers can offer in such places as Italy, Spain, and South America.

MILLINERY

The wearing of millinery for decorative effect, as well as warmth and protection, can be traced back through history for some thousands of years. Throughout the years, hairstyles, available materials, production skills, and the spirit of the times all have influenced women's millinery fashions. Historically, millinery has been an important segment of the fashion industry. Rose Bertin got her start in fashion's hall of fame as chief milliner, as well as dressmaker, to Queen Marie Antoinette of France.

Today's millinery industry in this country is largely a handcraft industry composed of small firms. Annual output in the mid-1960s was around $100 million at wholesale prices. By the mid-1970s, however, this figure had dropped below $50 million, although there were some indications of renewed interest in millinery.

The millinery industry has an active trade association, the National Millinery Institute, which engages primarily in sales promotion activities.

New York City is the principal market center for millinery. Major producers of both expensive and inexpensive millinery, and suppliers to the industry, maintain showrooms and often workrooms there.

The widespread rejection of hats is a phenomenon of the past two decades, during which time a casual look has been dominant. During this time the millinery industry in the United States has researched, publicized, and campaigned in an extensive effort to reverse the trend, but with little success to date. This situation serves as an example of one fashion principle: that no amount of sales promotional efforts can change the direction in which fashion is moving. Only renewed interest on the part of consumers can re-establish millinery as an important fashion accessory.

However, accelerated interest in a variety of fur head coverings for both men and women during recent years has improved and extended the market potential of millinery to a certain extent. Exploitation of this interest takes such forms as devising methods for creating quality fur hats at lower prices, using new and unusual furs, and introducing more creative designing.

OTHER ACCESSORIES

Various minor fashion accessories include neckwear, handkerchiefs, belts, umbrellas, sunglasses, and wigs. While once some of the industries producing these accessories were much larger, today they are relatively small. The output of industries producing these accessories tends to fluctuate in direct relationship to the fashion importance of each to the current popular look. The main showrooms of the producers are in New York City, although some larger firms also maintain showrooms in other domestic market centers.

Neckwear and handkerchiefs both used to be much more important accessories than they are today. Until the early 1950s, retail stores often had a neckwear department, a handkerchief department, and an umbrella department, each with its own buyer. Belts were usually displayed and sold in the handbag department. A small collection of sunglasses was carried in the costume jewelry department. Wigs were not then found in retail store inventories.

In the early 1950s, however, neckwear and handkerchiefs began to decline in fashion importance. When these categories of merchandise no longer produced enough retail sales to justify either the floor space allotted to them or the cost of maintaining separate accounting records, many retail stores combined these stocks with belts and umbrellas into a single "fashion accessories" department, which became the responsibility of a single buyer. When sunglasses began to show fashion importance, they also were added to this department. However, when wigs became an accepted fashion accessory, they usually were put elsewhere in the store, most often in the millinery department, for the primary reason that wigs, like hats, were worn on the head.

Neckwear

Until the early 1950s, neckwear producers turned out collar and cuff sets, dickies, and scarfs. As collar and cuff sets and dickies faded from the fashion picture, neckwear producers began diversifying into knit jackets, shrugs, shawls, and stoles, which, because they were made by neckwear manufacturers, were added to the assortments carried in the stores' fashion accessories departments. More recently, neckwear manufacturers have also added matching sets of knitted scarfs, caps, and gloves or mittens, as well as halter tops, to their offerings.

In recent years, scarfs have once more begun to play a more important role in the fashion picture.

In the last half of the 1960s, designer scarfs became fashion news. In the mid-1970s, because of the fashion to emphasize the head and shoulders, scarfs became the most important category in retail stores' fashion accessories departments. Producers turned out great varieties of scarfs, from the 12-inch squares, to the oblong 7- or 8-footers in a variety of fabrics, to shawls with long fringe.

Handkerchiefs

Once considered essential both for functional use and as a fashion accessory, handkerchiefs are today of relatively minor fashion importance.

In the days when handkerchiefs were important, only a few novelty handkerchiefs were domestically produced; by far the greater number were imported. In those days, Chinese embroideries were in greatest demand. Sheer cotton handkerchiefs, for both men and women, were imported from Switzerland, and linen handkerchiefs in more limited styles came from Ireland.

Then the tissue-paper handkerchief, of which Kleenex is the best-known brand, was introduced. Furthermore, trade with China was cut off. Today, handkerchiefs are still to be found in fashion accessories departments, but in very limited variety; initialed styles dominate the assortment for both men and women.

Umbrellas

Umbrellas for both men and women are produced by the same firms and carried side-by-side in most fashion accessories departments. Today, most umbrellas manufacturers produce both fashion or novelty and utilitarian items.

Fashion or novelty items include an increasing number of styles in new shapes, patterns, and color combinations. Also included in this category are rain accessories and umbrellas with coordinated rain hats, scarfs, capes, or handbags. Utilitarian items include not only traditional-type umbrellas but also a growing variety of styles for travel use.

Belts

Originally, women's belts were produced by manufacturers of men's belts. Today, nearly all women's fabric, leather, and plastic belts are still supplied by the men's belt industry, but many of the metal belts that have increased in popularity over the past decade are produced by costume jewelry firms. The industries' output of women's belts depends entirely upon whether the apparel styles currently in fashion or increasing in fashion acceptance require or lend themselves to the use of a belt.

Sunglasses

Aside from their purely functional use, in recent years sunglasses have become an important fashion accessory. Fashion has not only endorsed wearing them, both indoors and outdoors, but also made popular wearing them pushed back on the top of the head. One indication of their fashion importance: In 1974, sunglasses were the single largest income-producing item carrying the Dior name that was domestically produced under a license agreement with that well-known French firm. As sunglasses have continued to grow in fashion importance, manufacturers have increased both the variety of colors and styles in which sunglasses are available.

Wigs

Wigs have won a small but probably permanent share of the minor fashion accessories business. That period in the late 1960s and early 1970s, when wigs were regarded as a novelty, has passed; now the wig industry has settled into what it believes will be a pattern of modest but regularly increasing output and sales volume.

Some of the first wigs were made of natural hair; now nearly all wigs are made from man-made fibers. Improvements in these fibers, improved construction, increased fashion styling, and increased male interest in hair pieces all point to increased sales for the industry. Furthermore, producers are keeping the cost of wigs and hairpieces down by contracting to have production work done in countries where labor costs are lower, particularly in the Far East.

Semiannual market weeks are held in New York City under the auspices of the industry's trade association, the American Wig Association. Larger firms maintain permanent showrooms in that city.

MERCHANDISING VOCABULARY

Define or briefly explain each of the following terms:

Intimate apparel
Foundations
Lingerie
Loungewear
Last
Cosmetics
Brand-line representatives

Fine jewelry
Gemstones
Precious stones
Semiprecious stones
Costume or fashion jewelry
Reticule

MERCHANDISING REVIEW

1. Name the two major industries that make up what is referred to as the intimate apparel, or inner fashions, industry. What types of garments are produced by each? Why are they often regarded, and their products often merchandised, as a single industry?
2. Describe the various merchandising activities currently engaged in by the intimate apparel industries.
3. Name and briefly describe three methods of merchandising women's hosiery.
4. Discuss the merchandising activities of the domestic shoe industry, as these relate to (a) advertising, (b) maintenance of retail outlets, and (c) leased departments.
5. What is considered the most significant trend in the cosmetics industry today? Briefly discuss other trends of special importance to the cosmetics industry.
6. Name the two categories, or groups of merchandise, produced by the jewelry industry and describe the distinguishing product characteristics of each.
7. What are the major materials used in the production of gloves? Give several examples of how apparel fashions influence glove fashions.
8. Discuss the fashion importance of handbags. Of what materials are handbags made?
9. What categories of merchandise are usually to be found in fashion accessories departments today? Discuss the current fashion importance of each category.
10. What factors have contributed to the widespread popularity of wigs in recent years?

MERCHANDISING DIGEST

1. Discuss the following statement from the text and its implications for retail merchants of fashion accessories: "Fashion today emphasizes the total look, and accessories are an essential part of that look."
2. Discuss current trends in the intimate apparel industries as they relate to (a) mergers, (b) diversification of product lines, and (c) styling.
3. Discuss how changing fashions and technological advances have influenced the styling of women's hosiery.

10
FOREIGN FASHION MARKET CENTERS

One of the most interesting fashion developments in the second half of the twentieth century has been the emergence of new fashion market centers throughout the world. Each has strong nationally oriented characteristics; and, practically without exception, each has been strongly encouraged by various types of government patronage.

The development of these new fashion market centers has followed approximately the same pattern. Although Paris traditionally had been the Western World's foremost fashion center, World War II isolated France and cut off designers in other countries from their dependence on Paris as the source of fashion inspiration and materials. As a result, they had to rely on their own creative ability and make do with domestically available fashion materials.

After World War II, one way that each country rebuilt its economy was by stressing exports. Fashion designers in each country were encouraged to develop exportable products, provided the styles they featured used the fashion materials of that country. Thus, new fashion centers have developed and are continuing to develop throughout the world. Each tends to concentrate on styles and fashion materials characteristic of the country or region in which the center is located.

SHOPPING FOREIGN MARKETS

Now that exciting fashion news and merchandise may be found almost anywhere in the world, American fashion merchants have found it neces-sary to expand and diversify their methods for shopping foreign markets. Today retail stores may set up their own foreign buying division; or use foreign commissionaire organizations or agents; or send their buyers on foreign buying trips. Most frequently, all three methods are combined.

Major store organizations, such as Macy's, Gimbel/Saks, May Department Stores, the big chains, and one large buying office—the Associated Merchandising Corporation—have their own foreign buying divisions or subsidiary foreign buying organizations. The typical division is usually a network of offices staffed by company personnel in major foreign market centers. Commissionaire organizations may be employed to represent the firm in foreign markets where it does not maintain an office. Individual agents may be used in less important markets.

A commissionaire organization is the foreign equivalent of an American resident buying office. A commissionaire organization has its headquarters in a major city of a market area and is staffed by market representatives, each of whom specializes in a particular category of merchandise. These market representatives keep in constant touch with market developments; they work with visiting retail buyers who want to locate specific types of goods or simply want to see what the market center has to offer. The commissionaire does not make purchases for its store clients, however, unless authorized to do so by an appropriate store executive. However, the store pays the commissionaire a fee that is usually a percentage of the "first cost" (the wholesale price at place of origin) of any purchase made. In Europe in the mid-1970s, that percentage ranged from 5 to 7 percent.

Many store organizations also send retail buyers and merchandising executives on foreign buying trips. While the trips may be made throughout the year, most are timed to cover important fashion events. For instance, the most important European trip is likely to take place in October, when larger, fashion-conscious stores in this country may send from 2 to 20 buyers and store executives to cover the important Paris, Italian, and London ready-to-wear showings. Smaller stores, whose sales volume does not warrant the expense of a foreign buying trip, sometimes band together to make group purchases. In such cases, the stores send one executive from among their group abroad with authority to make purchases for the group.

One indication of the increasing interest of American fashion merchants and American consumers in foreign fashion goods is statistical: In 1960, the United States imported somewhat less than $500 million worth of foreign apparel and footwear; in 1972, the figure was up to $3 billion and rising steadily. An interesting indication in the mid-1970s of the eagerness of foreign countries to increase their exports to the United States was the discount travel and accommodation arrangements being offered to retail store buyers.

However, it is important to remember that American producers and retailers shop foreign market centers for fashion trends and fashion news as well as fashion goods. That is why, for instance, while French and Italian fashion goods imported into this country represent only a very minor portion of the total amount of fashion goods we import, the French and Italian fashion showings are considered very important. French and Italian style and design ideas still strongly influence fashion trends in this country, even if not quite as strongly as they once did.

FRANCE

The reputation of Paris as a prime source of fashion inspiration began to develop several centuries ago as the result of many interrelating factors. As an artistic center, Paris was considered ideal for creative apparel designers. Skilled seamstresses were abundant. Luxury fabrics were readily available, and their producers were willing to work closely with designers to create exclusive materials. Suppliers of high-quality trimmings—laces, embroideries, buttons, sequins, ribbons, and feathers—were plentiful.

Historically renowned for original and trend-setting high-fashion collections, today Paris is also an important fashion center for innovative ready-to-wear apparel. In fact, the traditional differences between the worlds of couture and ready-to-wear are fading, for reasons discussed below.

Paris Couture

A *couture house* is an apparel firm for which a designer creates original styles. The French term, *haute couture*, although literally translated as "fine sewing," conveys much the same meaning as our own term, "high fashion"; that is, it includes styles or designs accepted by a limited group of fashion leaders. In France, the term is used in connection with those houses that combine luxury fabrics and fine workmanship to create trend-setting styles.

The proprietor or designer of a couture house is known as a *couturier*, if male, or *couturiere*, if female. Most Paris couture houses are known by the name of the designers who head them, such as St. Laurent, Givenchy, Ungaro, Cardin. Sometimes, however, a couture house may keep the name of its famous designer even after that designer's death, as in the case of Dior and Chanel.

Charles Frederick Worth, an English dressmaker to Empress Eugènie, is generally regarded as the father of the Paris haute couture. Shortly after he established his headquarters in Paris, other couturiers began opening salons there. In 1868, an elite couture trade association, called the Chambre Syndicale de la Couture Parisienne, came into being. Membership in the Chambre Syndicale was by invitation only and was restricted to couture houses that agreed to abide by strict rules governing such matters as copying, timing and dates of collection showings, shipping dates, and issuing of press cards. However, not all Paris couture houses were members of the Chambre Syndicale. In 1970, for example, only 20 firms were listed as belonging. These included some of the best-known names in Paris, but not all of them; firms such as Cardin and Chanel were not members.

Today, drastic worldwide changes are taking place in the fashion industry. Interest in and patronage of couture has declined in favor of ready-to-wear. Couture houses are changing in order to survive, and so is the Chambre Syndicale. In 1973, its name was changed to the Federation Francaise de la Couture. A new group within the Federation, called the Groupe Mode et Creation, or "Fashion Group," made up of both couturiers and ready-to-wear designers, was organized to hold semiannual showings of ready-to-wear collections at the same

THE CAUTIONS

Dior: United States—about $2,400. Europe—about $800.

Ferand: $500 for two people; $150 for each additional person.

Givenchy: United States—Two models. Europe—Two paper patterns worth about $1,000.

Patou: To see collection once—about $560 for 1 person, about $700 for 3 persons. To purchase paper patterns—about $800 for 2 or 3 persons to get 2 paper patterns; about $960 for 4 persons to get 3 paper patterns; about $640 for 2 persons and only 1 paper pattern.

St. Laurent: $1,500.

Venet: United States—One model. Europe—One paper pattern worth about $300.

THE MINIMUMS

Dior: Cautions, as above.

Feraud: Four toiles—$1,000.
One model—$1,000.

Mme. Gres: Between $1,000 and $1,500.

Patou: Cautions, as above.

Venet: One dress—$800.
One suit—$1,000.

As shown in Women's Wear Daily, January 6, 1975.

time. Also, a Chambre Syndicale of couture designers of menswear was created within the new Federation structure with Pierre Cardin as its first president.

Couture Showings The major Paris couture houses show their semiannual haute couture collections in late January (for spring–summer) and in late July (for fall–winter). Four types of customers attend:

- Private customers who may select a model (garment) from a designer's collection and have it made up to individual measurements. (In 1974, Cardin had around 250 regular private customers; Dior had around 500.)
- Retail store buyers who may buy models from a collection for resale to their own customers or, in many cases, so they can have the model copied or adapted into ready-to-wear garments for their store's exclusive use.
- Ready-to-wear producers who may buy models for purposes of inspiration or adaptation when designing styles for their own lines.
- Pattern manufacturers who may buy models or paper patterns of models for reproduction as patterns for home sewers.

Private customers and the press are admitted free, although the latter have to apply for admission passes. Retailers and manufacturers, who must also apply for admission, are charged a stipulated "caution." A *caution* is a fee charged for viewing a couture collection. The caution may be stated as a dollar fee, or as an agreement to purchase a certain number of models, or as an agreement to purchase a certain number of paper patterns, or any combination of these three requirements. The amount of the caution usually varies with the importance of the couture house; less well-known houses usually require considerably lower cautions than do famous houses.

Other Couture Business Activities While the traditional haute couture collections continue to make fashion news, actual sales volume has steadily declined in recent years. More and more, private customers whose wardrobes previously might have consisted almost entirely of exclusive couture-made garments are now turning to ready-to-wear, partly because (1) many private customers have become impatient with the numerous and lengthy fitting couture garments require; (2) the figures of potential private customers now tend to be so slender and well cared for that they can easily be fitted with ready-to-wear garments; (3) general economic trends have made many long-time private customers balk at the money required to be dressed by the couture; (4) an increasing number of talented ready-to-wear designers are creating an increasing amount of fashion news.

As a result of these trends, Paris couture houses have been forced to change their methods of operation in an attempt to meet the challenge and competition of the flourishing ready-to-wear industry.

Couture Boutiques The first step in meeting this challenge was the creation of couture boutiques, usually located on a lower floor of the same building that housed the couture showrooms. These couture boutiques, which most well-known Paris couture houses now have, feature unusual and exclusive fashion accessories, as well as limited lines of apparel. Boutique items are usually designed by members of the couture house staff, sometimes are made in the couture workrooms, and all bear the famous couture house label. Couture boutiques can be as profitable as they are popular. For example, St. Laurent is said to have grossed well over $1 million in 1973 through sales in the boutique owned and operated as part of his couture house.

Couture Ready-to-wear Couture designers then went a step further—a very big step indeed. Most expanded their operations to include production of women's ready-to-wear. Styling of the ready-to-wear lines originally was the responsibility of the design staff of a couture house; but today more and more name designers are taking a hand in designing ready-to-wear styles bearing their labels. Although

production takes place in small outside workrooms, it must conform in quality to the exacting standards of the couture house.

Some couture ready-to-wear is sold in special shops operated by the couture house in major cities around the world. Large quantities are sold to department and specialty stores, which often set aside special departments or areas for displaying and selling couture-designed ready-to-wear and accessories.

Ready-to-wear operations have become major moneymakers for some couture designers. For instance, in 1973 St. Laurent's couture operation was said to have grossed about $1.5 million. That same year, St. Laurent Rive Gauche, the firm in which St. Laurent is a partner and which produces under the Rive Gauche label all the apparel and accessories carried in the more than 80 worldwide Rive Gauche boutiques, was said to have grossed more than $8 billion. In addition, St. Laurent is said to have realized some $600,000 in gross sales of his ready-to-wear lines produced in the United States under licensing arrangements.

Couture Licensing Agreements By the mid-1970s, a number of couture designers were not only selling their own accessories and ready-to-wear lines but also licensing the use of their names on a wide variety of other products made by other producers. These products ranged from apparel and accessories through bed, bath, and table linens to home furnishings, fabrics, and more.

A licensing agreement is a contract whereby the licensor usually agrees to pay the licensee a royalty (which is most often a percentage of the wholesale price of the goods sold) for the use of the licensee's name. The latter may or may not actually provide designs for the product and is not in any way involved in its production.

In 1957, the year Christian Dior died, his annual couture sales amounted to just over $8 million. In the mid-1970s, the House of Dior was reported to be grossing $85 million to $90 million a year, most of which came from some 180 worldwide licensing agreements.

Jean-Claude Givenchy, brother of Hubert and business manager of the couture house, was quoted as saying, "That we continue in couture is often a condition of the licensee contracts that we sign—and through these licenses, the couture can pay for itself." [1]

French Ready-to-wear

The ready-to-wear operations of Paris couture houses represent only a very small part of the burgeoning French ready-to-wear industry, or *prêt-à-porter* industry. In the mid-1970s, France was exporting somewhat over a quarter of its apparel output and was trying hard to increase the figure. At that time, the largest market for French apparel exports was other European countries, but the second largest market was the United States. Our imports of French apparel were growing slightly, but they still represented only a small fraction of our total apparel imports.

Designers Despite this fact, Paris ready-to-wear showings have become increasingly important to American fashion merchants as a source of fashion inspiration. New, young Paris designers, such as Karl Langerfeld, Emmanuelle Khanh, Sonia Rykiel, Kenzo Takada, and Issey Miyake, are making increasingly big fashion news with their trend-setting styles. French ready-to-wear firms such as Cacharel, Mic Mac, Dorothy Bis, and Chloe have become important resources for American fashion retailers.

Trade Shows By far the most important French trade show is the semiannual Salon du Prêt-à-Porter Feminin held in the Porte de Versailles, Paris. This trade fair brings together more than 900 exhibitors, not only from France but from all over the world. Fall–winter merchandise is shown in late March or early April; spring–summer merchandise is shown in October.

The Prêt-à-Porter is actually two shows in one: An international section features medium- to better-priced merchandise from producers throughout the world; and a boutique section brings together the latest boutique styles, boutique accessories, and ready-to-wear collections of well-known French couture houses.

The new strength and importance of the French ready-to-wear industry became obvious at the October 1974 prêt-à-porter showing. Although the fall–winter couture collections had been reasonably well attended in late July, many fashion merchants perferred to wait for the October prêt-à-porter showing of summer lines. That show brought 30,000 trade buyers, as well as the fashion press, to Paris. Producers were not only showing their lines on three floors of the Porte de Versailles and in their own Paris salons, but also in hotel rooms and even in theaters. Crowds of retail buyers jammed into the showings held by the better-known designers. One couture house issued 700 invitations to view its ready-to-wear line and had 2,000 people trying to get in. For the first time, the United States apparel industry was represented at the prêt-à-porter showings, by 27 firms whose participation was subsidized to a small extent by the United States Department of Commerce.

Export Efforts In an effort to promote the export of more ready-to-wear for both men and women, French apparel manufacturers, in the early 1970s, formed a trade association called the Federation Francaise des Industries de l'Habilement, roughly the equivalent of the American Apparel Manufacturers Association. In order to carry on its work, this association maintains offices in major countries throughout the world. These offices play a major role in helping member firms find agents for their products, assist in planning retail store promotions featuring French apparel products, and carry on a number of other related activities.

ITALY

Italy has long been a famous fashion market center, considered by many as second only to Paris in fashion importance for women's apparel. Italy's particular fashion strength is in its sportswear, knitwear, and fashion accessories, particularly handbags

Buyers from around the world flock
to the famous Prêt-à-Porter showings in Paris.

and shoes. It is also building a reputation for interesting ideas and styling in both men's apparel and accessories.

Italian Couture

Like France, Italy has long had couture houses named for the famous designers who head them, such as Galitzine, Valentino, Heinz Riva, Tiziani, Fabiani, and Andre Laug. These houses are all members of Italy's couture trade association, known as the Alta Moda Italiano. Unlike France's couture houses, however, Italy's are not all located in a single city. Many are in Rome, but others are in Milan, and a few are in other Italian cities.

Couture Showings Members of the Alta Moda show their high-fashion collections semiannually in Rome to private customers, visiting retailers and manufacturers, and the press. The showings are timed to take place just before the Paris couture-collection showings, so that foreign visitors can cover both important fashion markets in a single European trip. Italian couture houses not participating in the Rome showings usually arrange to show their collections either in their own salons or in some other location during the same period, for the convenience of foreign visitors.

As in Paris, foreign buyers and manufacturers are required to pay a caution to attend the Rome couture showings. Private customers and the press are admitted free, although cards of admission are required for the latter. In 1974, cautions ranged from $750 at Andre Laug, plus an agreement for European visitors to purchase two paper patterns or United States visitors to purchase one model, to a flat $4,000 a visitor at Valentino.

Other Couture Business Activities Many Italian couture houses, like their Paris counterparts, have set up boutiques to sell exclusive accessories as well as limited lines of apparel. The designs are usually done by the couture house staff, and the apparel and accessories are sometimes made in the couture workrooms. All items offered in the boutique bear the couture house label.

In addition, many Italian couture houses now have high-fashion ready-to-wear lines that they sell either in their own shops or to retail distributors throughout Europe, in the United States, and to an increasing extent in Japan. For example, in the mid-1970s, Valentino's ready-to-wear was being sold in more than 20 stores in the United States, and contracts had been signed for its distribution in Japan.

To an increasing extent, Italian couture designers also have licensing agreements with foreign producers. Some design and produce uniforms for employees of business firms, such as airlines. Some accept commissions to create designs for a wide range of fashion products, from menswear to home furnishings.

Italian Ready-to-wear

Italy began to develop both its women's and its men's ready-to-wear industries, separate from that of the couture, earlier than France did. As a result, it started exporting earlier, and today its economy relies heavily on its exporting program. In 1973, Italy shipped well over $100 million in apparel alone, at wholesale prices, to the United States.

Designers Innovative Italian ready-to-wear designers make their shows as exciting as the Paris ready-to-wear shows have become. Among the better-known Italian designers who may work for one or more ready-to-wear firms are Walter Albini, Gianni Versace, and Muriel Grateau. Among widely known designers who head their own firms are Emilio Pucci, Giovanna Ferragamo, and Rosita and Tai Missoni. Among well-known Italian ready-to-wear firms are Basile, Callaghan, Ken Scott, Cadette, Mirsa, Tiktiner, and Fendi.

Trade Shows and Market Centers Preparing a calendar of Italian showings of women's ready-to-wear was a fairly simple matter until the late 1960s. As interest in ready-to-wear grew, and Paris initiated its semiannual prêt-à-porter showings, Italian ready-to-wear producers followed suit. Since many of these were located in Florence—a city that already had an established reputation as a fashion center—regular, semiannual showings of both ready-to-wear and accessories began to be held in both the Pitti and Strossi palaces in Florence the week before the prêt-à-porter showings in Paris, for the convenience of foreign visitors.

In the early 1970s, however, a group of Milan-based firms began holding semiannual shows of their own, just before the Florence showings. The Milan shows have become regular events and are growing in fashion importance because of the increasing number of important firms who have decided to exhibit in Milan rather than Florence. Some firms exhibit in both.

Both the Florence and the Milan shows include, along with the exhibits and showings of regular ready-to-wear lines, some ready-to-wear collections of Italian couture houses, the latter being known as the Alta Moda Pronto.

Men's ready-to-wear shows are held in Florence in February and in September. These shows are increasing in importance because of the growing number of talented designers producing menswear apparel and furnishings.

Accessories

Italy is known for a variety of accessories, particularly those made of leather, such as handbags, shoes, and small leather goods. Leather products are a major export category of Italy. In 1973, it exported over $350 million in shoes alone to the United States. Each year a number of Italian accessories fairs are held. A few are mentioned below.

Couture Goods At the same time the Alta Moda couture collections are shown in Rome, a special accessories fair is held at the Grand Hotel in the same city, featuring handbags, gloves, belts, umbrellas, and hats to be worn with couture apparel.

Trade Goods There are always a cluster of accessory exhibits at every major ready-to-wear trade fair. In addition, certain of the accessories industries have their own fairs.

"Mipel" is the name of the trade show for Italian-produced handbags and accessories, such as luggage, belts, umbrellas, hats, scarfs. This im-

MILAN
26th MIPEL
ITALIAN LEATHERGOODS EXHIBITION

from 10th to 14th January 1975
at the Pavilion 30 (Piazza 6 Febbraio)
in the Milan Fair grounds

Sole and complete panorama of the Italian leathergoods production, in which all the Italian manufacturers meet twice a year with buyers from all over the world.

At the MIPEL are displayed: leather items for gifts, office articles, suit-cases, travelling bags, hand bags, belts, umbrellas, small leather items, wallets, sundries.

The only specialized market-show reserved exclusively for buyers.

There will be displayed the novelty samples for Spring/Summer 1975.

Apply in time for buyers' cards to:

SEGRETERIA GENERALE DEL MIPEL

**14 Via G. Leopardi -1-20123 MILANO (Italy)
Tel. 872 120 — 872 182 — 898 372**

Typical of trade show advertising that appears in Women's Wear Daily.

portant show is held in Milan twice each year, in January and in June. Because the timing of the Mipel show is too late for American buyers to place orders and be sure of receiving delivery by the start of the coming season, an earlier show, called "Europel," was instituted in 1974. This show concentrates on handbags and features exhibitors from all over Europe instead of only Italian producers. Although originally sponsored by the Italian handbag industry, "Europel" held its first show in Paris in November 1974; the second was held in Dusseldorf in April 1975.

The shoe fair held in Bologna in March is considered a very important trade show for foreign visitors because of the importance of Italy's shoe industry and shoe exports. The glove industry, centered around Naples, is represented in several fairs, as is ladies' neckwear, another interesting Italian export, whose producers are mainly in the Como and Milan areas.

GREAT BRITAIN

For many years, London was for menswear what Paris has been for women's apparel: the fountainhead of fashion inspiration. Although in recent years its dominance has diminished, London still remains the major fashion center for impeccably tailored custom apparel for men.

As a whole, however, British fashion strength lies in tweeds, woolens, and knitwear for both men and women. The materials for these garments come not only from the mills of the Midlands of England but also from Scotland and Northern Ireland. Britain is also a growing market center for leather apparel for both women and men.

London Couture

The fashion market center of Great Britain has always been London. Until very recent years, a small but important British haute couture group known as the Incorporated Society of Fashion Designers had headquarters in London. This group,

modeled after the Chambre Syndicale de la Couture Parisienne, showed semiannual collections by its members to private customers, foreign buyers, and the press just before or just after each of the Paris showings for the convenience of foreign visitors. For some years, two members of this group, Norman Hartnell and Hardy Amies, have had the distinction of being designated "Dressmakers to the Queen." Upon request, they take selections from their haute couture collections to the Queen and the royal family, who select models they may wish made up to their individual measurements.

Because British women's apparel styling had always been considered less trend-setting than that of France or Italy, London showings of haute couture collections attracted far fewer foreign visitors than did the Paris and Italian collections. As a result, in the early 1970s the Incorporated Society of Fashion Designers ceased to exist as a formal trade association. Several former members, however, continue to show their collections in their London showrooms for the convenience of foreign visitors to the French and Italian collections.

Like their Continental counterparts, most British haute couture designers are now producing high-fashion ready-to-wear lines. Some have entered into licensing agreements with foreign producers. Some design and produce uniforms for employees of business firms. One, Hardy Amies, has emerged in recent years as a trend-setting designer of menswear.

British Ready-to-wear

As England was long a nation in which people relied heavily on made-to-measure apparel, its ready-to-wear industry was of minor fashion importance both at home and abroad until after World War II. The British government is given credit for having played an active role in its growth. In fact, the British government has for many years been engaged in nurturing its apparel industries. According to one of England's best-known fashion authorities, Britain's Board of Trade has been "the fairy godmother to whom is due the survival of their couture and the rapid development of their large and excellent ready-to-wear trade."[2]

Women's Apparel Like its American and Continental counterparts, British ready-to-wear for women is divided into three categories: high fashion (usually high-priced), moderate-priced, and mass-produced (popular-priced). High-fashion ready-to-wear is usually the product of couture houses in Britain, but it rarely has been considered trend-setting. British moderate- and popular-priced ready-to-wear was considered of little fashion importance until the 1960s.

Early in the 1960s, however, a London designer named Mary Quant recognized an emerging youth trend and began designing clothes for the young. Other London designers quickly followed her lead, and almost overnight London became the world's fashion market center for junior apparel.

However, when the British ready-to-wear industry failed to follow the fashion trend in the early 1970s toward longer, softer, more romantic styles, London began to lose fashion importance again. But with the backing of the British government, and led by three London designers—Jean Muir, Zandra Rhodes, and Ossie Clark, who had sprung to prominence during the 1960s—a new group of young designers began to exert renewed impact on the London fashion scene.

London is the center of Britain's women's ready-to-wear industry, and the major manufacturers' trade associations have headquarters there. Most permanent showrooms of ready-to-wear producers are located there, although there also are showrooms in the Midlands and in Scotland. The major ready-to-wear shows take place in London. The International Fashion Fair, sponsored by the Clothing Export Council of Great Britain, is held each April and October; in the mid-1970s it featured lines from 150 to 200 British, Canadian, and Continental firms.

Menswear Both London and Harrogate are important market centers for menswear. The major trade associations are located in London. So are many of the permanent showrooms of menswear producers, although others are located elsewhere in England and in Scotland. One important trade show, the International Men's and Boys' Wear Exhibition, which had some 200 British and Continental firms exhibiting in the mid-1970s, is held in London in February. However, a bigger menswear show, the Menswear Association Convention and Exhibition, is held in Harrogate in September. At this show, around 300 exhibitors (90 percent British and 10 percent from the Continent, Australia, Japan, and Yugoslavia) showed their lines in the mid-1970s.

British Accessories

Most British accessories industries have their headquarters and permanent showrooms in London, and most accessories trade fairs are held there. The Leather Expo is usually timed for June; the London International Footwear Fair is held in September; there is a British Glove Fair in London in February; and a Millinery Guild Show in London in May and November. These are relatively small shows, however.

Although Britain does have some interesting accessories, particularly in leather products, they do not dominate the country's fashion goods offerings as they do in Italy.

SPAIN

Even though Spain's apparel offerings are, at present, only of limited interest to American retail buyers, Spain is one of the few countries that still maintains a haute couture group.

The couture group is known as the Alta Costura and maintains headquarters in Madrid. Member firms show their collections, either in Madrid's Palacio Nasional or in their own Madrid salons, in late July and in January. These showings are timed to precede those of Paris, so that foreign buyers will be encouraged to put Madrid on their travel itineraries. The best known of its fewer than 20 designers are Pertegaz, Elio Bernhanyer, Carmen Mir, Herrera y Ollero, and Pedro Rovira.

Spain's women's and children's ready-to-wear association is the Camara de la Moda Espanola, with headquarters in Madrid. Its member firms, however, are located in major cities throughout the country. Besides holding regular showings to the trade in Madrid in March and October, several members of this association show at fashion fairs throughout Europe.

Spain is an important fashion market for moderate-priced knitwear and leather products, particularly the latter. At times in recent years the United States has bought almost three-quarters of all shoes exported by Spain. There is increasing production of fur, leather, and suede garments in Spain. In accessories, gloves, handbags, travel items, and small leathergoods are of special interest to foreign buyers.

An important shoe fair is held in Alicante each year, and there is an annual handbag fair in Barcelona. "Iberpiel," the Spanish Festival of Fashion in Leather, is an annual trade fair held in Madrid each January.

SCANDINAVIA

The four countries that make up Scandinavia are closely grouped geographically but quite different in character. Sweden and Finland are the most closely allied, not only historically but also through joint business ventures. Denmark, generally regarded as the link between Scandinavia and the rest of the world, is in many ways more internationally oriented than the other Scandinavian countries.

While each country has its own fashion industries and specialties among fashion products, the four countries do form a single identifiable market center. This is partly because they tend to have the same basic materials with which to work: leather, fur, some wool, an increasing amount of textiles made of man-made fibers, some gold and silver. However, the main reason is that the four countries, while they do make individual marketing efforts,

hold major trade fairs and have a concentration of permanent showrooms in one central location: Copenhagen. Copenhagen is the dominant center of the Scandinavian fashion world.

Fashion Products

Conservative high-style wool apparel, including coats, dresses, and suits, has long been the specialty of the Danish apparel industry. Prices tend to be high, too.

Moderate-priced apparel is particularly strong among the Swedish, Finnish, and Norwegian offerings. Some is cotton knit, but man-made fibers and cotton blends are more common. Styling is often youthful; one Swedish sportswear producer is among those who claim to have introduced the string bikini to the United States in the fall of 1973.

Leather apparel, mainly menswear, is a popular Swedish product. Both Sweden and Norway are among the important suppliers of mink and other furs to countries around the world.

Scandinavia offers some interesting textile designs. Both American producers and American retail buyers, interested in finding unusual fabrics to have made up for special promotions, watch the Scandinavian textile offerings very closely.

Excellent jewelry in all price ranges is available in Scandinavia. The area has long been known for its clean-cut designs in gold and silver. Today, an increasing amount of costume jewelry and "fun jewelry" is being produced there, particularly in Sweden.

Trade Shows and Showrooms

Each Scandinavian country holds its own national fairs in the city that is considered the trade center of that country. For instance, Boras is the center of the Swedish textile and apparel industry; it has some permanent showrooms, and regular exhibitions of Swedish textiles and apparel are held there.

In addition, the Scandinavian countries encourage exports by taking their goods to show in other countries. For instance, Sweden and Finland cooperate in an annual Scandinavian fashion show in New York as well as in Canada.

However, the major market center for the whole of Scandinavia is Copenhagen. In Copenhagen is located the "Bella Centret," where the international Scandinavian trade fairs are held. In Copenhagen is the Scandinavian Fashion Center, where the major fashion producers from all the Scandinavian countries have their permanent showrooms. Copenhagen is also the city where producers of such accessories as jewelry and handbags have their permanent showrooms and hold their trade fairs.

The apparel fairs are organized by the Scandinavian Clothing Council, headquartered in Copenhagen and made up of representatives from the national clothing associations of each Scandinavian country. The important women's apparel fair, called the Scandinavian Fashion Week, is held semiannually, usually in March and in September. The menswear fair, called the Scandinavian Menswear Fair, is also held twice a year, usually in February and in September. Both draw exhibitors not only from all the Scandinavian countries but from a number of other countries as well.

OTHER EUROPEAN COUNTRIES

Hardly a country in Europe does not produce some type of fashion goods of interest to foreign buyers. Many goods, however, are produced by firms in widely separated geographic areas that a foreign buyer, on a short business trip, does not have time to visit. Other goods are produced in countries that are still in the development stage of their fashion importance; therefore, fashion buyers do not spend the time and money to explore their potential. For these reasons, European trade fairs have become important sources of fashion inspiration and merchandise, not only for American fashion retailers seeking goods to offer their customers, but also for American fashion producers searching for new resources for materials and contract production facilities.

Western Europe

There has always been considerable trade between the United States and Western Europe. However, until recently, American buyers looked only to France, Italy, and Spain for fashion inspiration and merchandise. Now other European countries, including Germany, Portugal, and Austria, are increasing in importance as fashion market centers.

West Germany   The Federal Republic of Germany is better known to American producers than American retail buyers. The huge Interstoff textiles fair held in Frankfurt each May and November is an important place to find new fabrics and new fashion ideas. Frankfurt is also one of the four big fur auction centers of the world, and its Fur Fair is held in April.

Germany is just beginning to increase its apparel exports beyond Europe. The center of its women's ready-to-wear industry is Düsseldorf, where four fairs a year are held, each with 900 to 1,200 exhibitors and attracting up to 30,000 retail buyers. There is also a newly established Fashion Fair in Munich each March, and an Overseas Export Fair in Berlin each September. The center of the menswear industry is Cologne, where major menswear fairs are held in February and August. There are numerous accessories fairs; the most important is probably the Leathergoods Fair held in Offenbach in February and August.

Austria   Austria has some interesting offerings in junior fashions and in accessories. Salzburg is the city where most apparel and accessories producers have permanent showrooms. It is also the city in which the trade fairs are held: the Leathergoods Fair in December, the Junior Fashions Fair in February, and the Jewelry Fair (fine and costume) in May.

Portugal   American retailers buy some Portuguese products, most of which are lower-priced knitted goods, such as women's knitted ready-to-wear and men's knitted sportswear. That country's knitwear industry is located mainly in the Oporto area.

Eastern Europe

As trade quotas and trade restrictions ease, more and more American producers and retail buyers are investigating market centers in Eastern Europe. One place to begin is at the big international trade fairs held by each country in its major industrial city on either an annual or semiannual basis.

Poland   Poland is already exporting to much of Western Europe and a small number of other countries of the West. The Polish government showed its interest in developing exports to this country by sponsoring a show of Polish-made apparel in New York in 1974—the first government-sponsored export show ever held here by an Eastern Europe country. Featured in this showing were budget-priced car coats, fake furs, leather jackets, corduroy pants and suits for men, and denim dresses for women. Poland may also be developing as an area where American producers can have contract work done. The international fair held in Poznam each year is an excellent showcase for Polish products.

Yugoslavia   Yugoslavia has also begun to actively promote its fashion products for export. In 1974, that country held the first of what is hoped will become an annual International Fashion Fair, to be held each August in Tragir. Both Yugoslavian and other Eastern and Western European producers had lines on display at the first Tragir fair. The Yugoslavian offerings were unique in that the styles chosen were selected by the votes of customers of the top department store in each of the 20 largest cities in Yugoslavia. Response to the show indicated that Yugoslavia has at least one designer of major foreign interest: Richard Gumzej, who showed higher-priced ready-to-wear with interesting folk-art touches.

ISRAEL

In terms of the overall dollar value of United States imports of apparel and accessories, Israeli products are not vital to our country's fashion merchants. In terms of Israeli exports, however, the United States is very important to Israel, and Israeli producers are eager to turn out products that appeal to American buyers.

Leathergoods, including handbags, belts, and suede jackets, are a category of fashion merchandise that American buyers find interesting. In addition, Israel is becoming a good source of lower- to moderate-priced knitwear and swimwear, in both cotton and cotton and man-made fiber blends.

Through the government-sponsored Israel Company for Fair and Exhibitions, Israeli producers have been promoting their lines aggressively in other countries as well as in the United States. In 1974, for instance, there were Israeli producers represented at the Paris Prêt-à-Porter, at the Frankfurt Interstoff, at the Milan Camis, at the Munich Fashion Week, as well as Israeli Fashion Week shows held in London and New York.

There are still some contracting facilities available in Israel, but not as many as there once were. Some firms are moving out of contract work and into the production of their own higher-styled, higher-priced lines. In general, Israeli fashion goods are on their way up in both styling and price.

LATIN AMERICA

Although French and Italian have been the traditional foreign languages of fashion, by the mid-1970s, Spanish and Portuguese, spoken in Latin American accents, were being added to the list. Fashion merchants began visiting such market centers as Rio de Janeiro, Buenos Aires, São Paulo, and Bogota just as routinely, if not as often, as they visited Paris and Rome.

Two factors encouraged fashion merchants in the United States to pay attention to Latin America, which includes Central America, South America, and the Caribbean. One was inflation. The other was the level of achievement reached by the developing nations of Latin America.

Inflation in the 1970s cut sharply into the American fashion merchant's traditional sources of textiles, apparel, and accessories. Because of in-

Signatures of some Israeli designers.
Israeli Trade Center

flation, Japan was temporarily priced out of its textile and textile products export business. American producers and retailers had to look elsewhere for goods at more reasonable prices.

Many countries of Latin America have reached a level of development where they can offer foreign buyers the goods they want at attractive prices. These countries have important raw materials, such as cotton, wool, leather, and the ingredients of man-made textiles. They have built networks of industries that are eager for export opportunities so that they can expand. These industries are being encouraged by their governments, because additional exports mean both an increase in gross national product and an increase in international trade status. These industries also have a good labor supply. Because the standard of living in these countries is not as high as elsewhere, the cost of labor is not as high.

As a result, Latin America has emerged in recent years as a market center for three different kinds of fashion goods. First, its most advanced countries already have industries producing a variety of internationally styled fashion goods. Second, many countries in this geographic area offer increasingly greater quantities of unusual fashion goods that reflect each country's national heritage in arts and crafts. Third, the countries' production facilities and labor can turn out a variety of fashion goods to the specifications of American producers and retailers at attractive prices.

Fashion Products

Important industries producing both women's and men's apparel already exist in Argentina, Brazil, Columbia, and Bolivia. Argentina is probably the largest South American producer of apparel in both the moderate and upper price ranges, with wool a very important fabric. Brazil is particularly strong in sportswear. Colombia is an important market center for menswear and, together with the Dominican Republic and most of the Central American countries, produces popular-priced lines of men's sports shirts, particularly of the shirt-jac variety. Bolivia has a somewhat smaller apparel industry than the other three major countries of South America, but it offers some unusual styles of excellent quality.

Handbag buyers are likely to go to Argentina for better-quality goods, to Brazil for moderate-quality goods, and to Colombia for inexpensive goods. Uruguay is another source of handbags, producing moderate- to high-quality goods.

Perhaps the single most important market center for shoes in Latin America is Brazil. Brazilian shoe manufacturers concentrate on producing well-styled merchandise in lasts that fit North American feet. For belts and small leathergoods, some of the major market centers are in Brazil, Argentina and the Dominican Republic.

Jewelry buyers find tortoise shell jewelry in Jamaica and both tortoise shell and amber jewelry in the Dominican Republic. For costume jewelry, the major market center is Brazil. A number of Latin American countries produce silver and gold jewelry of native design, with Ecuador and Peru having some of the most interesting offerings.

Fashion Production

For those producers or retailers who are interested in having contract work done in Latin America, there are many possibilities. Considerable contract work is already being done in Mexico, San Salvadore, Costa Rica, and Honduras. The Dominican Republic has five free zones, and contract work for United States fashion merchants is being done in each one of them. There is also a free zone in Colombia, and one Japanese firm has a plant employing 600 workers there.

Most of the countries mentioned above have facilities that specialize in high-volume, moderate-quality, and low-price goods. However, there are also opportunities for those who want to have top-quality work done. Ecuador, for instance, can only handle a small amount of contract work, but it specializes in producing top-quality goods.

Trade Shows

Probably the single most important market center in South America is São Paulo, Brazil. An international textile and textile products fair is held there every January and June, with exhibitors not only from Latin America but from other areas of the world as well. This trade show draws some 60,000 buyers from around the world.

Other important international fairs featuring textiles and textile products as well as fashion accessories are held in Bogota, in Lima, and in San Salvadore. All three are annual fairs.

THE FAR EAST

The United States imports more apparel from the Far East than from any other area of the world. However, nearly all the imports are products whose manufacture has been contracted for by American producers or retailers and which have been made to individual marketers' specifications. In general, the entire area is a source of low-price, moderate-quality, high-volume production. High-quality work at moderate prices is also available in some localities.

During the 1960s and into the 1970s, American buyers came to depend on this area as a source of low-cost production. When buyers found an interesting blouse or sport jacket in another retailer's stock, they could have a similar "development sample" made up and sent to a contract factory in the Far East for copying at low cost. Although contract prices have increased in some parts of the Far East, much of that type of work done for American producers and retailers is still handled there.

A retail buyer needs to know which areas in the Far East are best equipped to handle specific types of contract work. For instance, Japan was once one of this country's biggest contract-work markets. While prices have gone up in that country, it is still considered an important center for the manufacture of cut-and-sewn goods. To get knitted goods of low to medium price, producers and retailers go mainly to Taiwan and Korea. Other important areas in which considerable contract work is done include Hong Kong (which is now turning out goods of increasingly better quality), the Philippines, Indonesia, and Singapore. An important textile fair is held in Tokyo each year. In addition, GarmenTaipei, held in Taipei in the Republic of China each October, is an interesting showcase of what is being produced in the Far East.

In the future, the People's Republic of China may become one of the most interesting market centers of the Far East. As yet, only token buying is being done in China by American retailers. However, many retailers expect Chinese–United States trade to increase. In 1974, a department store executive was quoted as saying, "If China opens up for trade, cotton, silks, and such will come down in price. The manufacturer will get a break, I'll get a break, and the customers will get a break—and we all could use it."[3]

That break may well come in the second half of the 1970s. The People's Republic of China holds a very important semiannual trade fair in Kwangchow (formerly Canton), but admission is by invitation only and only a few hundred foreign firms are invited. However, in 1975, the Chinese Trading Corporation, which is government sponsored, brought a "mini-Kwangchow Fair" to the United States and spent two years touring 32 major cities of the country. United States trade with the People's Republic of China almost doubled between 1973 and 1974 and is likely to keep increasing.

REFERENCES
[1] *Women's Wear Daily*, September 17, 1973, p. 8.
[2] Garland, *Fashion*, p. 73.
[3] *Business Week*, September 21, 1974, pp. 102–109.

MERCHANDISING VOCABULARY

Couture house	Caution
Haute couture	Prêt-à-porter
Couturier, couturiere	

MERCHANDISING REVIEW

1. What are the three different methods that American retail stores may employ when shopping foreign markets?

2. Distinguish between a store's own foreign buying division and a commissionaire organization.

3. Name and describe the four different types of customers who attend the showings of couture designers.

4. Indicate four reasons why the sales volume of European couture houses has declined in recent years.

5. How have most Paris couture houses attempted to meet the growing challenge and competition of a rapidly developing ready-to-wear industry? To what extent have each of these business efforts been successful?

6. For what fashion products is Italy best known?

7. Discuss the developments of the British ready-to-wear industry. What designer is credited with making London the world's fashion market center for junior apparel?

8. For what fashion products is Spain best known?

9. What countries make up what is commonly referred to as Scandinavia? What city is the major market center of that geographic area? For what fashion products is it best known?

10. What countries are included in the geographic area referred to as Latin America? Name and discuss several reasons why Latin America has become an important fashion market center in recent years.

MERCHANDISING DIGEST

1. It is stated in the text that "The reputation of Paris as a prime source of fashion inspiration began to develop several centuries ago as the result of many interrelating factors." Identify those factors and discuss their importance in the development of any major fashion design center.

2. What major countries are usually included in the term Far East? Discuss the importance of that geographic area to producers and retailers of fashion goods.

11
RETAIL DISTRIBUTORS OF FASHION

The crucial moment in the fashion business comes when consumers inspect the assortments of merchandise offered by retail distributors. Success in the fashion business is achieved only when those consumers decide to make a purchase. Unless that decision is made, all the creative and productive efforts it took to put that merchandise in front of consumers were useless. Unless consumers buy, fashion design and production are merely exercises in futility.

The various techniques employed in the retail distribution of fashion merchandise are determined by the interests and lifestyles of the target customers of each retail firm. Changes in distribution patterns follow closely in the wake of changes in customer demand. This is why some fine department and specialty stores that once concentrated on offering high-priced merchandise to an elite group of consumers now have expanded their fashion assortments to include moderate price lines and erected branch stores in middle-class suburbs. Chains that once catered solely to customers with limited incomes are now upgrading both their fashion assortments and their upper price limits.

Adhering rigidly to time-honored ways of doing business in today's highly competitive economy spells doom for retail distributors of fashion apparel. Flexibility is the key to their success and growth. As the customer changes, so must retailers' methods of serving that customer change if they wish to stay in business.

HISTORY AND DEVELOPMENT OF FASHION RETAILING

The term *retailing* refers to the business of buying goods from a variety of resources and assembling those goods in convenient locations to resell them to ultimate consumers. Therefore, it logically follows that *fashion retailing* refers to the business of buying fashion-oriented merchandise from a variety of resources and assembling it in convenient locations for resale to ultimate consumers.

The term *merchandising* refers to the planning required to have the right merchandise at the right time, in the right place, in the right quantities, and at the right prices (that is, prices which the firm's customers are both willing and able to pay). It logically follows, therefore, that *fashion merchandising* refers to the planning required to have the right fashion-oriented merchandise at the right time, in the right place, in the right quantities, and at the right prices. Thus the merchandising function is the most important function in all retail organizations because, in almost all cases, it is the sole source of a store's revenue.

In this chapter, we will explore how various forms of retailing have developed and the means by which modern retail organizations seek customer patronage.

Early Retailing

Retailing began in the outdoor bazaars of the Orient and the marketplaces of the Mediterranean, where people came together to buy, sell, and barter goods of all kinds. The modern version of such bazaars and marketplaces is the shopping center.

Some early tradespeople were masters at their crafts, such as weavers, potters, and goldsmiths, who produced the goods they offered for sale to customers. Each of them was usually responsible for the training of a number of apprentices. They lived, worked, and maintained shops in their homes, which usually were located on a street or in an area crowded with other people who produced similar goods. Customers seeking a particular type of product would shop for it on that street or in that area. The modern descendant of those craft shops is considered to be the specialty store, whose staff is expected to be able to offer the same expert knowledge about specific types of merchandise that shoppers expected of those early masters and their apprentices.

Other early retailers bought, rather than made, goods for resale purposes, obtaining their stock from traders who brought the merchandise from distant countries by ship or caravan. Each offered, in one location, many different types of merchandise. The modern descendants of those early shops are considered to be department and variety stores.

Other early retailers deliberately sought out their clientele. These were peddlers, who purchased limited assortments of goods from a variety of tradespeople, carried the goods on their backs or on pack animals or in wagons, and called on customers who lived in sparsely settled areas far removed from the urban shops and facilities of that day in an effort to resell those goods. The modern version of the early peddler is the house-to-house salesperson.

Development of Retailing in the United States

Among the first explorers of North America were traders who set up trading posts to collect furs, bartering food, liquor, and jewelry with trappers and Indians for the prime pelts which they sold in European markets. Many of these early trading posts later developed into some of the larger cities on the continent, such as New York, Chicago, Detroit, and St. Louis.

Towns that soon developed along the eastern coast of North America had shops and stores much like those of European towns, but along the frontier and in sparsely settled farming areas, different forms of retailing developed. The *general store,* which carried a wide variety of consumer goods and took goods as well as cash in payment, became an important retail distribution center in those early days. Peddlers also played an important role, going from town to town and from farm to farm with their limited assortments of otherwise unavailable merchandise. Later, mail service became more reliable, and a third method of rural retail distribution developed: mail-order selling.

General Stores Many of the earliest general stores in America developed from fur trading posts. In the beginning, their stocks consisted solely of utilitarian items; fashion merchandise was not carried. As more farmers and ranchers settled along the frontier, however, the women in those pioneer families became eager customers for rudimentary fashion goods, and stores added basic sewing notions and bolts of fabric to the assortment they carried. Since money was a scarce commodity on the frontier, bartering remained the main way of doing business in general stores.

As the frontier pushed westward, and as larger communities and the beginnings of prosperity followed, there were more fashion consumers of relative wealth to be served, and the stores increased their stocks of fashion merchandise. Some of the wealthier sent away to stores on the East coast for their fashion purchases; others patronized local specialty shops that had sprung up as the frontier towns grew in size. In the rural areas, the country general store continued to thrive until the 1920s, when easier and faster transportation and communication brought more sophisticated resources for fashion goods within the reach of rural customers.

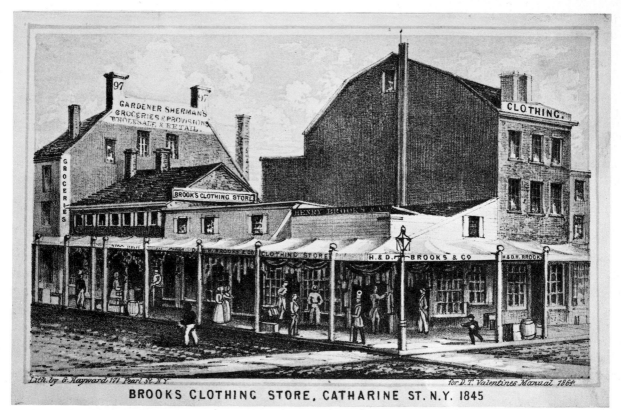

BROOKS CLOTHING STORE, CATHARINE ST. N.Y. 1845

An early store of Brooks Bros., today one of the country's best-known men's specialty stores.

Brooks Bros.

As the population expanded, many of the barter-type general stores switched to a cash-only basis, thus becoming strictly retailers of merchandise, rather than bankers and dealers in farm crops. Some of today's largest general merchandise and department store regional chains grew from just such "cash store" beginnings. R. H. Macy & Co. is an example.

Peddlers The peddlers who went from house to house along the country roads of America were often from the Northeast, and their packs held an assortment of such tools and materials of fashion as needles, pins, threads, combs, and ribbons and laces. In addition to supplying the utilitarian needs of the rural housewife, peddlers also served as a source of fashion information for consumers and as

a source of customer preference information for producers. But the peddlers' route invariably was a long and slow one, and sometimes it was a whole year before they returned to market centers to replenish their wares and report back to producers what they had gleaned from customers.

Door-to-door is still an effective way to sell some fashion products, particularly if the salesperson is a woman trained to offer fashion advice. Foundation garments and silk stockings once were sold rather extensively door-to-door. Today, however, cosmetics dominate the field, so far as fashion products are concerned.

Some of the largest retail organizations in this country were founded by early peddlers who, tired of traveling, decided to settle down and open retail stores. An outstanding example was Adam Gimbel, who set down his peddler's pack and opened a retail store in Vincennes, Indiana, in 1842. His descendants opened additional stores, established the Gimbel Brothers, Inc., department store organization, acquired the Saks 34th Street specialty store in 1923, and established, in 1924, the Saks Fifth Avenue specialty store which, in the following 50 years, became a national chain, a wholly owned subsidiary of Gimbel Brothers, Inc. Although ownership of the original Gimbel corporation passed out of the hands of the Gimbel family in 1973, the retail firm that Adam Gimbel formed in 1824 has today expanded into 37 Gimbel's department stores and 32 Saks Fifth Avenue specialty stores.

Mail-order Sellers As mail service became faster and more reliable in the latter part of the nineteenth century, a new form of retailing developed for those who had the cash but were not close to urban centers: mail-order selling. Montgomery Ward, founded in 1872, was the first in the field, followed in 1886 by Sears, Roebuck and Company.

Their mail-order catalogs brought descriptions of low-priced apparel and home furnishings into rural homes, permitting people to make their selection at leisure and place and receive orders through the mail.

Early mail-order catalogs had little variety or fashion excitement. Their styles were basic; there was no attempt to anticipate developing fashion trends. Compared to what the country general store had to offer, however, the pages of the mail-order catalog opened up a whole new world of fashion to rural customers at prices they could afford.

With the advent of the automobile, mail-order companies found themselves competing with city stores rather than country general stores for the business of rural customers. As a result, the larger mail-order houses began to open retail stores in the 1920s. In the 1930s, catalog centers were opened, to which customers could come and either write up their own orders or be helped by salespeople in making their selections of merchandise listed in the firm's catalog but not included in the store's stock.

The first Kinney store, established in Waverly, New York, in 1894, grew into today's nationwide chain of shoe stores.
Kinney Shoe Corporation

Today, customers can shop at any of the major mail-order companies in person, by mail, or by telephone.

The Retail Scene Today

Retailers exist to serve customers. As their customers change, so, too, must they change. Successful retailing of fashion, like fashion itself, depends upon customer acceptance. No one has ever been able to force a fashion upon the public or withhold one that the public demanded. And no distributors of fashion, not even the greatest and most prestigious, can survive for long if they do not, in the late Marshall Field's words, "Give the lady what she wants!"

Retailers have developed various forms of organization and methods of operation to give customers what they want. There are retailers who stock many different types of merchandise and retailers who specialize in limited types of merchandise. There are retailers who offer a variety of services and retailers who offer only a few. There are retailers who serve those willing to spend large sums of money casually for their fashions and retailers who concentrate on customers who watch every cent carefully. There are also retailers who own no retail outlets of their own but operate departments in the stores of others.

Today, there are some 110,000 retail organizations of various kinds in the United States that specialize in apparel and accessories. Since some of these are multiunit organizations, the actual number of individual stores selling apparel and accessories is higher. In addition, there are nearly 70,000 general merchandise organizations that include some apparel and accessories among their offerings. There are also many other retail firms specializing in other types of merchandise that also handle limited varieties of fashion merchandise, such as the food and drug stores that sell hosiery, toiletries, and cosmetics.

Some retail establishments that strive to meet the current fashion needs of customers have been on the scene for a long time. Others represent new forms of retailing that developed in the early and middle years of this century in response to customer demand.

ORGANIZATIONAL STRUCTURE OF RETAIL FIRMS

The organizational structure of retail firms does not follow the clean-cut lines of authority, coupled with responsibility, that one often finds in other types of business firms. Therein lies one of the strengths of retail firms. Management recognizes that retailing is a "people business"—a service to a firm's customers. A tightly structured and rigid organizational structure could inhibit the kind of creative awareness retail executives need to understand the changing needs of a store's customers and to respond effectively to them.

Organizational Chart

An *organizational chart* is a visual presentation of the manner in which a firm delegates responsibility and authority within the organization. A retail organization may adopt an organizational structure involving anywhere from two to six major functions or areas of responsibility. Each of these functions is headed by a top-management executive who is responsible to the chief executive of the firm, usually called the general manager, the executive vice president, or the president.

The organizational structure of most medium-size department stores today is based on a four-function plan, as follows:

- Finance and control division, with responsibility for the credit department, accounts payable, and inventory control
- Merchandising division, with responsibility for buying, selling, merchandise planning and control, and usually fashion coordination
- Sales promotion division, with responsibility for all advertising, display, special events, publicity, and public relations
- Operations division, with responsibility for main-

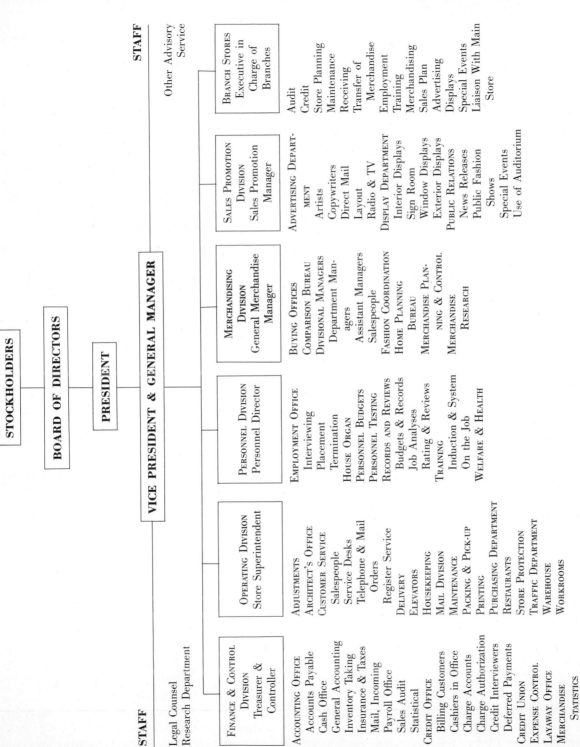

A typical organization chart for a large department store

Courtesy NRMA

tenance of all facilities, store and merchandise protection, customer services, receiving and marking, and personnel

The number of major functions established by a retail firm as a basis for its effective operation depends upon its sales volume, the number of employees it has, and how many store units it operates. The smaller the sales volume and the fewer the employees, the more varied are the responsibilities of each of its employees, including executives. The larger the sales volume and number of employees, the more specialized become the responsibilities of each employee.

In the smallest retail firms, an owner, a part-time bookkeeper, and a salesperson or two may handle all the work necessary to keep the firm operating successfully. In somewhat larger firms, an owner or manager is often responsible for both the sales promotion and merchandising activities, but turns over responsibility for financial and operational activities to one or two others in the firm who have experience in these fields.

Retail firms with larger than medium sales volume, a larger number of employees, and perhaps operating a few branches, usually find it necessary to increase their major functions from four to five. They remove responsibility for personnel from the operations division and elevate it to major functional status under the direction of a personnel executive. When this is done, personnel, as a separate function or division within a retail firm's organizational structure, is responsible for employment, training, employee records, executive recruitment and development, and related activities.

Retail firms with the largest sales volume and number of employees, and usually operating more than six branches, often add a sixth major function to their operating structure: branch store coordination. The executive responsible for this function is the link between parent and branch store executives and sees that the firm's merchandising, personnel, and public relations policies are carried out in the branches.

A chain's organizational structure is much more extensive than that of even the largest branch-operating retail firm because of the more complex nature of its activities. For example, in a branch-operating retail firm, transportation and warehousing activities are usually part of the operations function, while in a chain, these two activities are usually considered a major top-management function under the direct supervision of a top-management executive.

Overlapping authority and responsibility occur frequently in the retailing field. For example, salespeople are trained by personnel executives in ringing up sales, handling delivery requests, and charges; but they are given merchandise and fashion training by their buyer and often by the fashion coordinator.

Where there are several branches, overlapping can become even more complex. In an effort to adapt the merchandise assortments and presentations of each individual branch to the preferences of the community each serves, branch-operating stores can develop relationships within their organizational structure that defy charting. For example, in branch stores department managers are assigned to supervise merchandise assortments and selling activities in one or more merchandise areas. They also are responsible for reporting customer reaction to departmental assortments in their assigned areas to the appropriate parent-store buyers. A department manager's immediate superior in the branch store may be a group manager or the branch store manager, but he or she also works with and receives directions from the parent-store buyer of each department managed.

DEPARTMENT STORES

Department stores get their name from the fact that they seek to present many different kinds of merchandise, each in a separate area or department, under one roof. Department stores serve a broader range of customers than do most other stores.

In addition to acting as purchasing agents for the community, department stores are increasingly interested in finding ways to serve their local communities. If a department store can stage a fashion show for a local charity, or lend space for an art show or club meeting, for instance, it usually will do so gladly. Such community service not only generates goodwill but also, by creating an awareness of the store and its merchandise, increases the flow of fashion information among consumers quite apart from, and in addition to, what the store does specifically to publicize and sell its merchandise.

Definition

A *department store* is defined by the Bureau of the Census as one that employs 25 or more people and sells general lines of merchandise in each of three categories: home furnishings, household linens and dry goods (an old trade term meaning piece goods and sewing notions), and apparel and accessories for the entire family.

Organization for Buying and Merchandising

Department stores derive their name from the fact that they physically group together various categories of related merchandise into departments, such as notions, sportswear, or furniture. In most cases, a separate buyer is assigned to buy all stock for each department. In most nonchain retail organizations that have fewer than 12 branches, a department buyer is headquartered in the parent store and is usually responsible for purchasing stock for all branches as well as for the parent store. In addition, the buyer is responsible for departmental sales in all locations, for the merchandise training of all departmental salespeople, and for the profitable operation of the department as a whole.

Merchandising Policies

Merchandising policies are guidelines established by store management for merchandising executives to follow in order that the store organization may win the patronage of the specific target group(s) of customers it has chosen to serve. Each type of retail organization has its own characteristic merchan-

dising policies, different from those of all other types of stores. The following shows how a department store's policies, in each major area of merchandising activity, differ from those of other types of retail organizations.

Fashion-cycle Emphasis Small or moderate-size department stores place major emphasis in their fashion assortments on styles that are mainly in the late-rise and early culmination stages of their fashion cycles. Larger department stores, however, often expand their fashion offerings to include both prestige and budget departments as well. Their prestige departments feature styles in the early-rise stage of their fashion cycles; budget or basement departments feature styles that are well into the culmination stage or may even have begun their decline.

Price Ranges Small or moderate-size department stores tend to concentrate on merchandise assortments within moderate price ranges. However, larger department stores will feature higher price ranges in their prestige departments and lower price ranges in their budget or basement departments.

Depth and Breadth of Assortments A department store's policy in relation to fashion merchandise is initially to spread a broad, shallow assortment before customers and then to narrow and deepen the assortment to reflect those styles, colors, and prices to which customers show good response. As the terms are used in fashion merchandising, a *broad assortment* is one that includes many styles. A *narrow assortment* is one that includes relatively few styles. The term *deep* is applied to an assortment that includes a comprehensive range of colors and sizes in each style, while the term *shallow* refers to an assortment that contains only a few sizes and colors in each style.

Brand Policies Nationally advertised brands usually play an important role in a department store's fashion stocks and are prominently featured in its displays and advertising. In order to minimize competition from local stores that feature the same brands, department stores may seek items from branded lines that will be "confined," or exclusive with them in their own communities.

Customer Services   Department stores were pioneers in offering customer charge and return privileges. This willingness to accept merchandise returns was one of the foundation stones on which the late John Wanamaker built his business. His first store, opened in Philadelphia in 1876 in an old freight station, was a men's clothing store. A year later he had added such departments as ladies' goods, household linens, upholstery, and shoes, making a total of 16 departments in all. Wanamaker advertised that any article that did not fit well, did not please "the folks at home," or for any other reason was unsatisfactory could be returned for cash refund within ten days.

Today, department stores offer an increasing number of services because of increased competition for customers. In addition to the more familiar customer services such as a variety of credit plans, free local delivery, free parking at suburban branches, and alterations, new customer services may include travel bureaus, ticket agencies, post office facilities, art and needlework instruction, child-care centers, expanded telephone-order facilities, and extended shopping hours.

Selling Services   Modern department stores may offer a variety of selling services within a single store, depending upon the nature and sometimes the price level of the merchandise involved. In prestige apparel departments, a salon type of selling service often prevails. In this type of service, merchandise other than that used for display purposes is kept out of sight, and a salesperson chooses styles from the stockroom to bring out for individual customer's inspection. Self-selection is the type of selling service most commonly employed by department stores today, however. In this form of selling service, merchandise is arranged on open racks, counters, or shelves, for the customer's inspection. Salespeople are available to assist customers by

providing information about the merchandise and by completing the sales transaction once a customer has reached a buying decision. A few department stores may employ self-service with check-out counters for certain types of merchandise, but this is the exception rather than the rule.

Promotional Activities   Department stores engage in a moderate amount of promotional activity. For this reason, they generally are referred to as semipromotional stores. This means they regularly feature individual items in their advertising and displays and do a moderate amount of "special sale" and "special purchase" promotion, such as anniversary sales, end-of-month clearances, and traditional seasonal events such as White Sales and Back-to-School promotions.

Fashion Coordination   Department stores usually place only a moderate amount of emphasis on coordination of fashion accessories with apparel, other than in fashion shows and in window and interior displays. However, as competition increases, particularly from specialty stores and discount stores, department stores place greater emphasis on the coordination of their fashion assortments as a means of creating a distinctive fashion image.

SPECIALTY STORES

Specialty stores vary widely in both size and type. They range from the tiny *Mom-and-Pop store*, run by the proprietor with few or no hired assistants, to huge departmentalized institutions that resemble large department stores. Some are single-unit stores; some are units of chains; some are suburban branches of central-city stores or branches of a parent store located in a distant city.

Most specialty stores are individually owned, have no branches, and are not units of chains. The composite sales of these single-unit stores, however, represent less than half the total sales volume of all specialty stores. The larger share of business is done by multiunit specialty stores or local, regional,

Bergdorf Goodman's first branch, in White Plains, New York, emphasizes its high fashion image through its luxurious use of space.
Bergdorf Goodman, Inc.

or national chains. Saks Fifth Avenue, for example, is a specialty-store chain with units throughout the country.

Definition

According to the Bureau of the Census, a *specialty store* is one that carries limited lines of apparel or accessories or home furnishings. A shoe store, a jewelry store, or one handling only women's apparel

and accessories is classified as a specialty store. In the trade, however, retailers use the term "specialty store" to describe any apparel and/or accessories store that exhibits a degree of fashion awareness and that carries goods for men, women, and/or children.

Organization for Buying and Merchandising

In specialty stores, as in department stores, merchandise is usually grouped into separate departments. In departmentalized specialty stores, a buyer is assigned to purchase stock for each department and has the same responsibilities as does the buyer for a single or multibranch department store.

Smaller specialty stores, however, may not be departmentalized. In this case, all merchandise is usually bought by the owner or store manager, sometimes with the help of one or two assistants.

Like department stores, multibranch specialty stores generally merchandise their branches from the parent store. Specialty-store branches enjoy the same advantages over local competition that department branches do: a skilled fashion merchandiser who directs the operation from the parent store and a large stock from which to draw styles, colors, and sizes.

Merchandising Policies

Specialty stores generally concentrate on pleasing a specific, carefully profiled customer, rather than trying to serve a broad range of customers as department stores do. These are the merchandising policies most nonchain specialty stores employ in their efforts to win maximum customer patronage.

Fashion-cycle Emphasis The customer selected by the specialty store as its target may be high-fashion or budget minded, a fashion innovator or follower, a teenager or senior citizen, to give just a few examples. Each specialty store builds its fashion assortments around merchandise at the particular stage in its fashion cycle that is most likely to appeal to the majority of its target customers.

Price Ranges Although some specialty stores feature lower price ranges, many specialty stores carry only current and high fashions and feature moderate to high price lines. These latter stores are so widely known and function so effectively that consumers tend to associate the term "specialty store" with slightly higher prices and newer fashions than are found in department stores.

Depth and Breadth of Assortments The usual merchandising approach of specialty stores is to have broad and shallow assortments within the framework of what their target customers may be expected to accept.

Brand Policy Most specialty stores place major emphasis on their own store label or, in some cases, on designer labels. If specialty stores select merchandise from nationally advertised brand lines, they usually avoid the *Fords* (styles that are widely copied at a variety of price lines). Because they often buy only a few units of a given style, specialty stores can and do make greater use of smaller resources with limited production than can and do department stores.

Customer Services Customer services offered by specialty stores are similar in both type and number to those offered by department stores with equivalent sales volume.

Selling Services Self-selection selling is used in specialty stores where it is appropriate, but there is likely to be more emphasis on personal selling than in department stores. In the medium- to higher-price specialty stores, emphasis is placed on remembering what individual customers and their friends have purchased. The accent in such stores is on personal service.

Promotional Activities Advertising and display activities of specialty stores tend to be less promotional than those used by department stores. Rather than featuring individual items, moderate- to higher-price specialty store ads and displays tend

to feature designer collections, "looks," and trends in coordinated apparel and accessories. Lower-price specialty stores, and particularly those that are units of a chain, tend to feature in both their ads and displays the fashion-rightness of the styles carried in their assortments.

Fashion Coordination In most specialty stores, accessories are usually carefully related to apparel, and fashion coordination is stressed in their ads, displays, and selling services.

CHAIN ORGANIZATIONS

Chains that deal in fashion merchandise may be national, regional, or local. They may be department store chains, with only a portion of assortments devoted to fashion goods; or they may be specialty store chains, devoted exclusively to a limited range of fashion apparel and/or accessories. Some large department store chains that today distribute impressive quantities of fashion merchandise are Sears, Roebuck and Company, Montgomery Ward & Co., and J. C. Penney Co., Inc. Some well-known specialty store chains include Saks Fifth Avenue, Lerner Stores, Plymouth Shops, and Lane Bryant.

Definition

A chain organization is a group of 12 or more stores, centrally owned, each handling somewhat similar goods, and merchandised and controlled from a central headquarters office. The difference between a chain organization and a department or specialty store organization with multiple branches is that the former is merchandised and controlled from a central office, while the latter is merchandised and controlled from a parent store.

Organization for Buying and Merchandising

Centralized buying, merchandising, and distribution of fashion assortments prevail among retail chain organizations. Although the majority of chain stores

At the fashion distribution center of a major chain,
garments are stored on automated overhead racks
awaiting ticketing and distribution to units of the chain.

Boxed merchandise is moved through
the distribution center on conveyor belts.
Sears, Roebuck and Company

are departmentalized, a chain buyer located in a central buying office is usually assigned to purchase only a specific category or classification of merchandise, instead of all categories carried in a single department as a nonchain buyer does. For example, a sportswear buyer for a department or specialty store might be responsible for buying all the various categories of merchandise usually carried in a typical sportswear department, such as swimwear, sweaters, and slacks. In contrast, one chain organization buyer might be assigned to purchase swimwear, another to purchase sweaters, and so on. Category buying rather than departmental buying is necessary because of the huge quantities of goods in each category that are needed to stock all the individual units of a chain, which sometimes number in the thousands.

Centrally purchased merchandise is usually distributed to various units of a chain from central or regional distribution centers. Most larger chains have elaborate systems of supervision and reporting so that their central-office buyers are kept informed at all times of what is selling and what remains in stock at each of their many units.

Unlike single-unit or multibranch department or specialty store buyers, central buyers are not directly responsible for sales. These are the responsibility of the store manager of each unit in the chain and the designated department manager in that unit. Neither are central buyers responsible for the merchandise training of salespeople in each unit, although they do supply trend and other information to chain units about the merchandise distributed to them. And, since central buyers are usually responsible for providing stock in only one or limited merchandise categories, they are not responsible for the profitable merchandising of a department as a whole.

Merchandising Policies

A chain organization's merchandising policies depend upon the type of target customer the chain has chosen to serve. Most department store chains, with a few important exceptions, establish merchandising policies that appeal to customers with limited or moderate income. Most specialty store chains, on the other hand, mold their merchandising policies to attract customers with average to above-average incomes and usually above-average interest in fashion apparel and accessories.

Fashion-cycle Emphasis   Most department store chains do not try to be fashion leaders. Instead, they place emphasis on fashion styles that have reached the culmination stage of their cycles. Some large specialty store chains, such as the West Coast Joseph Magnin and Company, however, assert fashion leadership by offering styles in earlier stages of their fashion cycles at moderate prices.

Price Ranges   Most department store chains tend to emphasize consistent values and promotional prices in their fashion offerings, as do lower-price specialty store chains. Therefore, they feature prices in the low to moderate ranges. Specialty store chains with more fashion leadership, however, stress moderate to higher price ranges.

Depth and Breadth of Assortments   Both department and lower-price specialty store chains usually concentrate their assortments on a narrow range of proven styles with depth (in color and size) in each style. The fashion assortments of specialty store chains that stress greater fashion leadership tend to be broader and more shallow.

Rapid and accurate stock and sales reporting is essential to profitable chain operation. The "system," or method of reporting used, is looked on by a chain, large or small, as the vital artery that carries its lifeblood. For this reason, electronic systems now handle the tremendous flow of merchandising data in most chain organizations.

Brand Policy   Private labeling is used to a large extent by both department and specialty store chains. In offering its own brands, each chain can maintain certain quality standards and provide the merchandise characteristics most in demand by its customers. At the time, private labeling can ensure that the merchandise assortments are not readily comparable with the offerings of competing stores.

Customer Services Customer services are usually more limited in chain organizations than in most nonchain stores. Free delivery of fashion merchandise is rarely provided. The usual credit plans prevail, with greater emphasis on installment plans. Rarely do chain organizations accept credit cards other than their own. Chain organizations may take the lead or follow the lead of other prominent stores in the community in establishing business hours.

Selling Services With rare exceptions, selling services in department store and low- to moderate-price specialty store chain organizations are usually of a self-selection type. Clerks simply answer questions and ring up sales. In some instances, self-service may even apply. Higher-price specialty store chains, however, tend to place more emphasis on personal selling techniques.

The three major department store chains supplement floor sales in their retail outlets with catalog sales. A special catalog desk or counter is usually maintained in each retail store unit; customers may phone, mail, or come in person to order merchandise not regularly carried in that store's stock.

Each chain prepares seasonal catalogs which may number as many as five or six a year. Selection of fashion merchandise for catalog selling has to be done much further in advance than selection for store floor sales, because of the time required to develop and print catalogs. Central buyers for each chain's retail stores may assist in the planning and buying of catalog merchandise.

Today's catalogs differ vastly from those 20 to 50 years ago, especially in the case of fashion merchandise. More pages are now devoted to apparel and accessories for men, women, and children. Merchandise is more related to current fashion trends, and illustrations are usually in full color.

Promotional Activities Promotional activities of most chain organizations are coordinated with their central buying activities. The advertising staff

at a chain's central or regional headquarters prepares advertising layouts and provides display suggestions for all chain units in order to promote the fashion merchandise purchased by the central buyers for the various units.

Department store chains concentrate mainly on item advertising of fashion goods with frequent off-price promotions. Specialty store chains that carry higher-price fashion merchandise usually follow the promotional pattern of nonchain specialty stores operating at the same price level; they feature looks and trends in ads and displays.

Fashion Coordination Larger department and specialty store chains may employ the services of a fashion coordinator who searches both domestic and foreign markets for new fashion trends and for unusual styling that can be adapted or incorporated into their private label merchandise offerings. In the largest chains, a fashion coordinator has a staff of assistants, each assigned responsibility for a specific type of fashion apparel, such as dresses, sportswear, menswear, and children's wear.

The fashion coordinator of a chain, working closely with the central buying and merchandising staffs, is also responsible for periodic fashion reports to managers and staff of each unit. These highlight current fashion trends and coordination possibilities between apparel and accessories for the coming season. (For further details about fashion coordination in chain operations, see Chapter 20.)

DISCOUNT STORES

Discount stores are a twentieth-century development. Originally the term "discounter" applied only to dealers in durable or hard goods who sold merchandise below manufacturers' list prices. The procedure was considered illegal in those days, although the Fair Trade laws in most states have since been changed.

Every facet of discounters' operations were designed to keep costs low. They dealt only in low-risk merchandise. Their stores were situated in out-of-the-way locations where rent and real estate taxes were low. Minimum facilities and basic "pipe rack" fixturing were the rule. Sales were handled on a central-cashier basis that eliminated the need for a sales staff. They did little paid advertising, depending mainly on word-of-mouth promotion. As a result, they could price merchandise much lower than could conventional retailers and still operate profitably.

During the latter 1950s many of the early hard-goods discounters began adding limited lines of soft goods and fashion goods to their durable-goods offerings. At first these efforts met with only mediocre success because most discounters lacked this type of merchandising experience. As a result, a number of them turned over the merchandising of soft goods and fashion departments to leased operators, who had more expertise along those lines. By using lessors, the discount store owners also did not have to invest the firms' capital in high-risk inventory nor in the expenses involved in merchandising such inventories. Instead, they simply collected a share of each leased department's sales

volume as rent. Even today some discount stores are made up entirely of leased operations, with the firm's profit being derived from rented space.

In the last two decades, many of the old-line discount organizations have substantially expanded their fashion assortments, improved housekeeping and services, modernized facilities and fixturing, and upgraded advertising and display in an effort to establish a definite fashion image.

In addition, in recent years many conventional retailers and large ownership groups have entered the discount field with wholly owned discount operations as separate divisions of parent firms. For example, Target Stores is the discount operation of the prestigious Dayton-Hudson department store group, and K-Mart is the highly successful discount operation of the S. S. Kresge variety chain.

Although most discounters started as durable-goods merchants, a few started out as women's apparel fashion discounters and still retain prominence in that field. For example, Ohrbach's today has branches in the New York metropolitan and Long Island areas, as well as in the downtown and

Merchandise is stocked on self-service racks and tables in discount stores.
Two Guys

suburban areas of Los Angeles. Long known for its regular semiannual showing of domestically produced line-for-line copies of selected European couture models, Ohrbach's is perhaps the best known of this country's fashion discount operations. Alexander's, with its parent store in the Bronx and branches throughout the New York area, is also an important fashion discount operation. It carries men's as well as women's and children's apparel and accessories. Barney's, located in New York City, calls itself the world's largest men's store.

Today, a new type of fashion discount operation is making its appearance on the retail scene. These are stores that specialize in offering odd lots of higher-price fashion apparel, frequently designer-label apparel, at prices considerably less than those charged in conventional stores. One of the oldest, best-known, and largest of these is Loehmann's; it has a parent store in the Bronx and a number of branches in the Northeastern United States.

Creative merchandisers or dealers in producer overstocks, discount stores serve an important fashion function in selling enormous quantities of fashion goods.

Definition

A *discount store* is a limited-service, mass-merchandised retail firm selling goods below usual retail prices. It may be an independent store or a unit of a department, specialty, or variety store chain.

Organization for Buying and Merchandising

In departments owned and operated by a chain discount organization, buying and merchandising activities are basically the same as those previously described for chain organizations. Centralized buying prevails. Discount store buyers are usually responsible for buying for several departments rather than for only a single category of merchandise. The nonchain discount stores, which are far less numerous than chains, follow the same basic buying and merchandising pattern as that of similar volume nonchain department or specialty stores.

Early discounters searched the market for closeouts and special-price promotions. In many cases, their inventories consisted almost entirely of this type of merchandise. Today, however, the fashion stocks of many discounters consist of regular goods bought in either the low-end open market or special lines made up exclusively for discount operations by producers who sell their regular lines to conventional stores. Since most conventional retail firms will not allow their buyers to purchase fashion goods from producers who sell the same goods to mass-merchandised operations, many producers have found it profitable to create a second line for such customers because of the huge quantities of fashion goods they can use.

Merchandising Policies

Nearly every discount store has the same target customer: a person who wants value at prices lower than those charged by conventional retail stores. Discount store merchandising policies are designed to serve this kind of customer.

Fashion-cycle Emphasis   Most discount stores today concentrate on styles that are well into the culmination stage of their cycles. However, a few, such as Ohrbach's and Alexander's, offer some styles that are still in their early fashion stages.

Price Ranges   In most cases, discount operations feature lower prices than those offered by conventional retailers.

Depth and Breadth of Assortments   The fashion assortments of stores that buy mainly manufacturers' closeouts and discontinued styles tend to be broad and shallow. The fashion assortments of discounters that have goods made up especially for them and regularly buy low-end merchandise tend to be narrower in ranges of styles but greater in depth.

Brand Policy   Until recently, nationally advertised brands were usually not available to discounters. As a result, some producers made up secondary lines under different brand labels for distribution through discount firms. Recently, however, some nationally advertised fashion apparel and accessories may be found in discount store assortments at the same prices as identical merchandise is marked in competing conventional stores.

Customer Services   Transactions in discount operations are usually made for cash, although a number of such stores today accept checks or bank credit cards or offer credit plans of their own. Refund policies are generally liberal: money back if the goods are returned unworn in a specified number of days. Delivery service, if available, is usually restricted to bulky items and often involves an extra charge. Limited fitting-room service for trying on apparel may sometimes be found. Paperwork is kept to a minimum. The cash-register receipt often serves as a sales slip, and refunds are usually made in cash, eliminating credit slips and extensive bookkeeping.

Selling Services   In discount store selling, frills are eliminated. Merchandise is stocked on racks or tables and customers help themselves. Self-service prevails. Employees are present only to direct customers and straighten the stock. Customers make their selections and then take them to a cashier's desk where sales are rung up.

Promotional Activities   Today discount stores are highly promotional, putting emphasis on all types of advertising, including not only newspaper advertising but also radio and direct mail. Advertising always emphasizes low price and, in many cases, comparative prices.

Interior displays are used mainly to identify the location of merchandise; they play a relatively minor role in the store's promotional efforts. Window displays in some leading discount chains, however, are well planned and attractive.

Fashion Coordination   In spite of the gradual upgrading of some merchandising techniques, there is little evidence that discount stores try to coordinate their fashion apparel and accessory offerings.

VARIETY STORES

Variety stores once referred to themselves as "limited price variety stores," to underscore the fact that they carried a wide range of merchandise in a limited number of low price lines. Some literally were 5-and-10-cent stores, with all merchandise priced at either a nickel or a dime. Others sold goods priced up to a dollar. Fashion merchandise was represented in their assortments only by such utilitarian articles as socks and underwear, ribbons and buttons, simple hair and dress ornaments. Chain operations dominated the field.

In the 1930s, the larger variety chains began broadening their assortments and extending their price ranges. They grew into what are now known as "general merchandise stores," a term applied rather loosely by retailers to stores that primarily carry limited lines of apparel and accessories for men, women, and children, as well as limited assortments of home furnishings.

Definition

A *variety store* carries a wide range of merchandise in a limited number of low or relatively low price lines. Some variety stores are independent organizations, but most are units of chain organizations.

Organization for Buying and Merchandising

Since most variety stores are units of a chain, their buying and merchandising techniques are identi with those described for chain organizations above). These include centralized buying a tribution, handled by headquarters office p

Merchandising Policies

Variety stores serve a wide range of customers. They provide one-stop shopping for many different basic personal and household necessities, all relatively inexpensive. Following are the merchandising policies which make variety stores the convenience they are for many different groups of customers.

Fashion-cycle Emphasis The fashion apparel and accessories that variety stores carry are usually limited to styles that are well into the culmination stage of their fashion cycles.

Price Ranges The fashion assortments carried by variety stores are low or relatively low in price.

Depth and Breadth of Assortments Fashion assortments in variety stores tend to be narrow in range of styles carried and generally shallow in depth of size and color in each style.

Brand Policy Many variety stores use their own private labels on merchandise made to specification or bought from unbranded manufacturers.

Customer Services The earlier variety stores had bare wooden floors, no fitting rooms, and few, if any, customer services. Today, however, modern units of such variety chains as F. W. Woolworth Company or S. S. Kresge are well lighted, air conditioned, and carpeted or surfaced with resilient floor coverings. Only the larger chains, however, offer such customer services as charge privileges, ~~~ ~~~ery, and a basic kind of ready-to-wear fitting

~~~ervice, as a selling tech-
~~~ in variety stores, although
~~~ selling may be provided.
~~~lise is packaged, binned, or
~~~ inspection.

Promotional Activities Variety stores seldom, if ever, advertise fashion goods. Their promotion of fashion goods is largely limited to displays which, though mainly functional, attempt to bring out the important fashion points of the merchandise.

Fashion Coordination Variety stores make no attempt to coordinate fashion assortments since the styles they feature are already widely accepted. In units of the larger chains, however, a concerted effort has been made to feature coordinated apparel and accessories both in window and in interior displays.

Because the fashions that are featured have already proved successful before making an appearance in these stores, and also because of their low pricing policies, variety stores make their major appeal to lower-income customers who are fashion followers.

LEASED DEPARTMENTS

Department stores tend to lease both merchandise and service departments, as do chain and discount organizations. Specialty stores tend to restrict leased operations to services.

Services commonly leased include the beauty salon, shoe repair, and jewelry repair. Merchandise departments most frequently leased include millinery, shoes, fine jewelry, and furs. There are also some leased departments that handle women's apparel, but these are likely to be found in discount stores, and they usually concentrate on lower-price goods.

Definition

A leased department is a department in a retail store merchandised by an outside organization rather than by the store itself. That organization owns the department's stock, merchandises and staffs the department, pays for its advertising, is required to abide by the host store's policies, and pays the store a percentage of sales as rent. In general, the operator of a leased department is an expert in some merchandise or service that a retail store finds unprofitable to handle directly.

Organization for Buying and Merchandising

The operator of a leased department may be a local person, functioning in a single store, or a giant organization, doing business in hundreds of stores across the country. Central buying and merchandising prevail. In larger operations, traveling supervisors regularly visit their various locations to confer with both the host-store management and the department manager, to help them cope with problems that may arise, and to plan for future growth.

Leased-department operators are in a unique position with respect to the fashion industries. They are usually in daily contact with their markets and are sometimes established in a wide variety of stores. They can give impetus to incoming styles or clear producers' stocks of declining styles, according to the merchandising policies of their host stores. The successful, long-established operators sometimes know their industries better than the producers themselves. Such operators are equipped to give fashion guidance to their sources of supply as well as to the stores they serve.

Merchandising Policies

The fashion merchandising policies of a leased department are dictated by the terms of its lease and must conform to those of the store in which it operates. Assortments and services must be on a level with those of all other departments in the host store, so that customers have no indication that the department is not owned and operated by the host store.

Some larger leased-department organizations are immensely flexible in their approach to individual store policies and can function on almost any level of fashion and service that may be required. Others limit themselves to narrow fields, such as popular-price shoes, and they seek connections only with stores whose merchandise and service policies are compatible with their own.

TRENDS IN RETAIL FASHION DISTRIBUTION

A major trend in fashion distribution is movement toward bigness: in size of organization, in number of units, in breadth of assortments. This trend affects department stores, specialty stores, chain organizations, discount organizations, and all other forms of retailing. There is also a trend toward expanding assortments and improving their quality, as fashion customers become more knowledgeable and are both willing and able to spend more on fashions.

Growth of Large-scale Retailing

Both department and specialty stores in their early history were primarily single unit, independent, and family owned. In the 1930s, a trend toward bigness and mergers began, when Federated Department Stores, Allied Stores, and other corporate ownership groups were formed and began acquiring stores that were formerly independent. At that time the Macy interests owned several stores, each in a different city, as did the Gimbel family and May Department Stores. This trend has not only continued but accelerated; by the mid-1970s, only a few of this country's largest stores were still independently owned.

During the late 1920s and early 1930s, what formerly had been exclusively mail-order houses began opening store units. These retail units represented the entry of chain organizations into the retail distribution network.

Mergers and Acquisitions   Mergers and acquisitions in the retail field normally are carried out in the financial arena, through exchange of stock or purchase of controlling interests. The operations and image of the acquired store or chain itself remain apparently unchanged in the public eye.

For example, there is nothing about the operations of the New York–based Bergdorf Goodman or Dallas–based Neiman-Marcus specialty stores to indicate that they both are under the same corporate ownership (Carter Hawley Hale) as The Broadway department store chain based in Los Angeles or the Walden bookstore national chain. Most customers are unaware that the Bonwit Teller stores are among the firms owned by the many-faceted Genesco Corporation. The Bullock stores in California and the Burdine stores in Florida are among those owned by Federated Department Stores. New York–based Lord & Taylor, Los Angeles–based J. W. Robinson, and Phoenix–based Goldwater's are among the stores owned by Associated Dry Goods Corporation. Although operating under their original owner's names, Kaufmann's in Pittsburgh and G. Fox in Hartford are both owned and operated by May Department Stores.

Voluntary Associations   On another level, there is a growing trend among smaller stores to affiliate loosely with one another on a voluntary basis to exchange information as well as to secure certain group-buying advantages such as early delivery and sometimes lower prices.

In voluntary associations each store retains its own identity, and owners retain complete control of their stores. No financial joining is involved. However, the heads of stores that are affiliated in this manner get together regularly to compare methods and results, and feel such meetings result in better and more profitable storekeeping for all concerned. Affiliations of this type are often organized and guided by an accounting firm or by a management consultant firm that specializes in the retail field.

Chain Expansion   Chain organizations are continually replacing older, smaller units with larger, newer units that contain considerably expanded fashion assortments. They are also expanding into such foreign markets as Spain, Belgium, Italy, Canada, South America, and Japan.

Branch Expansion   Until recent years, branches were located principally in suburbs of the cities in which the parent stores were located. The trend today, however, is toward opening branches far

from the trading area of the parent store. Lord & Taylor, for instance, currently has branches in Pennsylvania, Massachusetts, Maryland, Connecticut, Illinois, Texas, Georgia, Virginia and New Jersey, with additional branches in other states in the planning stage.

Both branching and merging have not only increased the stores' volume, but they also have increased the stores' fashion impact. The trend in branch store operation today is toward ever larger branches, established at ever greater distances from parent stores, with branches being given increasing merchandising and operational autonomy.

Expanded Fashion Assortments and Services

Fashion retailers of all kinds are expanding their assortments and services in an attempt to encourage and facilitate one-stop shopping.

Assortments   Fashion assortments are being expanded to include merchandise not previously carried, for example: imports, multipurpose apparel (such as pajamas both for at-home and for social-occasion wear), and apparel for the most popular active sports of the day (such as tennis).

Assortments are also being expanded to include size ranges not previously carried, such as junior petites and special figure types.

There is also a trend toward expanding the number of price ranges carried. For instance, many stores traditionally known for higher price ranges are now adding lower price lines, as Bergdorf-Goodman and Bonwit-Teller have done. Some department stores that used to emphasize moderate price lines are now trading up to include fashion assortments in higher price ranges, such as The Broadway department store.

Services   The fashion services offered by retail organizations divide into two categories: those that are free and those for which a fee is charged.

Today, free services include a greater variety of consultant and demonstrator services, expanded mail and phone order facilities (some large-city stores have 24-hour-a-day, seven-days-a-week service), extended shopping hours (nights, Sundays, holidays), expanded parking facilities, and more in-store fashion shows and modeling.

Today, merchandised services, or those for which a fee is charged, include rental of a variety of apparel items, such as men's tuxedos and women's fur coats, jackets, and stoles. They also include beauty salons, charm courses, fur storage, and wardrobe repair services (in addition to the alterations service traditionally offered), and home sewing clinics.

Increasing Use of Automated Data Processing Systems

There is a steadily growing use of punch-card and electronic data processing systems in retailing, although the retailing industry, with its many small stores, has not moved in this direction as rapidly as have some other industries.

There are many areas of operation in which an increasing number of retailers are using automated data processing. However, in terms of fashion merchandising, perhaps the most important trends are in the expanding use of electronic cash registers and other automated methods for capturing sales information at point of sale. These enable retail executives to obtain faster, more accurate reports on sales and inventory. Further development of sales and inventory data processing systems are making greater use of manufacturer preticketing of merchandise purchases which should considerably reduce store marking and receiving expenses and make possible faster delivery of purchases to the selling floor.

Changing Retail Patterns

A theory expounded by Dr. Malcolm P. McNair, retailing authority and professor emeritus of Harvard University Business School, suggests that many retail organizations originate as low-price distributors of consumer goods, with strictly functional facilities, limited assortments, and minimum customer services. As time goes on, each successful firm begins to trade up in an effort to broaden its consumer profile. Facilities are modernized; store decor becomes more attractive; assortments become more varied and higher in quality; greater emphasis is placed on promotional efforts; and more customer services are introduced.

In this process of trading up, considerably greater capital investment in physical plant, equipment, and inventory is required. Operating expenses spiral. As a result, retailers are forced to charge higher prices to cover the increased costs of doing business.

As retail organizations move out of the low-price field and into the moderate- or higher-price fields, a vacuum is created at the bottom of the retailing structure. This vacuum does not long exist, however, because enterprising new firms move quickly into the vacated and temporarily uncompetitive low-price area to meet the demands of customers who either need or prefer to patronize low-price retail distributors. The pattern keeps repeating itself, with successful retail firms trading up and new firms moving into the bottom level of the retail price structure.

That pattern of movement is very obvious in today's retail scene. Department and specialty stores are expanding their facilities, services, assortments, and price-line offerings. Chain organizations are opening new and larger store units that feature expanded assortments, more services, and a higher quality of goods. Discount stores are trading up. As a result, a vacuum appeared at the bottom of the retail price structure, and is being filled by such forms of low-price operation as the outlet store, the warehouse store, and the catalog showroom.

The outlet store is the oldest form, having originated as an odd-lot, low-price factory-owned outlet in the early days of industrialization. Today, these outlets are growing in number, and many handle products of more than one manufacturer. The warehouse store, a newer development, handles mainly odd lots of major appliances and furniture. The catalog showroom, the newest entry in the low-price field, is set up like a trading-stamp redemption center, with merchandise catalogs for customers to study and samples of the merchandise on display in the showroom. Orders are filled from a stockroom on the premises, and customers take their purchases with them. Although there is still only a minimal amount of fashion goods offered in such catalog showrooms, it is likely that in the future more soft goods will be available.

MERCHANDISING VOCABULARY

Define or briefly explain the following terms:

Retailing
Fashion retailing
Merchandising
Fashion merchandising
General store
Organizational chart
Department store
Merchandising
    policies
Broad assortment

Narrow assortment
Deep assortment
Shallow assortment
Mom-and-Pop store
Specialty store
Ford
Chain organization
Discount store
Variety store

MERCHANDISING REVIEW

1. What are considered the modern retail versions of the following types of early retail distributors: (a) outdoor bazaars of the Orient and market-places of the Mediterranean, (b) medieval craft or guild shops, (c) tradespeople who purchased goods from traders for purposes of resale rather than producing such goods themselves, and (d) peddlers?

2. Name and briefly explain the characteristics and importance of three early forms of rural retail distribution in this country.

3. Describe the organizational structure of most medium-size department stores and the responsibilities of executives in charge of each major function.

4. How did department stores originally get their name? What are the four major responsibilities of a departmental buyer for an independent retail firm with fewer than 12 branches?

5. What is meant by the term "merchandising policies"? Who is responsible for establishing them? What important purposes do they serve?

6. Compare and/or contrast the merchandising policies of department and specialty stores in regard to the depth and breadth of assortments during a selling season.

7. Compare and/or contrast the responsibilities of nonchain departmental buyers with those of central buyers for chain organizations.

8. What is a leased department and how does it operate? Name the departments in a retail store that are frequently leased.

9. What stage or stages of the fashion cycle would most likely be emphasized in the fashion assortments of (a) a small or medium-size department store, (b) a higher-price specialty store, (c) a department store chain, (d) a discount store?

10. In which major type of retail store would you be most likely to find the following emphasized in its merchandise assortments: (a) nationally advertised brands, (b) private brands, (c) low-price branded or unbranded goods?

MERCHANDISING DIGEST

1. Discuss the following statement from the text and its implications for retail merchants: "As the customer changes, so must retailers' methods of serving that customer change if they wish to stay in business."

2. "The number of major functions established by a retail firm . . . depends upon its sales volume, the number of employees it has, and how many store units it operates." Discuss this statement from the text, citing specific examples of how these three factors not only affect the organizational structure of a firm but also the responsibilities of its various employees.

3. Discuss any two major trends in fashion distribution and how each reflects specific changes in consumer demand.

PART 3
RETAIL MERCHANDISING
OF FASHION

The essential activities involved in retail merchandising of fashion goods, as outlined by Dr. Paul Nystrom,[1] are discussed in detail in Part 3. Briefly, and in their sequential order, these activities include:

1. Analyzing what prospective consumers will want in a future selling period (Chapter 12)
2. Planning how to act upon those estimates of consumer demand (Chapters 13 through 16)
3. Selecting and buying goods in accordance with those estimates and plans (Chapter 17)
4. Promoting the sale of the goods for which orders have been placed in anticipation of demand (Chapters 18 through 20)
5. Meeting the difficult problems relating to increased competition (Chapter 21)

In handling day-to-day buying and selling activities and in implementing merchandising policies, the merchandising division of most retail organizations have a variety of staff aides upon which to call for information and advice. These include the fashion bureau, the comparison bureau, the unit-control bureau, the testing bureau, the research bureau, and the resident buying office.

The Fashion Bureau

A fashion bureau or office, discussed in Chapter 20, may consist of a single individual or a whole department. The fashion bureau's job is to collect and assess information on fashion trends from all available sources, both within and outside the store, and to make such information available to the store's merchandising, advertising, and display executives.

[1] Nystrom, *Fashion Merchandising*, pp. 10–12.

The Comparison Bureau

The comparison bureau or office, covered in Chapter 12, acts as the eyes and ears of the merchandising division, keeping track of and reporting on the store's competition. Comparison-bureau personnel are expected to compare both the merchandise and the services of the home store with those of its local competition, from the viewpoint of consumers rather than merchandising professionals.

The Unit-control Bureau

Unit control systems, as discussed in Chapter 15, are procedures for recording the number of units of merchandise bought, sold, in stock, and on order during a given period. From these records, periodic reports are drawn up to give buyers and merchandise managers up-to-date information about consumer buying trends and inventory positions.

The Testing Bureau

Some of the largest department stores, and most national chains, maintain special testing laboratories to examine prospective or in-stock merchandise in terms of its performance in use. This work may be done routinely, as a quality control of all goods purchased by the company's buyers; or it may be done at the request of a buyer who is considering a new type of merchandise or a new resource. The cost of the necessary equipment and staff makes a store operated testing bureau too expensive for any except the very large retail organizations. Other stores use commercial testing laboratories as the need arises.

The Research Bureau

Research bureaus, or research departments, serve every area of store operation. As a staff aide to the merchandising division, for example, the research bureau may analyze traffic patterns to improve departmental or store layout, or analyze departmental operating results in search of ways to improve profit.

The Resident Buying Office

Perhaps the most important staff aide to the merchandising division is the store's resident buying office, located in a major market area. The primary function of a resident buying office is to provide all types of merchandising assistance to member stores. Some offices also provide central merchandising facilities for client stores. How these offices are organized and how their activities dovetail with those of store buyers and merchandise managers will be discussed in Chapter 17.

12
INTERPRETING CUSTOMER DEMAND

Until the twentieth century, producers in the United States paid little attention to consumer preferences. The country was growing rapidly in population and personal income. Manufacturing facilities were concentrated on the production of industrial goods, and production of consumer goods was not equal to the demand for such goods. Manufacturers that did produce consumer goods turned out whatever kind and quality they felt their facilities, resources, and labor supply could produce most easily, at the least expense, and with the largest profit. Retailers had little choice when buying in the wholesale market. Consumers had little choice when making purchases from the limited assortments carried by retailers.

During the first three decades of this century, however, rapid technological advances, particularly those relating to the development of mass-production techniques, made increasing quantities and varieties of consumer goods available in the wholesale markets. In addition, new companies entered the manufacturing field, adding still more products to those already available. In the mid- and late 1920s, for the first time, supplies of consumer goods began to approach the level of *consumer demand* (customer needs and wants for consumer goods) for those goods. Competition among producers and retailers for customer patronage began to increase.

Then came the Depression of the 1930s—one of the most important periods in marketing history, the period in which marketing philosophy began to change from one that had been traditionally pro-

ducer oriented to one that was consumer oriented. Producers and retailers had ample goods to sell, but consumers had little money to buy. Competition for the consumers' dollars became intense. Advertising and other sales promotion efforts were sharply increased. Marketing efforts at all levels became more consumer oriented. Companies that produced or sold what was wanted survived the difficult years of the 1930s; those that ignored the trends in consumer demand did not.

This same period produced a strengthening of the consumerism movement, a movement that has existed as long as there have been buyers and sellers but which has only begun to have a major impact on marketing practices. *Consumerism* refers to the rights of consumers to have protection against unfair marketing practices. Because consumers of the Depression years had so few dollars to spend, they were more determined than ever to get good value for their money. Their demands encouraged Congress to pass the Robinson-Patman Act of 1936, which concerned unfair practices that tended to limit competition in the market place; the Wheeler-Lea Act of 1938, which outlawed fraudulent advertising of any products involved in interstate commerce; and, perhaps most important, the Food, Drug and Cosmetics Act of 1938, which required detailed and accurate labeling of food, drugs, and cosmetics and was a vastly improved version of the original Food and Drug Act of 1906.

Thus the 1930s saw the beginning of a new era in the history of marketing. The age-old philosophy of *caveat emptor*, or "let the buyer beware," had begun to give way to the philosophy of *caveat venditor,* or "let the seller beware."

After the 1930s, however, some producers and retailers failed to remember what those hard years had taught them. An artificial economy during World War II and the boom years immediately thereafter encouraged some of them to believe again that promotional efforts alone could get consumers to buy anything. Producers and retailers also believed that if they agreed on what was to be the fashion, consumers had no choice but to accept it. As a result, some promotions failed because the products concerned were not in line with demand; other promotions succeeded because they were on behalf of products consumers wanted and would have bought even without promotion.

Recent fashion history provides many illustrations of promotions that proved futile because they sought to launch unwanted fashions, as well as many illustrations of fashions that gained popularity virtually without promotion, simply because people wanted them. Classic examples of the inability of promotion to force unwanted fashions on consumers include the premature and unsuccessful introduction of the sack or chemise dress in the late 1950s and the more recent unsuccessful promotion of the midi-length skirt in 1970.

Today, however, fashion producers and retailers accept the fact that success in fashion retailing is the result of finding out what consumers want or need and supplying it. Against the background of fashion principles and knowledge of the factors that influence fashion movement and dissemination, merchants study customer demand as it relates to that particular segment of the total population they seek to serve. Only if retailers are prompt to recognize and act upon evident and even subtle changes in demand can they expect to assemble assortments of merchandise that will continue to meet the approval of their customers.

Consumers, not merchants or producers, decide which styles shall become fashions. Consumer preferences determine what goods should be included in a retailer's assortment, in what quantities, at what time, and at what prices. By accepting or rejecting what is available, customers indicate to retailers not only the nature of their present wants but also the direction their preferences are taking.

TIMING AND OBJECTIVITY IN MEASURING CUSTOMER DEMAND

The needs and wants of consumers, as discussed in Chapter 2, are influenced by various economic, sociological, and psychological factors. These environmental factors constantly change, and as they change, so do the needs and wants of consumers. For instance, American consumers today are vastly different from consumers a few decades ago. They have a higher standard of living, are better educated, enjoy a wider range of interests, travel more, and have greater social mobility. And they are continuing to change.

Because of the constantly changing needs and wants of customers, a merchant's job of identifying those needs and wants and interpreting them in terms of specific items of merchandise is a constant, continuing process. It cannot be a one-time or once-in-a-while research project; instead, it must be as much a part of day-to-day business operations as keeping sales or inventory records.

As merchants chart the trends in customer demand, they must be ready to change their goods and services in accordance with important changes noted. Such changes may require, for instance, the addition of new categories of apparel, such as ski wear or tennis outfits, or they may require the addition of lower price lines, or the introduction of luggage in patterns and colors related to apparel fashions. As changes occur in customers' interests or lifestyles, merchants must make corresponding changes in their assortments.

Among the changes most difficult for merchants to recognize are those that occur as a result of changes in taste. Since taste is a very personal thing, good merchants cannot let their own taste dominate their assortments. They must make every effort to recognize and cater to the tastes of their customers.

Adapting to the tastes of others is not always

easy, especially when that taste differs radically from one's own. Yet objectivity in choosing merchandise in accordance with the tastes of a store's customers is one of the most important qualifications a retail merchant, in general, and a retail buyer in particular, must develop. Buyers cannot buy according to their own tastes. They must constantly keep the customer's preferences in mind when making merchandise selections.

However, this does not mean that every fashion retailer should rearrange assortments to reflect every new fashion trend. How far a retailer should go in changing assortments to meet a new trend depends upon customers. When the fashion for crude colors and harsh lines was at its height in the mid-1960s, such designers as Balenciaga and Mme. Grès resisted the trend and continued to produce garments with the graceful lines and elegance that had always characterized their creations. Throughout the 1960s, when skirts rose to mid-thigh, Chanel refused to conform, and all her skirts remained one inch below the knee. Each of these great fashion houses retained its following among women whose tastes remained more conservative.

Some merchants, in that period of crude colors and harsh lines, edited available styles, eliminating from their assortments those that they considered in poor taste. Among their relatively conservative customers, this was acceptable. Other retailers, regardless of personal preferences, accepted even the most garish of the then-popular fashions, because they knew customers' tastes ran in that direction. Successful fashion merchants accept change only to the degree that they expect customers to accept it. Thus the key to successful merchandising lies in a continual study of customer demand and an objective interpretation of the precise nature and extent of that demand.

ELEMENTS OF CUSTOMER DEMAND

In determining the potential demand among a store's customers for fashion merchandise, the retailer must consider a number of factors. The mer-

Fashion magazines are a source of important trend information.

chandise itself must be analyzed in terms of the various elements and characteristics that may either contribute to or mitigate against its acceptance by customers. The merchandise must be studied in the light of customer buying motives, particularly those influencing a store's target customers in purchasing fashion merchandise. The store's own image, its regional location, and the season of the year must also be taken into consideration.

It is not enough for merchants to merely keep abreast of general fashion trends and general customer demand. They must carefully study and evaluate each item of merchandise offered in the market, in competing stores, and in their own inventory in terms of its particular appeal to customers. Fashion merchandise selected and offered for sale in any store must meet the fashion demands of its target customers in styling, in quality, and in pricing.

Selection Factors

Selection factors refer to the various characteristics or components of an item of merchandise that influences a customer's decision to purchase or not to purchase it. Customers make decisions to purchase or not to purchase items of fashion merchandise based upon the composite value each attaches to the various elements or characteristics of the individual items of merchandise. Listed below are the major selection factors that significantly influence a customer's choice when contemplating the purchase of most fashion goods:[1]

- *Silhouette* refers to the degree to which an item is considered moderate or extreme in form, as in relation to the currently popular silhouette.
- *Decoration or trim* refers to the presence or absence of buttons, bows, piping, ruffles, or other types of decorative trimmings. Some customers prefer strictly tailored apparel, while others prefer various degrees of decoration.
- *Material or fabric* refers to the "hand" of the material or fabric, its bulky or slenderizing effect, its weight when worn, its sheerness or opacity,

its fiber content, and its durability in use (Will it stand up under hard wear? Is it easily snagged? How likely is it to "pill"?).
- *Surface interest* refers to the roughness or smoothness of the material, the degree to which the material is dull or shiny, whether the surface is patterned (as in jacquard), plain, or deep (as in velvet or corduroy).
- *Color* refers to the actual color or color combinations used and the hue or value of each, the intensity of color, whether the item is solid or multicolored, whether the color or colors are complimentary to the wearer, and whether the color or colors blend with, mix, or match accessories or wardrobes already owned.
- *Workmanship* refers to the degree of quality in construction, stitching, shaping, finishing. Value judgment is often involved here. Not all customers have the same quality or value standards relating to workmanship.
- *Size* refers to accuracy of fit, degree to which the graded measurements of ready-to-wear apparel correspond to the actual body measurements of customers, the relative size of accessories in relationship to the size and shape of the apparel with which the former will be worn.
- *Sensory factors* refer to odors (such as the pleasant scent of leather or perfume, or the unpleasant scent of some leather substitutes) and sounds (such as the pleasant crackle of taffeta or the unpleasant squeak of a poorly made pair of shoes).
- *Ease and cost of care* refers to such easy-care and economical features as wash-and-wear and permanent-press finishes, as well as to the future expenses involved in fabrics that have to be dry-cleaned or furs that have to be both cleaned and stored.
- *Brand* refers to customer confidence or lack of confidence in a brand name because of previous experience with the brand, familiarity or lack of familiarity with the brand, and status or lack of status of the brand.
- *Utility* refers to the extent of usefulness of an item (such as the degree of warmth and protec-

tion provided by a coat, the support provided by a well-fitting shoe, the capacity and carrying devices of a handbag) and the number of different uses to which such an item can be put.

- *Appropriateness* refers to the degree of suitability and acceptability of an item for specific occasion use.
- *Price* refers to the value placed by an individual customer upon the above factors, plus any other factors that a customer may consider important, in relation to the retail price of the item. For example, in a child's swimsuit, a high quality of workmanship may not be as important as price because the suit may be worn only a few times one summer, then outgrown by the following season or two and discarded. On the other hand, a high quality of workmanship is usually important when purchasing work shoes, as they are likely to have to withstand long, hard wear.

Thus merchants have to start determining whether or not to stock a fashion item by examining a number of factors relating to the item itself. They have to look at the styling and detail, at how the item is constructed and finished, at its practicality, and gauge whether or not it would have appeal to customers at the price that must be charged for it.

Buying Motivation

In order to gauge an item's appeal to customers, fashion merchants must understand customer *buying motivation:* why people buy what they buy. One of the early marketing authorities to study buying motivation was Dr. Melvin T. Copeland. He divided consumer buying motives into two classes: rational motives, or those based on appeal to reason, and emotional motives, or those originating in instinct and emotion, representing impulse or unreasoned promptings to buy.[2] Rational motives, according to Dr. Copeland, included such factors as durability, dependability, comfort, economy of operation, and price. Emotional motives were thought to include such factors as imitation, emulation, quest for status, prestige, appeal to the opposite sex, pride of

appearance, the desire for distinctiveness, ambition, and fear of offending.

As a result of more recent market research and the findings of experimental psychology, it has become obvious that buying motives are neither so simple nor so readily categorized as formerly believed when the variety of available consumer goods was considerably less than today.

Jon G. Udell, director of the Bureau of Business Research and Services, University of Wisconsin, has developed a much more valid theory that buying motives arise out of both conscious and unconscious reasoning and can best be measured along a bar scale of motives.[3] Udell's bar scale runs from *operational satisfactions,* which are those derived from the physical performance of the product, to *psychological satisfactions,* which are those derived from the consumer's social and psychological interpretation of the product and its performance.

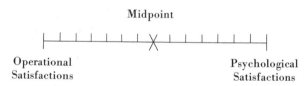

Midpoint

Operational Satisfactions   Psychological Satisfactions

Every purchase is made for a variety of reasons that can best be measured along a bar scale of motives

When selecting fashion goods, utility is seldom of as much concern to consumers as the psychological satisfactions to be derived from ownership and use of the product. Yet fashion buying decisions are not always clean-cut. Operational motives may also be present.

A typical example might be why people buy boots. Most boot purchases used to be made strictly on the basis of operational motivation. Shoe boots were worn in place of shoes and used primarily to keep feet and ankles dry and warm. They were both more attractive and more convenient than the traditional galoshes they replaced. During the 1960s, however, shoe-boot styles improved, and more and more people adopted them more for their fashion appeal than for their utilitarian value. Boots for year-round wear became available in a variety of heel heights appropriate for a variety of occasions, in a wide range of colors to match or complement a widening range of costume colors, and in a variety of lengths for wear with all types of apparel.

Even today, boots are still widely accepted as a fashion accessory. Although some people will continue to choose boots only in terms of the amount of protection they offer against bad weather, it appears likely that boots for both indoor and outdoor wear will continue to maintain their fashion importance for some time to come.

Patronage Motives

Fashion merchants, eager to collect an assortment that will please present customers and hopefully win additional customers, have to consider *patronage motives:* the reasons that induce customers to patronize one store rather than another, or why people buy where they do.

The distance one has to travel to make a specific purchase is one factor to be considered. For convenience items, such as cosmetics and inexpensive hosiery, people often patronize the nearest store, even if it happens to be a supermarket or drugstore with only a limited selection of basic styles. For fairly routine fashion purchases, such as moderately priced blouses, slacks, and sweaters, women customers are willing to travel farther, if necessary; suburban women can be counted on to travel several miles to shopping centers, where they can find a good selection of such items. For important fashion purchases, such as furs, fine jewelry, or evening clothes, people may travel many miles. People who live in the suburbs may go considerable distances to patronize stores in high fashion shopping centers or in the nearest large city. Those who live in small urban areas frequently make their fashion purchases in the major stores of nearby large urban areas.

As far as fashion merchandise is concerned, a customer's reasons for choosing one store in preference to another are likely to be based on the store's fashion reputation, the assortments it offers, its price ranges, and its merchandising policies. Other prime considerations are the services offered (credit, adjustments, delivery, parking) and the attitude of the salespeople. Finally, the customer includes the location of the store in relation to others, as well as the size and layout of the store.

Each successful fashion store has to offer fashion merchandise that reflects all facets of the fashion image that the store wants to project to its customers, for customers mainly base their fashion patronage on that image.

Variations in Demand

The geographical area where people live, their lifestyles, the prevailing climate, and numerous other factors influence both the type and the extent of customer demand. These factors explain, for instance, why two specialty stores—one in a metropolitan area of the Northeast and one in a Midwest city, both serving customers of approximately the same income group—cannot offer similar assortments. They also explain, in another example, why a nearby branch may need an assortment somewhat different from that of the parent store.

Regional Variations Variations in the composition of the population and in the prevailing climate bring about variations in the demand for fashion goods in different parts of the United States.

For instance, people in the Western states often are quicker than most to adopt new styles, especially if they are casual and informal. Sometimes regional preference in apparel come about as reflections of the racial stocks from which the population is mainly drawn. In the Great Lakes region, for example, many residents are of German and Scandinavian ancestory. Blue-eyed and fair-skinned, they are partial to the color blue, whether it is in or out of fashion.

Sometimes climate is responsible for variations in demand. San Francisco, for example, is famous as a "suit city," whether or not suits are fashionable elsewhere, and also as a city whose women never store their furs. The city's climate makes a removable jacket comfortable for daytime wear, and chilly evenings make the warmth of a fur stole welcome even in summer.

Urban and Suburban Demand Fashion demand in suburbs is usually different from that in central cities, and often there are notable differences in demand among the various suburbs of a single central city. Most retail stores find that, although branch customers may be in similar income brackets and have essentially the same taste levels as city customers, apparel preferences of the two groups differ. Living is more casual in suburbs than in cities.

When department stores first branched out vigorously into the suburbs in the 1950s, stores were small in size compared with today's giant branch stores. Because the first branches were small, merchandise selections were necessarily limited and often featured the store's higher price lines. As the population movement from cities to suburbs continued, stores found small branches inadequate and replaced them with larger units that were either free-standing or else served as anchor stores for new regional shopping centers. Because of the larger size of these new branches, the parent stores were able to increase the depth and breadth of the branches' assortments and offer a greater range of price lines.

To stimulate business in their branches and lend additional emphasis to the fashion image they wish to project, stores occasionally feature special fashion promotions at branch stores. This gives suburban customers the opportunity to attend fashion events that traditionally had been held only in center-city stores.

Perhaps the most important fact about consumer demand that branch store expansion has taught retailers is that people prefer to make fashion purchases from plentiful assortments. When a branch offers only a limited assortment, customers are more likely to visit several stores before making their purchasing decision, and the branch store runs a greater risk of not getting their patronage.

Seasonal Variations In areas where the change of seasons is strongly marked, the demand for warmer or cooler apparel follows the calendar. In regions like southern Florida or Hawaii, however, there is practically no seasonal climatic change and little reason for seasonal variations in the weight or type of garments offered for sale. Some Northern parts of the country have short springs and summers, and most of their fashion demand is for cold-weather clothes. In the South and Southwest the reverse is true; there is only a short winter season and little demand for warm clothes, and so fashion interest concentrates mainly on styles, materials, and colors that provide summer comfort.

The element of seasonality in the demand for fashion goods that are designed specifically for hot or cold weather, however, has been diminishing in importance in recent years. With improved heating and increased use of air-conditioning systems in homes, cars, and business, consumer demand for fashion merchandise tends increasingly to ignore the outdoor climate. In areas where summers are hot, air conditioning occasionally makes a sweater desirable when indoors. Where winters are cold, central heating can make heavy indoor clothing oppressive. Styles and especially materials that bridge the seasons are increasingly important factors in relation to consumer demand.

Another factor that upsets the traditional impact of the calendar upon fashion demand is the ease and speed of travel. Consumers can take a brief vacation—even a weekend trip—and quickly reach a climate radically different from the one at home. Today, customers who live in a mild climate turn to the stores they regularly patronize in search of warm clothing for a ski weekend; and customers who live in a cold climate and are planning a quick trip south descend upon their favorite store in midwinter looking for cool, lightweight apparel.

Successful merchants must provide at all times what their customers want. The timing and nature of customer demand today is subject to constant change and requires that fashion assortments be able to provide various types of merchandise that customers want, no matter when they want them.

Other Variations   More than weather and climate is involved in selling fashions, however. There are also selling seasons linked to holidays and certain times of the year when customers have come to expect special sales.

Special Occasions and Holidays   An obvious example of the fashion demand patterns determined by the calendar is the need for new clothes for children and young adults when schools open each fall. Stores recognize this natural peak of demand by preparing appropriate assortments, setting up special departments if necessary, and running special promotions for school wear. Thus, on a hot day in late August, stores are often filled with mothers outfitting their school-age children with warm dresses, suits, sweaters, and coats.

Holidays such as Easter, Christmas, and the New Year create a demand for clothes to wear for social events. In May and June merchants peak their assortments of wedding gowns and trousseau merchandise, as they do in such other favorite bridal months as September and December.

Vacations are another seasonal spur to fashion demand. Although winter vacations are increasingly popular, summer still remains the favored time for vacation trips. Stores try to time their offerings of travel clothes and equipment to conform to the vacation habits and resultant fashion demands of the customers they serve.

Special Sales Events   Because stores have established an annual pattern of promotions, customers have come to expect and patronize special preseason or postseason sales. These have little relation to the normal pattern of demand but have become traditional off-price sale periods. The merchant's need to stimulate sales during normally slow periods as well as to clear out odds and ends of old stock before bringing in new season styles has led to a traditional pattern of sales in many merchandise categories. Such categories range from bedlinens to furniture and include such fashion items as apparel, lingerie, and shoes. Even elegant shops whose policies are firmly against off-price promotions find it necessary to stage semiannual or annual clearances.

Another example of artificially stimulated demand is the summer preseason sale of winter coats and furs. The history of such sales goes back to the 1920s and perhaps even earlier, when coat factories had long layoffs between peak selling seasons followed by periods of intense activity and expensive overtime work. To reduce the need for overtime work and provide their workers with more regular employment, manufacturers made concessions in price to retailers who ordered and accepted delivery of goods in advance of the normal selling period. This enabled the retailers, in turn, to offer winter garments to their customers at lower than regular prices if they bought such garments in summer. In the days before air conditioning, a considerable price inducement was necessary to entice women into stores to try on winter coats in midsummer heat. Nonetheless, customers came and made their selections, and summer coat and fur sales became a tradition.

AIDS IN DETERMINING CUSTOMER PREFERENCES

The fashion sense of successful merchants is simply the fruit of hard work: checking their own stores' past merchandising records, determining general trends in consumer demand through every available source, and on occasion soliciting information on local demand from representative groups of their own customers. In fashion merchandising, instinct and intuition are no match for facts and conscientious research.

Although most stores base their fashion merchandise selections on systematic research, such research is particularly important in larger stores. In a small specialty store, the owner is usually also the merchandise manager and can collect customer preference information by studying stock and sales records, talking to customers, and listening to vendors. In larger stores, determining customer preferences is a more complex job of research. The number of customers served may be in the hundreds of thousands instead of just in the hundreds, and the number of fashion items offered and vendors involved may be multiplied proportionately. Smaller stores may need only pencil and paper to do a good customer research job from their sales and stock records. Larger stores often use electronic data processing systems to collect and analyze such customer demand information on a continuing basis.

Information From Store Sources

Any store that has been in business for more than a season has in its records a treasury of information about its customers' responses to previous merchandise offerings. This information, properly interpreted, shows what customers have bought and what has not interested them. It also indicates what fashion trends may be developing and what trends may be passing their peak.

It is assumed, of course, that the store or department being studied has a clearly defined target group of customers. These are not necessarily the same individuals month after month or year after year, but they are people of similar incomes and taste levels who prefer styles at approximately the same point in their fashion cycles. If a store's customers are too heterogeneous a group, or if a store has been shifting its sights, aiming first at one and then at another type of target customer, its past history will not be a reliable basis on which to build future plans.

Past Sales Records It can be assumed that those items which sold at the fastest rates in the past had the strongest natural appeal to customers. If fast sellers have some features in common, such as color, price, detail, or texture, these features can be an important indication of the nature of customer demand. For example, if the unadorned round neckline usually described as a "jewel neckline" is a feature of nearly all best-selling blouses, at several prices, in several colors, it can be assumed that the jewel neckline is gaining in demand

over other types. On the other hand, if beige blouses are the best sellers, regardless of neckline, then it is color that is influencing the customers and beige the color that is most important in the tide of demand.

Pretesting New styles are first bought in wide variety but in small quantities. Customer reaction and sales are then observed. Styles that sell promptly presumably are those with strong natural appeal to a store's customers; they are reordered, other similar styles are ordered, and the slow sellers dropped.

There are many other ways to pretest new styles, including staging fashion shows early in the season and observing customer reactions and noting purchases, showing vendors' lines to salespeople and inviting their comments, and preseason sales, such as the summer coat sales, that indicate which styles are most popular.

The *trunk show* is a form of pretesting that involves a producer's sending a representative to a store with a sample of every style in the line, and the store's exhibiting these samples to customers at scheduled, announced showings. People who attend see every style the producer has available, not just those styles the merchant has already chosen to stock. If customers see a style they want that is not carried by the store, they can order it. Merchants, meantime, have a chance to see how their selections from the producer's line compare with what interests their customers, so that they can tailor their assortments to more adequately reflect their customers' wants.

Markdowns Downward revisions in the selling prices of merchandise are "markdowns." Good retail practice requires that all markdowns be entered on a store record, and a reason given for each markdown taken. Since markdowns are often used to clear out slow-moving stock, an analysis of the styles that had to be reduced often shows what merchandise features failed to attract sufficient customers, thus indicating how the merchant should readjust the assortments in the future. For example, a line of particularly vividly colored vinyl jackets may do well in a high-priced version in a boutique setting and in a low-priced version in the budget department. A moderate-priced version offered in the regular sportswear department, however, may be such a slow seller that most of the stock ends up on the markdown rack. A logical assumption, then, is that the extreme in sport jackets, properly priced, is acceptable to the top and bottom strata of the store's customers, but the group in the middle, who are traditionally conservative, are not interested in this type of merchandise.

Want Slips   When a customer requests something that is not in stock, salespeople report the situation on forms known as *want slips.* (See Form 12-1.) These can be particularly interesting as a means of studying current customer demand, for they are one of the few indications a store has of what customers would buy if the store had it available. Study of these unfilled customer wants helps a merchant correct possible errors in filling demand for particular sizes, prices, colors, or types of items. A dress department, for instance, might stock only quite conservative styles in larger sizes, but want slips might show that customers wearing these sizes

would like to find more lively colors and youthful styles from which to choose.

Advertising Results   Stores try to determine the amount of business that is transacted as a direct result of advertising. This is often hard to determine, unless a customer arrives at the store with ad in hand or mentions the ad to a salesperson. However, if an ad promotes a particular line or item, increases in sales immediately after the ad appears are usually attributed to the promotion. The response to the advertising of a specific style is usually an indication of the degree of customer interest in the style, particularly if several styles receive equal advertising emphasis but show considerable differences in arousing customer interest.

In a departmentalized store, a buyer for one department sometimes can obtain valuable guidance from the results of advertising done by related departments in addition to the results of his or her own ads.

Returns, Complaints, Adjustments   When a store accepts a return from a customer or makes an adjustment on goods that failed to give satisfaction, all the details about the transaction are recorded. These records are warnings for store buy-

---

MERCHANDISE WANT SLIP

Department No. _42_   Name _Sara Davies_
Date _8/17/–_

The following Requested Merchandise is not in Stock:

Description (Item, Color, Size, Price)	No. of Calls	Buyer's Remarks
After Five #417, brown, 10, $40.00	2	On order

The following Stock is getting low:

Mfr., Style, Color, Price	Pieces On Hand	
Aiken, 6912, red, $26.00	3	Discontinued

SUGGEST A SUBSTITUTE

FORM 12-1

ers, telling them which goods have not been found acceptable by customers and why. For example, if customers return laminated fabrics because they separated in cleaning, then the buyer should consider finding a more reliable source for laminated fabrics. In addition, the buyer would have to accept the fact that a certain degree of prejudice might have developed against laminates, thereby influencing customer demand, and additional promotion, stressing the reliability of the new fabrics, might be needed.

Customer Surveys Many customers are quite willing to tell a retailer what they like and what they do not like about his store, what interests them in the merchandise assortment and what does not interest them. Such surveys can be quite informal, and yet provide a clear indication of trends. The buyer or store owner, talking with customers on the selling floor, observing expressions and listening to remarks made by the customers, learns a good deal about the nature of customer demand and how the store's assortment is viewed by the customer. Formal surveys can be made by mail or personal interview to determine, for example, what price lines are favored, what types of merchandise are wanted by regular or potential customers, and what services are expected.

Salespeople Because of their constant, direct contact with customers, salespeople usually can provide valuable information about what customers want. In larger stores, salespeople are really the stores' only links with their customers, for store buyers seldom can spend much time on the selling floor. Salespeople can report whether customers bought certain styles eagerly or reluctantly, and whether they asked for any particular items that were not immediately available. Sometimes the information gathered from salespeople is the first indication a store may have of a change in a trend; at other times, what the salespeople report will reinforce and amplify what a merchant may already have suspected from observations and from store records.

Information from Sources Outside the Store

Merchants also look beyond their own doors for indications of consumer demand. What they learn from outside sources may confirm what they deduce from their own experience—or it may indicate points they have missed, or perhaps misinterpreted. A typical case would be that of styles or items which a store has not yet stocked but which are enjoying good acceptance in other stores.

There are many specific sources to which merchants turn for information, including their competitors and suppliers. To alert retailers, however, everything has fashion significance. What people wear to the theater and restaurants, what important local people are wearing, and what national celebrities are wearing are among the many guides that help a fashion merchant identify current trends in customer demand.

Competitors Merchants and their buyers regularly study the advertising of other stores. They visit the selling floors of competing stores to see what is stocked, what is featured in displays, and what appears to be selling.

Some stores rely on their buyers and merchandise managers to do this job, but others prefer to set up a separate comparison bureau or office, believing that its staff can perform the work involved more extensively and more objectively than can the store's merchandising executives.

Comparison shoppers visit the stores of local competitors, check prices, assortments, services, and customer response; they then report their findings to executives in their own store for appropriate action.

Resident Buying Office The resident buying office that provides a store with representation in a major market area also provides that store with a steady flow of current information on general trends in consumer demand. Such information takes the form of market bulletins, reports on new items, fashion forecasts, and lists of styles and items that are best-sellers in other client stores. During periods when store buyers are in the market to view producers' lines, the resident buying offices hold clinics, or meetings, at which buyers from their various client stores can discuss fashion, merchandise, and merchandising. Separate clinics are held for buyers specializing in each category of merchandise, so that the discussions can be fully detailed; there are also group meetings for heads of stores and for merchandise managers.

In addition, individual store managers and their buyers may consult the market representatives of the buying office about vendors and best-selling items. At the resident buying office, buyers from many noncompeting stores meet informally, and frequently compare notes on consumer demand.

Manufacturers and Their Sales Representatives   The producers with whom a store deals can contribute information about the reasons why they sponsor certain styles and trends. Their lines have been planned to meet anticipated consumer demand and tested against the reactions and sales experience of many retail buyers. Well-prepared sales representatives usually are eager to provide retail buyers with detailed information not only about their line but also about response to it.

Some of the most accurate information about consumer demand comes from producers. Today, major producers in each branch of the fashion business are large enough to use modern electronic equipment in collecting and analyzing information about sales trends quickly. Such producers thus are in a position to tell merchants what styles are selling at what rate in each part of the country. They can give advice about the styles that might prove to be best for each store and the time when they should be offered. They can also give the buyer helpful details about ways other stores have presented similar merchandise and what the results have been.

Research Studies   Individual manufacturers, industry associations, publications, and government agencies occasionally make research studies in

which consumers are polled about what they want to buy, where and when they prefer to buy, and their reasons for buying or not buying. The purposes for which surveys are undertaken are varied, but each contributes some useful information about customer buying patterns.

Typical of such studies are the surveys made regularly by *Clothes* magazine. For instance, a typical survey concerned men's accessories and included information collected from both vendors and retailers. The result was statistical information about the various categories of accessories in terms of share of market by both units and dollars, plus a sales percentage breakdown for each category of merchandise by types of items. The article accompanying the statistics discussed the trends in men's accessories and pointed out what categories and what items within those categories would probably be the popular sellers of the next season.

Another typical survey was made by a foundation and lingerie producer to ascertain ages, heights, weights, and dress sizes of customers, as well as to gather information about the kinds of foundations, lingerie, and sleepwear they preferred.

A popular form of survey made regularly by some consumer magazines and sporadically by others is undertaken to determine how many of each of a list of items their readers buy per year and what they pay for each.

Consumer and Trade Publications   Fashion merchants obtain insights into consumer demand from publications, both those that are intended for the general public and those intended for readers within some specific sector of the fashion business.

Fashion news is reported in almost all consumer newspapers and magazines. Merchants keep track of this news, and also of the fashion advertising in such publications, so that they will know what influences may be creating or discouraging demand for certain fashion products among their customers. Magazines that give special emphasis to fashion, such as *Vogue* and *Harper's Bazaar*, or to fashions for specific groups of customers, such as *Glamour* or *Mademoiselle*, go to considerable

RETAIL NEWS BUREAU

'A *Confidential* Reporting Service'

ITEM (S)— MISSES DRESSES
SIZES 6-14
$ 90.00

Lord & Taylor

A graphic print

of American Indian
ancestry and soft rayon
challis make these some
of the prettiest pyjamas
around. Black print
on cream, 6 to 14,
90.00 Sports Dresses;
Fifth Floor
Lord & Taylor —
call WI 7-3300 And at all
Lord & Taylor stores

RESPONSE*			
FAIR	GOOD	STRONG	SELLOUT
	VERY	...X	

DM	**RESOURCE**

LUCRECIA FOR ERMAR
498 7TH AVENUE
NEW YORK CITY

REPORT NO. JG-MM07I8-I

STORE LORD & TAYLOR

PAPER POST 7/I7

AD. SIZE 7" BY 4

WEATHER WARM

* Shopped 3 Times

DETAILS: GRAPHIC GLORY.......

STYLE: # 375R: TWO PIECE PYJAMA OUTFIT IN BLACK PRINT ON
A CREAM COLORED BACKGROUND IN SOFT RAYON
CHALLIS. FOR SIZES 6-I4. $ 90.00.

ADVERTISED MERCHANDISE IS DISPLAYED ON T-STANDS IN LORD &
TAYLOR'S SPORT DRESS DEPARTMENT ON THE FIFTH FLOOR. THIS
IS LORD & TAYLOR'S INITIAL ORDER. OTHER STORES THAT HAVE
ORDERED THIS OUTFIT ARE SAKS FIFTH AVENUE AND BERGDORF
GOODMAN. DELIVERY IS 3-4 WEEKS.

Errors subject to correction

● MERCHANDISE REPORT OF **RETAIL NEWS BUREAU,** 232 MADISON AVE., NEW YORK N. Y. 10016 ●

Copyright 1976   An Independent Agency Reporting the News of Retailing—Promptly, Accurately, Completely.   MU 6-7134

Subscribing to an independent reporting service can give a retailer a steady flow of pertinent information on consumer demand.

Retail News Bureau

effort to keep fashion merchants informed about the merchandise to be featured in future editions. They also can provide assessments of fashion trends among the particular segments of the public that they serve, and with information about how best to influence their readers. Consumer magazines spend enormous amounts on research in order to know their readers better, and they are usually more than willing to share the results of these studies with fashion merchants.

Trade publications are expert in assessing fashion and market developments. Some of these publications are aimed primarily at retailers, telling them what merchandise is new and good, and how stores are promoting it successfully. Examples are *Intimate Apparel, Handbags and Accessories, Jewelers' Circular-Keystone,* and *Boot and Shoe Recorder.* Others, like *Women's Wear Daily,* address themselves to all branches of an industry, from the retailers to the sources of the primary materials used in manufacturing the products concerned. From both types of trade publications, a fashion merchant can get a highly professional assessment of consumer demand and the influences that are being exerted upon it.

Reporting Services There are services to which merchants can subscribe to keep up to date on store happenings, ideas, trends, and market news. For example, Retail News Bureau supplies regular reports on the ads run by New York stores. Other services include market forecasts, hot-item bulletins, general market news, a merchant's newsletter, and a variety of other bulletins and news releases about women's apparel and accessories. Another example is the *Fashion Calendar,* published weekly and available on a subscription basis, that lists and gives details about all upcoming openings, fashion shows, and other important fashion events. The same source also publishes a monthly fashion newsletter for retail executives called *Fashion International.* Similar market information is also available on a fee basis from Tobé Associates, Inc., one of the older services in the field, founded by the late Tobé Coller Davis.

Fashion Consultants Independent fashion consultants sell their expertise to merchants to supplement that of a firm's own executives. Fashion consultants may be hired by merchants on a regular retainer basis or to assist with a single project. Some consultants tend to specialize in certain areas of fashion, while others offer a wide range of fashion services. Most of these experts have years of experience in the fashion business.

One of the best-known New York–based fashion consultants is Estelle Hamburger, an outstanding authority on fashion promotion. Other important fashion consultants located in the New York City area are Mildred Custin, former president of Bonwit Teller; Mildred Finger, former import buyer for Ohrbach's and designer salon buyer for Bergdorf Goodman; Merchandising Motivation, Inc., headed by Marjorie Reich, former fashion director for R. H. Macy and Co.; Beryl Tucker Young, Inc., specializing in the youth market; and Letitia Baldridge Enterprises, Inc., headed by the former secretary to Mrs. Jacqueline Kennedy Onassis when she was First Lady of the United States.

Customer Advisory Groups

A third source of useful information for retailers is supplied by various customer groups organized by some stores. These groups give retailers a consumer's-eye-view of store policies, services, assortments, and fashions. In addition, they assure the store of a flow of favorable publicity among the circles in which group members move and also in the news media, if group members or their activities are considered newsworthy.

College Boards Perhaps the oldest and most firmly entrenched consumer advisory group is the college advisory board. A college board is made up of at least one upper-class student chosen from each college that is important to residents of an area. In the August and September selling rush, these young women and young men serve both as salespeople and as advisers to college-bound customers. They may also informally model apparel.

Teen Boards Stores often set up teen or high school boards. Activities of these boards differ from those of college boards in several respects. Actual sales work usually is not involved; activities are year-round, since the high schools are located in the store's trading area. Teen boards, unlike those for college students, often engage in activities beyond fashion merchandising alone. For example, working through their teen boards, stores may sponsor such projects as charm schools, dressing dolls for deprived children, club meetings, window decorating contests, record-playing sessions, and the preparation of fashion columns for school newspapers. Some stores have similar activities for pre-teens, but usually on a more restricted scale.

Accustoming younger age groups to visit a store regularly lays the foundation for making fashion customers of them in their college, career, and married years. And the store, having "watched them grow up," is better able to anticipate their wants and to encourage them to comment freely to management if the assortments or services are lacking in some respect.

Career Women Although many stores have special shops and special promotions for career women, relatively few have clubs or boards for this segment of their customers. More commonly, they reach career women through special programs and fashion shows. On these occasions, the merchants observe their reactions to the merchandise, invite orders, and encourage comments.

One store that does have a career woman activity runs a club for them with meetings devoted to informative programs emphasizing fashion. One club member is chosen by lot every second week to select and accessorize several stock garments she considers ideal for working women. Her selections are then featured in the store's boutique for career women.

REFERENCES

[1] Based on Wingate and Friedlander, *The Management of Retail Buying*, p. 92.
[2] Copeland, *Principles of Merchandising*, pp. 155–167.
[3] Udell, *A New Approach to Consumer Motivation*, pp. 8–9.

MERCHANDISING VOCABULARY

Define or briefly explain the following terms:

Consumer demand	Psychological satisfactions
Consumerism	Patronage motives
Selection factors	Trunk show
Buying motivation	Want slip
Operational satisfactions	

MERCHANDISING REVIEW

1. Trace the rise of the consumer movement and the practices, at both production and retail distribution levels, that gave the movement impetus.
2. In what respects is today's typical American consumer different from the typical American consumer of a few decades ago?

3. Name and describe any five elements or selection factors that significantly influence a customer's choice when contemplating the purchase of most fashion goods.

4. In what respects does Udell's theory relating to buying motives differ from an earlier and widely held theory? Do you agree or disagree, and why?

5. Name at least five reasons why customers patronize one store rather than another.

6. What factors are primarily responsible for (a) regional variations in demand and (b) seasonal variations in demand?

7. What factors, other than regional and seasonal differences, contribute to variations in customer demand? Give at least one example of each of these factors.

8. What sources in a merchant's store yield information about customer demand? Briefly note the specific type(s) of information provided by each source.

9. What sources outside a merchant's store yield information about customer demand? Briefly note the specific type(s) of information provided by each source.

10. Of what value to a fashion merchant, in obtaining relevant information on customer demand, are customer advisory groups? Give at least one example of how each group can provide a merchant with helpful information on demand.

MERCHANDISING DIGEST

1. Discuss the following statement from the text: "It is not enough for merchants to merely keep abreast of general fashion trends and general customer demand." What else should a merchant carefully consider when selecting and promoting fashion assortments?

2. Discuss the importance of price as a selection factor when making fashion purchases.

3. Discuss the following statement from the text and its implications for fashion merchants: "The element of seasonality in demand for fashion goods that are designed specifically for hot or cold weather . . . has been diminishing in importance in recent years."

13
THE DOLLAR MERCHANDISE PLAN

In earlier times, merchants' inventories were composed mainly of staple items with a smattering of apparel fabrics and sewing notions. Most apparel and accessories for the family were made in the home. Because they stocked only a few fashion goods, most merchants would order goods only twice a year, buying enough each time to cover their needs for a six-month period. Often such semiannual purchases arrived in a single shipment which was gradually sold off as a season progressed. Plans and budgets of how much should be spent for such purchases and what types of merchandise should be bought were often in merchants' heads rather than on paper.

Today, budgeting for a fashion department or store entails far greater risks and capital investment than ever before, for the following reasons:

- Fashion implies change, and retail fashion assortments must continually change to reflect changes in customer demand. Any notable difference between the change in customer demand that fashion merchants anticipate at the time they begin acquiring merchandise assortments and the change in customer demand that actually takes place almost certainly means lost sales, large markdowns, and decreased profits.
- Since stocks must be peaked in anticipation of peaks in customer demand, fashion merchants must risk considerable investment in acquiring an inventory with no assurance that the actual demand will be as great as anticipated.

- Customers are demanding expanded and well-coordinated fashion assortments from which to choose, thereby requiring greater capital investment in inventories.
- With vendors requiring longer periods for delivery of store purchases, fashion merchants must tie up considerable capital further and further in advance of the time that the merchandise ordered will actually be available for sale in the store.
- Branch store expansion, modernization of facilities, high taxes and interest rates, and rising operating costs require huge additional capital investment.

Today, there can be nothing hit or miss about how a store invests its money in fashion goods. Sound financial planning and control, together with sound assortment planning, are essential to a profitable operation.

RETAIL FINANCIAL MANAGEMENT

The only source of income for most retail stores is that resulting from the merchandising activities of its selling departments. This income, then, must be sufficient to pay not only for all merchandise purchases but also for all other costs incident to the operation of the business, while providing a reasonable rate of return on invested capital.

Financial management of retail firms requires careful advance planning of both the amounts of money that will be needed to finance a store's merchandise purchases and the amounts of revenue that can be expected from sales of that merchandise. Only by planning in advance can management provide for the financial needs of the business and seek to reduce the financial risks involved.

Goals of Dollar Merchandise Planning

The major goals of scientific dollar planning in retail merchandising are:

- To have at all times an inventory that is neither too large nor too small for anticipated customer demand
- To time the store or departmental purchases so that merchandise is available for sale neither too early nor too late for customer demand
- To keep purchases in line with the store's ability to pay for them
- To have funds available for the purchase of new goods when they may be needed

Tools of Dollar Merchandise Planning

The principal financial tools that retail merchants use to achieve these goals are the dollar merchandise plan and the dollar open-to-buy. The dollar merchandise plan looks to the future; it is drawn up to serve as a guide for a selling period that has not yet begun. The open-to-buy is concerned with the present; it is a control device to keep stocks in line with actual sales.

The Dollar Merchandise Plan The *dollar merchandise plan* is actually a budget, a projection, in dollars, of the sales goals of a merchandise classification, a department, or an entire store for a specific future period of time, and the amount of stock required to achieve those sales. The plan, or budget, indicates the rate at which money can be spent for purchases during a given period in order to maintain a desired relationship between dollar sales and inventory values.

The dollar merchandise plan is similar in purpose to a personal budget. It shows merchants the income expected and the expenditures anticipated during a particular period, just as a personal budget balances proposed expenses against expected income for a given time. In the same way that people have to check what they actually receive and spend against their budget, so must merchants check actual merchandising results against those projected in their plan. If actual sales are below those planned, they make every effort to improve merchandising techniques so that the planned figures will be achieved. If conditions differ from those that existed or were anticipated at the time the plan was drawn up, they revise the original estimates.

The Dollar Open-to-buy The term *dollar open-to-buy* refers to the dollar value of planned purchases for a given period minus the dollar value of all orders scheduled for delivery during that same period but not yet received. Planned purchases are defined and discussed later in this chapter. A detailed discussion of open-to-buy will be found in Chapter 16.

Use of Retail Figures

The majority of department stores and departmentalized specialty stores operate under an accounting system known as the *retail method of inventory* evaluation. In this system, all records of transactions affecting the value of a store, department, or merchandise classification inventory—such as sales, purchases, markdowns, transfers, and returns-to-vendor—are recorded at their retail values. Stores on the older "cost" method of inventory evaluation (usually only small stores) keep their records of purchases and other inventory changes on the basis of the cost of the merchandise, rather than the retail price at which each item is marked.

Stores operating under the retail method plan their merchandise budgets and assortments entirely on the basis of retail values. Since the majority of departmentalized stores use the retail method of accounting, all figures used in subsequent discussions of dollar merchandise planning are at retail values, unless otherwise indicated.

THE BASIC DOLLAR MERCHANDISE PLAN

As already defined, the merchandise plan or budget is a careful integration of a sales program and the stock needed to achieve those planned sales during a specific period of time.

In a small store, where the owner is in constant touch with all operations, a formal merchandise plan may be unnecessary. However, even in a small store with limited capital resources, some preplanning of purchases and other elements of the merchandising operation is necessary.

In large retail organizations a carefully detailed plan or budget is essential. The very size of the establishment requires the distribution of merchandising responsibilities among many individuals. The merchandising plan thus provides a guide for each of these individuals in their efforts to secure desired sales and profit results. In addition, a carefully prepared merchandise plan furnishes a standard against which store management can measure the performance of those executives charged with the responsibilities of the merchandising operation.[1]

Preparing the Plan

In a small organization, dollar merchandising plans for the store as a whole are usually drawn up. In larger stores, separate budgets are first developed for each department. Later these separate budgets are incorporated into a master plan at the divisional level, or the storewide level, or both.

The merchandise plan, whether for a single department or for a store as a whole, should be prepared in such a form that its significance becomes clear and its information plain to all who must work with it. While the format of the plan may vary considerably from store to store, both in scope and amount of detail, the ideal is a plan presented in the simplest form possible and in terminology familiar to everyone who will be using it.

The period covered by a merchandise budget may vary from one month to a year, but the usual planning period is six months. The spring season, February through July, is usually planned in one budget; the fall season, August through January, is planned in another. In most cases the seasonal plan is later broken down into monthly or, in some cases, weekly subdivisions.

Merchandise plans are drawn up several months in advance of the period to which they refer. The length of time varies from store to store, but plans are necessarily completed and approved before actual buying for the season begins.

Departmental buyers usually play an active role in the initial preparation of merchandise plans. First, a store's accounting department supplies each buyer with a planning form on which has been recorded the actual result figures from that department's merchandising operation during the corresponding season last year. Many stores, particularly larger ones, also include in their plans last year's actual and this year's planned figures for certain seasonal merchandising goals, such as gross margin desired, the number of stock turns desired, and certain departmental operating expenses. These seasonal merchandising goals are established by store management, not by departmental buyers. Form 13-1 is typical of a six-month merchandising planning form as it might be originally presented to a buyer of Misses' Dresses.

Then, within the framework of management's goal figures, armed with the previous year's actual result figures, and guided by specialized knowledge of market conditions, trends, and demand cycles, a buyer prepares anticipated sales, stock, markdowns, and purchase plans for the department in the upcoming six-month season.

When a buyer has completed work on the merchandise plan, it is reviewed with the divisional merchandise manager, who may make revisions before approving it. Next, the merchandise manager consolidates into a divisional plan the approved plans of all the departments supervised and submits the divisional plan to the general merchandise manager for review and approval. Finally, all plans are subject to review by the store's controller (or other chief fiscal officer) and usually the chief executive (the general manager or president); when approved,

SIX MONTH MERCHANDISING PLAN

Dept. Name _____ Misses' Dresses _____ Dept. No. ___ 42 _____

	PLAN (This Year)	ACTUAL (Last Year)
Initial markup (%)	48.5	47.5
Gross margin (%)	42.3	41.8
Cash discount (% cost purch.)	8.0	7.8
Season stock turnover (rate)	2.8	2.6
Shortage reserve (%)	1.5	1.8
Advertising expense (%)	2.8	3.0
Selling salaries (%)	8.0	8.5

SPRING 197— ~~FALL 197—~~		FEB. AUG.	MAR. SEP.	APR. OCT.	MAY NOV.	JUNE DEC.	JULY JAN.	SEASON TOTAL
SALES	Last Year	12,100	14,200	17,300	15,500	14,100	10,800	84,000
	Plan							
	Percent of Increase							6.0%
	Revised							
	Actual							
RETAIL STOCK (BOM)	Last Year	34,500	35,500	39,000	35,000	34,000	29,000	21,000*
	Plan							*
	Revised							
	Actual							
MARKDOWNS	Last Year	2,000	2,500	2,800	2,200	2,200	2,100	13,800
	Plan (dollars)							
	Plan (percent)							14.0%
	Revised							
	Actual							
RETAIL PURCHASES	Last Year	15,100	20,200	16,100	16,700	11,300	4,900	84,300
	Plan							
	Revised							
	Actual							

Comments

*Represents stock end of period.

Merchandise Manager _____   Buyer _____

Controller _____

FORM 13-1

departmental plans are combined into a master plan for the store as a whole.

Departmentalized stores with several large branches usually make separate merchandise plans for each department in each branch. These plans are usually drawn up by departmental buyers in cooperation with respective branch store managers. Separate branch plans may then be incorporated into the parent store's departmental plan; or individual branch store plans may be incorporated, together with the total parent store plan, into a companywide plan. Stores with only a few branches generally combine branch store merchandising plans on a department-by-department basis with the plans of each parent store department.

A good merchandise plan is both specific and flexible. Since the plan is an attempt to forecast customer demand and develop strategies far in advance of the period covered, the plan is not presumed to be completely rigid. As the season actually gets under way, figures in the plan are frequently reviewed, both in relation to actual results and in relation to more current information about the balance of the season. For example, if the supply of certain types of goods appears to be threatened by a lengthy strike, store management might decide to increase immediately their stocks of such goods, which would mean increasing beginning-of-the-month stocks in affected departments, which would increase purchases. Or if important business firms go on a reduced work week or lay off large numbers of employees or go out of business, retail stores in that area can probably expect a decrease in customer demand and may decide to reduce their sales plans and stock requirements. Such reductions in the seasonal plan would result in decreased planned purchases for the affected departments.

Elements of the Plan

Merchandise plans vary considerably from store to store in format, scope, and detail. The basic elements included in most seasonal merchandise budgets, however, are sales, stocks, markdowns, and purchases. In addition, as previously mentioned, the merchandising plan may include other seasonal goal figures affecting operating profit, such as initial markup, gross margin, reserves, stock shortage, cash discounts, and stock turnover. Also often considered essential in planning are such operating expenses as selling salaries and advertising expense.

Planning Sales The first step in the preparation of a merchandise plan is to make a realistic estimate of prospective sales during an upcoming season, based upon external factors, internal factors, and general fashion trends that are likely to influence a department's sales volume. Finally, sales goals are established for each month of the season being planned.

External Factors External factors—those outside of the store or its control—include employment prospects, general economic conditions, population changes, and the competitive situation. The opening of a new plant in an area, for example, is likely to increase spending power in the community. Conversely, the possibility of strikes or shutdowns among local employers means a potential loss of spending power in the trading area.

Optimism regarding the future encourages consumer spending; threats of new taxes, higher interest rates, or declines in economic activity tend to discourage spending.

Sales prospects are affected by the growth or lack of growth in an area's population, by changes in the proportion of high-income to low-income families, by changes in the age composition of a population. A new housing development for young families, for example, provides a potential increase in sales in children's, juniors', young women's, and young men's departments. A new, center-city high-rise apartment building appealing to older couples may favor departments selling higher-priced, more conservative apparel and accessories, as well as home furnishings.

The competitive effect of new or expanded stores and shopping centers in the trading area is evaluated; consideration is given to the possibility that stores in other communities, within easy traveling distance, may be gaining or losing power to draw off some of the local retail business. On the other hand, if any local competitors have closed up shop, or if new highways or parking facilities have made it easier for customers to get to the store, there is reason to anticipate sales growth.

Internal Factors Internal factors—those within the store or its control—include physical changes within the store that either enhance or diminish the sales prospects of individual departments, such as the opening of new branches, the general trend in store sales, and the number and extent of promotions the store's management expects to undertake during the season being planned.

Physical changes within a store can affect the sales prospects of various departments within the store. For example, if new escalators are being installed with landings at the entrance to department X, sales of that department presumably will benefit. On the other hand, if department Y had to be moved to a less prominent location or perhaps had its floor space reduced because of the alteration, department Y's sales may suffer. Not only do relocation, expansion, or contraction of a department's selling space affect sales, but so do the acquisition or elimination of display fixtures, a change of decor, and any change in its proximity to departments carrying related merchandise.

If a new branch is to be opened within the planning period, the additional anticipated sales in that branch should be taken into account. The fact that there may be a shift in the location of sales, with a possible decrease in the main store sales as a result of the transfer of some patronage from there to the new branch, should not be overlooked in the planning procedures.

If the store as a whole is enjoying expanded sales, each department within the store usually profits from the increased customer traffic. The reverse is true if the store as a whole is attracting less traffic.

A department's sales are also affected by the amount of promotion the store plans in its behalf. Its sales opportunities are enhanced if the store as a whole plans increased promotional effort, since this usually will bring increased customer traffic. Such efforts may be general, intended simply to bring more people into the store, or may be aimed at specific groups, such as career women, young mothers, or teenagers. In the latter case, only those departments in which the merchandise has particular appeal to the group being courted can expect significant sales benefit.

Fashion Trends Fashion trends are frequently the most important factor influencing sales. These usually affect the sales of several departments at one time, pushing up the sales potential of some and depressing the sales prospects of others. For example, if the trend is toward dressier apparel, dress departments can budget optimistically, but departments selling sportswear and other casual attire will plan more cautiously. Similarly, fashion trends in ready-to-wear affect the sales planning of other fashion departments. For example, a trend toward fitted waistlines undoubtedly will increase the sales potential of the belt department as well as that of the foundations department. A trend toward longer skirts places less emphasis on legs, thereby decreasing the sales potential of hosiery departments but increasing the sales potential of shoe departments, particularly among such merchandise as higher heels and styles to wear with longer skirts.

Monthly Sales Goals Retailers usually express sales goals in dollars and as percentages of increase or decrease in actual sales compared with the corresponding period of the previous year. The percentage of change, however, is not necessarily the same for each month of the season. Each month's sales goals are separately set within the framework of the seasonal plan, after careful consideration has been given to the previous years' sales for the same month, to that percentage which each month has normally contributed to total annual sales, and to any other factors influencing a department's sales potential.

Since the pattern of consumer demand varies both seasonally and monthly, this fact must also be taken into account when planning monthly sales goals. If there were no such variations, each month would contribute an equal number of dollars to the year's total sales volume. A glance at Table 13-1 will show this to be far from the case. In planning sales, merchants allow for the fact that not only do the number of business days vary from month to month but that there are some months in which customers buy more freely than in others.

Monthly sales volume, as a percentage of the total year's sales, also varies from department to department because of the seasonality of the merchandise that each handles and the curve of con-

sumer demand for that merchandise. For example, toy departments and often fur departments do the bulk of their annual business in a relatively few months of the year.

The pattern of monthly sales volume in many fashion departments may also be affected by Easter and by its variation in date from year to year. Table 13-1 illustrates this point. Compare the March and April shares of the year's business in 1975, when Easter was early (March 30), with those for 1974, when Easter was late (April 14).

Holidays and other special days, such as Valentine's Day, Mother's Day, and Father's Day, give rise to variations in demand. The extent to which each influences monthly sales planning depends upon the nature of the merchandise and the extent of the department's promotional plans.

In estimating the sales potential for each month, a buyer or store manager also considers any special circumstances that may have affected sales the previous year but that can be ignored in this year's planning. For example, some sales may have been lost in the previous year because of delivery delays. If no delivery problems are anticipated this year, sales may be appreciably better because of this one factor alone. Similarly factors affecting sales in previous years, such as unseasonable weather, special promotions held in competing stores, and special attractions that drew customers to one's own store, should be taken into account.

Most buyers keep some kind of personal notebook in which they list special conditions that have affected sales, such as weather, their own advertising and that of their competitors, and changing market conditions.

Another familiar device is a departmental "Beat Last Year" book, in which comparative daily sales are recorded for as many as five successive years. Notes like "rain," "parade," and "half-page ad" (noting the item advertised) remind the buyer of the story behind sales figures for each day.

In the case of a new store, a new branch, or a new department within an established store, past sales records are not available as a guide. Research,

TABLE 13-1
Estimated Percentage of Year's Sales Made in Each Month of Year, 1974 and 1975

Total Misses' Apparel and Accessories Departments (in Department Stores)

	1974*	1975†
January	5.8%	5.9%
February	5.6	6.0
March	7.5	8.7
April	9.0	7.8
May	8.0	8.1
June	7.0	7.0
July	6.3	6.2
August	7.4	7.5
September	8.7	8.8
October	9.3	9.4
November	9.8	9.4
December	15.6	15.2
	100.0%	100.0%

*Easter April 14.

†Easter March 30.

Source: Estimated and projected figures based on typical data collected and prepared by the Board of Governors, Federal Reserve System.

Dept. Name _Misses' Dresses_ Dept. No. __42__

SIX MONTH MERCHANDISING PLAN		PLAN (This Year)	ACTUAL (Last Year)
	Initial markup (%)	48.5	47.5
	Gross margin (%)	42.3	41.8
	Cash discount (% cost purch.)	8.0	7.8
	Season stock turnover (rate)	2.8	2.6
	Shortage reserve (%)	1.5	1.8
	Advertising expense (%)	2.8	3.0
	Selling salaries (%)	8.0	8.5

SPRING 197—		FEB.	MAR.	APR.	MAY	JUNE	JULY	SEASON TOTAL
~~FALL 197—~~		AUG.	SEP.	OCT.	NOV.	DEC.	JAN.	
SALES	Last Year	12,100	14,200	17,300	15,500	14,100	10,800	84,000
	Plan	12,500	17,500	16,000	16,500	15,000	11,500	89,000
	Percent of Increase	3.3	23.2	−7.5	6.5	6.4	6.5	6.0%
	Revised							
	Actual							
	Last Year	34,500	35,500	39,000	35,000	34,000	29,000	21,000*

FORM 13-2

formal or informal, combined with careful judgment, must take the place of experience. Market studies, consultations with other merchants or other buyers, and discussions with bankers and vendors are all helpful in arriving at sales goals for the new enterprise.

Form 13-2 indicates how the seasonal merchandise plan looks when seasonal and monthly sales goals have been set.

Planning Stock The next step in dollar merchandise planning is to estimate the amount of stock that will be needed to support the planned monthly sales. Such planning and control of stocks, in terms of dollar investment, constitute an essential part of the merchandise plan or budget.

The objective in planning a beginning-of-the-month inventory is to keep stocks in a desired ratio to sales planned for that month, thereby making possible the achievement of the seasonal stock turnover goal. At the same time, placing realistic limits on the beginning-of-the-month investment makes possible a steady flow of new merchandise into stock throughout the month as inventory is depleted by sales.

Considerations in Planning Since sales during any month can only be realized if the stock from which such sales are to be made is first provided, it is considered good practice to plan stocks for the beginning of each month rather than for the end of the month. In any event the planned beginning-of-the-month (BOM) stock is identical with the end-of-the-month (EOM) stock for the preceding month. Only such rare events or catastrophes as fire or extensive theft that occurred after the close

Dept. Name __Misses' Dresses__ Dept. No. __42__

SIX MONTH MERCHANDISING PLAN

		PLAN (This Year)	ACTUAL (Last Year)
Initial markup (%)		48.5	47.5
Gross margin (%)		42.3	41.8
Cash discount (% cost purch.)		8.0	7.8
Season stock turnover (rate)		2.8	2.6
Shortage reserve (%)		1.5	1.8
Advertising expense (%)		2.8	3.0
Selling salaries (%)		8.0	8.5

SPRING 197— FALL 197—		FEB. AUG.	MAR. SEP.	APR. OCT.	MAY NOV.	JUNE DEC.	JULY JAN.	SEASON TOTAL
SALES	Last Year	12,100	14,200	17,300	15,500	14,100	10,800	84,000
	Plan	12,500	17,500	16,000	16,500	15,000	11,500	89,000
	Percent of Increase	3.3	23.2	−7.5	6.5	6.4	6.5	6.0%
	Revised							
	Actual							
RETAIL STOCK (BOM)	Last Year	34,500	35,500	39,000	35,000	34,000	29,000	21,000*
	Plan	32,000	39,000	36,000	35,000	33,000	26,000	21,000*
	Revised							
	Actual							
	Last Year	2,000	2,500	2,800	2,200	2,200	2,100	13,800

FORM 13-3

of business on the last day of the month would affect this balance.

Two major considerations influence fashion merchants in planning BOM stocks. First, there must be an adequate opening assortment on hand, in sufficient quantity, to meet anticipated customer demand until stock replacements for goods sold can be secured. The best dollar stock plans for fashion departments are those built up from unit assortment plans, or model stocks, in which minimum quantities of each item needed are detailed by classifications, price lines, types, colors, and sizes. (Assortment planning is discussed in detail in Chapter 14.)

A merchant's second consideration is to plan BOM stocks in relation to anticipated sales so that a desired seasonal stock turnover may be realized, markdowns minimized, and a steady flow of new, interesting merchandise assured throughout the month.

The same external, internal, and fashion factors that influence the planning of monthly sales also influence the planning of monthly stocks, and must be evaluated accordingly.

Variations in Monthly Stock Goals In planning monthly stock goals, stocks should be brought to a peak just prior to the time when sales are expected to reach their peak. By peaking stocks before consumer demand reaches its crest, merchants are able to present maximum assortments and to avoid being out of needed styles, sizes, and colors when the public is in the mood to buy.

Similarly, beginning-of-the-month stock plans are reduced as a selling season approaches its close and demand decreases. Other factors help the merchant to reduce his inventory as the season ends: unsold seasonal goods are marked down; new goods that may be brought into stock are usually manufacturers' closeouts, which are purchased and resold at prices lower than earlier in the season.

Stock-Sales Relationships Departmentalized stores are guided in their stock planning by two stock-sales relationships: monthly stock-sales ratios and a desired rate of seasonal stock turnover.

- The first of these relationships, known as a *monthly stock-sales ratio*, is defined as the number of months that would be required to dispose of a beginning-of-the-month inventory at the rate at which sales are made in (or planned for) that month. The formula used for calculating this relationship is

$$\text{stock-sales ratio} = \frac{\$ \text{ BOM stock}}{\$ \text{ sales for month}}$$

Applying this formula to the February planned sales and stock figures appearing on Form 13-3,

$$\text{stock-sales ratio} = \frac{\$32,000}{\$12,500}$$

$$= 2.56$$

The stock-sales ratio is an important tool in stock planning in that it directly relates stock requirements to planned sales. Appropriate stock-sales ratios may be derived from a store's own experience or from the experiences of other stores as compiled by such trade associations as the National Retail Merchants Association, or from combinations of the two. Ratios will vary, of necessity, from month to month, from department to department, from one type of retail operation to another, and from one type of merchandise to another. They depend primarily upon the cycle of demand for various types of merchandise and the merchandising policies of an individual store. Once a sales goal has been set and a desirable stock-sales ratio is established, the stock needed at the beginning of any month can be determined as follows:

$$\$ \text{ BOM stock} = \$ \text{ planned sales} \times \text{ stock-sales ratio}$$

Using the figures from Table 13-2 as an illustration of the application of this formula, assume that a merchant plans February sales at $2,000 in each of three departments: Women's Dressy Coats, Lingerie, and Men's Furnishings. Applying the February stock-sales ratios listed in this table, the amount of stock at retail value that he should have on hand February 1 in each of these departments is found to be

Women's Dressy Coats	$2,000 × 2.6 =	$ 5,200
Lingerie	$2,000 × 4.6 =	$ 9,200
Men's Furnishings	$2,000 × 6.7 =	$13,400

- Unlike the stock-sales ratio, which is used in planning beginning-of-the-month stocks, *stock turnover* refers to the number of times that an average stock of merchandise (inventory) has been turned into sales during a given period. The formula for determining the rate of stock turnover during any given period is

$$\text{stock turnover} = \frac{\$ \text{ net sales}}{\$ \text{ average inventory}}$$

For example, using Form 13-3, we can find that the average stock for the spring season being planned is $31,714, by adding all six beginning-of-the-month stocks (February–July) to the end-of-

TABLE 13-2
Typical Monthly Stock-Sales Ratios

MONTH	WOMEN'S DRESSY COATS	LINGERIE	MEN'S FURNISHINGS
January	2.1	4.7	6.3
February	2.6	4.6	6.7
March	2.3	5.5	5.7
April	2.4	5.2	6.3
May	3.8	3.8	6.2
June	4.7	4.3	3.8
July	3.9	4.3	6.0
August	4.5	3.9	5.6
September	5.0	5.0	5.1
October	3.3	4.7	5.6
November	2.7	4.0	3.6
December	1.9	1.8	1.5

season stock ($21,000) and dividing that sum by 7 (the number of inventory figures used):

$$\text{average inventory} = \frac{\begin{array}{c}\$32,000 + \$39,000 \\ + \$36,000 + \$35,000 \\ + \$33,000 + \$26,000 \\ + \$21,000\end{array}}{7}$$
$$= \$31,714$$

Then, by dividing the season's total planned sales of $89,000 by the average stock of $31,714, a stock turnover rate of 2.8 is found for the six-month period:

$$\frac{\$89,000}{\$31,714} = 2.8$$

On a storewide basis, the typical stock turnover figure for all department stores is somewhat better than three turns a year. Rate of stock turnover, however, varies widely from one department to another within a given store, depending upon the type of merchandise handled, its price ranges,

and the depth and breadth of assortments carried.

In general, the rate of stock turnover is higher in women's apparel than in men's clothing or home furnishings, in departments featuring lower price ranges than in those featuring higher price ranges. Typical average turnover figures for various types of goods are widely used by retail merchants in evaluating the proficiency of their merchandising operations (see Chapter 16). The following average rate of stock turnover figures illustrate how the annual turnover varies on the basis of type of merchandise handled:

Misses' dresses	4.5 turns
Men's clothing	2.5 turns
Sleepwear and robes	7.8 turns
Millinery	6.5 turns

As an example of how the rate of stock turnover varies according to the price ranges of merchandise handled, the average turnover rate for budget dresses in 1972 was 4.6, compared with 4.1 for higher-priced dresses.[2] In departments in which the very nature of the merchandise handled requires that considerable depth and breadth of assortments be carried in relation to sales, turnover is low. As an example of this fact, the average stock turnover in women's shoes remains fairly constant at 2.0. This is because it is often necessary to stock as many as 100 pairs of women's shoes in a single style and color in order to have an adequate stock of the most popular combinations of length and width.

The rate at which stock is turned into sales directly affects retail profit objectives, since no income is realized until merchandise is sold. A direct attempt to achieve a desired rate of stock turnover is made by limiting beginning-of-the-month stock to a predetermined stock-sales ratio, as further discussed in Chapter 16.

Planning Markdowns Having planned monthly sales and beginning-of-the-month inventories, the fashion merchant is now almost ready to calculate the amount of stock that should be purchased throughout each month in order to achieve planned sales and stock goals. Before this is done, however, the merchant may decide to estimate the dollar value of markdowns it will be necessary to take each month, because markdowns reduce the retail value of the inventory just as sales do.

Purpose of Markdowns   Wise fashion merchants use merchandise markdowns to speed the sale of slow-moving, damaged, and out-of-season goods, in order to make room for new merchandise. Markdowns are also used as a means of meeting price competition and for adjusting retail prices to declining market values. Markdowns are most useful if regarded as a tool rather than as a curse. They help to release capital that would otherwise be tied up in stock and make funds available for reinvestment in more salable merchandise.

Because of rapidly changing consumer demand, markdowns are generally larger and of

Dept. Name __Misses' Dresses__   Dept. No. __42__

SIX MONTH MERCHANDISING PLAN		PLAN (This Year)	ACTUAL (Last Year)
	Initial markup (%)	48.5	47.5
	Gross margin (%)	42.3	41.8
	Cash discount (% cost purch.)	8.0	7.8
	Season stock turnover (rate)	2.8	2.6
	Shortage reserve (%)	1.5	1.8
	Advertising expense (%)	2.8	3.0
	Selling salaries (%)	8.0	8.5

SPRING 197—		FEB.	MAR.	APR.	MAY	JUNE	JULY	SEASON TOTAL
~~FALL 197—~~		AUG.	SEP.	OCT.	NOV.	DEC.	JAN.	
SALES	Last Year	12,100	14,200	17,300	15,500	14,100	10,800	84,000
	Plan	12,500	17,500	16,000	16,500	15,000	11,500	89,000
	Percent of Increase	3.3	23.2	−7.5	6.5	6.4	6.5	6.0%
	Revised							
	Actual							
RETAIL STOCK (BOM)	Last Year	34,500	35,500	39,000	35,000	34,000	29,000	21,000*
	Plan	32,000	39,000	36,000	35,000	33,000	26,000	21,000*
	Revised							
	Actual							
MARKDOWNS	Last Year	2,000	2,500	2,800	2,200	2,200	2,100	13,800
	Plan (dollars)	1,800	2,000	2,600	2,000	2,000	2,100	12,500
	Plan (percent)	14.4	11.4	16.3	12.1	13.3	18.3	14.0%
	Revised							
	Actual							
	Last Year	15,100	20,200	16,100	16,700	11,300	4,900	84,300

FORM 13-4

greater importance in departments devoted to fashion goods than in departments in which the merchandise is more staple, such as blankets or housewares. By using markdowns judiciously to clear out seasonal goods promptly, fashion merchants avoid the very considerable risks involved in carrying the goods beyond their normal selling period.

Markdown Terminology   As stated in Chapter 12, the term *markdown* refers to the dollar difference between the previous price and the reduced price to which merchandise is marked. To express the relationship between the value of accumulated markdowns and net sales for a given period, a markdown percentage figure is used. *Markdown percentage* may be defined as the dollar value of the net retail markdowns taken during a given period expressed as a percentage of net sales for that period. For example, Form 13-4 shows that February markdowns are planned at $1,800 and February sales at $12,500. Expressed as a formula, markdown percentage is calculated as follows:

$$\text{markdown } \% = \frac{\$ \text{ markdown}}{\$ \text{ net sales}}$$
$$= \frac{\$1,800}{\$12,500}$$
$$= 14.4\%$$

Retailers use the term ''retail reductions'' for all reductions that occur in the retail value of the inventory, including merchandise markdowns, discounts allowed to employees and other special customers, and stock shortages. Merchandise markdowns, however, constitute the major part of retail reductions and vary considerably from month to month, particularly with respect to fashion goods. These are the markdowns that are usually planned when seasonal budgets are drawn up. Estimates of special discounts may be included with merchandise markdowns or shown separately when planning the seasonal budget. Provisions for reductions caused

by stock shortages are made by setting up special monthly reserves for such contingencies.

Only merchandise markdowns and special discounts are included in the monthly and seasonal figures found in Form 13-4. Reductions caused by stock shortages appear separately as a percentage of each month's planned sales, the reserve percentage for which is found in the upper right-hand corner of this form.

Factors in Planning Markdowns   A certain percentage of any retail store's stock will always have to be marked down before it can be sold. Some stock may have to be marked down more than once. Since markdowns result in lowered gross profit (the difference between the cost of the merchandise and the price at which it is finally sold), they must be planned for and controlled.

Markdowns are usually planned as a percentage of each season's planned sales. They may then be allotted to individual months, according to the merchant's estimates of when and to what extent monthly markdowns are going to be needed to move the goods. In establishing the markdown estimates, the experience of previous seasons and of other stores is considered, together with the general business outlook for the period ahead.

The chief factors to be considered in establishing seasonal markdown goals are

- The past experience of the store or department
- Trends in wholesale prices (Markdowns tend to increase during periods of falling wholesale prices and decrease when wholesale prices are rising.)
- Comparative figures of similar stores
- Amount of old stock on hand at the beginning of a new season
- Changes in merchandising policies and methods that may have occurred since the previous year or that are about to occur

In allocating a season's markdown estimate to individual months, a merchant considers not only dates throughout the season when changes in customer demand are expected to occur, but also store policy in taking markdowns. Large stores tend to take markdowns while there is still sufficient customer demand to move the goods quickly at minimum price reductions. Small stores tend to postpone the taking of markdowns, preferring to clear their stocks only at the end of a major selling season.

Planning Purchases Having entered monthly sales, beginning-of-the-month stocks, and monthly markdown goals on the planning form, the merchant is now ready to calculate the value of the purchases that can be made each month if stocks and sales are to be kept in balance. *Planned purchases* is the term used to indicate the amount of merchandise that can be brought into stock during a given period without exceeding the planned inventory for the end of that period.

In most large stores, purchases are planned on a monthly basis. However, some smaller fashion merchants, particularly those who make infrequent market trips, budget purchases on a seasonal or market-trip basis. In either case, planned purchases are computed on the same basis. Planned purchases are derived from planned sales, stocks, and, when applicable, markdowns, by simple arithmetical computation.

The calculation of monthly purchases begins with planned sales for that month. To this figure is added planned markdowns for the month. These two figures represent the amount by which the beginning-of-the-month stock is expected to be decreased during the month. To these figures are added the planned end-of-the-month stock (the same as the BOM stock for the following month), because these three factors—planned sales, markdowns, and EOM stock—represent the value of the merchandise needed during the month in order to have on hand, at the end of the month, the amount of stock that has been planned. From the total of these three figures is subtracted the BOM stock for that month, which is the amount already available for sale. The remainder represents the purchases that can be made for delivery during that one month.

The formula for calculating planned purchases, then, is as follows:

$$\text{planned purchases} = \begin{array}{l} \text{planned sales} \\ +\ \text{planned markdowns} \\ +\ \text{planned end-of-month stock} \\ -\ \text{beginning-of-month stock} \end{array}$$

Applying this formula to the February figures given in Form 13-5:

$$\begin{aligned} \text{planned purchases} &= \$12{,}500 + \$1{,}800 \\ &\quad + \$39{,}000 - \$32{,}000 \\ &= \$21{,}300 \end{aligned}$$

Although most stores plan their purchases at retail value, as was done here, some smaller stores still use cost value. If desired, the equivalent cost value of retail purchases can be calculated easily by multiplying the retail value of the planned purchases by the cost complement of the planned markup percentage for the period. (The cost complement is 100 percent minus the retail markup percent.) For example, if the February initial markup is planned at 48.5 percent and February retail purchases are planned at $21,300, the cost value of the $21,300 retail figure may be determined as follows:

$$\begin{aligned} \$ \text{ cost} &= \$ \text{ retail value} \\ &\quad \times (100\% - \text{retail markup }\%) \\ &= \$21{,}300 \times 51.5\% \\ &= \$10{,}970 \end{aligned}$$

SUPPLEMENTAL ELEMENTS IN DOLLAR MERCHANDISE PLANNING

As previously stated, many retail stores, particularly large departmentalized stores, expand budgeting procedures beyond the four basic elements discussed above. They frequently include in the dollar merchandise plan goal figures for any of the several additional elements that directly relate to the profit

Dept. Name __Misses' Dresses__ Dept. No. __42__

		PLAN (This Year)	ACTUAL (Last Year)
SIX MONTH MERCHANDISING PLAN	Initial markup (%)	48.5	47.5
	Gross margin (%)	42.3	41.8
	Cash discount (% cost purch.)	8.0	7.8
	Season stock turnover (rate)	2.8	2.6
	Shortage reserve (%)	1.5	1.8
	Advertising expense (%)	2.8	3.0
	Selling salaries (%)	8.0	8.5

SPRING 197—		FEB.	MAR.	APR.	MAY	JUNE	JULY	SEASON TOTAL
~~FALL 197—~~		~~AUG.~~	~~SEP.~~	~~OCT.~~	~~NOV.~~	~~DEC.~~	~~JAN.~~	
SALES	Last Year	12,100	14,200	17,300	15,500	14,100	10,800	84,000
	Plan	12,500	17,500	16,000	16,500	15,000	11,500	89,000
	Percent of Increase	3.3	23.2	-7.5	6.5	6.4	6.5	6.0%
	Revised							
	Actual							
RETAIL STOCK (BOM)	Last Year	34,500	35,500	39,000	35,000	34,000	29,000	21,000*
	Plan	32,000	39,000	36,000	35,000	33,000	26,000	21,000*
	Revised							
	Actual							
MARKDOWNS	Last Year	2,000	2,500	2,800	2,200	2,200	2,100	13,800
	Plan (dollars)	1,800	2,000	2,600	2,000	2,000	2,100	12,500
	Plan (percent)	14.4	11.4	16.3	12.1	13.3	18.3	14.0%
	Revised							
	Actual							
RETAIL PURCHASES	Last Year	15,100	20,200	16,100	16,700	11,300	4,900	84,300
	Plan	21,300	16,500	17,600	16,500	10,000	8,600	90,500
	Revised							
	Actual							

Comments

*Represents stock end of period.

Merchandise Manager __T. J. Evans__   Buyer __Jane Dean__

Controller _____

FORM 13-5

of the operation. Important among these elements are initial markup percentage, cash discounts earned as percentage of purchases or sales, the rate of stock turnover desired, the gross margin, shortage reserves, and operating expenses as a percentage of net sales.

In most cases, only seasonal goal figures for these supplemental elements are planned. In fewer cases, seasonal and monthly dollar and percentage-to-sales goal figures are worked out. Goal figures of each of these supplementary elements of the dollar merchandise plan, together with the figures representing the previous year's actual performance, are supplied by the store's controller or fiscal division. Since such goal figures reflect the financial objectives of the store as determined by top management, they are rarely left to the discretion of departmental planners.

Guidelines in budgeting these additional elements of the dollar merchandise plan are obtained from the store's own experience, from the *Merchandising and Operating Reports* of the National Retail Merchants Association, and frequently from figures supplied by the store's resident buying office.

Markup

Markup is the difference between the cost and the retail price of merchandise. ("Markon" is a term used by some large retail stores as a designation of the difference between cost and selling prices.) Most stores express markup as a percentage of retail value, thus:

$$\text{retail markup } \% = \frac{\$ \text{ retail} - \$ \text{ cost}}{\$ \text{ retail}}$$

Some smaller stores and most manufacturers, however, calculate markup percentages on the basis of cost, or:

$$\text{cost markup } \% = \frac{\$ \text{ retail} - \$ \text{ cost}}{\$ \text{ cost}}$$

Even though most fashion merchants use the retail system of accounting and employ the first formula given here in their calculations, they need to be familiar with the second formula as well, since it may be used in discussions with suppliers and other retailers.

The dollar difference between the delivered cost of merchandise and the retail price placed on it when it is first brought into stock is called the *initial markup.* Retail stores plan initial markup percentage in order to ensure that the income derived from sales (the difference between the cost of goods and the retail prices at which they are marked) will be adequate to cover all expenses incurred in the operation of the business and also will yield a reasonable profit. In addition, this income must be sufficient to cover anticipated reductions in the retail value of the inventory, such as markdowns, stock shortages, employee discounts.

It is important to remember that some purchases may yield a higher or lower percentage of markup than planned, but that a buyer's aim throughout the season is to maintain an average markup on purchases no less than the goal figure indicated on the dollar merchandise plan. This predetermined average figure is intended as a guide for the buyer, not an arbitrary percentage figure which a buyer must apply to all purchases.

Gross Margin

Instead of initial markup percentage, or sometimes in addition to it, some stores plan gross margin of profit. *Gross margin* represents the dollar difference between net sales for a period and the net cost of merchandise sold during that period. Gross margin percentage is calculated by dividing the dollars of gross margin by the net sales for the period.

Gross margin is a very important figure in dollar merchandise planning. This is because it represents the amount of money left from sales income, after deducting the total cost of merchandise sold during a given period, with which to pay all operating expenses and taxes, and still yield a reasonable profit, or a return on invested capital.

Cash Discounts

Cash discounts are the percentages or premiums allowed by manufacturers off their invoices if payment is made within a certain specified period of time. Such discounts are given to encourage the prompt payment of invoices.

Cash discounts are an important source of additional income for a store or department, and for that reason are included in most dollar merchandise plans, either as a percentage of net sales or as a percentage of the cost of purchases. Cash discounts earned increase gross margin, because they reduce the actual cost of merchandise purchases.

Terms of Sale   *Terms of sale* refer to the combination of allowable discounts on purchases and the time allowed for taking such discounts. The percentage of cash discount allowed and the length of time allowed for the taking of that discount vary widely from industry to industry.

For example, in the women's apparel industry the usual terms of sale are 8/10 EOM (8 percent cash discount allowed if the invoice is paid within 10 days following the last day of the month in which the invoice is dated); in the handbag industry, 3/10 EOM; in the millinery industry, 7/10 EOM; in the glove industry, 6/10 EOM.

Anticipation   An extra discount granted by some vendors for the prepayment of their invoices before the end of the cash discount period is called *anticipation*. Because anticipation further reduces the cost of purchases, retail stores have traditionally made profitable use of their capital by taking anticipation whenever possible.

Stock Shortages and Overages

Stock shortages or overages represent the dollar difference between the book inventory (the value of inventory on hand as indicated by the store's accounting records) and the physical inventory (determined by taking a physical count). When the book inventory is greater, there is said to be a *stock shortage*. When the physical inventory is greater, there is said to be a *stock overage*. Stock shortages are experienced with consistent regularity by retail stores. Stock overages occur very seldom. Both are discussed in detail in Chapter 16.

Since stock shortages or overages can be determined only when a complete physical inventory is taken, which is usually only once or twice a year, most stores set up interim monthly reserves for tolerable, or anticipated, shortages. This means that a certain percentage of sales is reserved to offset the actual difference between the book inventory and the actual physical inventory when the latter is taken.

Shortage reserve percentages are usually based upon past experience. The allowable percentage is determined at the beginning of a season or year, and does not change from month to month. Actual differences between the value of the book inventory and the value of the physical inventory, as determined from an actual count, are compared with the accumulated shortage reserve when the physical inventory is taken. If the actual shortage is less than the reserve, gross margin is increased by the amount of the difference. If the actual shortage is greater than the reserve, gross margin is thereby reduced by an equivalent amount.

Since stock shortages decrease a department's profit and are essentially the responsibility of the buyer, many stores include seasonal shortage reserve figures in their dollar merchandise plans.

Operating Expenses

There are two kinds of expenses incurred in the operation of a selling department: direct and indirect.

Direct expenses are those that occur as a direct result of the operation of a specific department and that would cease if the department itself ceased to exist. Examples of such direct expenses are salespeople's salaries, buyer's and assistant's compensation, expenses incurred in connection with buying trips, advertising expenses, and delivery charges.

Indirect expenses are those that do not directly

result from the operation of an individual department, but are shared by all departments of the store, such as compensation of top management executives, utilities, maintenance, insurance, and receiving and marking expenses.

Many stores that include operating expenses as an element of the dollar merchandise budget make it a practice to plan advertising expenses and selling salaries separately as seasonal or monthly percentages of planned sales, since these expenses are most intimately related to the actual production of sales. The six-month plan in most stores does not include a budget for indirect expenses, but they are included in planning initial markup.

REFERENCES

[1] Barker, Anderson, and Butterworth, *Principles of Retailing*, p. 338.
[2] *Departmental Merchandising and Operating Results of 1972.*

MERCHANDISING VOCABULARY

Define or briefly explain the following terms:

Dollar merchandise plan	Initial markup
Open-to-buy	Gross margin
Retail method of inventory	Cash discount
Stock-sales ratio	Terms of sale
Stock turnover	Anticipation
Markdown	Stock shortage
Markdown percentage	Stock overage
Planned purchases	Direct expenses
Markup	Indirect expenses

MERCHANDISING REVIEW

1. What are the four major goals of scientific dollar planning in retail merchandising?
2. What are the two major financial tools that retail merchants can use to achieve these major goals? Describe the function of each.
3. What are considered to be the essential elements of any dollar merchandise plan, and why? What other elements are often planned, and why?
4. When are dollar merchandise plans usually drawn up? Why is it essential that they be flexible and subject to frequent review and adjustment? What provisions are made on the plan for making any necessary adjustments?
5. What specific factors or conditions should be carefully considered in estimating the sales potential of a department or a store in a given future period? How may each of these factors or conditions actually influence sales potential?

6. Why do fashion trends frequently have a more important bearing on a fashion department's sales potential than do business or economic conditions? Give examples to illustrate your answer.

7. What factors or circumstances should be carefully considered in establishing monthly sales goals? What planning aids or devices are helpful to buyers when they are developing six-month sales and stock plans?

8. Differentiate between the two types of stock-sales relationships that are of major importance in dollar stock planning. Why are each considered important? What is the formula used in calculating each of these two relationships?

9. What is meant by the term "stock shortage"? What provisions are usually made on a six-month merchandise plan for anticipated stock shortages?

10. Why should purchases be planned in advance of a selling season? What is the formula for determining planned purchases?

MERCHANDISING DIGEST

1. Discuss this statement from the text: "Today budgeting for a fashion department or store entails far greater financial risks and capital investment than ever before." Why are the financial risks greater today than in the past? Why is considerably more capital investment required today than formerly?

2. Discuss the responsibilities of each of the following retail executives with regard to drawing up dollar merchandise plans: (a) the departmental buyer, (b) the merchandise manager, and (c) the controller.

3. Discuss markdowns on the basis of the following: (a) their purpose, (b) factors to be considered in budgeting, and (c) their effect on profit.

14
PLANNING THE FASHION MERCHANDISE ASSORTMENT

A merchandise assortment that is well balanced in relation to demand is the most potent tool any retailer can use to attract and hold customers. Such factors as store location, layout, facilities, services, and promotional effort are also important; but the cornerstone of the entire customer-winning structure is the merchandise assortment. If people are to continue to patronize a store, the merchandise itself must at all times be what is wanted.

For decades, retailers have described good assortments as those containing the right merchandise, at the right time, in the right place, in the right quantities, and at prices that customers are both willing and able to pay.

Each merchant strives to build a merchandise assortment to conform with what is considered "right" by the store's target group of customers. Their merchandise preferences must be studied before guidelines can be established for the buying staff to follow in developing and maintaining assortments that are at all times balanced with demand.

The major objectives of assortment planning are similar to those of dollar planning, namely:

- To buy and assemble in inventory those styles, sizes, colors, and price lines that accurately reflect customer demand throughout a given period
- To time the delivery of purchases to the store so that each individual component of the inventory is available for sale neither too early nor too late for customer demand
- To keep purchases in line with the store's ability to stock, display, promote, and pay for those purchases

- To keep funds available at all times for the purchase of new or additional goods, when and as they may be needed
- To relate demand for each type of fashion goods to the demand for all other types of goods in an inventory so that similar fashion influences and price levels will be reflected throughout the entire assortment

CONSIDERATIONS IN ASSORTMENT PLANNING

The major responsibility of a buyer is to plan and maintain through purchases an assortment of merchandise so well balanced to the preferences of customers that sales goals will be achieved and a reasonable profit will result from the merchandising operation.

A *merchandise assortment* is a collection of varied types of related merchandise, essentially intended for the same general end use and usually grouped together in one selling area of a retail store. An *assortment plan* is a comprehensive and detailed listing of all items making up an assortment by type and price line. A *balanced assortment* is one in which types, quantities, and price lines of merchandise included in inventory during a given period of time are closely matched to the demand of target customers. A balanced assortment is the goal of all merchandising efforts.

To achieve balanced assortments, fashion merchants must always be guided by the merchandising policies of their stores. They consider the same factors that they weigh in drawing up the dollar merchandise plan, and they decide how each factor will affect the size and composition of their assortments. They carefully consider variations in demand—those arising out of the divergent preferences of different customer groups and those occasioned by seasonal change. They study and evaluate planning information from a wide variety of sources, and particularly information gathered from the market. Once they have given careful consideration to each of these factors, fashion merchants are then ready to plan assortments for the coming season, in dollars or units or both.

Store Merchandising Policies

Senior executives of a store are responsible for establishing and clearly defining a store's merchandising policies, which are detailed statements about how the store chooses to implement its specific business objectives. No retail enterprise can be all things to all people or supply all the needs of all people in a given trading area. Each store must select one or more specific segments of the area's total population that it wants to serve and then establish merchandising policies that best serve the interests and preferences of those target customers.

Merchandising policies are management directives to employees about how the store elects to carry on its business. These are drawn up primarily to serve as guidelines for buyers to follow in developing and maintaining merchandise assortments.

As discussed in Chapter 11, merchandising policies relate to:

- The degree of fashion leadership for which the store or department wishes to be known—fashion leader, fashion follower, emphasis on specific items such as fads
- The price ranges offered—high, moderate, popular, low
- Its quality standards—finest available, acceptable, unimportant consideration
- The depth and breadth of its assortments—shallow, deep, broad, narrow, or a combination
- Its brand policies—national, private, unbranded

- Exclusivity of merchandise—emphasized or non-emphasized
- Maintenance of basic assortments—always in stock, usually in stock, unimportant consideration

Factors Influencing Assortment Planning

In planning assortments, as in preparing the dollar merchandise plan, merchants review the probable impact of external, internal, and fashion factors. These factors affect not only how much customers may be expected to spend in an upcoming season, but also the types of goods they will purchase.

External Factors General and local economic conditions have a marked effect on merchants' planning of fashion assortments. If a retailer anticipates greater affluence in the trading area or a larger proportion of affluent customers than previously served, then an assortment should include more high-priced goods than before, as well as a larger proportion of new and relatively untried fashions, and probably a more generous representation of strictly "fun" apparel.

If, on the other hand, the community has suffered financial setbacks, or if a generally pessimistic attitude toward the future of the economy prevails, or if the unemployment rate is increasing, or if taxes, interest rates, and prices are escalating, then the assortment should feature styles that are versatile enough to make a limited wardrobe adequate for many varied occasions, and the most expensive goods included should involve minimum fashion risk.

The local competitive situation is also taken into account, since changes in that area may have a direct bearing on the components of a fashion assortment. If, for example, supermarkets and drugstores in a local trading area are prominently featuring limited styles of low-priced hosiery on self-service racks, the hosiery buyer for a local quality department or specialty store may decide to play down utility items and increase the offerings of finer quality and newer styles.

Internal Factors Internal factors also affect the assortment plans for any or all parts of a store's inventory. An enlarged and refurbished selling floor may be able to accommodate deeper and broader assortments than were previously possible. Relocating related departments so that they are next to each other may encourage each to plan larger assortments of matching colors and patterns.

The opening of new branch stores directly affects the planning of fashion assortments, for the merchandise preferences of potential customer groups in the new trading areas must be recognized and provided for.

The extent and type of promotional activities the store intends to engage in during the period for which fashion assortments are being planned also has a direct bearing on the components of those assortments. For example, if the store intends to increase its use of television presentations during that period, departmental fashion assortments should carry generous quantities of the merchandise that is to be featured. If a store's management has decided to embark on an advertising campaign stressing the values to be found in its merchandise offerings, then value must be of prime consideration when planning each department's assortment.

Fashion Factors Fashion trends, of course, exert a powerful influence on assortment planning for fashion departments. Fashion makes the difference between what was the right assortment yesterday and what can be expected to be the right assortment tomorrow. This is true of both apparel and accessory assortments for men, women, and children. Whatever the trend, fashion rarely affects one department in the apparel or accessories groups without influencing the assortments in all the others.

The degree to which a store's customers show a marked preference for fashions in the introductory, rise, culmination, or decline phases of their cycles becomes a prime factor in assortment planning for fashion departments. While many customers choose apparel and accessories at more than one phase of a fashion cycle, each tends to favor merchandise at one phase more than any other.

Fashion assortments should always be planned with such customer preferences in mind.

Variations in Assortment Planning

Assortments carried in similar departments will vary from store to store, depending upon the merchandising policies of each store, the preferences of each of its target group of customers, and often the geographic location of the store.

For a highly simplified example, consider two merchants who are planning assortments for college shops catering to similar groups of customers in similar geographical areas. Each merchant had identical sales of $6,250 in skirts, sweaters, slacks, and pantcoats the previous year. Table 14-1 shows two of the many ways in which that $6,250 could have been distributed among the four categories, assuming (for further simplicity's sake) that there were only two price lines carried in each category.

Shop A's customers showed considerable interest in pantcoats last year. Shop B's customers had little interest in these garments but showed considerably more interest in sweaters than did shop A's customers. Shop A's customers showed a fairly strong interest in lower-priced goods. Shop B's customers had a pronounced interest in higher-priced goods.

In developing assortment plans for a six-month period, the fashion buyer must always carefully consider the important selling seasons that will occur during that six-month period, and the effect of each on demand for a specific department's merchandise. Seasonal variation in demand is a primary consideration of fashion buyers as they undertake planning departmental assortments.

Sources of Planning Information

In collecting facts to guide assortment planning, fashion merchants study records of what they have bought, sold, and marked down in corresponding past seasons. They also seek information from buyers in similar but noncompetitive stores, from vendors, and from their store's resident buying office

TABLE 14-1
Foundation for Assortment Planning
Review of College Shop Sales for Previous Year

	SHOP A		SHOP B	
	UNITS	DOLLARS	UNITS	DOLLARS
Skirts at $10 each	30	$ 300	35	$ 350
Skirts at $15 each	50	750	40	600
Total skirts	80	$1,050	75	$ 950
Sweaters at $18 each	30	$ 540	25	$ 450
Sweaters at $25 each	40	1,000	70	1,750
Total sweaters	70	$1,540	95	$2,200
Slacks at $12 each	50	$ 600	30	$ 360
Slacks at $20 each	60	1,200	80	1,600
Total slacks	110	$1,800	110	$1,960
Pantcoats at $30 each	50	$1,500	18	$ 540
Pantcoats at $40 each	9	360	15	600
Total pantcoats	59	$1,860	33	$1,140
Grand Total	319	$6,250	313	$6,250

about what other customers, similar to their own, may be expected to purchase in the coming season.

At best, however, all indications of consumer preferences in the past can only serve as a rough guide to fashion merchants as they go about identifying future fashion trends, both in general and on the local scene. They compare notes with buyers of related departments. They analyze what they read about fashion trends in trade and fashion publications. They note what is to be featured in future editions of consumer publications and what fashion themes are being planned for future editorial coverage in those publications. If their stores serve customers who want to be first with the newest styles, in addition to covering the better domestic markets they may visit couture houses and ready-to-wear producers in foreign market centers for indications of incoming fashion trends.

METHODS OF SEASONAL PLANNING

There are two methods of planning sales and the amount of stock necessary to produce those sales during a given six-month period. The first method, known as dollar planning, has been discussed in Chapter 13 and is merely reviewed here. The second method, known as unit planning, is discussed in detail below.

Dollar Planning

For purposes of review: The six-month merchandise plan, based on the dollar value of anticipated sales, optimum stock levels, necessary markdowns, and allowable purchases, is an essential part of merchandise assortment planning for the following reasons:

- It indicates the minimum sales objectives of the store or department.
- It serves to guide management in planning for and control of the capital needed for inventory investment throughout the period.
- It serves as a guide in making purchases.
- It provides a base against which sales-related operating expenses can be measured.

- It serves as a guide in planning promotional expenditures.
- It provides management with a way of measuring the results of merchandising efforts by establishing seasonal goal figures such as planned sales, rate of stock turnover, and gross margin.[1]

Under the dollar method of planning, it becomes the responsibility of departmental buyers to provide a merchandise assortment, by classifications and price lines and within dollar limitations, that is at all times balanced to customer demand.

Unit Planning

However, dollar planning does not ensure assortments that are well balanced to demand because it does not pinpoint the nature and extent of customer demand at any point in time. For that reason, an increasing number of retailers are now combining dollar merchandise planning with unit planning, especially in fashion departments. Under the latter method, sales and beginning-of-the-month inventories are first planned in terms of units of merchandise by classifications and price lines. When these units are multiplied by their respective price lines, they yield dollar classification figures for planned sales and stock. Unit purchases are then planned in the same way that dollar planned purchases are determined.

The advantages of planning by units rather than dollars are

- It is more consistent with the way sales are actually made, since customer purchases are made in units of merchandise.
- It serves as a guide to the types and quantities of stock needed to produce specifically identified units of planned sales.
- It helps reduce inventory investment in slow-moving merchandise.
- It provides a base for developing monthly open-to-buy figures so that active classifications and price lines are not penalized because of the more sluggish ones.

- It helps to minimize departmental overbuying.

Table 14-2 illustrates how a casual dress department, with two major classifications, might construct its sales plan for February using this method. First, the number of unit sales anticipated at each price line within each classification are determined. Next, the retail value of the unit sales planned at each price line within each classification is computed. Finally, both the units and their dollar equivalents are totaled to produce the overall departmental planned sales for February.

In planning the stock needed at the beginning of each month or season, stock-sales ratios may be applied to the unit sales planned at each price line within each classification, and totals are derived in both units and dollars, as in sales planning. Finally, planned purchases in both units and dollars may be calculated for each price line in each classification, and for the department as a whole, using the procedure described in the explanation of dollar purchase planning in Chapter 13.

PRICING ASSORTMENTS

The first factor to be considered in planning assortments is the price structure around which the assortment is to be built. The second factor is the depth and breadth of merchandise assortments to be offered at each of the various price points within that structure.

The price structure of a store or department is determined by management and is designed to attract the customer groups which the store has chosen to serve. Therefore, the price structure of a store or department is a very important aspect of its overall image; it provides the foundation upon which all assortments should be based.

Price-related Terminology

For a clearer understanding of retail pricing and its importance in assortment planning, it is necessary to understand the meaning of several price-

Table 14-2 Unit Sales Plan

Dept.: __#40__   Season: __Spring 197–__

Name: __Casual Dresses__   Month: __February__

CLASS	PRICE LINE	DESCRIPTION	PLANNED SALES UNITS	PLANNED SALES DOLLARS
12301	$18	Dresses, misses'	30	$ 540
12302	24	Dresses, misses'	36	864
12303	30	Dresses, misses'	40	1,200
12304	36	Dresses, misses'	38	1,368
12305	42	Dresses, misses'	15	630
12306	48	Dresses, misses'	12	576
12300		Total, Dresses, misses'	171	$5,178
12801	$18	Dresses, juniors	25	$ 450
12802	24	Dresses, juniors	32	768
12803	30	Dresses, juniors	36	1,080
12804	36	Dresses, juniors	30	1,080
12805	42	Dresses, juniors	18	756
12806	48	Dresses, juniors	10	480
12800		Total, Dresses, juniors	151	$4,614
		Total, Casual Dresses	322	$9,792

related terms and their relevance in assortment planning.

Price-lining The term *price-lining* refers to the practice of determining the various but limited number of retail prices at which a department's assortments will be offered.

Price Line The term *price line* refers to a specific price point at which an assortment of merchandise is regularly offered for sale. For example, if a Casual Dress department regularly offers a selection of dresses in a variety of styles, colors, and sizes at $18, $24, $30, $36, $42, and $48, each specific price is known as a price line.

Price Range The term *price range* refers to the spread between the lowest and the highest price line carried. The price range in the Casual Dress department mentioned above is $18 to $48.

Price Zone The term *price zone* refers to a series of price lines that are relatively close to each other and that are likely to appeal to one particular segment of a store's or a department's customers.

The three most widely accepted retail price zones are

- Promotional (lowest price lines carried)
- Volume (middle price lines, where the largest volume of sales occur)
- Prestige (highest price lines carried, usually to lend importance to the assortment as a whole)

These three price zones normally prevail within any departmental price range, regardless of what or how many price lines may be included. They apply to the price structures of basement or budget departments, as well as to prestige or high fashion departments, as well as to moderate-priced departments.

For example, within the price range of the Casual Dress department mentioned above, the price lines included in the three typical price zones might be:

- Promotional (or lowest): $18, $24
- Volume (or medium): $30, $36
- Prestige (or highest): $42, $48

The number of units sold in each price zone, as a percentage of total department sales, will vary, however, from one department to another, from one store to another, and from one selling season to another. For instance, a department store tends to do 50 to 60 percent of its business in the volume price zone, 35 percent in the promotional price zone, and 5 to 15 percent in the prestige price zone. But in a high fashion specialty store, the largest volume of business would be done in the prestige price zone, a moderate amount in the medium price zone, and almost none in the lower price zone.

Considerations in Pricing

A departmental buyer is responsible for establishing specific price lines within the range assigned to a particular department. The buyer is also responsible for the pricing and repricing of individual items included in the assortment.

Establishing Price Lines   In establishing retail price lines, care should be taken to see that there is enough dollar difference between price lines so that customers can readily distinguish differences in quality that exist, or should exist, in the merchandise at various price lines.

While it is advantageous from the standpoint of customer goodwill to maintain the same price lines on a continuing basis, this is not always possible. Higher wholesale prices inevitably result in higher retail prices. Higher costs of doing business at the retail level inevitably result in a need for a wider spread between the wholesale price of an item and the retail price at which that item is marked.

Pricing Items   Once price lines have been established, a buyer usually "buys into" those price lines; that is, the buyer prices merchandise at the established price line that comes closest to covering the wholesale price of an item plus the initial markup which may be required. For example, if the wholesale price of an item is $10.75 and the initial markup required is 48 percent, the buyer calculates the item's retail price to be $20.67. Quite obviously $20.67 is not a customary retail price line. Assuming there are established price lines in the department of $20 and $23, the buyer would consider the item's sales potential at $20 and $23. Although it might first appear that the item should retail at $20, if the buyer thought the quality of the item was comparable to other items in stock at $23, the item might be retailed at $23, thus achieving a higher initial markup.

In addition to wholesale cost and quality, other factors influence retail pricing practices. These factors include:

- Competitors' prices for the same or similar merchandise
- Manufacturers' "suggested" retail price (for example, those of nationally advertised brands)
- The home store's pricing policies: low, medium, or high; its required correlation of prices between departments
- Nature of the goods: exclusive, high markdown risk, fragile
- Demand and supply

Best-selling Price Lines   Among each department's price lines there are always a limited number that account for the greater share of the department's dollar and unit sales volume. These are referred to as *best-selling price lines* and usually are to be found concentrated in the middle of the department's price range.

In planning assortments, a successful buyer clearly recognizes best-selling price lines and plans the assortments so that the greatest number of units, in the greatest variety of types, colors, materials, and sizes, are included at these price lines. Other price lines are then planned on the basis of the relative sales importance of each to the department's total volume.

CLASSIFYING ASSORTMENTS

As stated in the NRMA *Standard Classification of Merchandise,* a *classification* is "an assortment of units or items of merchandise which are all reasonably substitutable for each other, regardless of who made the item, the material of which it is made, or the part of the store in which it is offered for sale."[2]

Purposes of Classification

The major purposes in subdividing merchandise into classifications are (1) to more precisely define the nature and extent of customer demand so that merchandise is readily available to satisfy that demand, and (2) to provide better planning and control of the merchandising operation.

To achieve these aims, it must be clearly understood by the buyer, as well as by superiors and subordinates, that the department is composed of many different types of merchandise, each of which, although generally related, is intended for a somewhat different purpose. For example, a Men's Furnishings department usually is made up of such nonsubstitutable types of merchandise as dress shirts, sport shirts, underwear, hosiery, robes, hats, accessories, and so on. Each type, therefore, should be designated as a separate classification for assortment planning and control purposes.

Establishing Classifications and Subclassifications

Authorities agree that, as a first step in establishing classifications for assortment-planning purposes, every item at every price line that is currently in stock should be listed. In addition, the list should include items not currently in stock but which have been included in the department's assortment during the preceding 12-month period. The next step is to sort out the listed items by classification, or end use.

When broad classifications have been established on the basis of end use and nonsubstitutability, it then usually becomes necessary to set up subclassifications. These identify the merchandise within each classification according to various product characteristics so that specific areas of customer demand within the broad classification can be identified. It also may be necessary to indicate the seasons or months each classification and subclassification is carried, since many items, especially fashion goods, are quite seasonal in nature.

For merchandise planning and control purposes, each classification and subclassification is assigned a permanent identification code, usually a number. In most cases, the code for a classification consists of a fixed range of consecutive numbers, and each subclassification is assigned a specific range of numbers within the wider range assigned to the broad classification.

Careful study of the price lines at which each classification and subclassification will be offered is considered essential in assortment planning. This ensures that (1) all price lines within a department's price range are represented in the assortment plan; (2) the best-selling price lines are appropriately represented with the widest variety of types, colors, materials, and sizes; and (3) duplication of merchandise has been at least minimized, if not prevented.

According to a well-known authority on merchandise planning and control, the objective of all classification and assortment planning is to carry "stocks that provide the customer with the combination of [selection] factors that to [that customer] are most significant."[3]

ASSORTMENT PLANNING IN FASHION DEPARTMENTS

The assortment plan for a fashion department, like that for a staple or semistaple goods department, should be based on a well-conceived classification and price-line plan. However, planning ready-to-wear or accessories assortments involves considerably more study, time, and effort on the part of the buyer than does planning assortments for carpets and rugs or housewares, for the following reasons. In a fashion department:

- Both the rate and pattern of sales vary considerably within a given season and from one season to the next.
- Customer preferences vary dramatically from one season to the next and from year to year.
- Merchandise frequently cannot be reordered during a selling season.

For these reasons, a fashion buyer's major responsibilities with regard to planning and maintaining a well-balanced merchandise assortment are (1) to be able to estimate, with reasonable accuracy, the peaks and valleys in customer demand that will occur during the season being planned; (2) to be constantly on the alert for even the faintest sign of change in customer preferences; and (3) to continuously evaluate the assortment in terms of newly developing trends.

Classifying a Fashion Department

The principles of classifying and subclassifying items to develop balanced merchandise assortments can be applied to departments handling fashion goods as readily as it can to departments handling merchandise that does not vary so dramatically in type, styling, or color from one season to the next. The techniques used in applying the principles do vary, however, in several respects.

First, because customer preferences for product characteristics such as styling, color, and fabric usually vary from one season to the next and always vary from one year to the next, a fashion buyer can use past sales experience only as a rough guide in planning assortments for a coming season. Planning has to be based more on a determination of major fashion trends and an evaluation of those trends in respect to the store's target groups of customers. This is in sharp contrast to developing seasonal assortments for departments handling more staple goods, in which products carried in the assortment have longer demand cycles and style changes are far less frequent. In departments handling more staple goods, the rate of sale of most items can be plotted with reasonable accuracy, and the availability of merchandise remains fairly constant throughout a season and often from one season to the next.

Second, the demand for certain fashion classifications and subclassifications is highly seasonal; so is the availability of those types of merchandise. An effective classification system for fashion goods clearly indicates in which season or seasons of the year each classification or subclassification should be included in the assortment.

Third, since fashion assortments are often highly volatile in nature, an age limit, or length of time that each item should be allowed to remain in stock (before being closed out), should be established. This policy can be implemented by coding the day of receipt and age limit of each item on its price ticket for easy reference. For example, the age code for a dress received on April 25 to which a six-week time limit has been set might read, "4256W." For most other types of assortments, a regular season code, indicating the month and season of receipt of the merchandise, is usually considered sufficient.

Finally, price-line planning by classification and subclassification is as important, if not more so, for fashion assortments as it is for other types of merchandise. Because of the financial risks involved in acquiring merchandise that is so highly seasonal, fragile, and vulnerable to loss in value due to sudden change in demand, fashion merchants can ill-afford to have duplications in their stock or to have limited assortments at their most popular price lines. As one authority puts it,

Developing a classification plan for a fashion department involves the exercise of considerable imaginative effort prior to the start of each sea-

son, yet its creation is essential. It becomes in effect, the foundation stone upon which the entire structure of assortments and a store's "level of service" must perforce rest.[4]

Procedures in Seasonal Planning

Although classifications in fashion departments remain relatively unchanged from one season to the next, their subclassifications, or variables, and the resulting composition of the departmental assortment do not. For this reason, fashion buyers cannot make valid decisions about their seasonal assortments until they have thoroughly appraised what the market has to offer. In addition, they should become familiar with what related markets are offering. Once they have shopped the market, exchanged ideas with other fashion buyers in their own and noncompetitive stores, and learned what fashion themes their stores plans to promote during the coming season, they are in a position to start planning their assortments.

As a first step, a buyer might list all the fashion trends she has observed or learned about and list them in what she believes is their order of importance for her customers in the approaching season. Next, she might rank each fashion variable offered in the market—such as new styles, fabrics, colors, price lines, and any other significant characteristic—according to what she believes to be their prospective sales potential. Since past selling experience is only a rough guide for the buyer, planning an assortment for a new season must be primarily concerned with attempting to interpret when, and to what extent, newly developing fashion trends will be of interest to the store's target customers.

Based on their market work and considered judgment of the importance of each fashion trend to customers, fashion buyers can develop a preliminary seasonal classification plan—but only in broad terms. Final decisions regarding details of the departmental assortment plan can come only after a new season is underway. Customer demand alone will determine which styles should be reordered and which should be dropped, in which subclassifications selections should be increased or reduced, and which subclassifications should be eliminated from the assortment.

Evaluating Fashion Trends

All alert fashion buyers are well aware that their customers tend to purchase fashion goods when these are at a certain stage in their fashion cycles. Buyers, therefore, must carefully analyze the fashion trends observed in market offerings and decide when, and to what extent, their customers will be ready to accept new fashions.

For example, if a store's customers want only newly introduced fashions, they will not be satisfied with fashions once they are rapidly rising in popular acceptance. But if customers will not consider purchasing fashion goods until the goods have won widespread acceptance, they will look at, but not buy, fashions in earlier stages of the fashion cycle.

However, it is good merchandising policy for each fashion department to include in its assortment some merchandise that is in earlier stages of fashion development. The newer fashions may be just what the few fashion leaders or influentials among the store's customers are looking for, thus giving impetus to those fashions on the local scene. In any event, having a small percentage of merchandise in the assortment that is more advanced in styling, color, and fabric than that which appeals to most customers lends an aura of fashion leadership to the store's image. Moreover, it helps get customers' eyes used to new fashion features and prepares them to accept those features earlier than they might otherwise.

Components of a Fashion Assortment

It is essential to bear in mind that a classification represents merchandise in general demand for a specific end use. Subclassifications represent variable or distinguishing characteristics of merchandise within each broad classification.

Classifications As an example of classifying a fashion department, let us consider Misses' Dresses. The primary classifications into which such a department's merchandise might be broken down, on the basis of end use, are

- Casual
- Streetwear
- Late day
- Formal
- Resort

Other classifications, also based on a specific end use for which no classification had yet been made, could be added whenever a new type of misses' dress became important in the assortment.

Subclassifications Subclassifications, indicating fashion characteristics or variables of each class of dress, could then be made. There might even be sub-subclassifications, if the need for this information is worth the time and cost involved.

Just a few examples of possible choices of subclassifications and sub-subclassifications might be these:

- *Style:* basic, coatdress, costume (dress with jacket or coat), two-piece, jumper, princess, sheath, tunic, etc.
- *Neck:* bateau, jewel, portrait, scoop, square, V, cowl, etc.
- *Skirt:* circular, draped, gathered, gored, pleated, slim, tiered, wrap, full, etc.
- *Sleeve:* sleeveless, long sleeve, short sleeve, dolman, rolled, gathered, etc.

Sizing Size is one characteristic of fashion apparel that is unaffected by changing seasonal demand and for which there are no substitutes. What is known in the trade as "women's apparel" is manufactured in four basic size ranges:

- *Junior:* 5 to 15 (odd-numbered sizes)
- *Misses':* 4 to 20 (even-numbered sizes)

- *Women's half-sizes:* $12\frac{1}{2}$ to $24\frac{1}{2}$ (and sometimes larger, in even-numbered sizes)
- *Women's straight sizes:* 36 to 52 (and sometimes larger, in even-numbered sizes)

In recent years, some manufacturers are also producing what are termed "junior petites," "petite misses'," and "petite women's" sizes. Also there is some limited production of "tall girls," based on misses' size measurements, and of "chubbies," for more generously proportioned young women.

In any department where the merchandise is sized, size is often the determining selection factor, taking precedence over color, price, styling, or any other fashion variable. A woman who requires a size 14 dress can scarcely be expected to buy a size 10, even if that is the only size available in the style that attracts her. Neither can a woman whose foot requires a $6\frac{1}{2}$AA shoe be satisfied with the fit of a size $7\frac{1}{2}$AA, even if the style pleases her.

Not all sizes enjoy the same rate of sale, nor is any one color or color combination equally popular in each size in which it is made. Great care has to be exercised by a fashion buyer of sized merchandise to see that all sizes are at all times well represented in stock in proportion to the needs of target customers. There is a saying among retailers: "If you're out of a size, you're out of stock."

Alert fashion merchants have found they can bolster their store's fashion image and acquire faithful customers by including in their assortments a well-rounded variety of styles, fabrics, and colors in less popular sizes or in size ranges largely overlooked by competitors in the trading area.

Fashion Trends Fashion buyers are aided in planning their assortments by the knowledge that fashions are largely evolutionary rather than revolutionary in nature. Fashion change tends to be fairly gradual. While changes may occur in one or more fashion element (silhouette, detail of design, texture, and color) from one season to another, rarely does change occur in all four elements simultaneously. Actually, such change is readily predictable once fashion components are isolated and examined in detail. Fashion buyers who are well acquainted with fashion principles, as discussed in Chapter 1, and how fashions move and disseminate, as discussed in Chapters 3 and 4, are prepared to identify trends as well as gauge their future relevancy for their target customers and for the departmental assortment.

New Season Testing At the start of each new season, all fashion stocks should include testing quantities of newly introduced styles, colors, and fabrics. At this time, much of the speculative risk involved in merchandising fashions can be reduced by using only a conservative portion of the open-to-buy until customer preferences can be established more definitely. These preferences are established by customer acceptance or rejection of the choices of styles, colors, and fabrics offered in the opening assortments.

Once the most popular styles, colors, and fabrics become obvious, then these and similar merchandise should be bought in depth and aggressively promoted. At the same time, other components of the starting assortments, for which customers have shown little interest, should be either narrowed down or eliminated from stock.

Expanding and Contracting Fashion Assortments

Assortment planners must always consider the fact that sales in fashion departments vary considerably from month to month throughout a six-month planning season. This is because of the highly seasonal nature of fashion demand and the fact that more than one fashion selling season often occurs within a six-month budget season. The assortments in most fashion departments run a peak-and-valley course throughout a six-month season, and special consideration must be given to this fact when planning fashion assortments.

Early in a season, the variety of styles, colors, and often price lines in an assortment should be broad and in small quantities in preparation for the selling peak ahead. As this peak approaches, the variety of styles carried in inventory should gradually be reduced so that the assortment includes only those in most popular demand. At the same time, depth of stock (in sizes and colors) should be increased for each of the best-selling styles. As the peak is reached, buying for that season is discontinued, and stock on hand is sold off in order to have a substantially smaller stock once the peak has passed. When the peak is passed, only minimum assortments of basic styles, colors, and sizes, at the most popular price lines, should be continued in stock, and then only as long as reasonable customer demand prevails. All other merchandise from the just-ended season's assortment should be marked down and closed out. Then, broad and shallow assortments of new-season styles, colors, materials, and price lines should be introduced into stock, and the cycle of expansion and contraction of assortments begins all over again.

Reviewing the Plan

Planning, establishing, and maintaining a complete fashion assortment should be an ongoing program rather than one that is only undertaken when sales are down and inventories up. While formal, end-of-season reviews of departmental assortment plans—participated in by buyers and their merchandise managers—serve a very beneficial purpose for future planning, less formal reviews conducted on a continuous basis throughout each six-month season are essential in fashion departments.

Fashion is rarely static, and neither should a fashion assortment plan be static. Fads come and go; fashion trends follow a fairly normal pattern of development or fade quickly into obscurity; "hot items" appear unexpectedly. These and other changes in customer preference often take place after a planned season is underway. To be successful, a fashion buyer must keep constantly on the alert for, and receptive to, such changes.

FASHION ASSORTMENT PLANNING IN MULTIUNIT RETAIL ORGANIZATIONS

Multiunit retail organizations are of two types: (1) branch-operating department and specialty stores and (2) chain organizations. Although the two types of organizations traditionally have had almost opposing methods of merchandising and operating responsibility, each is gradually adopting some of the other's methods. While still very distinct, today they are not as different as they once were.

Branch-operating Department and Specialty Stores

Assortment planning and control in branch-operating department and specialty stores are essentially as described above, although planning techniques may vary from one retail organization to another, depending upon the number, size, and location of its branches.

Assortment Planning   In smaller retail organizations with only a few relatively small branches in nearby locations, responsibility for merchandising all stores in the group is vested in the parent store executives. Branches are considered "outposts" and concentrate solely on selling. Buyers and other executives of the organization are headquartered in the parent store. Communication with branches is maintained mainly by telephone and periodic visits by parent store executives. All merchandising records are kept in the parent store for the convenience of buyers and other store executives. Buyers are technically responsible for transmitting merchandising information to all sales personnel, wherever located, and for departmental sales results.

In operations of this size, seasonal departmental merchandise budgets are prepared by the parent store buyers and include figures for branches as well as the parent store. There is little formal planning of assortments for each of the branches, since branch and parent store stocks are usually considered as one.

In developing a preliminary seasonal assortment plan for all stores in the group, fashion buyers proceed as already described. They study records and reports on sales, stock, markdowns, and promotions in the corresponding season of the previous year. They carefully shop the market. They consider the different preferences of customers of each store in the group, through personal observation on visits to and discussions with store personnel at the branches. Guided by these considerations, they develop a preliminary assortment plan for their departments, regardless of where the merchandise will be located.

In this size of retail operation, fashion merchandise is usually tested only in the parent store at the start of a new season. Once the season has gotten underway, buyers rarely place merchandise orders for specific branches. Instead, they simply select from newly received shipments those styles, colors, sizes, and price lines most suitable for each branch, and the merchandise is transferred to that branch.

In larger retail organizations, with more numerous, larger, and often more distantly located branches, planning is much more formal. Usually separate merchandise budgets are prepared, separate assortments are planned, and separate unit controls are maintained for each branch. Since customer preference may vary widely from branch to branch, especially in the case of fashion goods, branch store managers, merchandise managers, and department managers are usually consulted when seasonal assortment plans are being developed.

While it is important that a branch-operating organization, no matter how widely dispersed its branches are, maintain its fashion image by always having in stock certain fashion assortments and price lines in keeping with that image, these need not make up the total fashion assortments of any one branch. Basic fashion assortments can be provided to all stores by the parent store's departmental buyer, while other components of a branch store's assortments should be more directly related to specific local demand at that branch.

There is a noticeable trend among large branch organizations to permit their individual branches greater autonomy in developing their own fashion merchandise budgets and developing and maintaining their own assortment plans. This has come about for one or more of the following reasons:

- Many branches today are as large or even larger than the parent store.
- Sales volume of branches now far exceeds that of most parent stores.
- Many branches are located at considerable distance from the parent store, thus complicating communication.
- Patterns of demand and competitive practices vary from branch to branch according to the trading area in which each is located.

In general, therefore, the more numerous a store's branches, or the larger their size, or the greater their distance from the parent store, the greater is the need for fashion assortments to be more precisely tailored to the needs of the customers of each branch.

Trends   Among branch-operating department and specialty stores, chiefly those with numerous large branches located at a distance from the parent store, there is a definite trend toward relieving buyers of responsibility for sales supervision in all store locations. Other trends include: (1) allowing individual branches greater autonomy in assortment planning and merchandise decision making; (2) increasing use of electronic data processing for merchandising purposes, particularly in inventory control; and (3) the adoption of an increasing number of the successful operating techniques practiced by chain organizations for many years.

Chain Organizations

Chain organizations have previously been defined as groups of retail stores that are centrally owned, each handling similar goods, and all merchandised from a national or regional headquarters office. There are chains of department stores, variety stores, and specialty stores. From the standpoint of location, chains are national, regional, or local. The number of store units in a chain may range anywhere from 12 (a minimum established by the Bureau of the Census) into the thousands.

Chain operation is chiefly characterized by central buying and merchandising. Individual units of the chain are engaged only in selling. Central buyers, located in major market areas or a headquarters office, are responsible for providing merchandise for all units of the chain. In contrast to departmental buyers, however, chain or central-office buyers are not responsible for sales results or supervision of sales personnel. Because of the tremendous quantities of merchandise needed to keep all chain units supplied with the varieties of stock needed, central-office buyers are specialists: They are responsible for no more than one classification of merchandise and frequently for only limited price lines within a classification.

Centrally bought staple merchandise is kept in warehouses and requisitioned from there, as needed, by the units of the chain. Centrally purchased fashion merchandise is usually sent to a distribution center, where merchandise is allocated and distributed to chain units.

Methods of planning fashion assortments for each unit varies from one chain to another, particularly with respect to the amount of autonomy granted individual units in determining the composition of their assortments. For example, in one chain, assortment planning for all units may be the responsibility of the national or regional headquarters office. In another chain, all regular assortments may be planned by the headquarters' merchandising staff, with store units permitted only to make decisions relating to the timing, type, and extent of promotions in which they may wish to engage. In yet another chain, what is considered to be a basic seasonal fashion assortment is detailed by the headquarters staff and suggestions are made in the form of a listing of other items, classifications, subclassifications, and price lines that are available through the buying office to round out and complete the seasonal assortments of each unit. In this case, complete descriptions and cost and retail prices of suggested merchandise are provided to assist the unit management in making selections best suited to satisfying the needs and wants of that particular store's customers. In such cases, the chain's district manager usually works with the store manager, the fashion (or soft-goods) merchandise manager, and the appropriate department manager in finalizing a seasonal fashion assortment plan.

Individual store merchandise budgets, seasonal assortment plans carefully detailed by classifications and price lines, and weekly or biweekly sales and stock-on-hand reports provide the framework within which fashion merchandise is distributed to each store unit. Chain operation depends, for its success, on the continuous and accurate flow of sales and stock information from its store units to its headquarters office. Only in this way can inventories be properly balanced with demand.

Chain organizations were pioneers in using automated data processing systems to control retail inventories. Only data processing can handle the tremendous flow of merchandising data generated in a chain's operation and rapidly convert that data into accurate and timely reports for decision-making purposes by the chain's executives.

Catalog Operation The three largest department store chains in the country—Sears, Roebuck and Company, J. C. Penney Company, and Montgomery Ward—sell impressive quantities of fashion merchandise through seasonal catalogs, as well as in their stores. Sears, Roebuck and Company and Montgomery Ward were originally mail-order retailers and sold merchandise only through catalogs until they opened retail stores in the late 1920s and early 1930s. The J. C. Penney Company, on the other hand, started as a retail store and fairly recently added a catalog operation.

In chain organizations, the planning of fashion assortments to be offered in various catalog issues is the responsibility of a separate catalog buying and merchandising staff, located in the headquarters office. The reason for maintaining separate fashion buying and merchandising staffs for store sales and for catalog sales is the timing of the offerings, although both staffs work closely with each other. Catalog assortments have to be decided upon many months before those that are offered in the chain's retail stores because of the amount of time involved in the projection of trends, the selection of individual items, the printing of the catalog, and the delivery of that catalog into the hands of the customers—all of which must take place before the peak of demand for the various merchandise offered in the catalog. Because fashion merchandise offered in catalogs has to be planned and priced so far in advance of its actual availability in the wholesale market, its planners not only have to excel in accurate prediction of fashion trends, but in most cases have to buy fabrics and have them made up to specifications. In addition, the catalog buying and merchandising staff has to make sure that stock of each item in the catalog will be available upon demand.

Trends Today, the major chain organizations are expanding their use of automated data processing equipment to include electronic cash registers. Almost error-proof, point-of-sale information can be fed into this type of register, either by punching the register's keys or by use of a "wand" that electronically "reads" a price ticket. This information is transmitted to a computer's memory banks, and the computer can produce, on demand, fast and accurate selected sales and stock reports that are essential in making good merchandising decisions about the inventories of individual store units, or regional divisions, or the chain as a whole.

At the same time that conventional retail organizations are adopting many chain store techniques for more profitable merchandising results, chain organizations have begun to adopt to an increasing extent some of the more successful techniques of traditional retail merchandising. In particular, many chain organizations are now allowing executives of store units more autonomy in merchandising and operating decisions.

Chain organizations are also becoming increasingly fashion-minded. They are devoting considerably more space in their stores, as well as in their catalogs, to fashions for men, women, and children. They are expanding and upgrading their fashion assortments. They are emphasizing fashion coordination more in their advertisements and displays. Their newer stores are bright, spacious, and colorful, with attractive fixtures, fitting rooms, and carpeting. Many have beauty salons and a variety of other fashion services. All indications point to a continuation of this trend.

REFERENCES

[1] Taylor, *Merchandise Assortment Planning*, p. 25.
[2] *NRMA, Standard Classification of Merchandise*, 2d ed., p. 15.
[3] Wingate, "What's Wrong with the Planning of Stock Assortments," *New York Retailer*, Oct. 1959, p. 6.
[4] Taylor, op. cit., p. 15.

MERCHANDISING VOCABULARY

Define or briefly explain the following terms:

Merchandise assortment	Price range
Merchandise plan	Price zone
Balanced assortment	Best-selling price lines
Price-lining	Classification
Price line	Season code

MERCHANDISING REVIEW

1. What are the major objectives of assortment planning?
2. To what factors should a fashion buyer give careful consideration when planning assortments? Briefly discuss the importance of each factor.
3. Name and briefly discuss five major areas of merchandising policy that importantly influence the composition of a store's fashion assortments.
4. Name at least five sources of information available to fashion merchants as they go about developing seasonal assortments. What kind of information does each source provide?
5. Name and briefly describe the two major methods of planning merchandise budgets and assortments. Which method is considered best for planning fashion assortments, and why?
6. What is meant by the price structure of a store or department? Why is it important in planning assortments? By whom is it determined? What factors must a buyer carefully consider when pricing goods?

7. In addition to the wholesale cost of an item, what other factors must a buyer consider in assigning a retail price? Briefly discuss how each factor might effect a buyer's decision in pricing an item.

8. Briefly discuss the reasons why assortment planning for fashion departments is more difficult than assortment planning for more staple goods.

9. Discuss the procedures involved in assortment planning of seasonal fashions.

10. Discuss the procedures for and importance of testing fashion merchandise at the start of a new selling season. Why are expanding and contracting fashion assortments implicit in fashion merchandising?

MERCHANDISING DIGEST

1. Discuss merchandise classification on the basis of the following: (a) purposes, (b) procedures in setting up a system, and (c) establishing subclassifications.

2. Compare and contrast fashion assortment planning in (a) smaller branch-operating department or specialty stores, (b) large branch-operating department or specialty stores, and (c) chain organizations.

3. Discuss the following statement from the text: "A merchandise assortment that is well balanced in relation to demand is the most potent tool any retailer can use to attract and hold customers." Why is a store's merchandise assortment the most important factor in attracting and maintaining customer patronage? What does this statement imply in relation to (a) types, (b) quantities, (c) prices, and (d) depth and breadth of assortments?

15
CONTROLLING FASHION ASSORTMENTS: UNIT CONTROL

Chapter 14 explained how merchants plan fashion assortments to reflect as accurately as possible the demands of a store's clientele. This chapter is concerned with a basic tool that helps merchants set up and maintain assortments in proper balance with the needs and wants of the store's target customers. That tool is *unit control,* which refers to systems for recording the number of units of merchandise bought, sold, in stock, and on order, and from which a variety of reports can be drawn.

Because of the rapidly changing nature of fashion demand, sales and stock records of previous years can serve only as rough guides in planning assortments for an upcoming season or in evaluating the assortments as the season progresses. Much more useful guides are current, detailed reports on unit sales, stock on hand, and stock on order, in terms of merchandise classification, subclassification, and price line. Fashion merchants can use this information to identify developing trends in customer demand and then to adjust their assortments accordingly.

Unit control systems are used to collect this kind of sales and stock information. They isolate and identify "centers of demand" around which properly balanced assortments can be built or reshaped. However, it is important to remember that unit control is a merchandising tool, not an inventory accounting procedure. As used in retailing, it does not and cannot serve as a substitute for regular inventory accounting procedures.

There is no standard unit control system. Systems vary in format from store to store and from one type of merchandise to another. They also vary widely in the methods used for collecting and reporting data, and in the amount of detail collected.

In a single small store, unit control is relatively simple and informal. A small store contains such a limited amount of stock that a merchant can often use "visual inspection" to see what is selling rapidly and what is selling slowly or not at all. As stores grow in physical size and sales volume, however, the need for a formal unit control system becomes increasingly vital. And as branches are opened, the need for a good unit control system that provides sales and stock information about all store units—regardless of their number, size, or location—becomes absolutely essential.

TYPE OF INFORMATION RECORDED

Regardless of the type of system used or the type of merchandise involved, a unit control system is set up to show:

- Net sales in number of units
- Stock on hand and on order in number of units
- Additional dissection of this sales and stock information in whatever detail is considered relevant, such as cost and retail price, style number, size, color, vendor, merchandise classification or subclassification

The kind and extent of details about sales and stock information collected depends upon the kind of merchandise involved and what a merchant needs to know to be able to gauge changes in customer demand properly. Systems used for staple goods, for instance, which are relatively slow to show change in styling or rate of acceptance, may be set up only to collect general information; yet they may be quite adequate for their purpose. Because fashion merchandise, however, is subject to rapid change in demand, systems usually are set up to collect information in considerable detail, so that the merchant will be alerted to the slightest change in demand for specific designs, colors, or other basic fashion factors.

Some fashion merchandise requires more detailed control than others. Inexpensive blouses, for example, may require only the recording of unit sales and stock figures by size, price line, and color. For moderate-priced dresses, on the other hand, a system probably would be set up to collect sales information in terms of sizes, colors, classification, vendor, and retail price for each individual style. In men's shirts, it may be necessary to keep sales and stock records by collar size, collar style, sleeve length, color, fabric, and price line or price range.

Each merchant seeks to develop a system that provides the essential facts needed to maintain an assortment that is well balanced to customer demand and yet that does not collect unessential details. The system has to give meaningful help in the form of current and accurate information if the assortments are to be kept adjusted to customer demand.

Forms used for the manual recording of unit control data vary from store to store. Those shown in this chapter are typical. Each store or department within a store needs unit control forms that meet its particular needs, which sometimes requires a merchant to examine a number of forms used by others and then draw up new forms that fit the store's exact needs. In actual retail practice, there are many variations of forms serving similar unit control purposes.

TYPES OF SYSTEMS

There are two basic types of unit control systems used to record fashion assortment data: perpetual (running or continuous) control and periodic stock count control. The types of merchandise for which each is best suited, and the procedures involved in maintaining each, are discussed below.

Perpetual Control

In a *perpetual control* system, purchase orders, receipts of merchandise, and sales are recorded for individual style numbers as they occur, and stock on hand is computed. This system eliminates the need for actual stock counts except for regular physical inventories.

Merchandise for which perpetual controls are best suited include goods that are subject to frequent style change, goods in which the degree of fashion acceptance of specific design features and color must be carefully watched, and goods that are high or relatively high in unit price. Examples of such merchandise are men's, women's, and children's ready-to-wear and outerwear; furs; and fine jewelry. Although the cost of maintaining a perpetual control system is substantially higher than that of a simpler unit control system, it is not high in terms of its value to fashion merchants who need and use its detailed information.

Procedures   A perpetual control record begins when an order is placed for merchandise requiring this type of control. A separate record is kept for each style in each classification. On this record, or form, notation is made of such identifying information as classification, style number, description of merchandise, vendor, cost and retail prices. When the order is placed, the number of pieces ordered and the date of the order are noted. When goods are received against this order, the number of pieces originally noted as "on order" is reduced, and an entry is made to show the total number of units received and their date of receipt. Sales, in units, are recorded as to the date on which they take place and the number of units remaining "on hand" is reduced. Returns to vendors, which decrease the stock on hand, are also recorded by date and number of units involved. Returns from customers,

Berry's COLOR AND SIZE UNIT CONTROL REPORT

Dept. 42 Three Days Ending 12/08/7- Page 3 01

SELLING PRICE	CLASS	VENDOR	STYLE	STORE NO.	NET STORE TOTALS	COLOR CODE	06	08	10	12	14	16
48.00	40	012	0555	2	-1	01				-1		
				1 3	2	01					2	
58.00	40	018	0699	4	1	01					1	
64.00	40	018	0753	3	1	01					1	
32.00	40	020	0401	1	3	01				1	1	1
				4 5	1	01					1	
32.00	40	020	0406	1	1	22				1		
				2 3	1	22						1
16.00	90	020	0422	3	1	50						1
16.00	90	020	0424	4	1	50					1	
				2 3	1	50						1
32.00	40	020	0458	1	1	01					1	
32.00	90	020	1120	1	-1	00						-1
				4	3	01		1		1		1
					1	47					1	
					3	01				1	2	
				5	-1	40			-1			
44.00	43	020	1206	1	1	15				1		
				0	-1	34				-1		
44.00	43	020	1217	1	1	01					1	
20.00	90	020	1401	4	2	34		2				
20.00	90	020	1403	4	1	01				1		
					4	34				2	2	
				3	1	00				1		
				7	1	01			1	1	-1	

FORM 15-1

Example of a computer-prepared color and size unit control report.

which increase the stock on hand, are also recorded by date. Thus, at any time, a buyer can tell from looking at the perpetual control records how many units of an individual style have been sold to date, how many were purchased, how many are on order, and how many remain in stock.

On most manually maintained perpetual control forms, a breakdown of each style by size and color can also be kept, if needed. A common practice is to indicate the number of units on order in each size and color with a penciled-in dot or diagonal line for each individual unit. When shipments are received against a purchase order, the number of units received in each size and color is indicated by inking a diagonal line over the penciled-in mark. As each unit is sold, the appropriate tally line is crossed off, making it easy to see how many of each size and color have been sold and how many remain in stock. Merchandise returned by customers is re-tallied by adding another diagonal line, usually in red this time, in the appropriate column on the form. Returns to vendor are indicated by circling the appropriate tally lines. Thus, it is easy to see at any point how many units, by size and by color, have been sold, are in stock, and are on order.

Branch Operations   Stores with only one or a few branches, which maintain a central unit control system, usually tally the number of units in each style, by size and by color, that are transferred to each branch. This may be done by using a different-color tally mark for each branch, such as brown for branch A, yellow for branch B, and so on. Branch store sales are then recorded by style, size, and color, from individual branch sales records received by the parent store.

Stores with larger and more numerous branches usually adopt a unit control form that permits them to keep, on a single form, separate sales and stock-on-hand information, by size and color, for each branch as well as the parent store. This enables merchandising executives of the parent store to calculate sales and stock data by style, size, and color at separate store locations, as well as total figures for all stores combined.

Forms   Form 15-2 shows how a manually kept perpetual control record of an individual style might look after the buyer has received into stock 72 pieces of that style. On August 15, 72 pieces were ordered, and at that time larger dots were made in pencil in the applicable color and size block for each unit ordered. When the merchandise was received on September 5, the "on order" entry was circled, to indicate that it had been received in full, and an entry was made to this effect in the "received" block. Penciled tallies of the units of sizes and colors ordered were then inked over with a diagonal line to indicate the exact number of pieces received by color and size.

Form 15-3 shows how the control card for the same style number might look after the style had been on sale for two weeks. Sales have been recorded daily, noting the total number of units sold each day as well as their size and color distribution. Customer returns have also been noted and re-entered into stock on hand by size and color. Then net sales for each week have been totalled. Any return to vendor has also been noted by date of return and the number of pieces involved, and lines corresponding to each size and color returned have been circled to indicate this action.

In this case, the buyer could see that the demand for larger sizes and for the color black was underestimated. When reordering the style, the buyer will note the date and the number of pieces in the "on order" section of the form, again making appropriate dots in pencil to indicate the number of units reordered in each color and size.

Unit sales summaries take various forms. They may be either manually or automatically prepared, based on the information available in the inventory control records. They may be issued to report the total number of units sold and on hand by department, classification, selling price, vendor, style, and store. In addition to these breakdowns, they may be further detailed in terms of color and size. Form 15-1 is a computer-prepared example of a color and size unit control report (see page 255). In fashion departments, sales summaries may be issued daily, twice a week, or weekly.

FORM 15-2: *The buyer placed an order for 72 units of a dress, in sizes 8 through 14, in three different colors. When the order was placed, this perpetual inventory card was prepared, with full details about composition of the order, the vendor, classification and style number information, cost price, and the retail price at which the units are to be sold. This is the way the card looked right after the order was received into stock. The receipt date has been entered, the "on order" number circled to show that the order has been received in full, and the original pencilled tally marks have been inked in.*

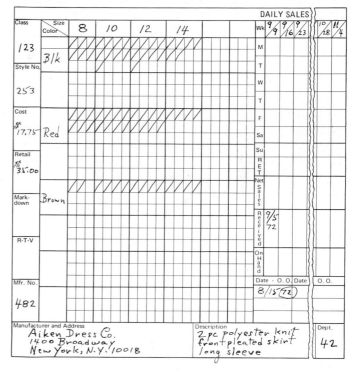

FORM 15-3: *Two weeks later this is how the inventory card might look. Sales by size and color have been entered daily by cross-hatching of the tally marks, appropriately noting any returns that have been made. Daily and weekly unit sales have also been entered so that stock on hand can be readily computed. The result is a detailed day-by-day record of how this style is selling by size and color. Dots have been entered to indicate additional merchandise on order but not yet received.*

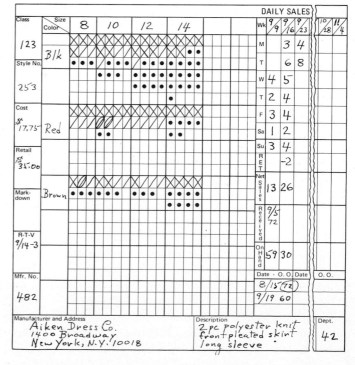

TABLE 15-1
Sales of Two Separate Styles

| | UNITS SOLD | |
	STYLE A	STYLE B
Week #1	10	2
Week #2	10	2
Week #3	10	2
Week #4	8	3
Week #5	7	5
Week #6	6	7
Week #7	3	8
Week #8	2	8
Week #9	2	10
Week #10	2	13
Total, 10 Weeks	60	60

Whatever the exact method, a perpetual control system enables a merchant to compare the total number of units sold of each style or group of styles from day to day and week to week, as well as to know the total number of units sold thus far in the season. The importance of this knowledge becomes apparent if one considers the example of two styles, each of which has had sales of 60 pieces during a ten-week period. If weekly sales figures are available, a situation like the one in Table 15-1 becomes obvious: One style is dwindling in acceptance, while the other is growing in popularity. Without such weekly figures, this very important difference could be missed.

Periodic Stock Count Control

A unit control system in which stock is counted and recorded at regular intervals and the results are used to compute sales for the intervening period is known as *periodic stock count control*. This type of unit control system is best suited for merchandise that is moderate to moderately low in price, that is subject to a degree of fashion change but not as much as is ready-to-wear, and/or that does not lend itself to easy tagging by multipart or print-punch tickets. Examples of this kind of merchan-

dise are children's socks, cosmetics, hosiery, and notions. This type of stock control is considerably less expensive to maintain than a perpetual control system.

Procedure   In periodic stock count control, sales are not recorded as they occur but are calculated from inventory changes occurring between the current count and the previous count. The results of this calculation are not as accurate nor as detailed as the results provided by a perpetual control system. However, they are sufficiently detailed and sufficiently accurate to indicate trends in demand and the rate of demand for less volatile merchandise; they also make it possible for a merchant to maintain stock levels consistent with the sales rate of individual items or groups of items.

In a manual periodic stock count unit control system, stock is counted at designated intervals. The number of units on hand and on order—by classification, price, style number, and size and color (if applicable)—is recorded. Also recorded are orders placed and receipts of merchandise since the previous count was taken. Unit sales can then be computed and recorded as follows:

$$\text{sales} = \begin{array}{l} + \text{ units of stock at previous count} \\ + \text{ merchandise receipts since previous count} \\ - \text{ units of stock on hand at present count} \end{array}$$

For purposes of periodic stock count control, a department's assortment is first divided into sections of related merchandise. Next, the buyer decides how often to count the stock in each section, with more active items being counted more frequently. Specific dates are established for each section's count. These must be adhered to faithfully if this system of unit control is to be effective. Responsibility for planning and carrying out counts of specific sections of stock is usually distributed among department personnel, with different dates set for different counts, so that no one person is overburdened and no one day finds the entire department in the process of being counted.

Forms   Forms used for a manual system of periodic stock count control differ from those used for manual perpetual control. The most widely used method for keeping the former is a loose-leaf notebook with a pair of facing pages assigned to each style or group of items. (See Form 15-4.) On the left-hand page are listed style numbers, classification codes, descriptions, vendor's name and address, cost and retail prices, and other information needed for writing up an order.

For instance, such information may include minimum packaging for each item, if that is more than a single unit. This is an important factor to consider in reordering because an item may be retailed individually but purchased by the half-dozen, the dozen, or the gross. Vendors may ship quantities as small as a half-dozen or dozen, but the cost of ordering and shipping charges on such small orders may make it wiser to order in lots of three or six dozen.

Also noted on the left-hand page are maximum quantities of each item that should be in stock or on order at all times during the item's selling season. Careful analysis of sales in previous corresponding seasons, plus specialized knowledge of current production and market conditions, guide a buyer in determining "coverage" of each item needed throughout a selling season. The term *coverage* refers to the maximum quantities to which each item's stock should be built after each regular stock count; it is expressed either in terms of a certain number of weeks' supply or a specific number of units or both.

In determining coverage needed for each item under periodic stock count control, buyers first estimate the weekly rate of sale of an item during a given selling season. Then they note the number of weeks already established between scheduled stock counts. Next they estimate the normal delivery period, in terms of weeks, required from the date of order to the date of actual receipt of the reorder. They also estimate, in terms of weeks, the safety or reserve stock needed at all times to allow for an unexpected increase in sales or an unexpected delay in delivery.

In terms of weeks' supply needed, coverage is calculated as the sum of the number of weeks between counts, the number of weeks required for delivery of reorders, and the number of weeks' supply estimated as a necessary safety or reserve factor. Unit coverage is determined by multiplying the estimated weeks' coverage by the estimated weekly rate of sale of each item.

For example, in Form 15-4, the weekly rate of sale of style 140, white, is estimated at six pairs. If the delivery period is estimated at two weeks, the interval between counts at two weeks, and the safety or reserve period at two weeks' supply, then the coverage needed is a six weeks' supply, or:

$$\begin{aligned} \text{maximum units to be} \\ \text{on hand and on order} &= 6 \times (2 + 2 + 2) \\ &= 6 \times 6 \\ &= 36 \end{aligned}$$

Stock counts should be checked immediately after they are taken and reorders promptly placed to bring the amount of stock of each item up to its designed coverage figure. At all times during a selling period, the quantity of an item on hand and on order should equal the maximum quantity established for that item. Only in this way can stocks be maintained in direct relation to anticipated demand.

The right-hand page of the control form lists the date and quantities of merchandise ordered, the quantities on hand on the dates assigned for counts, and merchandise receipts since the previous counts. On the basis of these figures, sales are calculated for the period between counts. The right-hand page of this form is often punched in both margins so that it can be turned and used on the second side. This page carries only the briefest identification of each item, often only a page number, since all necessary details are on the facing page.

The right-hand page is usually columnar, with blocks of columns available for successive counts and with space above each block for the date on

Department No. _15_

Vendor   Ricci Glove Company   **Ship via**   Lee Transport
             Gloversville, New York

Manufacturer No. _102_   **Terms**   6/10/E.O.M.

Class	Style	Cost	Unit Retail	Description	Color	Min. Pack	Coverage	
							Weeks	Units
268	140	17.50 dz.	$3.00	Stretch glove	White	1 dz.	6	36
268	140	17.50 dz.	$3.00	Stretch glove	Black	1 dz.	6	24
268	140	17.50 dz.	$3.00	Stretch glove	Beige	1 dz.	6	24

FORM 15-4 (*left-hand page*)

which the count was made. The columns are usually headed:

OH   Quantities on hand when count is made
OO   Date and quantity of any order placed since previous count was made
REC   Date and quantity of merchandise received since previous count was made
SOLD   Sales made between counts, a figure calculated by adding receipts to previous count and then subtracting present count

Reserve Requisition Control   For fast-selling, low-priced items, particularly those that are packaged, reserve requisition control is often used. *Reserve requisition control* is a form of periodic stock count in which the stock on the selling floor is considered sold and only the reserve stock is counted. A reasonable amount of stock is kept on the selling floor, but the main supply is kept in a stockroom. As the forward (selling-floor) stock runs low, more is requisitioned from the reserve.

Under this system, sales are calculated by adding up the requisitions and by considering as sold everything that has reached the selling floor.

Periodic stock counts are made, but only the reserve stock is counted, and that is considered "on hand."

The reserve requisition control system is especially useful in high-volume, small-unit sales departments, such as hosiery or notions. It is much faster, for example, to count one carton of 144 pairs of hosiery in the reserve stock than to make a count on the selling floor of 48 boxes, each containing from one to three pairs. And it is much easier and faster to record requisitions for 36 pairs of one style and 24 pairs of another than to record possibly 30 individual sales transactions involving the same 60 pairs.

Visual Control   What merchants call "eyeball control" or "visual control" is another form of periodic stock count. In *visual control,* a rack or bin is assigned to each style, size, or classification, and a periodic check is made to see whether one of these bins or racks looks too empty or too full. The merchant makes an on-the-spot judgment about action to be taken when the bins and racks are checked.

Fashion merchandise does not usually lend

Department ___15___

Manufacturer No. ___102___

			Date 5/3				Date 5/17				Date 5/31			
Class	Style	O.H.	O.O. 5/6	Rec. 5/14	Sold	O.H.	O.O. 5/20	Rec. 5/28	Sold	O.H.	O.O. 6/2	Rec. 6/10	Sold
268	140 White	20	(12)	12	10	22	(12)	12	12	22	(12)	12	
268	140 Black	20			8	12	(12)	12	4	20			
268	140 Beige	30			10	20			8	12	(12)	12	

FORM 15-4 (*right-hand page*)

itself well to visual control. Exceptions might be a very small operation in which the proprietor's memory serves as the record, or a boutique or specialty shop that never stocks styles in depth because its customers only want one-of-a-kind items or the newest and most unique styles. Still another exception might involve the stock of such special-purpose, lower-volume merchandise as cocktail dresses, theater ensembles, or party pajamas. In these cases, visual control, rather than more formal and detailed controls, might prove satisfactory for determining sales and stock-on-hand information.

SOURCES OF UNIT CONTROL INFORMATION

Unit control involves setting up procedures for collecting data on additions to or subtractions from stock, from the time an order is placed with a vendor through the time the item is sold to a customer. Principal sources of such information are purchase orders, sales records, merchandise transfers, returns from customers, returns to vendors, order cancellations, and price changes. The use of each in a unit control system is described below.

Purchase Orders

When a purchase order is placed, the original copy is given to the vendor, and the store owner or buyer retains one or more carbons for future reference and for making appropriate entries in the unit control records. (See Form 15-5.) The amount of information on each order that is entered in the records depends on the type of unit control system used. In general, however, the purchase order is the source of such important control information as

- Date of order
- Department number
- Classification of merchandise ordered
- Vendor's name and address
- Number and description of each style ordered
- Cost and retail prices of each style ordered
- Quantities ordered of each style
- Details of color and size, if any, in each style

Multiunit stores, such as department and specialty stores with several branches, usually prepare order forms with separate columns for each

Berry's

			STORE NAME	DEPT. NO.		ORDER NO.
			Berry's #1	42	M	184925

BILLING, PACKING, AND SHIPPING REQUIREMENTS
1. INVOICE MUST BE ENCLOSED WITH SHIPMENT, AND CARTON CONTAINING INVOICE MUST BE SO MARKED ON THE OUTSIDE.
2. MERCHANDISE FOR TWO OR MORE DEPARTMENTS, SHIPPED AT THE SAME TIME, MUST BE BILLED AND PACKED SEPARATELY, AND INVOICES AND CARTONS PLAINLY MARKED FOR THE SEPARATE DEPARTMENTS. HOWEVER, ALL SUCH SHIPMENTS MUST BE COMBINED UNDER ONE BILL OF LADING.
3. DEPARTMENT, ORDER NUMBER AND WEIGHT MUST BE SHOWN ON THE INDIVIDUAL CONTAINERS.
4. ALL GARMENT PACKAGES MUST CONTAIN COLOR AND SIZE LISTS BY STYLE NUMBER.

NAME Aiken Dress Co.
ADDRESS 1400 Broadway
CITY AND STATE New York, N.Y. 10018

TERMS 8/10 EOM
WITH ANTICIPATION FOR PREPAYMENT

DATE OF ORDER	DUE DATE AT STORE	CANCEL BY	HOUSE NUMBER	
8/15/7-	9/10/7- Complete	9/10/7- Will be cancelled or shipment returned at vendor's expense.	482	SHIP TO: Main Store Cincinnati, Ohio

STYLE NUMBER	CODE OR CLASS	DIS LETTER	DESCRIPTION	8	10	12	14			TOTAL QUANTITY	UNIT COST	TOTAL COST	UNIT RETAIL
				SIZES									
253	123		2 pc polyester knit										
			front pleated skirt										
			long sleeve										
			Black	6	9	9	6			30			
			Red	6	10	8	4			28			
			Brown	2	4	4	4			14			
										72	17 75	1,278 —	

ROUTING INSTRUCTIONS

FOLLOW OUR ROUTING - WE CHARGE BACK ANY EXCESS TRANSPORTATION COSTS TO YOU.

☒ F.O.B. STORE NAMED OR WAREHOUSE
☐ 1 TO 20 LBS. - PARCEL POST DIRECT TO STORE - DO NOT INSURE
☐ 21 TO 50 LBS. - REA EXPRESS DIRECT TO STORE - MINIMUM VALUE
    (SPECIFY COMMODITY TARIFF ON WAYBILL)

OVER 50 LBS. (TRUCK ROUTING) __IOU Service__
SPECIAL ROUTING INSTRUCTIONS __Hangars__
VALUATION EXCEPTION: NO DECLARATION OF VALUE IS TO BE MADE BY THE VENDOR EXCEPT ON FURS AND JEWELRY, IN WHICH CASE ACTUAL VALUE UP TO $1000 SHOULD BE DECLARED.

FORM 312 REV. 12-63

This order subject to conditions of purchase appearing on the reverse side and is a contract only when confirmed by merchandise office signature.

GRAND TOTAL COST	1,278 —
GRAND TOTAL RETAIL	
% MARK UP	

Jane Dean   DEPT. MGR.
T. J. Evans   DIV. MDSE. MGR.

FORM 15-5

store unit for which merchandise is purchased. In this way, a single order can cover purchases made in behalf of as many store locations as need to be served. On orders placed for distribution to specific branches, however, quantities and applicable details of color and size distribution are specified for each location. The more units to be served, the wider the form becomes. With such a form, however, a buyer can see when the order is placed if it results in a balanced assortment of styles, sizes, and colors for each store unit. Merchandise for specific branches may be sent directly to those stores, or the order may specify that all merchandise be delivered to the parent store.

RECEIVING RECORD					No. 16181			

Received From _Aiken Dress Company_

Address _1400 Broadway_ City _New York, N.Y. 10018_

Date Received _9/5/7–_

Department	Order No.	Transportation Charges		Buyers Approval or Remarks	Received Via			
		Total Paid	Charge Shipper					
42	M 184925	36.00		_Jane Dean 9/16_	I O U Service			

Invoice Date	Terms	Invoice Passed	Discount		Amt. of Invoice	Retail Value	Pkg's.	Pieces	Cartons
9/5/7–	8/10 EOM	9/12/7–	Date 10/10	Amount 102.24	1,278.00	2,520.00		72 (hangers)	

ATTACH INVOICE HERE

Received From _____

No. 16181

Vendor No.	Unit Cost	Color	Description	Size				Quantity		Class	Unit Price
				8	10	12	14	Amt.	Unit		
482	17.75	Blk	Style 253, 2 pc.	6	9	9	6	30	ea.	123	35.00
482	17.75	Red	Style 253, 2 pc.	6	10	8	4	28	ea.	123	35.00
482	17.75	Brn	Style 253, 2 pc.	2	4	4	4	14	ea.	123	35.00

Order Checked	Date	Mdse. Checked	Date	Price Tickets	Date	Mdse. Marked	Date	Cost Extension	Retail Extension	Merchandise Received/Date	
										Stock Room	Department
HLC	9/6	FBJ	9/6	MPR	9/6	mng	9/9	1,278.00	2,520.00	aJL 9/10	

FORM 15-6

Receiving Records

Good retail practice requires that a record be made of each unit of merchandise received by a store. (See Form 15-6.) A copy of this record is turned over to the unit control clerk, who updates the "on order" entry by indicating the number of units received and the date of receipt. If the total order is received, some systems merely circle the "on order" entry.

The many purposes served by receiving records can be observed by examining Form 15-6. The form shown is in two parts: one above and one below the horizontal perforated line. In the upper right-hand corner of both parts is a number, one of a consecutive series, that is assigned to an incoming shipment; it is used for all future identification of that shipment. The right-hand corner also has space for recording the number of cartons or packages in the shipment, the name of the carrier, and the date of delivery.

The upper left-hand section of the form provides space for a variety of information that will be needed by the accounting department in processing the invoice for payment, including the buyer's approval or exceptions. When this upper part of the receiving form is detached from the bottom part and attached to an invoice, it is designed as a *receiving apron*, a sequentially numbered form designed for complete information about each shipment of merchandise; it includes the signatures of persons handling the shipment that are required by the accounting department before it can enter an invoice for payment.

The bottom part of the receiving form provides space for the receiving clerk to indicate how many pieces of each size and color have been counted in the shipment. (Some forms have two or three printed size scales. The receiving clerk cancels those that do not apply; if necessary, the clerk cancels all three and writes in an appropriate scale.) From this information, the purchase order can be checked, and the work of making price tickets and affixing them to the merchandise can proceed. When this lower section, or a copy of it, is passed to the unit control clerk, it supplies the details needed to keep the style records up to date.

Sales Records

In manual perpetual control systems, the unit control clerk receives for every sale either a sales check or a price ticket stub identifying the specific article sold. This information is then recorded on the appropriate style record. In periodic stock control systems, sales figures are not recorded as they occur. Instead, sales for a specific period are calculated as the difference between one stock count and the next.

Merchandise Transfers

Departmentalized stores frequently transfer merchandise from one department to another or from one store or branch to another. Special forms are used to report such transactions. Transfers are equivalent to sales for the department or store unit releasing the goods, and equivalent to purchases for the department or store unit receiving the goods. The stock on hand of the former is reduced, and the stock on hand of the latter is increased.

Form 15-7 illustrates a report of the movement of merchandise between the various locations in a branch-operating store. An appropriate entry for all such merchandise transfers is made on the style's unit control record.

Merchandise Returns

When merchandise is returned by a store to a vendor, a form known as a "return to vendor" or "charge-back" is issued. (See Form 15-8.) A *return-to-vendor* is a store's invoice covering merchandise returned for cause to its vendor. A *charge-back* or *claim* is a store's invoice for claims against and allowances made by a vendor. In most stores, the same form is used for either returns or charge-backs. Copies of return-to-vendor forms go to the unit control clerk so that stock on hand of individual styles may be appropriately decreased on the unit control records.

Should a customer make a return to the store, a charge credit or cash refund is issued. A copy of these forms goes to the unit control clerk, who adds the returned article to the record of the total number of that style presently in stock.

All returns are carefully recorded on the forms used in perpetual control. If periodic stock count is the control method used, however, small adjustments like these are usually ignored. Only a transaction of major proportions, such as the return of an entire shipment from a vendor, is likely to be entered.

Cancellation of Order

A store may cancel an order for justifiable reasons, such as a vendor not shipping the designated merchandise by the shipping date specified, or a vendor eliminating a style from an order. When an order is cancelled in whole or in part, a covering entry must be made promptly on the appropriate unit control form so that whoever studies the control records will not mistakenly think that an additional supply of merchandise is still on order.

No. E 5 4 1 6 5

BRANCH STORE TRANSFER

From _____ *Main* _____ To _____ *# 6 – 42* _____

Dept. _____ *42* _____ Date _____ *9/9/7 –* _____

Class	Style	Description	Qty.	Retail Unit	Retail Extension
123	253	2 pc polyester	12	35 00	420 00
			8 10	12 14	
		Black 1 1	1	1	
		Red 1 1	1	1	
		Brown 1 1	1	1	
		Vendor: 482			

Written by _____ *Janet Bauer* _____

Checked by _____ *P. Anders* _____ Container _____ **38**

FORM 15-7

Price Changes

Unit control records indicate the retail prices at which merchandise is placed in stock, as well as any price changes that occur later. In most stores, a special form is required for reporting all upward or downward revisions in retail prices so that the retail value of the inventory may be adjusted ac-cordingly. (See Form 15-9.) Copies of these forms are routed to the unit control clerk as well as to the inventory control office for appropriate action. Most stores use a single price-change form for recording markdowns, markdown cancellations, or additional markups; a few provide a separate form for each type of price change.

Berry's

66375
REFER TO ABOVE
NUMBER IN ALL
CORRESPONDENCE.

BEFORE SHIPPING GOODS TO
A VENDOR ON A CLAIM.
DETACH ALL CARBONS. THE
FIRST THREE COPIES OF THE
CLAIM MUST ACCOMPANY
THE GOODS TO THE CLAIM
ROOM OR THE WRAPPING
DESK.

INVOICE

VENDOR: PLEASE FOLLOW CAREFULLY THE PROCEDURE CHECKED BELOW

| CREDIT: THIS MERCHANDISE IS RETURNED FOR CREDIT. DO NOT SEND A CREDIT MEMORANDUM UNLESS THERE IS A DISCREPANCY IN QUANTITY OR PRICE. | EXCHANGE: THIS MERCHANDISE IS RETURNED FOR EXCHANGE. SEND A NEW INVOICE TO COVER THE REPLACEMENT ON RECEIPT OF OUR PURCHASE ORDER. | REPAIR YOUR MDSE: THIS MERCHANDISE IS RETURNED FOR REPAIR. SEND A NEW INVOICE FOR THE MERCHANDISE WHEN YOU RETURN IT TO US ON RECEIPT OF OUR PURCHASE ORDER. |

ALL CLAIMS AGAINST THIS INVOICE MUST BE FILED WITHIN 60 DAYS

SEND TO: Aiken Dress Co.
1400 Broadway
New York, N.Y. 10018

CHARGE (IF OTHER THAN SEND TO)

STORE NO.	Main
DEPT. NO.	42
AS AGREED WITH	L. Salzman

TERMS	8/10 EOM
AMOUNT OF INVOICE	$ 1,278.00
DATE OF INVOICE	9/5/7-

| DATE | 9/14/7- |
| PER | M L. Smith |

| REGISTER DATE | 9/14/7- |
| REGISTER NUMBER | 66375 |

VENDOR: THIS IS AN INVOICE. WE ARE CHARGING YOUR ACCOUNT AS FOLLOWS:

CLASS	VENDOR	STYLE	DESCRIPTION	QUANTITY	KIND OF UNIT	UNIT COST		TOTAL COST		UNIT RETAIL		TOTAL RETAIL	
123	482	253	2 pc. polyester, front pleated skirt	3	ea	17	75	53	25	35	00	105	00

SPECIAL INSTRUCTIONS TO VENDOR	For credit only. Do not replace	TOTAL QUANTITY	3	SUB – TOTAL	53	25	TOTAL RETAIL	105	00
				SHIPPING CHARGES	1	24			
				TOTAL	54	49			

FORM 15-8

AUTOMATED UNIT CONTROL

Retailing has been slower than some other areas of business in investigating the value of automatic data processing in general and electronic data processing in particular. However, the 1960s and 1970s have seen a steady growth in interest among retailers in this newest way to handle the processing of information.

Large retail organizations were among the first to use automated systems and equipment. They started by automating the processing of accounts receivable. Once they had developed a system for handling this tremendous bookkeeping chore, they used the same equipment to automate other basic bookkeeping jobs, such as accounts payable and payroll. Then they began working out automated systems in the area of merchandise statistics, which

(X) TO SHOW TYPE		PRICE CHANGE			DEPT. NO. 42				B 29001				

(X) TO SHOW TYPE

X	MARK-DOWN
	CANCELLATION OF MARK-DOWN
	ADDITIONAL MARK-UP

DEPT. NO. **42**

B 29001

DATE *Aug. 10, 197–*

ISSUE SEPARATE SHEETS FOR MARK-DOWN CANCELLATION, MARK-UP, STOLEN, AND SALVAGE ITEMS.

SHOW REASON BY LETTER		ORIGINAL MARK-DOWN NUMBER	CLASS	ITEM DESCRIPTION VENDOR — STYLE	QUANTITY	SEA. LET.	VERIFIED QUANTITY	OLD RETAIL		NEW RETAIL		DIFFERENCE		AMOUNT	
A. PROMOTIONAL PURCHASE REMAINDERS	E	—	172	Cotton lace, 385 #1120	4	M5	4	26	00	18	00	8	00	32	00
	F	—	126	Sleeveless print, 482 #401	3	M6	3	22	00	15	00	7	00	21	00
B. SLOW MOVING OR INACTIVE STOCK															
C. SPECIAL SALES FROM STOCK															
D. PRICE ADJUSTMENTS															
E. BROKEN ASSORTMENTS AND REMNANTS															
F. SHOPWORN, SOILED OR DAMAGED															
G. ALLOWANCE TO CUSTOMER															
H. STOLEN															
J. SALVAGE															

DO NOT ENTER ANY PRICE CHANGES BELOW THIS LINE

DEPT. MGR'S SIGNATURE	DATE	MDSE. V. P. OR MGR'S SIGNATURE	DATE	MARKER'S SIGNATURE	DATE		TOTAL	53	00
Jane Dean	8/10/7–	T. J. Evans	8/10/7–	Ann Hogan	8/12/7–				

FORM 15-9

includes unit control systems. An automated unit control system is simply a mechanized version of a manually kept unit control system; the sales and stock records kept in the system's memory banks usually are updated daily or weekly. At any point the system can be instructed to print out periodic reports in as much depth as needed on a department's sales and stock by classification, vendor, style, and price line.

Today, a number of large retail organizations have electronic data processing systems that handle, among many other jobs, the automatic collection and processing of merchandise information. An increasing number of medium-sized and smaller stores are also benefitting from electronic technology because of the increasing number of independent computer service centers. These centers provide computer knowledge, standardized data processing programs (including unit control programs), and

computer time to companies not large enough to need or afford this expensive equipment, yet large enough to be able to make good use of it on a part-time basis.

Coding

An automated unit control system collects exactly the same kind of sales and stock information that a manual system does, although it often is programmed to collect more detail than is feasible by a manual system. The major difference, then, is that a manual system uses people to record and process data, while an automated system uses machines.

However, before merchandise information can be used in an automated system, that information has to be coded. This code consists of numbers, since mechanical equipment works only with numbers. Although no two retail organizations use ex-

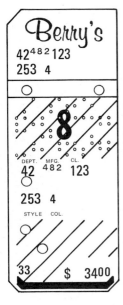

FORM 15-10

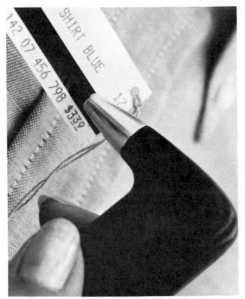

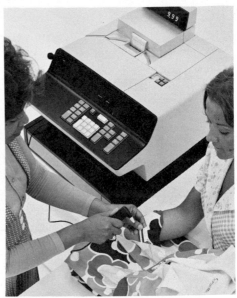

(1) Today's price tickets often contain detailed merchandise information. This information can be (2) "read" by a hand-held "wand" and (3) transferred to an electronic register that figures the transaction and relays information about it to the company's computer system.
IBM

actly the same coding system, most fashion merchandise is coded for unit control purposes to identify department, classification, vendor, style, color, size, and season in which received.

Take another look at the sample receiving record, Form 15-6. It shows the receipt by department 42 of six black dresses in size 8, classification number 123, style number 253, at $35 retail, from the Aiken Dress Company, which is vendor number 482. Classification, style, size, and vendor already are expressed in numbers. Suppose the color black is assigned the number 4, and the season code is 33. Then the code numbers appearing on the price ticket (see Form 15-10) of each of those six black dresses received into stock would be:

Department	42
Classification	123
Vendor	482
Style	253
Color	4
Size	8
Season	33

Whenever a sale of one of these dresses is made and that information fed into the system, one of those numbers is automatically removed from the "on hand" record and added to the "sold" record.

A growing number of large retailers today identify their merchandise with SKU numbers. A *stockkeeping unit* (or *SKU*) is either a single item of merchandise or a group of items of merchandise within a classification to which an identifying number is assigned and for which separate sales and stock records are kept. An SKU is the lowest level of merchandise identification and takes the form of a two- to four-digit number. Under this type of control system, an identifying SKU number is assigned within each merchandising classification to each item or group of items of merchandise on order or in stock that has specific characteristics which distinguish it from all other merchandise.

For a retailer working with an automated system, the code numbers or SKU number assigned a unit of merchandise is as descriptive as a handwritten or verbal description. But only code numbers can be processed by automated systems.

Value of Automated Systems

The automation of unit control systems offers retailers the same benefits as the automation of other data-collecting and data-processing chores. First, automated systems in general, and electronic computer systems in particular, are infinitely faster than manual systems. Second, automated systems are almost infallibly accurate, so long as the right information is fed into them. Third, automated systems can collect and process more detailed information than typical manual systems can, making it possible to produce more useful reports for evaluating merchandise assortments.

However, automated systems also bring several problems. First, they are expensive, even when the number of clerical personnel the system replaces is considered. Second, if inaccurate information is fed into the system—and this can happen, in spite of the elaborate controls such systems have—errors can be very hard to track down. Third, because of the tremendous capabilities that such systems have, store managements sometimes program the systems to turn out reports that contain far more detail than merchandisers need or can use. Too much information can be as confusing and misleading as too little. The key to a good automated unit control system, like the key to any good automated system, is accuracy in recording data and a program that produces reports which are as useful and as succinct as possible.

EVALUATING UNIT CONTROL

In evaluating unit control, it is usually helpful to remember that the word "control" is somewhat misleading. However, traditional trade terms do not change readily. A better term would be "unit records," since the various systems are set up to collect sales and stock information from which reports can be drawn. These systems do not exert control in themselves. They only provide information that merchants use to determine how closely their assortments meet customer demand and what they can do to improve that assortment.

Advantages

The major value of unit control is that the resulting records make it possible for a buyer to refer to a detailed analysis of sales and inventory while sitting at a desk or working in the market. The records are usually maintained by style numbers, and reports can be prepared that show departmentalized sales by classification, price line, vendor, size, color, or any other merchandise characteristics helpful to buyers. Thus a buyer can go into the market armed with such facts as: Most of vendor A's styles were reordered, while vendor B's had to be marked down before they sold; or fewer size 16s were sold this season than in the previous season; or the department sold as many $20 units this year as last year.

Facts are a much more reliable guide than memory about the nature of consumer demand, even in the immediate past. Facts, not guesses, are essential in keeping track of consumer demand.

Properly used, unit control systems contain a built-in reminder that encourages prompt action when conditions require it. Both periodic stock counts and periodic reports of sales by price line or other factors collected by a perpetual system serve as reminders to the merchant to check the assortment for completeness and balance in terms of current indications of consumer demand.

An assortment plan, like the dollar merchandise budget, is necessarily subject to change as often as conditions show that the original guidelines need adjusting. Unit control records and reports provide the means for regularly checking previously planned projections against actual results.

Problems Related to Unit Control

Unit control systems, however, are not always properly run or properly used. Moreover, they cannot be expected to do some jobs.

In working with unit controls, carelessness can result in inaccurate and misleading figures. As mentioned above, this is true even with electronic systems, since a computer can digest only the information fed into it.

Manual systems are slow, and sometimes the clerks handling them are so far behind in their work that their reports are of little use by the time buyers receive them. Electronic systems, on the other hand, are sometimes programmed to give so much detail and give it so rapidly that merchants are drowned in data, unable to digest it all, and therefore unable to make effective use of it.

Another problem is that it is difficult to estimate the true costs of unit control systems. A number of people are involved in some aspect of the unit control job—clerical workers, technicians, supervisors, buyers, assistant buyers, sales and stock people—yet no part of their salaries is charged to the unit control expense.

Cost, however, is a relative factor. In general, a merchant weighs the costs of maintaining a unit control system against the benefits derived from those systems. If a store provides its buyers with accurate and correct information and the buyers use that information to good advantage, then the cost is likely to be considered worthwhile. However, if the buyers do not use that information, the store has a costly system. On the other hand, if a buyer is deprived of useful information, the store is probably practicing a costly economy.

The last problem relating to unit control systems is that they cannot reveal one very important facet of consumer demand: what items, colors, and sizes customers wanted to buy but could not because they were not present in the assortments. To a point, unit control records may show unfilled demand, in that, for example, they may show that a certain style enjoyed brisk sales for a period, then was out of stock for a week or two, and when restocked resumed its brisk sales. But unit control systems are not set up to show the requests made by customers for merchandise that was never part of the assortment. The only means by which buyers can find out about unfilled wants of customers is through want slips, customer surveys, and comparison shopping, as discussed in Chapter 12.

REFERENCES
[1] Wingate, et al., *Retail Merchandise Management*, p. 4.

MERCHANDISING VOCABULARY
Define or briefly explain each of the following terms:

Unit control	Visual control
Perpetual control	Receiving apron
Periodic stock count control	Return-to-vendor
Coverage	Charge-back
Reserve requisition control	Stockkeeping unit (SKU)

MERCHANDISING REVIEW
1. What are the two basic types of information any unit control system is set up to provide? What additional types of merchandise information can it also provide?
2. Name the two basic types of unit control systems used for the recording of fashion data. How do they differ in method of operation?

3. For which specific types of merchandise are each of the above systems best suited, and why?
4. Name at least 10 kinds of information that can be recorded on most perpetual unit control forms.
5. In what ways do forms used for periodic stock count control differ from those used for perpetual control? How are sales determined in a periodic stock count control system?
6. What is meant by the term coverage? How is it determined? Discuss its importance in a periodic stock count control system.
7. Name at least five types of important unit control information that are obtained from a purchase order.
8. What is meant by "coding" as the term applies to automated unit control systems? Discuss its importance and give examples of its use in such systems.
9. What is meant by the term SKU? Discuss its use and advantages in automated or electronic data processing systems.
10. What are the major advantages and disadvantages of automated unit control systems?

MERCHANDISING DIGEST

1. Discuss the following statement from the text: "Some fashion merchandise requires more detailed control than others." Do you agree or disagree? Defend your answer.
2. Identify and discuss the kinds of unit control information that can be obtained from the following store records: (a) receiving records, (b) sales checks, (c) price ticket stubs, (d) merchandise transfers, (e) customer charge-credit and cash-refund forms, (f) price-change forms, (g) return-to-vendor forms, and (h) cancellation of order.
3. Discuss the major advantages of and problems relating to unit control systems.

16
CONTROLLING FASHION ASSORTMENTS: INVENTORY CONTROL

This chapter is concerned with the procedures and devices established by retail management for the ongoing control of dollar inventory investment and supervision of the merchandising function. All stores use the same procedures and criteria for evaluating the merchandising function in each selling department. Assortments of fashion merchandise, however, are highly volatile compared with other consumer products, such as furniture and housewares. The risks and rewards involved in merchandising fashion goods and services are correspondingly greater than those involved in merchandising more staple products.

Therefore, closer inventory controls, and the need for continuous evaluation of stock on hand in relation to customer demand, are essential to profitable fashion merchandising. Every merchandising executive involved with apparel or accessories has a special need to become thoroughly familiar with the inventory control procedures and various management tools discussed in this chapter.

DOLLAR INVENTORY CONTROL

Retailers plan their dollar investments in fashion assortments well in advance, as discussed in Chapter 13. Each seasonal plan or budget then becomes the base for evaluating actual results. Once the selling season gets underway, purchases of additional inventory are limited to and controlled by actual dollar sales and the dollar value of stock on hand as compared with the planned dollar sales and dollar value of stock on hand.

Retail Method of Inventory Evaluation

The accounting system used by most retail organizations today is known as the retail method of inventory. Under this system, unlike most accounting systems, all records of transactions affecting the value of inventory on hand—such as sales, purchases, markdowns, transfers, returns-to-vendor—are added to or subtracted from inventory at their retail values. Some small stores still use the older "cost method" of accounting, keeping their inventory records on the basis of the cost price, rather than the retail price, of each item in stock.

The retail method of accounting developed as a necessity for handling large departmentalized retail operations. Because of the huge quantities and varieties of merchandise handled by each firm, the wide range of cost prices of that merchandise, and the increasing number of store locations in which that merchandise is sold, it became impossible to keep track of each item in a large retail organization's inventory in terms of its cost price. The cost method is satisfactory only for nondepartmentalized small stores or shops that handle limited varieties of merchandise in fairly shallow depth.

The Book Inventory

Under the retail method, each selling department is a separate accounting unit for which separate records are kept. These records contain details relating to the cost and retail value of each department's inventory, as well as operating expense data.

Dept. _159_   **DEPARTMENTAL INVENTORY LEDGER**   Year Ending _Jan. 31, 197–_

Period Ending	Purchases and Transfers			$ Freight Costs (4)	$ Add'l. Markup (5)	Accumulated			Deductions at Retail					EOM Inventory		
	$ Cost (1)	$ Retail (2)	% Markup (3)			$ Cost (6)	$ Retail (7)	% Cum. Markup (8)	$ Net Sales (9)	Markdowns $ (10)	% Sales (11)	Shortage Reserve (12)	$ Total (13)	$ Cost (14)	$ Retail (15)	% Maint. Markup (16)
Beg. Inv.	32,276	52,227	38.2	—	—	—	—	—	—	—	—	—	—	—	—	—
Feb.	6,000	10,000	40.0	37	120	—	—	—	11,500	590	5.1	173	12,263	—	—	—
YTD	38,276	62,227	38.5	37	120	38,313	62,347	38.5	11,500	590	5.1	173	12,263	30,802	50,084	38.5
Mar.	7,200	12,000	40.0	45	—	7,245	12,000	39.6	13,000	650	5.0	195	13,845	—	—	—
YTD	45,476	74,227	38.7	82	120	45,558	74,347	38.7	24,500	1,240	5.1	368	26,108	29,571	48,239	38.7
Apr.																
YTD																
Oct.																
YTD																
Nov.																
YTD																
Dec.																
YTD																
Jan.																
Year																

KEY:

YTD = Year to Date
Column 1 = Billed Cost of Purchases
Column 2 = Retail Value of Purchases
Column 3 = $\dfrac{\text{Col. 2 − Col. 1}}{\text{Col. 2}}$
Column 6 = Col. 1 + Col. 4

Column 7 = Col. 2 + Col. 5
Column 8 = $\dfrac{\text{Col. 7 − Col. 6}}{\text{Col. 7}}$
Column 9 = Net Audited Sales
Column 10 = From Markdown Book
Column 11 = $\dfrac{\text{Col. 10}}{\text{Col. 9}}$

Column 12 = as % of Col. 9
Column 13 = Col. 9 + Col. 10 + Col. 12
Column 14 = Col. 15 x complement of Col. 8
Column 15 = Col. 7 − Col. 13
Column 16 = $\dfrac{\text{Col. 15 − Col. 14}}{\text{Col. 15}}$

FORM 16-1

The term *book inventory* refers to the dollar amount of inventory that should be in stock at any given time, as indicated by each department's accounting records. The figures used to compute the book inventory are derived from various records submitted to the accounting department that report additions to and subtractions from the inventory as these occur.

Systems for computing book inventories may be manual or automated. Under either method, figures relating to inventory value are usually shown as separate monthly and cumulative year-to-date totals. Form 16-1 shows how a manually kept mas-

ter departmental inventory ledger might appear after the first two months of a fiscal year. Responsibility for the initiation and accuracy of all records used by the accounting department in maintaining a book inventory is vested solely in each department's buyer and represents a major portion of a buyer's job.

Because entries are made in the book inventory as changes are reported to the accounting department, management can have a current evaluation in terms of the retail value of its inventory investment at any time—monthly, weekly, or whenever wanted—either for the store as a whole or for any accounting subdivision. In stores that use electronic data processing systems, inventory values are adjusted instantly when relevant figures are fed into the system. Reports can then be printed out as frequently and in as much detail as desired.

Beginning Inventory Under the retail method, a physical count of each department's merchandise is taken annually and sometimes more frequently, particularly in fashion departments. From this count of each item in the inventory and the listing of each by the retail price at which it is marked, the total retail value of the inventory is calculated. If the retail value derived from the physical count differs from the book inventory figure as of the same date, the physical count figure is accepted as correct, and the book inventory figure is adjusted to conform. The procedures for taking a physical inventory are discussed later in this chapter.

Inventory Transactions Once a beginning inventory has been established, all subsequent transactions affecting the value of that inventory are entered in a department's book inventory as they are reported to the accounting department.

Purchases Purchases are recorded at both cost and retail, a procedure that requires the unit retail price of goods to be entered on each invoice covering shipments received from vendors. For example, items purchased at a cost of $8 a dozen might be assigned a retail price of $1.25 each. The addition of one dozen of this item to a department's book inventory would be entered as a cost value of $8 and a retail value of $15.

To facilitate this bookkeeping procedure, most stores require buyers to *pre-retail* their orders, that is, to indicate the intended retail prices of all items on each purchase order. Thus, when goods are received at a store, the retail value of each vendor's invoice can be calculated, and the goods can be marked and placed on sale, even if the buyer is away from the store. This is important because, with the varied demands on buyers' time, particularly in large stores, it is practically impossible for them to be present to "retail" each shipment of goods as it arrives. Another advantage to having buyers pre-retail purchase orders is that invoices can be processed more quickly with less likelihood of a store's losing the opportunity of taking any cash discount offered by the vendor for prompt payment.

Sales Sales are recorded either on cash registers or sales checks. From register tapes or duplicate sales checks, a total sales figure for each department or classification is obtained daily and entered as a "credit" or decrease in the retail value of the book inventory.

Customer Returns Returns made by customers are recorded on sales credit forms, which are totaled daily and entered in the books as a "debit" or increase in the retail value of the book inventory.

Price Changes When price changes are made on merchandise after it has originally been placed in stock, a record of each such change is made on price change forms (see Form 15-9) and forwarded to the accounting department, which then increases or decreases the value of the inventory by an appropriate amount. Price changes may take any of the following forms:

- Additional markups or increases in retail prices above what the goods were marked when first received into stock
- Cancellations of additional markups previously taken and recorded
- Markdowns or reductions in the retail price of goods currently in stock
- Markdown cancellations, or increases in price to offset all or any part of previously taken markdowns (Such cancellations may occur, for instance, after a special sale for which goods from regular stock were briefly reduced.)

Net additional markups increase the retail value of a book inventory; net markdowns decrease the retail value of an inventory.

WEEKLY REPORT OF OUTSTANDING ORDERS

Department _42_   Date _3/17/7-_ Sheet No. _1_

Orders of $50.00 and over must be reported individually. Orders under $50.00 should be reported collectively under "Small Purchases." Report all cancellations in _Red_.

Order No.	Order Date	Vendor	Total Retail	March Cost	March Retail	April Cost	April Retail	May Cost	May Retail
91428	3/4	Aiken Dress Co.	450	252	450				
91478	3/11	Supreme Dress Co.	1,600			896	1,600		
91464	3/8	Lane Dress Co.	1,080	322	540	322	540		
91514	3/15	Casualaire	3,200					1,856	3,200
		Total Small Purchases	130	70	130				
		Total on Order	22,268	876	1,511	9,361	16,140	2,678	4,617
		Open to Buy			(261)		29,700		43,100

BUYER'S SIGNATURE
Jane Dean

MDSE. MANAGER'S SIGNATURE
T. J. Evans

FORM 16-2

Transfer of Goods Any transfer of goods from one department or accounting unit to another is recorded as a decrease in the inventory value of the issuing department and an increase in that of the receiving department. If there are branch stores, transfers of merchandise from one to another are similarly reported and entered on the inventory records. (See Form 15-7.)

Returns-to-vendor Merchandise returned to vendors for credit is reported to the accounting department on a return-to-vendor or charge-back form (see Form 15-8). A description of the merchandise being returned and the quantities are listed on this form at both unit and total cost and retail prices. The total cost value of each return-to-vendor decreases the cost value of the book inventory; the total retail value of the return decreases the retail value of the book inventory.

Some charge-backs are not concerned with actual return of merchandise but with claims or allowances, as when a vendor agrees to a lump-sum allowance toward transportation costs. In this case, the amount of the allowance reduces the transportation cost of purchases by a corresponding amount; there is no change in the retail value of the book inventory.

Merchandise on Order

Stores also keep careful records of the cost and retail values of outstanding orders placed for current as well as future delivery. Form 16-2 is an example of a typical, manually prepared report of a department's outstanding orders, indicating the date of each order, the order number, the vendor to whom issued, the total cost and total retail values of the order, and the month or months in which delivery of merchandise is intended. Stores with electronic data processing systems usually process departmental merchandise on-order reports on a weekly basis.

Merchandise on order does not affect the book inventory because it represents merchandise that has not yet been received in stock. But outstanding orders are kept on file and carefully watched, since they represent future upward revisions in inventory value as well as future financial obligations. If an order is cancelled by either store or vendor, equivalent cost and retail amounts are deducted from the on-order figure for the month in which delivery was expected.

The Physical Inventory

Errors inevitably creep into records, even those maintained by computers. Sales may be rung up at the wrong prices; price changes and transfers may be made for more or fewer pieces than were actually involved; transactions may be incorrectly identified as to department or classification. Real shortages also occur, through pilferage and shoplifting.

With the multiplicity of items and transactions involved, the book inventory is never exactly the same as the true marked retail value of all goods currently in stock. This is the reason for taking a physical count of all merchandise in a department at the end of each fiscal year or sometimes more often if a special situation, such as excessive shortage, warrants it.

Inventory Procedure The taking of a physical count of all merchandise on hand in a store or department requires a precise cut-off date on the handling of records affecting inventory. Every merchandise shipment received by that date must be counted, marked, and entered in the book inventory before an actual count takes place. Every sale, every return, and every price change up to that date must also be entered. This assures that the book inventory is updated to the exact time of the physical inventory.

In a physical inventory, every piece of merchandise belonging to a department must be accounted for. This includes not only merchandise on the selling floor and in the department's stockrooms but also merchandise on loan to the advertising department, the display department, in "will call," and in other selling departments. Furthermore, all items of merchandise should have been examined and carefully identified as to classification, season letter, and current retail price before the counting and listing starts. Care should be exercised to see that all items of stock are easily accessible for counting and listing. Guesswork is not compatible with a thorough physical inventory of stock.

The actual count is best made after store closing hours or on a holiday when the store is not open for business, so that selling does not confuse the stocktaking. Ideally, the count should be made by crews who do not normally work with the merchandise they are assigned to count and list. After the count has been completed, spot checks should be made to verify the original counts.

Inventory Forms Sheets or cards on which the counts are recorded are provided by each store's accounting office. These are usually sequentially numbered, and the department buyer is responsible for seeing that each issued sheet or card is accounted for at the conclusion of the inventory period. (See Form 16-3.)

In most cases, only a single classification of merchandise is listed on each sheet or card. A typical inventory form may require a listing, at the left, of an identifying style number for each item listed, or other identifying information. To the right of the description are usually columns in which the counter enters the exact number of pieces of each specific item by the retail price and season code as indicated on each item's price ticket. Each inventory sheet is also carefully identified as to department, classification, or other requested subdivision.

When the counts have been completed, the forms are returned to the accounting office. There, totals are calculated and compared with book

INVENTORY SHEET

FLOOR ☑
STOCK ROOM ☐
WAREHOUSE ☐

FIXTURE No. | SHELF No.
10 | A

No. 59987

DEPT. No. | CLASS.
201 | B

	Description	Number of Units	Kind of Unit (ea., pr., dz., etc.)	Selling Price per Unit Dollars	Cents	Season Letter	Check in Pencil	Inventory Signatures
1	SCORE PADS	42	ea	6 for 1	50	P	✓	Listed By N. Jones
2	BRIDGE COVER	10	ea	2	98	K	✓	
~~3~~	~~PLAYING CARDS~~	~~25~~	~~pr~~	~~2~~	~~49~~	~~A~~		Counted By J. Costello
4	GAME SET	4	ea	29	98	K	✓	
5	CHIP RACK	7	ea	11	98	M	✓	Merchandise Recounted By M. Murphy
6	SCRATCH PADS	11½	dz	1	29	B	✓	
7	PENS	13	ea	5	00	C	✓	Listing Checked By A. Pappas
8	PLAYING CARDS	27	ea	2	49	C	✓	Last Line Used Was Number → 8
9								
10								FOR OFFICE USE ONLY
11								AGE ANALYSIS
12								Age in Months / Dollars / Cents
13								Current
14								7 thru 12
15								Over 12
16								
17								GRAND TOTAL

FORM 16-3

inventory figures. If the two do not agree, the book figure is adjusted to bring it into agreement with the physical inventory figure.

Stock Shortages and Overages

In the normal course of business, the physical inventory rarely tallies precisely with the book inventory figure. If the physical inventory figure is less than that of the book inventory figure, the discrepancy is a stock shortage. If it is greater than the book figure, the difference is a stock overage.

Overages are rare; they are found most commonly among stores with several branches. For example, a stock overage is created by transferring merchandise to one branch while charging that merchandise to the inventory of another branch.

Shortages are common and are on the increase. In the past, whereas stock shortages might have averaged 1 to 2 percent of net sales, today this figure has more than doubled in many cases and is still on the rise.

Some departments, of course, have higher shortage percentages than do others, mainly due to the nature of the merchandise handled and the selling techniques employed. Open selling and self-service tend to increase departmental shortages because they permit greater opportunities for undetected theft. Some departments, such as jewelry and cosmetics, have higher-than-average shortages because their merchandise is more susceptible than others to theft, damage, and spoilage. In some fashion departments today, for example, shortages run well above 3 percent of net sales.

Stock shortages are an important factor influencing retail pricing. The initial retail price of merchandise must be set high enough to compensate for loss of income due to stock shortages.

Stores constantly strive to reduce shortage figures by stressing greater accuracy in taking physical inventory; by exercising more care in recording purchase, price change, and sales data; and by taking greater precautions against theft, such as using sensitized price tags, increased security staff, and so on. It is an old saying in the department store business that although shortages may not be directly the fault of the buyer in whose department they occur, more buyers have been fired for high shortages than for any other reason. Shortages reduce profits, and a profitable operation is the buyer's responsibility.

The two major causes of stock shortages and overages are clerical errors and physical merchandise losses. Common clerical errors include:

- Failure to take or record markdowns properly
- Mistakes in calculating retail values of invoices
- Mistakes in charging or crediting departments
- Mistakes in recording merchandise transfers
- Mistakes in recording returns-to-vendors
- Mistakes in recording physical inventory

Physical merchandise losses occur through:

- Internal theft (pilferage)
- Shoplifting
- Failure to obtain receipts for merchandise loaned
- Breakage and spoilage
- Providing samples of yard goods, perfume, etc., from stock

The Purchase Journal

In departmentalized stores, the accounting office issues to each department a monthly or semimonthly report known as a *purchase* or *merchandise journal*. On this report are listed all invoices for purchases, transfers of merchandise in and out, and returns to or claims against vendors that have been charged or credited to the department's book inventory by the accounting department during a stated period. (See Form 16-4.)

Entries made for each invoice include: department name and number; vendor name and number; receiving number and date; invoice number, date, and amount; freight costs; discounts earned; net cost; total retail; and markup percentage. Information on transfers and returns to or claims against vendors indicate: issuing department number; document number and date; name and number of department or vendor to which issued; details of transaction; total cost and total retail value of each document; and any transportation costs incurred.

Buyers are instructed to carefully check each item on those reports against their own copies of receiving aprons, transfers, and returns-to-vendor and immediately report any errors to the accounting office. Any undetected error on these reports represents a potential stock shortage or overage. For example, an invoice for merchandise received by department X, but incorrectly charged to department Y, represents a stock overage for department X and a stock shortage for department Y.

PERIODIC FINANCIAL REPORTS

Each buyer in a departmentalized store receives a number of periodic reports on the actual results of the merchandising operation in a department. The purpose of these periodic reports is to guide the

PURCHASE JOURNAL 01/31/7–											
Dept. 320 Fashion Accessories		Division 2								Page No. _1_	
Vendor		Type	Apron/KeyRec		Invoice			Freight			Total	
No.	Name	Trans.	No.	Date	No.	Date	Amount	Costs	Discount	Net Cost	Retail	M%
1140-1	Baar & Beards	Inv.	55504	01/06	7132	01/04	243.00		19.44	223.56	504.00	
	Vendor Total						243.00		19.44	223.56	504.00	55.6
1192-4	Ben Goodman	Inv.	54707	12/29	9211	12/27	360.00		28.80	331.20	720.00	
		Dum.	55155	12/28		12/28	3.00			3.00	6.00	
		Inv.	22823	01/10	9697	01/08	135.00		10.80	124.20	288.00	
	Vendor Total						498.00		39.60	458.40	1,014.00	54.8
1822-8	Glentex	RTV			3441	01/18	−183.31		−14.40	−168.91	−336.00	
		Inv.	52852	12/14	8761	12/12	360.00		28.80	331.20	672.00	
		Inv.	52852	12/14	8708	12/04	945.00	9.22	75.60	869.40	1,764.00	
	Vendor Total						1,121.69	9.22	90.00	1,031.69	2,100.00	50.4
2795-2	Regina Products	RTV			3439	01/18	−32.70		−.65	−31.05	−55.00	
		RTV			3438	01/18	−422.90		−8.46	−414.44	−706.00	
	Vendor Total						−455.60		−9.11	−446.49	−761.00	41.3
3013-9	Society Mills	RTV			3442	01/18	−72.49		−5.70	−66.79	−133.00	
	Vendor Total						−72.49		−5.70	−66.79	−133.00	49.8
				DEPARTMENT TOTAL			1,334.60	9.22	134.23	1,200.37	2,724.00	55.6

FORM 16-4

buyer in operating the department more profitably. The same reports go to top management and, in large stores, to appropriate divisional merchandise managers as well. Thus the figures are available to both buying and management levels for study and determination of what action should be taken to improve results, should the reports indicate a need for an improvement.

Four major types of financial reports are usually issued on a regular basis to departmental buyers in medium- and large-volume stores. Although varying widely from store to store in both format and extent of information presented, these reports are usually known as sales reports, sales and stock reports, departmental operating statements, and open-to-buy reports. Small stores may use similar reports, but they are usually more informal than those used in larger stores.

Sales Reports

As indicated in Chapter 13, sales constitute the basis of all merchandise planning and control. Therefore, actual sales results are studied closely to evaluate their effect on other elements of the merchandise budget. A number of sales reports are usually available to the buyer for this purpose.

Flash Sales Daily reports of sales, by department, are routinely developed from the unaudited saleschecks and cash-register tapes for the previous day. They usually include the dollar sales of the corresponding selling day in the previous year and are circulated early the following business day to all merchandise executives. These reports are generally referred to as *flash sales* reports. If a store has branches, sales of each branch are usually

BUYERS' SALES REPORT

Dept. **42**

3 Days Ending 12/18/7-

SELLING PRICE	CLASS	VENDOR	STYLE	STORE NO.	LAST 3 DAYS	THIS WEEK	ONE WEEK AGO	2 WEEKS AGO	TOTAL LAST 4 WEEKS	TOTAL TO DATE	ON HAND	INITIAL DATE OF RECEIPT	TOTAL CUSTOMER RETURNS	ACTIVITY INDICATOR
40.00	51	001	8527	1	1	2	5	4	23	26	31	11 13 7-		
				6			1	3	1	1		11 24 7-		
				5	−	1	−	1			1	11 17 7-		
				7					7	10	8	11 13 7-		
				2		1	1		3	4		11 13 7-		
				3		1	1	4	5	6	12	11 17 7-		
				T		5	8	11	39	47	52		7	SLOW 1
44.00	51	001	8533	1	2	2	1	3	9	35	8	10 06 7-		
				5						3		10 16 7-		
				7				4	3	9	9	10 06 7-		
				2						5		10 06 7-		
				3	1	1	1	3	7	13	12	10 06 7-		
				T	3	3	2	10	19	65	29		8	
44.00	51	001	8537	1	3	4	2	3	10	19	20	10 16 7-		
				6			1		1	1	13	11 13 7-		
				5							6	11 17 7-		
				7			1	1	2	3	7	10 16 7-		
				2	−	1	1	1	2	8	15	10 16 7-		
				3		1			1	3	6	10 16 7-		
				T	2	5	5	5	16	34	67		1	
40.00	51	001	8539	1	3	5	4	4	16	16	8	11 24 7-		
				2		1			1	1	5	12 11 7-		
				3			1	1	2	2	8	11 24 7-		
				T	3	6	5	5	19	19	21		2	
44.00	51	001	8540	1	2	5	4		11	14	1	11 13 7-		
				6					2	3	15	11 13 7-		
				5	1	2	1		3	3	3	11 17 7-		
				7	1	2	1		4	5	6	11 13 7-		
				2	2	3	3	1	7	7	4	11 13 7-		
				3	2	2			4	5	7	11 17 7-		
				T	8	14	9	1	31	37	36		1	
40.00	51	001	8541	1	1	2	1		2	13	15	10 06 7-		
				6						5		10 06 7-		
				5							1	10 06 7-		
				7		1		1	4	9	10	10 06 7-		
				2			1	1	1	7	13	10 23 7-		
				3					−	1		10 27 7-		
				T	1	3	2	2	7	34	38		8	
44.00	51	001	8542	1		1	1		1	2	2	7	11 24 7-		
				6							6	11 24 7-		
				5							4	12 18 7-		
				7	1	1				1	1	1	11 27 7-		
				2			1			1	1	5	11 27 7-		
				3			1			1	1	5	11 24 7-		

FORM 16-5

shown separately from those of the main store, and there is also a total sales figure for all locations.

Periodic Sales Reports More detailed sales reports are prepared on a one-day, three-day, weekly, or semimonthly basis. In large branch-operating stores, these sales recapitulations may show both main-store and individual branch-store sales and customer returns in units or dollars or both, by classification, price line, style number, and vendor. (See Form 16-5.) In smaller stores, departmental sales may be reported simply in units and dollars by classification.

Weekly reports give buyers a quick, on-the-spot review of sales at all locations and encourage earlier action than would be possible if sales were reported less frequently. In addition to the weekly sales summary figures, some reports, particularly those that are obtained from computers, sometimes show cumulative sales for the month or season to date and sales for the corresponding period of the previous year.

"Beat Last Year" Book The simplest form of daily sales record kept by a buyer is the "Beat Last Year" book, which may be a single-sheet monthly

WEEKLY SALES AND STOCK REPORT

DIV. *1* | DEPT. NO. *15* | DEPT. NAME *Handbags* | WEEK ENDED 01/07/7- | PAGE 6

CODE	CODE DESCRIPTION PRICE GROUP	PRICE	SEASON TO DATE SALES PLAN	THIS YEAR	TREND	BEGINNING ON HAND	ADJUSTED PHYSICAL INVENTORY	CURRENT WEEK SALES	RECEIPTS	ADJUSTMENTS PLUS	MINUS	ENDING ON HAND	INTRANSIT	COVERAGE PERIOD	SALES FOR COVERAGE PERIOD PLAN	BALANCE OF SALES FOR SEASON PLAN
241	DRESS PLASTIC															
	1 3.00	5.00	32	16	50-	15		4				11	24	9	29	6
	3 6.00	8.00	85	36	58-	13						13	36	5	11	1
	5 9.00	11.00	20	9	55-	32						32		8	6	
	7 12.00	999.00		1		1-						1-		8		
	9 4.97													7		
241	TOTAL UNITS		137	62		59		4				55	60		46	7
	TOTAL DOLLARS*		897	408	55-			16				440	324		249	31
242	CASUAL PLASTIC															
	1 3.00	5.00	8	11	38	20						20		9	13	1
	3 6.00	8.00	199	72	64-	24		3				21	24	5	11	2
	5 9.00	11.00	56	25	55-	25		1				24		8	6	
	7 12.00	999.00		6		6						6		8	6	
	9 3.97	4.97	49	10	80-	6-						6-		7		
242	TOTAL UNITS		312	124		69		4				65	24		36	3
	TOTAL DOLLARS*		2065	868	58-			29				504	168		255	17
352	FRENCH PURSES															
	2 2.00	3.00	22	3	86-	14						14		6	5	1
	3 3.50	UP	6	3	50-	21		1				20		7	5	
	9 .97			7		19		2				17		6		
352	TOTAL UNITS		28	13		54		3				51			10	1
	TOTAL DOLLARS*		87	27	69-			6				133			34	3
	DIVISION TOTAL															
	TOTAL UNITS		1191	536		92		46	48			94			193	1929
	TOTAL DOLLARS*		4807	2365				198				377			667	7409
	* CENTS OMITTED IN DOLLAR FIGURES															

FORM 16-6

record of daily sales or a three-year or five-year diary. Sales figures are entered day by day, and subtotals are inserted to show sales to date during the month. Special conditions affecting sales, such as bad weather, transit strikes, and ads or other promotional efforts, are usually noted as well.

Sales and Stock Reports

Sales alone tell only half the merchandising story. The other half concerns stocks. Therefore, retailers have developed reports that are supplied to buyers weekly, semimonthly, or monthly, showing sales for the period, inventory on hand and on order, planned sales and stocks, and the sales and stocks for the corresponding period of the previous year. In addition to the figures for the current period, some reports may show cumulative figures for the year to date. Others may show dollar purchases and markdowns for the current period and year or season to date.

If electronic data processing is available, reports may show not only departmental totals but also classification and subclassification totals. (See Form 16-6.) Thus a buyer whose total departmental sales and stocks are about at the level of planned figures may see that some classifications are far enough above or below plan to require corrective action. Similarly, where there are branches, a separate set of figures for each location may reveal a need for action at one or more sites, whereas overall figures for all stores combined would mask such a need.

Departmental Operating Statements

Buyers and their management also receive regular summary reports from the accounting office on the financial aspects of each department's total merchandising operation. (See Form 16-7.) The format of these reports varies from store to store, but most include actual and planned dollar figures for all phases of the merchandising operation, such as gross sales, customer returns, net sales, markdowns, purchases, gross margin of profit, operating ex-

penses, cash discounts earned, and so on. Departmental operating statements are usually issued monthly, but in some large stores a midmonth flash report is also provided. Figures are usually stated both in dollars and as percentages of net sales. Some stores also include the retail value of all merchandise on order; others include the number of transactions and the average gross sale for the month.

Open-to-buy Reports

For buyers and store management, the open-to-buy report is the most important merchandising tool in keeping the inventory investment in line with plans and a desired ratio to actual sales. (See Form 16-8.) When a promising new item or trend appears, the buyer who wishes to exploit it must move promptly, particularly if it is a fashion item. If the buyer does not have enough open-to-buy, purchase plans may be rearranged to make room for the new item or management may be asked for extra purchasing funds.

Open-to-buy, remember, refers to the amount of purchases that can be made for delivery in a given period, minus orders already placed for delivery during that same period but not yet received. Open-to-buy may be expressed in dollars or units or both. Dollar open-to-buy reports are usually issued weekly to departmental buyers and may cover future periods as well as the current period.

The following is an example of how open-to-buy is calculated at any point during a month.

Planned sales for balance of month	$1,000*
Planned end-of-month stock	2,000*
Total stock requirements for balance of month	$3,000
Stock now on hand	1,500
Purchases for balance of month	$1,500
Orders previously placed for delivery this month	1,000
Open-to-buy balance of month	$ 500

*From Dollar Merchandise Plan.

DEPARTMENTAL OPERATING STATEMENT

Department No. 20   Month _March_   Year _197-_

Line		This Month Plan $	%	Actual $	%	Year to Date Plan $	%	Actual $	%	Last Year $	%	Line
1	Gross Sales	38,000	108.0	39,476	108.6	69,120	108.0	71,396	108.2	72,669	108.3	1
2	Customer Returns	3,000	8.0	3,142	8.6	5,120	8.0	5,411	8.2	5,569	8.3	2
3	NET SALES	35,000	-9.3	36,334	3.8	64,000	-4.6	65,985	3.1	67,100	2.1	3
4	Beg. Stock @ Retail	66,500	39.6	65,816	39.6	82,800	—	81,950	39.5	86,520	39.2	4
5	Net Retail Purchases	60,200	40.0	58,960	40.0	76,400	40.0	76,102	40.0	78,559	39.5	5
6	End. Stock @ Retail	86,900	39.9	83,541	39.8	86,900	—	83,541	39.7	89,720	39.3	6
7	Markdowns	4,450	12.7	4,565	12.6	7,660	12.0	7,868	11.9	7,590	11.3	7
8	Employee Discounts	350	1.0	336	.9	640	1.0	658	1.0	669	1.0	8
9	Shortage Reserve	525	1.5	545	1.5	960	1.5	990	1.5	1,141	1.7	9
10	Workroom Costs	350	1.0	340	.9	640	1.0	690	1.0	672	1.0	10
11	Cash Discounts	2,890	8.3	2,830	7.8	3,667	5.7	3,653	5.5	3,707	5.5	11
12	GROSS MARGIN	13,056	37.3	13,446	37.0	22,912	35.8	23,092	35.0	23,322	34.8	12
13	Advertising	1,120	3.2	1,417	3.9	2,048	3.2	2,111	3.2	2,416	3.6	13
14	Special Events	210	.6	291	.8	384	.6	396	.6	537	.8	14
15	Buying Salaries	1,155	3.3	1,200	3.3	2,112	3.3	2,178	3.3	2,214	3.3	15
16	Buyer's Travel	175	.5	218	.6	320	.5	397	.6	402	.6	16
17	Selling Salaries	2,660	7.6	2,834	7.8	4,864	7.6	5,015	7.6	5,299	7.9	17
18	Stk & Cler. Salaries	280	.8	284	.8	512	.8	530	.8	604	.9	18
19	Supplies	70	.2	75	.2	128	.2	135	.2	135	.2	19
20	Delivery	140	.4	185	.5	256	.4	270	.4	268	.4	20
21	Other Direct Expense	1,050	3.0	1,091	3.0	1,920	3.0	1,982	3.0	2,015	3.0	21
22	TOTAL DIRECT EXPENSE (13 thru 21)	6,860	19.6	7,595	20.9	12,544	19.6	13,014	19.7	13,890	20.7	22
23	DEPT. CONTRIBUTION (12 minus 22)	6,196	17.7	5,851	16.1	10,368	18.2	10,078	15.3	9,432	14.1	23
24	Indirect Expense	4,095	11.7	4,178	11.5	7,488	11.7	7,586	11.5	7,851	11.7	24
25	TOTAL EXPENSES (22 plus 24)	10,955	31.3	11,773	32.4	20,032	31.3	20,620	31.2	21,741	32.4	25
26	OPERATING PROFIT (12 minus 25)	2,107	6.0	1,673	4.6	2,880	4.5	2,492	3.8	1,581	2.4	26

FORM 16-7

UNIT OPEN TO BUY REPORT

Dept. 42 Casual Dresses   WEEK ENDING FEB. 21, 197–

CODE	PRICE RANGE	E.O.M. INV. 1/31/7–	FEB. ON ORDER	AVAILABLE FOR SALE	PLANNED SALES	ANTICIPATED MARK DOWNS	PLANNED 2/28/7– INV.	OPEN TO RECEIVE FEB.	MAR.	ON ORDER APR.	MAY	JUNE-JULY	OPEN TO BUY MAR-JULY
700	14.00	771	100	871	500	40	750	419	300	800	1000	100	2885
702	18.00	621	85	706	425	30	900	649	500	1000	250	0	2625
704	22.00	1412	210	1622	800	70	1500	748	200	1400	1400	50	3410
706	26.00	3201	610	3811	1600	120	3000	909	800	800	0	0	4310
707	30.00	2120	350	2470	1000	80	2500	1110	1000	750	500	0	4820
708	35.00	1409	300	1709	600	50	1200	141	150	150	100	100	2530
TOTAL MISSY		9534	1655	11189	4925	390	8850	3976	2950	4900	3250	250	20580
710	14.00	494	500	994	700	50	1050	806	1000	1000	500	500	3405
712	18.00	1464	1000	2464	1000	80	1500	116	850	850	550	550	4460
714	22.00	2026	800	2826	1100	100	1700	74	1500	1200	700	0	4795
716	26.00	2251	100	2351	850	70	1500	69	1000	200	100	0	3620
TOTAL JUNIOR		6235	2400	8635	3650	300	5750	1065	4350	3250	1850	1050	17280
TOTAL CASUAL	15769		4055	19824	8575	690	15600	5041	7300	8150	5100	1300	37860

FORM 16-8

From the viewpoint of top management, the open-to-buy report reflects the buyer's competence and efficiency. The overly optimistic buyer tends to buy too heavily and to be chronically overbought, even when the selections are excellent. Another type of buyer who overstocks is the one whose selections tend to fall just short of being right and therefore sell more slowly than planned. Some buyers tend to underbuy, even though they have a gift for anticipating what customers will want and for presenting it to them temptingly. They may have too little confidence in their own judgment or too much confidence in the ability of resources to deliver additional stock in a rush. Accuracy in planning and skill in merchandising to the plan reveal themselves in a department that has adequate stocks yet always has some open-to-buy available for unexpected developments.

MANAGEMENT DEVICES FOR EVALUATING THE MERCHANDISING OPERATION

Management and the individual buyer use many other devices to measure the success of a department's merchandising operation and to guide it toward even greater accuracy in meeting consumer fashion demand. Among these are basic stock lists, age-of-stock reports, markdowns, analyses of customer returns, vendor analyses, stock turnover figures, and others. Each is a way of keeping track of or exploring the significance of some facet of the merchandising operation that affects that operation's overall profitability.

Basic Stock Lists

An item of merchandise is described by fashion merchants as being *basic* if it enjoys such consistent demand that it should be in stock in a complete range of sizes and colors at best-selling price lines throughout a year or season. A basic may be a specific item or a group of substitutable items, such as women's pantyhose in neutral shades, nurses' oxfords, women's white tailored slips, or men's white dress shirts.

When a store runs short of an item that enjoys consistent demand, customer goodwill, as well as sales, is at stake. Stores therefore encourage or require their buyers to list specific items in their departments that are considered basic each season and to set up periodic stock counts or similar ways of making sure there is always an adequate supply of these goods. Many stores require that a list of such items be retained in the merchandise manager's office. The latter may, at unannounced intervals, send someone into a department to check the basic stock and report any listed items that are not on hand or are in low supply. A buyer whose department repeatedly makes poor showings on such checks is subject to criticism.

To ensure adequate stocks of basic merchandise, some stores draw up two separate budgets for each department or classification: one for basics and one for fashion merchandise. Executives of such stores believe that an overstock elsewhere in a department should not deprive the buyer of needed open-to-buy for basics. Other stores have a policy of permitting basics to be reordered regardless of the state of the departmental open-to-buy. Still others leave the entire matter in the buyers' hands, expecting them to reserve part of their budget and enough of their open-to-buy for basics.

Prior Stock Reports

Retail stores usually place a code for the season on each price ticket. The season code, as previously defined, is a number indicating the month of the year in which the merchandise was received into stock. In fast-moving fashion categories, the season code may also include a numeral to indicate the week, in addition to the month, in which the article arrived in stock. Some stores put the complete coded date of receipt on the price ticket of each piece of fashion merchandise.

By flipping through the tickets on a rack of garments, a merchant can quickly see which ones have been in stock too long and should be given prompt attention. In some stores, and for some merchandise, a week is considered a long time; in other cases, a month may not be considered long.

PRIOR STOCK

Department No. 42
Sheet No. 1

Class.	Style No.	Article (List each classification separately)	Season Letter	Inventory Date 1/31/7-		First Month Date 2/28/7-		Second Month Date 3/31/7-		Third Month Date 4/30/7-	
				Qty.	Price	Qty.	Price	Qty.	Price	Qty.	Price
12301	1234	Dress	H4	5	14.00	2	9.88	0	—	—	—
	789	Dress	H5	7	14.00	4	9.88	1	6.88	0	—
	1401	Dress	H5	3	14.00	3	9.88	1	6.88	0	—
12302	239	Dress	H4	6	18.00	4	12.88	2	9.88	1	6.88
	141	Dress	H5	8	18.00	4	12.88	1	9.88	0	—
	984	Dress	H5	1	18.00	0	—	—	—	—	—
12308	957	Dress	H3	1	35.00	1	26.88	1	18.88	0	—
	245	Dress	H4	2	35.00	1	26.88	1	18.88	0	—
	698	Dress	H5	2	35.00	1	26.88	0	—	—	—
NOTE: These sheets must be returned to the Merchandise Office on the 5th of each month with all data shown complete.		Season	H3	27	462.00	14	226.00	3	36.00	0	—
		Season	H4	41	924.00	22	468.00	7	66.00	3	28.00
		Season	H5	64	1,579.00	31	740.00	11	118.00	3	44.00
		Total		132	2,965.00	67	1,434.00	21	220.00	6	72.00

FORM 16-9

Prior stock reports are reports that provide information in summary form of the amount of stock in units and in dollars in each of a number of prior seasons, as indicated by the season letter on each price ticket. Such reports may be prepared by the accounting office from data listed on inventory sheets or from special inventories taken of all or part of a department's stock for age-record purposes. The reports are created by dividing the listing of stock into age groups, totaling each group, and then showing what percentage of the total inventory each age group constitutes. Buyers are required to recheck these reports periodically, indicating what steps have been taken to dispose of prior season stock. (See Form 16-9.) Some stores, particularly those using electronic data processing equipment, run off actual lists of the specific items of merchandise that are "old." These lists are presented to the appropriate buyers for action.

Apparel departments for women and misses rarely have inventory that is more than six months old. One larger chain organization requires that all women's apparel remaining in stock 10 weeks after its receipt must be marked down.

Once it was common for management to record and pursue slow sellers until each item was finally eliminated from stock. With the faster pace of fashion and the higher cost of clerical help today, stores now tend to rely instead on spot checks and unit control records to make sure that buyers locate and act upon slow-selling fashion merchandise.

Markdown Analyses

Downward revisions in retail prices are reported to the accounting office whenever they are made. To provide data for further study, stores provide price change forms on which reasons for taking the markdowns may be indicated. Analyses of markdowns and reasons for them yield clues to a buyer's proficiency in gauging customer demand and indicate the quality of departmental supervision.

Markdown Causes The National Retail Merchants Association recommends using these classifications for causes of markdowns:

- Promotional purchase remainders
- Fabrics or quality
- Style or pattern
- Color
- Sizes
- Quantities (including overstock conditions as well as excessive quantities of specific styles)
- Special sales from stock
- Broken assortments, remnants, shopworn goods
- Price adjustments to meet competition, because of generally falling prices, or to consolidate or eliminate price lines
- Allowances to customers on adjustment claims[1]

Buyer Responsibility for Markdowns Hardest to recognize but most in need of correction are markdowns due to poor timing. These stem from offering merchandise too soon or too late for its normal selling season or for that stage of the fashion cycle to which the store's customers are attuned. Such markdowns may be reported under almost any of the headings above, but the discerning eye of an experienced merchandise manager will usually recognize them for what they are and search out the roots of the buyer's problem.

Errors in timing the presentation of merchandise to the customer are not always solely the fault of the buyer. There are occasions when tardy deliveries or uncertain weather conditions are to blame. Since late deliveries frequently represent potential markdowns, buyers are expected to weigh the advisability of accepting overdue shipments against the possibility of slackening customer demand.

Delay in taking markdowns or failure to take adequate markdowns, however, is definitely the fault of the buyer. Fashion merchandise deteriorates so rapidly that stores caution their buyers against postponing markdowns or making only timid reductions once they recognize that goods are not readily salable. Yet buyers often engage in wishful thinking; they postpone the inevitable and then have to slash prices drastically in the end. The markdown book records it all, and management finds in that book a vital index to the buyer's competence.

Customer Returns

The extent to which goods are returned in a fashion department is also an important index of the buyer's competence. If a large proportion of the goods sold is brought back for credit, there is something obviously wrong with the assortment, the merchandise, the selling techniques used, or a combination of all three. Sometimes, a persuasive salesperson or a low price may encourage a customer to purchase a dress. If the dress is unflattering, unfashionable, or poorly made, however, the customer is likely to have second thoughts about it after getting it home, and back it goes to the store.

The nature of the merchandise also affects the ratio of returns to sales. In departments devoted to women's and misses' apparel, the rate of returns to gross sales normally exceeds 10 percent. In departments devoted to men's and boys' wear, the rate of returns is well below 10 percent.

Vendor Analysis

A retailer rates suppliers in terms of how accurately their merchandise meets the needs of customers. Sometimes there is an affinity between one vendor's merchandise and the preferences of a store's customers that persists for seasons and even years. Sometimes the affinity is fleeting.

To help evaluate department's resources, a buyer may, with the help of the store's accounting office, maintain records of dealings with each vendor. Typical forms used for this purpose show ven-

VENDOR ANALYSIS

Dept. 444 CHILDRENS UNDERWEAR   **Division** 1   **Period Ending** 01/31/7-   **Page** 17

NUMBER	NAME	MARK UP %	RETAIL	COST	FREIGHT	DISCOUNT	$	%	RETAIL	COST	FREIGHT	DISCOUNT
	VENDOR		YEAR-TO-DATE NET PURCHASES				YEAR-TO-DATE MARK DOWNS		YEAR-TO-DATE RETURNS-TO-VENDOR			
3529-7	TRALEE								4000	2175	174	
3006-6	SMITH DISTRIBUTORS INC	34.2	1400	921								
2499-6	MODERN GLOBE INC	37.9	24600	14664	1173	613						
4484-9	BAGS BY MR ROBERTS	38.3	48600	30000	600		45	9.3		3000	60	
4439-3	CASSIE COTILLION	41.4	358800	205800	16464	4393	360	10.0	1500	825	66	
2184-9	KID DUDS	43.1	388800	217600	17408	3596	423	10.9				
3776-1	METRO NOVELTY CO	43.5	6000	3461	68		10	16.7				
4264-1	CHERRI LYNN	43.5	525000	296650	23782		420	8.0		640		
2142-3	K M T CO	44.4	513800	291228	5649		649	12.6	31000	19463	390	
3352-9	WILLIAM CARTER CO	44.4	574000	318575	6346	7039	341	5.9	49700	26710	535	
1002-2	A D SUTTON & SONS	44.6	129600	69450	1389	2319			3800	1320	26	
2140-7	K GIMBEL ACCESSORIES INC	44.7	34800	18730	370	512	52	15.0				
4274-9	SOFTSKIN TOYS	44.8	52200	27360	547	1431						
3187-9	TOM FIELDS INC	45.1	119500	66273	657		137	11.5	800	445	04	
1045-6	ALEX LEE WALLAU INC	45.5	143600	81157	3558	639	87	6.1	3300	2761	36	
2244-6	LE ROI HOSIERY CO	45.7	329200	180209	3603	2260	265	8.1	300	146	03	
4062-2	JUST ACCESSORIES	46.0	-36000	-18000		-1438						
4981-6	EARL BERNARD INC	46.1	12000	6600	132		30	25.1				
4272-2	PILLOW PLAYMATES	46.7	105000	52860	349	3098	120	11.4				
1622-5	EASTERN ISLES	47.4	784000	414076	32999	4838	975	13.3				
1557-1	DETERMINED PRODUCTIONS	48.6	99000	49950		924	259	26.2				
1931-3	HER MAJESTY IND INC	48.6	1390700	779030	65743	868	1529	11.0	70400	42403	3194	
1756-6	FREDERICK WHOLESALE CORP	49.9	945400	494158	31738	11692	756	8.0	87500	43958	879	
1618-7	E K WERTHEIMER & SON INC	50.0	36000	18000	540							
4207-2	GIANT UMBRELLA CO INC	50.0	72000	36000	1080		40	6.0				
2741-3	PYRAMID LEATHER GOODS CO	50.1	34800	17935	2044	1490	39	11.2				
3654-4	GAYSTONE PRODUCTS	50.4	14400	7355	216							
1862-7	GUILD LINGERIE OF CALIF	51.2	100800	53467	4296		187	18.6				
2759-6	R G BARRY CORP	51.4	248800	121344	2588	-379	278	11.1				
1755-8	FREDERICK ATKINS INTERNTL	51.7	40000	19340								
4233-1	A M A EXPENSE TRANSFER	51.7	-40000	-19340								
3531-9	VELVA SHEEN	53.5	143900	66975			156	10.8				
4920-4	HOLLYWOOD CHILDRENS DRESS	54.0	87600	43800	3504		98	11.2				
	DEPARTMENT TOTAL	47.7	7288300	3965628	226793	43895	7258	10.4	252300	143846	5367	

FORM 16-10

dor name and address, purchases at cost and retail, and the year's or season's total purchases. Vendor returns and claims, as well as markdowns, are also reported by season or year. Thus a buyer can see if a resource has added to the past season's profits or to its problems. (See Form 16-10.)

Buyers also consolidate and list the yearly totals for their principal vendors so that they can compare one with another. They rank them according to amounts purchased, initial markup, percentage of markdowns, or other criteria. The list of principal resources has another function. The management executives of departmentalized stores usually contact, at least once a year, the few best resources for each of their many departments. Often such contact between the heads of the store and the heads of the manufacturing firm leads to better understanding and to long-range planning that benefits vendor, store, and customer.

Stock Turnover

The more rapidly its retail stock is sold, the more profitably a store operates. Good turnover is the fruit of careful planning and wise management. Retailers are very conscious of the stock turnover in each of their departments.

As explained in Chapter 13, turnover rate, or stock turn, is calculated by dividing net sales for a year by the average retail value of the inventory for that year. A common error, however, is to use only season-end or year-end inventories, omitting the intervening months. At the end of a year or season, fashion inventories are at a low point. To base the average only on these lows would be to calculate a deceptively low average inventory, and therefore a deceptively high turnover rate, causing the store to congratulate itself on what actually may have been a poor performance.

Improving Turnover   The only sensible way to improve turnover is to examine the details of the assortment, identify the slow-selling classifications or items, and dispose of them through better display, better selling techniques, or as a last resort, markdowns. The buyer should then use the funds released through the disposal of slow sellers to build up stocks of fast sellers.

Turnover cannot be improved merely by slashing the buying appropriation, nor can elaborate classification and unit control data do more than direct the attention of the merchandising executive to those parts of the stock with the best and the worst turnover. The merchandise itself must be inspected. When the extremely slow-selling numbers are gathered on one rack and the really fast-selling ones on another, the differences between them generally stand out sharply. Buyers can see that their clientele is accepting certain lines, colors, and prices, and rejecting others. Better assortment planning then becomes possible, and better turnover results.

Not all causes of slow turnover are correctable, however. If imports must be bought and paid for long before they reach the selling floor, or if domestic merchandise in irregular supply must be bought well in advance in order to ensure timely delivery, turnover necessarily suffers. But the deliberate sacrifice of turnover to secure desirable merchandise is by no means an error of the same magnitude as the stifling of turnover through inept management of the fashion assortment.

Importance of Good Turnover   In explaining the value of good turnover, more than one merchant has likened fashion merchandise to fresh fish: both deteriorate rapidly! A good rate of turnover in fashion merchandise results in

- Minimum loss of sales appeal of merchandise
- Reduced hazard of soilage and damage from handling
- Increased open-to-buy and the opportunity to freshen assortments with new goods, especially important when the same customers visit a given store or department frequently
- Accelerated interest on the part of salespeople, most of whom become bored with lingering stock
- Increased interest of customers in constantly changing stock
- Reduced inventory investment (which, in turn, means a reduction in both interest costs and need for borrowed capital, reduced insurance rates, and reduced opportunities for pilferage)

Excessively High Turnover   Good turnover, however, is not always the highest rate obtainable. While fashion merchandise turns at a higher rate than more staple merchandise, there are disadvantages in an excessively high rate of stock turnover. Too high a rate of stock turn implies inadequate stocks, unbalanced assortments, and loss of goodwill when customers cannot find wanted styles, colors, and sizes. In addition, high handling and billing costs may have been incurred by placing many small orders rather than a few large ones. The added expense reduces operating profit.

Other Measuring Devices

Other devices used by retail management in evaluating a department's merchandising effectiveness include the number of its sales transactions, the average gross sale, and dollar sales per square foot. Each of these sheds light in its own way on one or more aspects of a buyer's competence and the efficiency of the merchandising operation.

Transactions   The more transactions a department rings up in a year, the more customers it is assumed to have served. If the number falls off from one year to another, this is a possible indication of failure to attract or sell customers. The transaction figure itself is not an index of major importance, but increases or decreases are useful guides when hunting for the strengths or weaknesses of a department.

Average Gross Sale On an annual or sometimes seasonal basis, stores divide the net sales of a department by the number of its sales transactions. The result is known as the *average gross sale*. A rising average gross sale may indicate rising prices, successful efforts to sell higher-quality goods, successful efforts to sell more than one item to a customer, or all three. A higher average gross sale, when compared with the previous year's figure, can mean a better merchandising operation or simply rising prices. When combined with a rising transaction figure, however, it usually means that a department really is pleasing its customers.

Sales per Square Foot Stores annually calculate the number of square feet of selling space assigned to a department and divide that number into the department's total net sales for the year. The resulting figure, dollar sales per square foot, is an index to how well the department has paid its "rent" to management. Most misses' and women's apparel departments in department stores have figures well above those of the store as a whole.

In departmentalized stores, management usually is amenable to expanding the selling area of a department or classification that shows exceptionally high sales per square foot. It may condense those departments that make a poor showing in this respect. Suggestions from buyers for rearranging their departments or installing new fixtures are more acceptable to management if there is indication that the change will result in increased sales per square foot.

REFERENCES
[1] *Buyer's Manual,* pp. 257–259.

MERCHANDISING VOCABULARY

Define or briefly explain the following terms:

Book inventory	Basic stock
Pre-retail	Prior stock reports
Purchase or merchandise journal	Average gross sale
Flash sales	

MERCHANDISING REVIEW

1. Why is the retail method of inventory, as an accounting procedure, better suited to large retail firms than the cost method?
2. To what does the term "book inventory" refer? What store department is responsible for keeping the book inventory? What general types of records are used in maintaining it?
3. What is the effect upon a department's book inventory of each of the following: (a) purchases? (b) customer returns? (c) returns-to-vendor? (d) additional markup? (e) markdowns? (f) transfers to other departments

or branches? (g) transfers from other departments or branches? (h) merchandise on order? (i) merchandise loaned to other departments?

4. What is a departmental buyer's responsibility with regard to stock shortages and overages? What are the two major causes of shortages and overages? Give at least four examples of each cause.

5. What is a purchase or merchandise journal? Why should it be carefully checked by a buyer or assistant buyer? What is involved in checking it?

6. Name and briefly describe the purpose of each of the four periodic financial reports commonly used today in departmentalized stores.

7. What is the primary purpose served by a departmental operating statement? How often is it usually issued? What specific information does it contain?

8. What is meant by the term "open-to-buy"? Why is it considered such an important merchandising tool? How is it calculated?

9. Why is age of stock a very important consideration in fashion merchandising? Discuss various ways in which old season or slow-selling fashion merchandise can be kept to a minimum.

10. What factors do retailers take into account when evaluating resources (vendors)? What purpose or purposes do such evaluations serve?

MERCHANDISING DIGEST

1. Discuss the taking of a physical inventory with respect to each of the following: (a) purpose, (b) necessary preparations, (c) procedures and (d) use of resulting data.

2. Discuss markdowns with respect to (a) major causes, (b) "poor timing" of merchandise offerings, (c) delays in taking, (d) size of markdown of individual items, and (e) departmental profits.

3. Discuss stock turnover with respect to (a) how a buyer can achieve a higher rate, (b) benefits resulting from an improved rate and (c) disadvantages of an excessively high rate.

17
SELECTING FASHION MERCHANDISE FOR RESALE

Planning procedures prepare the retail buyer or store owner for one of the most important jobs in fashion merchandising: the selection of the individual styles that will make up the merchandise assortment. Up to this point, the buyer's plans have been quantitative, in terms of how many units and dollars should be invested in apparel or accessories of given types. Up to this point, too, others at the store may have helped the buyer with the planning by supplying data, expressing opinions, or setting policies and limits on purchases. Now qualitative decisions must be made—by the buyer alone.

Buying for a fashion department is a continuous process that takes place anywhere from the buyer's desk to the market centers. Reorders of goods that have sold well may be placed at any time by mail, telephone, or teletype. New items may come to the buyer's attention and be ordered as a result of a visit by a vendor's representative or a visit by the buyer to regional showings in foreign or domestic market centers.

It is almost impossible to operate a fashion shop or department without at least two market trips a year. When and how often a buyer goes to market are determined by the size of the store, the volatility of fashion in the merchandise concerned, and how far away a store is from the market. A store that wants to build or maintain a strong fashion image may send its buyers to market many times a year, so that they will be aware of even the slightest changes in the market. Retailers who feature price above all else may also have buyers in the market frequently, but in search of special

advantageous buys. Plans for a special promotion may require buyers to make an extra market trip in search of special purchases for that promotion.

THE BUYING PLAN

A merchant or buyer on a trip to the wholesale markets leaves the store prepared to spend a considerable amount of money. To make sure this money is not spent haphazardly, and to show that there is need for the trip, most stores require a written buying plan to be drawn up and approved prior to departure. A *buying plan* is a general description of the types and quantities of merchandise a buyer expects to purchase for delivery within a specific period of time. It also sets a limit on the amount of money to be spent, so that purchases will be kept in line with planned sales and desired inventory levels.

The more enthusiastic a retail buyer is about fashion merchandise, the more the stabilizing influence of a written buying plan is needed. It is a constant reminder to avoid spending too much on the first new and exciting goods encountered, unless the budget and assortment plan permit buying freely while not neglecting other sectors of the assortment.

A buying plan makes all the difference, for example, between going to market to see what is offered in coats, and going to market to find coats at specific retail price lines, in specific quantities, with specific delivery dates—all in accordance with budget limitations, assortment plan, present inven-

BUYING PLAN

Page __1__

Dept. __42, Misses Dresses__ Date __Feb. 20, 197-__

Planned MU% __48.5__

Buying trip to: __New York__

From: __Feb. 24__　To: __Feb. 27__

Reason for trip: __Additional Easter Mdse;__
__Review Mar. – Apr. O.O.; New Mdse for__
__early Apr. delivery__

Mo. of Delivery	O.T.B. 2/20/7-	Planned Purchases	O.T.B. Balance	Actual Purchases	
				Cost	Retail
March	$9,300	$7,900	$1,400	_____	_____
April	13,600	6,700	6,900	_____	_____

APPROVED: GMM __ABD__ Date __2/22/7-__ DMM __TJE__ Date __2/21/7-__

(1) Class	(2) Unit Retail	(3) Description	(4) Actual Sales L.Y.	(5) Planned Sales T.Y.	(6) Planned Stock 4/15/7-	(7) Total (5+6)	(8) O.H. 2/20/7-	(9) O.O. 2/20/7-	(10) Total (8+9)	(11) O.T.B. (7-10)	(12) Plan to buy	(13) Purchases		
												No.	Cost	Retail
123	22		141	150	250	400	176	90	266	134	Mar 60 / Apr 60			
	26	Street, business and general occasion wear dresses	163	175	300	475	202	100	302	173	Mar 90 / Apr 80			
	30		155	160	225	385	162	80	242	143	Mar 80 / Apr 60			
	35		94	100	180	280	112	60	172	108	Mar 60 / Apr 42			
140	30		42	45	80	125	94	36	130	—				
	35	Dressy and after-5 dresses	30	35	65	100	80	18	98	—				
	40		19	25	50	75	60	18	78	—				

FORM 17-1

tory, present commitments, and sales potential of the coat department. Until a buyer or store owner actually inspects producers' lines, the buying plan cannot be completely explicit. To be without one, however, invites unplanned assortments, poorly related to customer demand.

The buying plan is part of the homework that every retailer undertakes before making any major commitment of funds to buy fashion merchandise. Department stores generally do not release travel funds to their buyers until a plan has been made and has been approved by the merchandise manager or senior store executive. Form 17-1 illustrates a simple buying plan that might be used in a moderate- or large-volume store.

Information Required for a Buying Plan

In addition to identifying data such as department number and name, date of trip, destination, and length of stay, a typical buying plan requires detailed information about a number of other points. These include various projections in either dollars or units of merchandise or both, based on both the department's merchandise budget and the merchandise assortment plan.

When a buyer has supplied all the information required in a buying plan, the merchandise manager or senior store executive is in a position to evaluate the need for the trip and also to bring greater experience and judgment to bear upon the tentative decisions that a buying plan represents.

Reason for Trip   The purpose of a buying trip may be to attend regular seasonal openings of vendors' lines, or to seek out special values for a forthcoming promotion, or to bolster a section of the assortment that is enjoying an unexpected burst of demand. The reason given for making the trip, as well as some of the other data in the buying plan, also shows management whether the trip is urgent or routine.

Open-to-buy   Open-to-buy, as discussed in Chapters 13 and 16, is the amount of merchandise that can be purchased for delivery during a given period minus outstanding orders scheduled for delivery during that period. The formula for calculating open-to-buy is

$$
\text{open-to-buy} = \begin{array}{l} \text{planned sales} + \text{planned mark-} \\ \text{downs} + \text{planned closing stock} \\ - \text{present stock} - \text{merchandise} \\ \text{on order for delivery during the} \\ \text{same period} \end{array}
$$

Open-to-buy can be calculated and shown on a buying plan either in dollars or in units of merchandise or both, usually by classification and price lines or ranges within each classification. The total dollar figure on the buying plan automatically shows management whether or not the proposed purchases are within the financial limits established in that season's merchandise budget. The unit figures are based on the season's unit assortment plan. In some cases, open-to-buy figures may be shown for one or more months into the future; this is a useful guide if the buyer is authorized to make commitments for delivery of goods beyond the current period for which buying is now being done.

Stock on Hand and on Order   For each classification of merchandise to be purchased, current merchandise on hand and on order for delivery during the period for which purchases are being planned are indicated on a buying plan. Usually each price line in each classification at which purchases are planned is entered separately, with the stock on hand and on order indicated in units or dollars or both. In moderate- and large-volume stores, unit price and total amounts to be purchased are shown at retail values, while smaller stores tend to use cost figures. By comparing these figures on the buying plan with those in the merchandise budget and the assortment plan, management can determine whether or not the intended purchases are within the budgetary limits set for the department or classification and are in line with its assortment plan.

Sales for the Period   The buying plan, prepared just before a market trip, includes the most recent sales estimates and reports available. These may be shown in units or dollars or both. If the buying trip is made before the start of a season, the sales figures in the plan will be those projected on the dollar merchandise budget and the merchandise assortment plan. If the selling season has already begun, these figures will have been adjusted to reflect anticipated sales for the balance of the period for which buying is to be done. If the merchandise budget and the assortment plan have been revised to meet current conditions, the revised figures are used. The important point is that the buying plan includes the most up-to-date sales, stock-on-hand, and stock-on-order figures available at the time it is prepared.

Planned Stock at End of Period The planned end-of-period inventory figures, in both dollars and units, are very important in planning the buying of fashion goods. Because demand rises rapidly to a peak in fashion goods, and falls off even more sharply after the peak has been passed, it is essential to keep the inventory within the established limits. If a fashion merchant brings in too much stock and has more than planned at the close of a selling period, it is likely that heavy markdowns will be needed to get rid of that excess stock.

If the buyer plans to make purchases for more than a month or two, then the planned stock for the end of that period is entered in the buying plan. If buying is short term, then only the current month's closing stock estimate may be needed.

Quantities to Be Purchased Based on their judgment of sales potential, availability of merchandise, market conditions, and other factors, fashion merchants indicate on their buying plans how much of each type of merchandise, in terms of both units and retail dollars, they want to purchase on this trip in order to maintain an assortment balanced to meet anticipated customer demand. Quantities to be purchased vary with the timing of a market trip, the store's merchandising policies, the type of merchandise, and delivery conditions. At the start of a selling season, perhaps only trial quantities are ordered, while larger quantities may be purchased with more assurance as the season advances. Most stores establish loosely defined percentages of the seasonal open-to-buy that may be purchased early. The experienced buyer saves a good part of both the unit and dollar open-to-buy for later in the season, for unexpected opportune purchases, for reorders, and as a hedge against changing customer demand that would require changes in the fashion assortment.

Additional Data Some plans provide space for the buyer to enter the amount of actual purchases after shopping the market. As illustrated in Form 17-1, these entries are usually placed alongside the approved, planned figures. A number of stores require the buyer to submit, at the conclusion of each trip, a detailed reconciliation of all orders placed, by classification and price line, with quantities approved on the original buying plan. Either of these procedures underscores the importance of adhering to planned figures unless there is good reason to do otherwise.

A few store managements require a list of resources the buyer intends to visit on the market trip. Such a list is usually expected to include the names of one or more resources with which the store has not yet had dealings, but whose potential the buyer will explore. It also includes resources with which the department has already dealt, sometimes for years.

This requirement serves a double purpose. It stimulates the buyer to make realistic plans as to which and how many producers to visit in the time available. In addition, it is a reminder to inspect the lines of resources that have proved successful in customer acceptance and yet it helps avoid the danger of going only to regular resources. Just as any business constantly seeks new customers, so an alert store seeks new and gifted resources to add fresh and interesting items to its assortments.

Some buying plans also include a figure provided by management representing a total dollar limitation for the market trip. This amount may be higher than the total of the planned purchases listed, and may actually exceed the open-to-buy, since it may include a provisional allowance for opportune purchases. In a store commited to fashion leadership, this leeway permits buyers more flexibility, should they find a new trend developing in the market. For stores serving bargain hunters, this extra money may permit buyers the opportunity to snap up good buys in the market without ignoring the needs of their regular assortments and without having to contact the store for permission to exceed planned figures.

Detailed descriptions of purchases to be made are not necessarily included on buying plans, since buyers, not knowing precisely what they may find, cannot be more specific than "skirts," "dress shirts" or "girls' 7–14 party dresses."

How a Buyer Plans

Before actually drawing up a buying plan, fashion merchants or buyers review the stock in several respects. They check their basic stock requirements; they study any overstock conditions; they note any items that are winning strong acceptance; they take upcoming sales events into consideration. This overall review is intended to give a good idea of exactly what is needed and what should be sought in the market.

Overstock   Any section of the assortment that exceeds its planned size requires analysis. The adjustments needed to reduce such overstocked conditions may affect buying plans for categories that otherwise are proceeding according to plan. For example, slow sellers in higher price lines may have to be marked down into lower price lines. In such cases, buying plans for the lower price line may have to be adjusted to take such additions to the existing stock into account. There also may be some common factor among a department's slow sellers which can be regarded as a warning against further purchases of a disappointing price line, color, fabric, detail, or other features customers have not favored.

"Hot" Items   Items, new or otherwise, that have demonstrated greater customer acceptance than was anticipated receive thoughtful consideration from the buyer. Even though they may not have been prominent in the original assortment plan for the season, it may be necessary to make an important place for them. To do that, buying plans for other items may have to be cut back.

If the "hot" item is one the buyer has heard about but has not yet actually had in stock, judgment on its sales potential may be reserved until it has been studied in the market. Then approved buying plans for the more predictable and familiar items may be adjusted, and the buyer may decide to add the hot item to the assortment.

Special Events   If the buying trip for which the plan is drawn involves preparation for a promo-

tional event, special sale, catalog distribution, or similar activity, the buyer is fortified with details on what was offered to and bought by the store's customers on similar occasions in the past. If a buyer is about to purchase children's gloves, for example, for the store's Christmas catalog, it is important to know how many of those sold from the previous year's catalog were knitted or leather, bright colors or neutrals, matched to caps and scarves or sold separately, and how many were sold at each price. Then this information has to be weighed against what appears to be this year's trends in children's gloves.

Importance of Complete Data   When drawing up a buying plan, the buyer is in the store. All the sources of information on present conditions and past experience, described in Chapters 13 and 14, are available. Once in the market, however, only the condensed data of the buying plan itself can be consulted. The more thoroughly the buyer checks while still at the store, the more valuable the capsulized data on the buying plan will be.

TIMING OF THE MARKET TRIP

Few fashion buyers feel they can function effectively if they do not get to the market to view manufacturers' showings for at least the two most important selling seasons of the year: spring–summer and fall–winter. In general, spring lines are becoming less important, but resort-cruise wear is becoming more important and extending into the traditional spring season. These showings are occasions for exhibiting new styles in their greatest variety and with the maximum of showmanship. To view a series of lines this way is both exciting and educational for the buyer.

The dates of such openings vary from one segment of the fashion industry to another, according to the lead time required for production and delivery of goods, the convenience of the market date for buyers, and the seasonality of consumer demand for the goods. In order for the retailer to have ample selections of fall goods in stock by

NEW YORK COUTURE
BUSINESS COUNCIL, INC.
OPENING DATES
SUMMER 1975

FOR COMPLETION MAY 31st, 1975

ADELE SIMPSON	Tuesday, Feb. 4th	10:00 A.M.
LEW PRINCE of ALDRICH	Monday, Feb. 3rd	continuous by appointment
ALPER SCHWARTZ	Monday, Feb. 3rd	continuous by appointment
ANDREW ARKIN	Wednesday, Jan. 29th	by appointment
GEOFFREY BEENE	Wednesday, Feb. 5th	12:00 NOON
BARON-PETERS	Monday, Jan. 13th	continuous by appointment
THE HOUSE OF BRANELL	Tuesday, Feb. 4th	continuous by appointment
CARLYE	Wednesday, Jan. 29th	continuous by appointment
DON LUIS de ESPANA	Monday, Jan. 27th	continuous by appointment
GENRE by GIL AIMBEZ	Monday, Jan. 13th	continuous by appointment
HALSTON	Thursday, Feb. 6th	3:00 P.M.
KIKI HART NEW YORK	Tuesday, Feb. 4th	continuous by appointment
JAMISON	Wednesday, Jan. 29th	continuous by appointment
NAT KAPLAN	Monday, Feb. 3rd	continuous by appointment
KAPPI	Thursday, Jan. 30th	continuous by appointment
HAROLD LEVINE	Tuesday, Feb. 4th	12:00 NOON
MAISONETTE	Wednesday, Feb. 5th	continuous by appointment
NANTUCKET NATURALS	Monday, Jan. 27th	continuous
OSCAR de la RENTA	Wednesday, Feb. 5th	2:30 P.M.
PARNES FEINSTEIN	Monday, Feb. 3rd	continuous by appointment
MOLLIE PARNIS		
BOUTIQUE	Tuesday, Feb. 4th	11:00 A.M.
RODRIGUES	Monday, Feb. 3rd	continuous by appointment
DOMINIC ROMPOLLO	Thursday, Feb. 5th	continuous by appointment
PAT SANDLER	Tuesday, Feb. 4th	1:00 P.M.
PAT'S PLACE	Tuesday, Feb. 4th	1:00 P.M.
ABE SCHRADER	Monday, Feb. 3rd	continuous by appointment
SCHRADER SPORT	Tuesday, Jan. 21st	continuous by appointment
STEPHAN CASUALS	Monday, Feb. 3rd	continuous by appointment
JERRY SILVERMAN	Tuesday, Feb. 4th	continuous by appointment
TEAL TRAINA	Monday, Feb. 3rd	1:00 P.M.
GRETA PLATTRY		
for TEAL TRAINA	Tuesday, Feb. 4th	3:00 P.M.
TRIGERE	Tuesday, Feb. 4th	4:00 P.M.

An ad appearing in Women's Wear Daily, January 21, 1975.

mid-August, manufacturers of better apparel show their early fall lines as early as the preceding April, and buyers come to the market at that time.

The ad above shows the dates on which certain vendors of women's better apparel began showing their lines for Summer 1975. The recent trend has been for earlier openings with a longer spread between showings and completed delivery dates. This allows more time to get the goods produced and into the stores when customers want to see them. By contrast, spring lines in the 1930s opened in January, and fall lines opened in July.

RESIDENT BUYING OFFICES

Most buyers of fashion merchandise, with the possible exception of those from the smallest and perhaps the most exclusive shops, make resident buying offices their first port of call on a market trip. A *resident buying office* is a service organization located in a major market area that provides market information and representation to its noncompeting client stores. These stores are usually fairly similar in size and class of trade but are located in different towns and cities throughout the country.

Nearly all resident buying offices have their headquarters in New York City; some have branches in other important market centers both in the United States and abroad. Most of the major offices cover the whole range of department store merchandise, from fashion accessories to home furnishings. A number, however, serve only specialty stores. A few restrict themselves to a narrow range of merchandise, such as infants' and children's wear.

Types of Resident Buying Offices

There are two major types of resident buying offices—independent offices and store-owned offices. An independent resident buying office actively seeks out noncompeting stores as paying clients, while the store-owned office is entirely owned by the store or stores it represents and works exclusively for them.

Independent Offices   Numerically there are many more independent resident buying offices than there are store-owned resident buying offices. The dominant type is the *salaried office*, or *fee office*, which is independently owned and operated

and charges the store it represents for the work it does for them. Such offices usually enter into annual contracts with noncompeting stores to provide market services in exchange for an annual stipulated fee or "salary" based upon each individual store's sales volume.

This type of office strives to familiarize itself with each client store's individual operation and needs and to meet those needs with a broad range of services, including development of private brand merchandise as well as group purchasing of merchandise, store equipment, and store supplies. Among the oldest and best-known offices of this type are the Mutual Buying Syndicate; Kirby, Block & Co.; McGreevey, Werring, & Howell; and S. Irene Johns, Inc. Also in this category are a number of specialized offices, such as the Youth Fashion Guild, which serves only children's shops.

Store-owned Offices   Resident buying offices that are owned and operated by the stores they represent, divide into three groups: private offices, associated or cooperative offices, and syndicate offices.

An office that is owned and operated by a single, out-of-town store organization and performs market work exclusively for that store is called a *private office*. Such an office is actually a staff bureau of the store, located in the market rather than in the store itself. Because of the investment involved and the high cost of operation, only very high volume department and specialty store organizations maintain their own private resident buying offices.

A second type of store-owned office is an *associated office*, which is one jointly owned and operated by a group of privately owned stores. Membership is by invitation only and is considerably more expensive than if the store were a client of a salaried office. Stores that belong to an associated office, however, usually are highly homogeneous as to sales volume, store policies, and target groups of customers, and as a result, their relationship is generally an intimate one, extending to

Mutual / new item

BUYING SYNDICATE, INCORPORATED

To: Merchandise Manager of Lingerie
     Buyer of Lingerie

Bulletin #677-EA-April 10, 1975

THE TEE SHIRT SAYS ... I LIKE YOU

The Tee Shirt ... season's favorite top ... now seen in a delightful,
Young Sleepwear style.

Attractive screen print decorates this tee top made of easy-care,
comfortable blend of 50% nandel and 50% polyester. Shirt
can easily see double duty as a jean or pant top.

Shirt has matching bikinis.

Style:	#432 – Short Sleeve
Sizes:	S-M-L
Colors:	Assorted: Blue, Mint, Maize, Coral
Packing:	4/12 per size
Cost:	$36.00 dz.

(Also available in tank top styling – Style #433 – same colors,
sizes, cost.)

Resource:	LISETTE LINGERIE
	148 Madison Avenue
	New York, N.Y. 10016

Terms:	8/10 eom
FOB:	Vidalia, Georgia
Delivery:	April 25th complete

EILEEN AHERN
Market Representative
Divisional Merchandise Manager

/rb

Buying offices provide their member stores with regular bul-
letins about current market news.
Mutual Buying Syndicate, Incorporated.

an exchange of operating figures and the sharing of merchandising experiences. The operating expenses of an associated office are allocated to each member store on the basis of sales volume and amount of services required. Typical of this type of buying office are the Associated Merchandising Corporation, Frederick Atkins, and the Specialty Stores Association. However, there are relatively few associated resident buying offices, and their number is steadily decreasing as more and more privately owned store organizations are being absorbed by syndicates and holding corporations.

A third type of store-owned resident buying office is generally known as a syndicate office. A *syndicate office* is an office maintained by a parent organization that owns a group of stores. The office performs market services for those stores that are owned by the syndicate or holding corporation. Some offices of this type have more authority than their counterparts in salaried or associated offices for the placing of merchandise orders to be delivered to member stores. In others, authorization from store buyers is required, despite the close corporate relationship. Examples of syndicate offices are those maintained by Allied Stores Corporation, Associated Dry Goods Corporation, and May Department Stores.

Some stores maintain a private office within the facilities of an independent, associated, or syndicate buying office to which they belong. In this way, a store has access to all the services of the larger office, while the private office also provides adequate working space for visiting buyers. Such an office is usually under the direction of a manager who is on the store's payroll and is directly responsible to the store's management.

Organization of the Resident Buying Office

The typical resident buying office is organized along lines similar to those of a department or specialty store. In the merchandising division, there are market representatives, whose positions parallel to a degree those of retail store buyers. There are also merchandise managers, who supervise groups of market representatives, just as store merchandise managers supervise a limited number of store buyers. There is a fashion coordinator who is responsible for information on the overall fashion picture. All of these specialists are available to store buyers who visit the market, although most of a visiting buyer's needs can be handled by the market representative alone.

Other executives in the typical buying office provide sales promotion ideas and aids to client stores, while still others provide assistance in the purchase of supplies and equipment. There is a personnel office responsible not only for selecting staff for the buying office itself but also for recruiting junior and senior executives for client stores. In most offices, there also are facilities for exchange of information on the retail operations of client stores. The latter are supplementary services, performed in addition to the resident buying office's primary function of keeping in close and constant contact with markets and merchandise.

The Market Representative

A *market representative* is a specialist who covers a narrow segment of the total market and makes information obtained about it available to buyers of stores served by the resident office. Market representatives "live" in their markets and make themselves authorities on supply, demand, styles, prices, deliveries, and any conditions affecting supply and service to retailers. They visit resources, see lines, check into general conditions of supply and demand, verify trends, seek new "hot" items, hunt up specific items requested by client stores, and follow up on delivery or other problems referred to them by client store buyers.

Although the market representative's responsibility is similar in many respects to that of a retail store buyer, it differs in one important aspect: Market representatives cannot place orders for client stores except at the explicit request of the appropriate store buyer.

The early hours of each working day are spent by the market representative at a desk, reviewing mail from stores, seeing items and lines brought to the office's sample rooms by vendors' salesmen, and being available to any store buyer who may be in the market.

Afternoons are usually spent in the market, tracking down items, reviewing lines in producers' showrooms, and keeping in touch with what is happening in the industries assigned for coverage. In the late afternoon, the market representative returns to desk work, often to prepare a special bulletin to the stores on something they should know about immediately. It might be an opportunity for a special buy from a manufacturer who is closing out remainders, for instance, or the discovery of a new and exciting item that buyers should have a chance to consider without waiting for a market trip.

Merchandising Services

The merchandising services provided by resident buying offices to their client stores include current market information, conducting buyer clinics, central merchandising facilities, arranging for group purchases, and order placement and follow-up.

Current Market Information The market representatives are responsible for keeping appropriate buyers and merchandise managers of client stores continually informed of developments and trends in the market or markets that they are assigned to cover. They usually do this by sending out descriptive bulletins about new items, best sellers, and special price offerings, as well as market surveys.

When buyers arrive in the market, they check in first with their store's resident buying office and review their buying plans with the appropriate market representative. In the light of current supply and demand situations, fashion developments, and other pertinent factors, the buyer and market representative determine what changes, if any, should be made in the buying plan.

A great deal of market time is saved for buyers through such early conferences, since the market representative can direct them to those resources best able to fill their needs. If the buyers come to market hoping to locate some item they have not yet seen but have heard about and hope to find, the market representative will either suggest appropriate resources or advise against hunting for it, depending upon the availability and marketability of the particular item.

Buyer Clinics Just prior to the start of major market weeks, the resident offices usually arrange a series of meetings or clinics for client stores' buyers of certain types of merchandise. These sessions are designed to give the buyers an idea of current fashion and market situations before they visit the showrooms of individual producers.

At such meetings the market representatives and other speakers discuss fashion trends, supply, retail prices and market conditions. Often samples of the new season's merchandise are put on display. Occasionally a manufacturer comes before such a meeting to present a line, or a new sales promotion program, or an idea for more effective product merchandising. In the course of such discussions, buyers may develop a new perspective in relation to their buying plans that enables them to make adjustments to improve the plans or they may emerge from the meeting with increased confidence in the advisability of following their plans.

Central Merchandising With the information that unit controls provide, even a knowledgeable outsider, remote from a store, can gain sufficient insight into the preferences of customers to be able to plan assortments and select merchandise for them. If a resident buying office is given this information about such fast-moving fashion categories as inexpensive dresses and budget sportswear, the buying office can perform this merchandising service for subscriber stores anywhere in the country. The advantage of a central merchandising operation of this type is that the buying office's representatives are in the wholesale markets daily and can make fresh selections or follow up on deliveries of orders constantly. This service, while not as extensively used today as it once was, is extremely valuable for smaller stores, because they usually cannot afford to send their buyers into the market more than twice a year, which is not often enough to keep a stream of fresh, newsworthy fashions coming into stock.

In such a central merchandising operation, each store provides the buying office with a dollar merchandise budget and an assortment plan, to which it adds general observations about its customers' preferences, such as "no sleeveless dresses" or "our people like wide necklines." Using these guides, the resident buying office orders the garments it considers appropriate for each store. The store regularly reports to the buying office all receipts of merchandise, sales, markdowns, and customer returns, just as if it were reporting to a unit control department under its own roof. The records are kept in the buying office, however, so that the merchandiser in charge of the central merchandising operation has a finger on the pulse of demand in each store.

Group Purchases Sometimes the market representative or the store buyer may suggest group action in a buying situation. Through *group purchase,* identical merchandise is bought by several stores at one time from a given resource, so that all participants may share in the advantages of a large-volume purchase. Such a group purchase might involve the development of special merchandise for the exclusive use of member stores, the pooling of purchases in order to obtain financial benefits, or the encouraging of production of a new fashion item not yet widely available in the market but in which the stores have confidence.

A buying office may organize a group purchase when a manufacturer offers closeout merchandise in a quantity that is too large for one store to handle but might be adequately apportioned among several stores. Another time when group purchasing may be used is when the office prepares a group catalog for such occasions as Christmas or back-to-school promotions. When the catalog is one that can be used by a number of stores, a substantial reduction

in printing costs can be realized by all the participating stores. Items selected for such a catalog, however, must be agreed upon by all the buyers, and each must plan to set aside sufficient open-to-buy for the styles chosen by the group. Thus participation in group purchases may, on occasion, involve adjustments in the planned assortments.

Order Placement and Follow-up Market representatives for resident buying offices, other than those maintained by syndicate or corporate holding companies, are not empowered to place orders for client stores. They may do so, however, at the request of store buyers. Frequently, a market representative will send out an illustrated bulletin on a new or "hot" item, suggesting that the appropriate buyer authorize a sample order for that store. Sometimes, store buyers may allocate a portion of their available open-to-buy to market representatives to be used at the discretion of the latter.

Store buyers often send special orders to market representatives for placement with vendors. This is done to ensure faster service. Vendors might be inclined to overlook an order for one or two pieces of merchandise placed by a store buyer, but they are less apt to do so when that order is personally placed by the representative of a resident buying office that may have hundreds of potential customers.

Some stores send copies of orders to resident buying offices for follow-up regarding delivery. Market representatives maintain tickler files on such orders and check with vendors to ensure that deliveries are made as specified.

OTHER SOURCES OF INFORMATION IN THE MARKET

Good fashion merchants are always hungry for fashion information. Armed with data about their own store's experience and guided by carefully developed buying plans, fashion buyers continue accumulating facts and opinions throughout their market trips. Their major sources of information are the experience of other buyers from the home store, fashion periodicals, manufacturers, trade associations and trade shows, and other noncompeting stores and their buyers.

Experience of Other Home-store Buyers

In addition to their own departments' experiences, department or specialty store buyers also call upon the market experiences of other fashion buyers within their own organization. Some retail merchandising executives make a point of having all fashion buyers confer at the end of each day in the market to exchange information and promotional ideas.

For example, a dress buyer's report that many varieties of the bulky-top look are being offered in the market will influence the coat buyer's selection of styles to carry out the bulky look. Furthermore, the fashion accessories buyer will be encouraged to stock varieties of long, bulky scarfs. Each buyer's evaluation of current market fashion trends helps the others evaluate what they find in their markets and helps project a more coordinated storewide fashion image.

Consumer Magazines

The editorial offices of consumer magazines, both those that devote themselves primarily to fashion and those for whom fashion is but one of many subjects of editorial coverage, are usually located in New York City and therefore are a good source of fashion information for visiting buyers. They are in a position to give advance information on the fashion trends to be featured editorially in upcoming issues and the specific styles to be used as illustrations of those trends. In addition, the fashion magazines share with the retailer their considerable knowledge of fashion itself and of the particular segment of consumers to which their pages are addressed.

The editors of these magazines, like the fashion buyers themselves, do not rely upon intuition to guide their selection of fashions. They study their readers carefully, often with the aid of elaborate consumer research projects, observing how their readers live, dress, work, and relax. Like successful fashion merchants, they are in such close rapport with their readers that they can forecast with a high degree of accuracy the styles that will win acceptance in the months ahead.

Editorial Credits   When a magazine editor selects a garment or an accessory item to be featured in a forthcoming issue, the usual policy is to invite one or more stores to permit their names to appear as retail sources for the merchandise that is being editorially featured. Such a mention is known as *editorial credit.* If a store decides to accept such a credit, or mention of its name, it is expected to stock the featured item in sufficient quantity to satisfy local demand. A well-chosen credit does not affect the buying plan, however, since such merchandise normally would be part of the regular assortment. Ideally, a credit simply highlights an item the store would have selected anyway on its own merits.

Trend Information   Buyers in the market who call at the offices of magazines usually can see photographs or samples of fashion styles to be featured in future issues. A talk with any fashion or merchandising editor will give the buyer information about the trends the selected merchandise exemplifies, reasons why these trends are important to the magazines readers, and suggestions about possible promotional tie-ins.

For example, in the mid-1970s, when longer, fuller skirts returned to the fashion scene, several fashion magazines ran articles illustrating what to look for in a skirt, how each woman could determine the right hem length for her own particular figure and height, and which blouse, sweater, and jacket styles should be worn with the new skirts to carry out the new look. This information was particularly useful to younger readers who had spent most of their lives in jeans, miniskirts, and pantsuits.

Resource Information Consumer magazines, as a matter of course, provide retailers with lists of those manufacturers who produce the garments and accessories to be shown in future issues. Their service to the retailer often goes beyond this point, however. As a result of having spent many hours in the market, the fashion editor of a magazine often can direct a buyer to resources for the particular merchandise sought.

Fashion News and Insights Whether or not retailers accept an editorial credit or seek suggestions as to resources, they still can profit by visiting the offices of those periodicals whose readers most closely resemble their own customers in tastes and interests. They are almost certain to come away with information and insights that aid their market work. If nothing else, in the case of publications whose impact is strong among their customers, they will know what merchandise and fashion news will be given magazine exposure in upcoming months, and they can plan to reflect similar influences in their assortments, if they choose to do so.

All this, of course, is in addition to the fashion buyer's required reading of periodicals devoted exclusively to fashion news in both consumer and trade categories. Magazines such as *Vogue, Harper's Bazaar, Glamour* and *Gentlemen's Quarterly Magazine* provide the buyer with a background on incoming fashions, as do such trade publications as *Women's Wear Daily* and *Men's Wear*. Regardless of the stage of the fashion cycle at which their customers buy, all merchants need to keep abreast of the newest trends. Only in that way can they evaluate the sales potential of their current stock and decide what purchases to make.

Manufacturers

There is much that producers of fashion merchandise can give buyers by way of useful information. If the manufacturer is a major one in the field and has fairly wide distribution, his experience, activi-

ties, and marketing plans provide invaluable assistance to buyers who are in the market to select merchandise.

Fashion Projections Top-ranking producers usually have carefully thought-out reasons behind their decisions to make up certain styles, to use certain materials and colors, and to ignore others. They can also indicate which numbers in their line are frankly experimental and possibly prophetic, which ones are new but nevertheless definitely expected to develop fashion acceptance, and which are carryovers of styles that are no longer new but remain in demand. Equally important is information explaining why they have perhaps ignored some of the ideas that others in the field have taken up. All this becomes part of the background data buyers process in order to arrive at decisions concerning their own assortments.

Store Experience Manufacturers often pass along valuable information about what other retailers have bought, promoted, and displayed and how they have trained their salespeople. For example, in a certain category of merchandise, a vendor may tell a buyer how one store achieved exceptional turnover and did many times the volume of equivalent stores elsewhere by keeping rigidly to a rule of frequent stock counts and fill-ins. In another instance, the buyer may be told the details of a spectacular promotion through which a store sold more units of higher-priced merchandise than it had ever previously sold. By picking up ideas about how other stores have achieved good results with a line or styles in that line, buyers may find a way to promote their own merchandise assortments more advantageously.

Promotional Plans The extent of promotional efforts that a vendor plans to invest in a line, style, or trend can have a bearing upon buying decisions. Buyers should weigh the possible impact of a particular type of promotion upon their own stores' customers. For example, a vendor may have plans

Buyers get useful information about fabric trends for the coming season from the fabric manufacturers.
Deering Milliken, Inc.

for a series of advertisements in various consumer magazines. If one or more of these publications is influential among the store's customers, this fact may cause the buyer to buy more freely of that line. On the other hand, if the buyer believes that the vendor's promotional program will have little effect upon the store's customers, it will have equally as little effect upon the amount purchased from that firm.

Occasionally, without attempting to relate the vendor's advertising directly to its impact on the store's customers, buyers may find their confidence in a certain style confirmed by the fact that the vendor has such confidence in it that an entire season's promotional outlay is planned around it.

Promotional Techniques Buyers are more likely to purchase radically new merchandise with greater confidence if they have some well-defined ideas for its display and sale. Manufacturers often can offer such ideas. For example, when stretch hosiery for women was first introduced in the

1950s, many buyers hesitated to purchase it because it looked quite unimpressive if shown to a customers in the usual way: by having the salesperson open a box of folded stockings and thrust a hand into the upper portions of the top stocking. When buyers were told of the successes achieved by stores that displayed the stretch hosiery on leg forms, some of them, confident that they had or could obtain a sufficient supply of such forms, were encouraged to buy more freely.

Tested Consumer Preferences A resource with national distribution is usually completely familiar with regional variations in timing of consumer demand for merchandise, color preferences, and other marketing matters. Certain apparel, for instance, may be purchased earlier and may enjoy a longer selling season in the South than in the North; certain colors may be perennial favorites in some areas, but may fluctuate in popularity in other areas. A buyer who is new to a store or department can obtain helpful guidance on such points from dependable manufacturers. Records left by the preceding buyer may not show clearly the reasoning that governed timing and assortment choice in the past, but a manufacturer often can clarify the situation in a few words.

Trade Associations and Trade Shows

Associations of manufacturers and of retailers assist fashion buyers in many ways. The nature and frequency of the assistance available, however, are not uniform throughout the fashion industries. Some associations offer more help to buyers than others, and buyers learn to familiarize themselves with the degree of assistance they may expect in the industries from which they buy.

Retail Buyers' Groups Associations or clubs for buyers of a single classification of merchandise provide an opportunity for the exchange of opinion with others. At the very least, such an opportunity aids buyers in clarifying their own ideas about fashion and market conditions. In some instances, groups of this kind provide a medium through which buyers can transmit to an entire industry their preferences in matters ranging from the dates when lines should be opened to the sizes of stock boxes to be used. Many such associations are subsidized by the industries concerned, or by trade publications, or both.

Trade Shows Retail or manufacturer groups, and sometimes independent organizations, establish trade shows at which a great many manufacturers in a given industry exhibit their lines under one roof and at the same time. "Under one roof" usually means a hotel, or two or three hotels, in which several floors are set aside for exhibit space. With a minimum of time and travel, buyers can see almost every line they want to see, can make comparisons, and can exchange opinions in "corridor talk" with other buyers from all over the country. The impact of seeing so many lines in so short a space of time is great, and a clear-cut impression of what the market offers can be readily gained. This is especially helpful in industries in which small firms predominate. The buyer can look in on dozens of them in one day at such a show, instead of trekking from building to building, up and down elevators, and possibly covering only four or five showrooms in as many hours.

Among the industries in which such shows are regularly staged for retail buyers are shoes, notions, piece goods, and men's sportswear.

Fashion Bulletins Many trade associations publish fashion bulletins for buyers, to alert them to fashion trends and to explain their significance in terms of retail opportunities. Since whatever helps the retailer to sell an industry's products also helps the industry itself, some of these associations retain experts in retail merchandising and promotion to contribute suggestions to buyers about advertising, selling, and display ideas related to current fashions. Especially noteworthy are the bulletins of some of the associations in the raw materials fields, which discuss colors and textures to be featured in coming seasons.

Retail Conventions Retailers' associations regularly hold conventions or meetings for their members. Some of the sessions are devoted to subjects of interest to fashion merchants and buyers, especially in areas that present unusual problems or opportunities. The National Retail Merchants Association, at its annual convention (always held in New York City in early January), devotes sessions to various selected categories of merchandise, whenever fashion developments (or the lack thereof) in the merchandise concerned make these worthwhile. For many years, also, a regular feature of NRMA conventions has been a discussion of outstanding retail fashion promotions during the previous year and the elements that made each successful.

Other Stores, Other Buyers

Buyers meet with representatives of noncompeting stores through the resident buying office. In the market, they find themselves in contact also with a host of other buyers. Informal conversations can become the medium for exchange of opinions and experience with other retailers.

In addition to such contacts, buyers visiting a market city make a point of looking over the merchandise and displays of local stores. Chatting with a local buyer about some of the new ideas or new merchandise seen in the department may prove stimulating and profitable to the visiting buyer.

Making the rounds of the stores in a large city also provides buyers with an opportunity to gauge the progress of a particular fashion. They can observe where it stands in its cycle and how much or how little emphasis is given to it in stores of varying degrees of fashion leadership. If a style is featured by stores whose clientele purchase at a later stage of the fashion cycle, the buyer has reason to be wary of that style. If a style is featured by stores whose clientele purchase at an earlier stage of the fashion cycle, that might suggest that it is something customers will want soon.

Visiting other stores is also a way to check how far the copying-down process has gone for styles that interest a buyer. Buyers for a medium-priced store, for example, may decide against ordering an otherwise acceptable style because they see that it has been "knocked off" and is already in basement departments and discount houses.

WORKING THE MARKET

It has been said that there are as many ways of shopping or "working" the market as there are buyers. Buyers develop their own techniques or procedures for covering a vast amount of ground and doing it with a minimum of physical strain and a conservation of mental energy. The primary purpose of the trip, the length of the trip, and the number of resources that have to be covered all influence the manner in which each buyer works.

In spite of the differences as to how each buyer shops a market, however, certain basic procedures should be followed. These have to do with the advance planning of each day's activities, note-taking, and writing up orders.

Order of Seeing Lines

Before setting out each morning, a buyer should have a tentative itinerary set up for calls to be made that day. The schedule cannot be too rigid, since delays are bound to occur. Nevertheless, some sort of itinerary helps a buyer to make sure that each day in the market produces its quota of calls.

Geographical Some buyers, keenly aware of time limitations, visit showrooms in what might be called geographical order: one building at a time. With dozens of vendors' showrooms in each skyscraper in Garment Town (an affectionate name for the area in which apparel and accessories showrooms are located), the calls made in one building alone can often constitute a good day's work for the buyer. On the other hand, the building-by-building technique may fail to produce an overall impression of trends, because each building tends to draw tenants dealing in the same type and price range of goods. To get a more general view, several buildings must be visited.

By Type and Price Lines   Other buyers, at some cost to themselves in terms of effort, ignore geography and instead concentrate their efforts on shopping as much of the market as possible for the specific types and price lines of merchandise in which they are interested. The advantage of this type of shopping is that buyers can compare one vendor's merchandise with that of others while impressions are fresh in their minds.

By Prime Resources   A third approach is to visit first *prime resources,* those from which their departments have consistently bought a substantial portion of merchandise needs in past seasons. Under normal circumstances, buyers can expect to continue to purchase an important share of their needs from these resources so long as the merchandise continues to meet the customer demand and quality standards of their stores.

Rapport between buyers and such resources is usually excellent, and the exchange of ideas and information fairly rapid. Hopefully, the buyers can find much of the merchandise for which they are shopping in the showrooms of their prime resources and can proceed to complete their market tour in a more relaxed frame of mind. Also, when they know what their prime resources are showing, buyers are in a better position to evaluate the styles they see later in other showrooms.

By Price Lines   Still another approach is by price line, or visiting the showrooms of higher-priced resources in each class of merchandise first, and then continuing the visits through successively lower-priced markets. Although this approach has obvious disadvantages, buyers usually find more fashion news, more original styling, and more fashion information among the higher-priced vendors than among those in the lower-priced brackets. Buyers who prefer this method point out that it gives them a quick overview of fashion trends as an important base for evaluation of all other lines to be seen during the remainder of the trip.

The choice of method is usually up to the buyer, unless the store has established a preferred method. In a store that strives for fashion leadership, buyers may be required to see the showrooms of the fashion leaders among their resources first, and then to meet with the store's other fashion buyers to evaluate what they have seen and to decide which fashions or "looks" appear right for their store. Only then are buyers free to go on with the rest of their market work.

Showroom Procedures

When important resources first show or "open" a new seasonal line for retail buyers' inspection, most buyers review the line in its entirety, usually taking notes on styles of special interest. Buyers of stores that are regular customers of individual vendors then usually make an appointment for a return showroom visit. At that time, they work with their regular salesperson in reviewing the vendor's line. Styles that originally impressed the buyer are again evaluated, as well as any others that the salesperson believes, because of past experience, would be of special interest to the customers of the buyer's store. Such showroom visits usually are quite time-consuming, and buyers have to plan accordingly.

As each season advances, buyers may make additional market trips for reasons previously discussed. They may visit vendors' showrooms to check on orders placed when the new line was opened but portions of which have not yet been delivered. This is done for the purpose of possibly revising undelivered orders in light of actual store sales experience. Or they may wish to reorder styles that have sold well. Or they may be searching the market for specific merchandise in line with their buying plans. Such showroom visits must of necessity be brief. Wise buyers see to it that they do not permit eager salespeople to take up more valuable time on this type of market trip than the buyer can afford. In the interest of maintaining good vendor relations, however, the buyer should never appear curt, impatient, or rude with either vendors or their sales staff.

Managements urge buyers to listen to the sales staff's comments and suggestions and to avoid

When working the market, buyers visit as many vendors'
showrooms as possible.
The Broadway-Hale Stores, Inc.

cutting off what might prove a source of useful information. They instruct them, also, to tell their resources about the success they have had with the line and to express appreciation of business courtesies extended—if only to prepare for some possible future day when they have to request a favor from the resource. Business, and especially the exchange of information about the fashion business, proceeds best in an atmosphere of mutual respect. And respect is what store managements expect their buyers to achieve in the market.

Taking Numbers

Normally buyers do not write up orders when they are looking at lines in vendors' showrooms. Instead, they take numbers. *Taking numbers* means writing an adequate description of each style the buyer is considering for possible purchase, including style number, size range, available colors, fabric, wholesale price, and any other details the buyer finds are relevant to the style.

It is important to note here that when buyers are viewing a vendor's line, they are mentally con-

verting the quoted wholesale price into an established retail price line at which that merchandise
should be marked if they are to maintain the average departmental markup required by their merchandising plans. They must also evaluate whether
the item under consideration compares favorably in
quality with the merchandise they now own or have
on order at the same retail price line. Furthermore,
they must consider whether the new item has a
limited or excellent sales potential in their stores.
Should the new item fail to meet any of the above
requirements, the buyer would be well advised to
postpone the decision about purchasing the item or
perhaps even eliminate the item from further
consideration.

   In some classifications, such as scarfs, gloves,
hosiery, or costume jewelry, the lines buyers view
may be very extensive, and they may find it difficult
to write a sufficient description of each number for
later recall. For such merchandise, a buyer separates the samples into three groups: desirable, less
desirable, and least desirable. Later, when the entire
line has been examined, the buyer takes the numbers of those styles of greatest interest.

   At the end of their trip, buyers compare descriptions of similar merchandise they have seen
during their market trip, eliminate duplications and
less desirable styles, and make their decisions as
to exactly which styles they wish to purchase. If
such restraint is not exercised, a buyer may order
too lavishly from the first few resources, leaving
no funds for possibly more desirable merchandise
later. Buyers retain for future references, however,
those numbers they have taken but decided not to
order at the time. These may serve a valuable purpose should the style the buyer did order be cancelled or customers request merchandise that was
seen but not ordered.

   After eliminating the less desirable styles and
developing what they believe to be the best possible
list of numbers from those they have seen, some
buyers work again with the buying office's market
representative, calling on the latter's intimate
knowledge of a specific market for further guidance
before actually writing up their orders.

*A buyer in the market sees all available lines
and "takes numbers" before making
a final decision about what to order.*
Halston

Writing the Order

Until an order has actually been placed, buyers are free to change their mind about what they want to order. Once they have placed an order, however, it is considered a contract between the store and the vendor, and buyers have committed their stores to take the merchandise. Any change of mind at some later date requires the written permission of the vendor with whom the order has been placed.

To ensure that an order covers all required points and to avoid committing the store to unacceptable conditions, buyers should write up orders only on the forms provided by their own stores (or, in some instances, on the forms of their resident buying offices) and not on the vendor's form. Prevailing practice is to write up orders after leaving the market and to have them countersigned by the merchandise manager or other responsible store official.

The typical store order form (see Form 13-6) requires the buyer to specify:

- The date of the order.
- The vendor's name and address, together with the shipping point, if different from the showroom address. (A vendor may maintain a sales office in New York City but produce and ship from elsewhere.)
- Shipping instructions, including the date by which all shipments should be completed or the order can be legally cancelled, the route by which shipments should be sent, and all arrangements relating to shipping costs.
- The terms of sale. (How soon after shipment the invoice must be paid, and with what discount.)
- The department for which the goods are purchased.
- The address of the store unit to which shipment should be made (if store wishes deliveries to be made to other than the main store).
- Any special directions about packing and shipping. (For example, a store with several branches may request each branch's goods to be separately packed and labeled, even though all merchandise is to be received at a central location.)

- Details of styles purchased, including classification, number, description, and cost price. Descriptions, depending on the article, should specify color, fabric, size, or other relevant points. There should be enough information to make it easy for the store's receiving department, as well as for the vendor's shipping room, to know exactly what the order specifies. Failure to include this information on an order leaves the vendor free to ship anything.
- The retail price (shown only on the store's copies of the order, not on the vendor's copy). The buyer indicates the unit retail price intended for each style number. Thus the total retail as well as the total cost value of each order can be calculated, and the initial markup percentage can be worked out. On copies of the order that are intended for the marking room, the column of cost figures is blacked out, and only the retail prices, needed for making up price tickets, are visible.
- Any special arrangements concerning the purchase. (For example, the vendor may agree to contribute a specified amount, on specified conditions, toward the advertising of a purchase; or as is sometimes the case, particularly in placing orders for such merchandise as furs and high-ticket jewelry items, the buyer may have the privilege of returning unsold goods by a specified date. This is known as *buying on consignment*.)
- Standard trade practices. Established many years ago by the National Retail Merchants Association, in cooperation with the associations representing the apparel trades, these practices are usually printed on the back of each store's order blank. The provisions spell out the obligations of buyer and seller to one another and define what constitutes fair or unfair practice in relation to an order.

Merchandising Notes

At the time they write up their orders, buyers also should write up brief notes about the merchandise ordered, the reasons for choosing it, and the overall impression gained from the market trip. From these notes they later prepare training talks for their salespeople about incoming merchandise and fashion trends. These notes also may serve as memos about the selling points of the goods for salespeople as well as for the advertising and display departments. If they do this work while the merchandise is fresh in their minds and while enthusiasm for it is strong, some of the excitement of the market trip will spread to everyone else at the store who will eventually be concerned with the sale of the merchandise.

TESTING NEW FASHIONS

Astute merchants avoid taking too many chances as to which fashion will be accepted by their customers and which will get only a cool reception. There is great risk in letting oneself be carried away by enthusiasm for a new fashion that has been seen in the market. The same risk is present when buyers assume that their own ideas of the right color, line, or texture are identical with that of customers. A mistake in judging the acceptability of a new fashion can be a costly error for merchants. They risk their fashion reputation in the community, as well as capital, every time they select a new style for stock.

Most merchants greet a new fashion with the sample-test-reorder technique. They buy in small quantities in a wide range of possibly acceptable styles to observe customer reaction. Then they reorder in substantial quantity those styles and colors that appear to have won an initial favorable reception; the rest are quickly marked down and cleared out. The customer casts the deciding vote.

For example, suppose that every indication points to a growing popularity of pale, neutral shades in wool dresses. A buyer may feel very strongly that off-white will be the season's preferred neutral shade and that shirtwaist types will be the preferred styles. Instead of buying off-white shirtwaists alone, however, the buyer will perhaps try white, off-white, and pale beige and will purchase each color sparingly in several styles. When the goods arrive at the store, customer comments as well as actual sales will determine which colors and styles are best received. The buyer may find that pale beige is as well received as off-white; therefore ample quantities of both colors should be ordered. The buyer may also find that shirtwaist styles with convertible collars are more acceptable than collarless styles and that cuffed sleeves are evoking better response than push-up sleeves.

At this point, the buyer places additional orders for the styles that have the most acceptable features. These may or may not be the same features originally thought to have the greatest sales potential. Actual experience now gives the buyer more confidence to purchase in larger quantities.

The testing procedure is not entirely risk-proof, however. In offering customers a wide range of styles at the start of the season, a merchant inevitably stocks certain numbers that will have to be marked down because they are hard to sell. In general, however, the losses that occur are far less than they might have been had no testing been done.

An increasingly difficult problem facing retailers today is the length of time it takes for manufacturers to deliver goods, particularly if they are of a highly seasonal nature. The fabric out of which the sample was made may not be available; production problems may arise; transportation strikes may occur. Nor can manufacturers always produce at short notice the styles that a buyer wants to reorder. This may be because the original fabric is no longer available or because other stores have not had similar success with the style and the manufacturer has not received enough reorders to warrant recutting.

Here is where experience and judgment come into play. While on a market trip, buyers should always determine from the vendor exactly when the latter expects to ship each style of merchandise that is being ordered. This is of utmost importance for two reasons. First, the buyer's open-to-buy is reduced by the retail value of all merchandise ordered for delivery each month. Second, the buyer needs this information in planning ads and other promotional activities.

MERCHANDISING VOCABULARY

Buying plan	Associated office	Editorial credit
Resident buying office	Syndicate office	Prime resources
Salaried, or fee, office	Market representative	Taking numbers
Private office	Group purchase	Buying on consignment

MERCHANDISING REVIEW

1. What factors usually determine how often buyers go to market? For what reasons, other than viewing seasonal lines, do buyers make market trips?

2. What are the major purposes served by a buying plan? What information, other than identifying data, is usually required on a buying plan?

3. In preparation for drawing up a buying plan, what specific aspects of the present stock assortment must the buyer carefully review?

4. What is the major function of a resident buying office? Name and describe the four major types of resident buying offices.

5. Name and briefly describe the five major merchandising services provided by resident buying offices to client stores.

6. What is a "market representative"? Distinguish between the responsibilities of a market representative and those of a store buyer. Name at least five activities engaged in by a market representative.

7. Name five valuable sources of fashion information available to a buyer when on a market trip. In what specific ways can each of these sources aid a buyer?

8. Why is it necessary for buyers, while on a market trip, to carefully plan their daily itineraries? What options do buyers have in working the market?

9. What is meant by the term "taking numbers"? What important factors must a buyer consider when viewing a line and taking numbers? Why is it advisable when working the market to take numbers rather than writing an order at once?

10. What is the sample-test-reorder technique? What are its advantages to fashion merchants and buyers?

MERCHANDISING DIGEST

1. Discuss the implications for a buyer of the following statement from the text: "Buying for a fashion department is a continuous process that takes place anywhere from the buyer's desk to the market centers."

2. Discuss the various reasons why buyers visit vendors' showrooms and the typical procedures involved in each case. What are the buyer's responsibilities with regard to vendor relations?

3. Discuss the legal aspects of a purchase order, the types of information required on most order forms, and the possible penalties resulting from not completely and accurately filling out an order form.

18
PROMOTING FASHIONS: ADVERTISING AND DISPLAY

Retailers have an adage: "Goods well bought are half sold." Half the process of selling fashion to the consumer, they believe, consists of analyzing wants and offering assortments that are geared in every possible respect to those wants. The remaining half of the selling effort is sales promotion, which is the business of arousing the consumer's buying impulses and requires just as much careful planning and precise execution as does the earlier half. Fashion merchants have never taken for granted that customers would come to their doors without encouragement or reminders. Everyone in the fashion business, from the designer with a new sketch to the merchant with new styles in stock, is anxious to talk about, show, and promote the sale of new goods. While this active effort is essential to a profitable operation at any marketing level, it is vital in the merchandising of fashion goods and services. Fashion moves at a fast pace today, and competition among fashion merchants is strong. Sales promotion is an essential weapon for both vendors and retailers in their battle for customer patronage.

The methods used by fashion merchants for promoting sales vary widely, since they each choose an approach suited to their own assortments and clientele. A small exclusive shop may rely entirely on word-of-mouth advertising, supported by an occasional call from the owner to a faithful customer about the arrival of new styles in the store. A large, low-priced retail organization may make extensive use of newspapers, throwaways, radio, and television to bring in crowds of customers.

Sales promotion can be subtle or obvious, but it must be continuous if fashion goods are to be sold before age withers their appeal and salability.

SALES PROMOTION DIVISION

In medium to large stores, there is usually a sales promotion division which is responsible for promoting sales through advertising, display, and publicity undertaken to attract customers to the store. In some stores, personal salesmanship is also considered part of this function. *Sales promotion,* therefore, may be defined as the coordination of advertising, display, publicity, and personal salesmanship in order to promote profitable sales.

Organization

In small stores where there is a relatively modest amount of promotional activity, there is usually a sales promotion manager who is directly involved in managing each and every one of these activities. Where the volume of promotional activity is too large for such an arrangement, there usually will be an advertising manager and a display manager functioning under the direction of the sales promotion director, who may handle publicity and its close relative, public relations. Very large stores have a publicity manager as well, who supervises special events, the activities of consumer boards, and so on, thus leaving the sales promotion director, often a vice president, free for policy making and for long-range planning.

Operation

The chief executive of the sales promotion division is responsible for preparing storewide sales promotion plans and budgets in conference with the advertising manager, the display manager, the publicity or special-events manager, the merchandise managers, and, if there is one, the fashion coordinator. Such plans and budgets are based on storewide sales goals, which have been developed earlier from six-month dollar merchandise plans (as explained in Chapter 13).

These storewide sales promotion plans indicate, by specific type of activity such as advertising, display, and special events, the extent to which the store intends to employ each in its effort to produce the total storewide sales planned for the upcoming season. Included in the master sales promotion plan are such regularly recurring events as anniversary sales, white sales, and back-to-school promotions, as well as other important and timely storewide, divisional, or departmental promotions relating to Easter, Father's Day, Mother's Day, and so on. Each department of the sales promotion division—advertising, display, and special events—then prepares its own seasonal plan and budget based on the amount of money allocated to it in the storewide promotional budget, and designating in general terms how that money shall be used to implement the master plan.

The percentage of planned dollar sales allocated to sales promotion varies from store to store, depending on the type of store and the policy of the store with respect to the nature and extent of promotional activities it chooses to employ. The percentage of departmental planned dollar sales allocated to sales promotion expense also varies from department to department, depending mainly on the merchandise involved and sometimes on the extent of local competition as well. Sales promotion budgets for fashion departments are usually higher than those for semistaple- or staple-goods departments. For instance, an active sportswear department may have a budget as low as 2 percent of planned sales, while a fur department may have a budget as high as 5 percent of sales.

By far the largest share of the sales promotion division's budget each season is allocated to advertising, and the major share of the advertising budget is usually allocated to newspaper space. In spite of the emphasis given to newspaper advertising, however, it is not the only promotional medium used by stores. Rarely does a fashion merchant rely solely on a single type of sales promotion technique. Instead, most merchants use every available method, and carefully coordinate their efforts.

Thus, when a newspaper advertisement is run, good retail practice implies that the same merchandise and its selling points be featured in departmental displays and possibly in window displays as well. It also implies that salespeople be briefed on what is being featured, as well as when and why. In addition, wherever possible, publicity is sought to back up sales promotion efforts. The effectiveness of a store's promotional efforts depends on the effectiveness of each separate activity in creating a motivational impact on customers.

FASHION ADVERTISING

The use of paid space or time in any medium—newspapers, shopping news bulletins, magazines, direct mail, radio or television broadcasts, or billboards—is known as *advertising*. All these media are used by retailers to promote the sale of fashion merchandise.

Types of Advertisements

There are two basic types of ads used by stores. One is designed to sell items, the other to "sell" a store's image.

A *merchandise* or *promotional advertisement* is one that endeavors to create sales of specific items. Goodwill, store image, and enhancement of the store's fashion prestige are incidental, although these are nevertheless considered when any such ad is planned and prepared. (See Form 18-1.)

FORM 18-1

A *prestige* or *institutional advertisement* is one that "sells" the store rather than specific merchandise. It may discuss a new fashion trend; it may point out the store's value as a headquarters for fashion news, for bargains, for clothes for the family; or perhaps it may publicize a community event. Any merchandise mentioned in the ad is usually considered incidental. The ad's value to the store is measured solely in such intangibles as prestige, goodwill, and enhanced store image.

Advertising Plan

An *advertising plan* is a forecast for a specified period of time, such as a season, quarter, month, or week, of the advertising that a store intends to employ in order to attract business. In general, such a plan outlines the dates on which advertisements will be used, the departments and items to be advertised, the estimated sales expected to result from such ads, the media to be employed, the amount of space or time to be used in each medium, and the cost thereof. The cost is usually estimated both in dollars and as a percentage of the sales expected to be realized.

The outlay for newspaper space, the most widely used medium among fashion retailers, amounts to more than 2 percent of the typical department store's annual net sales. In individual fashion departments, newspaper space costs vary; they amount to about 3.4 percent of sales in coat departments, 2.7 percent of sales in junior dress departments, and 1.9 percent of sales in handbag departments on an annual basis, although the amount of newspaper advertising done, expressed as a percentage of net sales, varies considerably from month to month throughout any given year.

Preparing the Plan The storewide advertising plan is a general guide to the timing and amount of advertising to be done by each department in the store during a specific season or other period of time. Exact dates, selection of media, decisions

as to size of ads, writing of copy, and other details are worked out later, closer to publication time.

Both the budget and the schedule of the general plan are prepared with the understanding that unforeseen developments may require sudden adjustments, just like those that merchandise plans sometimes require. An advertisement that produces spectacular sales results may be repeated promptly, even if the original plan did not call for a second run. Conversely, a planned ad may be scrapped if the merchandise to back it up is not in stock or for some other sound reason.

After the storewide advertising plan has been prepared, it is broken down first into seasonal plans for each selling department and then into monthly plans for those selling departments. The monthly plans are drawn up about a month in advance, and they specify the item or items to be advertised, the dates on which ads will appear, the size of each ad, and the medium in which it will appear.

Sources of Information for Planning Like the merchandise plan, the advertising plan is based on past experience, present conditions, and future expectations. The advertising department keeps careful records in scrapbook form of what was advertised last year, how it was advertised, at what cost, and with what results. Such a scrapbook contains tear sheets of all advertising previously run. On each ad is noted the dollar cost of the ad and the sales that resulted from it, as reported by the department for which the ad was run. When drawing up an advertising plan for a new season, the planner goes through the scrapbooks for similar periods in previous years and studies both the ads run and their sales results. Each season's plans incorporate as many features as possible of successful advertising used in the past, and avoid the features of that advertising which did not produce desired sales results.

The same factors that buyers and merchandise managers review when preparing their merchandise budget and plan are important in preparing promotional plans. These factors include conditions inside and outside the store; management's goals; indications of promotions planned by resources, publications, and competitors; and any other factors that might affect the store's own plans.

The experience of other retailers is also utilized in planning. In addition to the store's own advertising scrapbook, the advertising manager studies the advertising of other stores, particularly that of competitors whose advertising results have been observed and that of friendly noncompeting stores in other communities which are willing to exchange advertising information.

Through such sources as the store's resident buying office, the National Retail Merchants Association, and various trade publications, each advertising executive keeps in touch with the promotion experience of other stores. Reports of what is being advertised, shown, and sold in the country's top fashion stores are eagerly studied. So, too, are the advertising pages of consumer fashion magazines. Such reports are often a source of inspiration to advertising managers. They evaluate them, however, in terms of their own store's target group of customers. They know that the spectacular results from an ad placed by Saks Fifth Avenue, for example, might not be duplicated in their own stores if they placed an identical ad. Yet the approach used by another retail store may trigger an idea that can be used.

Finally, advertising staffs constantly need information from the merchandising division in order to develop effective copy and illustrations. They expect buyers and merchandisers to give the advertising department details about specific fashion trends and to indicate noteworthy features of items that are to be advertised.

Newspaper Advertising

Retailers use local newspapers extensively in promoting fashion merchandise because their customers are mainly from within the areas served by such newspapers. While producers whose fashion goods have national or at least regional distribution tend to favor national magazines for their ads, some may cooperate with their retail store customers by helping the stores pay for ads of their merchandise in local newspapers.

Newspapers are the retailers' preferred advertising medium because they provide immediate impact and broad local exposure. The time between preparation and insertion of an ad can be quite short, and last-minute changes can be handled readily. Compared with a monthly magazine whose ad pages "close" weeks before publication, a newspaper is virtually instant advertising. A daily paper normally can accept changes almost up to the moment that its presses begin to roll—and this is only a matter of a few hours before the edition is on the streets.

Speed is vital in promoting fashion merchandise. A newspaper ad can be prepared for new fashion merchandise even before the goods are in stock, provided the resource has made a firm promise of delivery and can be relied upon. Should there be an unforeseen delay in the availability of the merchandise, the ad can be pulled at the eleventh hour. The importance of this last-minute flexibility is obvious in view of the many kinds of sudden changes that can take place making it advisable to change advertising plans.

In a community where several newspapers are published, each attracts a particular readership in terms of income, education, and interests. Fashion retailers advertise in the paper that appeals to the readers who are most similar to their own clientele in fashion awareness and income level. In New York, for example, stores that feature fashions in the early stages of their cycles usually buy space in *The New York Times,* which reaches affluent, city-oriented, fashion-aware customers. Stores or departments that offer fashions at the peak and in the declining stages of their cycles have less reason to use the *Times,* and therefore rely upon other city or suburban papers. Occasionally an enterprising suburban or small-town store will advertise its newest fashions in a prestigious big-city paper that has circulation in its community. Much of the paper's

Berry's

ADVERTISED MERCHANDISE INFORMATION

Advertising information and the merchandise to be illustrated must be in the Advertising Department two weeks prior to the week in which the ad runs in the newspaper.

Department No. **74**

Date Ad Runs:
June 1, 197—

Paper(s):
Tribune

Space:
7-col. full

Item	Regular Price	Sale Price
Cotton canvas tote bags Matching webbing belts	Bags $11-18 Belts $6	No

List features in order of importance

1. Spacious, weightless, cotton canvas totes for town or travel

2. Five featured styles, wide assortment of colors, darks, neutrals, high shades

3. Webbing trim in contrasting colors, belts in cotton webbing matching bag trim

Sizes Roll: 17 x 10, #17, Kangaroo pocket, 17 x 12-1/2, #11; Shoulder: 11-1/2 x 10-1/2, #16; Ring: 11-1/2 x 10, #15; Maxi: 16-1/2 x 13, #18

Colors Roll: red, navy, black, natural; Shoulder: natural, tan, navy, red; Kangaroo and Ring: natural, black, navy, red, kelly green, pink, tan; Maxi: red, navy, black, natural, tan

Art Instructions Sketch woman's torso showing belt, bags, cascading down length of page

At What Stores At all stores

Submitted by Dorothy Smith, buyer

Date Received in Advertising Department May 15, 197—

Does manufacturer share cost of ad? Yes Is credit claim attached? Yes

Reason for Advertising:

- [x] New Line
- [x] Fashion News
- [ ] Sale
- [ ] Special Purchase
- [ ] Staple Stock
- [ ] Clearance

Quantity on Hand Date Ad Runs	Date Merchandise will be in Stock	Total Retail value of Merchandise	Use Trade Mark or Label	Is Manufacturer Paying for Ad?	Extra Delivery Charge?	Telephone Orders?	Mail Orders?	Mail Order Coupon?
250 pcs	5/26 complete	$3,750	Yes ☐ No ☒	Yes ☒ No ☐ 20 % of Payment	Yes ☐ No ☒ Amount? ___	Yes ☒ No ☐	Yes ☒ No ☐	Yes ☐ No ☒

FORM 18-2

circulation is wasted so far as such a store is concerned, but the use of a city newspaper dramatizes the store's fashion authority in the eyes of city-oriented members of its community.

Preparing the Ad The preparation of a routine ad begins with the buyer. Although a tentative decision has already been made about when and where the ad will appear and how much space will be used, it is the buyer who initiates a formal *advertising request.* (See Form 18-2.) The buyer gives a brief, carefully factual description of the style or styles selected for advertising, together with a few words that tell what is important and exciting about the goods from the customer's standpoint. These words are the key that the advertising copywriter needs to write attention-getting copy. In addition, the buyer includes on the advertising request such points about the merchandise as price, sizes, colors, fabric, and other pertinent information, such as quantities in stock, how and where available, and so on.

For example, a buyer may write: "Two-piece dress for multioccasion wear; ideal for travel because it's washable and wrinkle resistant; long-sleeved top modeled after a polo shirt, with wide gored skirt. Beige and brown nylon print; sizes 6 to 12; $85." The copywriter might write: "The Polo Shirt Swings Into Action! Here is a two-piece dress that will score points both at home and wherever you want to travel. The long-sleeved shirt tops a swingy gored skirt, both parts in a beige and brown nylon print that resists travel wrinkles and can be washed and ready to put on again without ironing. For sizes 6 to 12, $85." The fashion artist who sketches the garment may emphasize the currently popular styling features, which include the polo-shirt top and the wide gored skirt, and put some luggage or the suggestion of an airport into the sketch to underline the garment's usefulness as part of a travel wardrobe.

An important trend in fashion advertising in newspapers is toward greater use of descriptive copy, less "white space," and less reliance on art work alone to tell the fashion story. Chief exponent of this new type of advertising format in the mid-1970s was B. Altman & Co., New York, whose highly informative, personalized, and often amusing ads, presented in imaginative layouts, evoked widespread interest among retailers and customers alike. As a result, Altman's received a 1975 NoRAMA Award for outstanding creativity in copy, art, and design in fashion communication with the public. Annual NoRAMA awards are made on an international basis and are cosponsored by the National Retail Merchants Association and the Newspaper Advertising Bureau.

Manufacturers sometimes provide glossy photographs or sketches of their garments, suggested copy layouts, or mats, to assist in the preparation of retail ads. (A *mat,* short for *matrix,* is a paperboard mold on which picture or copy are impressed and from which a plate can be made for reproduction.) These advertising aids are given by manufacturers to the buyer, who may suggest their use for an upcoming ad of the merchandise they depict. The decision as to whether or not to use a specific aid, however, rests with the advertising department.

When an Ad Breaks At the same time that an ad is to be run, promotion plans may also call for window and department displays. In such cases, the buyer works with the display department to ensure proper presentation of the merchandise in the windows. It is also the buyer's responsibility to order appropriate signs (Form 18-3) from the store's sign shop, and to arrange for departmental displays of the advertised merchandise. Thus, on the day that an ad breaks, customers will find the item or items on display and properly identified.

Some stores mount tear sheets (clippings) of each day's ads on walls in or near elevators, escalators, restrooms, and other areas of heavy customer traffic for additional exposure. Each department usually exhibits its current ads on its own selling floor where customers may see them. Each buyer is responsible for making sure that her salespeople

SIGN REQUISITION

SIGN SIZES	QUANTITY
(1/16 = 5-1/2 x 7)	14
1/8 = 7 x 11	
1/4 = 11 x 14	
1/2 = 14 x 22	
FULL SHEET = 22 x 28	

- PLEASE PRINT PLAINLY
- ORDER SIGNS AT LEAST A WEEK IN ADVANCE
- ORDER ONLY ONE SIZE CARD ON THIS REQUISITION
- GIVE COMPLETE INFORMATION

FOR DEPT.	TEL. EXT.	DATE ORDERED	DATE NEEDED
74	3615	May 14, 197-	May 23, 197-

COPY:

CANVAS HANDBAGS
FOR
TOWN AND TRAVEL
$11 TO $18

REMARKS:

WHAT SPECIAL EVENT _Tribune ad June 1st_

CHECK APPROPRIATE BOX:

PROMOTION	CLEARANCE	SPECIAL PROMOTION	NEW LINE	FASHION NEWS
			X	X

ORDERED BY _Dorothy Smith_

APPROVED BY _H. L. Reiss_

FORM 18-3

know what is advertised, where it is stocked, and what the selling points are, so that they can talk intelligently to customers about the merchandise.

In stores that do a considerable amount of telephone order business, each day's ads are also posted in the order board area to aid the telephone operators. Today, many larger urban stores have their telephone-order boards manned 24 hours a day, 7 days a week, for customers' convenience.

Reporting Results Advertising departments generally request, for future guidance, a report from the buyer of the results achieved from each merchandise ad. (See Form 18-4.)

ADVERTISING RESULTS

Department ___74 - Handbags___

Date of Ad ___June 1, 197-___

Media ___Tribune___

No. of Stores ___5___

No. of Units Sold ___175___

DOLLAR SALES:

Advertised Item ___$ 2,625___

Total Department ___$ 7,824___

Note: *This form must be turned in to Merchandise Manager before noon the 4th day after ad has run. Merchandise Manager will initial and send promptly to Sales Promotion Manager.*

Buyer's Signature ___Dorothy Smith___

Merchandise Manager's Initials ___H.L.R.___

FORM 18-4

Advertising results of merchandise ads are measured in terms of net dollar and unit sales. Buyers are expected to report, usually on a printed form, such points as: how many advertised items were in stock before and three days after the ad ran; how many were sold; total dollar sales of the department for the three-day period following the ad; weather conditions; special display effort; and any other pertinent data that would help evaluate the ad's pulling power.

Buyers and advertising executives learn from such reports which items and approaches produce the most sales among the customers of the store and department concerned. Thus a sound basis for future planning is laid.

Planning in Smaller Stores Planning and reporting are less formal in relatively small stores where there is no advertising specialist to concentrate on promotions. Even in the smallest shop, however, good management demands at least a rough guide as to what is to be spent, in which media, for what merchandise, and with what expectations. A record of ad results also needs to be kept so that past experience can guide future decisions. Often all that is needed is a scrapbook of ads that have been run, with marginal notes about costs and results.

The store with no staff advertising expert or agency often finds that many aids in constructing ads are available free or at little cost. Part of the work on a market trip involves canvassing the possibilities of obtaining suitable advertising material, so that when the buyer or owner returns to the store they know not only what merchandise to advertise but also how best to present it in an advertisement.

Smaller stores often use media that larger ones may ignore. The cost of a newspaper ad looms large in the budget of a tiny establishment, so its proprietor often uses less costly media such as direct mail. Considerable use is also made of such resource-provided aids as low-cost statement enclosures, display cards, package enclosures, and the

Department __42__

NOTICE OF PAID ADVERTISING

Manufacturer's Name __Aiken Dress Company__

Attention of __Jack Shapiro__

Manufacturer's Address __1400 Broadway__
__New York, N.Y. 10018__

Newspaper Date __May 16, 197-__ Name __Tribune__

Date _____ Name _____

Describe Merchandise __Polyester dresses, styles 420, 674, 1060__

ADVERTISING AGREEMENT

Manufacturer Agrees to Pay:

☐ 1. Full Charge   4. Your Share as Agreed _____

☐ 2. One-half Charge   5. Up to Amount of _____

☒ 3. __25 %__ Charge   6. Other _____

Person with Whom Agreement Made __Jack Shapiro__ Date __Feb. 16, 197-__

Special Billing Instructions __Send tear sheet with duplicate of invoice.__
__Deduct from Aiken Dress Co. account payable__

Buyer's Signature __Dorothy Smith__

To Be Filled Out By The Advertising Department

Lineage, Total Ad __600__   Rate $ __2.20 /line__

Cost, Total Ad $ __1,320__   Amount to be Billed $ __330.—__

Treasurer's Bill No. __A61729__

FORM 18-5

"as advertised in" posters supplied by consumer magazines.

Cooperative Advertising

Retail advertising for which the costs are shared by the store and the producer of the merchandise on terms agreed to by both is called cooperative advertising. (See Form 18-5.) The practice offers advantages to both parties, but it also presents some problems or opportunities for abuse.

Advantages of Cooperative Advertising
Among the advantages to the fashion merchant of cooperative advertising are the following:

- More money is made available for advertising. Cooperative money is usually considered to be in addition to whatever amount the store has budgeted from its own funds for promotion.
- Additional advertising funds may enhance the impact of the store's advertising in two ways. First, larger or more frequent ads may be placed, thus increasing the impact of the store's name upon the public. Second, the additional space purchased with co-op money may help the store to qualify for a lower cost rate on all its advertising and thus be able to buy more space for the same cost. Newspapers usually give progressively lower rates as the total linage purchased increases.
- Cooperation from the producer in other respects is more certain, once he has invested funds of his own in the store's advertising. Prompt deliveries, assistance in training the selling staff, and other services are more likely to be available.
- If the advertised brand, or line, or item is new to the area, the producer shares introductory promotion costs with the store and thus shares the initial risk.

From the producer's point of view, the benefits include the following:

- The producer's money buys more advertising space than if the ad was placed directly. The retailer, as a consistent buyer of space, commands lower rates than a producer could earn with occasional advertising.
- The prestige of the store's name reinforces on a local basis the acceptance an item may enjoy on a regional or national basis—a fact especially valuable to lines or brands being introduced in a new area.
- The retailer, having invested funds in advertising the merchandise, can be more readily counted upon to carry adequate stocks, provide window and departmental displays, and brief the salespeople on the selling points of the goods.
- In large cities, where the manufacturer's line may be sold also through small neighborhood stores, the impact of a major store's advertising helps the sale of the line in the smaller stores as well.

Disadvantages of Cooperative Advertising
From the store's point of view, the major drawback in cooperative advertising is that buyers have been known to "buy" advertising rather than merchandise. Because of limited advertising funds and their own eagerness to see their departments promoted, some buyers pass up good merchandise for which there is little or no cooperative money available in order to buy what may turn out to be less desirable styles but for which there are cooperative advertising funds. This practice may result in poor assortments.

From the standpoint of the vendor, a major drawback of cooperative advertising is the danger of inadvertently discriminating against some customers in favor of others. Participation in the advertising of a well-known store that uses a big metropolitan daily may be worth much more to a vendor than participation in the advertising of a small shop that uses only a local suburban weekly, and yet, under the provisions of the Robinson-Patman Act (a section of the antitrust laws), a producer in such a situation might seem to be granting discriminatory allowances to the larger store. Rather than leave themselves open to charges of making offers for which only large stores can qualify, a number of apparel firms have simply abandoned cooperative advertising entirely.

Miscellaneous Fashion Media

Fashion retailers use a variety of media other than newspapers to promote sales. Among them are radio, television, direct mail, telephone solicitation, and magazines. The decision as to when and if any of these is to be used in behalf of a specific department's merchandise generally rests with the store's sales promotion manager. Buyers, however, familiarize themselves with the possibilities inherent in each medium, so that they can request those they consider useful. Conversely, in theory, buyers could conceivably ask to be excused from participating in promotional efforts involving some medium they consider inappropriate to their merchandise. In practice, however, the retail buyer who declines promotional efforts of any kind or in any medium approved by the store is rare or nonexistent.

Radio For certain segments of the population, radio advertising of fashion merchandise supplements or substitutes for newspaper space. The teenager's transistor radio and the car radio of the employed adult who drives to work make the medium useful for reaching these groups. Stores that cater to teenagers have found that radio is almost indispensable as an advertising medium, since these young customers are exposed to radio far more than to newspapers. Each store, each area, each clientele, presents a different situation so far as communications are concerned. Where radio reaches customers more effectively than newsprint, stores use it. There is no universal rule.

Television Television, and particularly color television, seems an ideal medium for showing fashion merchandise to the consumer. Fashion merchants, however, have been slow to use it. Until recent years, costs have been high, and production problems have been difficult. Lacking the expertise to

use the new medium effectively, many retailers tried it and then dropped it as unprofitable. There were exceptions, nevertheless. Burdine's of Miami, for instance, was proficient at television fashion shows by 1963, and was chosen in that year to stage a half-hour musical presentation of cotton fashions in conjunction with the National Cotton Council.

By the 1970s, several factors had brought a number of major retailers and many small merchants into TV advertising. The cost of prime time had become less expensive in relation to the rising costs of newspaper space; there was an increasing number of firms specializing in producing television shows and commercials for buyers of broadcast time; the pulling power of television was constantly being demonstrated to retailers by the broadcasting systems. Stores in areas served only by weekly newspapers found television a means of reaching their customers more frequently. Stores in large cities found that television enhanced the pulling power of their print advertising and helped them tell the fashion story more effectively. By 1969, several prominent retailers were committed to television, and the use of the medium was sufficiently common among retailers in general for the National Retail Merchants Association and the Television Bureau of Advertising to establish an annual competition for the best television commercials telecast by retailers. By the mid-1970s, many major department stores were routinely scheduling television spot advertising on a local basis, and the national chains, such as Sears, Roebuck & Company and the J. C. Penney Company, were buying prime time on national shows to tell customers around the country about their merchandise offerings.

Direct Mail Advertising sent to the individual consumer via mail lends itself readily to fashion promotion purposes. Small stores have used this medium in such simple forms as postcard announcements of sales or postcard illustrations of featured apparel. Both large and small stores use the colorfully printed statement enclosures provided by garment and accessories producers to show items in current assortments. Large stores, in fact, are offered so many such inserts that they turn away more than they use.

The effectiveness of the direct-mail medium is difficult for most stores to pinpoint, since customer response may take the form of a telephone order or a personal visit to the store. Occasionally, stores will advertise an item by direct mail only, to measure the medium's pulling power, but this procedure is not common practice.

Catalogs issued by department and specialty stores at Christmas and for back-to-school merchandise are familiar to everyone. The explosion of the specialty catalog has been one of the greatest sales promotion developments of all time. It is estimated that in 1975, there were some 1,500 catalogs devoted exclusively to clothing and accessories and some 3,000 for other types of merchandise.

Direct mail is a favorite medium for selling bridal fashions. Invitations to engaged women urge them to visit the bridal salon for advice on wedding plans and to select clothes for the wedding party.

A special form of direct mail is the personal note from a salesperson or specialty shop owner to individual customers to inform them of new styles and invite them to visit the store.

Mail-Order The use of a mail-order coupon in newspaper advertising is another way for stores to sell certain types of apparel and accessories. Fashion items that lend themselves especially well to such treatment are those which do not require trying on, such as some intimate apparel, classic blouses, hosiery, and handbags. The Sunday newspaper is a favorite medium for such coupon advertising. Customers are at home, the store may be closed, but pen, envelope, and postage stamp are almost always at hand.

Telephone Solicitation Department and large specialty stores use the telephone constantly to receive orders from customers, but they are cautious in using it to solicit sales. In most communities, solicitors for everything from carpet cleaning to calisthenics classes have overused the telephone to

The telephone order department in any large store is supplied with copies of current ads and recent catalogs for reference when taking customers' phone orders.
Sears, Roebuck & Company

such an extent that the fashion stores tend to avoid it. Usually the only kind of fashion promotion done by telephone is by salespeople who call a customer who knows and relies upon them. The risks of arousing resentment through indiscriminate calls are too great for most fashion retailers.

Magazines Retailers are generally best served by local advertising media, but there are occasions when they seek to augment their fashion prestige by placing ads in consumer magazines with national circulation. Preferred for this purpose are fashion publications, brides' magazines, and national magazines of general interest. Such advertising is rarely expected to sell the fashion item shown, although sales may well occur. Its purpose is to emphasize that the retailer's fashion message is sufficiently important to be carried in the pages of a publication whose fashion authority is nationally recognized. This prestige advertising is intended to emphasize the store's image: as a place to buy one-of-a-kind jewels, as a salon for the latest in high fashion apparel, as a headquarters for travel clothes and accessories, or whatever the case may be.

The merchandise selected for such treatment must be carefully chosen because of the length of time that elapses between the magazine's closing date (when all copy and illustrations must be in the hands of a publication) and its date of issue (when the magazine reaches the newsstands or the mailboxes of its subscribers). Apparel or accessories that are advertised in such magazines are either styles typifying incoming trends or timeless classics.

The impact of such advertising is that the shop or store, regardless of where it is located, is on a par with the country's best in fashion authority and desirable fashion assortments.

FASHION DISPLAY

A method of sales promotion widely used by all retailers of fashion is *display,* the impersonal, visual presentation of merchandise.

Unlike advertising, display has the advantage of addressing itself to customers when they are physically present inside or directly outside the store. It speaks to them when they are in, or almost in, a buying situation; hopefully, it encourages them to ask about and perhaps buy the merchandise displayed. The customers at whom display is aimed have already made the preliminary moves of leaving their home or place of business and approaching the store. Whether they are consciously on a buying errand, consciously examining what the stores are showing, or whether they are just moving along and idly watching displays, they are already on the retail scene. Effective display can make capital out of that proximity, arouse a buying impulse, and cause a sale to occur.

Window displays are intended to entice cus-

tomers into the store, and interior displays are intended to guide customers to specific departments and interest them in specific merchandise.

Window Display

To a fashion retailer, a store window is useful for selling merchandise, promoting an idea, or publicizing the store as a place to patronize. Its primary function, in one of retailing's puns, is "to make the passer buy." For this purpose it must be arresting and as dramatic as it can afford to be in the context of the store personality and the merchandise involved. Older stores were constructed with many display windows at street level. Newer, free-standing stores may have only a few or no windows at all. Stores in modern regional shopping malls have no separate display windows; instead, customers are presented with a sweeping view of an entire selling floor as they approach a store's entrance.

Fashion windows in stores that have street-level display windows are planned many months in advance, usually when storewide promotional plans are being drawn up. At that time, sales promotion and merchandising executives determine what looks, colors, and other fashion features they wish to promote during the coming season. The display department then draws up a seasonal calendar, based on the storewide promotional plan, indicating the dates on which specific themes and merchandise are to be featured and the number and location of windows assigned to carry selected messages. Departments compete for window space on the basis of how well their merchandise assortments convey the messages or themes the store has elected to promote during a given season.

Windows are rarely assigned to certain departments on a regular basis, although older stores, with many display windows, often allot certain banks of windows to certain store divisions on a fairly regular basis. For example, windows featuring ready-to-wear and accessories are usually to be found flanking the main entrance to a store because of the general interest of customers in these types of merchandise. Household textiles and home furnishings, on the other hand, are often displayed in window areas where there is less traffic. During special sales events, such as white sales, household textiles may be allotted windows in the areas of higher traffic as part of the store's promotional efforts.

As in the case of newspaper advertising, the store may require from the buyer a form stating what is to go into each window assigned to that department and what signs are to be used with the merchandise. If related items from other departments are used, the buyer or assistant may have the responsibility of selecting and signing for such items and seeing that they are eventually returned to the lending departments. Some stores have display coordinators who are responsible for securing merchandise to be used in displays.

Windows, like ads, are not always used for direct selling. They may be used to set the mood of a season, as are some of the merchandise-free windows that large stores install for Christmas. Some of the most famous of these are the banks of Fifth Avenue windows of Lord & Taylor and B. Altman & Company each December that usually are devoted to animated Christmas scenes. Windows that show Santa Claus bringing gifts or families opening packages on Christmas morning are quite commonly used by large stores during this period of the year. Rather than suggesting specific purchases, these windows remind customers that it is a gift-giving season and that the store is a place to buy gifts.

Types of Windows   Window displays are designed to convey one of several different kinds of messages to the customer. Window displays featuring fashion merchandise may be designed to show seasonal trends in fashion colors or looks, or to show how to wear specific fashion merchandise to achieve a particular "look," or simply to show what the store has available at what price.

Fashion Messages   Windows are an excellent medium for conveying a fashion message. They may be used to dramatize a new color, for example, by showing garments and accessories in a particular springtime yellow, or an autumn brown, or a bold print in which a certain color predominates. They can dramatize a new look, or skirt length, or season of the year.

Because the window should arouse interest and stimulate customers to refresh their wardrobes, the actual styles selected for display are usually more extreme and in earlier stages of their fashion cycle than much of the assortment inside the store. If the window merchandise is not too different from what already hangs in customers' closets, it cannot be stimulating. Arresting qualities are essential.

A familiar retail summary of this philosophy is, "Show royal blue; sell navy." The royal blue catches the customers' eye, but once inside the store, they buy their familiar, wearable navy. If navy alone had been in the window, their eyes might have glanced off it without receiving the message that it was time to buy some new spring clothes.

How-to-wear-it Windows   Windows are used also to tell customers how to wear or use fashion merchandise. The effective ones answer the shopper's unspoken question about how to wear a new fashion or what to wear with it. A window that shows a mannequin dressed in a new costume with hat, hosiery, shoes, and handbag makes it easier for customers to visualize themselves in the clothes than the window that presents merely one or two components of the current look. An excellent example was afforded by the long scarfs that came into fashion in 1974 and 1975, when the bulky top began to become fashionable. If displayed by themselves, the long scarfs had little appeal. But when shown on mannequins in the variety of ways they could be worn, such as over-the-head coverings or draped twice around the neck and shoulders, the window displays showed that scarfs played an important part in achieving the new bulky look.

A similar technique is used when new colors or color combinations are introduced. When "earth shades" became popular, stores devoted windows to examples of these shades, alone or in combination, in subdued as well as dramatic ways. Cus-

*Window displays may serve a variety of purposes. They may set the mood
of a season, as does the Christmas window, or tell a fashion story, as does
the window of the Honolulu unit of Woolworth's.*

Harzfeld's, Kansas City, Mo.; F. W. Woolworth Co., Irving Rosen, photography tomers, whatever their lifestyles or fashion interests, could relate to these colors not only because they were fashion news but because they had environmental overtones. Such window displays help customers translate a piece of fashion news into a personal interest in buying.

Direct-sell Windows   Window displays that aggressively try to make a sale also have an important function in promoting fashion merchandise. Not all customers are concerned with newness and glamour; most are concerned with price as well, particularly in times of economic stress. Thus many customers are drawn by the windows of less expensive stores that feature poster-size announcements saying that the dresses are "two for $20" or that any hat in the window is $7. Also for the price-conscious customer are the windows that present a veritable cornucopia of items: many kinds, many classifications, arranged with only the thought in mind of showing as much as possible in a small space. Display people who do windows for neighborhood shops of modest size are experts at such techniques; so are the display staffs of shoe, hosiery, and general merchandise chains.

The fact that windows of this type rarely convey fashion excitement should not in any way belittle their importance in the promotion of fashion merchandise. Vast quantities of apparel and accessories are sold as a result of such windows. These windows are the workhorses of fashion window display, and the merchandise they promote, even though it may be at or past the peak of its cycle, constitutes a substantial share of the total volume of fashion goods sold at retail.

Principles of Good Window Display   A window display is a work of art, created with merchandise and fixtures instead of paint or ink or clay. This is why window displays are usually the work of professionals who know the basic elements of art and how to use those elements to achieve specific artistic effects. However, there are also some principles completely divorced from artistic principles to which window displays, if they are to be effective, must adhere.

First, a window display should feature merchandise that is both timely and in current demand. Fashion merchants pick the newest and most dramatic items and "looks" in their fashion assortments to feature in their window displays. For the higher-priced merchant, these are the eye-catchers, the styles people have already seen in the fashion news but have not yet had a chance to examine in a store's assortment. For the more moderate-priced merchant, these would be the styles that have gained fairly wide acceptance but are still showing strong popularity.

Next, both the number of items shown and the way they are presented should reflect the fashion image of the store. Stores with higher-priced lines will often put only a single coordinated look or even only a single item in a window. That store will use a minimum of props, but both those props and the background decoration will carry out the "exclusivity" or "prestige" theme. A store with moderate-priced lines, however, will put a number of items in each window to show that they carry a wide assortment of currently popular styles.

Perhaps most important, the items chosen for window displays should be backed by adequate stock on the selling floor. If customers are drawn into a store by seeing an item in a window display, then those customers expect to find in the store's stock a good selection of that item. In higher-priced fashion stores, the assortment on the selling floor does not have to contain a large number of the exact item that is in the window display, but it should contain a reasonable number of items that are similar in their styling and fashion appeal. In more moderate-priced stores, the emphasis should be on having the featured item in a wide variety of styles, sizes, and colors.

Interior Display

Once customers have entered a store, the chances of converting their browsing activities into buying impulses can be enhanced by interior displays.

These may be true point-of-sale efforts at the spot where the goods are sold, or they may be displays in such places as overhead ledges, corners, platforms, or entrances to departments. Often they repeat a theme expressed in windows and once again drive home the message, whether it be the advent of a new season or the opportunity to buy a bargain. In large stores, such displays are again the work of professionals on the display staff.

Within a department, however, displays of fashion merchandise are usually the responsibility of buyers, their assistants, or the salespeople. In-

This interior display, which dominates the entire store, is a lavish floral tribute to spring.
Hess's Department Store, Allentown, Pa.

genuity, knowledge of the merchandise, and proximity to the point of sale make up for the absence of the professional's touch.

Types of Interior Displays There are several basic types of interior displays. These include displays that present a coordinated look, displays that suggest merchandise for a specific end use, displays that present a single item or an assortment of items, and displays arranged for easy selection.

Vignettes A product or group of products shown in use is a *vignette*. A typical vignette might display a mannequin in a nightgown and matching peignoir, wearing slippers of appropriate style and color, and seated on a boudoir chair to complete the suggestion of a woman preparing for bed. The impact of such a display at the entrance to a department is often enough to draw passing customers to its counters or racks.

Item Displays A single garment or accessory may be featured in an *item display*. The display may be created by putting one piece on a form, or by showing several versions of a style on a T-stand, a shoulder bag in several sizes, for instance, or a style of body shirts in several colors.

Assortment Displays Showing, identifying, and pricing one of each of the styles currently in a section of stock is an *assortment display*. Such a display is generally used for basic items and permits the customer to make at least a tentative selection while waiting to be served. A classic example is the usual wall display of white shirts behind a men's furnishings counter. The windows of shoe chains follow the same pattern, and their interior displays of slippers, boots, or shoes are also of this type. Scarf departments use assortment display when they fan out their folded stock of each price and type, permitting customers to see the entire color range at a glance.

Self-selection Racks Although they are not usually thought of as such, self-selection racks are definitely a type of departmental display. In order to emphasize the breadth of the color assortment, several garments, each in a different color, may be displayed on a rack or T-stand. To feature mix-match possibilities, as in sportswear separates, all of a style, pattern, or color may be grouped in one area. The first arrangement says, "Choose from our rainbow assortment." The second says, "See how many components we offer in each color." If the rack is merely a hodge-podge, the implication is that the assortment is broken or unplanned, as on a clearance rack. The buyer, within the framework of store policy, decides which message should be conveyed in departmental displays and instructs stock and sales personnel accordingly.

Other Types of Displays Interior display utilizes many additional small but effective aids: a counter card, extolling the virtues of the goods; a sign atop a rack of clothes, stressing a major selling point; a garment laid open across a lighted, glass-topped counter to emphasize its sheerness and perfection of weave; a sample article attached to a rack of packaged articles to invite the customer's examination. The little things that are done inside the store, as well as the big, dramatic windows, are all part of the effort to promote the sale of fashion merchandise by means of display.

Vendor Aids

Producers of fashion merchandise, from coats to cosmetics, have shown themselves keenly aware of the selling power of good retail display. Eager to help stores harness this effective tool in behalf of their merchandise, many vendors in the fashion business develop dealer aids, which they supply free or at modest cost to stores. Vendors may also provide speakers and demonstrators, to create a live display.

Counter and Window Cards Intended to be used in windows, on counters, or with interior displays of the vendor's merchandise, counter and window cards usually name the brand and recite the selling points of the item or brand. Cards of the "as advertised in" variety bear a mounted reprint of the producer's advertisement in the publication concerned. Smaller retailers are generally likely to use these to supplement their limited display facilities. Larger stores are likely to have a policy against the use of such cards, preferring that all announcements be made in their own sign shop and in the store's own style.

Forms and Fixtures   To facilitate the display of specific merchandise, resources sometimes offer stores free or inexpensive forms and fixtures on which to display their merchandise. This equipment often bears the brand name of the fashion producer who supplies it. Familiar examples are the bust and torso forms provided by makers of women's foundation garments and the self-selection racks in which packaged bras, gloves, or pantyhose are offered for sale.

The development of its own self-selection fixtures is a process requiring a large investment in research and design that only a large store is willing or able to make. Smaller stores, however, do not have capital available for such an investment. Instead, they may willingly use the forms and fixtures supplied by vendors. Vendors whose products are sold through many hundreds of stores, can profitably underwrite such an investment.

The fixtures developed by vendors generally prove to be very effective in displaying the merchandise, highlighting its sales appeal, and providing ample space for an orderly supply of stock on the selling floor. Some of these fixtures are almost boutiques in themselves, notably those developed for branded lines of personal leather goods, shirts, and related articles.

The fashion industries, although they are now quite active in this area, by no means pioneered the use of fixtures. That effort was made in earlier years by such industries as greeting card publishing, notions, and some branches of the housewares field. By the mid-1950s, however, prepackaging and self-selection had been adopted in many areas of the apparel and accessories fields, and by the mid-1970s, such selling techniques had become a way of life in retail stores.

Demonstrations and Exhibits   To help consumers understand the virtues of new materials, vendors may sometimes provide exhibits or demonstrations on retail selling floors. Experience has proved this approach an excellent one for getting the message across to the consuming public, for it brings out and answers questions that may be on the consumer's mind and promotes the sale of merchandise embodying the new idea.

Speakers and exhibit material supplied by vendors have been particularly useful to retail stores in explaining new fibers, fabrics, and finishes. When the first man-made fibers were developed for textile use, for example, some producers sent representatives into the stores to explain how their fibers were made and how they should be handled. Wash-and-wear apparel, stretch fabrics, durable press, and other fabric developments have also inspired store demonstrations organized by producers. So, too, have complexion care treatments, false eyelashes, new types of makeup, hair treatments, and wigs.

Recurring problems, such as the selection and packing of travel wardrobes, also prompt vendors to develop talks and demonstrations for use in retail stores. The retail selling floor provides an auditorium in which many fashion vendors are eager for a chance to perform.

MERCHANDISING VOCABULARY

Define or briefly explain the following terms:

Sales promotion   Advertising mat
Advertising   Display
Merchandise or promotional advertising   Vignette
Prestige of institutional advertising   Item display
Advertising plan   Assortment display
Advertising request

MERCHANDISING REVIEW

1. What activities are included in the term "sales promotion"? Describe the organizational structure of a large store's sales promotion division.
2. Discuss (a) how master storewide sales promotion plans and budgets are developed; (b) how each department of the sales promotion division prepares its plans; (c) why it is necessary to coordinate plans and budgets of the departments composing the sales promotion division.
3. What types of advertising media are used by retailers to promote the sale of fashion merchandise? Which type is most widely used, and why?
4. Name at least three sources from which fashion merchants may obtain helpful information in developing their advertising plans. What type of information does each source yield?
5. Discuss a buyer's responsibility in connection with running an ad.
6. What information is usually requested in an Advertising Results form? What purposes are served by this type of report?
7. Discuss the advantages and disadvantages of cooperative advertising.
8. Name at least three forms direct-mail advertising may take. Discuss the effectiveness of each for the advertising of fashion goods.
9. Name three types of window displays and explain the purpose of each. What type of merchandise lend itself best to each type?
10. Identify three types of vendor aids supplied by vendors, either free or at low cost, to stores selling their merchandise. Of what value is each of these to a retail merchant?

MERCHANDISING DIGEST

1. Discuss the following statement from the text and its implication for fashion merchants and buyers: "Goods well bought are half sold."
2. Distinguish between a merchandise or promotional ad and a prestige or institutional ad. What purpose or purposes are served by each? Clip one or more examples of each type of ad from newspapers or magazines and bring them to class for group discussion.
3. Assume you manage a small shop for women's apparel and accessories. What activities might you undertake in promoting the sale of sportswear? Of scarfs? Of handbags?

19
PROMOTING FASHIONS: PUBLICITY AND PERSONAL SELLING

Advertising and display by no means exhaust the list of tools available to fashion merchants in promoting the sale of merchandise. There are two other tools that play especially important roles: publicity and personal selling.

Publicity, like advertising, attempts to capture consumers' interest as they read their papers, watch or listen to TV or radio broadcasts, or even as they talk with friends and neighbors. Personal selling, like display, makes contact with them when they are already in a shopping situation. Publicity speaks to them as advertising does, in their capacity as consumers. Personal selling, unlike the other tools of sales promotion, is concerned with satisfying their individual wants and preferences.

Different as each tool is from the other, both publicity and personal selling are potent forces in promoting the sale of fashion merchandise.

FASHION PUBLICITY

The free and voluntary mention of a firm, brand, product, or person, in some form of media is *publicity*. Most publicity appears in print or broadcast media, although it may also be transmitted by word of mouth. The purpose of fashion publicity is to help in promoting the sale of fashion merchandise by making a trend, style, producer, retailer, or other facet of the fashion business better known to the public.

Because publicity is not purchased but is given free by the medium concerned, the medium, not the recipient of the publicity, determines how much time or space is to be allocated and what words or pictures are to be used. This is the essential difference between publicity and advertising, for the recipient of publicity does not have the privilege of saying when, where, and how the message will be disseminated, nor even be sure that it will be disseminated at all. The merchants or vendors who are the source of publicity information merely make the facts available to various media and suggest, in some cases, how those facts should be presented. They do have the privilege, however, of specifying a *release date* (a date before which an announcement is not to be made), even though they may have given such information to the news media weeks in advance of that release date.

The way in which fashion news is originated by designers, vendors, and wearers of fashion merchandise has been discussed in earlier chapters. This chapter is concerned with the efforts of retailers to publicize fashion in general and their own fashion assortments in particular.

Methods of Obtaining Publicity

Retailers call attention to newsworthy developments within their stores or actually create news by causing something newsworthy to happen, such as fashion shows or personal appearances of celebrities. Stores provide selected media with information about such events in hopes they will be of potential interest to the media's audiences. In turn, these media may then devote space or time to telling their readers or listeners about such happenings.

In their attempts to gain publicity, retailers make news available promptly and, preferably, in advance of the expected event. In addition, they refrain from flooding media with information that is not really newsworthy, for to overdo the publicity effort may cause print and broadcast editors to be less cooperative.

Following are several methods of passing fashion news along to print or broadcast media.

Press Releases Retailers may issue press releases before or after such newsworthy events as a visit to the store by a designer, the opening of a new department, or the introduction of a new fashion development. A *press release* is a written statement of news that has occurred or is about to occur, specifying the source of the information and the date after which its use is permissible. Press releases may originate with the store or may be provided to the merchant by vendors whose products are involved.

Photographs Vendors frequently send directly to newspaper fashion or women's page editors glossy photographs of a model dressed in one of the styles in the vendor's line. Attached to each of these glossies is a short description of the style, the fabric in which it is made, the color and sizes in which it is available, occasionally some information about the designer, and often the local store or stores where that particular style may be found. Reproduction of such a photograph, accompanied by its description, fashion importance, and where it may be purchased locally, often results in favorable publicity for both the vendor and the local store customers of that vendor. Unfavorable publicity, however, may result if an editor does not check with the credited local store or stores as to the actual availability of the style and its selling price before printing or broadcasting the related publicity. No customer enjoys making a trip to a store and not finding the publicized style in stock, or finding it in stock but at a higher price than stated in the publicity.

Telephone Calls Sometimes retailers may alert news media to happenings with only a telephone call. If the store is staging a fashion show to raise funds for charity, a call to the editor of the fashion or women's page of the local newspaper may bring a photographer and a reporter to the show.

Fashion Consultations Fashion merchants often make their expertise available to the media to encourage accurate and stimulating publicity for their store. Retailers do this by welcoming questions on fashion subjects from the press and answering them as completely as possible, thus encouraging editors to check with them on the accuracy and completeness of fashion news from other sources. Merchants can also achieve some of the same results by being available to speak on fashion subjects before school or consumer groups. In each case, they help stimulate the public's fashion interest in general and in the fashion assortments of the store the merchant represents.

Media Used

Retail merchants look to both print media and broadcast media when seeking fashion publicity. Most retailers find that the publicity given their activities by local newspapers engenders greater consumer interest than any other media they use. Magazine publicity can be of considerable value, but often lacks the newsy quality and local impact of newspaper coverage. Radio and television publicity also can be very useful, but again, the approach may not be as localized as newspaper publicity—and no one can preserve radio or television publicity for future reference.

Newspapers As a consistent user of advertising space in local newspapers, a retailer often gets preferential treatment in obtaining publicity. For maximum effect from publicity, the retailer selects the paper that seems most likely to reach the readers who will be interested in the particular publicity message. Which paper appeals to which group of readers is something the retailer already will have learned in the course of selecting media for advertising.

Newspapers are also generally more receptive to store requests for publicity than are other media because of the frequency of their publication. Fashion editors and women's page editors have daily pages to fill and Sunday features to prepare, and usually welcome being informed about store events that have local news value.

The local fashion publicity efforts of retail merchants gain strength from such industry efforts as the semiannual Press Week showings in New York and Los Angeles, described in Chapter 7. If fashion editors or women's page editors of newspapers have attended either or both events, they have seen the lines of the sponsoring vendors well in advance of their presentation to the public by retail stores. They have brought back with them the vendors' press releases and photographs of styles the individual vendors consider the most prophetic. Such editors are not only conversant with fashion trends as a result of their Press Week experience, but have also become somewhat personally involved in helping these trends develop on their local scenes. With this background and this attitude, they are more receptive than they might otherwise be to the fashion publicity efforts of local merchants.

Magazines Fashion and consumer magazines make a practice of showing fashions editorially and of mentioning one or more stores as sources for purchasing that merchandise. These mentions, discussed in Chapter 17, are known as editorial credits. The decisions to offer an editorial credit to a store rests with the publication. The decision to accept or decline the credit is made by the store, which takes the following factors into consideration:

- The value to be derived in terms of publicity among its customers and in the market of accepting a credit in the periodical concerned. Not every periodical has equal value in these respects.

- The confidence the store places in the style that is being considered for credit. If the sales potential of a style does not warrant purchasing, displaying, and promoting it on its own merits, a store will undoubtedly decline the credit. The store may still carry the style, but simply prefer not to give it the merchandising and promotional emphasis that are implied with the acceptance of a credit.

- The crediting of other stores. Some merchants prefer not to accept a credit if other stores also are mentioned, or if the other stores mentioned are of an appreciably different type from their own.

- The importance of the vendor to the store. A store may accept a credit as a means of strengthening a relationship with a new vendor. Conversely, it may decline a credit rather than share editorial mention with a resource not otherwise important to it.

- The number of concurrent credits the store may have already accepted in other publications. Too many credits appearing at approximately the same time can upset the store's own assortment and promotion plans.

Accepted and acted upon, an editorial mention publicizes the store and its fashion merchandise among readers of the magazine who are within its trading area. Properly managed, such credits enhance the prestige of both periodical and retailer among consumers and producers.

Advertising credits are also available in most magazines. They are mentions of one or more store names, in connection with the advertisement of a vendor, as being retail sources for the merchandise advertised. Such an ad might also include the names of fiber and fabric sources or other appropriate producers whose products contributed to the featured item of merchandise. The factors a store considers in accepting or rejecting such a credit are much the same as those considered in the case of editorial credits.

Radio and Television A retailer who is a consistent user of radio and television advertising sometimes enjoys preferential treatment in obtaining broadcast fashion publicity from local stations, just as is the case with newspapers. And just as each newspaper has special appeal to certain groups of readers, so does each radio and television program or station have special appeal to more or less clearly defined groups of listeners.

Retailers become familiar with the nature of such specialization through observing the results their own advertising have achieved. They augment what they have learned from their own experience by studying the research material prepared by each broadcast medium to indicate the number and kind of people who tune in to its programs. Then, to achieve maximum benefit from fashion publicity placed with broadcast media, fashion retailers seek to obtain mentions from those stations and programs whose listeners they believe will be most responsive to their message.

Sources of Fashion Publicity Material

Fashion publicity material may, and often does, emanate from a wide variety of sources. Chief among such sources is a store's fashion coordinator or ranking fashion authority. Other sources include fashion shows, visits to stores by fashion designers and vendors or their representatives, the efforts of vendors themselves, and the efforts of trade associations or the public relations or publicity agents for such associations.

The Fashion Coordinator In any retail organization, much of the fashion publicity obtained is a result of the fashion coordinator's activities. The *fashion coordinator* is the store's ranking fashion authority. The coordinator's duties, which are discussed in detail in the next chapter, include such publicity-generating activities as staging fashion shows, in or out of the store, and arranging clinics or demonstrations at which visiting designers or vendor representatives will speak. The coordi-

nator may also represent the store as a speaker on fashion before consumer or business groups in the community.

Fashion Shows Whether the retailer's store is a high fashion New York salon or a small shop on Main Street, there is nothing that tells the fashion story to customers quite so clearly and excitingly as does a fashion show. The usual presentation employs models, music, and a commentator, making it possible for the audience to see and to hear about fashion merchandise. Simpler ways of running shows are possible, of course, and some very effective presentations have been done by commentators who simply hold up each item in turn as it is being discussed. The glamour treatment, however, is more likely to draw larger audiences and win more publicity, and this method is the one stores usually like to use.

Such fashion shows may be held to benefit a local charity or to highlight the store's own assortments. In the former case, admission is charged and the proceeds are turned over to a designated charitable organization. In the latter case, admission is free and may be open either to the general public or only to those who have been invited to come.

Fashion shows may be held on a selling floor or in the restaurant or auditorium within the store, or they may be held outside the store, according to the occasion and the facilities required. Some shows feature the fashions of a single vendor or designer; in others the styles of several vendors are modeled. Shows may be general in nature, appealing to a cross section of the store's customers, or planned for specialized audiences, such as teenagers, college or career men or women, prospective brides, expectant mothers, or people with special interest in travel or sports.

Ways in which retailers assemble audiences for these shows are as varied as the kinds of shows they stage. If the event is on behalf of a charity, the sponsoring organization sells the tickets and usually offers the services of some of its members as models. If the event is geared to a relatively

*The formal fashion show is one of the most exciting
and dramatic ways to promote fashion.*
The Fashion Group, Inc.

small, special-interest group, such as brides or expectant mothers, personal invitations may be mailed out. For across-the-board audiences, announcements may be placed in the store's advertising, in its windows or in its elevators, or on radio broadcasts, inviting the attendance of all interested persons.

Cooperation in the staging of a fashion show may be provided by a consumer publication, a merchandise vendor, a fiber or fabric producer, or any other organization with a reason to help the retailer put across a fashion message.

Publicity is achieved by word-of-mouth and by informing the press and broadcast media, through direct contact or through press releases, about an upcoming event and why it is being undertaken. Occasionally fashion shows are so original in some aspect that the publicity lingers on long after the fashions themselves have gone. Such has been the case in recent years when a New York department store staged career fashion shows in a nearby park or when models displayed the fashions of a famous New York specialty store on moving escalators in a newly opened suburban branch of that store.

Visits from Designers or Vendors A visit from a designer, a vendor, or their representatives can often help a store earn considerable publicity for itself, for the vendor, and for the particular fashion area involved. Some representatives are capable speakers and appear on local television shows or give press interviews on fashion trends. These fashion authorities may address groups of customers or school groups, or act as commentators for store fashion shows, or hold clinics and act as consultants to individual customers.

In periods of economic uncertainty and increased competition, higher-priced vendors or their designers tend to schedule more trunk shows and increase the number of their visits to customer stores in large urban areas throughout the country. A trunk show, as described in Chapter 12, is a presentation by a designer, vendor, or vendor's representative, of samples of the line, held in the store's department featuring that line. The representative brings samples of the complete line to the store, puts on several scheduled showings, and takes special orders from any customers who choose styles, colors, and sizes not in the store's stock. In this way, designers or vendors' representatives have an opportunity to pinpoint regional variations in fashion demand, to get customer reaction to the vendor's overall fashion philosophy, and to more accurately gauge trends in demand from face-to-face customer contact than can be determined within the narrow limits of a design room or in a vendor's showroom.

Advance announcements about trunk shows are made in press releases and store ads. During and after the event, word-of-mouth publicity inevitably grows out of the customers' excitement over the special treatment accorded them. Further opportunities for publicity may be created by hav-

ing models show selected styles informally in the store's tearoom, or by showing the line on models at a special breakfast or luncheon show for the benefit of a local charity. Interviews with the visiting vendor or representative may be arranged with print and broadcast media, if the vendor is considered an authority on some special aspect of fashion or is otherwise newsworthy.

Maximum publicity benefits result from such vendor visits if the buyer or merchant who is handling the visit discusses the possibilities at an early date with the store's publicity staff. The publicity executive needs to know why the visitor is newsworthy and can participate productively in press conferences, television interviews, and the like. Arrangements for such supplementary appearances have to be made well in advance, not only with the press but also with the visitor. If a vendor knows, for example, that he will have five or ten minutes on television, he may bring along a special group of unusually photogenic style numbers to show, and possibly one or two highly photogenic models.

Vendor Publicity The fashion publicity efforts of stores are frequently supplemented by the work of the vendors' own publicity staffs. Sometimes the latter channel their publicity efforts through the stores, by making available suggested press releases and glossy photos of the styles they consider important. Sometimes they issue the publicity material directly to the news media, as described above. On occasion, producers may circulate reproductions of magazine pages on which appear either their advertising or editorial mention of their styles, at the same time pointing out the local stores that have received advertising or editorial credits.

When such publicity is channeled through the store, the store's fashion coordinator and publicity staff have the opportunity to evaluate it in terms of their own scheduled promotional efforts.

Trade Groups and Associations Buyers and merchants who keep in close touch with the indus-

Vendors often organize exhibits and clinics for store customers.
Simplicity Pattern Co., Inc.

tries from which they purchase fashion goods are in a good position to coordinate their own store publicity efforts with those of trade associations serving those markets. Such associations frequently release publicity to print and broadcast media on new developments in their particular areas of fashion, and relate these developments to current trends. Some of the fashion industry trade associations have fashion publicists on their staffs or retain the services of public relations firms, such as the one headed by Eleanor Lambert, originator of the New York market's Press Week.

When an industry trade association launches a drive to publicize its fashion message or its merchandise, or both, the buyer or merchant usually receives in the mail suggestions for tying in with such publicity efforts: ideas for press releases, photographs, recommendations for fashion events. If such material is passed along to the store's publicity staff and discussed with them, it often is possible to work out ways to benefit locally from the national publicity efforts of these associations.

FASHION SELLING

Effective use of advertising, display, and publicity brings a customer to the store ready to make a fashion purchase. At this point, a salesperson usually steps into the picture.

Modern retail sales ability is conceived of as a service that helps customers to make satisfactory purchases. Some authorities define it as "the business of helping people to understand their needs and of showing them how those needs can be satisfied through the purchase of merchandise and service."[1] Retailers have their own succinct definition of good sales ability: selling goods that won't come back to customers who will.

Fashion selling requires a more sophisticated type of sales ability than is required by most other consumer goods, since fashion decisions center around personal taste rather than more readily measured qualities such as durability and utility. Fashion salespeople need all the qualities that are required for success in selling goods of other types, but in addition, they need to be able to point out with confidence the fashion features of the merchandise they are selling and the personal satisfactions to be gained from ownership of those goods. By responding quickly and surely to their customers' needs and preferences, fashion salespeople should be able to help each customer make purchases that are fashion-right, becoming, and appropriate for their purposes.

Techniques of Selling Fashions

Modern retailers have a wide range of selling techniques at their command. The choice of the techniques or methods used is made by store management, depending upon the type of goods, the degree of fashion leadership the store or department wishes to assert, the price lines of the merchandise, the shopping preferences of the store's customers, and any other relevant factors.

Among the most commonly employed techniques are personal selling, simplified selling, and mail and telephone selling.

Personal Selling In this selling method, a salesperson actively assists customers in choosing articles suited to their individual taste and needs, and seeks to do this in such a way that the customers will return to the store or department for future purchases. The goodwill engendered by pleasing customers and serving their interests, by helping them identify and satisfy their wants, is the foundation upon which fashion stores or departments build continued patronage.

Salon Selling The most exacting type of personal selling is *salon selling*. It is most frequently used in stores or departments that offer higher-priced styles in the introductory or early rise stages of their fashion cycles. In salon selling, little or no stock is exposed to customers' view except that which is

brought out for inspection by the salesperson. Close rapport is needed between customer and salesperson if this type of selling is to be successful. An advantage of this method is that, once a mutual understanding has been developed, the customer usually comes back to the store to be served by the same salesperson, who understands the customer's wants and how to satisfy them.

Since salon salespeople are apt to develop a personal following of customers who return to them repeatedly and trust their suggestions, many maintain card files on their regular customers, noting merchandise previously purchased, style and color preferences, sizes worn, price lines preferred, and other pertinent personal information. Salespeople then use these files to inform customers about new styles as they arrive in stock and about other fashion developments designed to keep alive the customers' interest in both the store and its fashion assortments. Many specialty stores employ salon selling and encourage salespeople to keep records on their personal followings. Department stores, on the other hand, rarely employ salon selling except in their high fashion departments.

Over-the-counter Selling A less exacting type of personal selling is employed in many fashion departments in both department and specialty stores, as well as occasionally in chain and discount organizations. For over-the-counter selling, selected portions of the stock are kept in glass display cases, often with some merchandise displayed on top of the cases. Most of the stock, however, is kept on shelves or in drawers below and behind the display cases. Sometimes a free-standing "island" or "square" is formed by three or four glass display cases, with the center of the island or square being occupied by departmental stock and a cash register.

In over-the-counter selling, while some merchandise may be available for customers to personally examine, salespeople are needed to take the merchandise out of the display cases, or off the shelves, or out of the drawers so that a customer can inspect it. This type of selling requires that a salesperson be thoroughly familiar with the departmental stock, well aware of the fashion points and importance of each item, and able to speak tactfully but with authority about differences in quality that exist between similar items at different prices.

Over-the-counter selling is the personal selling method most stores prefer for merchandise that is high priced (such as fine jewelry), or which is easily soiled (gloves or better lingerie), or which requires more specialized knowledge of the product (cosmetics and shoes), or which is fragile (fragrances and some types of costume jewelry).

Simplified Selling There has been a significant trend in recent years among mass distributors of fashion goods to employ simplified, less costly selling methods in preference to highly personalized selling service. The trend has its origins in rising costs of labor and other operating expenses, tremendously increased competition, decreasing store loyalty among customers, and the preference among large segments of the shopping public for methods less formal than the traditional types.

Self-selection Selling In *self-selection selling*, merchandise is displayed and arranged so that customers can make at least a preliminary selection without the aid of a salesperson. Open wall racks, T-stands, display shelves, bins, and tables are among the fixtures most commonly used in self-selection departments. Salespeople are available to answer customers' questions about the merchandise, to check for styles, sizes, and colors not on the selling floor, to assist in the fitting room if requested, and to complete the sale once the customer has made a buying decision. This is the most prevalent fashion selling technique today, and it is found in stores and departments handling all types of fashion merchandise, except those at higher price lines, where personal selling usually prevails.

Self-service In *self-service selling*, customers not only make their selection from the goods on display but also bring their purchases to a check-out counter where they make payment and where their purchases are prepared for take-out. Most self-service

operations have stock personnel on the floor to keep the merchandise in order and to check, when requested by customers, for sizes and colors not on display, but there are no salespeople as such to give the customer fashion information and advice.

Self-service is the selling method most favored by discount operations and others whose low prices require holding services to a minimum. Self-service techniques, however, may be employed by stores of the traditional type in some of their fashion departments, particularly those handling prepackaged, brand-name goods, such as pantyhose and brassieres.

Although self-service is usually equated with savings and bargain opportunities, this method of selling fashion is by no means used exclusively for low-priced merchandise, closeouts, and "distress" merchandise. Both medium-priced and high fashion goods have also been sold successfully by this method. Ohrbach's and Alexander's, two discount fashion operations based in New York, make extensive use of self-service. Yet buyers from both these retail organizations visit the domestic and foreign couture showings, as well as accessories and ready-to-wear fashion markets. Both stores have bought couture styles abroad, either for resale as imports or for line-for-line copying. Ohrbach's has been especially successful in attracting women of wealth and distinction (and publicity value) to its showings of couture imports and domestically produced line-for-line copies. These fashion leaders attend an invitation-only preview of the styles which they may buy or order before the goods go on public sale.

Mail and Telephone Selling A store can sell fashion products successfully by mail or telephone only when customers have firm confidence in the store's assortments, in its fashion position, and in its understanding of customer wants and tastes. Readiness on the part of the store to accept returns is essential; returns of goods purchased by mail or telephone are much higher than on goods selected by the customer in person. Since customer returns reduce net sales and indirectly reduce profit, mail and telephone selling is usually restricted to merchandise whose markup is large enough to offset the cost of a high rate of returns. In addition, mail and telephone selling is usually restricted to classic styles and to merchandise that does not involve size and fit. Hosiery, some classifications of intimate apparel, and leisure apparel are typical of the kinds of fashion goods that may be profitably sold by mail or telephone.

Requirements for Success in Fashion Selling

Customers prefer to buy their fashion merchandise from stores whose decor and assortments reflect their own current fashion and taste levels. They also prefer to buy from salespeople who themselves represent these same fashion and taste levels in appearance, manners, speech, and method of presenting the goods.

Selection of the right type of salespeople is important for success in fashion merchandising. Their appearance, their grounding in fashion information, and their approach to their work are of deep concern to the fashion merchant or buyer, for the salesperson is the ultimate and most personal link between the store and the customer.

Personal Qualifications There are certain essential attributes that a buyer or merchant seeks in fashion salespeople. Selling is greatly aided when salespeople have developed such personal qualities as:

- Attractive appearance, scrupulous cleanliness, businesslike dress, careful grooming
- Good manners and good business etiquette
- Animation, alertness, promptness in attention to customers
- Ability to form a quick estimate of customers and their preferences, as well as a sympathetic appreciation of their problems
- Ability to speak well, a pleasing voice, a lively and intelligent expression, clarity of speech, and a knowledge of when to talk and when to listen
- Orderliness in thinking, talking, working; accuracy in handling records, reports, and other paperwork

- A good memory for faces and names
- A friendly, tactful manner and, above all, sincerity[2]

Fashion and Merchandise Knowledge Fashion salespeople need to know not only the fashion points of the merchandise they have been assigned to sell, but also what fashion really is, how it works, and what the current fashion trends are and the direction in which they are going. Those who sell apparel need to be knowledgeable about the fitting of garments and the characteristics of the materials used. Whatever is being sold, salespeople should be able to guide customers in selecting related apparel and accessories, both in their own and in other departments, that will achieve the desired look. Above all, fashion salespeople need an appreciation of the fashion values of merchandise, so that they can state the price of the merchandise with confidence and respect.

Success in fashion selling often depends upon the ability of a salesperson to convey to customers the various intangibles that make up an essential part of the value of fashion goods. Equally important is the ability to understand and sympathize with the problems of individual customers, and to exercise patience and diplomacy in aiding a faltering customer to overcome objections and obstacles to making a favorable buying decision.

It is taken for granted that successful fashion salespeople are thoroughly familiar with all the pertinent facts about the merchandise they are selling: its quality, materials, and so on. A thorough knowledge of merchandise is basic to successful retail selling. Selling fashion goods, with all the intangibles that go to make up their value, presents by far the greatest challenge.

The Individual Approach One of the most important points in selling fashion merchandise is the necessity of individualizing each sale, of avoiding any attempt to handle either the merchandise or the customer in an impersonal or routine way. Probably no other experience in the business world creates so much animosity or ill will as treating someone as just one of the masses rather than as an individual. When that person is a customer, such treatment can mean a lost sale.

In fashion selling, personal taste is an all-important factor in making a buying decision. Success in selling fashion merchandise, therefore, depends upon a salesperson's ability to cater to that personal taste and treat each customer as an individual.

This need to individualize fashion customers is among the major problems confronting retailers of fashion merchandise today. Mass production and mass merchandising have made low prices possible, but often at the expense of the individualization of both merchandise and services offered to customers. The retailer's problem, for which there appears to be no easy solution, is to continue to give customers the attention and service fashion goods require, and yet to cope with rising costs of operation and with profit margins that are being continually narrowed by competition. This is not exclusively a problem of large stores. Even in a tiny shop, the proprietor is hard put to provide individual services to customers and yet find time to perform all the many chores involved in running the business, or else to achieve the profit margin out of which to pay for others to perform these chores.

Training of Fashion Salespeople

Good fashion salespeople can be trained through thoughtful, unending efforts. In order to sell any merchandise well, a salesperson must be well acquainted with the goods, their uses, their selling points, and any special care they may need. In order to sell fashion merchandise well, a salesperson also needs to know the fashion picture as a whole and the significance of those elements that directly concern the merchandise he or she is responsible for selling. For example, to sell the Naive Chemise, the covered-up look, calf-length skirts, and the ruffled petticoats of the mid-1970s, the fashion salesperson needed to understand the nostalgia for the 1950s look that was then popular. Only when salespeople

understand the total fashion look can they explain to customers how its various components are related to one another. And only then can they anticipate the coordination problems each new look presents and help customers solve them, making acceptance of the new styles easier.

Not all salespeople can be expected to be expert fashion consultants, although such a state of affairs would surely be a happy one for the fashion business. But it should be clearly recognized that lack of fashion information and merchandise information on the part of salespeople causes considerable customer dissatisfaction. When salespeople acquire such fashion information, from the buyer, from fashion publications, from employee fashion shows and fashion training bulletins, they are better equipped to serve as consultants to customers. When salespeople radiate assurance and fashion authority, customers buy with more confidence. That is why the late Hector Escabosa, then president of I. Magnin and Company, San Francisco, besought merchants to "pamper, love, and cultivate" fashion salespeople, because "in their effectiveness rests our fate."[3]

Small Stores In small shops, informal training of salespeople goes on in the course of the day-to-day operation of the business. Fashion points of the merchandise are explained to the sales personnel by the buyer or store owner as the goods come into stock. In the relatively small store, that buyer or store owner often is on the selling floor for much of the day and can answer any questions posed by customers and salespeople alike.

Frequently, salespeople in small stores are invited to view lines shown by visiting representatives of the store's resources and to express opinions with respect to the salability of the merchandise. They may be encouraged, moreover, to ask questions and to discuss the merchandise with vendors or representatives. The latter, in turn, may be asked by a store owner or buyer to hold meetings with the sales staff to discuss fashion features of the line each represents. Such a presentation often is made to all salespeople in the store, not only those who sell in the department that handles that vendor's goods. This is because smaller stores are more likely than large ones to ignore departmental barriers and to train their salespeople to sell in all departments, helping the customer to assemble his or her entire outfit—ready-to-wear, innerwear, furnishings, or accessories—to achieve a desired look.

Multiunit Store Organizations In large, departmentalized stores, fashion training is more formalized than it is in small stores. Seasonal fashion reports, in the form of illustrated leaflets or color slides or closed-circuit television shows, are prepared by the store's training department in conjunction with the fashion coordinator and shown to salespeople in all the firm's store units. Buyers, and sometimes merchandise managers, hold meetings for salespeople upon their return from market trips, to report on the fashion trends they observed and to describe the merchandise they have purchased. In each department, the buyer or assistant holds weekly meetings, at which the sales staff is told about scheduled advertising for the upcoming week, the fashion points of the merchandise to be featured in these ads, and anything else that will help them do a more informed, fashion-conscious job of selling.

In chain organizations, the fashion coordinator usually prepares a seasonal summary of fashion trends in both ready-to-wear and accessories. This summary is sent to all stores in the chain at the start of each season. In addition, the central buyers of fashion goods alert the appropriate fashion department managers in the various units of the chain to current fashion developments. The usual medium is a fashion bulletin, which features sketches of items, swatches of the materials in which they come, and detailed descriptions, including colors and sizes available. Still another form of fashion training occurs when new styles are sent by the central buying office of the chain into some or all units for testing purposes, together with pertinent information about the fashion features and selling points of the merchandise.

Employee Fashion Shows One of the most effective devices for briefing a fashion sales staff is the presentation of a special fashion show for them. The employee fashion show may be as formal and elaborate as one staged for customers, or it may be a show taped in the parent store for future viewing in the branches, or it may be casual, using salespeople as models and substituting give-and-take conversation for prepared commentary. In some cases, it may consist simply of fully dressed and accessorized mannequins, displayed with explanatory signs in employee lounges or cafeterias. The basic idea, however, remains the same: to show concretely what lines, colors, or combinations thereof are expected to prove acceptable to the store's customers, and to call attention to points of difference between last year's or last season's styles and those of the new fashion season.

Employee fashion shows in a large store are likely to be planned and carried out by the fashion coordinator or any buyer whose fashion sense and knowledge have the respect of the store staff. Shows are also often carried out, on a less ambitious scale, by buyers of related departments for the benefit of their combined sales forces. A foundations buyer and a lingerie buyer, for example, might use the show technique to explain coordination in intimate apparel and to prepare their staffs to sell in either department, if this should be necessary in order to offer customers the complete coordination package. Similarly, a group of accessories buyers might work with a dress or coat buyer to explain how the new season's scarfs, belts, or jewelry can be combined effectively with new styles and colors in apparel.

Vendor Aids Obviously, it is to the interest of vendors of fashion merchandise to do what they can to maintain a high level of retail salesmanship on behalf of their merchandise. Among the steps they take to assist stores in this area are giving talks, distributing promotional literature, and showing products in use.

Talks to salespeople may be given by the vendors' sales representatives who call upon buyers. Often these talks are given in meetings held before

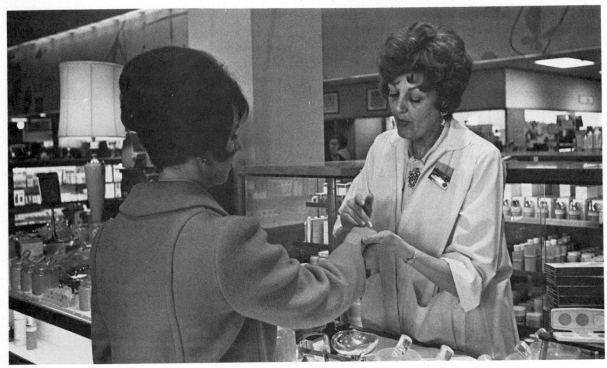

Cosmeticians are experts in over-the-counter selling.

the store opens, but sometimes a vendor may invite the entire sales staff, the buyer, and other store executives to dinner and an evening meeting outside the store. The vendors' presentations made at the latter meetings are often quite elaborate, with charts, slides, film, or modeling.

Sales literature, in the form of brochures, is often given to salespeople for study and reference. Typical literature might be a booklet of a coat manufacturer on how to care for a leather coat or jacket, a fiber or fabric producer's leaflet about a new textile development, a foundation maker's explanation of figure types and how to fit them, or a lingerie or hosiery producer's color chart.

Many vendors train people to instruct salespeople in the use and benefits of their products. Demonstrators visit stores to conduct customer clinics, to assist in the training of salespeople, or both. The representative of a wig firm or a new cosmetic line, a hairstylist, or the instructor sent from a fiber or fabric source to explain the use and care of new products are typical visiting demonstrators. Some demonstrators become regular members of a store's staff. These appear to be in the store's employ but are paid, at least in part, by the producer who trains them to sell and stock a firm's goods. In large stores, representatives of major nationally advertised cosmetic brands are likely to be permanent demonstrators.

Other Sources of Information Retail selling efforts are also of vital interest to others who may be several steps removed from direct contact with consumers. These include fiber sources, both natural and synthetic; leather and plastic processors; fabric finishers; associations dedicated to publicizing the merits of fibers, fabrics, leathers, or other fashion materials; and consumer periodicals. From these outside organizations may come a battery of aids in helping to train salespeople: talks and demonstrations, exhibits, leaflets, and film and slide presentations.

Everyone in the fashion business, from the producers of fibers to the makers of finished goods, has a vested interest in improving the quality of retail selling. The reason is plain: If goods move only sluggishly across retail counters, the supply lines all the way back from retailer to manufacturer to source of raw material become choked with unsold goods. Often the fashion salespeople seem to be the focus of all eyes in the trade: unless they perform their function well, little is sold to customers. Nothing happens in the fashion business until something is sold.

In addition to all those who cooperate in the training of retail salespeople at no charge to the merchant, there are also professionals who sell their training services. Some come into stores, hold rallies, hold workshops on the art of selling, and generally try to stimulate people to sell more goods. Others offer film presentations to achieve the same ends. Although these services are usually concerned with retail salesmanship in general, their impact upon fashion salespeople is as important as upon those in nonfashion merchandise departments.

The Buyer's Responsibility for Selling

In departmentalized stores, the buyer or department manager shares with the store's training department the responsibility for salesmanship in the department. The training staff teaches store systems and procedures to new employees before sending them to the selling floor. Thereafter, unless asked to help, the training department leaves merchandise training of salespeople to the buyer or assistant buyer, intervening only with storewide efforts to increase accuracy, encourage courtesy, discourage unnecessary deliveries, and so on. On-the-job supervision of salespeople, for example, is generally the responsibility of the buyer in small stores or the buyer's assistant in large stores. Although storewide or divisionwide efforts to present current fashion information or teach basic merchandise information may sometimes involve the store's training staff, as

a general rule each buyer is responsible for providing the sales force with merchandise information and with developing good selling techniques.

Merchandise Information As the fashion authority for a department, the buyer is the primary source of information about merchandise carried in the department. The buyer is expected to alert the sales force to current and anticipated trends and to indicate how they will affect sales prospects.

The buyer is also expected to relay to the sales force information about the quality and value of the department's merchandise assortment. Specific selling points of an article should be pointed out, emphasizing to the salespeople the features that might make the merchandise more desirable to individual customers.

Sometimes buyers may also have to teach salespeople how to arrange the merchandise in stock: how to fold slips, how to place dresses on hangers, or how to replace shoes in boxes. Or, they may have to point out to salespeople the most effective way to display merchandise to a customer. For example, they might show how a dress can be held against one's body to achieve a realistic effect, or demonstrate the many ways in which a customer can wear a scarf.

Selling Tips Because of their fashion expertise, buyers can also provide salespeople with effective selling tips. They should supply facts relating to the use and care of merchandise which the sales force can then pass on to customers. Or they may coach salespeople on proper size and fit.

Buyers may also tell salespeople what related items—even from other departments—to suggest in order to enhance customers' enjoyment of a purchase. For instance, they may show how to suggest to a customer that extra belts give variety to a dress or skirt that comes with its own belt. Or, how a dress neckline may seem more flattering if just the right kind of jewelry or scarf is suggested for wear with it. By briefing salespeople on such suggestions, buyers make it easier for them to close the sale on a major item of apparel or on an important

Buyers supply salespeople with merchandise information and display ideas.

Jack J. Morris Associates Advertising, Washington, D.C.

accessory. Moreover, it helps salespeople to impress upon customers the idea that the store is a headquarters for fashion advice.

Training Methods

The salesperson may be the ultimate link between the store and the customer, but it is the buyer's training and supervision that makes that salesperson a strong, productive, profitable link for both store and customer. As more part-time salespeople are employed in fashion departments, more branches are opened, hours are expanded, and buyers have less and less time to devote to the selling floor, the proper training of salespeople becomes an increasing problem. In order to convey needed merchandise information to salespeople, buyers or their assistants employ a variety of techniques.

Departmental Meetings   Each week, usually before the store opens, buyers, their assistants, the department managers, or the sales managers hold departmental meetings to review new or incoming merchandise and upcoming ads, to give pep talks, and to report any departmental problems or changes. Ideally, these are discussion meetings, but often the pressure of time makes them a series of rapid-fire announcements. Some fashion stores, to dispense with formality or avoid the atmosphere of a stereotyped, dull session, use instead a daily five-minute "huddle" just before the opening bell.

Fashion Shows and Reports   In addition to what may be done on a storewide basis, buyers may present fashion shows for their own salespeople to bring out the fashion and selling points of the department's merchandise. They may also provide informal market reports, written or oral, telling their salespeople what they have seen and heard on their latest market trip, what fashion trends appear to be shaping up, and what they have purchased for future delivery.

Miscellaneous   Leaflets, clippings, and other matter related to the department's merchandise may be posted on conveniently located bulletin boards. Commendation for special selling achievements, appropriate announcements, and bits of cartoon humor may also find their way to such bulletin boards.

Other training media may include posted reprints of ads that have been run or preprints of ads that are to be run by the department, and posted or circulated printed material such as fashion magazines and information received from vendors.

REFERENCES

[1] Robinson, Robinson, and Zeiss, *Successful Retail Salesmanship*, 3d ed., p. 2.
[2] Nystrom, *Fashion Merchandising*, pp. 187–188.
[3] Escabosa, "Heartbeat of Retailing," *Readings in Modern Retailing*, p. 395.

MERCHANDISING VOCABULARY

Define or briefly explain the following terms:

Publicity	Fashion coordinator
Release date	Salon selling
Press release	Self-selection
Advertising credit	Self-service

MERCHANDISING REVIEW

1. Differentiate between advertising and publicity. What is the purpose of publicity?
2. Name and describe four methods of obtaining publicity, or ways of passing fashion news along to print or broadcast media.
3. What is the medium most favored by retail merchants for obtaining publicity? What other media may be used?
4. Differentiate between an advertising credit and an editorial credit. What are the advantages of these credits for a retail store?
5. What factors are considered by a store when deciding whether to accept or reject an editorial credit or an advertising credit?
6. Who is considered the main source of retail store publicity? Name at least three sources of fashion publicity material and discuss the nature and importance of publicity emanating from each.
7. Differentiate between personal and simplified selling techniques. Name and describe the two major types of personal selling and the two types of simplified selling. For which types of merchandise is each best suited?
8. Discuss the importance of mail and telephone selling in relation to fashion merchandise.

9. Name at least ten essential personal qualifications of a successful fashion salesperson.
10. Discuss employee fashion shows as a training device.

MERCHANDISING DIGEST

1. Discuss the following statement from the text: "Fashion selling requires a more sophisticated type of sales ability than is required by most other consumer goods," from the following standpoints: (a) fashion knowledge, (b) merchandise knowledge, and (c) customer approach.
2. Discuss the training of fashion salespeople in (a) large stores, (b) small stores, and (c) chain organizations.
3. Discuss the following statement from the text: "As the fashion authority for a department, the buyer is the primary source of information about merchandise carried in the department." Point out the various types of information buyers are responsible for providing to salespeople and the means they may employ to this end.

20
FASHION COORDINATION

Retail fashion coordination demands teamwork of the highest order. If the customer is to be able to find compatible apparel and accessories in a store's stock, that store must see to it that the assortments in each of its fashion departments are related to those in all of its other fashion departments. Not only must these assortments be of the "right" type for each store's customers, but they also must be presented at the "right" time, the time when customers want to buy. Important to fashion coordination, therefore, is the timing of fashion merchandise offerings to coincide with varying levels of fashion demand.

From sales promotion director right down to part-time salespeople, everyone in the store must be able to convey the store's fashion story with the proper emphasis, with perfect timing, and in a way that induces the store's regular and prospective customers to buy.

Fashion coordination begins with the selection of the merchandise and the building of assortments. From there it extends to the training of sales personnel, the effective use of advertising and display, the staging of promotional events, and the garnering of favorable publicity.

THE FASHION COORDINATOR

In spite of fashion's long history, the job of fashion coordinator did not exist until the 1920s. When women made their own clothes or had them made by a dressmaker, "fashion dolls," fashion plates, and other types of illustration provided the details of various fashion looks. But when women began buying ready-to-wear apparel in stores, retailers gradually realized that they needed help in determining customer needs as well as in charting fashion trends and interpreting them in terms of the stores' assortments.

Development of the Coordinator Function

Tobé Coller Davis is given credit as being the first "stylist," as fashion coordinators were first called. It is said that Franklin Simon, impressed by her enthusiasm and energy, hired her in the period right after World War I and told her to find a way to make herself useful in his store. She found that what the store needed most, and an area in which she could be most useful, was someone to chart and anticipate fashion trends and help the store's buyers to select and coordinate their assortments to reflect all the elements of each new fashion look as it became popular.

Other retailers soon added "stylists" to their staffs. These early stylists gradually began meeting together to share problems, ideas, and fashion information. These meetings were the beginning of The Fashion Group, which today has a membership of over 5,000 women executives representing all facets of the fashion business, with chapters (called "regional groups") in 24 cities in this country and in a number of foreign countries, and with additional chapters in the process of being organized. The Fashion Group's meetings, fashion shows, and fashion "spectaculars" have become important events not only in the fashion apparel field but also in the accessories, home furnishings, and textile areas.

Today, in all but the smallest stores, a staff executive is usually assigned responsibility for fashion coordination. This executive is generally known as the fashion coordinator, but in some stores may have the title of fashion director, fashion administrator, fashion consultant, or stylist. The duties of this executive vary from store to store, depending on (1) the firm's fashion image, its management structure, and the responsibility allocated at each of its executive levels; (2) the amount of fashion authority and responsibility taken over by the store's top-level management; and (3) the amount of creativity, originality, and vision the fashion coordinator possesses.

Range of Responsibilities

The major responsibility of the fashion coordinator is to assist in promoting sales of fashion merchandise throughout the entire store. In this capacity, the fashion coordinator is responsible for analyzing fashion trends, for advising merchandising executives in relation to the buying of coordinated and related fashions, for helping devise the most effective presentation of fashion merchandise to customers, and for building a fashion reputation for the store.

Although a fashion coordinator may be a man or a woman, in most retail organizations today this position is held by a woman. The coordinator functions in an advisory capacity, as a staff aide to store management (see Introduction to Part 3), who achieves the goals of fashion coordination by being stimulating and persuasive in working with other store executives rather than having any authority to approve or reject their merchandising decisions. She works with nearly everyone in the store, advising on buying, selling, advertising, publicity, and display activities, to coordinate the timing and emphasis of all fashion assortments so as to present a distinct fashion image to the store's customers.

Briefly stated, the coordinator function in-

volves three major areas of responsibility: merchandising, sales training, and sales promotion.

Merchandising Responsibilities   The basic merchandising responsibilities of the fashion coordinator (or of any store executive who is responsible for the coordination function) are:

- To evaluate current fashion trends in terms of the store's clientele, image, and merchandising policies
- To alert management and buyers to incoming fashions, even before they become important to the store, so that appropriate action can be planned well in advance
- Conversely, to supply early warning about fashions currently in the store's stocks which appear likely to wane in customer interest soon
- To assist buyers, when requested, in selecting for their respective departments merchandise that reflect those fashion trends that the store has decided to promote
- To assist buyers, when requested, in correlating their merchandise with that of other departments of the store

When this job is well done, the store's fashion merchandise is well coordinated, and its customers can select from its various departments apparel and accessories that go well together. Obviously, customers buy more readily under such circumstances, much more readily than when each item under consideration poses a problem of what to wear with it or where to find suitable related items.

The basic merchandising responsibilities of the fashion coordinator can be divided into three areas: market work, developing coordination within the store, and fashion forecasting.

Market Work   To get the information she needs to carry out her merchandising tasks, a fashion coordinator visits all the major markets—not to buy merchandise for the store but to get a clear picture of the currently popular fashions and to scan the fashion horizon for possible future changes, so that she can advise management and buyers on trends in the overall fashion picture.

Market work may take the fashion coordinator to showrooms not covered by the store's buyers, to fabric, fiber, and leather producers from whom can be obtained opinions about incoming trends. She may be in the market before the store's buyers, or with them, or both. She also regularly visits the offices of fashion and consumer magazines that are important to her store's customers in order to assess their themes in upcoming issues and the value to various departments of the store of the editorial and advertising credits offered to each.

With this broad background of information, the coordinator is in a position to offer meaningful advice to individual buyers about offerings in their markets. Although she may not know any one market as thoroughly as does the buyer who covers it for the store, she will know, for example, what colors will be important in apparel during the forthcoming season, and can relate this information to the hosiery and shoe buyers so that they have appropriate colors available in their respective assortments. She may not know which producer has the best accessories, but she will know the ideal sizes and shapes to go with the new dresses and coats for the coming season. She advises, recommends, and informs; the rest is up to the buyers.

Developing Coordination   In order to achieve successful coordination among the various fashion departments of a store, top management first must make certain storewide decisions. The degree of fashion leadership for which the store wishes to be known must be determined, as well as the extent of the merchandising and promotional efforts to be undertaken.

The fashion coordinator consults first with the store's management about what fashions should be promoted, to what extent, and when. Next, she works with store executives responsible for carrying out such decisions, and assists each of them in implementing management's decisions.

For example, if management has decided that the bulky look is one of those that the store intends to sponsor, each buyer will select styles, colors, and silhouettes with that theme in mind. The handbag buyer may choose much larger handbags. The coat buyer may add capes with hoods to her assortment. The fashion accessories buyer will see that her assortment includes long, bulky scarfs, knitted hats, and matching knitted gloves. The sportswear buyer will look for bulky, hip-length sweaters with shawl collars.

In another season or in another store, the romantic look may be another one that will affect its assortments, fashion art, displays, store decor, advertising copy, and special events. The services of the fashion coordinator are available to any and all departments in achieving an effective interpretation of whatever promotional themes the store chooses.

Within the framework of the fashion themes the store has chosen to promote, there is often opportunity for a coordinated promotional effort within a single merchandising division. An accessories division may stage a promotion of its own with no direct tie-in with the apparel division. If neutrals are strong in apparel and highlights of bright color are to be introduced by accessories, these latter departments may join in promoting shoes, handbags, jewelry, scarfs, and blouses in a variety of colors, or in featuring accessories in a single bright accent color, such as royal blue or emerald.

The prime objective of the fashion coordinator, whether she suggests ideas or merely assists in carrying them out, is to help make sure that the assortments and presentations of each department are in harmony with the fashion image that the store seeks to present. She also may be called upon to advise buyers on items to feature in their department displays, in store windows, and on those to be featured in advertisements. She confers with display staff, advertising people, and salespeople about how to show and what to say about the merchandise, and acts as liaison between apparel and accessories departments, in furthering the store's efforts to give the consumer a clear, consistent picture of how to achieve the looks currently in fashion.

Fashion Forecasting After the fashion coordinator has collected all available fashion information, she carefully and objectively evaluates the data in terms of developing fashion trends. Then she decides which trends she believes are suitable for promotion in her particular store: which seem promotable on a storewide basis and which seem more appropriate for departmental promotion only. After completing this evaluation, she prepares both a written and an oral report for store management about the trends she believes the store should actively promote during the coming season. If this report presents the trends in order of their importance, at least in the fashion coordinator's judgment, then management can decide whether to adopt all of her suggestions or only the ones at the top of the list, basing that decision not only on the fashion coordinator's conviction regarding the relative importance of each fashion trend but also on store budgetary considerations.

The fashion coordinator's forecasts cover such

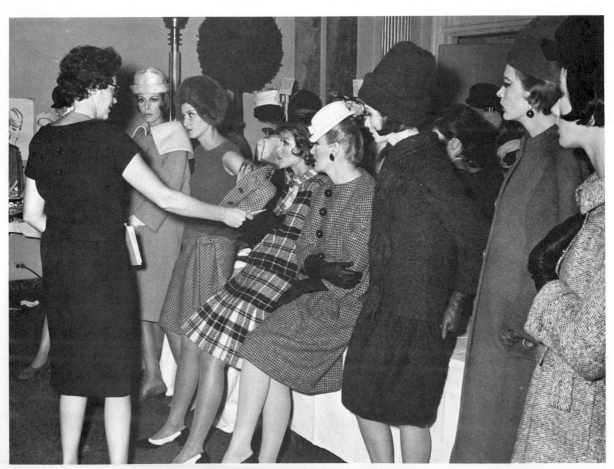

The fashion coordinator gives last-minute instructions to fashion show models.
The Fashion Group, Inc.

points as trends in silhouette, details, colors, textures—in short, the look or looks that are expected to be accepted by the store's customers in the coming season. Such a forecast may indicate, for example, that the longer, wider look in skirts requires higher, more slender heels on shoes. Or it may indicate that the heirloom look in jewelry goes well with certain nostalgic styles in dresses and blouses. The forecast may define whether favored colors in the coming season will be contrasts or monotones, bright or subdued, and whether or not some specific range of colors is featured above others. From such forecasts, knowledgeable buyers are able to proceed with more assurance, promotion executives can begin planning events, and display people can decide upon the "props" to look for in their own markets. If, for example, the fashion trend is toward delicate colors and dainty fabrics, the fashion coordinator's forecast alerts the display department to the need for backgrounds that will be suitable.

Forecasts are supplied by the fashion coordinator as often and in as much detail as management specifies. Usually, however, they are made on a six-month basis, just as merchandise plans are. In some cases, such as Easter or back-to-school, forecasts may be made for shorter periods of time.

Sales Training Responsibilities A fashion-educated selling staff is a major asset to any store that sells fashion goods. In each individual selling department, the buyer is the source of all merchandise information. However, for the overall fashion picture and for information on combining elements to achieve the currently fashionable look, the fashion coordinator may be called upon for training aid. Working with the store's training director, she often prepares seasonal fashion presentations for the salespeople.

Such presentations may take the form of fashion shows, sketch-and-copy pamphlets, talks illustrated by merchandise from stock, color slides, taped closed-circuit television shows or any combination of these that is suitable to the store and its facilities. So important is this aspect of fashion

coordination and promotion that some large, multi-unit stores have a policy each season of preparing a fashion show for all employees, as noted in Chapter 19. Initially, the show may be presented to buyers and branch store managers who assemble at the main store for that purpose. Repeat performances then may be staged in the main store until all employees concerned—salespeople, display staff, advertising staff, and so on—have attended. Finally, the show or a tape-recording of the show "goes on the road" to the store's branches. At each showing, those who attend may be given a brochure to help them remember what they have seen. Selling sentences, suitable for the salespeople to use in talking to customers, are usually worked into the show's commentary and repeated in the booklets.

Sales Promotion Responsibilities The advertising and display staffs look to the buyers for merchandise information about the specific goods to be featured in ads or windows. For background information on how the featured merchandise relates to fashion trends and how to present them, the fashion coordinator can be of great help.

Although the fashion coordinator may not write a line of advertising copy or sketch a fashion figure, she may be expected to see that the copy, merchandise illustration, and related items shown in an ad are all compatible with one another and in line with the store's fashion story. Similarly, she may never set up a display in a window or department of the store, but she may be called upon for advice by those who do the displays, about how to put the various elements of an outfit together, down to such fine points as the right spot for a pin or the right way to drape a scarf on a mannequin.

When stores stage promotional events featuring their fashion assortments, the fashion coordinator is very much in the picture. She may suggest the events, organize and supervise them, or simply stand by to see that the details of the fashion story are correctly presented.

Fashion shows for customers may be held in or out of the store, as direct sales builders or as public relations efforts to assist charitable and civic causes. They may be held in branch stores to enhance the fashion images of those stores. They may be formal, using models on a runway, or informal, with models strolling about a restaurant or departmental selling floor. Stage-managing such fashion shows, as well as coordinating the outfits and preparing the commentary, is usually the responsibility of the fashion coordinator.

Many other events also may be used to underline the importance of fashion coordination. There may be talks and discussion meetings for customers of a particular type, such as teen-agers, home sewers, or expectant mothers. There may be occasions to talk to women's clubs and similar groups outside the store about current fashions and fashion trends that are of special interest to each particular group. In all such cases, the fashion coordinator is usually involved.

The coordinator also works with visiting fashion experts in staging their presentations. For example, a producer of active sportswear may send a golf or tennis pro to a store to give a demonstration and to participate in a question-and-answer session with customers. Or a producer of patterns or sewing notions may send a representative to a store to hold one- or two-day clinics. Or a magazine may stage a fashion presentation on a theme it is currently sponsoring. The store's fashion coordinator, in such instances, makes sure that the presentation is in line with the store's fashion policy, assists in tying in all advertising, display, and personal selling, and helps secure as much publicity as the particular type of event warrants.

FASHION COORDINATION IN RETAIL ORGANIZATIONS

The primary objective of all retail fashion coordination is the same, regardless of store size or type: to create and maintain a definite, specific fashion reputation for the store. Achieving this objective involves advice, aid, and assistance in merchandising, sales training, and sales promotion areas.

The manner in which this objective is achieved however, as well as the personnel, skills, and responsibilities connected with the achievement of such coordination, varies widely with the size and type of store.

Large Multibranch Stores

The job of presenting coordinated fashion assortments in large, multibranch retail organizations is an awesome one indeed. Not only must the fashion assortments in the various branches meet the diverse needs of local customers, but also they must reflect the distinctive fashion image of the store organization as a whole. Dozens or even hundreds of fashion departments and their respective buyers must be considered and served; hundreds or even sometimes thousands of employees must be trained.

To accomplish this gigantic task, a large retail organization maintains a well-staffed fashion office to assist its coordinator. Members of the fashion staff are often assigned certain specific areas of responsibility. For example, one may be charged with the responsibility for coordinating all special events. Another may be in full charge of all fashion shows. Still another may work with one or more of the store's consumer boards.

The fashion coordinator for a large store usually attends all market openings, both at home and abroad; maintains close contact with local newspaper and national magazine editors; attends charity balls and first nights at the theater and opera, and frequents newly discovered and fashionable resorts and other "in" gathering places, in order to observe at firsthand what fashion leaders are wearing for such occasions. Through these observations, the coordinator seeks advance indication of fashion trends that have or may in the future have meaning for her store's customers. For example, if at these events she sees a number of women wearing evening pajamas with a full, graceful sweep, she suggests to appropriate buyers in her store that full, ankle-length apparel could be promoted for evening wear. If the chemise style is the outstanding feature of the leading Paris couturiers' collections, she can advise her store's dress buyers to look for styles that are looser and less figure-defining.

The fashion coordinator for a large retail organization is responsible for suggesting suitable seasonal fashion themes to be promoted throughout the store and for coordinating all sales promotional efforts toward this end.

Chain Store Organizations

The fashion coordinator of a national general merchandise or specialty store chain has many of the responsibilities of a coordinator in a multibranch organization, plus others that are unique to chain store operation.

Chain organizations largely restrict their fashion offerings to proven styles, those that have arrived at the culmination stage of their individual cycles. Fashion rightness, quality, promotional prices, and private labels are stressed in their advertisements, displays, and other sales promotion efforts. In recent years, major chains, such as Sears, Roebuck & Company, Montgomery Ward, and J. C. Penney Company, have made gigantic strides toward upgrading both the breadth and quality of their fashion assortments. Catalogs of these chain organizations also reflect an increased awareness of the power of fashion to move huge quantities of apparel and accessories. This is attested to by the increased number of pages devoted to illustrations of fashion apparel and accessories, as well as by the use of color to further emphasize the fashion features of their assortments.

The fashion coordinator of a chain organization usually attends both domestic and European fashion market openings in order to keep abreast of fashion trends. She also visits other foreign markets for additional fashion inspiration. On such market trips, she may buy for copying purposes several original models that incorporate certain new details of design she believes should be featured in the fashion assortments offered by her firm in its stores, catalogs, or both. She also may arrange to have internationally famous designers create exclusive models, which, after consultation with the firm's merchandising executives, may be reproduced by domestic manufacturers to the specifications and under the private label of her firm.

After viewing the major collections, the coordinator prepares detailed market reports which go out to the manager of each store unit in the chain. Such reports serve to keep both store managers and their fashion sales staffs abreast of current trends in fashion apparel and accessories.

The fashion coordinator also carefully evaluates the fashion trends that she has observed and, in close cooperation with her firm's merchandise managers, central and regional fashion buyers, as well as other merchandising executives, attempts to pinpoint customer preferences and determine the best means of achieving coordinated fashion presentations throughout the chain.

The major responsibility of the chain organization fashion coordinator is to expedite mass distribution of fashion goods on the basis of their wide appeal, good taste, quality, and moderate price. This responsibility is in direct contrast to that of the coordinator for a large specialty store, for example, who seeks to build and maintain her firm's reputation for fashion leadership.

Medium-size Stores

The coordination of fashion assortments in medium-size retail organizations does not require as much experience or training as in larger volume firms. Former buyers frequently become fashion coordinators in medium-size stores, as do young and ambitious former assistants to large store fashion coordinators.

In stores of this size, with few branches or none, with fewer fashion buyers, fewer departments, and fewer employees than in giant organizations, the fashion coordinators may perform their function with only a small staff or, in some

JULY through OCTOBER

hot fashion themes

july...
big shirt trend
continues across the board
- shirts, dressy and casual
- shirt on shirt
- shirtjackets with dresses and pants, also as separates
- shirtcoats; from rainwear to layaway winter styles
- shirty sweaters for all members of the family

august... the
wardrobe concept
continues from dress, sportswear and suit markets
- either multiple pieces in related color or pattern sold at one price
- or separates that harmonize or are compatible
- or actual dyed to match

forest green ...strong
promotional color emerging as part of the classic, well-bred look; important as a solid and in plaids, patterns and backgrounds

september...
sweaters are the single most
important category for increased sales and profits
- sweaterjackets edging out wovens
- basic pullovers with pants and skirts
- twins; long and short, bulky and fine gauge
- Sloppy Joe returns; fisherman cables worn longer, looser
- sweaterdresses, dresses with sweaters
- new yarns, stitches, patterns, combinations

tannery leathers and suedes,
real and pseudo

october...
pile up
includes rugged and luxury piles, men, women, children
- shaggy for sports and casual
- plushy or sleek for dressy
- fur and contrast pile trims
- novelty colors and effects

The chain store fashion coordinator prepares seasonal fashion market reports that are sent to each unit in the chain.

cases, even alone. If the store is at a distance from major fashion markets, she may attend openings in those markets only once a year, relying for her fashion knowledge on the observations of fashion editors, fashion reporting services, her store's buying office, and the observations of her own store buyers after they have completed a market trip.

Fashion coordination in medium-size stores is far less complicated than in larger stores for several reasons:

First, each fashion buyer in a medium-size store is responsible for merchandise in a larger number of classifications than is a buyer in a larger store. Thus buyers in the medium-size stores are already more alert to the coordination aspects of the many classifications for which they buy. For example, one buyer in a medium-size store may be responsible for all intimate apparel, whereas in a larger store that same merchandise may be segmented into several separate departments, such as foundations, sleepwear, daywear, and loungewear, each with its own buyer. One buyer in a medium-size store might be responsible for coats and suits in all size and price ranges, whereas in a larger store such merchandise may be segmented into several departments, each featuring separate types, sizes, and price ranges and each having its own buyer.

Second, effective training of salespeople is more easily accomplished in medium-size stores than in large stores because, in the former, buyers are on the selling floor more frequently. Thus they are in a better position to motivate their sales personnel and, at the same time, provide them with pertinent fashion information about the various kinds of merchandise they have been hired to sell.

Third, coordination among the fashion assortments offered by related departments is easier to achieve in medium-size stores than in their larger counterparts mainly because there are fewer buyers involved. With fewer buyers there are fewer personality conflicts, and there is easier exchange of information about what is selling and what is not selling.

Small Stores

Ideally, every store should have a fashion office or a fashion coordinator to assist it in building and maintaining a fashion reputation through better coordinated assortments. There are many small retail firms, however, that either cannot afford to hire a full-time fashion specialist or for other reasons are obliged to achieve coordination without a full-time executive to take charge of this important store function. In such cases, responsibility for fashion coordination may be delegated to one of the store's buyers or to a merchandise manager, or it may be assumed by the store's manager or owner.

The Buyer as Coordinator The fashion buyer in a relatively small departmentalized store is usually responsible for merchandising a larger number of related classifications than is the buyer for a medium-size or large store. For instance, in a smaller store, one buyer may be responsible for buying all types of merchandise in the accessories group, whereas a medium-size store would have several accessories buyers, and in a large store there would be even more buyers, each highly specialized as to type of merchandise.

The same factors that aid buyers in the medium-size store in matters of coordination are even more influential for buyers in the smaller store. The buyer for a group of departments or classifications in a smaller store becomes responsible for coordinating several pieces of the fashion picture as a normal part of the job when planning purchases, promotions, displays, and in the training of salespeople. In addition, not only is such a buyer in close daily contact with the salespeople, but salespeople in small stores often sell in more than one department and thus are more aware of coordination than if they were narrowly specialized.

Coordination in the small store is also easier to accomplish because very few buyers are involved. If only a few buyers cover the entire apparel and accessories fields, it is a simple matter to get them together either in the store or in the market to work out coordinated fashion themes for the store. In the market or at the store, it is easy for one buyer to exchange fashion ideas with another over lunch or on a coffee break. In a small organization, simple shoptalk often takes the place of much of the liaison work that a fashion coordinator does in a larger store.

Other coordinating procedures also are simpler in a small store than in a large one. Because the departments are usually physically close, displays of accessorized costumes benefit both apparel and accessories departments: Customers who like what they see on display can buy the entire outfit, if they choose to, right on the spot. Salespeople are more apt to keep one another informed in the same way that their buyers do; they chat about merchandise and fashion during breaks in their workday and while doing their personal shopping. There is also likely to be less regimentation in a smaller store and more feeling of belonging and of personal interest in the store and its merchandise.

The Merchandise Manager as Coordinator

It often happens that the head of a fine specialty shop, or the apparel and accessories merchandise manager of a small department store, takes over many of the functions that a fashion coordinator might normally perform. Sometimes this is done because the store has no budget for a coordinator; sometimes the reason is that fashion is the merchant's first love, and the merchant refuses to be divorced from it.

Many merchandise managers who have worked their way up from a buying job refuse to lose contact with fashion resources. Like the fashion coordinators of other stores, they visit fiber, fabric, and leather firms, talk to merchandising executives of fashion and consumer publications, and maintain personal contact with the key resources of each of their principal fashion departments. Against this background, such executives can readily coordinate the merchandising and promotional efforts of their fashion departments. It is usually also part of the normal routine for such executives to counsel their buyers regarding sales training and other phases of fashion coordination.

The Owner as Coordinator

In the smallest stores, those run by the owner with perhaps a salesperson or two, the owner is buyer, coordinator, merchandise manager, and sometimes even housekeeper. In such stores, there is little need for liaison activities.

The demands on the time and energies of owners of small shops are enormous. As a result, many such shop owners concentrate on serving only one very narrow group of customers, seeking out and remaining faithful to those few resources whose merchandise has proved to be of exactly the right character for the selected clientele. Or sometimes a tiny store may divorce itself entirely from the coordination problem and specialize in dresses, sportswear, furs, or accessories. Such a shop will attempt to key its offerings to the tastes of the community it serves, suggesting in general terms other components of the costume which customers will have to go elsewhere to buy.

An Example of Retail Fashion Coordination

Fashion coordination is a very important factor in the kind and clarity of fashion image a store projects, and thus in its success in selling fashion goods. Saks Fifth Avenue's fiftieth anniversary celebration, held in the fall of 1974, was a good example of this fact. Careful and thorough fashion coordination of all store activities, from assembling merchandise assortments through preparing ads and displays to the briefing of sales personnel, helped the chain organization repolish its fashion image, not only in its New York store but in its units throughout the country.

Saks Fifth Avenue began its anniversary planning nearly two years before the target date. A steering committee was formed, made up of the heads of the advertising, publicity, and display divisions and the fashion director; an independent public relations expert was hired to head the committee. The committee met regularly, mapping out the kind of benefits and events the celebration would feature and then hunting for an appropriate theme for the celebration. In late 1973, a year before the event, with a publicity program already worked out, the committee finally decided on a theme.

In 1973, fashion nostalgia was at its height. Many styles of earlier decades were being revived, including those of Art Moderne, or Art Deco, as it is sometimes called. The first Saks Fifth Avenue store had opened its doors in New York and began developing its fashion image during the Art Moderne period of the late 1920s. During its first years in business, the merchandise featured by the store, the ads and displays, even the decor of the store had strongly reflected the design ideas of Art Moderne. So, in celebration of its fiftieth anniversary, it was decided to transform the store, according to the press releases, "into something of a mecca of Art Moderne with nostalgic glimpses and contemporary adaptations of that specific style which emerged from the Paris Exhibition of 1925, only a few months after the store's opening." The fashion statement was to be made "through both specific merchandise presentations from literally every department of the store and the magic of display."

In January 1974, the tremendous job of coordinating the various parts of the fashion promotion began. That job continued right up to the official

During its fiftieth anniversary, Saks Fifth Avenue's windows featured the Art Moderne theme.

Saks Fifth Avenue

start of the celebration in September 1974, and involved the following activities:

- Extensive research was undertaken, with the help of the costume department of the New York Public Library and the Costume Institute of the Metropolitan Museum of Art, as well as other sources of historic costume information, to determine exactly what looks and design details dominated the Art Moderne period, and to decide which of these should be featured.
- Vendors were contacted about producing special fashion merchandise, in a wide variety of categories, that would reflect the Art Moderne look and yet be contemporary in appeal.
- Within the store organization, merchandise managers were carefully briefed about the fashion theme the store intended to present, and they in turn were responsible for briefing each of their departments. The training department was enlisted in an effort to ensure that all store personnel would be familiar with the Art Moderne theme. Special signs, shopping bags, and "Fifty Years of Fashion" badges to be worn by all store personnel were designed. Each of the chain's store units were also briefed on plans, and ways they could tie into the anniversary celebration were discussed.

By February, all advertising and sales promotion efforts had been planned and coordinated. Ads, displays, and special events were designed to contribute to the overall fashion statement.

By late spring, merchandise selections had been completed, and in June, special "showings" were held in the store's fashion office. On display were samples of specially selected or designed merchandise from every division of the store, showing how each merchandising department planned to tie in its assortment with the Art Moderne theme. Store merchandise managers and buyers attended these showings, so that each could become familiar with the total Art Moderne fashion picture that was going to be presented to the public.

On September 15, 1974, Saks Fifth Avenue officially opened its "Fifty Years of Fashion" celebration. In the New York store, all windows featured the Art Moderne theme, as did the interior displays. A battery of Art Moderne–styled ads appeared in New York newspapers. Contemporary adaptations of Art Moderne merchandise were featured in every department of the store. Even the telephone operators answered the phone with "Saks Fifth Avenue, Fifty Years of Fashion!"

The entire fashion effort was carefully coordinated not only in the New York City store but in all the 31 other units of the chain as well. From Palm Beach to Beverly Hills, from Detroit and Chicago to Phoenix and Houston, every Saks Fifth Avenue store celebrated "Fifty Years of Fashion." Each ran local newspaper ads in the same Art Moderne style, and each devoted some window and interior display space to the theme. Each used the same specially designed signs, badges, and shopping bags. Each carried at least some Art Moderne merchandise, the amount and type depending on the nature of the trading area in which each store was located.

The major publicity effort, however, was centered in New York City, where the first Saks Fifth Avenue store had opened 50 years before. A number of charity benefits and special events were held in October and November, such as a black-tie dinner for the New York Public Library and a party and fashion show for the Museum of the City of New York. A cocktail party for vendors, retailers, and the press was held on opening day in the lower plaza of Rockefeller Center. A series of art and photographic exhibitions were held in the Fifth Avenue store. And most exciting for the fashion-minded public: Nearly every day for almost a month, a different celebrated designer made a personal appearance at the store, with informal modeling of his or her designs. They included Oscar de la Renta, Michael Moreaux, Ernst Strauss, Anna Beltrao, Adolfo, Frank Smith for Evan-Picone, Judith Leiber, Clovis Ruffin, Don Kline, Calvin Klein, Pat Sandler, Marc Bohan for Christian Dior, Jerry Feder for Francini, Noriko, Michael Gordon for Koret, Elie Jacobsen for Dorothee Bis, Steve Brodie for Cadoro Jewelry, Bill Blass, Suzanne Dache, Luba, and Ilie Wacs.

Saks Fifth Avenue executives and staff put many hours of planning time into coordinating activities related to the anniversary celebration. In addition, the store organization put a sizeable amount of money into special events. The results were excellent:

First, the chain received widespread fashion publicity, a proper tribute to its long history of fashion importance.

Second, although sales of its specially stocked Art Moderne merchandise were not a major goal, the chain sold at least as much as it had planned to, with sales particularly strong in Art Moderne–styled accessories in general and millinery in particular.

Third (and perhaps most important in terms of the future), Saks Fifth Avenue found it had increased its fashion prestige and rejuvenated its fashion image well beyond expectations. Although

always known as a fashion authority, the chain had developed into somewhat of an "institution." The anniversary celebration made the store seem more lively, more approachable, more up to date, more adventurous. It not only reconfirmed the chain's fashion leadership to those who had always shopped Saks Fifth Avenue, but it also brought in a flood of new, younger customers, many of whom were to become regular Saks customers. These results were noted both at the New York City store and at other Saks stores throughout the country. The coordination effort was so thorough and so effective that it not only brought together all the pieces of the Art Moderne fashion picture but also enabled every store unit in the organization to project the same fashion image.

SHOP MERCHANDISING

It can take a customer considerable time and fashion knowhow to put together all the various items

Shops are distinguished from the rest of the store by their merchandise, decor, and atmosphere.
Hess's Department Store, Allentown, Pa.

of apparel and accessories needed to achieve a desired fashion look. A customer may have to go from store to store, or from department to department within a large store, making perhaps a dozen different purchases, each from a different salesperson, to assemble all the elements of the outfit wanted.

A relatively new approach to fashion merchandising recognizes this problem and attempts to solve it by offering the fashion customer a special kind of one-stop shopping: the shop. A shop offers the very essence of fashion coordination. Here are assembled all the components of a particular fashion look or costume or special-purpose outfit. Because the assortment is so carefully coordinated, selection is simplified. Because the goods offered are grouped in one small area, customers, with the help of a single knowledgeable salesperson, can purchase all the components of whatever outfit they are seeking in one single transaction.

Some of today's shops are separate enterprises, entire stores devoted to serving the fashion needs of a special type of customer. Others are set up as separate areas within a large store or as special areas within certain departments of a large store. These shops are distinguished from the rest of the department or store not only by their merchandise but also by their decor and atmosphere.

The Shop Concept

Special shops, either as independent operations or as departments within departmentalized stores, have existed for many years and continue to be established in increasing numbers as the means of presenting coordinated apparel and accessories to special groups of customers. For example, teen shops within department stores date back to the 1930s, and those set up as separate enterprises are not much younger. College, maternity, and bridal shops have also been long familiar.

Among fashion merchants, a *shop* refers to a small store or a small area within a large store that is stocked with merchandise for special end uses, intended for customers with specialized interests. These are the customers whose fashion requirements differ sufficiently from those of the general consumer to make it worthwhile for the merchant to assemble appropriate merchandise in a separate store or in a separately designated area of a large store.

Types of Shops Typical of such shops are those devoted to country clothes, ski or tennis or golf wear and equipment, maternity clothes, contemporary fashions, college clothes, and clothes for young women with couture tastes but ready-to-wear budgets.

In each such shop, the atmosphere, merchandise, selling techniques, and fashion coordination are all geared to the interests of the particular customer to be served. Teen shops, for example, are informal, lively, and often noisy places, with high-decibel renditions of popular recorded music. In department stores, teen shops are usually set aside from regular departments for the dual purpose of providing an area where young customers can feel at ease and of screening more mature customers from the sometimes wearying exuberance and group shopping habits of the young.

One of the special shops most frequently encountered in retail stores today is that devoted to the bride. A skilled bridal consultant assists the bride in the selection of her gown and those for the members of her wedding party. Services offered usually include answers to questions on etiquette and dress, and a visit by the bridal consultant to the bride's home just before the wedding to make any necessary last-minute adjustments in her costume. In addition, if the bride wishes to be photographed in her wedding gown before the day of the ceremony, the bridal shop usually can make arrangements for this as well.

The bridal shop in department and large specialty stores is capable of bringing added business to other departments of the store. Because the customer comes into the store for fittings, advice, and reassurance, she tends to purchase much of her trousseau there as well. Moreover, the bridal shop is usually located so that the bride and members of her wedding party, on their way to and from the salon, pass through departments featuring other fashion merchandise and are subjected to the appeal of their displays.

Assortment Selection and Coordination

Buying for shops is done in either of two ways, depending upon the nature of the shop. Shops that are permanent in nature and feature apparel and accessories of year-round interest usually are assigned their own buyer. This buyer covers many different kinds of markets to gather the particular types of apparel and accessories needed. Because a single person can do just so much work, a buyer relies heavily on information from other buyers, from the store's resident buying office, and from the store's fashion coordinator. Yet it is often the items that a buyer finds being offered by out-of-the-way and unusual resources that give the assortment its special appeal.

On the other hand, shops featuring merchandise of a seasonal nature, such as swim shops, may present merchandise contributed by buyers of several different departments in the same store. For instance, a swim shop might offer swim suits in every style from the covered-up look to The String, beach cover-ups, beach hats, beach bags, sandals, sand chairs, beach towels, sun umbrellas, casual jewelry, sunglasses, picnic baskets, and drink containers. In such shops, the display props that create the special-department atmosphere are removed when the peak of demand has passed; the merchandise is distributed among the departments whose buyers purchased it; and the salespeople are reassigned.

Almost as important as the selection of the merchandise is the selection and training of the salespeople who staff the shops. These need to have a thorough knowledge of both the merchandise in the shop and its coordination possibilities, as well as an understanding of the type of customer for whom the merchandise is intended.

The Boutique Concept

"Boutique" is the French word for "shop." In the fashion business today, *boutique* has come to mean a shop associated with few-of-a-kind merchandise, generally in very new or extreme styling, with an imaginative presentation of goods.

Boutiques got their start in France. They originally were small shops operated by famous designers to sell the often specially designed accessories to be worn with the designers' apparel creations. Like the more common kind of shop, they offered a kind of one-stop shopping, limited as to categories of merchandise but of a very highly coordinated nature. The boutique bearing a designer's name was (and still is) the place where that designer's clientele could find the appropriate accessories needed to achieve the total fashion look created by the designer.

The Boutique Image Today, there are many shops called boutiques simply because they follow this tradition of newness, exclusivity, and few-of-a-kind designs. Occasionally a style that gets its start in a boutique later becomes a popular best seller. When this happens, boutiques usually lose interest in the style. This emphasis on newness and exclusivity, as well as the lack of depth of assortments, is what usually distinguishes a boutique from a shop.

Boutiques are not new but they are far more numerous and important in today's more affluent, fashion-alert society than they were a generation or two ago. There have always been some shops in which well-to-do women could find distinctive, well-coordinated apparel and accessories. And in large department and specialty stores in major cities, there have been corners, galleries, or alcoves set off from the general flow of traffic and devoted to merchandise more expensive and of higher fashion appeal than that offered elsewhere in the store.

What is new about today's boutiques is that many of them are dedicated to people whose tastes run to extremes in styling. Such boutiques are gen-

Correges, New York City

Abracadabra, New York City
Boutiques emphasize coordinated assortments, exclusivity, and few-of-a-kind designs.

erally strikingly different from other departments on the selling floors of their stores; even their decor is dramatically keyed to the individualized merchandise they carry.

Selecting and Coordinating Boutique Assortments   Buying for a store's boutique may be done by one buyer who covers several markets in search of appropriate merchandise or, as is more often the case in departmentalized stores, the responsibility may be shared by buyers for several of the store's regular departments. In the latter case, each participating buyer selects for the boutique such unusual styles as seem suitable for it, reserving for the regular department other styles that have wider, less individualized appeal. The salespeople in a boutique are carefully chosen and trained to understand its target customers, its merchandise, and its coordination possibilities.

The prosperity of a boutique does not depend entirely upon the ability of the merchant to judge correctly the needs and tastes of special groups of customers. Some, although skillfully operated, have a relatively brief life, simply because interest in the special fashions to which they have been devoted is not yet strong enough, is declining, or has ceased to exist.

MERCHANDISING VOCABULARY
Define or briefly explain the following terms:

Shop
Boutique

MERCHANDISING REVIEW
1. Discuss the historical development of the coordination function in retail stores from its beginning up to the present time.
2. What is the major responsibility of a fashion coordinator? Into what three major areas of responsibility are a coordinator's duties divided?
3. What are the five basic merchandising responsibilities of a fashion coordinator? Into what three general areas do these merchandising responsibilities fall?
4. Describe what is involved in a fashion coordinator's "market work."
5. Describe how a fashion coordinator goes about developing coordination within a retail organization.
6. Describe the activities of a fashion coordinator in carrying out fashion-forecasting activities.
7. Name and briefly describe three methods commonly employed by large stores for achieving fashion training of its employees. Discuss the coordinator's responsibility with respect to each.
8. Name several retail promotional activities with which a fashion coordinator may be directly concerned, indicating the extent of responsibility with regard to each.

9.   Give three reasons why fashion coordination in medium-size stores is less complicated than in large stores.

10.   Differentiate between a shop and a boutique, and cite specific examples of each.

MERCHANDISING DIGEST

1.   Discuss the following quotation from the text, with respect to its implications for the merchandising of fashion goods and services: "Retail fashion coordination demands teamwork of the highest order."

2.   Discuss the coordination responsibilities and activities of (a) a buyer, (b) a merchandise manager, and (c) an owner in small retail firms that do not have a full-time fashion specialist.

3.   Discuss the shop concept of merchandising fashions from the standpoint of (a) its advantages for customers, (b) how assortments are selected and coordinated, (c) atmosphere and decor, and (d) the selling techniques employed.

21
DEVELOPING A FASHION IMAGE

Fashion retailing is a highly competitive business. One of the most important ways in which an increasing number of retail merchants are meeting competition today is by developing a distinctive fashion image as a means of attracting customers to their stores. Retailers, of course, have a wide range of other tools to use for this purpose: price, location, service, hours of business, and credit terms, to name a few. But when they compete with each other by using fashion itself as the attraction, they are matching their respective abilities to understand consumers' fashion preferences, to shop hundreds of markets in search of goods that represent those preferences, and to present those goods to consumers in well-coordinated assortments that encourage patronage. In this type of competition, each fashion merchant seeks to project a store image, and a fashion image within that store image, that will attract the kind of customers each wants to serve.

A *store image* is the character or personality that the store presents to the public. In the words of a well-known fashion merchant, Stanley Marcus, of Neiman-Marcus in Dallas, an image is "an honest reflection of what the store actually is. It should accurately mirror what the store stands for in service, values, quality, assortments, taste, aggressiveness, and citizenship."[1] A store image, then, is not something that merely has been dreamed up in the minds of its management and held up to the public for admiration. Rather, it is the opinion that the public has of the store as a result of the store's policies and activities, the sum total of whatever

makes one store individual and different from others in the community.

A store's *fashion image* is that aspect of its store image that reflects the degree of fashion leadership it strives to exercise, and the stage of the fashion cycle that its assortments represent. The merchandising activities discussed throughout Part 3 play the major role in creating a fashion image, but all phases of store operations contribute to the total effect.

PROFILING TARGET CUSTOMERS

The first step in creating a fashion image is to define the store's target customers, those people for whom the merchandise assortments, the services, and the whole atmosphere of the store are planned. Only when a store has a clear-cut and definite profile of the customers who constitute its target group can it create a successful fashion image.

A store relates its merchandising, promotion, decor, selling techniques, services, participation in community affairs, and even its housekeeping to that target customer it seeks to serve. Elegant fashion merchandise cannot be offered against a background of dusty displays and untidy fitting rooms, nor do customers expect to find bargain-priced shirts or skirts in departments with thick carpets and highly attentive salespeople.

Stores serving areas in which the preferences of potential customers are fairly similar tend to adopt somewhat similar fashion images, but stores with a variety of target groups to choose from have a variety of fashion image possibilities open to them. For instance, a small town in which a university is located probably would have two basic customer groups—the younger university students and the more adult faculty and townspeople. A small city serving as the only metropolitan center in a large geographic area, and with limited business and industrial interests, would likely be dominated by people having fairly similar general interests, thereby forming an homogenous target group of customers. In large metropolitan areas, however, the diversity of business and industrial interests and of lifestyles create a variety of different customer groups to be served, each with distinct and separate needs and wants. A sampling of some of the fashion images projected by stores in the New York City area shows how diverse that variety can be.

Abraham and Straus describes its target customers as "a diverse group of people who shop A & S for various reasons: wide assortments, convenience of buying many things under one roof, services, price, credit facilities, friendliness." To attract these diverse customers, A & S tries "to project an awareness of current lifestyles, and do it in a way that indicates that, while we're with it, the customer still will find a warm neighborly atmosphere in our stores."[2] Henri Bendel is a very different kind of store: "either the biggest boutique or the smallest specialty shop in town; a store of individual shops, devoted to the iron fashion whim of a very special creature—the most sophisticated, aware, small-sized, and free-wheeling of New York women."[3] The Lane Bryant stores serve women with fuller figures, whatever their age. Bergdorf-Goodman caters primarily to people with ample funds and a keenly developed fashion sense. Saks Fifth Avenue tries to provide "medium to better fashion quality merchandise," a "high quality level in all merchandise regardless of price," and "fashion news and leadership in every classification of accessories and apparel for both men and women of every age group."[4] The stores and catalogs of such chains as Sears, Roebuck & Company or J. C. Penney Company have as their target groups for fashion merchandise those customers from low to middle income who, although not necessarily experimenters in fashion, are fashion-conscious and demand good value in the merchandise they buy.

Each store or group of stores in these examples develops its own character through its merchandise assortments, decor, advertising, and display. It would not be difficult, given the descriptions above and a few days in which to inspect these stores and review their assortments and advertising, for someone completely new to the city to identify each by its merchandise, its ads, its windows, and the behavior of its sales staffs. Not only is the merchandise different in each store, but the whole atmosphere of each store is different. Each store has developed the atmosphere most natural and most comfortable to the target group of customers that the store wants to attract.

ELEMENTS OF FASHION MERCHANDISING POLICY

Once a store has defined and studied its target group or groups of customers, it then develops and maintains that fashion image it hopes will attract those customer groups through its fashion merchandising policies. A policy is "a settled, clearly defined course of action or method of doing business deemed necessary, expedient, or advantageous. Policies are to business what sailing charts are to a seaman."[5] A fashion merchandising policy is a long-range guide for the fashion merchandising staff, spelling out the store's fashion aims, standards of quality, price ranges, attitudes toward competition, and any other elements that may be considered pertinent.

While fashion merchandising policies constitute a store's instructions to the buying staff, they are also of concern to the nonmerchandising executives who are responsible for keeping their areas of operation in line with the store's merchandising aims.

For example, if it is a policy to carry goods of superlative quality, the store's wrapping and packing materials would also be of excellent quality,

A&S played up its large assortments with a series of ads repeated in many languages, this time Hawaiian.

and its adjustment department would be expected to take a liberal attitude toward customer complaints. On the other hand, if the policy is to have quality that is merely adequate, wrapping and packing may be of minimum quality and the adjustment office may take a tougher line with customers who have complaints. Another example: If there is a policy to emphasize newness, there may be a company rule against running ads featuring clearance merchandise, except for discreet twice-a-year announcements. If the policy is to emphasize bargains, however, there may be numerous price promotions, mention of comparative prices in advertising, and general assurances that the store will not be undersold.

Fashion merchandising policies, therefore, are closely intertwined with almost every activity of the store, so that the image presented to the public is consistent throughout.

The Merchandise Assortment

Basic to a store's fashion merchandising policy is a determination of the degree of fashion leadership that its merchandise assortments will show. The composition of its assortments is influenced not only by the type of styles brought into stock but also by the length of time they are permitted to remain in stock.

For example, if the store chooses as its target customers those who want to be first with the new-

est, store buyers will be instructed to assemble assortments that consist primarily of "prophetic" styles, those that incorporate one or more incoming trends. Buyers probably will be required to apply a high initial markup to their merchandise in order to compensate for the risks involved when fashions are at the early experimental stages of their cycles. They will also be allowed quite liberal markdowns, because these are almost inescapable in such an operation. They will be expected to mark down nonstarting styles promptly, and clear out promptly any styles that have been copied into lower price lines or that show signs of being already well on the rise in their cycles of demand.

By way of comparison, a store that caters to women who want to be in fashion but not necessarily among the experimenters will offer an assortment made up primarily of securely established styles. Such assortments may contain several versions of any particularly good style, or they may contain mainly classics with a sprinkling of forward-looking styles. Policy may specify that a few pieces may be purchased above the normal price range of the store or department and ahead of the store's normal position with relation to the fashion cycle. This procedure lends prestige to the regular assortment and provides exposure to styles probably too new for the firm's clientele but likely to prove acceptable somewhat later. "Getting the eye used to it" is one way to prepare customers for incoming fashions.

A store of this type will not require initial markups as high as those in a store carrying more experimental styles, since risks are not so great at this stage of the fashion cycle. Its policy on markdowns may not be especially liberal, unless the store has a policy of refusing to be undersold and therefore requires its buyers to price everything as low as (or lower than) similar merchandise in competing stores.

Large stores often offer customers a choice in degree of fashion leadership by having two or more departments, each of which features styles for identical end uses but at different stages in their fashion acceptance and therefore at different price levels. In such cases, each department may have a different merchandising policy. The prestige department may have a policy of immediately clearing out any styles that have been copied down into lower price lines. The medium-priced department may have a policy of doing the same with any of their styles that have found their way into the stock of the store's basement or budget departments. When an individual style, a total look, a color, or a detail moves into a lower price level, the fashion merchandising policy of these stores usually requires its higher-priced departments to clear their stocks of similar merchandise.

Sales Promotion and Selling Techniques

Sales promotion and selling techniques take their cues from the degree of fashion leadership evident in a store's merchandise assortments. Each has to be coordinated with the overall fashion image if the target group of consumers is to be attracted and turned into customers.

Stores that wish to be known for their fashion leadership are among the first to promote new colors and styles, stressing them in their advertising and displays. Their ads emphasize themes and looks. Both window and interior displays underline the advertised themes and looks. Price is played down, and designers' names are played up.

Stores catering to the vast middle group of customers avoid advertising extremes in styling, although such stores may have a policy of showing a few prestige numbers in their displays. In general, their advertising and displays stress the rightness of the promoted styles rather than their newness. Price is given prominence only in proportion to its importance to the particular group of customers.

Stores in the mass-merchandising category give strong prominence to price in their advertising. Since the fashion leaders and the middle group have already proved the importance of the fashions concerned, these stores concentrate on promoting their availability at budget prices. Their assortments usually contain quantities of nearly identical merchandise, thus reinforcing the idea that a particular fashion has made its mark.

Selling techniques are keyed to the fashion image the store wants to project in much the same way. In prestige stores, salespeople are coached to speak with authority about fashion, to present new ideas with confidence, and to give full service to the customer. Stores catering to the middle group of customers usually display their merchandise on open racks, but salespeople are present to answer customer questions and assist them in finding the desired styles in the right colors and sizes. Self-service fixtures dominate the mass merchandisers' selling floors, with store personnel limited primarily to stockclerks and cashiers.

Many experts believe it is at the point of sale that a store either succeeds or fails in its attempt to establish a particular fashion image—and that the salespeople are the key to that success or failure. Herbert Wittkin, former head of Stern Brothers, New York, explained it this way:

We can spend literally millions of dollars in merchandise investments; we can spend many millions more on display and merchandise presentation and advertising; we can spend unlimited energy and time in trying to influence people to think well of us—only to have it all go down the drain because of a surly sales clerk. . . . Our salespeople talk to our customers and convey a feeling with everything they do—in the way they look—the way they smile—the way they shrug their shoulders—in short, they project our image more forcefully than any other element in the store. If they are warm, friendly, alert, fashionable, efficient people, our customers make the equation that our store is all of those things. If they are brusque, short-tempered, curt, unpleasant, their impact is deadly and frequently permanently damaging. . . .[6]

Other Essential Elements

There are still other important elements to be considered by a store's top management when establishing its fashion merchandising policies. Clear-cut decisions must be made as to the quality of the merchandise it will handle, its pricing policies, and its position relative to the depth and breadth of its assortments, to exclusivity of products, and whether private or national brand goods will be featured. Each of these elements must be in harmony with the overall fashion image the store wishes to create and maintain.

Quality Standards   A store sets its quality standards in terms of those of its customers. In prestige stores, durability of merchandise may be of minor importance, but fineness of material and care in workmanship may be important. Among stores catering to the middle group of customers, both durability and good fit in merchandise may be important, the latter because of the high cost of alterations in relation to the price of the garment. Customers of mass merchandisers may evaluate each piece of merchandise in terms of the price asked for it, and stores of this type may have no set standards of quality other than that the goods be represented honestly.

Grades   Some types of fashion merchandise, such as hosiery and shoes, are graded by the producer either as "perfect" or as "irregulars" or "seconds." Less-than-perfect goods are graded "irregular" if they have defects that may affect appearance but not wear. "Seconds" are factory rejects that have faults that may affect wear. Depending upon its clientele, store policy may exclude anything except perfect goods or it may permit irregulars and seconds to be offered in special promotions or by basement departments. It is what customers want and expect that determines policy, in this as in the many other phases of fashion merchandising. If customers demand perfect goods, the store offers them; if they accept slight irregularities at concessions in price, the store follows the lead and makes such goods available when possible.

Prices   There are a number of facets to any store's price policy on fashion merchandise. These facets include:

The Selling Price   Store policy usually specifies whether prices should be rounded off to or placed at a point a few cents below an even-dollar figure. Today, both prestige stores and those catering to the middle group of customers have even-dollar prices, while mass merchandisers, as a rule, price their merchandise a few cents below the even dollar mark.

The Price Range   The difference between the highest and lowest price at which merchandise is regularly offered for sale in a department or a store is referred to as its price range. Price ranges in prestige stores tend to be moderate to high. In stores catering to the middle group of customers, prices range from moderately low to moderately high. Mass-merchandising stores tend to feature prices ranging from low to moderately low.

The Price Lines   The price points at which balanced assortments are offered are known as price lines. In stores that permit similar merchandise to be carried in several departments, each catering to a different level of income, policy may prohibit overlapping of price lines between departments or may allow some overlapping of price lines so long as there is no duplication of merchandise.

Depth versus Breadth Assortments   The degree of fashion leadership the store has chosen to

After 50 years in men's clothing Barney's has finally arrived at a fashion point of view.
All of them.

Once upon a time it was very easy for a man to be in fashion. He simply wore what everybody else wore.

Today, that's no longer the case.

Today there are literally hundreds of different ways in which a man can express himself.

And no one style or "look" is more fashionable than the other.

In 1973, the man who wears a traditional vested glen plaid suit with wingtip shoes and shirt with button-down collar is just as fashionable as the man who wears a Pierre Cardin suit with suede shoes by Rosetti of Rome.

And today, it's very often the same man.

Where do you go when anything goes?

The idea that you have to go to one store for the "conservative look" and another store for designer styling or some other store for something else is no longer fashionable.

Who has the time? Or the patience?

Today, the most fashionable store is the store that has the most.

And that store is Barney's.

We don't know what you want. But we've got it.

Barney's has never been a know-it-all when it comes to men's fashion. For fifty years our goal has been to have-it-all.

And we have never been closer to achieving that goal than we are this fall.

The Madison Room at Barney's is steeped in traditional fashions. Here you'll find the biggest names in the softly constructed natural shoulder look.

In designer clothing, no one tops Barney's International House. Our collection is five stories tall.

Neither traditionalist nor designer devotee can fail to find merit in the quiet elegance of English clothing. We've just opened an entire floor of suits, coats and sportwear by DAKS, Kilgour, French & Stanbury, Rodex, Burberrys and Aquascutum.

If your taste runs to something more far-out, you don't have to go far to find it. Just go down to Barney's Underground.

All in all, Barney's has 21 shops and dens which contain the most comprehensive collection of men's fashion you'll find anywhere in the world.

One area where Barney's remains unfashionable.

Although we're flexible on fashion, Barney's does have a point-of-view you won't find around much anymore.

It's called value.

At Barney's you always get your money's worth. Not only in the price you pay, but in the quality you get for the price.

In the little things too. Like free alterations and free parking.

Isn't it nice to know that a store that could be so fashionable in one respect, can be so old-fashioned in another?

Barney's
7th Avenue and 17th Street
Open 9 A.M. to 9:30 P.M. We honor the American Express Card.

Barney's concentrates on promoting its breadth of assortments, saying "We don't know what you want. But we've got it." Above, an ad run by Barney's on its fiftieth anniversary.

Barney's, New York City

project usually determines how deep and how wide its assortments will be. Broad, shallow assortments, presenting a large variety of styles but not a large stock of any one style, are characteristic of prestige stores and departments. In stores catering to the middle group of customers, assortments are usually broad and shallow early in the season, when new styles are still being tested for acceptance, but relatively narrow and deep later in the season, once the trend of demand has become clear. Mass merchandisers concentrate on narrow, deep assortments of proven popular styles. Some large stores, with the space to carry wider assortments, may have broad, shallow stocks on the outer fringes of demand and narrow, deep stocks where demand is clearly defined.

Exclusivity "Exclusivity" is an important selling point for stores that cater to fashion leaders. Stores serving the middle group of customers also welcome exclusivity as a competitive weapon. Exclusive styles may come from several sources: foreign markets; small factories; new, young designers; sometimes large manufacturers who prefer exclusive distribution and sell to only one store in an area. Some stores consider exclusives so important that their buyers are expected to work with producers toward having special styles made up for the store.

Brands   A private or store brand, meeting standards specified by the retailer, belongs exclusively to that store and is used to ensure consistent quality of product or to meet price competition, among many other purposes. A national brand, sold by many stores across the country, can give stores and customers alike a consistent guarantee of quality and fashion correctness. Prestige stores tend to feature their own store labels and designer names. National brands are the backbone of assortments found in department stores. Chain and mail-order companies consistently feature private brands. National brands are sometimes offered by mass merchandisers, but as a rule these stores tend to feature unbranded merchandise.

CHANGING A FASHION IMAGE

Stores sometimes find it either necessary or advantageous to shift their sights and to aim for a different target group of customers than the one for which their fashion image was originally created. Such a change may be necessary if the character of the community the store serves undergoes a marked change. Such a change may be advantageous if the store wants to reach out for additional groups of customers not previously served, or to fill a merchandising need temporarily left unfilled by competing stores, or even to retreat from a merchandising area in which the competition has become too fierce.

The classic case of the necessity to change an image is that of the neighborhood store whose original customers have moved out of the area and have been replaced by people of other income or ethnic groups. If the store is to continue to do business at its old location, it must adjust its fashion image to attract the new potential clientele flowing into the area. If, on the other hand, the store wants to retain its original image, it must move to a different

area where it can find enough customers of the original type to support it.

Department stores in the years since World War II have been faced with such problems of adjusting to shifting groups of customers. In many cities, there was a flow of middle-class and well-to-do families from the cities to the suburbs in the 1950s. Center-city stores have followed them there with branch stores, but had to reconcile themselves to the loss of some of their downtown store demand for medium- to higher-priced goods. In recent years, however, there has been somewhat of a return flow of moderate- to higher-income customers to the city, as well as a general change in the income and taste levels of almost all types of customers. As a result, department and specialty stores had to readjust their central-city images once again, in atmosphere as well as merchandise, to a level attractive to these customers.

Changing an image, once it has been established, is not easy and is usually a slow and gradual process. The store has to teach its customers to forget the old familiar face it has turned to them for years and to become accustomed to a new face. Some stores that have changed successfully have taken a decade or more to complete the process. A gradually changing assortment, a gradually changing tempo in promotion, a gradual shift in the quality of selling and other services—all permit a store to replace the customers it has lost or no longer wishes to serve with new customers year by year.

One of the most sweeping image turnabouts in recent years occurred when discounters added fashion apparel to operations that formerly had been concerned only with hard goods. Starting with what might be called a negative image as nonfashion retailers, these merchants used assortments, displays, and advertising in their attempts to get people to consider them as apparel and accessories outlets. Some fumbled and ruined their businesses, but there have been some spectacular successes.

A few of the discounters, originally well entrenched in the fashion field at its lower levels, have successfully moved up the ladder toward the earlier stages of the fashion cycle and toward higher-priced merchandise. Ohrbach's and Alexander's, in New York, are especially noteworthy in this respect. Each made the change by opening a store in an area of the city with greater fashion prestige than the store's original home enjoyed. Ohrbach's abandoned its original location entirely. Alexander's retained its existing stores but gave some of its new units impressive lighting, wide aisles, and glittering chandeliers to convey a higher fashion image. No one facet of the operation in either store carried the whole burden of changing its image; merchandising, publicity, promotion, display, and selling techniques all worked together to produce an upgraded image.

TYPES OF FASHION IMAGES

Based on the target group of customers it seeks to win, each store works to create its own distinctive fashion image. This image may be anything from fashion leadership to bargain headquarters, from the immensity of a huge department store to the intimacy of a tiny boutique.

In general, a store's fashion image is a composite of its degree of fashion leadership, its relative size, and its type of operation.

Degree of Fashion Leadership

Although the degree of fashion leadership a store chooses to assume can be at any point along a graduated scale, stores can be divided generally into three categories: those who project a high fashion image, those who project a middle-of-the-road fashion image, and mass marketers of widely accepted fashions.

Fashion Leaders Those merchants who elect to deal in high fashion, who cater to customers who want to be in the forefront of fashion, have a relatively straightforward course in creating a fashion image. The styles they feature must be new and prophetic; every assortment in the store must be coordinated with all others; and the customer, whether she wants bras, shoes, handbags, or slenderizing treatments, must have her wants understood perfectly. This is easily said, but it involves a superlative job of coordinating the market work, the merchandise selections, the emphasis, and the promotion of every component of every new look in fashion that the store chooses to offer. Dresses must relate to coats, and slips must relate to dresses; loungewear must relate to ready-to-wear; all accessories, from bedroom slippers to bath salts, must be in tune with the current fashion trend.

Stores that achieve such fashion leadership in their merchandise assortments have such distinctive advertising that their ads can be easily recognized even without the store name. Their promotions are usually around a theme rather than concerned with specific items of merchandise. They speak of looks and themes, rather than of individual styles of dresses, shoes, or handbags. When they do advertise a specific item, it is promoted not as an item alone but as a necessary component of a currently acceptable fashion theme. Prices are mentioned almost as an afterthought and never prominently.

Salespeople in such stores are extremely well trained in fashion and coached in how and when to advise customers. If necessary, they are expected to leave the departments to which they have been assigned in order to help customers assemble a total outfit, from foundations to furs. Alterations to improve the fit of garments are made with meticulous care; returns are accepted no matter what the reason. Physical surroundings are compatible with what customers are accustomed to at home: rich carpets; beautifully upholstered chairs and sofas; expensive draperies, wall treatments, and lighting fixtures.

Public relations activities of such stores are likely to be of the played-down type. The head of the store may give parties that rate society-page mention to select groups of customers and friends. Fashion shows may be small and intimate, run by a store executive who knows everyone in the audience by name and who probably has a good idea which favorite designer's clothes are in the closet of each one. Publicity on behalf of the store is likely

Should you spy a **very** petite well dressed woman zipping through customs and looking fit as a fiddle after an eleven hour flight, chances are you've just caught a glimpse of Adele Simpson. Adele is one of America's most **indefatigable** designers and one of Altman's super-reliable resources for the kind of fashion coverage our woman likes and needs **(desperately)**.

We asked what she had been up to in the past months and she told us that just since January 1st she had attended **65 lunches,** given 31 parties, turned   two collections, and clocked about 75,000 miles on Pan Am.

With this kind of super-charged life, Adele says she has plenty of time to reflect on what woman do, think, wear, and want. She says she is a **"people watcher".** That's probably why she dresses so many important women who travel a lot, speak a lot, work a lot, committee a lot, and play a lot. Adele Simpson understands them.

And we might add that Mrs. Simpson never misses a trick—an example: one Sunday, while relaxing in her Greenwich hideaway (if you can call gardening, sketching, **snipping** fabrics, coordinating colors, and writing a jillion letters relaxing) she spied a petal on an **anemone** in her greenhouse. Quick as a bunny, she sent off a note with the petal to her Italian print man. This was precisely **the** red she wanted. She got it. She could have settled for his red, but Mrs. Simpson wanted her own. It's that kind of care, energy, and keen eye that make her clothes well worth **"springing"** for.

Take the dress we sketched here. it's just one of Mrs. Simpson's new Hothouse prints and any woman will feel superbly dressed in it whether she's dining penthouse-style or zipping into the Union Club for a gala dinner. It has a wrap skirt **(Hello, Carmen Miranda)** and a V-neck wrapped bodice which is bare, indeed, but properly bare. The print is a mélange of pink, white, black and "that red" from the greenhouse.

Well, if Mrs. Simpson can watch people, it's your turn to watch Mrs. Simpson. Her whole marvelous print collection will be in our **Fifth Avenue** windows all this week.

Oops, we forgot, the dress is 240.00 and comes in sizes 6 to 14.

B. Altman & Co

An image of fashion leadership is often achieved through ads featuring designers.
B. Altman & Co.

to be in terms of having dressed well-known people or of the store owner's personal participation in community projects.

Mass Retail Marketers At the lower end of the price and fashion scale, the method of creating a fashion image for a retail store is equally as direct as that of the fashion leaders. The image that mass merchandisers strive for is one of bargains in fashions that have become widely accepted. Target customers of such a store do not expect individual service; they are satisfied to wait on themselves, try on garments in crowded fitting rooms; and stand in line at a cashier's desk to pay for their purchases. Crowds do not bother them; instead, a crowd implies that the bargains must be good to draw so many shoppers. Little or no luxury is evident in the surroundings; only the simplest and most functional of furnishings and lighting are used.

Coordination of an outfit in mass-merchandising stores is strictly a customer's job. Although the store may have provided the related accessories to go with its clothes, it is up to the customer to collect them unaided from the assortments and to put the right pieces of the fashion look together. This task is not difficult, however, since the fashion looks with which she is concerned are familiar by the time they reach the mass level of acceptance and price. Coordination of apparel and accessories has been worked out, tested, and widely worn before the fashion has reached that peak or waning stage at which the customers of such stores usually make their purchases.

The Middle Retail Marketers Retailers who operate between the two extremes in fashion leadership have the advantage of serving the largest customer group, but they have the problem of marking out the particular segment of that total group they plan to serve and then developing their merchandising, services, and promotion policies accordingly.

Timing of merchandise presentation is a major challenge to stores that wish to project a middle-of-the-road fashion image. It is not as easy for them to judge the precise stage of the fashion cycle in which their customers are interested as it is for those retailers whose customers are always fashion leaders or those whose customers are always content with fashion in its late stages. Instead, their customers are the ones who are neither first nor last to adopt the new. They are the customers who looked with interest at displays of colored bed sheets for a long period before they actually bought anything but white. They are the customers who were outraged at the early miniskirts but, two years later, let their own skirts creep above the knee. To judge the precise moment when such customers are ready to test the new, and to know how much emphasis to place upon the new in assortments, promotion, and personal selling, is a challenge to the merchandising skill and fashion knowledge of the retailer.

Another challenge to the middle marketers is devising ways to suggest the appropriate combinations of apparel and accessories to their customers. These customers do not buy with the sure touch of fashion leaders, nor have the fashions they are buying become so familiar that coordination is almost automatic. Since selling techniques cannot be as personalized as they are in prestige stores, and since their customers resist being pushed into spending more than they planned, there is a limit to what can be done by the salespeople. Advertising and display usually do an important job in this respect, showing how, for example, the right scarf, necklace, or pin will set off the neckline of a coat or dress.

These are the stores, too, that face the most plentiful competition, and they function in an area in which one store's merchandise tends to look much like that of another. In their quest for distinction, some stores of this type make a point of managing their stocks to keep them complete at all times. Their image then becomes that of the store that "always has something for me." Some seek distinction by offering special services. "Smiling service," for example, is the philosophy of one store whose management insists upon friendly greetings, cheerful acceptance of returns, and even pleasantness in efforts to collect overdue bills, as a way of making the store stand out from others with similar merchandise, similar services, and similar appearance.

Service and atmosphere that have no direct connection with fashion also help build a distinctive image for an individual store. Some stores are so meticulous about every detail of service that their customers feel reassured about the care that has been devoted to assembling their fashion assortments. Others lend luster to their image by using distinctive wrappings and boxes that customers are proud to be seen carrying. (The implication is that the smart wrap encloses equally smart merchandise.)

Some stores do things with such finesse that people automatically link their names with fashion excitement. Neiman-Marcus, the well-known Dallas specialty store, indulges in such delightful irrelevancies as offering "his and her" airplanes in one of their Christmas catalogs and an elaborate one-of-a-kind "mouse ranch" for $3,500 in another. The natural reaction of the public is to assume that a store whose customers can afford such spectacular gifts is a good place to shop—not only for a $15,000 fur coat but for a $5 fashion gift as well.

Size and Type of Organization

Very large and very small stores, because of their size, have both problems and opportunities in establishing and maintaining their fashion image that are unlike those of medium-volume stores. In addition, multiunit retail organizations have unique challenges to meet in creating and maintaining a distinctive fashion image throughout all of their many units that single-unit stores do not have.

The Giants   Giant retailers have special image considerations because of their size. Some of them sell to such a broad range of the public that they need to segment their overall image, presenting one face to those customers who are fashion leaders and another to those who are fashion followers. They often handle this through special departments or

shops, each one establishing an image for a specific group of customers: teens, tall girls, expectant mothers, sports enthusiasts, wearers of country clothes, and career or college people. The huge size of such stores permits them to engage in shop merchandising, whereas smaller stores, with more limited floor space and assortments, cannot set up such shops quite so freely.

Large stores often make capital of their bigness. They stage promotions on a spectacular scale. Instead of devoting one or two windows to a new fashion, they devote block-long batteries of windows to an idea. They hire display executives who are highly creative and whose windows and interior displays are remembered for years. They turn their main floors into flower shows, as Macy's in New York City and Hess Brothers in Allentown, Pennsylvania, do each spring. Or they regularly run ads that stress the vastness of their assortments; New York's Abraham and Straus has, using humor to make the point that one should never say something cannot be found unless one has first tried that store.

Many large stores have special facilities, such as auditoriums, that they lend to civic groups for community events. Often the auditorium is used by the store for a fashion show or demonstration that is expected to draw large crowds.

The Small Independent   At the opposite end of the size scale is the small, independently owned shop in which the proprietor is likely to be the merchandiser, policy maker, and promotion expert. Such stores, even though they may employ several salespeople, cannot afford and may not need the amount of advertising space that large stores use to enhance their image.

Small operations have their own special tools for image building, based on the personal approach. Salespeople and proprietors know customers by name; they suggest apparel to coordinate with what is already owned; they send personal notes to customers when new merchandise of suitable type has arrived. They have coins readily available for parking meters; they gift-wrap beautifully and individually; they provide innumerable friendly, person-to-person small services that cannot be offered practically by large stores.

In their merchandising, some small stores even capitalize on their smallness. They buy only a few pieces, or even single pieces, of a style. The customer who purchases a dress or coat from such a store can be certain that she will not meet herself on the street, at the bus stop, or at the club luncheon.

Chain Organizations Units of apparel chains and general merchandising chains often use image-building tools of both large and small stores. Among the large-store techniques used by a general merchandise chain, for instance, might be the establishing of special shops within its stores to feature a particular look, such as country casuals. Or an apparel chain may run a continuing series of newspaper ads of an institutional type, such as those run by a few years ago by a women's apparel chain,

featuring wardrobe components for "a certain type of customer."

Other chains find ways to offer some of the personalized service characteristic of small stores. One, for example, instructs its telephone operators to give their names to customers so that customers can be made to feel that there is a "special" operator who knows them and is interested in them. Salespeople may be encouraged to obtain customers' names for notification of special sales or new merchandise. Customer files may be kept to facilitate coordinating future purchases with what is already owned. Although the merchandise in one unit of a chain may not differ markedly from what is offered by another unit of the same organization, nevertheless it is possible for the staff of each unit to develop warm, friendly relations with customers. In this way, all customers feel they are receiving personal attention and advice when making fashion purchases.

REFERENCES
[1] *Stores,* January 1960, p. 17.
[2] *The Fashion Group Bulletin,* Oct. 3, 1972.
[3] Ibid.
[4] Ibid.
[5] Nystrom, *Fashion Merchandising,* p. 195.
[6] Wittkin, "An Image Is a Multi-faceted Thing," *Readings in Modern Retailing,* p. 230.

MERCHANDISING VOCABULARY

Define or briefly explain the following terms:

Store image   Fashion image

MERCHANDISING REVIEW

1. Clearly distinguish between the terms *store image* and *fashion image.* Do you think it is possible for a store to have a favorable store image and an unfavorable fashion image, or vice versa? Defend your answer.

2. Why is it important for a store to clearly define or have a clean-cut profile of its target group of customers before attempting to establish and implement its fashion philosophy?

3. Name and briefly discuss the two major elements of a store's fashion merchandising policy.

4. Name at least four other essential elements of a store's fashion merchandising policy. Briefly describe the implications of each for the store's fashion image.

5. For what specific reasons might a store seek to change its fashion image?

6. What are some of the things a store can do to achieve a distinctive fashion image if it is neither a fashion leader nor a mass merchandiser?

7. Describe the merchandise, selling, and promotional characteristics you might expect to find in a store whose image is one of fashion leadership.

8. Describe the merchandise, selling, and promotional characteristics you might expect to find in a mass-merchandising store.

9. Describe the merchandise, selling, and promotional characteristics you might expect to find in a store with a middle-of-the-road fashion image.

10. What are some of the image-building devices available to an independent store that may be too small to do much advertising?

MERCHANDISING DIGEST

1. It is stated in the text that "stores serving areas in which the preferences of potential customers are fairly similar tend to adopt somewhat similar fashion images, but stores with a variety of target groups to choose from have a variety of fashion image possibilities open to them." Discuss this statement and its implications, citing examples to illustrate your opinions on the subject.

2. Discuss the following statement from the text: "Changing an image, once it has been established, is not easy and is usually a slow and gradual process." What factors are involved? Why should change be slow rather than abrupt? Do you know of any store that has undertaken to change its previous image? If so, explain how such change was brought about.

APPENDIX: CAREER OPPORTUNITIES IN FASHION

Fashion is fun; fashion is excitement; fashion is big business. Fashion is also a seemingly endless parade of career opportunities for those who want them and prepare for them. The fashion field is so vast, however, that beginners need a guide to the path that will lead them to their goals in fashion work, whether the goal be merchandise manager or photographer, fashion model or designer, copywriter or boutique owner.

This Appendix offers such a guide. Its brief description of the areas open to those interested in fashion may save beginners some initial uncertainty and direct them to that part of the fashion field in which they will be most capable and feel most content.

Whichever part that may be, it is sure to be an exacting and stimulating place to work. Some fashion careers are more rewarding than others in terms of money and recognition, but whatever career is chosen, it is certain to develop an awareness of people, to leave no room for boredom, to provide a quantity of hard work, and to give full satisfaction for that work.

SCOPE OF THE FASHION BUSINESS

The size and influence of the field of fashion cannot be measured in dollars alone—but, indicatively, out of every dollar of personal consumption expenditures in the United States each year, about 10 cents is used for such direct manifestations of fashion as apparel, accessories, and personal adornment.

Nor can what is included in the fashion field be readily defined. Fashion is a reflection of the consumer's way of life, and it manifests itself in cars as well as clothing, in houses as well as hats, in any commodity or service in which the consumer exercises personal choice.

The "fashion industries" are considered to be those engaged in producing apparel and accessories for men, women, and children, including the merchandise categories known as "boys" and "girls." In this Appendix, as throughout the book, any reference to "fashion industries" means these, unless others are specifically mentioned. The term "fashion business," however, tends to include all industries and services connected with fashion: manufacturing, distribution, advertising, publishing, and consulting—any business concerned with goods or services in which fashion is a factor.

In the earlier part of this century, some industries went along for years with little regard for consumer preferences and little consumer demand for style change. But as preferences and demands became more diverse as a result of fast-changing lifestyles, most industries came to accept the fact that consumers alone make fashions by their acceptance or rejection of offered styles. To the career seeker, the spreading influence of fashion to industries unrelated to apparel and accessories means this: Experience gained in the primary fashion industries has useful application to almost any other industry serving consumers.

The person who embarks on a fashion career today enters a field that is far-flung and many faceted. This field provides freedom: freedom to grow, freedom to change jobs or direction, freedom to move to different cities or even to different countries without having to begin anew in an unrelated type of work.

International Character of American Fashion

The American fashion business today is international. Raw materials, such as furs, hides, and fibers, are imported from remote areas of the world. Manufactured goods, too, including both apparel and accessories items, are imported from all over the world. Also imported are ideas and inspiration, not only from the couture houses of Europe but from any part of the world where general news or fashion news is being made. Even outer space is within fashion's territory, as evidenced by jumpsuits and other apparel inspired by astronaut gear.

American goods and ideas are exported. Many American manufacturers contract to have their lines produced abroad under franchise agreements. American fashions are produced in foreign countries to the specifications of American firms. Producers in other countries send their young people to Seventh Avenue and to the fashion industries' technical schools in the United States to prepare them for fashion production careers. Sometimes the producers themselves seek United States know-how to help them establish or improve their fashion business in their home countries. In addition, the United States exports its know-how in fashion retailing. Stores from all over the world are members of the National Retail Merchants Association. Foreign delegates attend NRMA conventions as special guests, and the NRMA has sent delegations of domestic retailers to visit foreign stores and participate in workshops with executives of those foreign firms.

Within the borders of the United States, fashion activity is everywhere. Seventh Avenue in New York City remains the heart of the apparel-producing industries, but there are also creative centers in Los Angeles, Dallas, Miami, and cities of the Midwest. Even in some seemingly unlikely small towns, there are mills and factories that need people to guide their output along current fashion lines. And there are retailers of fashion in every major city, in every suburb, and in every small town.

In planning a career in fashion, these facts mean that geography need not fence a person in. Almost any location in this country and throughout the world is one in which fashion work of some sort can be found or created.

Facets of Fashion Activity

Not only is fashion work ubiquitous, but its activities are varied enough to attract people with widely differing interests and capabilities. Some activities, such as designing, advertising, and display, demand a high degree of creativity and originality. Others, such as fiber and fabric research and development, require a scientific bent. Still others, such as plant management and retailing management, call for business acumen and administrative skills.

Strong feet and outgoing natures are indispensable in retail or wholesale selling, and also in the market work of retail buyers, buying office representatives, magazine editors, and their assistants. Writing, photography, and sketching are much used in the fashion field, and there is demand for those with appropriate skills. Sewing skills, even when they are not coupled with a designer's creativity, can lead to such interesting work as sample making. Teaching ability has its place in personnel work, in supervisory work, and in the schools devoted to fashion training.

Natural endowments, such as a good face and figure, sometimes make a modeling job possible, and through it perhaps an entry into other phases of the fashion field. Theatrical training has its place, too, especially in planning more sophisticated fashion shows, such as when a fiber company introduces a new product to retail audiences.

For others, such talents as orderly work habits and willingness to please, if coupled with an interest in fashion, can add up to a stimulating assignment as a receptionist, an assistant, or a secretary to an executive in one of the many branches of the fashion industry. Such jobs often offer the opportunity to discover and develop hitherto unrealized abilities in the fashion field.

CAREERS IN MANUFACTURING

The principal manufacturing industries in the fashion field require fashion-oriented and fashion-trained people to guide their production, reinforce their selling efforts, and disseminate fashion information to their customers and to the consuming public. In addition, these industries also require technical experts of many kinds, skilled and unskilled factory labor, and office workers of various types.

Fashion-related careers to be found in manufacturing include those among raw materials producers, the apparel trade, suppliers to the apparel trade, the accessories trades, and the home sewing industry.

Raw Materials Industries

The greatest number and variety of fashion careers in the raw materials field are found among the producers of fiber and fabrics. This is not only a big field but also a field that is very much interested in and keeps close contact with all phases of the fashion business. Similar positions, but in smaller number, are also to be found with other raw materials producers, such as leather and furs, and their respective industry associations.

Fashion Expert Fiber producers and fabric firms have fashion departments headed by individuals with a variety of titles who attend worldwide fashion openings, keep in close touch with all sources of fashion information, and disseminate the fashion story throughout their respective organizations. Candidates for such positions either may have already acquired fashion expertise in other areas of the fashion business or are presently employees of

the firm who have demonstrated an ability to handle such responsibilities.

The fashion department's activities usually require personnel with the ability to coordinate apparel and accessories, to stage fashion shows, to work with the press, to assist individual producers and retailers with fashion-related problems or projects, and to set up fashion exhibits for the trade or for the public. These extremely varied demands made upon all who work in such departments constitute an excellent training school, and even at the clerical level the beginners in such a department learn much about fashion and, if sufficiently motivated, are in the position to train themselves for promotion.

Fabric Designer While it takes technical skills to produce a fiber, it takes both technical and artistic skills to produce a fabric. Fabric companies employ designers who have both technical knowledge of the processes involved in producing a fabric as well as artistic ability and the ability to successfully anticipate fashion trends. The fabric designer, who works far in advance of the apparel trades, needs fashion radar of superlative quality. Some designers are allowed to concentrate on their own ideas, while others are expected to work out special fabric designs for certain customers. In either case, the chief designer for a fabric mill makes fashion decisions that can involve vast capital investments every time a new season's line is prepared.

Fabric Stylist Many fabric companies employ a fabric stylist to revise existing fabric designs for a new seasonal line or adapt them for specific markets. Some people find this job a career in itself; others use it as a steppingstone to the more creative job of fabric designer.

Fabric Librarian Most major man-made fiber sources maintain libraries of fabrics that are made from their fibers. These libraries consist of fabric swatches clipped to cards on which detailed descriptions and sources of supply are recorded.

The librarian in charge is expected to be thoroughly capable of discussing fashion and fabric matters with interested designers and manufacturers and knowledgeable not only about the firm's products but also about the market in general.

Educational Consultant Most of the fiber producers and some of the fabric houses maintain departments to convey technical information about their products to apparel producers, retailers, and consumers. Educational departments answer inquiries, prepare exhibits, address groups of retail salespeople or consumers, and stage demonstrations. In addition to a knowledge of both the technology and the fashion influence involved, graciousness is a must in this work, along with an ability to talk to people at all educational and social levels.

Industry Consultant Most of the fiber companies and some of the fabric houses assign executives to study the needs of the individual industries in which their products are used. These executives act as a liaison between their firms and the industries in which they specialize. If a company is about to introduce a new fiber, fabric, finish, or treatment, its industry consultants work closely with consumer goods producers, encouraging them to try the new product and helping them to solve any problems related to its use. The help these consultants give may also extend to the retail level, assisting retailers in launching fashions that employ the new product.

Publicity Executive In both fiber and fabric companies, the publicity staff keeps in close touch with technical as well as fashion matters and makes information about company products readily available to the trade and consumer press. Usually product stories can be tied to fashion information, enhancing their appeal to editors and readers alike.

The publicity executive in charge of the department generally has a thorough understanding of fashion and journalism, along with a pleasing personality and a good memory for names and faces. These attributes are essential in preparing press releases, working with photographers who provide illustrative material for those releases, and working with members of the press who seek help on feature stories or who want background information. Skill in subtle selling is useful in placing unsolicited publicity, when an editor has to be convinced of the value and interest of the story to the publication's audience.

In the major fiber-producing companies, there may be a corps of publicity executives, each specializing in one or two closely related industries. One may concentrate on the use of specific fibers in apparel fabrics, for instance, while another may specialize in the use of the company's fibers in rugs and carpeting. In smaller organizations, there may be only one such executive. In any case, there are usually typists, secretaries, and assistants—and a beginner who starts in any such capacity is in an excellent position to learn the art of fashion publicity.

Other Areas Both fiber and fabric industries offer career opportunities in sales, market research, and promotion. These are not always fashion jobs, however, and rarely are they open to beginners. Some experience within the company and some specialized skill in the field are likely to be more important than a knowledge of fashion alone in getting such jobs. Advertising, including its more exciting aspects such as the production of television shows, is often handled by advertising agencies rather than by the company's own advertising department.

Apparel Trades

For creative people, the fashion plum of the apparel trades is the designer's job. But the climb to this top job is often laborious and uncertain, and the footing at the top may be slippery. New talent is always elbowing its way in, and even the most successful couture designers are haunted by the prospect of a season when their ideas do not inspire, do not have customer appeal.

Personal interviews are an important part of getting a job.
The Broadway-Hale Stores, Inc.

Designing So much of an apparel firm's life depends upon the styling of its line that the designing responsibility is rarely entrusted to a beginner, even a fantastically talented one. There are matters of cost and mass production techniques involved, for example, and unless one is working in a couture house, there is also the business of judging accurately the point in the fashion cycle at which the firm's customers will buy.

For moderate-priced and mass-market producers, the designer's job may be one of adapting rather than creating. Immense skill may be required, nevertheless, to take a daringly original couture idea and modify it so that it appears bright and new but not terrifyingly unfamiliar to a mass-market or middle-income customer.

The beginner, aside from offering designs on a free-lance basis, can seek a number of jobs below the designer level and hope to work up to that top level. Entry-level design jobs are:

- *Assistant Designer* As a member of a large designing team, the assistant works under a head designer. Designing talent, indicated by submitted samples, and good technical knowledge are expected so that the assistant can help the designer in every aspect of the latter's job. Also highly desirable are a good disposition and the ability to accept and learn from criticism. In the tensions and frustrations that surround a head designer's job, corrections and suggestions may not always be made with the utmost tact.
- *Patternmaker* From the designer's sketch or sample, a pattern is made from which a sample garment is cut. The sample is tested for fit and appearance, and adjustments or even a new pattern may be required. Once acceptable results have been achieved and production of the new style decided upon, the patternmaker "grades" the pattern, that is, makes up a separate pattern for each of the sizes in which the style will be produced. The need for patience and technical skill is obvious, and these should be coupled with an understanding of sketching, draping, construction, and good workmanship.
- *Sketcher* From the designer's rough drawings working sketches may be made for the information of the sample maker and also for illustrations to be used in the showroom book. The showroom book includes fashion sketches of each style in a line, together with swatches of the materials used for each style illustrated.
- *Sample Maker* An all-around sewer is expected to construct a garment from a sketch or pattern. If it is to be modeled, the sample maker adjusts it to fit the designated model perfectly. The job of a sample maker is a particularly instructive

one for future designers, since it provides training in the fundamentals of design, sketching, pattern making, and construction.[1]

Advertising and Publicity An advertising manager, with possibly an assistant or two, may handle the advertising and publicity for an apparel manufacturer. Whether or not the firm is large enough to hire the services of an advertising agency (and most are not), there may be occasions on which ads are placed in cooperation with retailers or in cooperation with fiber and fabric sources. Publicity, usually a part of the advertising job, involves sending out press releases, interesting consumer publications in some of the firm's new styles, and so on. Promotion kits for retailers are prepared under the direction of the advertising manager, as are statement enclosures and other direct-mail pieces offered for retail use. Aspiring assistants in this job have a distinct advantage if they have had enough retail advertising experience to be able to draw up rough layouts and suggest copy for store use.

Sales Opportunities The sales representatives who call upon retail stores should know the fashion points as well as the value points of their merchandise. Nowadays, sales representatives are expected to be able to address retail salespeople, if invited to do so, or even to take part in forums and clinics for consumers.

Showroom sales are sometimes handled by a junior sales representative who is awaiting the opportunity to cover a territory alone. At other times, a showroom assistant, with good disposition, good feet, and a good memory, is hired. The assistant is expected to greet customers, understand their requirements, show the line, and help them place orders. Good appearance is especially important here, since the showroom assistant sometimes has to substitute for a model.

An understanding of retail merchandising, promotion, and fashion coordination is extremely helpful in all sales jobs in the apparel field. When selling to retailers, it is important to understand their needs, problems, methods of operation, and what stage of the fashion cycle is of major interest to their customers. With such a background, sales representatives can present a line more effectively and, moreover, can collect and develop sound retail merchandising and promotion ideas for their accounts.

Suppliers to the Apparel Trades

Belts, buttons, zippers, and other minor but necessary components of garments are produced and sold by companies that range in size from one-person operations to large national firms. A great deal of business with apparel producers is done by tiny firms that offer little opportunity to the outsider. Some of the larger producers, however, offer job opportunities in selling to the apparel trades or to retailers, working either for one firm or as a commission representative for several firms.

Fashion trends cause ups and downs for producers in this field, with consequent variations in selling opportunities. When fashion favors the industrial zipper, for example, no amount of sales ability is likely to create a market for delicate buttons or ruffling; when shifts are in, the most persuasive salesperson is balked in efforts to sell belts. In this field, a knowledge of fashion is important if producers are to know what products to offer and when to resign themselves to temporarily diminished sales prospects.

Sales representatives calling on the apparel trades should know, in addition to the fashion significance of what they offer, something about garment production, for the mechanics of production play as much a part as fashion does in a line's profitability. Representatives calling on the retail trade usually find themselves selling to the notions department, whose buyer may not be strongly fashion-oriented, and they must be especially skilled in presenting the fashion story of their wares, not only to the buyer but also to the salespeople. A notions department carries such a miscellaneous assortment of goods, from shoe polish to swim caps, that the fashion aspects of some of its assortment are often overlooked in sales training programs; the

representative who can help the department on this point becomes doubly welcome.

Some of the larger producers of such items as buttons and zippers keep close track of fashion's impact on their business. Among these firms it is not unusual to employ a fashion expert who analyzes trends to guide production toward the most salable types, sizes, and colors. The same expert also may have responsibilities in such other areas as publicity and promotion. In a large button firm, for example, the fashion expert may work out new and acceptable ways to use buttons to highlight the current fashion features of garments. These uses may then be publicized to apparel producers, notions departments, and to the press; displays may be worked out that help retailers sell the company's buttons to the over-the-counter customer. Such fashion specialist jobs are few in number, but they are fascinating for those who like widely varied activities. Entry is through the understudy route or through acquiring sufficient fashion experience in other fields to be hired from the outside as a full-fledged expert or consultant.

Accessories Trades

For the artistic person, designing of accessories is a huge field in which a talented beginner or an experienced free-lancer can find exciting creative opportunities. Many of the firms in the field are small; they depend upon free-lance designers to style their lines and upon their industry trade associations to promote and publicize their products.

A background in apparel fashions is necessary to design accessories that coordinate with the related garments, and a knowledge of production procedures and problems is essential—designing for commercial purposes has to result in a practical as well as a fashionable style.

The larger firms and the large industries in the accessories field offer some positions that combine fashion coordination and publicity functions. Similar jobs also exist in some of the trade associations serving these industries. Those firms that do national advertising, such as the better-known makers of shoes, handbags, and hosiery, have advertising departments that work with agencies and suggest or develop tie-ins for retailers.

Selling jobs require fashion knowledge. The sales representative or the showroom assistant who can give the retail buyer the fashion background of the merchandise has a natural advantage over the one who knows only quality and workmanship points.

A particularly interesting field of work is among the millinery syndicates, which are so close to their industry that they are almost a part of production. In these syndicates, the fashion staff works closely with both producers and retail stores, not only on millinery trends but on overall fashion trends and fashion coordination as well. Entry to these fashion staffs is usually through the assistant route or from an allied field as an already established expert.

Jobs in the accessories field can lead to other fashion fields, too. One of the country's most successful fashion coordinators, who headed the coordination work at a major buying office for years, got her start as a fashionist for a millinery syndicate. She won the job because she looked better in hats than other aspirants—but she succeeded because she brought to the job an excellent mind and sound training in fashion fundamentals.

Home Sewing Industry

The 40 million girls and women in this country who make clothes[2] are quite as fashion-conscious as those who buy ready-to-wear—and often more so. Some sew for the pleasure of it; others, to have garments of better quality than they could otherwise afford; still others, because their fashion ideas are a jump ahead of what they can find in the stores.

The industries that serve these home sewers include the sewing machine companies, the notions producers, the pattern companies, and the over-the-counter divisions of fabric companies. All these industries have learned—some of them the hard way—that fashion is a more effective spur to home dressmaking than either the economy or figure problems. All the industries use fashionists who can interpret fashion trends in terms of what the home sewer wants and can accomplish. Designers for the pattern companies are as much in step with fashion as those for apparel producers, but with an emphasis on finding ways to achieve currently important effects without taxing the skills of the average sewer or demanding too much time in the production of the garment.

The fashion staffs of industries serving women who make their own and their children's clothes have to learn the art of making instructions simple and clear. They work with photographers and sketchers to achieve illustrations that will show both how to make the garment and how the finished garment will look. Particularly in the fabric and pattern fields, members of fashion staffs have to be able to stage fashion shows for stores and give talks to consumers describing and illustrating how easily fashion can be created at home.

Working with schools and with schoolchildren is also vitally important, for if this effort is allowed to lapse, the industry may lose a generation of home sewers. Sewing used to be learned at home, but many families have relinquished this training to the schools.

For those with designing ability, pattern companies offer jobs for people to begin as assistants and work up. For those with a flair for fashion coordination, publicity, sales, or a combination thereof, excellent career opportunities are offered by the pattern companies, the sewing machine companies, and some of the larger firms in the sewing notions field. Entry can be as an assistant, or as an established expert with experience gained in a related field.

CAREERS IN RETAILING

One unique element of retailing is that there is scarcely a fashion career goal that cannot be reached through a retail organization. Even designing has its chance for expression among the few stores that still have custom workshops and their own designers. For the most part, a retail career demands a keen interest in merchandise, an equally keen interest in people, the sort of business acumen that recognizes the importance of attention to detail as well as long-range planning, energy, and a keen understanding of fashion.

Every phase of retailing demands the ability to deal pleasantly with people: customers, suppliers, and fellow workers alike. One of the earmarks of the successful buyer, merchandiser, or fashion coordinator is the ability to win the cooperation of subordinates as well as superiors. A much-admired and successful department store buyer was fond of saying that she was so fortunate in the cooperation she received from salespeople, publicity director, her fellow buyers, and others who worked with her, that she would not do a thing to complicate their jobs. Her subordinates and her colleagues told the story differently: She was so thoughtful and considerate that there was nothing they would not do to help her.

Merchandising Careers

The starting place for most merchandising careers is in selling. Here one experiences face-to-face encounters with customers and the problem of anticipating what they will want.

From a selling job, the next move up the promotion ladder may be to head of stock, a position in which one may do some selling but is mainly responsible for replenishing stock in the selling area from the stock room, reporting "outs," noticing and reporting slow sellers, and advising the buyer on unfilled customer wants. In branch stores, this position is usually handled by a department manager who acts as liaison between salespeople and buyer and may be responsible for more than one related department. Both the head of stock in a large store and the department manager at a branch may do some of the more routine reordering, subject to the buyer's approval.

The assistant buyer's job is the next step upward. As an understudy to the buyer, the assistant buyer may be called in to view the line of a visiting sales representative or taken occasionally to the market on a buying trip. Usually, however, the assistant relieves the buyer of floor supervision, helps to train and supervise salespeople, processes branch questions and requests, or writes up reorders for basic stocks subject to the buyer's approval. The assistant buyer may verify prices on incoming merchandise, telephone resources in another city to expedite merchandise on order, verify advertising proofs, post advertising tear sheets in the parent store department and dispatch other copies to the branches, run a meeting with salespeople on new merchandise or fashion or sales ability, schedule hours for sales and stock help, among other tasks.

Buyers are virtually in business for themselves, in the sense that they have to budget and plan their expenditures, select the actual merchandise for resale, and decide what is to be advertised or displayed, and why. The job usually involves from two to a dozen or more market trips a year. The buyer must have the ability to teach and train subordinates and the ability to work well with advertising, display, personnel, and other divisions of the store.

Usually, the merchandise manager, whether a general merchandise manager or a divisional merchandise manager, is either a former buyer or a graduate of a school of retailing or business administration, or both. He or she has sufficient knowledge of budgetary controls and principles of management to supervise buyers. The merchandise manager coordinates the efforts of a group of departments, with or without the aid of a fashion coordinator, so that the fashion picture each department presents to the public is related in theme, timing, and emphasis to those presented by the others.

The final merchandising career level is top management, which demands, in addition to fashion and merchandising know-how, an understanding of every phase of store operation, from housekeeping to finances. To travel the road from selling up to policy making is not impossible, but neither is it easy—a store may have hundreds or thousands of employees, but it has only a few people on its top management team.

For those interested in retailing as a career, well-qualified beginners may be recruited on college campuses or selected from among store employees who have demonstrated executive potential. For such people, large stores conduct formalized junior executive training programs. Total store orientation is provided through rotating job assignments in all phases of store operation and through regularly scheduled classes, usually conducted by heads of the various activities of the store. Those who successfully complete the training program qualify for junior executive positions, and they are assigned according to the talents and abilities they have shown during the training period.

The other way into large department and specialty stores is through their personnel departments, which interview, screen, and train desirable applicants 52 weeks of the year. A personal visit, with a preliminary mail contact, if the store is in a distant city, is advisable. First, however, anyone interested in a retail merchandising career should examine a store's advertising, display, and merchandise before making an application; unless one feels at home in a particular store, it might be wise to look to other retail establishments for employment opportunities.

Smaller stores are necessarily less formal in their interviewing, hiring, training, and promotion procedures. Openings are fewer, and advancement may come more slowly than in a larger store. In a small organization, however, there is little chance of being overlooked for promotion, and there is ample opportunity to learn every phase of store operation as part of each day's work.

As a general rule, those who enjoy administrative work and prefer to function within the framework of clearly defined responsibilities are well advised to investigate the larger retail organizations for the start of their careers. Those who enjoy a shirtsleeves atmosphere, who are versatile, and who get pleasure in dealing with all kinds of challenges (from digging out after a snowstorm to working up a spectacular fashion display), will probably enjoy the variety of work in a smaller store.

Sales Promotion Careers

The career opportunities in sales promotion include jobs on the advertising staff, the publicity and public relations staff, and the display staff.

Copywriters and artists who begin in retailing usually enjoy a tremendous advantage ever afterward. If they leave the field and go into advertising agencies or go to work for producers, they carry with them an understanding of consumer reaction that can be learned in no better school than the retail store. There is something exciting about a lineup of customers waiting for the store to open, and by their presence telling a copywriter that the ad in last night's paper was good. Even if the merchandise offered was a real "door buster" special, the size and temper of the waiting crowd tell the copywriter just how effective the words were.

Publicity assignments usually grow out of copywriting jobs, although outsiders are sometimes hired for this work. Involved are such diverse activities as alerting the local press to newsworthy happenings, arranging for television interviews of visiting celebrities, and working up elaborate events—whether in the name of fashion, community, or charity—that will brighten the store image. Writing ability and the ability to handle contacts are important, but in a large store the ability to keep track of details is even more important. If a department store undertakes to stage a fashion show, the publicity person assigned to the event may be responsible for checking on invitations, press and broadcast coverage, notices posted outside the store, notification of all store personnel, and so on.

Display executives usually start as assistants, with a willingness to work hard. They advance in position if they demonstrate artistic sense, a knowledge of fashion, the ability to speak in visual terms to the store's customers, and the ability to pick up important selling points about merchandise. Because there is a great deal of heavy physical work and after-hours work involved, many women have not entered this field in the past, although some have become display directors in smaller stores or

A store's advertising staff works to create ads that will capture the customer's interest.
The Broadway-Hale Stores, Inc.

have done excellent display work in the course of selling in or managing small shops.

Fashion Coordination Careers

Partly merchandising and partly promotion, the fashion coordination job is ideal for people who love fashion, know how to work with others, and are tireless. The job involves working with a great many people, from merchandise or fashion information resources to store staff to customers, and its goals are accomplished through recommendations and advice rather than direct orders. A store's fashion coordinator may have worked up through the merchandising or promotion staffs, or come into the store with sufficient outside experience in fashion to qualify as a store's top fashion authority.

The fashion coordinator's evaluation of a fashion trend or any aspect of it must be right, for he or she is making recommendations to experienced merchandisers who know their particular markets best. Each buyer is staking part of the budget on the coordinator's judgment when the recommendations are followed. Every ad that is written in line with these suggestions and every sales training session that is staged with the coordinator's help is done on the assumption that she or he knows how to read fashion's future. A beginner who has a chance to work as an assistant to such a fashion coordinator soon learns that intuition is no match for systematic checking and rechecking. A considered opinion arrived at by one fashion expert alone is not always as safe a base for merchandising and promotion operations as the combined thinking of a store and a market full of expert watchers.

Sales-supporting Careers

Retail stores have openings in fields not directly related to the buying, selling, and promoting of merchandise. These activities, which may involve more than half the employees of a store, include personnel, employment and training, accounting, customer services, and adjustments, among many others. Even in the rapidly growing area of data processing jobs, fashion knowledge can be a valuable asset. For instance, add a knowledge of fashion merchandising to an understanding of computer programming, and the result is the kind of background that can lead to a career in computer program design for fashion-oriented companies.

Of the many sales-supporting job opportunities, training is the field in which a fashion background is most likely to be of direct use. Large stores with well-staffed training departments sometimes assign one training executive to each merchandise division to assist buyers in training salespeople. A training executive assigned to a group of fashion departments, for instance, might compile a reference library of basic information on fashion merchandise and also collect and route current information on fashions. Another assignment might be setting up courses to teach salespeople and prospective buyers the basic elements of fashion, or devising contests and quizzes to keep salespeople alert, or to encourage them to sell related items.

A background in fashion aids materially in this work, not only in the apparel and accessories departments but in any others that find themselves becoming part of "the fashion business."

Chain and Mail-order Careers

Chain and catalog firms offer careers that are similar to those offered by independent stores, with this important exception: Buying, merchandising, publicity, and fashion coordination are usually handled by the headquarters staff rather than by the individual store itself.

Career advancement up the retail management ladder, if one starts in a unit of a chain or catalog organization, is from selling to department manager; to merchandise manager; to store manager; to district, regional, or central management. Those interested in such fields as buying, fashion coordination, promotion, catalog preparation, merchandising, and quality control start as assistants in regional or central headquarters, where central buyers and merchandise managers are located.

Many highly specialized jobs in the chain and catalog companies call for intimate knowledge of the fashion business. For instance, the quality-control department of one chain was called upon by the merchandising division to devise a size range for girls who fell between two size ranges currently offered by the children's market. The chain then made its new size range measurements available to any producers who wished to adopt them, whether or not they were resources of that chain.[3]

Whatever special assets the beginner presents— apparel production techniques, laboratory know-how, copywriting or art experience, selling, buying, coordination—the chain and the catalog companies can use them, but not always in the city or region where the applicant lives.

Resident Buying Office Careers

Fashion careers in resident buying offices center around market work. Market representatives "live" in their markets, see every line that is important (and many that are not), and know supply and delivery conditions in those markets as well as they know the fashion aspects of the merchandise. Market representatives also learn to work with any number of bosses: their own supervisors, the heads of the client stores, and the buyers in the stores they serve.

Entry into the market representative's job is by the apprentice route. Beginners work as assistants, literally running errands in the market all day. If the smile, the ability to remember, or the arches are weak, the career may never develop. The major job of an assistant is to follow up on details, to check with resources on deliveries and other questions that may arise, and spare the time of the market representative. In the process, the beginner gets to know the markets, the buying office routines, and the needs of the client stores. If the work is done against a background of fashion training, it is more easily mastered and promotion is apt to be more rapid.

Buying office people demonstrate tremendous physical and mental stamina in attending showings, handling mail and telephone calls, and working with visiting buyers. But they have no selling departments to oversee, no branch stores to visit, no weekend or holiday work, and no sales goals to meet. Their responsibilities are limited to specific markets.

Fashion coordinators in buying offices must function with an especially sure touch. Any errors of judgment on their part can mean wrong advice given to a number of client stores. They tour the major market sources to collect information, check their findings with appropriate market representatives, and consider what fashion publications have to suggest.

A fashion coordinator for a resident buying office usually has a secretary and an assistant, at least one of whom is trained in fashion or sketching.

In either job, a beginner with fashion training can quickly learn a great deal about fashion forecasting, markets, and coordination, all of which knowledge is needed to advance in the field.

Promotion staffs in resident buying offices are fairly small. In offices serving large stores, their function may be little more than reporting on what other stores are doing or what the New York stores are promoting. In offices serving small stores, they may draw up ads for the stores to use and send them out in the form of either rough layouts and copy suggestions or mats. The smaller the stores served by the office, the less likely it is that these stores will have full-fledged advertising departments and the more important it is for the buying office to supply them with such special assistance.

To find a place on the promotion staff of such an office, it is necessary for an applicant to have retail advertising experience or to show examples of how to prepare a retail ad. Sketching and a flair for layout are helpful; writing ability is essential.

It is possible eventually to establish one's own buying office, provided one starts small, with a few client specialty shops and a versatile staff. Specialty shops have fewer departments, and they need fewer—but very capable—market representatives than department stores need. The outlay in capital, office space, and staff is relatively small if one starts with only the fashion departments.

ADVERTISING, PUBLISHING, CONSULTING, TRADE ASSOCIATIONS

There is a wide variety of careers in those organizations that service the fashion business, including jobs in advertising agencies, on publications, at consulting firms, and at trade associations. Each area has its own requirements, but there are important jobs in each area in which an understanding of fashion is vital.

Advertising Agencies

Beginners, even those with special skills, often have a hard time entering the agency field. College graduates complain that they go to dozens of agencies and are offered nothing more exciting than a mailroom or receptionist job. A solution to the beginner's problem may be to avoid the biggest and best-known agencies and seek a starting job in those of modest or small size. There the pay is likely to be small, the office tiny, and the future problematical, but the opportunities to work and learn are good, and they provide the experience to qualify later for a good job in a major agency.

Among the careers in advertising agencies in which a fashion background can be useful are:

Account Executive   The man or woman who solicits accounts, who acts as liaison between client and agency staff, and who plans campaigns and calls upon the technical skills of the agency staff to develop them is known as an account executive.

Copywriter   These creative people are idea people, capable of originating campaign copy. Starting spot: copy cub. Top spot: copy chief.

Artist   Artists not only have creative talent and artistic ability but also understand the graphic arts, can specify type faces and sizes, and know the problems of reproducing material in various media. One starts with a skill and learns on the job.

Fashion Coordinator   Agencies handling fashion accounts need personnel to guide campaigns, assist in client contacts, and provide the fashion background that other specialized agency executives may lack. Even an agency that does not handle fashion accounts may have a fashion consultant on the staff to make sure that the figures in illustrations and television commercials are wearing currently acceptable apparel, accessories, and hairstyles.

Other Possibilities   Clerical, secretarial, and various technical jobs abound in large agencies, and can offer the beginner a foothold. For example, the media department is a haven for those who understand statistics, since this department is responsible for measuring the worth of a publication's or broadcast station's audience in terms of cost and increased exposure of the client's product. The research department investigates available information to guide the client's marketing and advertising efforts and often does some related studies on its own. The traffic department follows up on production schedules and makes sure that deadlines for advertising insertions are met.

Essential for any agency job is the ability to work well under pressure. Agency people do not acknowledge the word "impossible" in meeting deadlines.

Consumer Publications

Nearly all consumer publications carry some sort of fashion material, and some are devoted exclusively to fashion. Career opportunities with such publications are immensely varied, ranging from editorial work to those numerous behind-the-scenes activities that go into the publishing of a magazine or newspaper.

Editorial   When fashion is presented in a publication, that publication's fashion judgment must be authoritative. Whether the publication is devoted entirely to fashion or whether it simply runs a fashion section, the editor's job is to discover what the reader responds to, locate those fashions in the market, and illustrate examples of them at the right time. The editorial job can be all the more complicated because of pressures from publicity-hungry producers. An editor may cover the entire fashion market or just one segment of it, depending on the type of publication it is and the size of the publication's staff.

Large fashion staffs generally can absorb a few inexperienced assistants. For small pay, these people perform the necessary legwork in the market and do a thousand other chores. They learn how to select and how to work with models, photographers, and an art department. They learn how to cut down a lengthy description of a new style to a dozen words, if that is all the space allowed for a caption. Fashion know-how, the ability to meet

A new area of employment where fashion knowledge can be put to work is computer programming.

The Broadway-Hale Stores, Inc.

deadlines, and the ability to work with people are vitally important—at times, even more important than writing or sketching skills.

Small fashion staffs, like those on newspapers in small cities, do no market work but depend on press releases that come from the wire services and from producers and local retailers of fashion merchandise. Spending time as a general assistant in such a fashion department, which may also cover society news and garden-club activities, is useful preparation for big-city, big-publication jobs.

Merchandising Behind the scenes, the merchandising editors of national publications and their staffs work to make sure that readers anywhere in the country can buy the merchandise that is featured editorially. They do this by reporting to retailers in advance of publication the details of what is to be run, why it is important, and from what resources it is available. With their formidable knowledge of markets, merchandise, and retailing, these editors are also well equipped to offer retailers practical suggestions about how to merchandise, promote, and display the editorially featured items successfully.

Developing a following among retailers is good sales strategy for a magazine that sells advertising to producers. Therefore, the merchandising staffs are required to be extremely knowledgeable and often quite creative about retail promotion. Some work up storewide or divisional promotional ideas that stores can use—even quite large stores with their own capable promotional staffs. A typical "package" for a store may begin with a theme that ties in with a forthcoming issue of the magazine. To promote the theme, the publication's staff suggests merchandise and resources for it, as well as suggesting advertising copy for various types of media. If the merchandise lends itself well to fashion shows or displays, the retailer may receive scripts, posters, display diagrams, and even the offer of an editor's services as a commentator. Many of the awards given by NRMA for outstanding retail fashion promotions are captured each year by just such packages developed by publications.

Merchandising staffs of consumer publications are usually large enough to absorb a beginner. Tirelessness and willingness to learn are essential; so is versatility. The beginner may be combing markets for weeks; then acting as host in a temporary showroom where future styles to be featured editorially are being shown to store buyers; then drafting copy for a suggested retail ad; then acting as liaison with outside experts hired to work up displays or the design of boutiques that have been suggested as part of a special promotion.

Advertising Sales   Selling advertising space is the major source of revenue for a publication. The many aspects of selling accommodate various talents. Those who like selling deal with producers and their advertising agencies. People with a flair for research help the sales representatives to sell advertising space in the publication by supplying facts that indicate the ability of that publication to enlist retail cooperation or that measure the buying power of the publication's readers. Those with a flair for persuasive writing may find a place on the advertising promotion staffs, where they work out presentations to help the sales representatives conduct meetings with prospective advertisers.

Fashion background, sketching ability, and writing ability are aids to the beginner. Personality and contacts are vital in selling jobs, after one has become familiar enough with the publication to be entrusted with such assignments.

Trade Publications

Some trade publications are very narrowly specialized, such as *Handbags and Accessories* and *Hosiery and Underwear Review,* and are likely to be published monthly. Some are less narrowly specialized, such as *Clothes* and *Men's Wear,* and tend to be published semimonthly. A few, such as *Women's Wear Daily* (covering the women's apparel field) and *Daily News Record* (covering the menswear and textiles fields), provide in-depth coverage of a specific field and are published five days a week, Monday through Friday, except for holidays. All may offer opportunities for beginners with an interest in fashion.

Editors of trade publications spend part of their time in the market or investigating other sources of information and part of their time preparing material for publication. Assistants and secretaries to editors may be beginners learning how to make market calls, select new products for illustration, and write up what they have learned.

Trade publications hire beginners who are trained in publication procedures or journalism. Typing is indispensable, as is a durable smile for contacts with the trade and a good memory for names, places, and people. Knowing a particular industry is helpful, and knowing retailing even more so, because there is a regular need for articles for and about retailers. A good deal of rewriting is done from correspondents' reports and publicity releases.

Consulting Services

The most glamorous of the consulting services involved in the fashion field is, of course, the fashion consultant. Of these, the oldest and best known is the Tobé service, founded in 1927 by the late Tobé Coller Davis. As a young woman, she was hired to advise a retail store on its fashion merchandise by bringing the customers' point of view to bear on merchandise selections and promotions. From this start, she developed a syndicated service to which stores all over the country subscribed. With what is now a large staff, the firm continues to cover and interpret fashion news in such a way that buying, merchandising, and coordination executives can be guided by the views of skilled observers in every important fashion center. Reports, bulletins, clinics, and individual advice are the subscribers' diet.

Some of the other services, like Amos Parrish & Company, combine general advice on store operation with the availability of some fashion information advice. Others exist primarily to make the skill of an expert in fashion promotion, such as Estelle Hamburger, available to interested stores. Still others, such as the Retail News Bureau, offer a wide range of consultant services that may involve any subject from merchandise resources to advertising results.

In approaching any enterprise of this kind, the beginner is wise to offer other qualifications in addition to a background in fashion: typing, writing or sketching ability, or some retail experience. Some of the "graduates" of these services have gone on to become fashion coordinators for major retailers, buying offices, or producers. The opportunities to learn are great, if one has the stamina, ambition, and ability to work under pressure.

Some public relations and publicity consultants perform free-lance services in manufacturing and retailing. Writing skills, resourcefulness, and a knowledge of how to handle contacts of many kinds are basic equipment for job applicants to such firms. The beginner can enter as a secretary or copywriter to learn the techniques of getting product publicity and favorable mentions for client firms.

Television

Fashion-oriented specialists are beginning to find exciting careers in television. Many advertising agencies today engage outside companies to create fashion commercials for client producers or retailers.[4] The high cost of television time and production limits its appeal to retailers, but some make good use of television to present fashion. A fashion background alone is not sufficient to provide a beginner with an entry into this field. Some understanding of the technical aspects of the medium is vital.

Trade Associations

One of the more interesting areas of employment in the fashion field is trade association work. Industries, retailers, and professionals of all types form associations and hire executive staffs to do research, publicity, public relations work, handle legislative contacts, run conventions, publish periodicals, run trade shows, or perform any other services members may require. Small or large, a trade association affords great variety of work to its staff. Versatility is thus a paramount requirement. An assistant entering trade association work will find a background in the specific field served helpful, but the ability to communicate well is just as important.

The Millinery Institute, EMBA (organized as the Eastern Mink Breeders Association and now nationwide), and NRMA (National Retail Merchants Association) are only three of the many trade associations active in fashion or retailing fields. Other trade associations include local chambers of commerce, local and regional industry and merchants groups, and many others. Shopping centers have merchants' associations that employ promotion executives to keep the centers in the public eye.

Producers in regional markets, like those in the New York and Los Angeles fashion markets, as well as traveling salespeople, sometimes form associations to establish and publicize seasonal market dates.

Each year, tens of thousands of people seek fashion-related jobs. Those who win those jobs, and whose jobs turn into satisfying careers, are those who have that very important asset: fashion knowhow.

REFERENCES

[1] Brockman, *The Theory of Fashion Design*, p. 7.
[2] Brenner, *Careers and Opportunities in Fashion*, p. 25.
[3] "The Story of Penney Tweens," *Stores*, March 1965, p. 28.
[4] Brenner, op. cit., p. 125.

GLOSSARY

Adaptation A design that reflects the dominant features of the style that inspired it but is not an exact copy.

Advertising The use of paid space or time in any medium—newspapers, shopping news bulletins, magazines, direct mail, radio or television broadcasts, or billboards.

Advertising credit A mention of one or more store names, in connection with the advertisement of a vendor, as being the retail source(s) for the merchandise advertised.

Advertising mat, matrix A paperboard mold on which picture and/or copy are impressed and from which a plate can be made for reproduction.

Advertising plan A forecast for a specified period of time, such as a season, quarter, month, or week, of the advertising that a store intends to employ in order to attract business.

Advertising request A form prepared by a buyer stating when and where an ad will appear and how much space will be used. The form also requires a brief factual description of the style(s) selected for advertising and of what is important and exciting about the goods from the customer's standpoint.

Age-of-stock reports Reports that summarize information on the amount of stock in units and in dollars in each of a number of prior seasons, as indicated by the season code on each price ticket.

Alloy A blend of two or more metals.

Anticipation An extra discount granted by some manufacturers for the prepayment of their invoices before the end of the cash discount period.

Apparel contractor A firm whose sole function is to supply sewing services to the apparel industry.

Apparel jobber A firm that handles the designing, the planning, the purchasing of materials, and usually the cutting, the selling, and the shipping of apparel, but does not handle the actual sewing of the garments.

Apparel manufacturer A firm that performs all the operations required to produce a garment.

Assortment See **Merchandise assortment**

Assortment display A display created by showing, identifying, and pricing one of each of the styles currently in a section of the stock.

Assortment plan A comprehensive and detailed listing of all items making up an assortment by type and price line.

Average gross sale Net sales of a department divided by the number of sales transactions in that department.

Balanced assortment An assortment in which types, quantities, and price lines of merchandise included in inventory during a given period of time are closely matched to the demand of target customers.

Basic stock An item of merchandise that is in consistent demand throughout a year or season.

Best-selling price lines Those limited number of price lines within an assortment that account for the greater share of the department's dollar and unit sales volume.

Book inventory The dollar value of inventory that should be in stock at any given time, as indicated by each department's accounting records.

Boutique A shop associated with few-of-a-kind merchandise, generally in very new or extreme styling, with an imaginative presentation of goods.

Brand-line representative (cosmetics) A trained cosmetician who advises customers in the selection and use of a specific brand of cosmetics and handles the sales of that brand in a retail store.

Buying motivation Why people buy what they buy.

Buying plan A general description of the types and quantities of merchandise a buyer expects to purchase for delivery within a specific period of time.

Cash discount The percentage of premium allowed by a manufacturer off an invoice if payment is made within a certain specified period of time.

Caution A fee charged for viewing a couture collection.

Chain organization A group of 12 or more centrally owned stores, each handling somewhat similar goods and merchandised and controlled from a central headquarters office.

Charge-back A store's invoice for claims against and allowances made by a vendor.

Classic A style or design that remains in fashion acceptance for an extended time.

Classification An assortment of units or items of merchandise which are all reasonably substitutable for each other, regardless of who made the item, the material of which it is made, or the part of the store in which it is offered for sale.

Commissionaire The foreign equivalent of an American resident buying office.

Conglomerate A group of companies that may or may not be related in terms of product or marketing level but which are owned by a single parent organization.

Consignment selling An arrangement whereby a manufacturer places merchandise in a retail store for resale but permits any unused portion, together with payment for those garments that have been sold, to be returned to the wholesale source by a specified date. (**Buying on consignment:** A buyer's placement of an order with the privilege of returning unsold goods by a specific date.)

Consumerism The rights of consumers to have protection against unfair marketing practices.

Converter, textile A producer who buys fabrics in the greige and contracts to have them finished (dyed, bleached, printed, or subjected to other treatments) in plants specializing in each operation.

Cooperative advertising Retail advertising the costs of which are shared by a store and a manufacturer on terms agreed to by both.

Cosmetics Articles other than soap that are intended to be rubbed, poured, sprinkled, or sprayed on the person for purposes of cleansing, beautifying, promoting attractiveness, or altering the appearance (as defined by the Federal Trade Commission).

Costume jewelry Mass-produced jewelry made of plastic, wood, glass, brass, or other base metals, and set with simulated or nonprecious stones.

Cotton A vegetable fiber from the boll of the cotton plant.

Couture house An apparel firm for which a designer creates original styles.

Couturier (male) or **couturiere** (female) The proprietor or designer of a French couture house.

Coverage The maximum quantities to which each item's stock should be built after each regular stock count. Expressed either in terms of a certain number of weeks' supply, a specific number of units, or both.

Customer demand Customer needs and wants for consumer goods.

Dating The period of time allowed by a vendor for the taking of cash discounts.

Department store A store that employs 25 or more people and sells general lines of merchandise in each of three categories: home furnishings, household linens and dry goods (an old trade term meaning piece goods and sewing notions), and apparel and accessories for the entire family (as defined by the Bureau of the Census).

Design A specific or individual interpretation or version of a style. In trade usage, sometimes referred to as a "style" or "style number" or simply a "number."

Designer (fashion) A person who creates styles, thereby giving concrete expression to fashion ideas.

Details The individual parts that give form to a silhouette or make up its structure. These include trimmings, skirt length and width, or shoulder, waist, and sleeve treatment.

Direct expenses Those expenses that occur as a direct result of the operation of a specific department and that would cease if the department itself ceased to exist. Example: expenses incurred in connection with buying trips, advertising, and delivery charges.

Discount store A limited-service, mass-merchandised retail firm selling goods below usual retail prices.

Discretionary income The money that an individual or family has to spend or save after buying such necessities as food, clothing, shelter, and basic transportation.

Display Impersonal, visual presentation of merchandise.

Disposable personal income The amount a person has left to spend or save after paying taxes. It is roughly equivalent to what an employee calls "take-home pay" and provides an approximation of the purchasing power of each consumer during any given year.

Dollar merchandise plan A budget, a projection, in dollars, of the sales goals of a merchandise classification, a department, or an entire store for a specific future period of time, and the amount of stock required to achieve those sales.

Downward-flow theory The theory of fashion adoption that maintains that to be identified as a true fashion, a style must first be adopted by people at the top of the social pyramid. The style then gradually wins acceptance at progressively lower social levels. Also called the "trickle-down theory."

Dual distribution A manufacturer's policy of selling goods at both wholesale and retail.

Editorial credit The mention, in a magazine or newspaper, of a store name as a retail source for merchandise that is being editorially featured by the publication.

Environment The sum of the conditions that surround and influence a person.

Erogenous Sexually stimulating.

Fad A short-lived fashion. Fads usually affect only a narrow group within the total population and generally are concerned with some minor detail of design.

Fashion The prevailing style accepted and used by the majority of a group at any given time.

Fashion coordinator The store's ranking fashion authority. Sometimes referred to as fashion director.

Fashion cycle The rise, widespread popularity, and then decline in acceptance of a style. **Rise:** The acceptance of either an original design or its adaptations by an increasing number of consumers. **Culmination:** That period when a fashion is at the height of its popularity and use. The fashion then is in such demand that it can be mass produced, mass distributed, and sold at prices within the reach of most consumers. **Decline:** The decrease in consumer demand because of boredom resulting from widespread use of a fashion. **Obsolescence:** When revulsion has set in and a style can no longer be sold at any price.

Fashion image That aspect of a store's image

that reflects the degree of fashion leadership the store strives to exercise and the stage of the fashion cycle that its assortments represent.

Fashion influential A person whose advice is sought by associates. An influential's adoption of a new style gives it prestige among a group.

Fashion innovator A person quicker than his or her associates to try out a new style.

Fashion merchandising The planning required to have the right fashion-oriented merchandise at the right time, in the right place, in the right quantities, and at the right prices.

Fashion merchandising policy A long-range guide for the fashion merchandising staff of a store, spelling out the store's fashion aims, standards of quality, price ranges, attitudes toward competition, and any other elements that may be considered pertinent.

Fashion retailing The business of buying fashion-oriented merchandise from a variety of resources and assembling it in convenient locations for resale to ultimate consumers.

Fashion trend The direction in which fashion is moving.

Fiber A hairlike unit of raw material from which textile fabric is made.

Fine jewelry Jewelry made of such precious metals as gold and all members of the platinum family (palladium, rhodium, and iridium) and which may be set with precious or semiprecious stones.

First cost The wholesale price of merchandise at place of origin.

Flash sales reports Daily reports of sales, by department, developed from the unaudited sales checks and cash-register tapes for the previous day.

Foundations The trade term for such women's undergarments as brassieres, girdles, pantygirdles, garter belts, and corselettes.

Fur farming The breeding and raising of fur-bearing animals under controlled conditions.

Gemstones Natural stones used in making jewelry. Precious stones include the diamond,

emerald, ruby, sapphire, and real pearl. Semiprecious stones include the amethyst, garnet, opal, jade, cultured pearl.

Going public Turning a privately owned company into a public corporation and issuing stock for sale.

Greige goods Unfinished fabrics.

Gross margin The dollar difference between net sales for a period and the net cost of merchandise sold during that period.

Group purchase The purchasing of identical merchandise by several stores at one time from a given resource so that all participants may share in the advantages of a large-volume purchase.

Haute couture The French term for high fashion.

Hides Animal skins weighing over 25 pounds when shipped to a tannery.

High fashion Those styles or designs accepted by a limited group of fashion leaders. In general, high-fashion styles or designs are newly introduced and are produced and sold in small quantities, generally at high to fairly high prices.

Horizontal-flow theory The theory of fashion adoption that holds that fashions move horizontally between groups on similar social levels rather than vertically from one level to another. Also called the "mass-market theory."

Horizontal integration The joining of companies that function at the same level of production, such as the merger of two fabric producers.

Indirect expenses Those expenses that do not directly result from the operation of an individual department but are shared by all departments of a store, such as compensation of top management executives, utilities, maintenance, insurance, and receiving and marking expenses.

Initial markup The difference between the delivered cost of merchandise and the retail price placed on it when it is first brought into stock.

Inside shops Menswear manufacturers who perform all the operations required to produce garments.

Intimate apparel The trade term for women's foundations, lingerie, and loungewear. Also called "inner fashions" or "body fashions."

Item display A display created by showing a single garment or accessory or several versions of a garment or accessory.

Kips Animal skins weighing from 15 to 25 pounds when shipped to a tannery.

Lapidary Gemstone cutter.

Last (shoe) A wooden form in the shape of a foot over which shoes are built.

Leased department A department ostensibly operated by the store in which it is found but which is actually run by an outsider who pays a percentage of sales to the store as rent.

Leisure suit A man's suit consisting of a matching jacket and slacks designed in a casual style.

Licensed trademark A trademark used under a licensing agreement whereby the use of the trademark is permitted only to those manufacturers whose end products pass established tests for their specific end use or application.

Licensing An arrangement whereby firms are given permission to produce and market merchandise in the name of a licensor, who is paid a percentage of sales for permitting his or her name to be used.

Line A collection of styles offered by vendors to their customers, usually on a seasonal basis.

Line-for-line copy An exact duplicate of an original style using less expensive materials, machine stitching, and standard measurements.

Linen A vegetable fiber from the woody stalk of the flax plant.

Lingerie A general undergarment category that includes slips, petticoats, panties of all types, nightgowns, and pajamas. Slips, petticoats, and panties are considered "daywear" while nightgowns and pajamas are classified as "sleepwear."

Linters Very short fibers that remain on the seed of the cotton boll after ginning. Used mainly in the manufacture of rayon and for such non-fashion products as paper and absorbent cotton.

Long-run fashion A fashion that takes more seasons to complete its cycle than what might be considered its average life expectancy.

Loungewear The trade term for the intimate apparel category that includes robes, bed jackets, and housecoats.

Man-made fibers Fibers produced in chemical plants.

Markdown The dollar difference between the previous price and the reduced price to which merchandise is marked.

Markdown percentage The dollar value of the net retail markdowns taken during a given period divided by the dollar value of net sales for that period.

Marker (apparel manufacturing) A long piece of paper upon which the pieces of the pattern of a garment in all its sizes are laid out for cutting.

Market (1) A group of potential customers. (2) The place or area in which buyers and sellers congregate.

Market representative A specialist who covers a narrow segment of the total market and makes information about it available to client stores.

Marketing The performance of business activities that directs the flow of goods from producers to consumers.

Marketing process The series of activities involved in converting raw materials into a form that can be used by ultimate consumers without further commercial processing.

Markup The difference between the wholesale cost and the retail price of merchandise (sometimes called "markon" by large retail stores).

Mass fashion Those styles or designs that are widely accepted. Such fashions usually are produced and sold in large quantities, generally at moderate to low prices. Also called "volume fashion."

Mercerizing A finishing process by which cotton yarn is made stronger, more lustrous, and more receptive to certain dyes.

Merchandise assortment A collection of varied types of related merchandise, essentially intended for the same general end-use and usually grouped together in one selling area of a retail store.

Merchandise assortment, broad A merchandise assortment that includes many styles.

Merchandise assortment, deep A merchandise assortment that includes a comprehensive range of colors and sizes in each style.

Merchandise assortment, narrow A merchandise assortment that includes relatively few styles.

Merchandise assortment, shallow A merchandise assortment that contains only a few sizes and colors in each style.

Merchandising The planning required to have the right merchandise at the right time, in the right place, in the right quantities, and at the right price.

Mom-and-Pop store A small store run by the proprietor with few or no hired assistants.

Merchandising policies Guidelines established by store management for merchandising executives to follow in order that the store organization may win the patronage of the specific target group(s) of customers it has chosen to serve.

Natural fibers Fibers derived from plant and/or animal sources.

Number, style number See **Design**

Open-to-buy, dollar The dollar value of planned purchases for a given period minus the dollar value of all orders scheduled for delivery during that same period but not yet received.

Operational satisfactions (customer) Those satisfactions derived from the physical performance of a product.

Organizational chart A visual presentation of the manner in which a firm delegates organizational responsibility and authority.

Patronage motives (customer) The reasons that induce customers to patronize one store rather than another; why people buy where they do.

Pelt The skin of a fur-bearing animal.

Personal income Total or gross amount of income received from all sources by the population as a whole. It consists of wages, salaries, interest, and all other income for everyone in the country. (See also **Disposable personal income** and **Discretionary income.**)

Periodic stock count control A unit control system in which stock is counted and recorded at regular intervals and the results are used to compute sales for the intervening period.

Perpetual control A unit control system in which purchase orders, receipts of merchandise, and sales are recorded for individual style numbers as they occur, and stock on hand is computed.

Planned purchases The term used to indicate the amount of merchandise that can be brought into stock during a given period without exceeding the planned inventory for the end of that period.

Pre-retail The practice of indicating the intended retail prices of all items on each purchase order.

Press release A written statement of news that has occurred or is about to occur, specifying the source of the information and the date after which its use is permissible.

Prestige or institutional advertisement An advertisement that "sells" the store rather than specific merchandise.

Prêt-à-porter French term meaning ready-to-wear.

Price line A specific price point at which an assortment of merchandise is regularly offered for sale.

Price lining The practice of determining the various but limited number of retail prices at which a department's assortments will be offered.

Price range The spread between the lowest and the highest price line carried.

Price zone A series of somewhat contiguous price lines that are likely to have major appeal to one particular segment of a store's or department's customers.

Prime resources Those producers from whom a department consistently has bought a substantial portion of its merchandise in past seasons.

Promotional or merchandise advertisement An advertisement that endeavors to create sales of specific items.

Prophetic fashions Particularly interesting new styles that are still in the introductory phase of their fashion cycles.

Psychological satisfections (customer) Those derived from the consumer's social and psychological interpretation of the product and its performance.

Publicity The free and voluntary mention of a firm, brand, product, or person in some form of media.

Purchase journal, merchandise journal A monthly or semimonthly report listing all invoices for merchandise received, transfers of merchandise in and out, and returns to or claims against vendors that have been entered in a department's book inventory during a given period.

Ready-to-wear Apparel made in factories to standard size measurements.

Receiving apron A detailed record of a shipment of merchandise received that is attached to the vendor's invoice covering that shipment.

Release date A date before which a publicity announcement is not to be made.

Reserve requisition control A form of periodic stock count control in which stock on the selling floor is considered sold and only the reserve stock is counted.

Resident buying office A service organization located in a major market area that provides market information and representation to its noncompeting client stores.

Resident buying office, associated One that is jointly owned and operated by a group of independently owned stores.

Resident buying office, private One that is owned and operated by a single, out-of-town store organization and performs market work exclusively for that store organization.

Resident buying office, salaried A resident buying office that is independently owned and operated and charges the stores it represents for the work it does for them. Also called a "fee office."

Resident buying office, syndicate A resident buying office maintained by a parent organization that owns a group of stores and performs market work exclusively for those stores.

Retail method of inventory A method of inventory evaluation in which all records of transactions affecting the value of a store's or department's inventory (such as sales, purchases, markdowns, transfers, and returns-to-vendor) are recorded at retail values.

Retail reductions All reductions that occur in the retail value of the inventory, including merchandise markdowns, discounts allowed to employees and other special customers, and stock shortages.

Retailing The business of buying goods from a variety of resources and assembling these goods in convenient locations for resale to ultimate consumers.

Reticule A small drawstring bag introduced in the late eighteenth century for carrying money and other small objects. Forerunner of the handbag.

Return-to-vendor A store's invoice covering merchandise returned for cause to its vendor.

Sales promotion The coordination of advertising, display, publicity, and personal salesmanship in order to promote profitable sales.

Salon selling The most exacting type of personal selling: Little or no stock is exposed to the customer's view except that brought out for the customer's inspection by the salesperson.

Sample hand A designer's assistant who is an all-round sewer.

Sample-test-reorder technique A way of testing the acceptability of a new fashion by buying in small quantities in a wide range of possibly acceptable styles, observing customer reaction, and then reordering in substantial quantities those styles, sizes, and colors that appear to have won an initial favorable reaction.

Season code A code indicating the month and season of receipt of merchandise. The code appears on the price ticket of an item and is used to determine how long the item has been in stock.

Section work The division of labor in apparel manufacturing whereby each sewing-machine operator sews only a certain section of the garment, such as a sleeve or hem.

Selection factors The various characteristics or components of an item of merchandise that influence a customer's decision to purchase or not to purchase it.

Self-selection selling The method of selling whereby merchandise is displayed and arranged so that customers can make at least a preliminary selection without the aid of a salesperson.

Self-service selling The method of selling whereby customers make their selections from the goods on display and bring their purchases to a check-out counter where they make payment and their purchases are prepared for take-out.

Shop A small store or a small area within a large store that is stocked with merchandise for special end-use purposes; intended for customers with specialized interests.

Short run The production of a limited number of units of a particular item, fewer than would normally be considered an average number to produce.

Short-run fashion A fashion that takes fewer seasons to complete its cycle than what might be considered its average life expectancy.

Silhouette The overall outline or contour of a costume. Also frequently referred to as "shape" or "form."

Silk An animal fiber from the cocoons spun by silkworms.

Skins Animal skins that weigh 15 pounds or less when shipped to a tannery.

Slop shops A name associated with the first shops offering men's ready-to-wear in this country.

Specialty store A store that carries limited lines of apparel or accessories or home furnishings (definition of the Bureau of the Census). In the trade, retailers use the term to describe any apparel and/or accessories store that exhibits a degree of fashion awareness and carries goods for men, women, and/or children.

Spinerette A mechanical device through which a thick liquid base is forced to produce fibers of varying lengths.

Stock-sales ratio The number of months that would be required to dispose of a beginning-of-the-month inventory at the rate at which sales are made in (or planned for) that month.

Stock overage The condition existing when the physical inventory is greater than the book inventory.

Stock shortage The condition existing when the book inventory is greater than the physical inventory.

Stock turnover The number of times that an average stock of merchandise (inventory) has been turned into sales during a given period.

Stockkeeping unit (SKU) A single item of merchandise or group of items of merchandise within a classification to which an identifying number is assigned and for which separate sales and stock records are kept.

Store image The character or personality that a store presents to the public.

Structured apparel A garment whose construction involves many different hand-tailoring operations that give it a shape of its own when not being worn.

Style A characteristic or distinctive mode of presentation or conceptualization in the field of some art. In clothing, style is the characteristic or distinctive way a garment looks, the sum of the features that make it different from other garments.

Sweat shops, sweaters Early apparel factories known for poor working conditions, long hours, and low wages.

Tailored clothing firms Those menswear firms that produce structured or semistructured suits, overcoats, topcoats, sport coats, and/or separate trousers in which a specific number of hand-tailoring operations are required.

Taking numbers Writing an adequate description of each style the buyer is considering for possible purchase, including style number, size range, available colors, fabric, wholesale price, and any other relevant details.

Tanning The process of transforming animal skins into leather.

Taste An individual's ability to recognize what is and what is not attractive and appropriate. Good taste in fashion implies sensitivity not only to what is artistic but also to what prevailing fashion says is appropriate for a specific occasion.

Terms of sale The combination of allowable discounts on purchases and the time allowed for taking such discounts.

Textile fabric Cloth or material made from fibers by weaving, knitting, braiding, felting, crocheting, knotting, laminating, or bonding.

Texture The look and feel of all types of material, woven or nonwoven.

Trunk show A form of pretesting that involves a producer's sending a representative to a store with a sample of every style in the line, and the store's exhibiting these samples to customers at scheduled, announced showings.

Unit control Systems for recording the number of units of merchandise bought, sold, in stock, and on order, and from which a variety of reports can be drawn.

Upward-flow theory The theory of fashion adoption that holds that the young—particularly those of low-income families, as well as those in the higher income groups who adopt low-income lifestyles—are quicker than any other social group to create or adopt new and different fashions.

Unstructured apparel A garment whose construction involves few if any hand-tailoring operations and which often lacks padding, binding, and lining; it takes its shape in part from the person who wears it.

Variety store A store carrying a wide range of merchandise in a limited number of low or relatively low price lines.

Vertical integration The joining of companies at different levels of production, such as the merger of a fiber mill with a fabric mill.

Vignette A display showing a product or group of products in use.

Visual control A form of periodic stock count in which a rack or bin is assigned to each style, size, or classification, and a periodic check is made to see whether one of these bins or racks looks too empty or too full. Sometimes called "eyeball control."

Volume fashion See **Mass fashion**

Wool An animal fiber which is from the hair of sheep.

Want slip A form on which a salesperson reports the request by a customer for something that is not in stock.

Yarn A continuous thread formed by spinning or twisting fibers together.

BIBLIOGRAPHY

Alderfer, E. B., and H. S. Michl. *Economics of American Industry,* 3d ed. McGraw-Hill Book Company, New York, 1957.

American Marketing Association. "Report of the Definitions Committee." *Journal of Marketing,* October, 1948.

Anspach, Karlyne. *The Why of Fashion.* Iowa State University Press, Ames, Ia., 1967.

Arnold, Pauline, and Percival White. *Clothes and Cloth: America's Apparel Business.* Holiday House, Inc., New York, 1961.

Barker, Clare Wright, Ira Dennis Anderson, and J. Donald Butterworth. *Principles of Retailing,* 3d ed. McGraw-Hill Book Company, New York, 1956.

Beaton, Cecil. *The Glass of Fashion.* Doubleday & Company, Inc., New York, 1954.

Bell, Quentin. *On Human Finery.* The Hogarth Press, Ltd., London, 1947.

Bender, Marilyn. *The Beautiful People.* Coward-McCann, New York, 1967.

Bennett-England, Rodney. *Dress Optional: The Revolution in Menswear.* Dufour Publishing Co., Chester Springs, Pa., 1968.

Binder, Pearl. *Muffs and Morals.* George G. Harrap & Co., Ltd., London, 1953.

Brenninkmeyer, Ingrid. *The Sociology of Fashion.* Librairie du Recueil Sirey, Paris, 1963.

Brockman, Helen L. *The Theory of Fashion Design.* John Wiley & Sons, Inc., New York, 1965.

The Buyer's Manual, rev. ed. Merchandising Division, National Retail Merchants Association, New York, 1965.

Cobrin, Harry A. *The Men's Clothing Industry.* Fairchild Publications, Inc., New York, 1970.

Collier, Ann M. *A Handbook of Textiles.* Pergamon Press, New York, 1971.

Contini, Mila. *Fashion: From Ancient Egypt to the Recent Day.* Odyssey Press, New York, 1965.

Corbman, Bernard P. *Textiles: Fiber to Fabric,* 5th ed. McGraw-Hill Book Company, New York, 1975.

Corinth, Kay. *Fashion Showmanship.* John Wiley & Sons, Inc., New York, 1970.

Crawford, Morris DeCamp. *One World of Fashion,* 3d ed. Fairchild Publications, Inc., New York, 1967.

Cundiff, Edward W., and Richard R. Still. *Basic Marketing,* 2nd ed. Prentice-Hall, Inc., Englewood Cliffs, N.J., 1971.

Dardis, Rachel. "The Power of Fashion." *Proceedings of the Twentieth Annual Conference, College Teachers of Textiles and Clothing, Eastern Region,* New York, 1966.

Daves, Jessica. *Ready-made Miracle.* G. P. Putnam's Sons, New York, 1967.

Davidson, William R., and A. F. Doody. *Retail Management,* 3d ed. The Ronald Press, Inc., New York, 1966.

Departmental Merchandising and Operating Results of 1972. Controllers' Congress, National Retail Merchants Association, New York, 1973.

Duncan, Delbert J., et al. *Modern Retailing Management.* Richard D. Irwin, Inc., Homewood, Ill., 1972.

Dunlap, Knight. "The Development and Function of Clothing." *Journal of General Psychology,* 1:64–78, 1928.

Edwards, Charles M., and Russell A. Brown. *Retail Advertising and Sales Promotion.* Prentice-Hall, Inc., Englewood Cliffs, N.J., 1959.

Eicher, Joanne B., and Mary Ellen Roach. *The Visible Self: Perspectives on Dress.* Prentice-Hall, Inc., Englewood Cliffs, N.J., 1973.

Escabosa, Hector. "The Heartbeat of Retailing." *Readings in Modern Retailing,* National Retail Merchants Association, New York, 1969.

Fashion Group Bulletin. The Fashion Group, Inc., New York, October 3, 1972.

Ferry, J. W. *A History of the Department Store.* Macmillan & Co., New York, 1960.

Flügel, J. C. *The Psychology of Clothes.* International Universities Press, New York, 1966.

Foley, Caroline. "Fashion." *Economic Journal* (London), 3:458, 1893.

Garland, Madge. *The Changing Form of Fashion.* Praegner Publishers, New York, 1971.

———— *Fashion.* Penguin Books, Inc., Baltimore, Md., 1962.

Gold, Annalee. *How to Sell Fashion.* Fairchild Publications, Inc., New York, 1968.

Gore, Bud. *How to Sell the Whole Store as Fashion.* National Retail Merchants Association, New York, 1970.

Hall, Max. *Made in New York.* Harvard University Press, Cambridge, Mass., 1959.

Hill, Margot H., and Peter Bucknell. *The Evolution of Fashion.* Holt, Rinehart & Winston, Inc., New York, 1968.

Horn, Marilyn J. *The Second Skin.* Houghton-Mifflin Co., Boston, Mass., 1968.

Howell, L. D. *The American Textile Industry.* Economic Research Report No., 58, Department of Agriculture, Washington, D.C., 1964.

Hurlock, Elizabeth B. *The Psychology of Dress.* Reprint of 1929 ed., Benjamin Blom, New York.

Jabenis, Elaine. *The Fashion Director: What She Does and How to Be One.* John Wiley & Sons, Inc., New York, 1972.

Jarnow, Jeannette, and Beatrice Judelle. *Inside the Fashion Business,* 2d ed. John Wiley & Sons, Inc., New York, 1974.

Kelly, Katie. *The Wonderful World of Women's Wear Daily.* Saturday Review Press, New York, 1972.

King, Charles W. "Fashion Adoption: A Rebuttal to the Trickle-Down Theory." *Proceedings of the Winter Conference,* American Marketing Association, New York, December, 1963, pp. 108–125.

———— "The Innovator in the Fashion Adoption Process." *Proceedings of the Winter Conference,* American Marketing Association, New York, December, 1964, pp. 324–339.

Kleppner, Otto. *Advertising Procedure,* 5th ed. Prentice-Hall, Inc., Englewood Cliffs, N.J., 1966.

Kroeber, A. L. "On the Principles of Order in Civilization as Exemplified by Change in Fashion." *American Anthropologist,* 21:235–263, July–September, 1919.

Kybalová, Ludmila, et al. *The Pictorial Encyclopedia of Fashion.* Crown Publishers, Inc., New York, 1968.

Landsberg, Hans H., Leonard Fischmann, and Joseph L. Fisher. "Clothing and Textiles." *Resources in America's Future,* Johns Hopkins Press, Baltimore, Md., 1963.

Laver, James. *The Concise History of Costume and Fashion.* Harry N. Abrams, Inc., New York, 1969.

———— *Dandies.* Weidenfeld and Nicholson, Ltd., London, 1968.

———— *Dress.* John Murray, Ltd., London, 1966.

———— *Modesty in Dress.* Houghton Mifflin Co., Boston, Mass., 1969.

———— *Taste and Fashion,* rev. ed. George G. Harrap & Co., Ltd., 1946.

MacSwiggen, Amelia E. "Early Textile Mills." *The Town Crier,* Weed Publishers, Inc., Marblehead, Mass., April 14, 1965.

McClellan, Elisabeth. *History of American Costume.* Tudor Publishing Company, New York, 1969.

Milton, Shirley F. *Advertising for Modern Retailers.* Fairchild Publications, Inc., New York, 1974.

Morton, Grace Margaret. *The Arts of Costume and Personal Appearance,* 3d ed. John Wiley & Sons, Inc., New York, 1964.

Murphy, Michelle. *Two Centuries of French Fashion.* Brooklyn Institute of Arts and Sciences, The Brooklyn Museum, Brooklyn, New York, 1949.

Murray, Anne W. "Four Centuries of Dress in America." *Proceedings of Eastern Region, College Teachers of Textiles and Clothing,* College Park, Md., 1965, pp. 26–34.

NRMA's Standard Classifications, 2d ed. Merchandising Division, National Retail Merchants Association, New York, 1969.

Nystrom, Paul H. *Economics of Fashion.* The Ronald Press, New York, 1928.

———— *Fashion Merchandising.* The Ronald Press, New York, 1932.

Picken, Mary Brooks. *Fashion Dictionary.* Funk & Wagnalls, Inc., New York, 1973.

Readings in Modern Retailing. National Retail Merchants Association, New York, 1969.

Richardson, Jane, and A. L. Kroeber. "Three Centuries of Women's Dress Fashions: A Quantitative Analysis." *Anthropological Record,* 5(2), 1940.

Roach, Mary Ellen, and Joanne Bubolz Eicher. *Dress, Adornment, and the Social Order.* John Wiley & Sons, Inc., New York, 1965.

Robinson, Dwight E. "The Economics of Fashion Demand." *The Quarterly Journal of Economics,* 75:376–398, August, 1961.

——— "Fashion Theory and Product Design." *Harvard Business Review,* 36(6):126–138, November–December, 1958.

——— "The Importance of Fashions in Taste to Business History: An Introductory Essay." *Business History Review,* 37(1,2):5–36, Spring/Summer, 1963.

——— "The Rules of Fashion Cycles." *Harvard Business Review,* November-December, 1938, pp. 62–67, 113–117.

Robinson, O. Preston, Christine H. Robinson, and George H. Zeiss. *Successful Retail Salesmanship,* 3d ed. Prentice-Hall, Inc., Englewood Cliffs, N.J., 1961.

Roscho, Bernard. *The Rag Race.* Funk & Wagnalls, Inc., New York, 1963.

Rosencranz, Mary Lou. *Clothing Concepts.* The Macmillan Company, New York, 1972.

Rudolfsky, Bernard. *The Unfashionable Human Body.* Doubleday & Co., Inc., New York, 1971.

Ruhm, Herman D. *Marketing Textiles.* Fairchild Publications, Inc., New York, 1970.

Sapir, Edward. "Fashion." *Encyclopedia of the Social Sciences,* Vol. 5, 1968, pp. 341–345.

Schwartz, James. *The Publicity Process.* University of Iowa Press, Iowa City, Ia., 1969.

Seidel, Leon E. *Applied Textile Marketing.* W. R. C. Smith Publishing Co., Atlanta, Ga., 1971.

Seventy-five Years of Menswear Fashion: 1890–1965. Fairchild Publications, Inc., New York, 1965.

Seventy-five Years of Women's Fashions. Fairchild Publications, Inc., New York, 1975.

Sharpe, Deborah. "Sociological and Psychological Communications Through Color." *Proceedings of the Twentieth Annual Conference, College Teachers of Textiles and Clothing, Eastern Region,* New York, October, 1966, p. 10.

Simmel, George. "Fashion." *American Journal of Sociology,* Vol. 94, No. 1 (July 1, 1964), pp. 24–30.

"Story of Penney Tweens." *Stores,* March, 1965.

Survey of Current Business. Office of Business Economics, U.S. Department of Commerce, Washington, D.C.

"Tailored Sportcoats: Falling Behind." *Clothes,* May 15, 1974, pp. 65–69.

Tarde, Gabriel. *The Laws of Imitation.* Henry Holt and Company, New York, 1903.

Taylor, Charles G. *Merchandise Assortment Planning.* Merchandising Division, National Retail Merchants Association, New York, 1970.

Taylor, John. *It's a Small, Medium, and Outsize World.* Hugh Evelyn, London, 1966.

Udell, Jon G. "A New Approach to Consumer Motivation." *Journal of Retailing,* 40:6–10, Winter, 1964–65.

U.S. Industrial Outlook. Business and Defense Services Administration, U.S. Department of Commerce, Washington, D.C.

Veblen, Thorstein. *The Theory of the Leisure Class.* New American Library of World Literature, Inc., New York, 1963.

Vecchio, Walter R., and Robert Riley. *The Fashion Makers.* Crown Publications, Inc., 1968.

Ware, Caroline F. *The Early New England Cotton Manufacture.* Johnson Reprint Corp., New York, 1966.

Weitz, John. *The Value of Nothing.* Stein and Day, Inc., New York, 1970.

Wilcox, R. Turner. *Five Centuries of American Costume.* Charles Scribner's Sons, New York, 1963.

Wingate, Isabel B., Karen R. Gillespie, and Betty G. Milgrom. *Know Your Merchandise,* 4th ed. McGraw-Hill Book Company, New York, 1975.

Wingate, John W. "What's Wrong With the Planning of Stock Assortments." *New York Retailer,* October, 1959.

Wingate, John W., and Joseph S. Friedlander. *The Management of Retail Buying.* Prentice-Hall, Inc., Englewood Cliffs, N.J. 1963.

Wingate, John W., Elmer O. Schaller, and F. Leonard Miller. *Retail Merchandise Management.* Prentice-Hall, Inc., Englewood Cliffs, N.J., 1972.

Winters, Arthur, and Stanley Goodman. *Fashion Sales Promotion,* rev. ed. Fashion Institute of Technology College Shop, New York, 1972.

Wittkin, Herbert. "An Image Is A Multi-Faceted Thing." *Readings in Modern Retailing,* National Retail Merchants Association, New York, 1969.

Young, Agnes Brooke. *Recurring Cycles of Fashion: 1760–1937.* Harper & Brothers, New York, 1937. Reprinted by Cooper Square Publishers, Inc., New York, 1966.

Young, Kimball. *Social Psychology,* 3d ed. Appleton-Century-Crofts, Inc., New York, 1956.

INDEX

Abraham and Straus (A & S), 370,
    371, 379
Accessories:
    careers in, 388–389
    fashion cycle of, 37
    industries, 136–156
Actors and actresses, influence on
    fashion by, 53, 60
Adaptations, definition of, 34
Advertisements:
    merchandise or promotional,
        definition of, 314
    prestige or institutional, definition
        of, 316
Advertising, 314–326
    in apparel industries, 113–114, 129
    careers in, 394–395
    cooperative (see Cooperative
        advertising)
    in cosmetics industry, 147
    definition of, 314
    direct mail, 324
    magazine, 325–326
    mat, definition of, 319
    newspaper, 316–323
    radio, 324
    request form, definition of, 319
    results form, 321
    sign requisition, 320
    in smaller stores, 321
    telephone, 325
    television, 324
Advertising credit, definition of, 336
Advertising plan, 316–317
    definition of, 316
Afro styles, 23–25
Alexander's, 190, 376
Allied Kid Company, 94
Allied Stores, 193

Alta Moda Pronto, 165
Altman, B., and Company, 319, 327
Amalgamated Clothing Workers of
    America, 122
American Indian styles, 25
Amies, Hardy, 124, 166
Anticipation, definition of, 233
Apparel fashion game, 43–45
Argentina, 172
Arrow Company, 124
Associated Dry Goods Corporation,
    194
Assortment:
    balanced, definition of, 236
    definition of, 236
Assortment plan, definition of, 236
Assortment planning, 236–251
    classifying assortments, 243
    considerations in, 236–239
    in fashion departments, 243–247
    and fashion image, 171–172,
        373–374
    methods (dollar, unit), 239–240
    in multiunit retail organizations,
        248–251
    objectives of, 236
    pricing assortments, 243
Austria, 169
Automated data processing, 46–47,
    117–118, 195, 250–251
    in unit control, 266–270
Automation (see Technical advances)
Average gross sale, definition of, 289

Baldridge, Letitia, Enterprises, 214
Balenciaga, 203
Barney's, 190, 374
Basic, definition of, 284

Basic stock lists, 284
"Beat last year" book, 223, 281
Beaton, Cecil, 23
Beene, Geoffrey, 52, 107, 125
Bell, Quentin, 16, 59
Bendel, Henri, 370
Bergdorf-Goodman, 184, 193, 370
Bikini, 6, 45, 140
Blass, Bill, 52, 107, 125, 363
Bolivia, 172
Bonwit Teller, 194
Book inventory, 272–275
    definition of, 273
Boots, 22, 36, 205–206
Boredom as an influence on fashion
    demand, 28, 40
Boutiques:
    buying for, 367
    couture, 161
    definition of, 365
    image, 365–367
Branch organizations:
    assortment planning in, 248–249
    organization of, 180–181
    unit control in, 256, 261–262
Brand-line representative, definition
    of, 148
Brands:
    as factor in customer selection, 204
    and fashion image, 375
    importance of: in cosmetics,
        146–148
        in handbags, 153
        in hosiery, 142
        in shoes, 145
    merchandising policy concerning: in
        chains, 187–188
        in department stores, 182–183
        in discount stores, 191

Brands (*Cont.*)
  in specialty stores, 185
  in variety stores, 192
Brazil, 172
Broadway, The, 194
Brooks, Donald, 140
Brooks Brothers, 120, 177
Bullocks, 194
Burdine's, 194
Burlington Industries, 85
Burrows, Stephen, 140
Buyer:
  advertising responsibilities of,
    319–321
  buying responsibilities of: central,
    185–187, 190–193
    departmental, 182, 184
  career as, 390
  display responsibilities of, 330–331
  and dollar merchandise planning,
    217–234
  as fashion coordinator, 359–360
  and the market trip, 295–311
  and merchandise assortment
    planning, 236–251
  preparation of buying plan,
    291–295
  sales training responsibilities of,
    347–349
Buying motivation:
  customer, 205–206
  definition of, 205
Buying plan, 291–295
  definition of, 291
  how a buyer plans, 295
  information required, 292–294
Buying power, consumer (*see* Income)

Cardin, Pierre, 124, 159, 160
Care labeling, 85–86
Careers in fashion, 382–399
Caribbean, 170–172
Carter Hawley Hale, 194
Cash, Emmett, 125
Cash discount:
  definition of, 233
  and dollar merchandise planning,
    233
Cashin, Bonnie, 52
Cassini, Oleg, 125
Catalog operations, 178–179, 250,
  325
  careers in, 393
Caution, definition of, 160
Celanese Corporation, 75

Central America, 170–172
Chain organizations, 185–188
  assortment planning in, 249–250
  careers in, 393
  definition of, 185
  fashion image in, 370–380
  merchandising policies of, 187–188
Chambre Syndicale, 159–160
Chanel, Coco, 203
Change as a fashion intangible, 9–10,
  14
Charge-back, definition of, 264
Chemise dress, 6, 26, 38, 202, 344
Chicago, 113, 128, 176
China, 47, 53, 155, 173
Claim (*see* Charge-back)
Class structure (*see* Social structure)
Classic:
  definition of, 6
  fashion cycle of, 37–38
Classification:
  definition of, 243
  establishing, 243
  of a fashion department, 244–246
  purposes of, 243
Clothing Manufacturers Association,
  128
Coding, 267–268
College boards, 214
Color:
  as customer selection factor, 204
  as fashion component, 7–8
  fashion cycle of, 37
Colombia, 172
Commissionaire organization, 158
Communications as an influence on
  fashion demand, 22
Companionship, desire for, as an
  influence on fashion demand, 30
Comparison bureau, 200, 211
Conglomerates, definition of, 115
Consignment:
  buying on, definition of, 310
  selling, definition of, 98
Consulting services, fashion, 398
Consumer buying cycle, 38–39
Consumer demand:
  definition of, 201
  interpreting, 201–215
Consumer income, 17
Consumer publications, 212–214,
  302–303, 325–326
  careers in, 395–397
Consumer use cycle, 38–39
Consumerism, definition of, 201
Contractor:
  definition of, 103
  in menswear manufacturing,

Contractor (*Cont.*)
  121–122, 127–128
  in women's apparel manufacturing,
    105
Convention as an influence on fashion
  demand, 29
Cooperative advertising:
  definition of, 77
  in fiber industries, 77
  in jewelry industry, 150
  in retail stores, 323–324
Copeland, Melvin T., 205
Cosmetics:
  definition of, 146
  door-to-door sales of, 177
  industry, 146–149
  men's, 126
Cost method of inventory, 218
Cotton, 22, 70, 73–74, 138, 140
  definition of, 70
Cotton, Incorporated, 76, 85
Couture house, definition of, 159
Couturier and couturiere, definitions
  of, 159
Culmination stage, fashion cycle,
  definition of, 35
Curiosity as an influence on fashion
  demand, 28
Custin, Mildred, 214
Customer advisory groups, 214–215
Customer demand:
  interpreting, 201–215
    aids in determining, 208–215
    elements of, 203–208
    variations in, 206–208
Customer surveys, 211
Cycle (*see* Consumer buying cycle;
    Consumer use cycle; Fashion
    cycle)

Dallas market, 110–112, 128, 383
Dardis, Rachel, 28
Daves, Jessica, 63
Davis, Tobé Coller, 351, 398
Dayton-Hudson Corporation, 189
Decline stage, fashion cycle, definition
  of, 35
Denver market, 112
Department stores, 181–183
  assortment planning in multiunit,
    248
  definition of, 182
  and fashion image, 370–380
  history of, 176

Department stores (*Cont.*)
  merchandising policies of, 182–183
Design, definition of, 4
Design inspiration, sources of, 52–53,
    107
Designers:
  careers as, 384, 386–387
  definition of, 51
  of fur apparel, 99
  influence on fashion trends, 50
  menswear, 124–125
  role of, 51–53
  store visits by, 339
  types of, 51–52
  women's apparel, 52, 109
  (*See also* names of individual
    designers)
Details, definition of, 7
Dior, Christian, 10, 14, 36, 44
  House of, 62, 148, 156, 160–161,
    362
Direct mail advertising, 324–325
Disasters (*see* Wars and disasters)
Discount stores, 188–191
  definition of, 190
  and fashion image, 370–378
  merchandising policies of, 190–191
Discretionary income (*see* Income)
Display, 326–332
  careers in, 391–392
  definition of, 326
  interior, 329–331
  window, 326–329
Disposable personal income (*see*
    Income)
Diversification of product:
  in foundations industry, 138
  in intimate apparel industry, 140
  in jewelry industry, 151
  in menswear industry, 131–132
  in textile industries, 85
  in women's apparel industry, 116
Dollar inventory control (*see*
    Inventory control, dollar)
Dollar merchandise plan, 217–234
  definition of, 218
  elements of, 221–234
    planning markdowns, 227–230
    planning purchases, 230
    planning sales, 221–224
    planning stock, 224–227
  goals of, 218
  preparation of, 219–221
  tools for, 218
Dollar open-to-buy, definition of, 218
Domestic market centers (*see* Market
    centers)
Door-to-door selling, 176–177

Downward-flow theory, 56–57
Dual distribution:
  definition of, 121
  in menswear, 121, 128–129
Dynamics, definition of, 1

Economic factors as an influence on
    fashion, 16–22
  consumer income, 16–18
  population, 19
  technical advances, 19–22
Editorial credit, 302, 336
  definition of, 302
Education as an influence on fashion,
    39
Endangered Species Act, 99
England (*see* Great Britain)
Environment:
  definition of, 16
  as an influence on fashion, 16–31
Erogenous, definition of, 43
Escabosa, Hector, 29, 344
European couture, 58, 146
  (*See also* individual countries and
    cities)
"Europel," 166
Exclusivity and fashion image,
    374–375
Expenses:
  direct: definition of, 233
    and dollar merchandise planning,
      233–234
  indirect: definition of, 234
    and dollar merchandise planning,
      234

Fabric:
  definition of, 78
  processing of, 22
Fabric industry, 78–86
  careers in, 384–385, 389
Fads:
  definition of, 6
  fashion cycle of, 38
Far East, 172–173
Fashion:
  birth of a, 50
  components of, 6–8
  definition of, 4
  followers of, 61–62
  and individuality, 63–64
  intangibles, 8–13
  misconceptions about, 3
  principles of, 13–14
  terminology of, 3–6
Fashion adoption, theories of, 54–59

Fashion bureau, 199
Fashion Calendar, 214
Fashion consultants, 214
Fashion coordination, 351–367
  careers in, 384, 388, 389, 392–393
  in chains, 357
  fashion coordinator, 337, 345,
    351–356
    definition of, 337
    in different types of store
      organizations, 356–359
    history of job, 351–352
    responsibilities of, 352–356
    in large multiunit stores, 356–357
    in medium-sized stores, 357–359
    Saks case history, 360–363
    and shop merchandising, 363–367
    in small stores, 359–360
Fashion cycle:
  breaks in, 36
  definition of, 33
  influencing factors in, 39–41
  length of, 35–38
  stages of, 33–35
Fashion forecasting:
  identifying trends, 46
  importance of timing, 48
  interpreting factors for, 47–48
  as job of fashion coordinator,
    354–355
  sources of data for, 46–47
Fashion Group, Inc., 351–352
Fashion influentials, 59–60
  definition of, 57
Fashion innovators, 59–60
  definition of, 57
Fashion International, 214
Fashion leaders (individuals), 59–61
Fashion leaders (stores), 376–377
Fashion merchandising, definition of,
    175
Fashion retailing:
  definition of, 175
  trends in, 193–196
Fashion shows:
  for employees, 345, 348
  fashion coordinator's responsibility
    for, 355–356
  as store publicity source, 337–339
Fashion trends:
  predicting movement of, 45–48
  (*See also* Fashion forecasting)
Federal Trade Commission (*see*
    Government regulations)
Federated Department Stores,
    193–194
Fiber:
  definition of, 69

Fiber (*Cont.*)
  processing of, 22
Fiber industries, 69–78
  careers in, 384–385
Field, Marshall, 179
Financial reports, periodic, 278–284
  departmental operating
    statement, 281
  open-to-buy reports, 282–283
  sales and stock reports, 281
  sales reports, 279–281
Finger, Mildred, 214
Flammable Fabrics Act, 85–86
Flash sales report, 279–281
  definition of, 279
Florence (*see* Italy)
Flügel, J. C., 43, 56, 62–63
Food, Drug, and Cosmetic Act, 146,
    201
Fords, definition of, 185
Foreign market centers (*see* Market
    centers)
Fortrel, 75
Foundations, definition of, 137
Foundations industry, 137–138
Fox, G., and Co., 194
French apparel industry, 159–162
  couture, 159–162
    activities other than showings,
      160–161
    history of, 159–160
    showings of, 160
  ready-to-wear, 162
Fur farming, 95–96
  definition of, 95
Fur industry, 94–99
Fur Products Labeling Act, 99

Galanos, James, 52
Garland, Madge, 43–45
General store:
  definition of, 176
  history of, 176–177
Genesco Corporation, 194
Germany, Federal Republic of, 169
Gimbel Brothers, 158, 178, 193
Givenchy, Hubert, 148, 159, 162
Glove industry, 151–152
Going public, definition of, 115
Goldwater's, 194
Government regulations:
  for cosmetics, 146, 149
  for fur industry, 99
  general, 201–202
  for leather industry, 94
  for menswear industry, 134
  for textile industries, 75, 85–86

Grades (quality), 373
Great Britain:
  accessories, 167
  couture, 166
  ready-to-wear, 166–167
Greige goods, definition of, 79
Grès, Mme., 203
Gross margin:
  definition of, 232
  and dollar merchandise planning,
    232
Group purchase, definition of, 301

Habit and custom, effect of, on
    fashion, 40–41
Halston, 120, 140, 148
Hamburger, Estelle, 214, 398
Handbag industry, 152–154
Handkerchiefs, 155
Head, Edith, 53
Herman, Stan, 140
Hess's Department Store, 379
Hides, definition of, 90
High fashion, definition of, 4
Holidays:
  and customer demand, 208
  effect of, on dollar merchandise
    planning, 233
  sales promotion for, 314
Hong Kong, 105, 116, 173
Horizontal-flow theory, 57–58
Hosiery industry, 140–143, 177
"Hot" items, 295

Image, 369–380
  fashion, 369–380
    changing a, 375–376
    definition of, 369
    merchandising policy elements,
      370–375
    profiling target customers,
      369–370
    types of, 376–380
  store, definition of, 369
Income:
  definitions of, 17
  effect of, on fashion, 16–18, 39, 44
Industrial Revolution, 21, 119
Inside shops, definition of, 121
International Ladies Garment Workers
    Union (ILGWU), 102–103
Internationalization:
  in cosmetics industry, 148
  in leather industry, 94

Internationalization (*Cont.*)
  in menswear industry, 133–134
  in textile industries, 85
  in women's apparel industry, 116
Intimate apparel, definition of, 136
Intimate apparel industries, 136–140
Introduction stage of fashion cycle, 34
Inventory control, dollar, 272–278
  book inventory, 272–275
  merchandise on order, 275–276
  physical inventory, 276–277
  purchase journal, 278
  stock shortages, overages, 277–278
Israel, exports to the United States
    from, 170
Italy:
  accessories, 165–166
  couture, 165–166
  ready-to-wear, 164–165
Ivy League suit, 10, 124

Japan, trade with, 173
Jeans, 6, 13, 25, 52, 58, 131
Jewelry:
  costume, definition of, 150
  definition of, 149
  and fashion cycle, 37
  fine, definition of, 150
  industry, 149–151
Jobber:
  definition of, 103
  in women's apparel industry,
    104–105

K-Mart, 189
Kaufmann's, 194
Kennedy, Mrs. John F., 61, 62
King, Charles W., 57–58, 60
Kips, definition of, 90
Klein, Calvin, 52, 362
Korea, 116, 173
Kresge, S. S., 189, 192
Kroeber, A. L., 42–43

Lambert, Eleanor, 340
Lane Bryant, 185, 370
Last, definition of, 143
Latin America, 170–172
Lauren, Ralph, 125
Laver, James, 5, 43, 45, 56
Lawrence, A. C., Leather Co., 89
Leased department, 192–193
  definition of, 98
  furs, 98
  jewelry, 150
  merchandising policies of, 193

Leather:
  use of: in gloves, 151
    in handbags, 152
    in shoes, 143
Leather industry, 88–94
Lee, H. D., 131
Leisure suit, definition of, 123
Leisure time:
  effect of, on customer demand, 208
  as an influence on fashion, 23, 39
Lerner Shops, 185
Licensed trademark, definition of, 75
Licensing, 75, 116, 148, 161
  definition of, 116
Line:
  definition of, 53–54
  seasonal, lessening emphasis on, 116
Line-for-line copies, definition of, 34
Linen, 72
  definition of, 70
Lingerie, definition of, 138
Lingerie industry, 138–140
Linters, definition, 70
Loehmann's, 190
Logan, Jonathan, 106
Long-run fashions, definition of, 36
Lord and Taylor, 194, 327
Loungewear, definition of, 138
Loungewear industry, 138–140

McCardell, Claire, 109–110
McKinley, William, 20
Macy, R. H., and Co., 158, 177, 193, 379
Magazine:
  advertising, 325–326
  publicity, 336
Magnin, I., & Co., 344
Mail-order selling, 178–179, 250, 325, 342, 343
  careers in, 393
Man-made fibers, definition of, 69
Man-made fibers industries, 69–78
Manhattan Industries, 132
Manufacturers:
  careers with, 384–389
  definition of, 103
  influence on fashion trends, 50–51
  as source of market information, 303–305
  types of, 50
  (See also Vendors)
Markdown:
  as aid in determining customer demand, 209–210

Markdown (Cont.)
  analysis of, 285–286
  buyer's responsibility for, 286
  causes for, 286
  definition of, 229
  and dollar merchandise planning, 229–230
Markdown percentage, definition of, 229
Marker, definition of, 109
Market, definitions of, 68
Market centers:
  domestic, 109–113
    gloves, 152
    hosiery, 142
    intimate apparel, 138–140
    jewelry, 150
    menswear, 128
    millinery, 154
    miscellaneous accessories, 152–156
    wigs, 156
    women's apparel, 109–113
  foreign, 158–173
    Far East, 172–173
    France, 159–162
    Great Britain, 165–167
    how to shop, 158–159
    Israel, 170
    Italy, 162–166
    Latin America, 170–172
    miscellaneous European, 169–170
    Scandinavia, 168–169
    Spain, 167–168
Market representative, 299–300
  definition of, 299
Market trip, 295–311
  market information sources, 297–306
  resident buying office, 297–301
  timing of, 295–297
  working the market, 306–311
Marketing, definition of, 67
Marketing process:
  chart, 67
  definition of, 67
Markup:
  definition of, 232
  initial, definition of, 232
Marts, apparel/trade, 110–113
  Atlanta, 113
  California, 112
  Carolina, 112–113
  Chicago, 113
  Dallas, 110–112
  Denver, 111–112
  Kansas City, 113

Marts (Cont.)
  Miami, 112
  Northeast, 113
  Radisson, 113
  San Francisco, 113
Mass fashion, definition of, 4
Mass merchandisers (see Chain organizations; Discount stores)
May Department Stores, 158, 193, 194
Men's Fashion Association of America, 131
Menswear:
  categories of, 122–123
  and changes in fashion, 72
Menswear industry, 119–134
  careers in, 385–388
Merchandise assortment, definition of, 236
  (See also Assortment)
Merchandise journal, 278
Merchandise transfers, 264
Merchandising:
  definition of, 175
  retail careers in, 390–391
Merchandising Motivation, Inc., 214
Merchandising policies:
  and assortment planning, 237
  in chains, 187–188
  in department stores, 182–183
  in discount stores, 190–191
  and fashion image, 370–375
  in leased departments, 193
  in specialty stores, 184–185
  in variety stores, 192
Miami Mart, 113
Middle class, the, fashion demand among, 27
Midi, 14, 202
Millinery industry, 154
Miniskirt, 6–7, 26, 44, 141
Minority groups:
  change in status of, 23–25
  as an influence on fashion, 25
"Mipel," 165–166
Mirror of the times, fashion as a, 11
Mom and Pop store, definition of, 183
Monsanto, 76
Montgomery Ward and Co., 178, 185, 250, 357
Multiunit organizations:
  fashion assortment planning in, 248–251
  fashion coordination in, 356–357
  sales force training in, 345
  types of, 175–192

Multiunit organizations (*Cont.*)
(*See also* Branch organizations;
Chain organizations)

National Association of Men's
Sportswear Buyers, 128–131
National Cotton Council, 77
National dress, abandonment of, 16
National Retail Merchants Association,
72, 145, 226, 232, 243, 306,
310, 317, 319, 324, 383, 398
Natural fiber, definition of, 69
Natural fiber industries, 69–78
Neckwear industry, 155
(*See also* Scarfs)
Nehru jacket, 6
Neiman-Marcus, 193, 379
New Look (Dior), 10, 14, 36, 44
New York City:
and accessories industries, 137–154
and apparel industries, 103–105,
115, 121
as domestic fashion center, 110,
128, 383
Newspaper:
advertising, 316–323
publicity, 335–336
Newspaper Advertising Bureau, 319
Norell, Norman, 62, 148
North Carolina, 112–113
hosiery mills in, 141
Nylon, 140
Nystrom, Paul H., 1, 3–5, 47, 199

Obsolescence stage of the fashion
cycle, definition of, 35
Ohrbach's, 189–190, 376
Open-to-buy, 282–283
definition of, 218
formula for, 293
Operating expenses and dollar
merchandise planning, 233–234
Operating statements, departmental,
281, 283
Operational satisfactions, definition of,
205
Order (*see* Purchase order)
Organizational chart of retail
organization, 180
Overstock, 295

Pantsuits, 5, 22–23, 26–27, 29, 46,
48, 50, 62, 146
Paris, 101, 109, 139, 159–162, 357
(*See also* French apparel industry)

Patronage motives, definition of, 206
Patternmaker, 108
Peddlers in the United States,
176–178
Pelt, definition of, 95
Penney, J. C., Co., 185, 250, 324,
357, 370
Periodic stock count control, 258–261
definition of, 258
Perpetual control system, 254–258
definition of, 254
Personal income (*see* Income)
Physical inventory, 276–277
Planned purchases, 230
Plymouth Shops, 185
Poiret, Paul, 14, 52
Poland, 170
Population:
age-mix of, 19
size of, 19
Portugal, 169
Pre-retail, definition of, 274
Press release, definition of, 335
Press Weeks/Previews:
publicity for, 336, 340
menswear industry, 131
women's apparel industry, 114
Prêt-à-porter, definition of, 162
Pretesting as aid in determining
customer demand, 209
Price:
and fashion image, 373
relationship of, to fashion, 13–14
as selection factor, 205
Price changes, 265
Price lines:
best-selling, definition of, 242
definition of, 241
establishing for assortment
planning, 242
and fashion image, 373
Price-lining, definition of, 241
Price range:
definition of, 241
and fashion image, 373
Price ranges:
for chains, 187
for department stores, 182
for discount stores, 190
for specialty stores, 185
Price tickets, 268
Price zones:
definition of, 107
wholesale, in women's apparel,
106–108
Prime resources, definition of, 307
Prior stock reports, 284–285
definition of, 285

Product diversification (*see*
Diversification of product)
Prophetic styles, definition of, 47
Psychological factors as an influence
on fashion, 28–31
boredom, 28
companionship, desire for, 30
curiosity, 28–29
reaction to convention, 29
self-assurance, 29–30
Psychological satisfactions, definition
of, 205
Publicity, 334–340
careers in, 391
definition of, 334
media used, 335–337
in menswear industry, 129
methods of obtaining, 334–335
sources of material, 337–340
in women's apparel industry, 114
(*See also* Sales promotion)
Purchase journal, 278
Purchase order, 261–262
cancellation of, 264
writing the, 310
Purchases, planning of dollar, 230
Purchasing power:
consumer, 17–18
and fashion marketing, 18

Qiana, 77
Quality standards, 373
Quant, Mary, 167

Radio:
advertising, 22, 324
publicity, 337
Rayon, 72, 140
Ready-to-wear, definition of, 101
Receiving apron, definition of, 264
Receiving records in unit control,
263–264
Recurring fashions, 41–43
Reed's, Jacob, Sons, 120
Release date, definition of, 334
Religion, effect of, on fashion change,
41
Renta, Oscar de la, 52, 125, 362
Reporting services, fashion, 214
Research bureau, 200
Reserve requisition control, definition
of, 260
Resident buying offices, 200, 211,
297–301
careers in, 394
definitions of, 297–299

Resident buying offices (*Cont.*)
market representative, 299–300
merchandising services, 300–301
organization of, 299
types of, 297–299
Retail method of inventory, 272
definition of, 218
Retail News Bureau, 213–214, 398
Retail reductions, 229
Retailing:
current trends in, 193–196
definition of, 175
early history of, 175–176
U.S. history of, 176–179
Reticule, definition of, 152
Retirement (*see* Senior citizens)
Return-to-vendor, definition of, 264
Returns, 210, 264, 286
Rise stage of fashion cycle, definition
of, 34
Robinson, Dwight E., 46, 56, 57
Robinson, J. W., Co., 194
Robinson-Patman Act, 201
Rome (*see* Italy)

St. Laurent, Yves, 62, 125, 148, 159,
161
Saks Fifth Avenue, 178, 184, 185,
317, 360–363, 370
Sales events, special, 208
Sales goals, planning, 221–224
Sales per square foot, 289
Sales promotion, 313–332, 334–349
activities: in chains, 188
in cosmetics industry, 147–148
in department stores, 183
in discount stores, 191
in fabric industry, 82
in fiber industries, 76–77
in glove industry, 152
in hosiery industry, 142–143
in intimate apparel industries,
138–140
in leather industry, 93–94
in menswear industry, 129–130
in shoe industry, 145
in specialty stores, 185
in variety stores, 192
in women's apparel industry,
113–115
careers in, 385–394, 399
definition of, 313
division organization and operation,
313–314
and the fashion coordinator,
355–356
and the fashion cycle, 14, 40

Sales promotion (*Cont.*)
and fashion forecasting, 47–48
and the fashion image, 372–373
Sales records:
as aid in predicting trends, 47
and customer demand, 209
as evaluation device, 288
use in unit control, 264
Sales reports, inventory control,
279–282
Salespeople:
buyer's responsibility for training,
347–349
qualifications for, 343–344
training of, 344–349, 355
Salon selling, definition of, 341
Sample hand, definition of, 108
(*See also* Sample maker)
Sample maker, 387
Sample-test-reorder technique, 311
Sapir, Edward, 4, 56, 62, 63
Scandinavia:
fashion products, 168
trade fairs in, 168–169
Scarfs, 22, 37, 155, 327
Sears, Roebuck & Company, 178,
185, 186, 250, 324, 357, 370
Season code, definition of, 244
Seasonal change:
effect of: on customer demand,
207–208
on fashion cycle, 40
Section work, definition of, 105
Selection factors, definition of, 204
Self-assurance as an influence on
fashion demand, 29
Selling, 340–349
careers in, 387–399
and fashion image, 372–373
services: in chains, 188
in department stores, 183
in discount stores, 191
in specialty stores, 185
in variety stores, 192
and store image, 372–373, 377–380
techniques, 341–343
training of salespeople, 344–349
Senior citizens, fashion demand
among, 19
Services:
customer: in chains, 188
in department stores, 183
in discount stores, 191
in specialty stores, 185
and store image, 370–371,
377–380
trends in, 194–195
in variety stores, 192

Sexual appeal of apparel, 43–45
Sheppard, Eugenia, 62
Shoe industry, 143–145
Shopping centers, 176
Shops, 363–367
boutiques, 365–367
buying for, 365
definition of, 364
types of, 364–365
Short run, manufacturing, definition
of, 122
Short-run fashions, definition of, 36
Silhouettes:
basic types of, 6–7
definition of, 6
fashion cycle of, 6–7, 36–37,
42–43
as selection factor, 204
Silk, 70–71, 140
definition of, 70
Simmel, Georg, 56, 63
Simpson, Adele, 52, 148
Size ranges:
and assortment planning, 246
in men's suits, 127
in shoes, 145
in women's apparel, 106, 246
Skins, definition of, 90
Slop shops, 120–121
Social classes (*see* Social structure)
Social structure:
fashion as reflection of, 11–12
mobility within, 26
Sociological factors as an influence on
fashion, 22–28
South America, 170–172
Soviet Union, 16
Spain, 167–168
Specialty stores, 183–185
assortment planning in multiunit,
248
definition of, 184
fashion image and, 370–379
history of, 176
merchandising policies of, 184–185
Spinerette, definition of, 73
Sports professionals, 60–61
Sportswear:
influence of leisure time on, 23
men's, 123, 125, 127–128
Stevens, J. P., 85
Stock averages:
definition of, 233
and dollar merchandise planning,
233
inventory control of, 277–278
Stock-sales ratios,
definition of, 226

Stock-sales reports, inventory
control and, 282
Stock shortages:
definition of, 233
and dollar merchandise planning,
233
inventory control of, 277–278
Stock turnover:
definition of, 226
as evaluation device, 287–288
use of, in dollar merchandise
planning, 226–227
Stockkeeping unit (SKU), definition
of, 268
Strauss, Levi, 121, 131
Style:
acceptance of a, 8–9
definition of, 4
Sumptuary laws, 11, 41
Sweat shops, 122

Tailored clothing industry, 122–127
definition of, 123
Taiwan, 116, 173
Taking numbers, definition of, 308
Tanneries, definitions of, 89
Tanning, 88–92
definition of, 88
Tarde, Gabriel, 56
Target Stores, 189
Taste:
definition of, 5
effect of, on fashion forecasting, 48
relationship of, to fashion, 5–6
Technology:
advances in, 19–22, 37
effect of, on fashion cycle, 39–40
in hosiery industry, 140, 143
in intimate apparel industry,
138–140
in leather industry, 89, 93
in menswear industry, 132–133
in shoe industry, 143
in textile industries, 83–84
in women's apparel industry,
117–118
(See also Automated data
processing)
Teen boards, 215
Television, 22
advertising, 334
careers in, 398
publicity and, 337
Television Bureau of Advertising, 324
Terms of sale, definition of, 233
Testing bureau, 200
Testing new fashions, 311

Textile converter, definition of, 81
Textile fabric (see Fabric)
Textile fiber (see Fiber)
Textile Fibers Products Identification
Act, 75
Texture:
color and, 7
definition of, 7
fashion cycle of, 37
as selection factor, 204
silhouette and, 7
Tickets (See Price Tickets)
Tobé Associates, Inc., 214, 398
(See also Davis, Tobé Coller)
Trade associations:
careers in, 398–399
in foundations industry, 137
in fur industry, 99
in glove industry, 152
in handbag industry, 153
in leather industry, 92–93
in millinery industry, 154
as publicity source, 339–340
in shoe industry, 145
as source of market information,
305–306
in textile industries, 76–77
Trade publications, 212–214, 303
careers in, 397
Travel:
changes in, 27–28
as an influence on fashion, 27–28
Trends:
industry: in accessories, 138–156
in fur, 99
in leather, 93–94
in menswear, 131–134
in textiles, 83–86
in women's apparel, 113–118
in retail fashion distribution,
193–196
Triangle Shirtwaist Factory, 103
Trunk show, 209, 339
definition of, 209
T-shirts, 6, 138

Udell, Jon G., 205
Umbrellas, 155–156
Unions, 102–103, 122
Unit control, 200, 253–270
automated, 266–269
definition of, 253
evaluating, 269–270
sources of information, 261–266
types of information recorded,
253–254
types of systems, 254–261

Upward-flow theory, 58–59

Valentino, 148, 164
Variety stores, 191–192
definition of, 191
history of, 176
merchandising policies of, 192
Vendor analysis, 286–287
Vendors:
advertising aids from, 331–332
and publicity, 339
sales training aids from, 345
store visits from, 339, 356
Vignette, definition of, 331
Visual control, 260–261
definition of, 260
Volume fashion (see Mass fashion)

Want slip, definition of, 210
Wars and disasters:
as influences on fashion demand,
30–31, 36
as influences on women's fashions,
25–26
Wear-Dated, 76
Weitz, John, 125
Wheeler-Lea Act, 201
Wigs, 38, 45, 156
Window display, 326–329
Wittkin, Herbert, 372–373
Women:
apparel fashion game and, 43–46
effects on fashion by changes in
status of, 25–27, 39
Women's apparel:
categories of, 106
size ranges of, 106
wholesale price ranges of, 106–107
Women's apparel industry, 101–118
careers in, 385–388
Women's Wear Daily, 214
Wool, 70, 73–74
definition of, 70
Wool Bureau, 76, 77, 85
Woolworth, F. W., Co., 192
World War I, 25
World War II, 10, 25, 99, 109, 113,
140, 143, 202
Worth, Charles Frederick, 159

Yarn, definition of, 79
Young, Agnes Brooke, 42
Young, Beryl Tucker, Inc., 214
Youth, fashion demand among, 19
Yugoslavia, first annual International
Fashion Fair in, 170